THE SECRET HISTORY
OF THE CIA

BOOKS BY JOSEPH J. TRENTO

Widows (with Susan Trento and William Corson)

Prescription for Disaster (with Susan Trento)

The National Aeronautics and Space Administration
(with Richard Hirsch)

THE
SECRET HISTORY
OF THE
CIA

JOSEPH J. TRENTO

CARROLL & GRAF PUBLISHERS
NEW YORK

For Susan Trento,
who helped me uncover and make sense
out of this secret history

THE SECRET HISTORY OF THE CIA

Carroll & Graf Publishers
An Imprint of Avalon Publishing Group Inc.
245 West 17th Street
11th Floor
New York, NY 10011

AVALON
publishing group incorporated

Copyright © 2001 by Joseph J. Trento

First Carroll & Graf edition 2005

Library of Congress Cataloging-in-Publication Data is available.

ISBN: 0-7867-1500-6

9 8 7 6 5 4 3 2 1

Printed in the United States of America
Distributed by Publishers Group West

CONTENTS

INTRODUCTION TO THE 2005 EDITION

THERE WAS FOR ME an awful irony that the *The Secret History of the CIA* was first released the week of the 9/11 al Qaeda attacks on New York and Washington. We had just suffered the greatest intelligence failure in American history. The topic of my book was the CIA's cold war history of intelligence and counterintelligence failures. As the National Commission on Terrorism's 9/11 report so ably demonstrated, the intelligence mistakes made before 9/11 were precisely the same kinds of mistakes made again and again during the cold war.

So why had we not learned of key lessons from the mistakes in our intelligence history? In my view the main reason is that much of that history has been kept from the public. The idea that intelligence disasters can be kept from citizens in the name of national security has been a shield that has protected the intelligence bureaucrats for far too long. The pattern to bury mistakes began again right after 9/11 when Vice President Dick Cheney visited Senator Bob Graham and asked him not to undertake a 9/11 investigation because it would be a distraction from the war on terrorism. President George W. Bush took the same tack when he at first refused to establish the 9/11 Commission. Bush was trying to protect the CIA in the 9/11 aftermath which for me brought back memories of how the Agency was protected in previous scandals throughout the fifty-seven year history that is told in the book.

Another lesson from history is how the FBI and CIA bureaucrats distrusted each other to the point of mutual impotence. It was made clear in the aftermath of 9/11 that the lack of cooperation has continued. I received a personal preview of what we were to learn from the 9/11 Commission concerning the CIA/FBI relationship. A week after the attacks, a young FBI agent came into my office at the Public Education Center. He was upset and full of frustration. He had been working the 9/11 case and was already running into political problems with his bosses. He was told not to follow-up any leads connecting suspects in the attacks with Saudi officials, or with bin Laden family members living in the United States without clearing it with headquarters first. While he waited for approval, he watched key witnesses and even possible participants fly out of United States jurisdiction. The agent said early indications were that the CIA had deliberately withheld the identities of two of the hijackers who commandeered American Airlines Flight 77 and crashed it into the Pentagon. He was told that the CIA was "protecting sources and methods." The agent asked me if this sort of behavior between the FBI and CIA was something new. I explained that the problems he was encountering had haunted U.S. intelligence for its entire modern history. I gave the agent a copy of *The Secret History of the CIA.*

The next time I saw the agent, some months later, the naiveté was gone. In its place was a more cynical attitude who could not wait to get back to chasing bank robbers and kidnappers and hoped he would never work again on a national security case. I asked him why. He said: "Because when you are chasing street criminals, thieves and robbers they are more likely to tell the truth than the people at the CIA or even my bosses at the FBI."

My young friend's experience with the CIA and its employees is not unusual. The kind of ass-covering bureaucratic diversion of blame was not invented at either the FBI or CIA. The truth is many thousands of exemplary Americans toil with great patriotism for the CIA and a relative few, sometimes in alliance with self-interested politicians, are largely responsible for the damage that has been done. What is different, of course, is that under the guise of national security the mistakes and embarrassments can be hidden away for decades. So when reporters, historians, and investigators get bits and pieces of the truth, we citizens need to take advantage of the lessons the information offers. It is my hope that *The Secret History of the CIA* will give the reader a sense of why and how the CIA failed as an institution and what we can learn to make certain we don't keep repeating the mistakes.

9/11 was a transforming failure for Americans because it killed so many of our fellow citizens. But we need to realize for hundreds of thousands around the world, the effect of earlier CIA failures has been as profoundly felt and just as deadly. East Germany, Korea, Hungary, Vietnam, Chile, Haiti, Afghanistan, and other venues left the men and women of the CIA with blood on their hands amid consequences that were never intended. I hope this book will help allow those who did not live through this period understand how the incompetence of United States intelligence made our failure to detect the al Qaeda attacks sadly predictable.

The unanimous recommendations to reform our intelligence community by the 9/11 Commission remain mired in Congress. The Pentagon refuses to give up control of billions of dollars in intelligence money. Newly appointed CIA Director Porter Goss, who played the role of Agency cheerleader instead of providing oversight, is stuffing his DCI's office with political types instead of people who actually understand the intelligence business. George Tenet, who left the CIA even less credible then he found it, has decided to write a book. Perhaps for his $5 million dollar advance he will share with us how he managed to approve outsourcing to Saudi Arabian intelligence the role of hunting down al Qaeda while the same royal family was funding it. As the clock ticks toward the next attack Osama bin Laden's visage appears yet again, a few days before the 2004 Presidential election, to show us he is in a comfortable studio and remind us recruiting is better than ever. The CIA can't find him but he keeps finding us. That is the ultimate definition of an intelligence calamity.

PREFACE

―――――※●※―――――

HIS STORY IS ABOUT the men and women who were chosen to do hidden battle with the Soviet Union after World War II. They were from what we now call "the greatest generation" that won a world war and saved the United States from Nazi totalitarianism. Many of the best of them came together in the Central Intelligence Agency to fight the Cold War and, once again, save freedom—only this time they did it secretly.

These men and women of the CIA were trusted to do their work without any real accountability or oversight. This book is about how, left on their own, they broke the rules again and again. It is about mistakes the U.S. intelligence services consistently made and the damage that resulted. Sadly, one thing we learned is that no generation is "the greatest." Some individuals may be brave, but others may be cowardly and arrogant. Many World War II heroes went on to CIA careers that produced no real victories and many tragedies.

The Secret History of the CIA is not about America conquering godless Communism and winning the Cold War. It is more about ambition and betrayal than about patriotic achievement. It is about what happened when an age of fear caused us to turn extraordinary power over to a government agency run by human beings with weaknesses that we all share. It is about careerism, callousness, self-interest, and hubris.

From the very day the CIA opened for business, its management risked the lives of mostly innocent people who were not combatants in the spy wars. Over the course of the Cold War, hundreds of thousands of people died in a series of proxy wars and secret operations, often for purposes that had little to do with our national interest.

Delving into this less romantic side of covert operations stirs up resentment and anger among those who want to perpetuate the myth that the

CIA won the Cold War. Yet some men and women who served in the CIA recognize its flaws and spoke to me out of a desire to set the record straight.

This book could not have been researched or written without the co-operation of former CIA Counterintelligence Chief James Jesus Angleton. For some, Angleton is the poster boy of the anti-Communist paranoia that infected the U.S. for so many years. The allegation that he saw Commies and KGB agents everywhere and ruined innocent lives has an uncomfortable kernel of truth, as we shall see, but it is one of the great oversimplifications about the CIA.

In December 1974, CIA Director William Colby ended what he called Angleton's "pointless quest" to find the mole in the CIA by firing him. Colby's view, and that of a handful of writers, about the CIA was that there were no moles, no traitors—that the CIA was never penetrated by the KGB or any other intelligence service. After all, they thought, the CIA was the best of the best and invulnerable.

With Angleton defenseless and thoroughly discredited, that mistaken version of history stood. It suited the old boy network in all areas of American intelligence, including elements of the Justice Department, the International Division of the Bureau of the Census, and a host of other government agencies. However, with the arrest of CIA counterintelligence officer Aldrich Ames in 1994, the myth collapsed dramatically. Ames's arrest set off a wave of horror stories about suspected moles in the military, the Energy Department, the State Department, the FBI, and the CIA. But what is the context? What does all this mean?

The Secret History of the CIA is the record of what happens when a free society engages in an activity that is totally alien to its character. This book is the culmination of hundreds of interviews and 30 years of journalism covering the men and women who were the Agency during the Cold War. It collects and preserves an unofficial institutional memory about events that have been turned into mythology.

I came to write this story because I realized the intelligence service has more to do with how the United States behaves around the world than any other government agency. In some ways, the CIA exerts more power than the Pentagon. Its analysis of the world is crucial in determining the weapons we develop and in defining the threats to which we respond. Presidents come and go, but the intelligence bureaucracy remains in place as the real ruling class in our political system.

Recent presidents have learned that the commander-in-chief does not necessarily get to learn all the secrets. If the presidents do not ask the right questions, they will not get the right answers. Richard Nixon and Jimmy Carter both learned this the hard way. Even the director of Central Intelligence can be frozen out when operations turn questionable or illegal.

The emotional center of the CIA is the Directorate of Plans, Operations, Covert Action, or whatever name the spies call themselves at any given moment. During the Cold War, these men considered themselves so important to the survival of our country that they thought ordinary rules did not apply to them. That sort of elitism has haunted the CIA throughout its entire history. A feeling of exemption from rules and regulations is the norm. No career required as much abandonment of personal morality by an individual as a career in the CIA or, across the world, in the KGB.

My CIA lessons began when Dr. William R. Corson called me in 1976, after I had known him for six years. I was a newspaper reporter covering national security, and he was a source who seemed to me to have access absolutely everywhere. He was the author of a column on politics and the military. He was both a scholar and a Marine who had fought in three wars. He never worked for the CIA, but he did work directly for four presidents. He had studied physics, played minor league ball, fought at the Frozen Chosin in Korea, frolicked with JFK, and killed for him. Colonel Fletcher Prouty once told me, "For Bill Corson, the CIA was support staff. He needed to know; they didn't."

In the 1970s, *Penthouse* magazine began hiring reporters to do big investigative stories. Knowing I wanted to write some of those stories, Bill Corson took me under his wing. He was maddening to deal with, because he seldom told me anything directly. Just like "Deep Throat" during Watergate, he loved the drama of making me figure out what he was talking about as he hinted at dire events and tantalizing incidents. Each time I was ready to throw him over for another source, he always came through with the piece of paper or the hard information I needed.

He made me earn his trust. If I wrote a story and got the slightest detail wrong, he ignored me for weeks. I watched him destroy the careers of reporters he deemed "dead" because they were careless or, as he put it, "had been tamed by the Agency." Slowly, we became friends, and in some ways, I guess, he became my "case officer."

Corson walked away from his Marine Corps career in 1968 because his high-level access at the White House and the Pentagon convinced him that many more American soldiers would die needlessly in Vietnam. Risking court martial, he wrote *The Betrayal,* a bestseller that changed America's perception of the men fighting the war.

Compactly built and an intellectual, Corson grew up in Al Capone's Chicago. He lacked the Ivy League pedigree that was the usual ticket into the intelligence community, but he had another ticket that was almost as good: His father was one of the original disciples of General Ralph Van Deman, the father of Army intelligence. Corson's speech was filled with jargon from the secret world in which he lived. People who worked at the Agency were "from up the river." If someone was dead, they had "gone to the heavy side." As I wrote my stories, many of them embarrassing to the CIA, he and I worked closely together. We lunched weekly at the Hay-Adams Hotel in Washington, D.C., across from the White House.

One day, Corson said to me, "I want you to meet Angleton. You barely know enough, but it is time you talked to him." Corson sipped his double martini and put his flaming Zippo to yet another cigarette and said laconically, "You've got to get to know him before he drinks and smokes himself to death."

Coincidentally, Angleton called me on his own just a few days later. An article I had coauthored about the CIA's using the news media as cover had caught his attention. "Mr. Trento," he said, "my name is Jim Angleton, and I saw that in your article about the CIA and the news media you did not reveal the names of the CIA men. I would like to buy you lunch." With that call in June 1976, I prepared to meet the man whose code name, "Mother," Aaron Latham enshrined in his wonderful novel, *Orchids for Mother.*

Angleton's thinness was legendary. When I saw him for the first time at the old Army and Navy Club, he had an ethereal, unreal quality. We met in the lobby, and he escorted me up to the main bar. He got us a table in a padded and quiet corner, and he sat so he could see everyone coming into the room. By that time, he had been unemployed for two years. I suspected he had decided to talk to me because the only other reporter who regularly covered intelligence was Sy Hersh, and Hersh had run a story fed to him by Colby that created the excuse to fire Angleton.

That luncheon began a tumultuous relationship. For the next 11 years, Angleton treated me as confidant, enemy agent, sounding board, and in the end, as lung cancer overcame him, confessor. He was difficult, and he could be dour. He gave me major stories and then was furious when they were published. One day, I had news for him. I had learned that his old CIA colleagues, wanting to destroy his reputation once and for all, had reopened the hunt for a KGB mole in the Agency—only this time he was the target. Angleton shot the messenger. He was so angry at me for bringing him this news that he cut me off for a year. In court testimony related to the assassination of President Kennedy, he accused me of being a "KGB disinformation agent." Then, as if nothing had happened, he began calling me again.

At that point, he introduced me to his friend and former colleague, Robert T. Crowley, also a close friend of Bill Corson. Crowley was as much a headquarters guy as Corson was a field guy. He was one of the tallest men ever to work in the CIA. He was always in top-level staff jobs and possessed a personal magnetism and charm that made him a great espiocrat.

Crowley's main job was liaising with corporations like ITT, which the CIA used as fronts for moving large amounts of cash. He was deeply involved in U.S. efforts to overthrow Salvador Allende in Chile. Before we met, stories I had reported had gotten Crowley into a lot of trouble, including several invitations to appear before a federal grand jury investigating the Chile cover-up. Once he retired from the CIA, however, Crowley decided to take Angleton's and Corson's advice and begin talking to me.

After Angleton's hard death from lung cancer in May of 1987, Corson and Crowley began to give me access to files they had kept in trust for their old friend. The only promise I made was that I would publish nothing until Angleton had been dead 10 years. That time has now come.

Corson himself was diagnosed with lung cancer in late 1999. After his death seven months later, I came into possession of all his files, tapes, and writings.

Bob Crowley, also a smoker, suffered lung cancer and then terrible senility before his death a few months after Corson. His extensive files—and those of James Angleton—were also turned over to me.

Corson, Angleton, and Crowley generously provided me with introductions to former colleagues. Many of them cooperated as sources for this book, although some have asked that their names be left out. This book rests on the memories and papers of hundreds of men and women who toiled on the American, British, and German sides of the Cold War, plus several dozen who worked for the KGB and some who still work for the SVR (the post-Soviet Russian intelligence service) or the GRU (Russian military intelligence).

Beginning in 1990, one other source became invaluable in understanding the character of CIA leadership during the Cold War. John Sherwood, a wartime Army officer and a brilliant linguist, joined the CIA after World War II with great hope. Raised in Denver, Sherwood became an infantry platoon leader in Germany and joined the military government after the war. After graduating from the University of Chicago and starting to teach, he became a willing recruit for the CIA. "I'd barely heard of the place at the time. I wanted to go in the State Department, but the McCarthy mania had put a hiring freeze on the place. I have a feeling my credentials were slipped over the transom at the Agency."

Sherwood believed that the "relatively young old boys" from the OSS were looking to replicate themselves with their new recruits, and he had the right résumé. "So I went through Junior Officer Training and joined the Directorate of Plans. Having been a rather adventuresome youngster, I took one look at the endless challenge to all possible skills offered by the DP, and thereby hangs the tale of yet another wasted life, to wit my own." Beginning in 1990, Sherwood shared his memories and insights on the CIA with a candor and honesty that reporters seldom enjoy.

Weeks before this book went to print, John Sherwood, 76, rode his bike into the night and went up a mountain near his home in Colorado. The next morning, police found his body near the road below, with a suicide note apologizing to the emergency medical service for leaving such a mess behind. He died a year to the day after his friend Bill Corson. John Sherwood had been tormented by what he saw and did in the CIA.

Hundreds of people shared their lives with me, but it was Corson, Crowley, Sherwood, and Angleton who truly made this book possible. I also must add a word of thanks to a handful of friends at the SVR who risked their own careers by providing me with information that neither the Russian or U.S. intelligence services cared to see released.

WITH APPRECIATION

⟶⋙◆⋘⟶

T RUTH, WHEN TALKING about the CIA, is relative," James Angleton
told me. That caveat taken, any mistakes found in this book are mine.

This book could not have been written without the cooperation of
four complicated men who died while the work was being researched and
written. The late James Jesus Angleton cooperated under the condition
that I publish none of his words until a decade after his death. Robert T.
Crowley made himself totally available until illness claimed his health,
mind, and life. His wife, Emily, turned over Bob's remarkable files to help
fill in the blanks. John Sherwood, honest to a fault, provided me with insights into the human costs of intelligence work. His willingness to face
the past was my light in trying to work my way through the maze.
Dr. William R. Corson, with whom I enjoyed a long friendship, and who
had been my co-author, never relented in his search for answers.

The Igor Orlov story could not have been told without access to still
classified material, both in the United States and Russia. I want to thank
those sources for their help.

Eleonore Orlov, the ultimate Cold War survivor, shared the darkest
secrets of her life and Igor with openness and candor.

Crowley and Corson, the headquarters man and the ultimate field
man, provided me with an education and a sense of reality to what can
easily become an arcane academic exercise. In a sense, both men have
been, along with the late Justin O'Donnell, the closest thing we have had
to a conscience in the intelligence community.

I want to thank the late George Kisevalter who we also lost during
the writing of this book. He gave me an authentic sense of what it was
like being at the center of Cold War operations. His revelations about
SR-9 lifted the fog from that strange place.

Paul Garbler demonstrated an honesty and courage about his career that few men in his position would dare. His constant good grace as he shared his story is deeply appreciated.

Special thanks to Edward M. Korry and his wife, Pat, for their help in telling the story of what happened in Chile and the reality of being caught up in the world of the CIA.

Then there are the "boys" from Berlin who spoke to me on and off the record. Special thanks to Wally Driver, Anita Poctki, Sam Wilson, the late C.G. Harvey, Donald Morris, the late Lucien Conien, David Chavchavadze, Etta Jo Weisz, and scores of their colleagues.

I would also like to thank David Wise, the late Alan Lightner Jr., Geiselle Weisz, Susanne Gottlieb, Peter Kapusta, the late Teddy Kollek, Tulluis Accompura, Quintin Johnson, the late John Bross, Robert and George Orlov, the late Frank Steinert, Joe Bulick, Hank Knocke, Edward Petty, Donald E. Denesyla, Robert Maheu, Ricardo Canete, L. Fletcher Prouty, the late John A. McCone, James Wooten, Samuel Papich, Pete and Ellie Sivess, the late William Branigan, Courtland Jones, the late Bruce Solie, Ewa Shadrin, Richard Copaken, Leonard V. McCoy, the late William E. Colby, Alfred McCoy, Frank Snepp, Orrin Deforrest, Ralph Dungan, William Zylka, Felix S. Bloch, Milton Wolfe, Robert Kupperman, the late Admiral Harvey Lyon, Tom Issacs, Samuel T. McDowell, Leonard M. Brenner, Sherry Cooper, Dale Young, Herbert Kouts, Sarkis Soghanalian, Peter Stockton, William Bartells, the late General Richard G. Stilwell, Britt Snider, Tom Tucker, Nikki Weisz, Tom Sippell, Gwendolyn Jolly, and Dr. Hormez R. Guard. There are hundreds more who have asked that I leave their names out and I will honor that request.

I want to extend my deep appreciation to the team at Prima Forum: my editors, Steve Martin and David Richardson; the all-patient manuscript editing team, Cathy Black and Libby Larson; and Linda Bridges, who provided great help in making the manuscript more accessible to the reader.

I want to recognize the help of my colleagues at the Public Education Center's National Security News Service. Jeff Moag has been especially helpful. I want to also thank my toughest critic and editor, Susan Trento, for leaving her writing projects to help me get through the secret history.

If you want to communicate with me after reading this book you can either write to the publisher or e-mail me at *Trento@publicedcenter.org*.

CHAPTER ONE

BERIA AND STALIN

————▸◀————

I N THE SOVIET UNION in 1942, the Germans were on the offensive
in the Caucasus, and there was no end in sight to the siege of
Leningrad. On a cold morning in September, news of an even more disturbing event reached Laventia Beria, head of the People's Commissariat
for Internal Affairs, the NKVD.[1]

Watching his boss, Beria's senior assistant[2] correctly guessed Beria's
reaction to the classified cable he had just handed him. Beria's face went
from pink to dead white when he read the urgent message from his top
intelligence agent, a man who had penetrated British intelligence and even,
for a time, the staff of Hitler's Gestapo.

Beria's show of emotion was brief. In a moment, his face returned to
its normal pink. He rose and gestured to his assistant with a sweep of his
hand to clear the classified file from his desk.

Laventia Beria was a small man with no discernable neck. He had a
bald head and a large peasant's face on which his small nose and mean
mouth seemed out of place. He wore wire-rimmed glasses that did nothing to soften his dark eyes. His assistant had often watched those eyes
glint as Beria summoned teenage girls. At first, the small man would attempt to charm the young women, but if they did not yield quickly, he allowed his compulsion to rape overcome him. "Beria," the assistant later
wrote, "was more monster than man." Now, he disappeared into his private bathroom.

Through a mixture of ruthlessness and cunning, Beria had risen to a position at Stalin's right hand in charge of Soviet intelligence and Stalin's terror apparatus.

Beria's NKVD headquarters, the Lubyanka, was the center of terror in the Soviet Union. It was the repository for all the gossip on each and every Soviet citizen that was fed to the secret police by the Communist system of rats and snitches. The building also contained a prison with torture chambers, interrogation rooms, and dungeons where confessions were extracted from enemies of the state.

The Lubyanka was also the headquarters from which the NKVD pursued anti-Soviets living in exile—particularly the czarist White Russians and Ukrainians for whom Stalin nursed a special hatred. The destruction of these enemies had been the driving force behind NKVD activities before the war. Beria's henchmen had located thousands of these people, used their relatives to lure them back to the motherland, and then imprisoned or killed them. The war disrupted the bloody business of destroying them but did not stop it.

Stalin was determined to cleanse all disloyalty from his regime. He examined every political level of the revolution and ordered disinfection wherever he felt necessary. Beria, Stalin's fellow Georgian, was his willing instrument. In all the years the assistant had labored at the Lubyanka, he had never met a crueler man than Beria, who killed and tortured just to calm Stalin's fears.

But the NKVD chief was not the only monster in Moscow. The assistant knew only too well that he himself was just another cog in Stalin's killing machine. Not particularly courageous, the assistant had allowed old friends to be executed in order to enhance his own career. To be sure, he was not alone. No one lasted in the NKVD without betraying family, friends, or colleagues. Betrayal was the measure of trust. The joke at Moscow Center was that God had been eliminated so that no one in the NKVD would go to hell.

The assistant understood that his own and others' need to betray stemmed from Joseph Stalin's fears. He also understood that the Soviet leader had reason to be afraid. Even his so-called allies were against him: Before America got into the war, it was doing business with his German enemies, and the British had repeatedly tried to kill him and destroy his dream of a revolutionary workers' state. Furthermore, there were two and one-half million émigrés who had fled the country rather than submit to Stalin's rule, and Stalin feared that the West was exploiting these émigrés to undermine his government. Political opponents who remained inside the country only increased his rage and paranoia. The purges had started following Stalin's ascent to power and had now been going on for years.

By 1939, the cleansing had reached Beria's own secret police and intelligence organizations. Stalin's purging of the brilliant networks that the Revolution's Cheka intelligence service had built throughout Europe began with the execution of five capable Russian NKVD spies who were members of the Berlin Section of the "Red Orchestra" or Rote Kapelle[3]. At the very time Stalin was beginning diplomatic negotiations on a non-aggression pact with Hitler, Beria, on Stalin's orders, was ruthlessly eliminating virtually every secret Soviet operative in Germany. By the time Hitler and Stalin signed their nonaggression pact in August 1939, the Soviet Union was blind, deaf, and dumb to all intelligence from Germany. Stalin had recalled to Moscow and shot dead the very agents who could have warned him of Hitler's decision to invade Russia.

When the German invasion came in June 1941, Stalin was forced to make an alliance with Britain and the United States. His temporary need for the alliance did not blur his memory of the activities of Britain's greatest agent, Sidney George Reilley. The brilliant Secret Intelligence Service operative had cultivated relationships with the czarists and then penetrated the revolutionaries as a friend, while spying for His Majesty to kill Stalin and the other Soviet leaders and overthrow the Communist system. The United States and Britain, two countries that had most enthusiastically made common cause with the anti-Soviet émigrés, were now Stalin's only hope for survival.

Meanwhile, Stalin's short-lived alliance with Hitler had caused hundreds of the Soviet Union's foreign-born spies, who were largely motivated by idealism, to abandon Moscow in disillusionment. The price for the torture, purges, and executions was an extreme shortage of talented intelligence officers. Beria and Stalin had ruined what was once the world's greatest intelligence service, a legacy of Peter the Great.

To complicate matters, Stalin refused to allow Beria to recruit new intelligence agents from the families most loyal to his regime. The most promising candidates among the offspring of the *nomenklatura*—the elite caste that ran the military, the factories, the government, and the secret police—were protected from dangerous overseas assignments in order to promote their families' loyalty to Stalin.

It did not matter to Stalin that the ordinary Soviet people were exhibiting levels of courage unheard of in the annals of war. He would not transfer to the war effort the resources he was using to maintain his dictatorship over the nation.

All this was in the mind of Beria's assistant as he hurried to return the papers to the proper folders. He worked quickly, gathering up the files and organizing them for the car ride that was to follow. It was part of his daily routine.

Beria emerged from the toilet holding out his arms to be helped on with his coat. Every day it was the same. Beria never bothered drying his hands.

Stifling his repugnance at his boss's hygiene, the assistant walked behind Beria to the private elevator, and they descended to street level, where Beria's car was waiting. The assistant dared not speak to Beria in the halls of the Lubyanka: no one did unless Beria spoke first. There were plenty of security guards on duty, but neither Beria nor the assistant was under the illusion that they were there to protect Beria. Beria understood that the guards represented Stalin's ability to end his life at will. Like everything else at NKVD headquarters, the guards were there to protect Stalin, his family, and his friends.

An NKVD driver opened the car's rear door for Beria. Beria rode in the back seat alone, while the assistant rode up front with the driver. To the assistant, the fall colors on the trees seemed out of place in wartime Moscow. There was little traffic, and the black car made the short trip quickly. They entered the Kremlin gate and pulled into the parking area reserved for those cleared to see Marshal Stalin.

Two Red Army guards waited to escort Beria and the assistant. The assistant noticed that the guards were getting younger and younger as more and more men of military age were needed to fight the war.

Beria maintained his silence as they made their way through the halls of the Kremlin to the marshal's private wing. The assistant sensed something in Beria that he had never before detected in his brilliant and brutal boss: fear. It was the same fear he had seen in many once important men summoned to the Lubyanka, knowing they would never emerge alive. The assistant enjoyed Beria's discomfort. After all, it was Beria who had made fear the new religion of the soulless Soviet Union.

As they entered Stalin's suite, their escort stopped and remained outside. An efficient-looking young female Red Army officer rose from a desk and accompanied the two men in silence into the marshal's large office.

Stalin was on the telephone. The two men could hear enough of the conversation to deduce that the person on the other end was President Roosevelt's assistant, Harry Hopkins. The female officer escorted Beria and the assistant to a glass-covered conference table that abutted the marshal's desk. Tea glasses were in place for the daily meeting of the War Cabinet with Vyacheslav Molotov, Georgi Malenkov, and Kliment Voroshivov that was to follow this intelligence briefing.

As Stalin finished his phone conversation, the assistant noticed Beria staring at a photograph of Stalin and a general. The leather-framed picture was one of a dozen showing the marshal pinning medals onto protruding chests. This particular one showed Lieutenant General Andrei Andreyevich Vlasov, a member of the Red Army since 1919 and a survivor of Stalin's purges. As commander of the 20th Red Army, he had saved Moscow from the invading Germans in June 1941. After that unexpected victory, Stalin declared Vlasov a hero of the Soviet Union.

Then in June of 1942, the assistant recalled, Beria had brought Stalin the news that the Germans had captured Vlasov and much of his army at Volkhov. Now, as the Russian winter approached, Beria was bringing his patron even worse news about Vlasov.

Stalin hung up the telephone and looked up at Beria. As always, he ignored the assistant's presence.

"Roosevelt will train more pilots in Alaska," the Marshal announced. Beria could not stop staring at the picture. Stalin, ever suspicious, said, "You have news of Vlasov?"

Beria did not hesitate. Hesitation in presenting bad news could be fatal. "Our source in London reports, and the Americans have confirmed, that Vlasov signed a petition calling for members of the Soviet Red Army to surrender and form, under his leadership, a Russian Army of National Liberation."

The assistant expected a harsh reaction from Stalin. But he just listened. Beria went on to explain that this anti-Stalinist army was to be filled with exiled Russians, Ukrainians, and Georgians who, with Germany's help, hoped to reclaim Russia.

Stalin showed not a hint of emotion. He asked Beria about reports from the OSS—the United States' wartime intelligence service—about large-scale Red Army surrenders in recent weeks. Beria now realized that his report about Vlasov was not news to Stalin. Beria looked into Stalin's thick face and said: "Members of the Red Army surrendered by the tens of thousands to fight with Vlasov after he made it clear that his only use for the Germans was as a means to reclaim freedom for his own country from you."

Beria added that earlier in the month British intelligence reported the Germans had established a training facility called the Russian Leadership Center at Dabendorf. It was clear that Dabendorf would be used to train the counterrevolutionaries. By making Stalin's ouster an issue, the Germans hoped to win the support of the Russian people and thus undermine the Soviet government.

Stalin's demeanor changed abruptly. The Marshal, looking directly at the assistant, demanded the number of Vlasov's forces.

The assistant was prepared. "Marshal, General Vlasov has organized between 130,000 and 150,000 Russian troops into 176 battalions to fight us along the European front."

"The traitors will cost Moscow the war," Stalin said.

Beria attempted to reassure Stalin by saying that the Germans would never truly trust Vlasov: "They will suspect that he is on a mission for Moscow and that he and his men will turn on them. They will never use him or his men in a critical battle because of that fear."

Stalin seemed beyond anger. "Their reward from the Germans will be a German puppet state in Moscow. We know how good Hitler is at keeping his word."

Beria nodded and then spoke of his own failure: "Every attempt to penetrate the traitors fighting for Germany has failed. The few army or NKVD agents who have gotten into the partisan units in Germany are at so low a level that no worthwhile intelligence is coming back."

But he quickly offered a solution. "We have the perfect man to bore into Vlasov and his friend Reinhard Gehlen's operation." (Gehlen ran Germany's anti-Soviet intelligence effort.) The assistant already had his hand on the agent's file. But Stalin was uninterested in any details concerning the man who had been selected to infiltrate the traitor's army. Beria would not have to use the elaborate cover story he had prepared to hide the real background of the man he had chosen—a precaution he had taken because the man was Russian, and Georgian-born Stalin was so suspicious of Russians that he would never knowingly allow this agent to be sent on such an important mission.

That night, the assistant returned to his tiny apartment and prepared to repeat the dangerous procedure he had been undertaking every week for the past two years. The next morning, he awakened early to write his report in a simple letter code the Americans had taught him. On his way to work at the Lubyanka, he left the report in a hollowed-out rock at the base of a wall on a nearby street. The next day, as he walked to his bus stop, he noticed that a few fallen leaves had been cleared from in front of the drop site. This indicated that either the information had reached the Americans or the NKVD had found it, and he would soon die.

The information the assistant provided was handled on the American end by a small private intelligence operation set up for the sole purpose of making certain that what Stalin was telling FDR through Harry Hopkins had some basis in fact. President Roosevelt believed that the entire war effort depended on the Soviets defeating Germany. He had deep fears that the poor relationship between Stalin and Churchill could endanger that effort, and he did not trust reports passed to the United States by British intelligence. Using military attachés in the U.S. Embassy in Moscow as well as Americans with business covers there, FDR had established his own informal network to give him some assurances about Stalin. Beria approved the contacts but distanced himself from them to give himself deniability in case Stalin learned of them. What Beria's deniability meant for his personal assistant was that he was the one who would be shot if he were caught passing information.

The assistant's code of ethics allowed him only to report the contents of the morning briefing. He never passed on operational files or revealed the names of operatives. As the Americans realized, he was a patriot who passed on information because he believed it would help defeat Germany, not because he wished to undermine the Soviet system. Thus he never reported to the Americans the name of the man selected to penetrate Vlasov's army. Neither he nor anyone else had any idea of the titanic force that Beria was about to unleash on the West.

CHAPTER TWO

ENTER SASHA

———⟶●⟵———

THE SOVIET TRANSPORT PLANE flew high to evade German anti-aircraft fire. Standing at the jump door in the howling wind of late October 1943 was the young man Beria had personally approved to penetrate Vlasov's Army.[1] The plan was for the agent to be captured by the Germans, become a collaborator with Hitler's forces, and provide information of such value to the German General Staff that he would become a trusted German officer. In time, he would be in a position to send intelligence back to the NKVD.

It was an audacious plan with seemingly little chance of success. But Beria was willing to risk one of his most promising agents on this mission because of the danger posed by scores of anti-Communist Russian and other ethnic armies rising up against Stalin in the Soviet Union with Hitler's support and funding. Beria was also willing to take his time: The parachute jump took place more than a year after he had first suggested this mission to Stalin. Four previous attempts had been scrubbed because of mechanical problems or weather.

The man waiting to jump into the sky over Poland was known to his intelligence colleagues as Lieutenant Igor Grigoryevich Orlov. The NKVD had procured the name from a dead soldier from Kiev whose father, a Russian general, had been killed early in the war. Beria created the Orlov legend for his special spy because of Stalin's paranoia about "Great Russians." As a Georgian, Stalin was suspicious of any Russian who might have vestiges of loyalty to the czar or any element of Russian royalty.

Beria was a realist. Failed mission after failed mission using Ukrainian and Georgian agents convinced him that a non-Russian could not hope to fool the Germans or penetrate Vlasov's operations. Having a Georgian or a Ukrainian imitating a Great Russian had not worked. Since the Germans and the émigrés had uncovered and eliminated all the agents Beria had sent, Beria decided to risk deceiving Stalin and send an agent who was ethnically convincing.

"Lieutenant Orlov" was Beria's best chance for success. The real name of this darkly handsome agent was Aleksandr Ivanovich Navratilov. His natural aristocratic bearing was not an act he had learned at the NKVD or at the military school in Novosibirsk. Navratilov—known as Sasha, the Russian diminutive for Aleksandr—was directly, although distantly, descended from the Russian royal family. Sasha Navratilov was, in more senses than one, a "great" Russian. He eventually became the most effective agent to operate in the West since Peter the Great began dispatching agents at the end of the seventeenth century.

Sasha Navratilov was born in 1918—not 1922, as he told his classmates. He was an NKVD captain, working undercover in the NKVD as a fresh-faced lieutenant. The NKVD kept three files on him. Beria kept the one containing his real background in his personal, locked safe. A second file contained the records of Lieutenant Igor Orlov and was the file in the assistant's briefcase in September 1942 when Beria sought Stalin's approval for the mission. A third operational file was opened under the name Lieutenant Aleksandr Grigoryevich Kopatzky after this night's mission proved successful. The Kopatzky dossier eventually contained tens of thousands of pages, broken into many files. This dossier remained one of the Soviet Union's last great Cold War secrets.[2]

Sasha Navratilov earned Beria's trust through a ruthless action typical of the Stalin era. Sasha's father, Ivan Navratilov, was one of hundreds of loyal Communists who had worked their way up through the old Cheka, the NKVD's predecessor organization. Ivan had shown his loyalty to the state by his own brutality. He had a stellar secret police career. Then came Stalin's purges of the 1930s and Beria's control of the intelligence service.

The knock at the Navratilov's door came one midnight. Sasha, conveniently home on leave from the Red Army, let the security officers into the apartment. His father, Ivan, instantly understood the meaning of the visit. Midnight arrests were scenes of fear and horror that Beria's men repeated again and again all over the Soviet Union.

"Why are they here?"[3] Ivan's wife (Sasha's mother) asked as she watched her husband dress quickly.

"I don't know why," Ivan told her as he rushed to the small parlor where the men were waiting with his son.

When all three members of the family were present, the ranking NKVD officer spoke without hesitation and without emotion. His silent associate wrote down everything everyone in the room said.

"Comrade Ivan Navratilov, you will be taken to a reeducation center. . . ."

Anna Navratilov was a longtime party member and knew the rules. Angry, she asked, "Who denounced my husband?"

The senior man opened his orders, read them, and politely answered, "Comrade Aleksandr Navratilov provided evidence."

Both Anna and Ivan were breathless for a moment. They stared at their son. *Sasha* had betrayed them?

"Sasha?" Anna finally said.

Her son did not reply to her. He looked at his father. "You accused Marshal Stalin of being a traitor,"[4] he said.

His father said nothing.

Sasha and his father left with the NKVD men. At the Lubyanka prison, Sasha saw his father for the last time. Ivan Navratilov refused to denounce any colleagues even after he was sent to a labor camp.

The record shows he died in Siberia in 1940.

By betraying his father, Sasha earned his way onto the bottom rung of the NKVD ladder. A young man who would send his own father to Siberia offered Beria the sort of raw material he was looking for. The fact that in denouncing his father he also denounced an experienced Soviet intelligence officer made Sasha especially valuable. He was the ideal for Beria to point to as he and Stalin cleansed the old intelligence organs and replaced them with a new breed at the NKVD.

Sasha's cunning and his loyalty to Beria earned him an excellent military education. He already spoke passable English and strong Polish and German before he entered the NKVD.

He was the perfect NKVD con man. He was a consummate actor, possessed abundant charm and poise, and had proved he did not flinch at betrayal. A photograph taken in his late twenties shows a man with continental good looks, piercing blue eyes set in a finely chiseled face, a perfect nose, and thin lips. Although he was barely five-foot-three, his body was well proportioned and well muscled.

Sasha had a way with women, a talent respected by the insatiable Beria. He made a specialty in his work for the NKVD of recruiting the female relatives of exiled White Russians. Sasha's operational debriefings contain case after case where he charmed the daughter, sister, or wife of a suspected anti-revolutionary living in exile. As the affair proceeded, Sasha would gain the woman's confidence and find out where the exiled relative lived and who his associates were. Eventually, Sasha would "turn" the target and use her to lure the émigré home. If the woman would not cooperate, she was tortured or imprisoned until she did.

In some cases, Sasha convinced the women to denounce other family members and friends. Sasha was so effective that he turned some of these women into career NKVD operatives. To his colleagues in the NKVD, this ambitious and handsome young man with the soul of a sociopath seemed destined for big things.[5]

Meanwhile, by the fall of 1942, more than a dozen agents had died trying to penetrate the German military in various operations. Gradually from these failures, the Soviets learned how the Germans interrogated their prisoners. They used this knowledge to prepare Sasha for his mission.

As soon as Stalin gave his approval, Sasha's NKVD bosses pulled him from his domestic spying activities and gave him special physical and mental training. The aim was to turn him into a one-man counterrevolutionary wrecking crew.

His German, English, and Polish were constantly tweaked and improved. He exercised vigorously under the direction of a coach from the Bolshoi Ballet, until he was effectively a trained acrobat. His case officer brought him into a torture cell at the Lubyanka and selected the NKVD's toughest interrogators to simulate the sort of going over he might face during his mission. Sasha withstood the torture again and again.

Beria's men did everything possible to create a plausible background for Sasha that would withstand German intelligence's stiffest test. According to his file, more than a year before the mission, the NKVD repatriated his mother to Kiev to teach in an orphanage, the location and job that was held by the real Igor Orlov's mother.

On this cold October night in 1943, all of what had come before flashed through Sasha's mind as he waited for the order to jump. He patted his pocket to check again that his identity papers were there, confirming that he was Igor Orlov, born in Surozh in Bryansk Oblast in January 1923.

For Sasha, this mission held the balance for his future. If he succeeded, he would become an NKVD staff officer. If he failed, it really did not matter whether he was killed. He would probably die fighting the Germans anyway—just later, in another, less glorious engagement. Regardless of the outcome, his mother would finally understand he was a Soviet hero. She would receive a cable telling her that he was missing in action against the Germans. Before he left on his mission, he approved the wording of the cable announcing his valor.[6] Young Lieutenant Orlov carried into the dark sky that night the strong belief that Russian partisans fighting against the Soviet government had to be stopped. If they were not, he believed that socialism, weakened by the long war, would disappear from the Soviet Union. There is no greater threat to an enemy than a young man willing to die for his country. And that is exactly what Igor Orlov was.

The order from Moscow finally came over the plane's radio. As his case officer dutifully recorded, at the predetermined spot Orlov began the mission precisely as instructed. Using his sidearm, he shot into the backs of two dead bodies lying on the floor of the plane; the NKVD hoped that when the plane crashed the bullet-ridden bodies would bolster Orlov's believability to the Nazis as a defector to the anti-Soviet cause. Then the pilot looked through the cabin door and gave the signal. Orlov stepped from the airplane into the cold Polish sky. It was a high jump. As the noise from the plane's engines receded, Orlov saw that the protective cloud cover of earlier in the night was gone. He caught a glimpse of the moon and realized it lit up his big parachute like a searchlight. As he listened to the rustle of the parachute's silk against the wind, he feared the moonlight would make him a target for sharpshooters before he landed.

Orlov did not waste time worrying. Instead, he tried to memorize every second of the descent, because he knew he would be asked to recount every detail if he ever made it back to NKVD headquarters.[7]

The first sensation he felt was the cold—he had never been so cold as he was that night. A moment later he saw the pilot's parachute open. Then he saw flashes. A short space later, he heard gunfire, a strangely detached sound. The Germans were firing at both parachutes. Sasha lost sight of the pilot's chute.

Hanging from the silk, he was helpless to avoid the bullets he could hear but not see. He thought about using the poison capsule he had been issued, but quickly dismissed the thought. "I knew I would never commit suicide," he told the CIA years later. Instead, as trained, he detached himself emotionally. It was not easy, but he focused on the legend created for him. He later told the German authorities that he thought about his father while he descended: not the real father he had betrayed, but Orlov's father, a "Hero of the Soviet Union" and a Russian general, who had been shot from the sky early in the war by the Germans. The man jumping into the Polish night was aware of the irony of facing the same fate as his ersatz father. Then he thought about his own mother—would she be alone in Kiev?[8] His logical mind made him concentrate: *She teaches in an orphanage. After this war there will be many orphans. She will be very busy.* Later, Orlov recalled that he had steeled his emotions by simply willing himself to survive. He pretended the jump and the bullets were just another training exercise.

Orlov was so detached that he did not remember the first bullet hitting him in the leg, but he never forgot the pain of the second and third bullets tearing through his thigh and mid-torso. His parachute caught in a tree. With the physical training he had received, he was able to avoid being impaled by the branches, and he swung, dangling from the silk. A few moments later, he heard troops approaching, shouting in German.

Despite the pain and his blood pouring onto the snow, Orlov realized he had successfully completed the first step. If the Germans reached him before he bled to death, he had every confidence he would make it to the second. As he had done countless times in the past, he went over in his mind what he would say when he came face-to-face with his targets. Then he blacked out. As his captors approached, Orlov regained consciousness and greeted them in Russian-accented German: "I am a Russian intelligence officer and I am prepared to provide valuable information in exchange for immediate medical attention."[9] The lie was so ingrained in him that he embellished and improved upon it as he fell in and out of consciousness. He never asked to be treated according to the rules of the Geneva Convention.

After receiving medical attention, Orlov was visited by an SS interrogation team. He began by saying, "I am prepared to help General Vlasov free my country." The German captain in charge of his debriefing was unmoved, staring down at him without expression. A corporal took notes in precise shorthand. Orlov understood this was the key moment in his mission. "My father was a general. I had no need to risk my neck in that jump to get to Germany to fight."

"We assume you are here to spy," said the German captain, in Russian.

"You think so?" Orlov asked. "Then why would I be prepared to expose the NKVD agents in Vlasov's ranks—and in his liberation armies? I am prepared to cleanse these forces of NKVD trash."

By this point in the war, the SS were less skeptical than they might have been earlier. At the time, Hitler and Heinrich Himmler, the head of the SS, were engaged in one of their frequent debates about Hitler's hard-line view that Vlasov was really Stalin's agent and was just waiting for the right moment to turn his forces against Germany. Himmler, like Beria, had to deal with a paranoid head of state. He had gathered massive intelligence that proved Vlasov intended to destroy Stalin's government, but he could not get Hitler to accept it and unleash Vlasov's forces on the Russian front. Himmler's men had been told that any information concerning Vlasov's authenticity should be passed up the SS chain of command.

In the course of his interrogation, Igor Orlov said nothing about "killing" his air crew. If events went according to the NKVD's plan, the SS would find the wreckage and conclude that Orlov had killed the air crew before he jumped. The danger, of course, was if the pilot survived the crash, was captured, and cracked under hostile interrogation.

The Germans treated Orlov as a patient and a POW. It was obvious to him, however, that he was getting unusually good treatment and food. In January 1944, a captain working for German Military Intelligence's Special Soviet Unit began visiting Orlov in the hospital chaplain's office. The captain spoke fluent Russian and interrogated Orlov with quiet, precise expertise. His visits each lasted three to four hours, and went on for a week.

On a Sunday afternoon, the captain finally asked Orlov why he had killed the flight crew. Orlov asked if any of the crew survived. When the captain shook his head, Orlov answered carefully, "Because I was defecting,

trying to defect. The crew was trying to verify my orders. I was not authorized. They were contacting Moscow for instructions."

The captain smiled. As if on cue, the door to the office opened, and a
Wehrmacht general with large ears walked in. The senior officer had a
small tight mouth, a square chin, and dark eyes. From photographs he
had seen in Moscow, Orlov immediately recognized General Reinhard
Gehlen.

Gehlen was head of Branch 12 of Foreign Armies East, in charge of
all intelligence on the Soviet Union. Although he had held this post since
1942, Orlov's arrival was Gehlen's first major intelligence case. An aide
handed the general a box; he opened it and offered its contents to Orlov.
Orlov retrieved his sidearm. He understood the gesture meant the SS had
cleared him to work for German intelligence. Gehlen said in perfect Russian, "Lieutenant Orlov, we have a great deal to do, and you will have
ample opportunity to prove your claims."

CHAPTER THREE

HUMAN POKER

⊷

S ASHA'S PREPARATIONS PAID OFF. He succeeded in creating the persona of a Soviet intelligence officer so disillusioned with Communism that he was willing to commit murder to join Vlasov's Army. More tests lay ahead for Igor Orlov, but he had passed the first one.[1]

After spending several months recovering from his wounds in a military hospital in Bonn, Orlov began providing the Germans with counterintelligence assistance. To convince his SS captors and the untrusting Vlasov officer corps that he was genuine, Orlov employed an espionage technique the Russians had used starting with the Cheka spy organization in the early days of the Revolution. The NKVD, well aware that its previous missions had failed because the penetration agents were unconvincing and offered little to the Germans, authorized Orlov to give them legitimate information that betrayed real NKVD agents operating inside Germany. Some of these agents were idealistic German Communists the NKVD considered expendable. Others had escaped Beria's purge of the Red Orchestra but were so ineffective as agents that their loss would be of little consequence. Beria and his mission planners authorized the sacrifice of authentic NKVD agents to convince the Germans that Igor Orlov was real.

Before Sasha left Moscow, his NKVD case officer gave him the operational and personal files of NKVD agents operating in Germany. Sasha spent hours memorizing every detail about their families and personal weaknesses. Once he set to work in Germany, he used this information to maximum effect. According to Vlasov Army veterans, Orlov did not crudely blurt out the names of the agents he was betraying. Instead, he intimated to a unit commander that someone in his battalion was a possible traitor. Though Orlov already knew the identity of the man he was accusing, he created the illusion of a detective hunt by pretending to have only clues like a nickname, rank, or hometown and then working with the unit commander to tirelessly interrogate the unit's members. After weeks of this, Orlov and the Vlasov authorities together were able to "identify" the traitor. These subtle methods gave Orlov credibility among the partisans and allowed him to learn a great deal about the soldiers in each unit he targeted.[2] By the time he finished, Orlov had a complete dossier on the personnel in every Vlasov unit he encountered.

Orlov's use of this cunning and coldhearted approach on an unsuspecting NKVD agent named Akaki[3] is particularly telling. A low-ranking agent, Akaki was one of the many Georgians used by the NKVD to penetrate the White Russian forces. Because the White Russians held him in suspicion, he took months to get information, and what he finally got was marginal, according to his NKVD file. When Orlov approached Akaki, he asked an NKVD recognition question, "How do you feel about Russian vodka?"

"I prefer Polish," Akaki properly answered.

Turning on his abundant charm, Orlov then handed Akaki some letters from his home in Petrograd. Akaki was suitably impressed by Orlov's air of authority and surprised by his seeming personal concern. Orlov then began several days of debriefing Akaki. Orlov's Vlasov handlers gave him free rein to pursue his investigation.

Orlov told Akaki that he needed details of any weaknesses he had uncovered in his unit, to send back to Moscow Center. Akaki told Orlov the names of half a dozen Vlasov members he believed were spies or involved in illegal activity. After a few weeks, Akaki trusted Orlov to the point where he began to share intimate details about his family in Petrograd. He told Orlov of his father, a low-level bureaucrat with the Communist Party, and described how he had helped Akaki get his NKVD post.

After draining Akaki of all his personal and intelligence information, Orlov warned him that he had been under suspicion for some time. Orlov suggested that to make things look good, he needed to "sweat" Akaki. The Georgian was alarmed but was reassured when Orlov said that all he had to confess was some black-market smuggling. Orlov also urged him to name someone in the unit who might have tried to recruit him to work against Vlasov.

"But why?" Akaki asked.

"Because that is how you will be spared on the smuggling charge."

"But I *didn't* smuggle, Lieutenant."

"I'll give them the name after roughing you up," said Orlov.

Akaki was kept in a damp tent with only a bucket for sanitation. For three days, Orlov subjected him to hostile questions. Finally, thoroughly exhausted, Akaki broke down and signed a confession, believing he was admitting to smuggling. In fact, the document he signed was a confession that he was a spy for the Soviets. Orlov, in triumph, handed over the confession to high-ranking members of the Vlasov Army and announced that Akaki was an NKVD plant. The Germans allowed the Vlasov officers to execute Akaki immediately.

This case enhanced Orlov's credibility with both the Germans and Vlasov's officers and gave him broader scope to conduct his investigations. He began by suggesting to the Vlasov officers that Akaki might have been recruited into the NKVD from within the unit. Orlov subsequently reported to Moscow that he personally tortured two other men in the unit who admitted to supplying Akaki with information. However, this time Orlov "concluded" that they had done so innocently and exonerated them. Word quickly spread among the soldiers that Orlov was not a rat sent in by the Germans, but was fair and serious about protecting the Vlasov Army.

Not all his Vlasov colleagues trusted him, however. Georgi Lasnov, then an enlisted man in the Vlasov forces, was later interviewed by the NKVD[4] about Orlov. "He made three visits to our unit. . . . On the last visit two soldiers were taken away. . . . What happened to them, I don't know."

Nevertheless, the Vlasov officers were convinced that Orlov was a serious and effective counterespionage man and allowed him to travel freely among the units. He was tireless in interviewing troops and commanders—and incidentally learning the details of their operations for the NKVD. His timing was impeccable. Every few weeks, Orlov "uncovered" another NKVD agent, who was promptly tortured and shot or imprisoned. As he created his network, he worked higher and higher up the Vlasov command structure until he reached the pinnacle. From that time on, he was able to send back to Moscow detailed reports on what Vlasov and his top associates were doing.

Orlov also remembered to use his memorized list of Vlasov soldiers who still had families in the Soviet Union. Now when he approached these men, he made it clear to them that if they failed to cooperate, their families would be harmed. To Orlov, blackmail remained a powerful operational tool, just as it had been in his early days with the NKVD in Moscow. As he built dossiers on the Vlasov soldiers, he recruited the ones he deemed most trustworthy as couriers to carry information across the lines to his Soviet controllers.

Orlov never told these couriers, or his snitches within the units, that he was working for Moscow. The information he asked for was always supposed to help keep the Vlasov forces clean of NKVD penetrations. "That is the real danger of having a double agent who is involved in counterespionage and intelligence," a former chief of CIA counterintelligence explained. "If the guy guarding the chicken house is stealing the chickens, it is a very hard thing to figure out. It gave Orlov enormous freedom to operate."[5] In fact, debriefing reports show that no German counterintelligence officer ever suggested the possibility that the NKVD was sacrificing real agents just to establish Igor Orlov's bona fides. More than two dozen of his NKVD intelligence colleagues were executed because Orlov named them. To Igor, they were the poker chips that allowed him to play in a higher-stakes game: a chance to win General Gehlen's confidence.

In April 1944, just three months after he first met General Gehlen, Igor Orlov succeeded beyond his wildest dreams. Gehlen was so impressed by him that he brought Orlov into the planning of intelligence operations against the Soviets. Igor Orlov was now at the center of his enemy's intelligence staff. The German Army gave him a full commission as a lieutenant and paid him a special pension for the wounds he had suffered during the parachute drop. Orlov even convinced Gehlen and his staff that, because of his military and family background, he would be an excellent intermediary between the German General Staff and old friends of his father in Vlasov's Army. Gehlen agreed and approved Orlov for the appointment.

Thus, for the last year of the war, Orlov was a liaison officer between the Germans and Vlasov's Army.[6] His major intelligence accomplishment in this phase of his career was to undermine Gehlen's trust in the Vlasov forces. By reporting to Gehlen that the Soviets were planning to activate spies high up in Vlasov's ranks to betray Berlin, Orlov confirmed Hitler's paranoia and deterred Himmler and others from making full use of the Vlasov Army. In turn, Orlov was able to report to Moscow, using his Vlasov "scouts," that Hitler would never allow the Vlasov Army to be used for frontline operations.[7] This knowledge freed the Soviets to concentrate their resources elsewhere.[8]

On November 14, 1944, in a last-ditch effort to rally support, Vlasov's Committee for the Liberation of the Peoples of Russia (KONR) gathered in Prague with Igor Orlov among the five hundred delegates. From this meeting, Orlov collected enough intelligence on KONR personnel that the Red Army was able to hunt down its most important members.

In Moscow, as Beria and his team prepared for the war's end, they recognized the role that Orlov had played. It was in large part thanks to Orlov that the Germans never allowed Vlasov to operate in any theater that mattered. Orlov's mission for Beria delivered intelligence and exerted influence in the German high command on a level far beyond Moscow's expectations.

In January 1945, largely out of desperation, Heinrich Himmler finally decided to use Vlasov's Army more substantially against Stalin's forces. On February 10—three months before Germany surrendered—Vlasov was permitted to confront the Russians in a single large-scale battle in Czechoslovakia. The permission came too late either to save the Third Reich or to defeat the Soviets. Orlov learned of it in advance and reported to Moscow that Vlasov's operations would soon be concentrated inside Czechoslovakia. Vlasov's fate was sealed.

Facing defeat, a handful of Vlasov's generals fled across Russian lines to Bavaria to surrender to the Americans, but Vlasov himself did not surrender. On May 11, on a road west of Hanover, Stalin's forces captured him along with a half-dozen members of his command. Vlasov and his officers underwent a brutal interrogation at NKVD headquarters in Moscow and were then put on trial. A military tribunal of the Soviet Supreme Court found them guilty of "treason, espionage, and terrorist activities against the USSR as agents of the German espionage service." Vlasov, along with Generals Malyshkin, Zhilenkhov, Trukin, and seven lower-ranking generals, was sentenced to death on August 12, 1945. Meanwhile, in the Yalta treaty with Stalin, Roosevelt and Churchill agreed to repatriate all Russian POWs to the Soviets, including those who had fought in the counterrevolution. The British and Americans kept this agreement through "OPERATION KEELHAUL," sending tens of thousands of anti-Soviet Russians to be executed or imprisoned in "rehabilitation and reeducation" camps.

The Vlasov executions did not dampen the fervor of anti-Soviet forces still fighting fiercely in southwestern Ukraine and eastern Poland after Germany's surrender. Operating with former German SS officers, these ragtag units attacked the Soviet Army throughout the "liberated" regions of Eastern Europe. For the next two years, they fought the Soviets at every opportunity. In addition, armies of liberation were forming in other Soviet-dominated areas, including the Balkans. The war had unleashed opposition to Communism that had been successfully controlled since the Russian Revolution in 1917. Stalin's deepest fear that the Soviet Union could split apart from within seemed very real in the aftermath of a war the Soviet Union had paid heavily in human lives to win.

A CRUCIAL PLAYER on the postwar intelligence scene in Europe was the Nazi general, Reinhard Gehlen. More than a year before the war's end, Gehlen had begun preparing himself for Germany's defeat.[9] The dedicated Nazi was able to reinvent himself as a senior officer with anti-Nazi credentials. Gehlen knew that if he and his men fell into Soviet hands, they would be executed for their roles as patrons of Vlasov's Army. He also foresaw that the United States would be facing a voracious Stalin waiting for his rewards and retributions for defeating Germany. Gehlen recognized that his experience against the Soviets was worth huge currency to the West in the postwar world. He began playing high-stakes poker.

On April 28, 1945, he put into operation a plan to offer his best intelligence officers, his vast collection of documents, and his knowledge of the Soviet Union to the United States. Gehlen buried three complete sets of documents in separate locations near Mount Wendelstein.[10] Of all the information that Gehlen had compiled during the war, none was more important than his files on Soviet agents who had switched sides.

Gehlen successfully got a message to America's wartime intelligence service, the Office of Strategic Services (OSS), in London. (British intelligence, MI6, thwarted by a new postwar government, had decided to let the United States take the lead on anti-Soviet operations.) Allen W. Dulles, second in command of the OSS, sent a young colleague, Frank Gardiner Wisner, to accept the surrender of Gehlen and several hundred of his officers and their families.

Through Wisner, Gehlen convinced Dulles that the United States must provide protection for thousands of high-ranking Nazis who would otherwise fall under Soviet control. "Nothing was more important than the recruitment of these Nazis who had escaped all over Europe," said Robert T. Crowley, who played a significant role in managing the Nazis for the United States. "You have to remember they were considered the ultimate anti-Communists."[11]

Gehlen signed an agreement with the Americans that turned his organization into a U.S.-controlled intelligence asset. Years later, in 1956, it became the intelligence service for the new West German government. This partnership between the ex-Nazis and the OSS/CIA dominated U.S. activity against the Soviet bloc for the next three decades.

Gehlen convinced his new American masters that the surviving refugees from Vlasov's Army and other anti-Soviet agents had the greatest motivation to see the Soviet Union defeated. The Americans accepted his assessment and asked Gehlen to put together a list of Russians in displaced persons camps who should be recruited. Igor Orlov's name appeared at the top of Gehlen's list. Before the last shot had been fired against Germany, the U.S. Army Counterintelligence Corps was scouring the camps searching for Igor Orlov.[12]

Meanwhile, as the Soviets moved toward Berlin in the last days of the war, Orlov's NKVD supervisors summoned him to a location east of the city. It was his first direct meeting with his bosses in two years. After being escorted through the Soviet lines, Orlov learned just how important his work had been to Moscow. The NKVD colonel addressed him as "Lieutenant Colonel Orlov."[13]

The NKVD colonel shared news from headquarters and told Orlov of colleagues and friends killed in the war. Orlov was not a sentimental man, but at that historic moment, he was ready to return to Moscow and share in the victory. Instead, the NKVD colonel supplied him with new identity papers and gave him new orders. Impatient, Orlov asked why he could not return home to a job at headquarters.

"There is a new enemy," the colonel replied.

"Who is the target? Orlov asked.

"The Americans," the colonel answered.

CHAPTER FOUR

THE AMERICANS

———◆———

B Y LATE 1944, the men in charge of American intelligence operations were coming to the same conclusion as Igor Orlov's NKVD
colonel: The alliance between the United States and the Soviet Union,
based only on a common wartime enemy, was bound to break up.

The two men at the top of the OSS, "Wild Bill" Donovan and Allen
W. Dulles, were convinced that Stalin was planning to insulate the Soviet
Union with a cordon of puppet states that would prevent direct military
attacks on his country.

For his part, Stalin had never trusted his alliance partners, especially
the men who ran the intelligence services. Donovan and Dulles were both
Wall Street lawyers, and Dulles's law firm, Sullivan and Cromwell, had
enjoyed extensive business dealings with numerous German companies
and banks that had supported the Third Reich. Dulles himself had
brought much of that business into the firm.[1] Stalin's fears that the United
States would exploit anti-Soviet émigrés after the war were based, in part,
on the backgrounds of the men who ran the United States' intelligence
services. The OSS's decision to embrace Gehlen was a clear signal to
Stalin that, on this point at least, he was right.

Dulles and Donovan did not have the clear support of President
Roosevelt for their Gehlen operation. There was broad division within
the Administration over what to do about postwar Germany. Secretary of

the Treasury Henry J. Morgenthau proposed a drastic plan to reduce Germany to a rural economy without any major industry, thus preventing a German resurgence and also punishing German industrialists for using slave labor and participating in crimes against humanity. Others, like Dulles and Donovan, wanted to turn Germany into an anti-Communist bulwark. Dulles and Donovan wanted to exploit leading Nazis and incorporate them into postwar U.S. intelligence operations. Roosevelt inclined toward Morgenthau's view of an agrarian state. He understood the scale of the Soviet sacrifice to defeat Germany and believed that the Soviets would never accept anything less than a neutered Germany. While President Roosevelt was convinced that the Soviets had expansionist aims, he also understood that Stalin was extremely sensitive about the fact that he was not being treated as a full partner among the Allies. In long tirades directed at FDR aide Harry Hopkins, Stalin openly blamed Churchill for his status as a junior partner among the Big Three. [2]

Dulles and Donovan's concerns about the Soviets were based on the work of America's first Cold War covert operator, Frank G. Wisner, the man who accepted General Gehlen's surrender. Wisner was a seemingly easygoing man with a steel-trap mind. He would have a profound effect on U.S.–Soviet relations.

Like Dulles and Donovan, Wisner was a Wall Street lawyer, working before the war at Carter, Ledyard and Milburn, Franklin Roosevelt's old firm. Although he had a keen legal mind, Wisner, a Southerner, always felt like an outsider in New York society. He did well enough financially (in later years, he was so unconcerned about money that his paychecks languished in his desk drawer for a year or more), but, operating in an old-money atmosphere among Harvard and Yale men, Wisner felt he would never be admitted to the old boys club no matter how brilliant his work. When the war came, Wisner joined the U.S. Navy and became a censor. Eventually, in 1943, he got into the OSS and was assigned to Cairo Base as a reports officer. In less than a year, he turned Cairo's loosely run operation into a top intelligence center. In 1944, the OSS reassigned him to Istanbul, where he took over for an OSS base chief who, to say the least, paid little attention to security.

Wisner traveled to Turkey, taking great pains to remain undercover. The base chief he was replacing, Lanning "Packy" MacFarland, shocked Wisner by greeting him at the Istanbul train station with a brass band.

The clueless MacFarland invited Wisner to meet him at a hotel ballroom later that same night. When Wisner entered the ballroom, he saw the base chief standing on the stage under a spotlight in front of a full orchestra, singing the tune, "Boop boop . . . baby, I am a spy."[3]

Wisner soon learned that security problems in Istanbul were not limited to the base chief's odd sense of humor. The entire OSS spy ring operating in the Balkans was thoroughly penetrated by German intelligence. Under the most difficult circumstances, Wisner successfully built a new spy network. He had found his calling. On August 26, 1944, he cabled the OSS in Cairo that he was prepared to penetrate Bucharest, Romania. For two months, Wisner and his men outsmarted the Soviets and pre-empted the Germans in the Balkans. Working with Marshall Tito, Wisner helped arrange the release of eighteen hundred Allied airmen in POW camps throughout the area. Wisner's reports about Soviet behavior in the Balkans provided the first hard evidence that Stalin was using his forces to expand the Soviet sphere of influence. Wisner helped reinstall Romania's King Michael in power as the Nazi puppet regime fled.

In March 1945, Wisner left the Balkans, believing that the United States would press the Soviets to stop devouring the region. But while the U.S. stood by, Stalin ordered the brutal removal of eighty thousand Romanians to the Soviet Union on open boxcars to work as slave labor. Wisner was shocked at the brazenness of Stalin's self-awarded human war reparation. He became passionately involved in trying to get the Roosevelt Administration to save King Michael's regime. He even used FDR's stamp-collecting hobby as an excuse to make a personal written appeal to the President. Through Donovan, Wisner sent Roosevelt a collection of Romanian stamps courtesy of King Michael. Roosevelt's health was deteriorating, and there was no response to Wisner's effort.

Wisner seemed, to colleagues at the OSS, to be tired and suffering great stress over the Soviet tactics he had witnessed in the Balkans. "He was in a state of anger that seemed to go beyond the normal frustrations of his job," James Angleton later said. "What Frank witnessed out there made him a vehement anti-Communist. It really affected him." What Angleton was seeing in his OSS colleague manifested itself later as clinical depression. Wisner's mental illness would cast a shadow over his life and career. His intelligence and Southern charm mitigated in the eyes of his colleagues his willingness to exceed orders and circumvent authority in

his passion for his cause. Had his personality had a harder edge, his illness might have drawn attention earlier. Instead, Wisner was admired as a
man whose passions were inflamed by the experience of going up against
the Soviets. Dulles and Donovan believed Wisner to be supremely competent and ignored his outbursts and tantrums.

Wisner became the flawed prism through which the Americans saw
the ambitions of the postwar Soviet Union. The old boys finally anointed
Wisner a member of their club because his views about the Soviets fit
their agenda. Wisner may not have realized it, but the establishment he
had so resented when he was on Wall Street was using him again. This
time, his experiences in the Balkans were used to sell the Congress and
the President on a new civilian intelligence service.

Wisner was awarded the Legion of Merit for his work in the Balkans.
He became a top aide to Dulles as the Allies moved successfully into Germany. After arranging the surrender of Gehlen and his men, Wisner traveled throughout postwar Europe using the remnants of Gehlen's operations
to set up a stopgap intelligence network for the United States. Wisner's recruits for the new organization in Poland, Czechoslovakia, and Germany
were former SS officers on the run.

Thus the United States, through men like Donovan, Dulles, and Wisner, allied itself with the defeated Nazis in its campaign against the new
enemy, the Soviet Union. This alliance was the first of three fatal weaknesses in American postwar intelligence that the Soviet Union exploited.
No matter how brutal the Nazi regime, no matter how much slave labor
their society had used and destroyed, the American authorities were willing to recruit any useful Nazi. The Army, the OSS, and every other U.S.
agency committed to fighting the Soviets began finding these Nazis at the
various postwar tribunals and spiriting them to safety at sites inside and
outside Germany.

The second weakness of Wisner and his colleagues was paper. They
believed that large quantities of written reports proved that hard intelligence was being collected, and valuable activity was taking place. Wisner's reports became the templates a successful intelligence officer
followed. In just a few months after the war, he and his team produced
thousands of pages of "intelligence." Dulles promoted his agents and case
officers based on the number of reports they submitted. According to the
late William R. Corson, who worked with Dulles and Wisner, "No single

practice Wisner implemented in the U.S. intelligence community caused more damage. He created an atmosphere that would haunt us throughout the Cold War and burn us again and again. In the end, when all the intelligence was examined and digested, 99 percent of it was paste. People died because we acted on it."[4]

This was worse than wasted effort. The priority that Donovan and Dulles placed on any information at all about the Soviets gave the NKVD an opportunity to steer U.S. intelligence in the direction they wanted. Throughout Europe, the NKVD developed paper mills filled with double agents feeding massive amounts of false information to the new American intelligence establishment. The reports sent back by Wisner's staff contained a great deal of this false, NKVD-produced material.

The third weakness was a repeat of an OSS failing during the war: a lack of counterintelligence. Even OPERATION PAPERCLIP, the OSS's effort to find and recruit "useful" Nazis, did not take the time to investigate whether a particular Nazi's life had been spared by the Soviets because he had agreed to act as a double agent for them.

While the Roosevelt Administration continued to debate the fate of postwar Germany, Donovan and Dulles secretly threw in America's lot with the worst of the Third Reich. America was actively recruiting Nazis—not simply scientists, but high-level military and civilian officials of the Hitler regime. The American Army even recruited and evacuated the head of the Gestapo, Heinrich Mueller. To prevent later accusations that the United States government was employing the notorious Mueller, the Americans used Gehlen's organization to finance his work.[5] Gehlen and his men spent 10 months at an Army base outside Washington, D.C., laying the groundwork for what was to come.

Through Gehlen's organization, U.S. taxpayers paid the salaries of thousands of Gestapo, Wehrmacht, and SS officers. Among the hard-line Nazis in Gehlen's senior management was Holocaust organizer Alois Brunner, Adolf Eichmann's top assistant.[6] "We knew what we were doing," James Angleton recalled. "We did it because Gehlen was a shortcut to intelligence wherever the Nazis had a puppet government."

James Critchfield, the Army officer who worked with Gehlen, told colleagues at a fiftieth anniversary conference celebrating the founding of the CIA: "What we had, essentially, was an agreement to exploit each other, each in his own national interest."

Aside from the moral blindness it showed, this choice set up the new American intelligence service for decades of failure. "Our dependence on Gehlen made us sitting ducks for disinformation," said former Covert Operations Executive Robert T. Crowley. "The more paranoia he could foster among U.S. officials, the more dollars and power for himself. Gehlen, to a certain extent, told us what we wanted to hear. In the process, we let his group become the lifeline for escaped Nazis."

"Because these Nazis were already behind the Iron Curtain, in some cases secretly working in governments Moscow controlled, our efforts to recruit them and get them out were fraught with problems," Angleton admitted. "The biggest difficulty was that we had no way of knowing if they had been revealed to Moscow and forced to work for Soviet intelligence."

MEANWHILE, THE RED SCARE was spreading at home. A new generation of politicians was taking over Congressman Martin Dies's 1930s crusade against the Red Menace. An aging General Ralph Van Deman, who had spent his entire career hunting down American Communists, shared his secret files with politicians he trusted. The result: Americans turned on each other in fear and anger at home, even as Communism advanced around the world.

Despite anti-Red sentiments, counterintelligence did not play a serious role in America's postwar intelligence plans. Almost as soon as the war was over, the United States disbanded much of its wartime intelligence infrastructure. Many agents who had served with distinction in the OSS and in military intelligence returned home and resumed their prewar lives.

For those left in the American intelligence community, the battle centered on what kinds of resources they would have and who would control them. As early as 1944, Donovan and Dulles divided their efforts between defeating the Nazis and trying to convince President Roosevelt to continue the Office of Strategic Services after the war as a civilian spy service. Yet by that time, the OSS was coping with a seemingly endless series of compromises and penetrations. For one thing, Dulles's top industrial source inside the Third Reich had to be quickly removed from Germany when his name appeared in OSS message traffic. This kind of mistake reinforced FDR's doubts about continuing the intelligence service in peacetime. Donovan lobbied President Roosevelt with dire predictions about the Soviets' bad intentions. In reply, Roosevelt, knowing the OSS's own problems with double agents and penetrations, kidded Donovan about "his leaky umbrella of a spy service" and asked for more convincing evidence.

Matters did not improve for Donovan and Dulles after Roosevelt died and Harry Truman became president. Truman was not sympathetic toward the idea of a powerful intelligence service with the capability of conducting covert operations. He also had great reservations about American corporate influence on the wartime intelligence effort. He was very suspicious of the Wall Street businessmen who had dominated the OSS and treated their concerns less seriously than he might have. Despite a massive lobbying effort by former OSS officials, President Truman rejected the notion that the OSS and its fourteen thousand employees should immediately take the lead against the growing Soviet threat. On September 20, 1945, he ordered the OSS disbanded. For Donovan and Dulles, it was a brutal blow.

CHAPTER FIVE

THE COUSINS

━━━━◆━━━━

FOR ALL HIS CULTIVATED English manners and affectations, James Angleton, who would become the dominant force in U.S. counterintelligence, was, in reality, a son of the American West. His father, James Hugh Angleton, called Hugh, was a strapping outdoorsman from Illinois and part Apache. Hugh had served in the U.S. Army under General John J. "Black Jack" Pershing and fought with him to defeat Pancho Villa in the Mexican border wars early in the twentieth century. It was in Mexico that Hugh Angleton met Carmen Moreno, who became his wife. She was breathtakingly beautiful.

The couple moved to Boise, Idaho, where, now a civilian, Hugh became a salesman for the National Cash Register Company, and lugged the heavy machines on muleback from town to town making sales. The Angletons' son, James, was born on December 9, 1917. Carmen Angleton, a devout Catholic, gave him the middle name Jesus.

Young Jim Angleton loved the outdoors, especially fishing and hunting with his father, a life that changed when he came down with tuberculosis at age 12. His family moved to Arizona to help him recover. There, his father taught him to be an expert fly fisherman. When he was too sick to fish, he spent hours learning to tie flies. The patience he developed making lures for fish and learning how to fool fish played a major role in forming his character and his talent for espionage. In Arizona, he also experienced bigotry for the first time when he was teased about being half

Mexican. Jim hated the desert and welcomed the family's move to Italy in 1933, when he was 16 years old.

Hugh, stuck in a dead-end sales job at NCR, went to Italy to see why the company was doing so poorly there in the booming Fascist economy. In hopes that he could turn the Italian franchise around, he made a deal to buy it. He did not tell his family that if he failed, he would lose his investment and his job. His franchise was successful, and by the late 1930s, Hugh had cultivated a warm relationship with the Fascists who were running Italy. Hugh hoped Jim would join him at NCR after he completed his education.

To prepare himself for college in the United States, Jim was attending a series of schools in England, and the experience had a profound effect on him. "I became English," Angleton recalled. "I even spoke with an accent when I returned home." After graduating from Malvern College in England, he went to Yale in 1937.

Friends from Yale recall that Angleton seemed embarrassed by his Mexican background, and this was why he cultivated an English sensibility. Actually, at just over six feet tall and painfully thin, he looked English.

Even Angleton admitted that he spent his life recreating himself to disguise his personal history. "In some ways I tried to make up for my shortcomings by being someone else," he said. "I borrowed from the way other people lived their lives so that I could fit in. I designed myself like an architect might design a house. I was a self-creation. I pretended to be more important, more interesting, and more mysterious than I ever really was."

Angleton was a terrible student in most subjects except for poetry, which began to fascinate him in England. In 1938 he convinced the controversial Fascist poet Ezra Pound, an acquaintance of the family in Italy, to come to Yale for a visit.[1] The poet later spoke of young Angleton as a literary genius. "Something that was wildly overblown," Angleton said. "I never knew as much about literary subjects as I was credited with knowing." It did not matter. The legend of Angleton as a great man of letters had started.

After Angleton graduated from Yale in 1941, he entered Harvard Law School where he met the socially connected Cicely d'Autremont, then a pretty 19-year-old Vassar student from Minnesota. "We were absolutely madly in love almost from our first date," she recalls. "He was a completely enthralling and romantic man."[2] Hugh Angleton opposed their marriage on the supposed grounds that Jim had no job and no way to support a wife. Years later, Jim Angleton said that his father believed "we were just not suited for each other." Jim defied his father and married Cicely in 1943, a few weeks after the U.S. Army drafted him.

His father, with his army background, was already a colonel in the OSS in Italy and "pulled strings to get me out of the regular Army and into the OSS. He thought the war would not last long, and I could go into business with him after the war," Angleton said. That didn't happen. By the time the war ended, Jim Angleton had become totally devoted to the craft of counterintelligence.

The OSS routinely sent its most promising recruits to England for training by the topflight officers of British Secret Intelligence Service (SIS), better known as MI6 (Military Intelligence, Department 6). From the beginning, the Americans consciously patterned their intelligence service on their British "cousins." This pattern would haunt the Americans: The OSS and its peacetime successor, the CIA, demonstrated the same strengths—and weaknesses—as the older MI6.

In London, the men of the OSS enjoyed the company of the legendary MI6 Officer Harold "Kim" Philby. Like Igor Orlov, Kim Philby was an actor. Like Orlov, he skillfully used his ability to play whatever role furthered his objectives. The human toll of his actions on friends, family, and colleagues was never a factor to him. His only concern was accomplishing the mission.

Philby was born in Ambala, India, in 1912. His eccentric civil servant father nicknamed him Kim after the character in a Kipling novel about intrigue in colonial India. After graduating from Trinity College, Cambridge, Philby toured Austria and Germany, where he observed firsthand the persecution of the Jews. He was in Germany in 1932, when Hitler and a number of his fellow Nazis were elected to the Reichstage. When Philby returned to England, he had physical scars from fighting alongside German Communists against the Nazi Brownshirts. His friends welcomed him like a conquering hero as he told stories of being beaten by Nazis.

Philby was a pragmatic idealist. Already impressed by the arguments for Communism he heard at Cambridge in the late 1920s, he became angry at the British of his own class, because so many of them had climbed into bed with the Fascists for their personal gain. "To understand Kim," Angleton said, "you need to know that under his charm and intelligence was a resentment toward the British upper class that produced a passion for reform."

Back in England, Philby became a reporter and discovered that journalism provided the perfect outlet for his passions. His first big assignment was the Spanish Civil War. Using a cover called the Anglo-German Fellowship, Philby, along with Guy Burgess, a friend from Cambridge, penetrated Fascist organizations in England that were raising money to support General Franco. Flags with swastikas were openly displayed at the groups' functions. Privately, Philby was sickened by what he saw. Publicly, he worked to cultivate Nazis and Fascists and eventually became one of the few reporters with direct access to General Franco. Franco allowed Philby to travel with his forces throughout Spain. On this tour, Philby discovered members of the Republican opposition to Franco who actually were traitors to the Republican cause.

When the opposition collapsed in 1939, Philby was sent to Germany as a correspondent for the *Times* of London. His Fascist cover worked perfectly to get him access to the Third Reich. When the war broke out, the British Army sent Philby to France with its expeditionary force, where he enjoyed total access to the British commanders.

When the Nazis overran France, and the British retreated across the Channel, Philby reconnected with Cambridge chum Michael Straight, now working in MI6. Philby agreed to join the intelligence service. He was assigned to deal directly with the Soviets on Allied spying operations against the Nazis, run through Switzerland. Using a ring set up by the brilliant Soviet spy, Sandor Rado, Philby got remarkable intelligence concerning German military secrets. His work against the Abwehr (German intelligence) so enhanced his reputation with the British government that in 1942 when he returned to London, he became the unofficial liaison to the OSS.

This was where he first met and entertained the founding fathers of American intelligence, Wild Bill Donovan, the head of the OSS, and Allen Dulles and Richard McGarah Helms, both future CIA directors. These men were all Anglophiles, who admired Philby for his wit and social standing.

Soon, the younger members of the OSS were coming to Philby's offices on Ryder Street to study at his feet as if he were a great philosopher. "He had taken the Nazis and Fascists head-on and penetrated their operations in Spain and Germany. His sophistication and experience appealed to us," Angleton recalled.[3] Philby's cluttered office was a floor below the OSS office in a building in London's West End. The American "cousins" learned from Philby how to conduct interrogations, how to work with their Soviet allies, where to get hand-tailored uniforms, and how to behave like British gentlemen.

There was one American who stood out to Philby: the 26-year-old James Jesus Angleton. Angleton's personality—quiet and a little sad—appealed to Philby. More important, when they first met, Angleton questioned Philby about the British class system. Philby decided that Angleton was the only non-pretender of the bunch.[4] He later wrote that Angleton "had earned my respect by openly rejecting the Anglomania that disfigured the young face of OSO (the CIA's Office of Special Operations)."

Angleton, in turn, admired Philby's anti-Nazi operations and believed that Philby was a British patriot with a social conscience. Angleton said that he came to look upon Philby as almost an older brother. [5]

Philby took the young American under his wing and began to teach him everything he knew about counterintelligence—everything, that is, except its most basic precept: *Trust no one*. This training turned James Angleton into one of the greatest, and most deeply flawed, intelligence officers of the twentieth century.

Because of Jim Angleton's background, his father's contacts, and his knowledge of the culture and language, the OSS sent him to Italy for his first assignment, which was in counterintelligence (X-2). Angleton used his father's old business connections to tap into and aid the underground network smuggling Jews out of Europe into Palestine.[6] Through this network, Angleton got firsthand reports on the Holocaust. He repeatedly passed these along to his OSS superiors, but Allen Dulles's Bern Station stopped them from reaching Washington. "I came to the conclusion that Washington did not want to officially know because Roosevelt wasn't in a position to help," Angleton said.[7]

Involved in this human smuggling network were some of the bravest men and women of the war, and Angleton was profoundly affected by their courage. These were the men and women who, after the war, founded Israel, and the personal relationships he developed with them molded his whole career. [8]

In early August of 1945, with the war in Europe ended, the head of MI6, Sir Stewart Menzies, summoned Kim Philby to discuss a very important matter. Konstantin Volkov, an NKVD officer based in Istanbul, had told British agents that he wanted to defect. Volkov was prepared to name two Soviet spies in the British Foreign Office as well as a Soviet spy in MI6 counterintelligence. Philby, now chief of MI6's Soviet Section, fearing exposure by Volkov, decided to handle the case himself. He convinced Menzies to send him to Istanbul to retrieve Volkov. He delayed his arrival in Istanbul after warning the NKVD of the potential danger to his own security. Philby did not go directly to Istanbul. Instead, he made several stops along the way. He was in Cairo when the Soviets arrested Volkov and returned him to Moscow, where he was later shot.

Philby continued on to Istanbul and gathered the information he needed to write the damage assessment on the case. In that report, Philby got a British embassy official in Ankara to admit that he had indiscreetly used Volkov's true name on an open phone line. Philby successfully blamed the loss of the agent on that incident.[9]

On his way back from Istanbul, Philby decided to visit James Angleton in Rome. The Communists found fertile ground in Italy immediately after the war, and Angleton had agreed to remain there to operate against them. After Mussolini's defeat, he assumed responsibility for all counter-intelligence operations in Italy, which included running X-2 networks throughout southern Europe.

At the OSS office on the Via Archimedes, Angleton confided in his old friend about a personal problem: the effect his work was having on his marriage. As Angleton later put it, "I left Cicely at home with our first child to do this work. I felt guilty about it. So he helped me think things through."

Cicely and Jim Angleton appeared to families and friends to be very much in love. But "once I met Philby, the world of intelligence that had once interested me consumed me. The home life that had seemed so important faded in importance," Angleton admitted. Angleton nearly ignored the birth of his son, James. He wrote faithfully to Cicely, but he did not come home. Cicely decided that their marriage was "no longer viable," although she continued it anyway.

Unlike Wisner and Dulles, Angleton did not find joy in his work. He never took a moment out to celebrate the victory in the war or his Legion of Merit for his work in Italy. "I had this ability to see dangers that others ignored. Some people called this a phobia. Maybe I just have seen too much," Angleton said. Plagued with insomnia ever since his days at Yale, he was sleeping but a few hours a night and worrying. He told whoever would listen that the Soviets would try to devour the West.

At the close of the war, Churchill used Kim Philby to monitor the Soviets' increasingly suspicious activities. Churchill also approved Philby's suggestion to create a new division of MI6 called "Section 5," a unit to monitor Soviet activity against Great Britain and the United States. Philby used his new role to get to know high-ranking Soviet officials.

During the first postwar year, Philby's work for Churchill entailed frequent trips to the Continent, including regular visits to Angleton. Philby loved Rome, and Angleton offered the kind of company he enjoyed. Philby teased Angleton about naming his cultivated intelligence agents after plant life (Fig, Rose, Tomato, etc.). The two men shared a passionate interest in a Jewish state, which MI6 opposed. Philby helped Angleton penetrate and work against the Communist Party in Italy, an effort that became a pattern for operating against the Soviets through surrogate political parties around the world.

"Looking back on it, Kim taught me a great deal," Angleton said later. "He taught me never to assume anything; nail it down."[10] Philby taught Angleton well. Angleton's reputation for catching and exposing Axis spies made him a star in the OSS. His work with Jews, encouraged by Philby, created for him a world of new connections and sources throughout Europe and the Middle East.

Angleton later came to believe that Philby wanted him to succeed and get to the highest possible level of American intelligence because it suited his own career. Robert T. Crowley, a friend and colleague of Angleton's, had a far different view: "I think that Philby thought he had found a political soul mate in Jim. . . . Philby liked Jim for his idealism and intellect, but he did not understand that Jim was so fundamentally American."

CHAPTER SIX

THE BATTLE TO CONTROL AMERICAN INTELLIGENCE

W HEN WILD BILL DONOVAN and Allen Dulles lobbied President Roosevelt on behalf of a postwar civilian spy service, they assumed that they would be in charge of it. J. Edgar Hoover, the legendary head of the Federal Bureau of Investigation, had other ideas. Hoover hated the OSS, and he believed the FBI's wartime success in breaking Nazi spy rings in the United States and Latin America put the Bureau in a perfect position to expand into a new worldwide role.

However, in 1945, Hoover had a political mess on his hands. Communist spy rings seemed to be operating at will in the United States, sending government secrets to the Soviet Union. The all-powerful FBI seemed helpless to stop them. Four years earlier, Hoover had ignored important evidence that the Soviet Union was operating against the United States on a major scale.[1] Now he had to make up for lost time. Luckily for Hoover, he had an agent who seemed up to the job: William King Harvey.

Bill Harvey was one of three agents in the FBI's newly created Security Division. The picture in his FBI file shows a rotund version of John Barrymore. Unfortunately, Harvey and Barrymore shared more than a physical resemblance. Like the famous actor, Harvey was a philanderer and a heavy drinker. He also fought endlessly with his wife, Elizabeth. Although he affectionately called her Libby and she called him Big Daddy, Harvey spent many nights with other women. At times the marriage even degenerated into violence.[2]

Harvey came from a prominent Midwestern family. While still in law school at Indiana University in 1936, he ran as a Democrat for prosecuting attorney in Hendricks County, Indiana. However, even the endorsement of his grandfather's newspaper could not prevent him from suffering a close defeat. He then went into the practice of law just across the river, in Maysville, Kentucky, but, unable to endure the small talk or tolerate stupidity, he alienated many clients. In December 1940, Bill Harvey, now married to Libby, gave up his law practice and joined the FBI's Pittsburgh field office at a salary of $3,200 a year. He was not in Pittsburgh long before the FBI transferred him to its expanding New York City field office.

Harvey first caught J. Edgar Hoover's attention when he cracked the TRAMP case. TRAMP was William Sebold, who ran a central radio transmitting point on Long Island for a Nazi spy ring. Sebold received messages from other Nazi spies, including several in Latin America, and transmitted them back to Germany. After Harvey caught Sebold, he turned him into a double agent and ran him for a year. Hundreds of false messages were fed back to German intelligence before the network finally collapsed.

In September 1945, the FBI sent Harvey to question a dark-haired, heavy-set woman named Elizabeth Bently, who had confessed to being a courier for a major Soviet spy ring. Twenty-seven of the people she named to the FBI worked for the U.S. government. Elizabeth Bently told Harvey that an aide to Secretary of State Edward R. Stettinius, a man named Alger Hiss, was in fact a Soviet agent. Harvey knew that two others had given the FBI the same information: Whittaker Chambers, years earlier, and, just recently, an NKVD officer in Ottawa, Igor Gouzenko. Hiss was a Harvard graduate, a former law clerk for Supreme Court Justice Oliver Wendell Holmes, and a friend of Dean Acheson, then Truman's undersecretary of state. If he were a Soviet spy, it would be devastating.

Without telling Harvey, and before Bently's assertions could be proven, Hoover sent a top-secret message to President Truman, telling him that the FBI had information that government officials were working for the Soviets. Hoover, who had dismissed similar allegations a few years earlier, moved quickly because he was locked in a heated battle with Donovan and Dulles over who would control the postwar civilian intelligence service.

For Hoover, the biggest bombshell in the Bently material was that, out of 12 government employees suspected of working for the Soviets, five had worked for the OSS. This information, he hoped, would persuade President Truman that the FBI, and not the OSS, should take over international intelligence and espionage.

Bill Harvey worked the Bently case for Hoover for the next two years, investigating 51 individuals. The frustrations of working on so sensitive a case, coupled with physical exhaustion, took their toll. Harvey worked impossibly long hours and saw little of Libby and their only child, an adopted son named Jimmy. But the worst strain came from the dirty knowledge he held.

Bently told Harvey that Harry Dexter White, the assistant secretary of the Treasury, and Lauchlin Currie, a White House aide to Truman, had also been Soviet agents. Harvey was in a politically impossible position. His investigations into Bently's allegations came when the country was becoming hysterical over the Soviet threat. Harvey well understood that Hoover had created the tiny counterespionage branch only as a political ploy in his battle with Donovan and Dulles. Now the stakes were higher. If Harvey made a mistake or Bently was wrong, Harvey would end up the goat. That very scenario began to develop.

After Hoover's sensational message to Truman about Soviet spies in the government, the FBI was under pressure to give prosecutors in the Justice Department enough evidence to name names and to indict and convict. Yet despite two years of effort, Harvey could not prove a single allegation of spying. In the end, Harvey came up with tantalizing information, much of which later proved true, but it was not enough evidence to stand up in court. No arrests were made. Rumors at the Bureau began that Hoover was in trouble with Truman, and that Harvey was in trouble with Hoover and knew it.

Hoover's failed promises destroyed any chance the FBI may have had to establish a new American intelligence agency. Truman was not inclined to trust the man who had made so many unproven accusations about people in his administration. In the end, Hoover and Donovan cancelled each other out. President Truman decided on an independent new agency to take over intelligence instead of turning to either the FBI or old OSS. Truman and his aides agreed that the State Department, the Army, and the military intelligence services would handle operational intelligence responsibilities until the President and Congress could produce legislation to create a postwar intelligence apparatus.

ALLEN DULLES'S EGO never surprised Bill Donovan. Donovan was listening one day in the antique-paneled and leather luxury of the soundproof "Dulles room" at the Council on Foreign Relations, as Dulles, private citizen and bored corporate lawyer, laid out a scheme to operate an intelligence service outside the government. To one witness, Dulles's eyes twinkled as he proudly laid out his plan to outwit both Truman and Stalin.[3]

Donovan thought Dulles had lost his mind. "Our war is over, Allen," he told the most single-minded man who had ever worked for him.[4] Dulles then shocked Donovan by telling him that unauthorized operations were already underway.

Dulles had decided not to leave the future of an intelligence service in the hands of the President and Congress. On his own authority, he organized a spy organization clandestinely and planned to present it to President Truman as a fait accompli. By the time Truman discovered what Dulles and his cohorts had done, Dulles argued, Truman would have no choice but to accept it.

"Uncle Allen," as his staff called him, was already fighting his own private war against the Soviets. Using the Council on Foreign Relations as his base, he organized a three-pronged attack. First, he formed a privately run and privately controlled shadow intelligence service. Second, he placed those loyal to him in government positions to work with the front groups he controlled. Third, he used the media to mold public opinion in his favor.

Among other things, Dulles used his connections in the press to help create domestic fears that the Soviet Union was on the march in Europe and China. Dulles's plan worked. Truman was already seeing reports that the military, the State Department, and other government agencies had a small number of Communists in sensitive positions. He had no choice but to take action. The combination of bad publicity and the real threat forced Truman to accept Dulles's quasi-privatized operation.[5]

AFTER HIS WORK in the Balkans, Frank Wisner returned to Wall Street as a war hero. With his frontline experience in Cairo, Istanbul, and the

Balkans with the Soviets, Wisner joined the Council on Foreign Relations at Allen Dulles's behest. He took part in the sessions in the soundproof room, plotting ways the group could sell a civilian intelligence agency to Congress.

However, back at his old law firm, Wisner encountered the same frustrations he had faced before the war. When the opportunity arose in the fall of 1945, he left the law and joined the State Department as Deputy Assistant Secretary for Occupied Countries. His boss was another Wall Street type, Charles Saltzman. Dulles arranged the job for Wisner, who quickly turned it into an intelligence power base.

Wisner was situated in the middle of all U.S. planning involving Germany, Austria, Korea, Japan, and Trieste. He was working directly with General Lucius D. Clay, the military governor of Germany, and Robert Lovett, the undersecretary of state. Wisner was also in a position to work with Reinhard Gehlen, whose surrender he had accepted. Gehlen was in a class by himself in the amount of up-close knowledge he held about the new Soviet enemy, and it was his knowledge Wisner used to run his operation.

By 1946, both the FBI and the OSS had officially lost the battle to be America's Cold War intelligence service. President Truman had already dissolved the OSS in 1945, and now, in January 1946, he approved the creation of a temporary civilian entity called the Central Intelligence Group (CIG). When Truman dissolved the OSS, John J. McCloy, then High Commissioner of Germany, advised him to move much of its covert operations capability to the War Department. That capability was now transferred to the first director of central intelligence, Rear Admiral Sidney Souers, whom Truman felt he could trust. In reality, the OSS had not lost. Since the new CIG was not permitted to conduct covert operations, its personnel spent their time debriefing refugees, examining economic reports, and clipping news stories while they waited for a mission. It was Wisner and Dulles who had the exclusive right to covert operations.

Nevertheless, Dulles was not satisfied. He continued to apply pressure in the media and in Congress for a full-fledged government agency to handle intelligence. The Red Scare so inflamed public fear that in 1947 Congress passed and Truman signed the National Security Act, which created both the National Security Council (NSC) and the Central Intelligence Agency.

With all his manipulation, Dulles managed to create an agency where, from the start, the war against the Soviet Union was based on deception and lies. In a curious way, his backdoor operation suited Truman perfectly. The president, while not comfortable with a government clandestine service, had no compunctions about private fronts and foundations hiding government covert activities. Truman's concerns about corporate influence on intelligence evaporated in the face of the growing Soviet threat. His new NSC retroactively legalized the Dulles team's transgressions against U.S. laws and World War II treaties with a series of secret directives. NSC Directive 10/2 was one such directive, which allowed Allen Dulles, out of the government since the OSS was disbanded, to operate clandestinely through business and charitable entities. The White House, too, began deceiving the American public.

WISNER'S BUREAUCRACY within the State Department, the Office of Policy Coordination (OPC), was enormous. While officially the OPC was concerned with refugee affairs and worked in conjunction with the International Red Cross, in reality it was authorized by the new National Security Council to conduct sabotage and other covert operations against the Soviets.

By late 1947, Wisner, in an underhanded way, wielded vast power in the State Department bureaucracy. He never asked permission to conduct his operations. Rather, he played a deceptive double game in which he informed either Secretary of State George Marshall or Secretary of Defense James Forrestal that the other secretary had approved his operation. Then he went ahead and carried it out.[6]

With help from the U.S. Army, Wisner's OPC quickly created a U.S. intelligence network manned by anti-Soviet Russian émigrés and refugees concentrating on searching Eastern Europe for Nazis to use against the Soviet Union. The OPC supervised Gehlen's operations, now relocated to Munich, and it was engaged in quietly transporting Nazi war criminals, including rocket scientists, mathematicians, engineers, and doctors, into the United States.

The OPC's employees were largely handpicked by Wisner and included former OSS intelligence officers, European-born Jews with language skills, and a few paramilitary types. Wisner convinced Secretary of State Marshall to offer huge salaries and jumps in grade to entice former agents who had returned to civilian life. Because Wisner had special permission to bypass regular hiring practices and other civil service rules for his operation, resentment began to build within the rest of the government toward this elite cadre. This resentment haunted U.S. intelligence for the duration of the Cold War: Agencies declined to share information with each other, and this allowed Soviet spies—not least, Igor Orlov—to survive and prosper.

UNDER THE GUISE of refugee administration, Wisner ran his covert operations. Dulles ran Wisner from his Sullivan and Cromwell law offices. The go-between for the two men was Carmel Offie, a savvy operator who was always in the right place at the right time.

There are secrets which even presidents are not told. These darkest secrets are often actions that break laws and treaties and violate religious and moral acceptability, and they need a particular kind of person to carry them out. Carmel Offie was such a man.[7]

He was a tough and brilliant State Department infighter. He was the man Dulles relied on when his Free Europe Committee had to interact with the government and discuss his most sensitive operations. It was Offie who talked Dulles into setting up Radio Free Europe and to hire émigrés from the countries occupied by the Soviets to broadcast behind Cold War lines. Radio Free Europe was a successful propaganda tool for the West pretending to be a private organization. It raised money through charitable contributions from patriotic Americans who never understood that it was a government front from the very start.

Barely over five-and-a-half-feet tall, with a startlingly dark complexion and a thick mustache, Offie looked out of place among the Anglo-Saxon Protestants who dominated the State Department. An Italian-American from a poor family, he had overcome his background and achieved power. Yet he was under no illusions about his standing within the intelligence community. Offie told friends he was, figuratively, the man Dulles and Wisner "hired to clean out the toilets."

He was also homosexual. Like many gays living a secret life in Washington in that era, he made certain to ingratiate himself with those he worked for. He was the kind of ambitious assistant who reminded the boss of his wife's birthday. He took care of the boss's children and made sure the wife had events to go to and activities to keep her busy, especially when the family was stationed in a far-off land. His survival technique was to make himself indispensable in a million ways.

By the time Offie went to work with Wisner, he no longer hid the fact that he was gay. He reveled in the power he had earned and had sufficient confidence in his status to live openly.

Carmel Offie believed he could carry out any task, and now Allen Dulles gave him the worst task of all. Offie had to make his fellow public servants' moral sensitivity disappear when it came to coddling Nazis. The United States had signed a series of agreements and treaties and passed laws forbidding the government to protect war criminals. Offie's job was to get law-abiding officials and clerks to break these rules.

To do his job, Offie needed Frank Wisner's support. Offie targeted Wisner the way an intelligence officer targets a potential source. In doing so, he contributed to the burden that eventually destroyed Frank Wisner's soul and drained his sanity. He made Wisner complicit in protecting the most notorious and despicable war criminals of the twentieth century.

Offie worked his way into Wisner's confidence. He took care of Wisner's wife, Polly, and their children until he was loved and trusted like an old family retainer. He also became the mentor Wisner desperately needed. Offie had learned to overcome the most severe social handicaps to lead an amazingly successful and influential public life. Wisner, like Offie, was brilliant but erratic. Offie taught Wisner how to bury his erratic side and to always *seem* reasonable. "Offie was a world-class sophisticate who could put a stiletto in an opponent and offer him a treatise on the cognac he was serving him at the same time," James Angleton said of his colleague.

Wisner and Offie became great friends. The two men shared an evangelical zeal for taking on the Soviets. Both were prepared to do anything necessary to fight for freedom in Europe—even the secret protection of the Nazi establishment.

WHILE OFFIE AND WISNER pursed Dulles's agenda, Igor Orlov also followed orders. At the meeting outside Berlin in the spring of 1945, the NKVD colonel had told him not to travel back to the Soviet Union with captured German troops but to pass himself off, using his new identity papers, as Alexander Kopatzky, a Polish national forced to fight with the Germans. He should make his way to a displaced persons camp near Munich.

The Soviets created the Kopatzky cover for Orlov in order to make a renewed penetration of the West. They had not anticipated how much help they were to get from Reinhard Gehlen.

After the meeting with his colonel, Orlov, under his Kopatzky name, traveled to Munich as a displaced person. He survived in the camps by selling black-market items. He was hoping the U.S. Army would arrest him, so that he could demonstrate his competence as an intelligence resource in exchange for his freedom.

The scheme worked. In May 1945, the U.S. Army arrested him for black marketeering. Very quickly, however, the Army Counterintelligence Corps (CIC) discovered from his former Nazi colleagues that "Kopatzky" was really Igor Orlov, the liaison between the German General Staff and Vlasov's Army, the man they were looking for. Orlov realized that they knew his identity when the questions they were asking all centered on Soviet intelligence matters, not about his background or where he had fought. Later that summer, Orlov told the Americans he was half Russian and had worked for the NKVD before defecting to Germany to serve Vlasov.

David Murphy, an ambitious Army counterintelligence officer, became Orlov's first American case officer. Murphy spoke fluent Russian. He had married his Russian teacher, Marion, the daughter of a White Russian who had emigrated first to Shanghai in the 1920s and then to San Francisco.

Murphy's job was, first, to protect the Army from penetration and then, assuming that Orlov was not a Soviet agent, to determine how he could best be used. Murphy was no match for Orlov, a genius at getting personal details from people. Trying to put Orlov at ease, Murphy made a crucial mistake when he mentioned that he was married to a White Russian. Orlov instantly realized that the White Russian probably had family back in Russia, and that gave the NKVD a way of pressuring Murphy if the need should arise.

Beginning with Murphy, Orlov put together intelligence dossiers on America's first Soviet case officers. These dossiers proved invaluable to the Soviets over the coming years as these men rose to important positions. Orlov urged Moscow Center to gather material on Americans married to Russians and other Eastern Bloc citizens as quickly as possible. The NKVD had its foot soldiers canvassing the world to collect this extremely valuable biographical material.

By 1947, while the President and Congress were still trying to settle their deep divisions on forming an intelligence agency to face the Soviet threat, Alexander Kopatzky, or "Sasha"[8] to his friends, was thriving in Munich, working for the U.S. Army's counterintelligence office and for Gehlen's organization.

As Wisner's OPC sought to exploit anti-Soviet factions, Orlov once again played a key role in "helping" to organize anti-Soviet activities among the veterans of the old Russian and Ukrainian counterrevolutionary armies. According to his American case officers, Orlov frequently recruited for the OPC by entrapping Russian or Ukrainian partisans in his black-market schemes and then blackmailing them into working for the Americans. At the same time, he was reporting to Moscow Center that recruitment of the old Vlasov and other anti-Soviet forces was a top priority for the United States, which was planning to use them in the Soviet Union, Poland, and East Germany to foment revolution against the Soviet state.

Orlov then ratcheted up the stakes another notch. Using the same techniques that had proved so successful with the Nazis, and with Moscow's permission, he blackmailed some of the anti-Soviet Russian émigré groups working for the OPC, manipulating them to act as double agents. He then exposed them to the Americans as Soviet spies. Slowly, carefully, and brilliantly, he built up his own credibility, one body at a time.

CHAPTER SEVEN

GEORGE WEISZ

M ANY NAZIS ESCAPED to East Germany, Hungary, and Poland and assumed new identities. To find them, Carmel Offie needed men who had the stomach to make a devil's pact. The searchers were to inform the Nazis that their war crimes would be overlooked if they agreed to work for America as agents in place and help win the new Cold War against the Soviets.

Offie's plan had two elements. First, he had to find the Nazi engineers and scientists who remained in Soviet puppet states. He wanted them separated out and brought to the United States so the Soviets could not exploit their talents. Second, and a harder task, Offie wanted to find the most cunning Nazi collaborators—the ones who had hidden themselves in government and finance in the occupied countries.

The search for this talent ran from the Baltic to the Balkans. It involved a complicated and audacious plan, but the ever-confident Offie told his superiors he could implement it. And so, OPERATION PAPER-CLIP, and later NATIONAL INTEREST, were born, run out of Offie's suite on the supposedly non-existent thirteenth floor of the old I. G. Farben headquarters in Frankfurt. Both programs recruited Nazis deemed "crucial to U.S. national interests": PAPERCLIP targeted scientists and technical experts; NATIONAL INTEREST targeted Nazis who could be "politically useful" in operating against the Soviet Union.

Offie understood that German collaborators in the Soviet-occupied countries were deathly afraid of the Soviets and hard to find. A good case officer was needed to hunt them out and recruit them for the West. The case officer had to understand that their agreement to work for the United States need not be voluntary. Offie sold Wisner on the idea but never shared with him just how far he was willing to go to put Nazis on the U.S. payroll.

The man waiting to see Carmel Offie one spring day in 1945 was wearing civilian clothes. Offie's pretty WAC secretary (Offie always hired pretty secretaries because he felt they put people at ease) thought the man looked like the movie actor Charles Boyer. She guessed he was in his late thirties. He was of medium build and impeccably dressed. He was carrying Hungarian and German newspapers, and he had a European courtliness but no trace of an accent. The day before, the WAC had delivered his classified file to Offie. Had she taken a look, she would have learned that the man's name was George Weisz.[1]

Weisz was born to Jewish parents in Miskolc, Hungary, on August 27, 1918. He came to the United States with his family—father, mother, and sister—in 1932, when he was thirteen years old[2] and spent his adolescence in a Hungarian neighborhood in Manhattan in the midst of the Depression. After graduating from Stuyvesant High School with honors in 1937, Weisz, a vivacious young man who loved the arts, began college at Cooper Union.

"Georgie was afraid we would not have enough money; his father was not fond of working," his mother, Gizelle, told the investigator working for Carmel Offie. "So George worked on the side and helped support us." Despite the extra responsibility, George was fond of his handsome father. George used the European charm his father had taught him to great effect with the women he met in New York.

Family friends included a wide variety of Hungarian immigrants. "Georgie inherited my personality. He was sunny, open. . . . He had Dad's way with women," Gizelle Weisz said. The Weisz household was a place where people came to eat and drink and carry on lively conversations. Suzanne, George's younger sister, teased him about all his different girlfriends: "Georgie made many friends who were not Hungarian immigrants. He studied, but school came easily for him."

Though the family was Jewish, they were not particularly religious. George learned at an early age that to survive outside his immigrant community, he should avoid discussing his religion.

At Cooper Union College, George studied sculpture and painting, but soon realized a life in the arts could not supply his family's monetary needs. Since his family depended on the income from his part-time jobs, he decided to take more practical business courses and transferred to New York University, where he started preparing for a professional career.[3]

In the fall of 1941, with the United States not yet in the war, George, then just 23, joined the U.S. Army and left for Officers' Candidate School in Kentucky. He scored brilliantly on language and intelligence tests. His cultural background and his test scores clearly indicated that he was suited for intelligence work. As an intelligence office in early 1944, the Army sent Weisz to Fort Ritchie, Maryland, where he received special training in how to break a suspected enemy agent.

A classmate at Fort Ritchie said that Weisz was a natural at trapping even very skilled people into making mistakes. "He was brutal in his approach. He would win your confidence, make you think he believed you, and then break you. He was the quickest study in class." After D-Day, the Army sent Weisz to Europe, where he saw action as an intelligence officer for the 14th Armored Division, and later, the 28th Infantry Division inside Germany. His fitness reports were sparkling.

In his letters home to his mother and sister, Weisz mentioned nothing of the dark side of his job. He wrote about the art, the gardens, and the charm of European women. "George loved being in Europe close to the center of where things were happening," his sister recalled.

At the end of his first stint overseas, Weisz went home and regaled his family and friends with his adventures. He brought home pictures of himself with Soviet soldiers on tanks, smiling and waving in victory.

Weisz spoke to his family about just how bad things were in Europe, and for the first time he discussed the threat from the Soviet Union. "He never cared much about politics before," his mother said. Now, he was genuinely proud that the United States had liberated Europe and that he had played a small role. But despite his positive demeanor, his sister noticed a marked difference in George. "He was not as carefree as he used to be. He still loved women, he still had a good time, but there was a difference in him. His joy seemed to be not so near the surface." When she asked him if something was wrong, he said no.

Waiting for his appointment with Carmel Offie, Weisz ignored the pretty WAC. He was absorbed in a two-week-old Hungarian newspaper when the door to the inner office finally opened. Another pretty WAC led him through a maze of temporary offices into a small, bare conference room.

Carmel Offie was already a legend among intelligence and diplomacy insiders, and Weisz recognized his slicked-back hair and thick black mustache. Offie escorted Weisz through half a dozen makeshift offices. In a larger room with no windows, Offie left Weisz alone again with his newspapers and went into another office. There, Frank Wisner was reading Offie's file on Weisz.

Wisner was looking for the right man for their Nazi recruitment effort in Hungary. He read in the file that the Army had successfully used Weisz's well-developed charm as an intelligence weapon. He also learned that Weisz, with his language abilities and his cultural sensitivity, could get Germans to reveal their highest-ranking Nazis and most useful bureaucrats. He never revealed he was a Jew.

The file described one colleague's shock at Weisz's interrogation tactics with a local official. "Weisz caught the official in a series of lies about his connections to the Nazi Party. Weisz was very calm, very friendly, and then he just eviscerated this guy. Within an hour he gave up the identity of every high-ranking Nazi in the region. . . . Because George could be so charming, his toughness in these situations was a little shocking. He had a way of tapping into that German emotional reaction to an authoritarian figure. George could become very authoritarian, very intimidating."

Offie understood that Weisz's sophistication, combined with his experience as a hostile interrogator, was rare among Americans. Only in his midtwenties, Weisz had the air of a man of the world in his forties. He was one of a very few Army officers who spoke Hungarian or even had a rudimentary knowledge of Hungary. For all those reasons, Weisz was the man Offie and Wisner wanted for their mission of grilling and then recruiting the worst offenders of the Third Reich. It never occurred to either Offie or Wisner that they would be sending a Jew to offer deals to the same men who had tried to kill every Jew in Europe, especially in Hungary, his home country.

Offie and Wisner left Wisner's office and returned to Weisz. Offie said to Weisz, "I'd like to introduce you to Frank Wisner from the Department of State, Office of Policy Coordination." Awed, Weisz shook the hand of the man who controlled all of America's covert operations.

For Weisz, meeting Wisner was like meeting the crown prince of the intelligence establishment. For Wisner, meeting Weisz was one of a dozen such introductions in his day. Nevertheless, he seemed genuinely pleased to meet Weisz.

After this interview, Weisz joined the many men and a few women on Wall Street, inside corporations, on military bases and university campuses whom Wisner's and Offie's team recruited for OPERATION PAPERCLIP and OPERATION NATIONAL INTEREST.

Needing a cover job for Weisz, Wisner and Offie assigned him to the war crimes tribunal at Nuremberg. This assignment gave Weisz an opportunity to question and interview German Nazis about their work in Hungary. He asked where their files were located and where Hungarian Nazis might be hiding and how they were disguising themselves.

From Nuremberg, Weisz, armed with this information, went to Hungary. For his cover, Wisner gave him an appointment as negotiator with the new Communist government over the issue of displaced persons. Weisz, operating very much like Igor Orlov, began by sacrificing a score of useless Nazis who were in hiding. This served two purposes: First, Weisz bought credibility with the Soviet-backed regime in Budapest by uncovering and turning over Hitler collaborators. Second, and more important, the pro-Nazi underground in Hungary quickly learned that Weisz was ruthless and would give a recruiting target to the Soviets if he did not like the target's answers. As with Orlov, Weisz's most important weapon was fear.

Weisz ingratiated himself with regular Hungarians to the point where they were arranging meetings with relatives and providing first-class travel for him. No U.S. official had better contacts in Hungary than Weisz.

Weisz used some of the men and women he recruited to set up paramilitary operations that gave the United States economic and military information about Soviet movements in the country. However, his main job was to find "useful" war criminals and get them safely out of Europe to the United States or Latin America. To earn their trust and cooperation, he promised them U.S. citizenship and cash awards. Under the statute that created the CIA, one hundred individuals could be exempted from immigration laws with the approval of the director of the CIA.

IT IS HORRIFYING to contemplate the situation in which Weisz found himself. Many of his Hungarian relatives and friends had been slaughtered or had gone through unbelievable suffering and pain at the hands of the Nazis. Weisz's assignment now was to reward some of these same Nazis and make them secret allies of the United States. What Offie and Wisner saw as detachment and competence during interrogations was, in fact, Weisz managing his anger. He directed it now at the Hungarians who had collaborated with the Nazis, forcing them to tell him where the Nazis he wanted to recruit were hiding. It was as if Weisz, through these hostile interrogations, could personally assign blame to the Hungarian government for its complicity in the destruction of Hungarian Jews.

Weisz's methods grew increasingly more brutal. He played a dangerous game with local Communist officials. From the beginning, he let it be known he was a Nazi hunter and a Jew. For every Nazi he uncovered and successfully recruited, he took a less desirable Nazi and turned him over to the Communist authorities. That way, the officials looked good and so did he.

Weisz was so good at ferreting out and recruiting his targets that his colleagues gave him the nickname "the Black Knight."[4] To find the Nazis, he started with displaced persons. Once he found the most useful Nazi sympathizers in a designated region, he plucked them from among the other suffering refugees and got them either under his control or to the United States. If he found useful Germans hiding among the Hungarians, he offered them good jobs with the United States government. One of Weisz's colleagues, Clara Grace Follich, who was also working for the Army in PAPERCLIP and NATIONAL INTEREST, explained, "We were getting the scientists out and the scientists' families out. . . . I used to fly black flights [secret flights that supposedly could not be traced] from Wiesbaden to Andrews Air Force Base with the families of the men who were doing the space program. The Russians had warned them that they would be thrown out [of the plane] as we flew over the Atlantic Ocean. They were all scared to death, so I always got on and stayed with them."[5]

Clara Grace, who preferred to be called C.G., confirmed that Weisz went after higher-level Nazi collaborators: "His targets were bankers, businessmen—people who made Hungary run for the Nazis." As she explained: "The Russians were trying to take them and ship them to Moscow, and we would try and get them and bring them back to the U.S." C.G. had no moral hesitation about bringing Nazis into the United States, even if some of them were war criminals: "They were the guys who got us to the moon and got the Russians up in space. . . . The Germans were the ones that had the brains, the know-how, and the ability because they had been working on the buzz bombs."

During this period, Weisz invited his mother to visit him in Europe. What she found in her son shocked her. The young man so full of happiness, who had embraced life with such joy, was now filled with hate. Weisz told his mother he hated the Hungarians for protecting the Nazis. He insisted to his mother that Hungarian must never be spoken among the family in his presence again. "He hated Hungary," Gizelle Weisz recalled. "He didn't let me say one word of Hungarian. When the two of us were walking and talking, he didn't let me. He, months later, wouldn't let me go back to Hungary [after I moved to Berlin]."[6]

His sister, Suzanne, agreed: "Number one, he hated the Hungarians because of what the Hungarian police and Hungarian people did to the Jews."[7]

Three veteran counterintelligence officials who have studied the life of George Weisz all conclude that it was during the period that Weisz was assigned to Hungary that he began to live a double life.[8] The fact that Offie and Wisner overlooked in Weisz's résumé that he was born a Hungarian Jew is precisely the kind of biographical detail that Moscow Center jumped to exploit. Weisz's family connections to Hungary made him an instant Soviet recruiting target.

The NKVD assigned a rare Jewish Soviet case officer, Hungarian by birth, to recruit him. The case officer, who was thirty years older than Weisz, got to him through his relatives in Hungary, who introduced the officer to Weisz as an old friend.

As Weisz went through the agony of dealing with the moral challenge he faced every day, this capable NKVD specialist became his mentor and friend. The NKVD man, in what is called a "false flag" recruitment, sold himself to Weisz as a Zionist activist trying to break up the Odessa, an underground escape route for high-level members of the Third Reich. He and Weisz talked about the immorality of what the United States was doing. The case officer succeeded in convincing Weisz that there was nothing traitorous to America about hunting down for the Zionists the Nazis the United States was protecting. America was conspiring not only with her former enemy but also with those who had killed tens of thousands of Weisz's fellow Hungarian Jews.

Weisz occasionally passed a name to his Zionist friend. He apparently never suspected that the man his relatives had introduced him to was an NKVD officer. However, some in the intelligence community believe Weisz was too smart not to realize what was happening to him.[9] In any case, the first time Weisz fed information to his new Zionist friend, he started down a path with no easy return.

Weisz achieved incredible access inside the Hungarian Communist state. Wisner and Offie did not question why he was able to go into Hungary, pluck Nazis out from under the Soviets' noses, and then be welcomed back the next time by local Communist officials to do it all over again.

On one occasion when Weisz was returning to Germany from New York, he stopped off in Frankfurt. There he got to know Etta Jo McEndree, one of the pretty young WACs he had met the day Carmel Offie interviewed him in 1945, who was now also working for PAPERCLIP and NATIONAL INTEREST.[10] George and Etta Jo dated for a couple of years in a relationship that was not love at first sight. "That was the funny part about it," Etta Jo later said. "For some unknown reason we were at each other's throats constantly. I don't know why we kept seeing each other, really."[11]

One reason Weisz kept up the relationship, despite frequent public arguments, may have been that Etta Jo provided him with a connection, stability, and a cover for his duplicity. In the professional intelligence career in which Weisz hoped to excel, it was imperative that he marry someone already accepted by the intelligence community. More important, he should not marry a foreign-born Jew like himself. George Weisz had to keep up appearances.

In 1947 George married Etta Jo and, despite what he had told his mother and sister of his feelings about the Hungarian people, he took her to Hungary for their honeymoon. Etta Jo recalled that everyone wanted to get into Hungary, but the new Communist government was not letting anyone in. Yet George had no trouble getting visas.[12] Furthermore, U.S. intelligence officers at that time were not supposed to travel to Communist countries without specific orders. Even more, there were standing orders that no spouse or family member should travel behind the Iron Curtain. "That should have raised immediate security questions," according to the counterintelligence officer William R. Corson. "He should have been brought in for a debriefing and every moment of his contacts and trips accounted for. That never happened, because Wisner's people were untouchable. There were no rules for them."[13]

By 1948, Weisz had moved from the military to a foreign service cover job with the OPC. After a stint on the staff of German High Commissioner John J. McCloy[14] in late 1949, Weisz went to work with Dr. Erhard Dabringhaus, a top Army intelligence operative and the control officer for several important Nazi war criminals, including the infamous Klaus Barbie.[15] According to Dabringhaus, Weisz was assigned to recruit one of Barbie's networks, which included SS Colonel Gunther Bernau.

By the time Weisz returned to the United States in 1951 for a new assignment at the Pentagon, he had become even more secretive than before. According to his sister, when old friends contacted him, he refused to return their calls. Except for his immediate family, he turned his back on his prewar past, renouncing his Hungarian heritage and his friends. Suzanne remembered how shocked she was at the change: "He had a wonderful sense of humor. . . . He was a social butterfly. We used to go out and dance and sing and drive around . . . and then he went back to Europe, and he got involved with whatever work he was doing, and it was like Dr. Jekyll and Mr. Hyde. He no longer smiled. He no longer danced. He no longer sang. He became very serious."[16] Weisz's work for Wisner and the OPC had changed him forever. He had witnessed and performed incredibly inhuman deeds. He had become hardened, cold, and tough.

George Weisz did not stay in the United States long. Soon he returned to Germany, where he and Etta Jo worked for the CIA in Berlin. There he met a young man whom some people called Alexander Kopatzky, and others called Igor Orlov.

CHAPTER EIGHT

ORLOV:

THE INDISPENSABLE MAN

———⟶•◀———

IGOR ORLOV intuitively understood how to make use of the trust that came when General Gehlen vouched for him to U.S. authorities. Because so many American intelligence agencies turned to Orlov for help in their operations, he was able to provide the Soviets with information on almost everything the United States was trying to do against the Soviet Union in Europe. And he was able to end the speculation at Moscow Center about what Wisner and the U.S. Army worked out with Gehlen and his team during the 10 months they were at Fort Hunt, Maryland, being integrated into U.S. intelligence.

Through some of Gehlen's men he had befriended during the war, Orlov learned that a huge new underground base was being built for Gehlen at Pullach, outside Munich. Orlov's information about the long-range plans for Gehlen and his men permitted the Soviets to select several Nazi officers under their discipline to penetrate and infiltrate the Pullach base. With the patience that the Soviet intelligence service always demonstrated, they methodically put in place the people best able to compromise Gehlen's operations.

In Munich, Orlov quickly learned that personal relationships were the key to getting along with his American handlers. Some of the men he befriended, like David Murphy, were destined to reach important positions in U.S. intelligence.

Orlov's cunning and style helped him infiltrate operations outside of his assignments. Moscow Center ordered him to offer up some low-level Nazis to get access to OPERATION PAPERCLIP. The NKVD gave him the locations and aliases of several Nazis who were hiding in Germany. Following instructions, Orlov approached the Nazis and offered to make a deal on their behalf with the Americans. His American case officers were delighted and accepted Orlov's Nazis without question. More important for Moscow, Orlov was then given lists of higher-ranking Nazis to locate on behalf of his American handlers. These Nazis were much more crucial to the United States, and the Soviets immediately moved to get them under their control.

As he had done so successfully during the war, Orlov blackmailed some of the anti-Soviet Russian émigrés and manipulated them to act as double agents: ostensibly working for Frank Wisner's OPC, but in reality working for the NKVD. He then exposed them to the Americans as Soviet spies. Slowly, carefully, and ruthlessly, he worked to gain the Americans' confidence at higher and higher levels. His methods never changed over the years, and his technique was seamless.

Orlov increased his access by becoming a bon vivant in the émigré community. He took up with a coterie of White Russians working for Carmel Offie's Radio Free Europe, the U.S. Army, the OPC, and even British intelligence. Orlov used and eventually betrayed every one of these "friends." Their only purpose was to provide information and to establish Orlov's credibility.

Igor Orlov's ability to manipulate people extended to his personal life. Like George Weisz, he chose a wife to strengthen his position with the Americans. They knew that someone loyal to the Soviet Union would never marry a Nazi.

In early 1947, the Army CID asked Orlov for a favor—one that presented him with a unique opportunity. A few days before, local police had arrested two young Germans named Baladini and Stirner. The German police, under U.S. Army supervision, carried Baladini's interrogation too far, and he wound up dead. Igor's Army friends feared that Baladini's family would turn his death into a major international incident. Stirner, who had survived the incident, came from a well-connected Nazi family. His sister had been dating Baladini. The Army asked Orlov to help defuse the situation.

Orlov decided to target Stirner's sister. He had her dossier pulled and learned that she had been a minor celebrity as an Olympic-class swimmer for Hitler's "Aryan" team. When the war broke out, she became a leading member of the Hitler Youth.

One afternoon on Munich's number 8 streetcar, Orlov and an émigré friend, Boris, appeared as Eleonore Stirner was lugging two big bags of potatoes aboard. Eleonore had dark hair, a trim figure, and a flirtatious nature.

"Boris and I are Russian ballet dancers," Igor told her.

"I think you are more interested in the ladies than dancing," Eleonore replied.

Eleonore later said, "I did think they were ballet dancers when I first saw them. Igor was very much a lady's man."[1] The two men chatted with her until her stop on Elisabethstrasse in the artists' section of Munich and helped her carry off the bags of potatoes. When she tried to thank them, Igor said, "You can't get rid of us so easily. We will carry your potatoes home for you."

"I liked the attention," Eleonore recalled. When the three of them arrived at her home, Eleonore thanked the young men again and said goodbye. "Igor said, 'No, we are staying for dinner.' He was charming, and so was Boris." She introduced them to her mother, who asked if they worked for the Americans. Igor said he did. Mrs. Stirner burst into tears, telling him that her son was under arrest and Eleonore's boyfriend had been killed. Could Igor free her son?

When he asked for details, Eleonore took him to an upstairs apartment to meet her dead boyfriend's father, a college professor. The elder Baladini told the story Igor already knew. A black marketeer on his way to ski in the Alps, his son had been involved in a shooting incident with a German policeman. The U.S. Army had arrested him and, while in U.S. custody, he had been beaten to death.[2] Eleonore told Igor that she now feared for her brother's life. "Igor said he would help," Eleonore recalled.

Igor's flattering attention occurred simultaneously with the trauma of her boyfriend's death: "I slept with him the first night to survive," Eleonore explains. "You don't know what was happening in Germany. Hundreds of thousands of people died. . . . I did not want to starve." Handsome Igor Orlov seemed to offer Eleonore a ticket to a better life, a chance of reclaiming some of the stature she had enjoyed before the war. She had no idea that she was being used in an intelligence operation.

It took Igor only a few days to make her brother's problems with the police disappear. He offered to help in other ways, too. Mrs. Stirner was impressed with his kindness and his ability to find scarce items like sugar, meat, and bread. "My mother encouraged the relationship because Igor was generous," Eleonore said.

Through the Stirners, Igor gained access to middle-class Germans for his spying operations. He was able to pick up information about seemingly mundane matters like the American construction project for the Gehlen facility at Pullach. If Igor had asked his American colleagues about the project, they might have been suspicious. But because Igor was one of the family, and because he had worked with the Nazis during the war, the Stirners' friends shared gossip, rumors, and information with him freely.

Igor's first formal date with Eleonore was at the wedding of one of his friends, Knabe Urov. "Urov wore a monocle, and when I got to the wedding I was surrounded by Russian counts and countesses. I found myself looking for Anastasia," Eleonore joked.

Over the next few months, Urov told Eleonore more about Orlov than he had ever divulged himself, including the news that they had served in German intelligence together. The two men also had a friendly competition about who was braver. As Eleonore recounted, "He told me Sasha may be very brave, but he was much braver. If there is something to be shot at, he said, Igor hid under the bushes and Urov came out and shot the people." But when she repeated this to Igor, he told her that Urov "did not know which end of the gun to use."

Eleonore also met another Russian friend of Orlov's, Vladimir Kivi. "They always stuck together," Eleonore said. "Igor had nice friends, funny, kind, gentle, and great fun. One of the reasons I fell in love with him was because his pals were such interesting people." Eleonore's reaction was precisely what Orlov had planned to elicit from her by cultivating men like Knabe, Boris, and Vladimir.

In July 1948, Eleonore became pregnant with Igor's child. Her mother was furious that Igor and Eleonore had not taken precautions and insisted they marry. When the young couple hurriedly attempted to get married, "the Lutheran Church would not marry us because Igor told them he was Catholic . . . and the Catholic Church wouldn't marry us because I was Lutheran." They finally used forged identity papers provided by American intelligence to get married before a magistrate on July 14, 1948. It was only after they were married that Igor told Eleonore the forged papers had been given to him on condition that she undergo an abortion.

"I was crushed and confused. Igor told me his American bosses were not happy, and they demanded the abortion," she said. "Igor told me he would be fired if I had the baby." His case officers all later said Igor never discussed Eleonore's pregnancy with any of them. Evidently, Orlov felt that having a child might limit his operational capability. Eleonore had the abortion. It was the first of many sacrifices.

Even so, Eleonore was happy with her life with Igor, taking joy from small things like purchasing a new bicycle. "Our life seemed very good. I was married to a charming man and we were getting away from the hard days after the war."

The newly married couple rented a room on Elisabethstrasse. Eleonore found a job as translator at the Droemer book publishing company. Igor worked both for his American "friends" and for Droemer as a shipping clerk, and he spent long evenings socializing with exiled Ukrainians associated with Radio Free Europe.

One day in 1949, Orlov told Eleonore that he had to go meet an agent for the U.S. Army and would be gone a few days. Instead, he traveled by train to East Berlin and by car to Baden-Baden to meet with his old NKVD control officer from Moscow. On his arrival, Orlov learned that he had been promoted to full colonel in the NKVD.[3]

When Igor returned to Munich, the Army gave him the specific task of spying on the Russian émigré community, to see who might be spying for Moscow. Orlov's official émigré connections were with the National Labor Union (NTS), an anti-Soviet and anti-Nazi organization first formed in Belgrade, Yugoslavia, in 1930. The NTS had supported the Vlasov movement, and, like Vlasov, had anti-Nazi credentials because its leadership had run afoul of Hitler. Of 60 NTS leaders sent to concentration camps, only half survived. After the war, more than a hundred thousand Russians managed to avoid being repatriated and joined the NTS.

The NTS was secretly planning a covert war against the Soviets and was funneling funds to Ukrainian leader Stephan Bandera to set up a "tradecraft and sabotage school" for NTS agents infiltrating the Soviet Union in the flood of refugees returning home after the war. NTS members had the Russian-language ability much needed by the West. More important, they hated Stalin's Soviet Union. Since the British and the Americans agreed to use the NTS as a means of organizing anti-Soviet Russians, Igor Orlov was able to report everything—names, dates, even minutes of meetings—back to Moscow Center.

In the meantime, the Americans provided Orlov with a new cover job. He became a newspaperman for an NTS weekly propaganda sheet called *Sponya,* designed to encourage anti-Soviet Russians by exaggerating news of victories in the struggles against Stalin in the motherland. As a reporter for a paper largely funded by the U.S. Army, the "little man," as Orlov came to be known, could operate with amazing freedom.

One of the more bizarre events that Orlov was involved with was Frank Wisner's massive "Stay Behind Program," costing tens of millions of dollars. Fearing a Soviet takeover of Europe, the United States first trained Soviet refugees in guerrilla warfare techniques and then buried large amounts of arms, food, and cash in secret locations all over Western Europe. The plan was to activate the "stay behinds" in the event of a Soviet invasion, but Orlov and others gave most of the food stocks to local gangsters, and the "future partisans" sold off the armaments.

More realistically, the Americans planned to reinvigorate the old Vlasov movement and use its men to assist anti-Soviet partisans in the Carpathian Mountains. The plan was for the partisans to live in caves during the winter so the Soviet Army could not follow their tracks and hunt them down. When weather permitted, the United States would drop equipment and supplies to them.

All that the NKVD and Red Army needed was to know in advance when and where the drops of men and equipment were to take place. That information was easy for Orlov to get and pass along. Under the Americans' noses, he used Wisner and Offie's Radio Free Europe to send his messages back home in code. One of the first operations Orlov betrayed was a program in 1951 to send NTS agents behind Soviet lines. The infiltration program involved sending Russians, Czechs, and Poles by parachute with radio equipment into their respective countries where they would operate as agents. A. I. Osmanov, a 23-year-old Red Army deserter who had served with Vlasov, and F. K. Saratzev, a 25-year-old corporal who had been taken prisoner in 1943, were among the first to parachute in.

The planning for the drop was meticulous. Gehlen's people and the U.S. Army carefully crafted legends for both men, equipped them with the latest in small radio transmitters, East German–made bicycles, and gold and Russian rubles to buy supplies. Their flight took off from Greece on August 18, 1951. The men jumped out over the Carpathian Mountains in Moldavia, a region between Romania and Ukraine. A few radio transmissions were received—and then silence. The few freedom fighters who were not captured starved to death. The Soviets claimed that those captured had been executed.

Long before their flight, while both men were still training at Fort Bragg in North Carolina, Igor Orlov provided the Soviets with their names. Six months after the drop, Radio Moscow announced that they had been executed. Scores of other agents who parachuted into the area faced the same fate. Thousands more died fighting Stalin's troops. Peter Kapusta, who worked for the operation in Germany during this period, later said, "It was clear that the infiltration program was compromised from the very start. Most of the transmitters never were turned on. . . . Our carelessness killed many, many people who thought they were fighting for freedom."[4]

By 1954, all of these agents had been captured and executed.

Orlov's treachery continued undetected as the body counts increased.

CHAPTER NINE

BERLIN:
THE NEW FRONTLINE BASE

B ERLIN'S UNIQUE GEOGRAPHIC LOCATION totally within Eastern Germany made it inevitably an espionage center in the Cold War. Soviet military and civilian intelligence operatives swarmed over the Saint Antonius Hospital in the Karlshorst section of the city, turning Karlshorst into little Moscow. Karlshorst became the forward base for all Soviet intelligence activities in the occupied countries.

After the war, the Soviets returned captured German officers and enlisted men to the Eastern Zone and started a massive education effort to train Germans as Communist leaders. Their aim was to build an infrastructure in the Zone (later East Germany), including an intelligence service as good as the NKVD. A German Stalinist, Erich Honecker, became the head of the Young Communists.

Although Allen Dulles did not really believe Berlin would ever play a major role in postwar intelligence, he countered the Soviet move by picking out a handsome if decadent old mansion that had once been a German military facility in the Dahlem section and setting up the first Berlin Operating Base (BOB) for the OSS. Technically, he was the first chief of BOB, but he soon appointed one of his protégés, Richard M. Helms, as his replacement and Captain Peter Sichel, another protégé, as head of intelligence.

Always able to spot a dead-end job, Helms left Berlin after six months and returned to Washington. Dana Durand replaced him, and with Sichel continuing as deputy, he tried to keep BOB operating.

As Dulles and Frank Wisner successfully outflanked President Truman with their quasi-private "Project X" operations, Berlin Base languished under the U.S. Army's care. It did not have the authority to do much more than collect information from interviews with incoming refugees. The mainstays of the Base were German-born Jews with wonderful language skills and scientific training who hunted for useful information buried in the refugee interviews. Meanwhile, a dozen American case officers—mostly members of the Army Counterintelligence Corps, plus a few OSS types—tried to do a job for which they had very little training and almost no experience.

The number of refugees from the Eastern Zone throughout the late 1940s and the 1950s was staggering. In all, some four million people escaped to the West before the Berlin Wall went up in 1961. Berlin Base case officers attempted to talk to the most interesting of these refugees, those who had relatives with good access to government or scientific information behind Soviet lines, but the sheer numbers made their job very tough.

Berlin Base maintained offices at the Marienfelde Reception Center, a refugee relocation camp, for recruitment and interrogation. Using false names, the dozen case officers interviewed refugees all day long and then returned to the old mansion in Dahlem to write their reports. Promising leads were turned over to Wisner's OPC.

The house in Dahlem was hardly the best location for a secret operation. Although it had alarm systems and bars on the windows, tight security was difficult to maintain. The house overlooked a major street, and Soviet agents could easily photograph anyone entering or leaving the building. Since many senior Berlin Base employees lived in Dahlem, following them home and establishing their real identities was not difficult.

GENERAL WALTER BEDELL SMITH became the fourth director of the young CIA in August 1950, replacing Rear Admiral Roscoe H. Hillenkoetter. He saw that changes had to be made. In particular, he was concerned about Wisner. While technically Wisner's OPC was under the CIA, Wisner was in fact running his own show. Smith felt he had to get control of all intelligence operations.

At first, President Truman was reluctant to listen to Smith's pleas for control of Wisner and the covert operations. Smith continued to press, finally telling Truman, "Mr. President, either this group comes under the real control of my office or I shall resign." Smith had plenty of ammunition to make his case to take control of covert operations. It could be summed up in one word: failure.

The CIA had no inkling about two major events in 1949: The Soviets exploded their first atomic bomb, and the Communists took control of China. These twin blows to the United States were of such consequence that Secretary of Defense James Forrestal suffered a nervous breakdown. He subsequently committed suicide by jumping from the fourth floor of Bethesda Naval Hospital where he was being treated for depression.

To make matters worse, in June 1950, North Korea invaded South Korea. U.S. intelligence was totally surprised. Neither the CIA's overt operations nor Wisner's OPC had a hint of the attack. Hundreds of thousands, including tens of thousands of Americans, died because of the intelligence failure.

Not all the OPC's failures could be laid at Frank Wisner's feet. Wisner had been forced to quadruple his staff in a six-month period. By the time General Smith took over as Director of Central Intelligence (DCI), Wisner's organization was in an open feud with the CIA. Still, Smith hated the fact that he was ultimately responsible for the OPC's faulty intelligence and that Wisner, as its head, could bypass him and go directly to the secretaries of State and Defense. Furthermore, Smith could not understand why Wisner was not taking on the Soviets in Berlin.

Smith finally persuaded Truman to end the OPC's independence and combine the operations. "It took General Smith's almost entire tenure at the CIA to get control of Wisner's operations," according to William Corson.[1] Ironically, by moving to get Dulles and Wisner's operation under control, Truman finally gave Dulles what he wanted. The United States had a truly integrated civilian intelligence service at last.

Smith started by converting Wisner's OPC into the new Clandestine Services of the CIA. Wisner remained as head of Clandestine Services, but Smith knew that if he, as DCI, was going to have true control of all Agency operations, he had to make certain that people loyal to him were playing the major roles. Because the Soviets had beefed up their intelligence and military operations in Karlshorst, Smith decided to turn Berlin Base into the most important operations base in the CIA.

Peter Sichel went from deputy to chief of base. Sichel was born in France to an American mother and a French father whose family was famous for their wines. Peter served in the U.S. Army, joined the OSS, and was recruited by the CIA after the war. A jovial, easygoing man, Sichel ran Berlin Base with a firm but kindly hand.

A young man named Wally Driver arrived in Berlin as a junior officer just before Thanksgiving in 1951. He liked Sichel immediately, especially his sense of humor. When Driver asked Sichel, who was Jewish, about recruiting members of the German resistance, Sichel looked at him and said, "Yeah, there were Germans in the resistance. They didn't pay their taxes."[2]

When Sichel became overwhelmed with recruitment, according to Driver, "he decreed everyone was to do name traces," one of the most tedious tasks in the intelligence business. "From November until Christmas Eve, I and my roommate, Lucien Conein . . . were doing these traces. . . . We were literally living in our bunks." Late on Christmas Eve, when Driver was ready to collapse, Sichel found him. "Wally, do you have a German driver's license?"

"No, sir," Driver replied.

"Can you drive?"

Wally said he could. Could he read a map? By this point, Driver's adrenaline was pumping. He thought he was finally going to get a chance to prove himself as an operative. He eagerly assured Sichel he could read a street map. Then Sichel gave him the assignment: "You see that big box of Christmas presents over there? . . . Get yourself a car out of the motor pool and deliver them."

ONE AFTERNOON IN March 1951, Eleonore Orlov answered the door at her Munich apartment. A tall, blond man introduced himself as an employee of the CIA. He never used his real name, William Sloane Coffin, nor told Eleonore that he was Igor's control officer.

After coffee, Coffin announced to the young couple that Igor's newspaper job was being transferred to Berlin. "The man said my husband was going to Berlin," Eleonore recalled. "I said, 'No way. I won't go.' But Coffin said that Igor had to go to Berlin 'immediately.'" Eleonore did not know that Igor and Coffin had planned the entire conversation. Igor knew his wife would never voluntarily move away from her family in Munich.

Coffin's job was to step up the initiative against the Soviets by recruiting exiled Russians such as Orlov to hunt targets in Soviet-controlled ter ritory. In *Soyuz bor'by za osvobozhdeniia narodov Rossii,* or the Union of the Struggle for the Liberation of the Peoples of Russia (SBONR), the CIA thought it finally had an émigré group that could be trusted. But for some inexplicable reason, some of the men working in the "Secret Section" of the SBONR—including the section chief, Orlov's good friend Knabe Urov—persisted in behaving irresponsibly. CIA case officers were at their wits' end trying to keep the SBONR's relationship with the CIA secret, while members routinely talked about secret operations in public places, became involved in barroom brawls, and tried to confront the Soviets directly. After a few months, the CIA was ready to give up. Orlov seemed the only useful professional operative out of the SBONR group.

One month after Igor arrived in Berlin, he sent Eleonore a message asking her to visit him there for a few days. Eleonore agreed. He gave her instructions on where to go for her flight. "When I got on the special military flight for Templehof [the airport in Berlin]," she recalled, "they told me I would not be permitted to return to Munich. The CIA men told me that I had married a stateless person, and now I, too, was classified as stateless. To remain alone in Munich, I would have to report every week to the police." It turned out that the forged identity papers Igor had manipulated Eleonore into using for their marriage had made her stateless, giving him enormous control over her.

When Eleonore arrived in Berlin, Igor told her, "I cannot have the Americans looking for you; it is too dangerous for me."[3] For the first time, Eleonore began to suspect that her husband did more than newspaper work for his American friends. She did not know for years, however, how much more he did and for whom.

Meanwhile, Chief of Base Sichel was delighted to get Orlov. At least, Sichel thought, a man with Orlov's vast experience had a chance of recruiting agents to work against the Soviets. He was right about one thing: Orlov was the most experienced intelligence agent at Berlin Base.

CHAPTER TEN

THE FBI MAN IN THE CIA

———❖———

B Y THE SUMMER of 1947, the Red Scare had taken root in America, thanks to politicians like Richard Nixon and Joseph McCarthy. While most of the Red-baiting was overblown, there was enough truth behind the headlines to cause the public to question the direction of the country and to ask what was wrong with American intelligence. Chiang Kai-shek's Nationalists were losing ground to Mao Tse-tung's Communists in China, the Soviets clearly had no intention of giving up the sector of Germany they controlled, and it was public knowledge that Moscow had acquired atomic secrets from the Manhattan Project.

Rumors were floating around FBI headquarters that J. Edgar Hoover was not happy. The focus of his displeasure was said to be the man he had turned to in his battle against Donovan and Dulles, William King Harvey.

Bill Harvey's career and his marriage were both floundering when a bizarre incident brought matters to a head. On July 11, Harvey attended what was later described in FBI documents as an "all-male stag party" in Virginia. Harvey was unusually quiet that evening; he seemed moody and had little to drink. A fellow agent who left the party at about the same time as Harvey said he saw Harvey's car getting onto the Rock Creek Parkway heading for home around 12:20 A.M.

The next morning, an angry and worried Libby Harvey called FBI headquarters to complain that Bill was missing. She told the head of the security division that "Daddy had been despondent and discouraged . . . and moody." Agents began searching the route Harvey had taken. Half an hour later, Harvey came home. He told the Bureau he had not gotten drunk—he only had two cans of beer at the party. He explained that his car had stalled after going through a puddle and that he had slept in the car until 10:00 A.M.

This incident set off a remarkable series of events. The FBI brought Harvey up on an obscure charge of failing to be at a telephone number where he could be located within two hours—an FBI regulation that had never been enforced. A subsequent investigation by Hoover's aides cleared Harvey. Over at the new CIA, word was that Hoover needed a scapegoat for the allegations he had made to Truman in the Bently fiasco, and Bill Harvey was taking the fall. It looked like that was the case when Hoover transferred Harvey to Indianapolis for "general assignment."

The public story was that Hoover's order and the transfer were crushing to Harvey. Before this incident, he had never received anything other than an "excellent" rating in his seven years at the FBI. Telling colleagues he was not very good at fighting bureaucratic battles, he wrote a gracious letter of resignation and left the Bureau.

Bill Harvey told friends that he had no real savings and did not want to turn to his family for help. With the hundred days of accumulated FBI pay he had to live on, he set out to find a job. The new CIA urgently needed to establish a counterespionage and counterintelligence capability against the Soviets, since the wartime OSS had operated with the Soviets, not against them. The CIA needed someone like Bill Harvey, and Bill Harvey needed a job.

That was the accepted story of how Harvey left the FBI and went to work for the CIA. According to William R. Corson, later a counterespionage colleague of Harvey's, the real story was very different. "Bill Harvey was Hoover's mole in the CIA," Corson later said. "He started off as a plant or a spy. Both Hoover and Harvey realized that many of the old OSS crowd recruited by the CIA had personal histories that would make them vulnerable to recruitment [by the Soviets]."[1] Hoover knew Harvey would not be accepted in the CIA unless he had left the FBI, its rival, under a cloud.[2]

Harvey shared Hoover's distrust of the OSS and of the new CIA. Disloyalty seemed endemic in the upper classes, and he had actually found Soviet agents in the OSS. He knew he had to keep up his guard.

His behavior changed dramatically when he went to work for the Agency. His straightforward and professional demeanor changed to a pulp-detective personality. "He seemed to do everything to accentuate the background differences between him and other CIA officers," recalled Paul Garbler, a CIA officer who later worked for him.[3]

Meanwhile, the Harveys were under social pressures they had never before experienced. Bill's family may have been prominent in the Midwest, but now he was working with Wall Street lawyers and bankers—men from old families and the new rich who had prospered from the war. This period was particularly hard on Libby. With little formal education, she found herself surrounded by snobbish CIA wives. Because of Bill's continued dalliances, Libby was already drinking during the day. Now she also had to face the pressures of a world of pseudo-sophistication she did not understand.

Kim Philby, in his autobiography, vividly described the differences between FBI and CIA men: "The men of the FBI, with hardly an exception, were proud of their insularity, of having sprung from the grass roots. . . . They were therefore whisky-drinkers, with beer for light refreshment. By contrast the CIA men flaunted cosmopolitan postures. They would discuss absinthe and serve Burgundy above room temperature. This is not just flippancy. It points to a deep social cleavage between the two organizations."

Harvey possessed a toughness that few others at the CIA had. "The edge Bill Harvey had over those folks was that he had been up against the enemy and they hadn't," Corson recalled. "He understood the ruthlessness. To Harvey, the NKVD and later, the KGB, were criminals. . . . He was a cop and he had a cop's view of counterespionage."[4]

"Bill Harvey was the right man for the counterespionage job at the right time," Corson insisted. It was the right time because the United States Army Security Agency (the forerunner to the National Security Agency) was beginning to break a Soviet code called VENONA. The message traffic confirmed some of the allegations Elizabeth Bently had made to Harvey that the Soviets had been spying on America and England during the entire wartime alliance.

Harvey understood better than any of his new colleagues that the Soviets had targeted the CIA for penetration. He did not know that they had already been successful and that the penetration would have a profound effect on his future.

Harvey was put in charge of the new CIA's Office of Special Operations (OSO), a small counterespionage and counterintelligence unit called "Staff C." Harvey's office was located in rat-infested temporary buildings on the Mall, not far from the Lincoln Memorial. One of Harvey's new colleagues was a tall, thin young man recruited from the OSS Station in Rome, James Jesus Angleton.

The two men were totally different. Physically, they looked like Mutt and Jeff. Harvey was stout and short (Philby nicknamed him "the pear" behind his back), he wore his hair slicked straight back, and he had bulging eyes caused by a thyroid condition. Angleton looked taller than his six-feet-one inch, and he was, according to Philby, "the thinnest man I ever met." Both men enjoyed poetry, but Harvey went for Kipling, Angleton for Yeats. One of Angleton's proudest friendships was with Ezra Pound; Harvey thought Pound was a traitor, a Fascist, and a loon.

Despite their differences in class and interests, at first Harvey and Angleton liked each other. Angleton later said, "[Harvey was] full of bravado . . . but he had an exceptional mind. I think what I most remember about him was his ability to remember details of cases he had worked on. His first months at the CIA were sessions where we would listen to Bill recite relevant cases he worked on from Bureau files. . . . Hoover would not give us anything in those days. . . . We had Bill and that was just as good."[5]

Harvey's first impression of Angleton was that he was a typical Eastern snob. He later learned that Angleton had grown up in the West and that his mother was Mexican. Although Harvey was impressed by Angleton's counterespionage experience in the OSS, it was Angleton's friendship with superspy Kim Philby that most fascinated and disturbed him.

In 1949, when the United States broke the VENONA code, the British sent Philby to Washington to work with the CIA and the FBI on the names of double agents revealed in the intercepted messages. One of the code names the Soviets used was HOMER; another was STANLEY. MI6 assigned Philby to work on uncovering the identity of HOMER, who had helped manage the theft of Manhattan Project secrets for Russia. The British and the Americans believed HOMER was serving in the British Embassy in Washington.[6]

Angleton and Philby, reunited in Washington, were the closest of friends. CIA security records show, and former Angleton aides recall, that Philby visited Angleton several times a week. Angleton himself confirmed that "We ate lunch together on a regular basis."

Philby also had social contacts with Allen Dulles—who had just left Wall Street to become General Smith's deputy director for intelligence—and with Frank Wisner in Clandestine Services. Philby had access to the CIA's most classified facility at the time, the "L Building."

Harvey grew suspicious of Philby and expressed his concerns to Angleton and to anyone else at the CIA who would listen. But he was unable to prove his suspicions or to convince Angleton. It did not help that he had never managed to make any arrests on the basis of the Bently information.

Harvey's suspicions also fell on Philby's Cambridge classmate Donald Maclean, who was serving in Washington for the Foreign Office. Harvey was convinced that Maclean was HOMER. As it turned out, he was right. In fact, Maclean was still supplying Moscow with nuclear secrets as late as 1948, when he served on several joint U.S./British operations.

Before Harvey could make his case that Maclean was HOMER, the British promoted Maclean to their embassy in Cairo. In the meantime, Philby and his pregnant wife, Aileen, settled into a large rented house near the British Embassy with their four children. Then another of Philby's Cambridge classmates, Guy Burgess, was suddenly posted to Washington. "Hoover had informed Harvey that Burgess was having a series of homosexual affairs and was a serious security risk," according to Corson. Burgess was also a heavy drinker.

Harvey was astonished to see Angleton lend Burgess money. It also bothered him that Philby had direct access to the VENONA "take" at a small office kept for him at the FBI. Harvey's suspicions increased as many CIA operations began to go sour.

All too typical was the fate of the Albania operation. This involved an attempt by the United States and Britain to actually take back a country under Soviet control. The ever-optimistic Frank Wisner believed the plan would begin the collapse, like dominoes, of Soviet puppet states in Eastern Europe.

Hundreds of Albanian émigrés were trained on the island of Corfu. In December 1949, small boats carrying the rebels landed on the Albanian coast. But it quickly became apparent that Moscow knew about the entire operation before it was even launched and had warned the government in Tirana, the Albanian capital. Dozens of the rebels were captured and executed; in the end, several hundred Albanians were killed. Similar anti-Soviet operations in Latvia, Lithuania, and Estonia failed in much the same way.

Had Harvey done some checking among Angleton's Israeli friends, he might have been able to convince Angleton that Philby, Maclean, and Burgess were not to be trusted. In 1936, Philby had married Litzi Friedman, a young Austrian Jewish girl who was an avowed Communist. Among the guests at their Vienna wedding was Teddy Kollek, who became a legendary mayor of Jerusalem.[7] A year before his death, Kollek insisted that he had warned Angleton about Philby.

Kollek recalled that he went to CIA headquarters in September 1950 for a meeting with Angleton. Walking down the hallway after the meeting, he was shocked to see Philby. Kollek said he turned around, walked back to Angleton's office, and demanded to know what Philby was doing at CIA headquarters. Angleton told him, "Kim is a good friend of ours and is the British MI6 representative in liaison with the Agency." Kollek insisted that during this conversation he told Angleton about Philby's Communist connections. As Kollek later put it, "Philby moved in Communist intellectual circles, and people I knew to be committed Communists were among his closest associates."[8] Angleton never said a word about the incident to Harvey or made any note of it that could be found in his records.

Angleton also kept secret his relationship with Israeli Intelligence (Mossad) because of State Department fears that public cooperation with the Israelis would complicate Arab and British relations. According to a former CIA official who served as chief of station in Tel Aviv, "You have to understand that no one at the State Department or CIA was anxious to have an open relationship with Israel. Israel was a country made possible by the Soviet Union introducing a United Nations Resolution, 181, which allowed the partitioning of Palestine. . . . Moscow ordered Czechoslovakia and Yugoslavia to supply Israel armaments and train her pilots. Israel was a collectivist socialist state that had a very cozy relationship with the

Soviet intelligence services. . . . No bureaucrat was going to stake a career on that in the middle of McCarthyism."

This official believes that Moscow ordered Philby to strengthen the relationship between the CIA and Mossad. In any case, that is precisely what took place. Reuven Shiloah, the first director of Mossad, urged Israel to abandon its public ties to Moscow and align itself with the new American intelligence service.[9] The official cooperation agreement was signed in 1951. Among other things, it called for Israel and the United States to refrain from spying on each other—perhaps the least-adhered-to element of the agreement.

Relations between Harvey and Philby were cool from the start, but an incident at a dinner party at Philby's home led to open hostilities. Angleton, Bill and Libby Harvey, and other FBI and CIA people were finishing dinner when a drunken Guy Burgess arrived. Libby, also drunk, begged Burgess, who had a reputation as a sketch artist, to do a portrait of her. He quickly sketched her with her legs spread and an exaggerated bare crotch. Bill Harvey, another inebriated guest, emerged from an alcoholic stupor long enough to take a swing at Burgess and miss.

After that evening, Harvey more than distrusted Philby and Burgess. Harvey's nerve endings, his bloodhound investigative nose, and his desire for revenge meant the end of Philby in America. In his autobiography, Philby wrote, "Apart from Angleton, my chief OSO contact was a man I shall refer here to as William J. Howard. He was a former FBI man whom Hoover sacked for drunkenness on duty. The first time he dined in my house he showed that his habits had remain unchanged. He fell asleep over his coffee and sat snoring gently until midnight when his wife took him away, saying: 'Come now, Daddy, it's time you were in bed.' I may be accused here of introducing a cheap note. Admitted. But, as will be seen later, Howard was to play a very cheap trick on me, and I do not like letting provocation go unpunished."[10] Harvey's "cheap trick" was accusing Philby of being a Soviet mole.

On May 25, 1951, Guy Burgess and Donald Maclean disappeared. It was the beginning of their odyssey to the Soviet Union, and they did not officially surface for another five years.

General Smith ordered every CIA officer who had come in contact with Burgess, Maclean, and Philby to write a memorandum explaining their connection. The two most important memos were Angleton's and

Harvey's. Angleton's was dated June 18, 1951 and contained a disjointed account of his relationship with the British. The memo reported a series of incidents involving Burgess, including the one with Libby Harvey and another episode in a Georgetown restaurant, when Burgess appeared drunk and dirty and asked Angleton for a loan. In writing the memo, Angleton seemed to take pains to avoid the real issue. There was no mention of the warning about a Communist connection from Teddy Kollek.

Bill Harvey, after reading Angleton's memo, wrote across the top, "What's the rest of the story? OSOD." (OSOD was Harvey's shorthand for Oh Shit Oh Damn.) Harvey's own memo had been written a week earlier. It detailed Philby's entire history and concluded that Philby was a Soviet agent, in league with Burgess and Maclean and possibly others. Harvey told a colleague in Berlin a few years later that his concerns about Philby, Burgess, and Maclean came while he was getting his weekly haircut. "I realized that Philby really distrusted the British establishment. He wasn't really part of it. That's when I understood," said Harvey.

The memos pitted Angleton and Harvey against each other for the first time. Harvey could not understand Angleton. He confided to one colleague that he suspected that either there was a homosexual relationship between Angleton and Philby, or that the two were such good friends that Angleton just could not bring himself to face the possibility that Philby was a spy.

The bitterness between the two men exploded publicly one day. Harvey accused Angleton of covering up for Philby. Angleton insisted on taking a polygraph examination. The Office of Security complied, and Angleton passed, but the relationship between Harvey and Angleton was never the same again.

Meanwhile, the conclusions Harvey came to in his memo were shaking the very foundations of the American and British intelligence communities. General Smith wrote the director of MI6 asking him to remove Philby from Washington. MI5, the British counterintelligence service (the equivalent to the FBI), began to build a case against Philby. For Harvey, the victory was bittersweet. Once again, as with the people accused by Elizabeth Bently, there was not enough evidence to really move against the double agent. Once again, the bad guy got away. Philby was never a power in MI6 again, but Harvey believed the ring was bigger and included more double agents. He greatly resented "the boarding school crowd" at MI6 for not delving into the case with more force.

Although Harvey should have been a hero at headquarters, he was not. His dogged efforts to expose Philby, instead of advancing his CIA career, crippled it. Men like Allen Dulles and Richard Helms were the CIA's future. The CIA hierarchy "was the British system. Friendship, OSS, and the old boy network were at work," according to William Corson, who worked for Allen Dulles. "That is precisely how Dulles measured people."

In fact, to the CIA leadership, Philby was still a member of the club, whereas Harvey never would be. He was an embarrassment at dinner parties, and no one was comfortable with his on-the-record treatment of Angleton. "They wanted Bill out of headquarters," Corson said, "and he knew he could never operate in headquarters. . . . That's why he took Berlin."

Technically, the CIA's Berlin Base was under the control of Frankfurt Station, but General Smith assured Harvey that as new chief of Base, he would be in charge. He would be given the freedom to hire whomever he wanted and run the Base as he saw fit. It was an opportunity for Harvey to start fresh. He was to be the symbol of a new, tougher, braver CIA, facing the Soviets head on. "Harvey was really the only one the CIA had who understood how the Soviets operated . . . ," according to Corson, "and he [Smith] trusted Harvey. . . . Smith thought he had common sense. They were not friends, but Smith liked Harvey because he could get straight answers out of him. . . . He needed straight answers."[11]

Harvey went to visit Frankfurt Station, still located in the old I. G. Farben complex. There, he met a tough-minded, attractive foreign service officer and former WAC who worked for Carmel Offie and Frank Wisner on OPERATION PAPERCLIP along with her friends, Etta Jo and George Weisz. C.G. Follich was perfect for Harvey. She was instantly protective of him and realized that there was much more to him than the bravado and street lingo he had turned into an art form. For his part, the trip reminded him there was more to life than Ivy League snobs at headquarters and his unhappy marriage at home.

In 1952, Bill Harvey divorced Libby and took their five-year-old son, Jimmy, to Frankfurt.

Harvey's departure from Washington left a huge void in the CIA's counterintelligence operations at home. There was now no one with any real experience protecting the Agency from penetration by the Soviets. How that job was filled is one of the darkest episodes in CIA history, and one that had a major effect on Harvey's Berlin tenure.

Harvey left Frankfurt in January 1953 to take over Berlin Base from Peter Sichel. There he worked with his future wife, C.G., with George and Etta Jo Weisz, and, of course, with the prized Berlin agent, Igor Orlov.

CHAPTER ELEVEN

COVER-UP AND PROMOTION

———⊶●⊷———

THE BRITISH SECRET SERVICE welcomed the 39-year-old Kim Philby back to England in May 1951 with a protracted hostile inter-rogation, the first of many, about his friendship with Guy Burgess. Over the next five months, Philby admitted that he and Burgess were occa-sional lovers. At one point, Philby got so upset under questioning by an MI6 lawyer that he regressed into a boyhood stutter. But he never broke down in the interrogations or police interviews, and no hard evidence emerged showing that he was anything but a loyal British subject.

Still, as the MI5 report put it: "Guilt unproven but suspicion remain-ing." General Smith's devastating letter to Sir Stewart Menzies demanding that Philby be removed from operational duty in Washington had an ef-fect. After 10 years of service, Philby agreed to resign. However, he suc-ceeded in planting the idea at MI6 that Harvey's accusations were without factual basis and typical of a Hoover FBI agent. Harvey had never been part of the OSS that had gathered at Philby's feet to hear the wisdom of a master spy, and so, as William Corson put it, "No matter what smoking gun Bill Harvey had, they would never allow Harvey to nail Philby."[1] Many of Philby's colleagues believed he was being sacrificed to placate the Americans' fear of Senator McCarthy.

After he left MI6, Philby went into a deep depression. He had an ill child, his marriage was deteriorating, and he had lost a job he loved. He never forgave Bill Harvey for pointing the finger at him.

Harvey's failure to find proof that Philby was a traitor gave Philby's allies time to block further investigations. His warnings about Soviet penetration of MI6 also went largely unheeded. Although General Smith officially limited all American contacts with British intelligence—even at the risk of damaging the alliance—his orders were not followed. Allen Dulles maintained close contact with MI6, and, as a top Soviet expert for the CIA recalled, Dulles "put the word out to the cousins that Kim was all right and Harvey too anxious and too personal. London was quickly able to make a joke of Harvey's suspicions."[2]

Bolstering Philby's cause was the fact that Harvey was sent away from headquarters to run Berlin, while Philby's protégé and friend, James Angleton, was now a top official in foreign intelligence. Angleton had an office overlooking the Lincoln Memorial, a staff of six assistants, and he kept his role as the Israelis' main contact. He seemed destined for the career that Harvey would never achieve in his new field job.

Philby had been living on a small government pension and a handful of odd jobs. In 1955, his wife now dead and his family in tatters, he returned to his journalism career and began writing for a London newsletter.

GENERAL SMITH'S POSITION as head of the CIA was short-lived. Harry Truman did not run for reelection in 1952, and Dwight David Eisenhower coasted to victory over Adlai Stevenson. With men like Allen Dulles privately criticizing Smith, the new president did not reappoint him. Instead, President Eisenhower established the Dulles brothers, John Foster at the Department of State, and Allen at the CIA, as men of enormous power and influence over American foreign policy. Seven years after his conversations with Bill Donovan in the wood-paneled room at the Council on Foreign Relations, Allen Dulles realized his dream of becoming the spymaster of the United States.

In January 1953, as Bill Harvey was taking over Berlin Base, Allen Dulles settled in at the director's office in a sealed naval compound across the street from the State Department. His new position at the heart of the government was very different from the informality of the secret world he had created out of his and Foster's law offices at Number 44 Wall Street. He was thrilled with his new job, even though early in his tenure he received some very bad news.

For all its flaws, the new CIA had some accountability. Sheffield Edwards, who ran CIA security, was the symbol of that accountability, and he suddenly had a problem: Allen Dulles. The new director of central intelligence was not only a womanizer, he had brought other big baggage with him from the OSS.

Edwards, Dulles, and General Lucien Truscott, the intelligence advisor to President Eisenhower, gathered one day in Dulles's office. The meeting opened with a solemn announcement by Edwards: "Mr. Director, we have a serious problem that I have already briefed General Truscott on."

Dulles, who paraded around his office in brown slippers with foxheads on the toes, asked Edwards to go on.

"Sir, six of the men you have brought over from OSS into the CIA are serious security risks."

Dulles asked Edwards what made them security risks.

Before Edwards could speak, Truscott answered for him: "Jesus, Allen, they are homosexuals. Just like goddamned Carmel Offie. I can assure you that if we know, the Soviets know. What the president is concerned about is, does McCarthy know? Because if he finds out, we have serious problems."[3] McCarthy had earlier learned from J. Edgar Hoover that Offie had made advances toward a military officer. This information had forced Wisner and Dulles to put Offie into a lower-profile position.

Dulles asked for a list of names and pledged to Edwards and Truscott that he would see to it that neither the Administration nor the CIA was compromised. "It was devastating news to Dulles. He did not know," according to Robert T. Crowley.[4]

The list had one especially disturbing name on it: James Speyer Kronthal, a brilliant young deputy of Dulles's in Bern Station during the war. As one of the original 60 people Dulles brought to the CIA, he had not had to take a polygraph exam. Now, Dulles asked Edwards for the entire file on Kronthal.

The next day, Dulles asked Kronthal to come to dinner at his Georgetown home to talk about what they would do together at the CIA. Kronthal, who lived just a few blocks away, walked to Dulles's home with the anticipation of being named a top CIA official. But instead of the friendly, avuncular "Uncle Allen" he expected to find that evening, Kronthal met a side of Allen Dulles he had never before seen.

Dulles dismissed his maid and served himself and his guest the roast beef dinner she had prepared. Unknown to Kronthal, two security officers listened to the entire discussion from the kitchen. "Dulles put Kronthal at ease by offering him wine and a little shop talk before he got into it," Robert Crowley reported. "Then he asked a series of seemingly unrelated questions. Kronthal did not suspect he was being confronted. Allen told Jim that he should have come to him with his personal problems. Then Allen would remind him to eat."

After dinner Dulles brought out his favorite brandy and lit his pipe. He then asked Kronthal: "James, if you were not working for me, what would you be doing?" Kronthal fumbled for an answer.

As Corson related, "Allen then gave a sad speech about how personal compulsions destroy careers. He never directly confronted Kronthal. Allen said that everything he had built could be destroyed. Allen then said, 'James, sometimes there is no way out. Sometimes the right thing to do is to step aside. You need to think about that, because if you don't take this opportunity, things could be very ugly.' Allen never referred directly to Kronthal's homosexuality.

"Allen was brilliant at breaking people," Corson continued. "My supposition from reading the Kronthal file and doing the damage study was that it was based on a gentlemen's discussion. Dulles never determined if Kronthal had been turned. We did not find that out for two years. Having had to do similar interrogations, my guess is that Kronthal was relieved when his mentor let him know he understood the truth."[5]

Kronthal walked home to 1662 Thirty-Second Street, Northwest, a little after midnight. He prepared three sealed letters and one note. One of the letters was to Dulles, another to Richard Helms. The note was to his housekeeper, asking her not to disturb him in the morning since he had worked very late.

When "the State Department," as Mrs. Lavina Thomas later put it, called the next morning and interrupted her chores asking where Kronthal was, she repeated his instructions. At 9:30 A.M., two security officers, McGregor Gray and Gould Cassal, arrived. Over Mrs. Thomas's protests the two men entered Kronthal's bedroom and discovered his fully clothed body on a daybed. He had not undressed from dinner. An empty vial was on the floor by the bed.

"Allen probably had a special potion prepared that he gave Kronthal should the pressure become too much," Crowley conjectured. "Dr. Sidney Gottlieb and the medical people produced all kinds of poisons that a normal postmortem could not detect. Kronthal, from a powerful family in New York, could not bear having his secret homosexuality become a new case for Senator Joseph McCarthy."

Lt. Lawrence Hartnett of the Metropolitan Police handled the cover-up for the CIA. Instead of opening the letters, he delivered them personally to Dulles and Helms. Harnett made certain the press and the public thought the suicide resulted from depression linked to exhaustion. One letter got past Harnett, however. Kronthal had also written to his sister about his homosexuality and "the difficulties it posed in his professional life." His sister never understood the last line in her brother's letter: "I can't wait till 1984. Jim."[6]

The Kronthal case demonstrated just how careless Dulles and Wisner were about their early recruitments. As the CIA investigators later found, Kronthal had led a dark life in the art world, working with the Nazi regime during the war in fencing art stolen from Jews. It was during this period that German intelligence caught him in a homosexual act with an underage German boy. However, his friendship with Herman Goering prevented his arrest and saved him from scandal. Kronthal had every reason to believe the incident had been safely covered up.

When the Soviets took Berlin, they found all of Goering's private files, which included Kronthal's records. When Kronthal replaced Dulles as Bern Station Chief in 1945, the NKVD prepared a honey trap based on the information they had obtained. Chinese boys were imported and made available to him, and he was successfully filmed in the act. "His recruitment was the most well-kept secret in the history of the Agency," James Angleton said. The entire time Kronthal worked for Dulles and Wisner, he was reporting every detail back to Moscow Center. Kronthal was the first mole in the CIA. He served the Soviets for more than five years.

Dulles soon learned that the Soviets had several other of his closest associates from the OSS under their control. However, he treated what amounted to an intelligence catastrophe as a political problem, not a counterintelligence problem. His first concern was what would happen if Senator McCarthy learned that the head of the CIA had promoted a homosexual who had become a Soviet agent. Instead of going after the remaining traitors, he used his influence to remove from power the men, like Harvey, who might want to uncover the suspect agents and others they may have recruited.

For James Angleton, embarrassed by Harvey over the Philby affair, the Kronthal incident was a chance for redemption and power. After Harvey left for Germany, Angleton spent most of his time on the new Israeli "account," building a strong relationship with Mossad. Now Dulles was about to offer him a portfolio with influence that would reach far beyond the CIA.

A tough-minded colonel, Donald Galloway was the head of counterintelligence for the CIA. Like Sheffield Edwards, Galloway did not play political games. Angleton had enough information on the Kronthal mess to understand why all those involved—especially Dulles and Richard Helms, Kronthal's other close friend—would have reason to be grateful to him if the matter were handled with discretion. Somehow or other, Angleton managed to replace Galloway as head of counterintelligence.

"No one knows precisely how Angleton forced his way into the counterintelligence job," said William Corson, who examined the Kronthal case files, "but the effect was that the Kronthal damage assessment was never completed. It is my view that Angleton understood he was getting the counterintelligence slot in exchange for not pressing an Office of Security investigation of Kronthal and Dulles." Angleton, the man who never caught on to Guy Burgess and Donald Maclean, was now in charge of protecting the CIA from Soviet penetration.

The schism between those who collect and operate spies and those who protect the spying institution from penetration is a source of constant tension for any intelligence service. Like the internal affairs department of a police force, those responsible for counterintelligence often seem to the officers in the field to be nothing more than witch hunters. Angleton, with 120 people working for him, soon became the most feared man in the CIA.

In fairness, as former acting DCI Hank Knoche explained, Angleton's job was one of the toughest there is: "You almost have to be 100 percent paranoid to do that job. You always have to fear the worst. You always have to assume the worst of your enemies. You always have to assume, without necessarily having the proof in your hands, that your own organization has been penetrated, and that there's a mole around somewhere. It creates this terrible distrustful attitude." [7]

In Angleton's case, these difficulties were exacerbated by his personal quirks. Berlin case officer George Kisevalter always found Angleton strange. Once, when some visitors from British intelligence came to Washington, Angleton's Counterintelligence Division threw a party at a Chinese restaurant. Kisevalter was one of the guests. Trying to compliment Angleton about his background, Kisevalter mentioned that Angleton had gone to Yale. To Kisevalter's great surprise, he said Angleton yelled, "'I never went to Yale.' . . . He yelled it like that in front of the British. I looked at him and said, 'Do you want me to show you the yearbook or what?'"

Relations between Harvey in Berlin and Angleton in Washington went from bad to worse as soon as Angleton took over counterintelligence. Angleton sent Harvey a never-ending barrage of cables. "We had a lot of trouble with him [Angleton]," Berlin Base veteran Don Morris recalled. "It would be crazy things. One defector came out and had a notebook with about 15 names in it. . . . Angleton got this and fired a cable off to the station saying, 'Have this man arrested immediately!' And Harvey went back and said, 'Look, we can't just ask the Germans to arrest anybody; they have got to have bloody good reason before they go in. It is worse than the States. Will you have the proof out here in 24 hours? . . .' And the answer from Angleton was: 'Have him arrested before he gets away.' So the police were told to arrest him. They arrested him, and, of course, he had absolutely nothing to do with anybody, and Angleton never said anything again. He left everyone hanging in thin air."

According to Morris, incidents like this happened so often that people at the Base began to worry: "There is an old expression used by field hands: They don't like to be told on what corner to meet their agents. And Angleton was always trying to mastermind things from back home, with frequently disastrous results in the field." According to Morris and others, Angleton's counterintelligence staff developed a terrible reputation. As Morris put it, "It was the dumping ground for incompetents. When you had a married couple and the wife was worth her weight in gold and the husband was a dud, he went to the CI staff."

Making matters worse was the Philby connection. Through Philby, the Soviets were already well aware of Angleton's attitude and personality, and they knew that Angleton, as chief of counterintelligence, had access to almost every secret communication, operation, and document the CIA had. The Soviets believed that CI was the shortcut to important secrets.

Meanwhile, Angleton's knowledge of the Kronthal affair meant that for two decades he had a level of job security almost unknown in the intelligence business.

CHAPTER TWELVE

TOUGH GUY IN BERLIN

———⤐◆⤇———

B ILL HARVEY'S ARRIVAL in Berlin in January 1953 "was like a bucket of cold water on the place," according to Wally Driver. Harvey found the Base disorganized and so used to playing second fiddle to the military intelligence organizations and Wisner's OPC that it "was close to being worthless from an intelligence point of view."[1]

Harvey began restructuring Berlin Base into an activist intelligence organization engaging the Soviets face-to-face. Dulles had made it clear to Harvey that, to survive, the CIA needed to be successful in Berlin. "In a world where irrational fear of Communism had swept over the United States," as one top Soviet case officer put it, "our government had few tools to really understand what the Soviets were up to."[2] Another top case officer said, "Harvey saw his responsibility as finding out what was going on in Russia from BOB. He felt that if the military and KGB could be penetrated at Berlin, there was a chance at developing real intelligence."[3]

If Harvey was not happy with what he found in Berlin, the feeling was mutual. He gathered the Berlin staff together and announced to them that the Soviets "are criminals and we are cops." He lectured his subordinates on how the NKVD operated in the United States. He asked them if they "packed heat." When he got confused looks from his uneasy audience, he promptly pulled an ivory-handled pistol out of his pocket and held it up.

[93]

To the shock of his new subordinates, Harvey did not speak a word of German and seemed to have no plans to learn. Because of his experience chasing Nazi spies and the stories of German brutality during the war, he absolutely detested "the damn Krauts," as he called the Germans. Because of that attitude, he would not learn German. "He just refused to do it," Wally Driver said. Driver, who spent most of his years in Germany under deep cover as a magazine photographer, found this incomprehensible: "Normally, you just can't operate without it—but somehow Harvey managed." According to his subordinates, Harvey operated the way many British colonialists had—he simply spoke English loudly and expected to be understood.

Bill Harvey's first goal was to replace the café atmosphere at Berlin Base with a sense of urgency. His reforms went into effect quickly. The Base was put on a 24-hour schedule with a senior case officer assigned "the duty." To impress upon his subordinates how important this was to him, Harvey located the "duty station" in a small room next to his office.

The room had a cot, a telephone whose number was given to all agents, and a desk. The desk had two small file boxes on it. One box contained the names of case officers and their aliases; the other contained the names of agents and their aliases. Anyone who had the duty could easily put an agent and his case officer together. Harvey gave standing orders that any case officer could be called at any time.

Case officers meeting the new chief for the first time were in for a real experience. Like remembering where you were when President Kennedy was shot or when the *Challenger* blew up, Berlin Base veterans remembered their first meeting with Bill Harvey.

Paul Garbler, a Navy pilot who made his way to Berlin after a stint in Naval Intelligence in Korea, recalled his first encounter with Harvey in vivid detail. "Inside his outer office was Joan, his secretary. She was very plain, but she was very smart. . . . She was kind of a dragon at the moat. I realized that there would not be a way for me to see him without going through her."[4]

The secretary greeted Garbler, offered him coffee, and invited him to sit down. After Garbler had a refill on the coffee, the door to Harvey's office opened and a tall man walked out. After he passed, Joan looked at Garbler and said that he could go in. Garbler was lost in thought trying to figure out how many people were at the Base. Joan jolted him back to attention by repeating: "Bill will see you now."

Harvey's office was not particularly large. It was furnished with two overstuffed chairs covered with leather, a leather sofa, and a wooden coffee table with German publications on it. Garbler did not yet know that Harvey could not read German. Harvey's desk was three feet back from the doorjamb, flush against the wall, so Harvey could see visitors before they spotted him. The walls were decorated with undistinguished watercolors of birds.

Garbler was a little taken aback when he first saw Harvey. Harvey's head, almost neckless, was vast and pink, and when he was sitting, it seemed like a dome fixed on a large pear. That pear-shaped body was encased in an expensive salt-and-pepper Harris tweed suit. Harvey's eyes— larger than walnuts and the color of a Weimeraner dog—bulged from his face but did not blink. Harvey wore his hair so slicked back and so short that it blended into the top of his head. Under a strong nose was an almost invisible line of hair, a mustache that subordinates joked must have been grown to some old FBI specifications.

Harvey dropped a black fountain pen on a large thick ledger in which he had been writing. Garbler guessed correctly that Harvey's FBI experience made him a compulsive note-taker. Harvey offered Garbler one of his large hands. Garbler expected a crushing handshake but, instead, got a friendly one. Harvey seemed genuinely pleased to have him in Berlin. "Welcome aboard, Garbler. Please sit down," he said.

Garbler soon surmised that Harvey was in many ways a self-creation. His deep gruff voice and street-detective jargon did not seem natural. In fact, Garbler thought he detected a high-pitched voice underneath—not a falsetto, but almost. John Sherwood, another Berlin Base veteran, agreed. "He was a man with an ersatz voice," is the way Sherwood put it.

Harvey, who smoked, offered Garbler a cigarette. Garbler caught on that he was being put through a series of small tests. Harvey, already on the phone to Joan, said: "How about some coffee?" Garbler later learned that this was always the prelude to the big question: "So, you speak Russian?" Garbler answered that he spoke enough to run an operation. Harvey then asked about German. Garbler shook his head. Harvey pounced on him: "What the hell are you doing here? Go out and learn German and don't come back until you know it."

When Harvey raised himself out of his chair, he seemed bigger than Garbler, although Garbler was a good deal taller. Another CIA officer, who knew both Harvey and General Douglas MacArthur, said, "You know, MacArthur was only about five-foot-nine, but ask anyone and they all would guess him over six feet. Harvey had that kind of presence."

Harvey reached for his gun and put it on the desk. He looked at Garbler and asked him if he had ever used one. Garbler said that he had, during the war. "In Berlin, we all carry heat," Harvey told him. Garbler almost winced at the slang.

Several years later, when Donald Morris, a ramrod-straight Annapolis graduate, arrived in Berlin, Harvey had not mellowed. Morris had high hopes that his career would prosper with the Berlin assignment. Excited, he wore his Naval uniform for his meeting with Harvey and arrived half an hour early. When Morris walked into Harvey's outer office, he was greeted by Rita, one of the glamorous twin secretaries who had replaced the conservative Joan. These two very attractive women, the Chapwicki sisters, were blonde and very tall and the subjects of male case officer fantasy.

Faced with a half hour to kill, Morris decided to pass the time in the men's room reading the newspaper. "I was reading away and somebody walked in, got into the stall next to me, and I heard the usual sounds of the belt and a zipper. All of a sudden there was a crash, and a .44 Lugar came skittering across into my stall. It was followed by five large fingers each the shape of a small banana groping for the gun. I put my foot on it and shoved it over toward the stall. The hand closed on the gun and a voice way down said, 'Thank you.'"

Twenty minutes later, Morris recognized the banana-like fingers as Harvey offered him a handshake.[5] Morris took note of a photograph on Harvey's office wall featuring a statue of two nude Greco-Roman wrestlers. "One of them has got a hold of the other guy," Morris recalled, "and is in the process of throwing him over his shoulder, unaware that the man has a firm grip on his penis. This had a sign underneath that read: Staff Guidance."

When Bill Harvey arrived in Berlin, the Base was still located in the old mansion Allen Dulles had selected. Besides being in a bad location, the building was too small for Harvey's plans for Berlin Base. Within weeks of his arrival, renovations were underway on a large three-story building inside the U.S. Mission compound half a mile away. Harvey knew full well that Frank Wisner's OPC had operated out of the compound, and he wanted everyone to understand that there was, as he put it, "a new sheriff in town."

For his home, Harvey chose a beautiful old house in the Steglitz area on Lepsius Street. The house became the social center for BOB. In the summer, Harvey's guests could gather in the garden and cool off in the very deep swimming pool. Drunken parties were not unheard of. Etta Jo Weisz told of the welcoming party the Harveys gave in 1954 when she and George came to Berlin Base. Harvey said, "'Jo, let me make you one of my famous martinis.' I didn't know him then. And he gave me one martini and I set the glass down on the table. What I didn't realize is that he kept filling the glass." When it was time to get up and go to dinner, Etta Jo could not stand up.

Harvey had no difficulty getting people to move to Germany to work for him. By now, everyone accepted that Berlin Base was the CIA's premier operating base. Especially for a case officer who had not been to Harvard or Yale or served in the old OSS, Berlin Base was the punch needed for his ticket to the top of American intelligence. It meant that he had served with the best, that he had looked the enemy in the eye and not blinked. That was the myth that became the mind-set of Berlin Base.

Harvey, trained in counterespionage, had no experience in positive intelligence. He had no real knowledge of how to vet operations or sources. Still, when he arrived in Berlin, he set doggedly to work trying to determine what assets had been generated—what agents, companies, and government officials were available to U.S. intelligence. He went over with the case officers the Base's very short list of agents. The only promising agent Harvey found on the list was one who had been transferred from Munich. He was a Russian POW named Igor Orlov who had stayed in Germany after the war, and he had what Harvey considered a great idea: a plan to penetrate Karlshorst, the Soviet military ghetto in East Berlin.

Karlshorst was a closed enclave within a closed society. Orlov's idea—as his case officer, Sam Wilson, related it to Harvey—was to open Karlshorst up with sex. He would mount a major operation to entrap Soviet officers by offering them Berlin's best-looking hookers. The young women's mandate would be to determine if the officers were married and, if they were, to entice them into meeting an "uncle" in the American sector. The uncle, of course, would be a CIA officer, who would blackmail them into working for American intelligence.

Harvey loved the idea and insisted on meeting this imaginative agent. Sam Wilson, a decorated World War II hero who had worked with Orlov in Munich, drove Harvey to a nearby safe house and introduced him as "Mr. Ross" to the diminutive young man with piercing blue eyes called "Franz Koischwitz," formerly known as "Alexander Kopatzky."[6]

CHAPTER THIRTEEN

A MISSED CHANCE

I N JANUARY 1953, as Bill Harvey arrived in Berlin, East Germany was becoming a key concern to Stalin and Beria. They had concluded that the East German state they had created was, in fact, a very expensive sham. Massive numbers of refugees were leaving, bleeding the region of its professionals. The local Communist authorities were ineffective. Stalin instructed Beria to replace these generals and intelligence officers in the hopes of making the state less costly and more useful.

Since the end of the war, Beria had found Stalin less and less manageable. One of their major disagreements was what to do about Raoul Wallenberg, the Swedish diplomat who had produced fake Swedish identity documents that saved thousands of Hungarian Jews. Stalin ordered his execution, but Beria repeatedly delayed the order. In early 1947 Stalin became hysterical and insisted his order be carried out. Beria worried that this execution of a foreign national and a potential hero would cause an international investigation that might expose all the crimes of the Stalin regime. In sheer numbers, the deaths ordered by Stalin and Beria exceeded the six million murders Hitler had committed. As things turned out, there was no international investigation. It was not until decades later that the cause of Wallenberg's death was definitely proved.

Then, suddenly, Stalin was felled by a massive stroke. As Beria and another of Stalin's would-be successors, Nikita Khrushchev, watched by his bedside, Beria shocked Khrushchev with the hatred he demonstrated for the man he had served so long. Khrushchev wrote in his memoirs that whenever Stalin showed signs of recovering, Beria "threw himself on his knees, seized Stalin's hand, and started kissing it. When Stalin lost consciousness again and closed his eyes, Beria stood up and spat."

Stalin succumbed on March 5, 1953. Beria acted quickly. He put his own people in control of the domestic police forces, he installed a man loyal to him, Lieutenant General Vasili Stepanovich Ryasnoy, as head of the Foreign Directorate of the NKVD, and he quickly reorganized the intelligence services into the new, all-powerful MVD.

He also ordered big changes in the intelligence services in East and West Germany. Residents of the Soviet ghetto in East Berlin became filled with apprehension and fear as hundreds of key staff people were recalled to Moscow. Beria had learned nothing from the Red Orchestra experience in Berlin in the late 1930s. He was repeating all the same mistakes. The difference is that, unlike Hitler's men before the war, United States Intelligence in Berlin missed everything that was going on.[1] Bill Harvey's arrival was of more interest to Berlin Base than its Soviet targets.

Igor Orlov was one of those who watched Beria's overhaul of Karlshorst with alarm. As Moscow recalled hundreds of officers, Orlov feared he was next. He was also surprised that neither his CIA case officers nor "Mr. Ross" ever asked him what was going on. Igor could not imagine the United States' failure to understand just how weak Moscow's hold on East Germany was. Puzzled, he dutifully reported back to Moscow the lack of response at BOB.

BOB was also completely out of touch with what was happening in the rest of East Germany (although so was the man in charge of Karlshorst, General Fadeykin). The East German people, awarded to the Soviets at Yalta, were fed up. Warning signs had been evident for a year, especially after price increases for meat and other food went into effect. But CIA promotions were not being given for discovering that grocery prices were too high. This was always the problem with Berlin Base—and with CIA headquarters in Washington. The fact that Berlin Base reported very little about day-to-day life in East Berlin did not seem to upset top CIA officials back home. As John Sherwood put it: "Running whores was more interesting for a case officer than finding out how much a loaf of bread costs. But generally the price of bread is more important to people than the price of a woman."

The Eastern Zone was a mystery to the men who ran Berlin Base. With rare exceptions, case officers were not permitted to venture into the Zone, although their wives, against all the rules, did sneak over to shop. In the mid-1950s, a kilo tin of Russian caviar cost only a few dollars in the Eastern Zone. That was the extent of what Berlin Base could reliably tell headquarters about life in the East—the cost of caviar. Had the officers at Berlin Base listened to the refugees flooding into the West about the dramatic increases in food prices, the severe shortages of basic necessities, and the new work quotas, they would have been prepared for what happened in June 1953. But they were not interviewing refugees to get such mundane information.

The trouble really started in the spring of 1952, when the Communist regime increased work quotas a staggering 10 percent. When in April 1953 food prices were also increased, spontaneous demonstrations broke out. The government had to back off on the work quotas, but the dissatisfaction simmered.

On June 16, fifty thousand workers began rioting in the streets of East Berlin. They tore down Communist Party symbols. They attacked the feared and hated Vopos, the East Berlin police, with rocks and homemade weapons.

The leader of the East German Communist Youth, Erich Honecker, prepared to defend party headquarters from an attack from the streets. Honecker had spent World War II imprisoned by Hitler with other Communists. Now he was a trusted aide and political adviser to Walter Ulbricht, the Soviet-installed dictator of East Germany.[2] Honecker was prepared to fight to the death from Communist Party headquarters. However, Moscow's control over East Germany was so tentative that the Soviets decided it was better to evacuate the German Communist leadership than risk a fight they might lose.

If the West were going to liberate East Germany, there was no better time. Yet the West did nothing. What unfolded was a dramatic American intelligence failure with the worst consequences.

On June 16, as summer drizzle dampened Berlin, East German radio carried only traditional Austrian music. But RIAS, a West Berlin radio station controlled by the U.S. State Department, started reporting that strikes had broken out in East Berlin. RIAS's German broadcasters and reporters wanted to tell the full story, but the station's management received orders from Washington to keep the broadcasts low-key to avoid antagonizing the Soviets.

Berlin Base was tuned in to RIAS. Their intelligence sources in the Eastern sector were so poor that the Americans knew little more than what they heard on the radio. The fact that the Communist regime was facing a full-scale counterrevolution from its own workers never dawned on any American official except the German-born deputy chief of base, Henry Hecksher.

Unprepared, Base case officers quickly contacted the few agents they had to try to get more information. They learned little. One of the few to report in was Igor Orlov, who described events in the East as only a minor disturbance when, in fact, Karlshorst was in an uproar. Moscow was so convinced that the end was near for the Soviet-backed regime that its officers began shredding classified documents and preparing to evacuate their people. Beria was notified in Moscow that the puppet government was on the verge of falling.

In the demonstrations on Tuesday, June 16, workers marched on the House of Ministries. Ulbricht ignored the crowds until Wednesday morning when the workers staged a general strike. While Berlin Base debated what to do, the Soviets moved decisively. At 10:00 A.M. Wednesday, the Soviets ordered in T-34 tanks and dispatched two armored divisions.

At Potsdamerplatz, on the border between the American and Soviet zones, a huge crowd gathered. No American military force was present, but a number of Berlin Base officers were on the scene. They believed that this was the center of the action. One Base officer present was David Chavchavadze, who was there with his pregnant wife, Nell, watching the peaceful crowd chanting for freedom. The Soviets then raised the curtain on their little play. To the shock of the crowd, tanks began rumbling into a line of people and, without warning, began firing their huge guns above the crowd. Chavchavadze recalls, "I don't know that they actually crossed the border, but they opened fire into West Berlin. The crowd began to run, except for those with infantry training, who hit the dirt. So did I, bringing Nell down with me. . . ."[3]

The Soviets were bluffing. They were creating an East-West drama at the border to divert attention from a much more brutal game going on behind the scenes. The Soviets were convinced the West would do nothing as long as the trouble was confined to East Berlin, and they were hoping this diversion on the border would give them enough time to crush the revolution inside the Zone.

Belatedly, Berlin Base sent Washington a string of cables reporting the unrest. At CIA headquarters in Washington, it became clear that the foremost intelligence base in the CIA's constellation really did not know what was happening. The Base's inability to recognize the signs of unrest months earlier, and now its inability to confirm the severity of the riots, led to a series of decisions based on wrong assumptions about Soviet strength in East Germany. Even more serious was the fact that since the Base had done such a poor job of identifying opposition leaders in the East, the Americans knew no one in a position of responsibility to work with.

Only Deputy Chief of Base Hecksher, the tough German native, argued that a revolution was at hand, and, with support from the West, could be won. He felt that any material or moral support to the revolutionary workers might be enough to force the puppet regime out for good. He pleaded for the CIA to immediately supply the rioters with weapons to fight the Soviets. Although there was not a heavy American military presence in Berlin, there was a stockpile of weapons the CIA had put in place for just such an event. Hecksher argued that the Base should immediately cable Allen Dulles for help. But Dulles was not there. On what was probably the most important day in the first six years of CIA history, the boss was traveling and unreachable.

Harvey rolled his protruding eyes in response to Hecksher's plea to send the cable. He was well aware that in Dulles's absence, the appeal would go to John Bross, then chief of the CIA's Eastern European Division,[4] and on to Frank Wisner, who was running all secret operations. Harvey intuitively understood that a decision to help the East Berliners fight would be considered too daring and too difficult. "What he really understood," according to William Corson, "was that neither Bross nor Wisner was about to risk a career by recommending to the White House that we take real action."

Finally, Harvey gave in and approved a cable, drafted by his deputy, requesting permission to distribute stun guns, rifles, and grenades. As Harvey expected, a cable came back from Bross denying the request. In the end it did not matter. The reply cable arrived too late to do anything even if the answer had been yes.

At a meeting that afternoon, a Berlin Base counterintelligence officer actually stood up and suggested that the revolt had been staged by the Soviets. Harvey, fed up first with Washington and now with the stupidity of the comment, rose from his chair and said: "That's enough—I have been up to my ass in midgets all day."

Meanwhile, on the streets of East Berlin, the leaderless protesting workers were chased down and shot by machine-gun-carrying Soviet security forces. Had Berlin Base had a single intelligence agent at a hospital in East Berlin, they would have known that the emergency rooms and morgues were overflowing. The East German secret police—the Stasi—reported that 25 people were killed and 378 wounded. In fact, the CIA later reported that some three hundred were killed and over a thousand injured.[5]

Berlin Base never understood that if the Soviets could be shown up as frauds, economic vampires, and political charlatans, the whole system would collapse and blow away. "The Soviets played chicken with us, and we gave in," Harvey later told his colleagues. It was much worse than that. In a pattern that established a modus operandi in countries around the world, the CIA settled into an internal mind-set about what kind of intelligence was important. The intelligence they selected had very little to do with the actual experiences of everyday people.

To make matters worse, the time lost cabling back and forth between Washington and Berlin allowed the Soviets to develop a plan, blaming the United States for inflaming the "dissident minority" with the RIAS broadcasts. Because of this intelligence failure, an opportunity to roll back the Iron Curtain early in the Cold War was lost. The Soviets, having quashed the East German revolt, returned the puppet leadership that had fled East Berlin for the countryside to power. It lasted another 36 years. Harvey and the others at Berlin Base did not see the East German uprising as an intelligence failure. Instead, it strengthened their resolve to operate intensely and boldly against the Soviets.

WITH CONTROL RESTORED, Lavrenti Beria immediately flew to East Berlin to find out firsthand what had gone wrong. Beria spent several days consolidating his power and ending careers at Karlshorst. While there, he went to a government guest house outside Karlshorst for a very special meeting.

Igor Orlov was summoned from his bar in Karlshorst without notice or warning. He believed that he was finally to be at the receiving end in Beria's purge of German operations. He knew the history of the Red Orchestra, when loyal agents had been summoned home and executed.

In the backseat of the staff car that fetched him was a huge box. Inside the box was the uniform of a lieutenant general. Orlov's fears evaporated. He put on the uniform with its oversized cover and arrived for the meeting.

Caviar and the best vodka were waiting for him. Beria entered the room with Orlov's old case officer from Moscow, congratulated his most successful agent, and told him that the reports he had filed on Berlin Operating Base were the only accurate intelligence Beria had seen since the disaster started.

This was Orlov's first meeting with his patron and benefactor. Beria hardly seemed fearsome. The entire meeting lasted about an hour. At the end of it, they posed for pictures, Beria said his good-byes, and Orlov returned the uniform to his case officer for safekeeping. The case officer told him, "Under orders from Comrade Beria, you have been assigned an office in Karlshorst where this will be kept for you. You are to wear it while traveling in fraternal countries."

Orlov asked if there might be an opportunity for him to return home to visit his ailing mother. The case officer laughed and said, "Be grateful. This is no time for you to go home."[6]

Orlov returned to his bar in Karlshorst at 2:00 A.M., two hours late for his check-in with Sam Wilson. Resourcefully, he called a friend in the Berlin police department, who in turn called the duty desk at BOB. The cooperative policeman reported that Orlov had been arrested for disorderly conduct and public intoxication. The CIA duty officer contacted Orlov's case officer, Wilson, who reprimanded Orlov and later placed a note in his file about his errant behavior but there was no indication in the file that he had independently checked Orlov's story.

Beria, meanwhile, called Moscow and learned, to his surprise, that an emergency meeting of the Soviet Presidium had been called. He was assured his presence was not needed, but taking no chances, he ignored the assurances and flew home for the meeting. Filled with outrage over what he had seen in East Berlin, he made a presentation on East Germany that shocked his colleagues. According to Andrei Gromyko, who was there, a sneering and dismissive Beria told the Presidium, "German Democratic Republic? What does it amount to, this GDR? It's not even a real state. It's only being kept by Soviet troops, even if we do call it the German Democratic Republic."

Beria's remark was a huge mistake. He should not have spoken the truth to a group of men who had built their careers and lives on lies. Immediately, Vyacheslav Molotov—one of Beria's fellow deputy premiers— moved to object to Beria's words. One by one, his fellow members rose in criticism.

Unaware of the depth of political damage he had done to himself, Beria, after the meeting, went to his house on Vspolny Pereulok to enjoy the young women his underlings had procured for him. He did not know that Khrushchev was gathering evidence against him. Beria, who had spent his life watching others, did not realize he himself was being watched.

Beria was not the only one operating blind. Long before 1953, his assistant, the mole who had been reporting information to the United States, had cut off all communications to the Americans after the war. With the loss of this source, the Americans had no reliable information. In 1953 the CIA did not even operate a station or a base in Moscow. The United States essentially had no intelligence coming from the capital of the Soviet Union as almost a civil war broke out among the Soviet leadership.[7]

In the weeks following Stalin's death, Nikita Khrushchev had approached members of the Presidium he trusted to determine their support for Beria's removal and arrest. They all reminded him that Beria had a detailed file on each of them. Nonetheless, Khrushchev began to collect intelligence on Beria's activities. He got a break from an unexpected source when a number of the Jews whom Beria had purged from the MVD, the successor to the NKVD, came to Khrushchev and his allies with evidence against Beria.

On June 26 Khrushchev called a special meeting of the Presidium. With a gun in his pocket for protection, he told his colleagues: "There is one item on the agenda: the anti-party, divisive activity of imperialist agent Beria. There is a proposal to drop him from the Presidium and from the Central Committee, and hand him over to the court martial. Who is in favor?"

One after another, the members of the Presidium denounced Beria and urged his removal from power. Then the Minister of War, Nikolai Bulganin, entered with a group of armed officers and arrested Beria. His fate was not publicly known for several weeks. On Christmas Eve 1953, the Supreme Court of the Soviet Union publicly convicted Beria of a plot to "revive capitalism and restore the rule of the bourgeoisie." Additional convictions for mass murder and rape were not made public.

After Beria's ouster, Khrushchev consolidated the Soviet Union's intelligence organs into the Committee for State Security, the KGB, the best known in the series of Soviet intelligence services. The military intelligence organs, especially the GRU, operated sometimes in concert and sometimes at odds with the KGB. In many ways the GRU gave the generals and the admirals a check on the KGB.[8]

The CIA missed it all.

CHAPTER FOURTEEN

MURPHY AND FRIENDS

B Y 1953, IGOR ORLOV'S old case officer from Munich, David Murphy, had made the big time. He wangled the second most important job at Berlin Operating Base, Soviet Branch Chief.

This was a plum assignment, a rung on the ladder to the top of the CIA. To get a job like that, someone like Murphy—with no important social ties, no Ivy League credentials, no pipeline to Allen Dulles—needed a sponsor, or in CIA old boy parlance, a "rabbi." Murphy's rabbi was one of the old boys, a brilliant case officer and a favorite of Allen Dulles, Edward Snow. It was Snow's patronage that propelled Murphy's CIA career.

According to James Angleton, Harvey did not know Murphy's controversial history when he arrived in Berlin. "Murphy's behavior before he got to Berlin caused many of his colleagues to wonder about his sense and even his loyalty," Angleton said. He mused: "Had Harvey known, I am not certain that Murphy would be in charge of every activity against the Soviets in Berlin."

David Murphy hailed from Brooklyn's Williamsburg Heights Section. He later told his CIA colleagues that he picked up his lifelong interest in Russia from the Russian immigrants in his neighborhood. He took intensive Russian language training at the University of California in an Army program. One of his instructors was a Russian Jewish émigré, Marian, who had lived with her parents in Shanghai until the outbreak of World War II. They began dating and eventually married.

Veterans of Berlin Base remember Marian Murphy as strong-minded and tough. "She was a seagoing ton of bricks," George Kisevalter recalled. "She tried to push him. She was jealous as hell of any gal he made a pass at, which was plenty."[1]

After Murphy's stint in Munich with the Army at the end of the war and his early encounter with Igor Orlov, the Army Counterintelligence Corps (CIC) transferred him to Japan. When the CIA began to operate in the Far East in 1949, it was desperate for people with decent language skills and sought out those who spoke Russian. David Murphy responded to the CIA's search. "He just slid across the street from the Army Counterintelligence Corps to the CIA in Tokyo," Robert Crowley recalled. "He came in as a GS-5 [entry-level Civil Service grade] or something. He was not a luminary. He had been a Jeep driver." Because of the severe shortage of translators, Murphy easily worked his way into the center of operations. He impressed his bosses with his ability and his desire to please. "Murphy was like a camel who puts his head in the tent and ends up owning the tent," former Army colleague Colonel Tulluis Accompura said.

After the war, Tokyo was nearly as busy an intelligence center as Munich, with the CIA and the Army CIC both trying to cope with huge numbers of Russian refugees and returning Japanese prisoners of war. Before resettling the Japanese, the Army tried to determine how many of them had been recruited by the Soviets while they were held in Soviet POW camps. Several key Soviet staff officers who had defected to the United States prior to the war were now working for American intelligence and debriefing Soviet-held Japanese prisoners of war.[2] Before long they were joined by a White Russian, Arseny (Andy) Yankovsky.

To James Angleton, one of American intelligence's great mistakes was its heavy reliance on White Russians. "We needed people with information and language ability. We did not have the resources to check out bona fides.[3] We certified people we thought could help us or could enhance our careers. The Soviets understood how to exploit our weakness for the Whites. Andy Yankovsky was the classic case," Angleton said in 1981.

Yankovsky was a colorful man from a colorful Vladivostok family that had received its status from the Czar. In 1920 their czarist connections finally caught up with them, and they were supposedly driven from their home and, traveling overland, reached North Korea. There is no question that Andy's father, George Yankovsky, fought with the Whites against the Communists. What is not clear is how 30 family members plus horses and cattle all managed to get out of Russia and end up in the Chongjin region of North Korea. Eventually, the family settled in Chuul.

Andy Yankovsky defected to the Americans in 1948 and brought with him fabulous tales of his family. He claimed that his father had been a famed hunter and that his two brothers had hunted tigers and wild boar and trained reindeer. His father was even a renowned butterfly expert. Yankovsky arrived speaking Russian, Korean, English, and Japanese. According to Peter Kapusta, a CIA man stationed in Tokyo at the time, Yankovsky was modest about his language abilities. Accompura agrees: "That guy, who went by the name of Andy Brown, could speak at least 16 languages."

Yankovsky claimed that, when the Soviets came into North Korea, they again went after his family. He told Murphy that his father and two brothers were arrested, and he had to escape on foot. He said he had to leave his wife and stepdaughter behind. It was a sad and dramatic story. The problem was that he left out some key parts.

Nevertheless, the Army quickly accepted Yankovsky as a genuine Soviet refugee and put him to work in Tokyo with David Murphy. "Yankovsky and Murphy first got together in Tokyo—all of this is then very informal," Accompura explained. Murphy and Yankovsky became friends and began working operations together.[4] Murphy's wife, the White Russian from Shanghai, had much in common with Yankovsky. Eventually, Murphy and Yankovsky were transferred to Korea, where they began running agent networks in the South.

Captain Alan D. Bogardus headed the 24th Army CIC unit in Korea and was directing agents into North Korea. Almost immediately, Yankovsky, only a recent defector, was included in sensitive intelligence operations. "Andy ate daily at the officers' mess and came to learn the identity of all our agents and case officers," Kapusta recalled. Murphy and Yankovsky began recruiting agents out of the growing number of anti-Soviet Russian refugees in Seoul, sending them back into the Soviet Union as agents. In the course of this operation, Murphy came up with the idea of sending counterfeit North Korean currency into the North. The idea was to ruin the North Korean economy with inflation. "He took the lousiest paper God put on earth," said George Kisevalter, "and he falsified North Korean currency."

Tragically and mysteriously, as soon as Yankovsky and Murphy joined Bogardus's operation, North Koreans started killing American-controlled agents. "Agents are dying at incredible rates—like a hundred percent," Accompura said. He was not exaggerating. Every single agent who was sent into North Korea by Army intelligence was lost during the time Yankovsky worked with Murphy.[5] To Kapusta, the slaughter was too wholesale to be coincidence. It was "obvious we had a leak." Kapusta recalled that Captain Bogardus was livid when he returned to Tokyo from a counterintelligence meeting in Seoul. Bogardus told his colleagues that as soon as Yankovsky showed up on the scene, "all of my agents start getting killed." "He was fuming," Kapusta remembered.

Yet in terms of Murphy's career, his problems with lost agents could not have come at a better time. What was attracting the attention of Washington, and therefore of the Far East Command, was a scandal rocking Hongo House, the U.S. Army CIC headquarters in Tokyo. The scandal involved male Russian defectors, CIC agents, and Army officers who were found having homosexual encounters. One man was even beaten to death in the facility. Since Hongo House was at the center of Far East intelligence, being discovered in a homosexual liaison there was far more career-threatening than losing scores of agents in North Korea.

In 1949, the loss of China to the Communists increased the importance of both Korea and Japan to the United States. Murphy, in turn, became increasingly influential.

Then, as Accompura tells it, "All of a sudden, Yankovsky's wife and daughter come paddling their way from North Korea on a fishing boat." Yankovsky's "wife," Olga Sokolovskaya, whom he claimed to have married in 1934, and her 22-year-old daughter, Nata, wanted to defect to the West. Murphy was the "Soviet expert" who debriefed the two women. He quickly certified and established their bona fides, setting aside any questions about holes in Nata's story. Nata was renamed Anna Yankovsky, and Murphy arranged a job for her as a translator in Seoul. The Yankovsky family now had complete access to U.S. intelligence's Korean operations. When North Korea invaded South Korea, the family was moved to Yokusuka, Japan, where they continued to work for U.S. intelligence, this time for the new CIA. According to Angleton, Yankovsky and his family were hired and cleared solely on the recommendations of David Murphy.[6] Murphy's defenders point out that the pressure to provide agents with detailed knowledge of Soviet operations was enormous, and there was never sufficient time or information to allow the CIA and Army to vet every agent thoroughly.

The large number of failed operations in Korea should have put an end to Yankovsky's intelligence career. However, according to Quentin Johnson, a former high-ranking CIA official, "What sealed Yankovsky as an informant and expert was his prediction that the North Koreans would invade the South," even though the CIA didn't act upon this information. Angleton confirmed that Yankovsky's correct prediction staved off increasing pressure for an investigation into breaches in security over failed Korean operations.

Yankovsky's "family" should also have been under suspicion from the start. Nata had a brother, Slava. According to Angleton, "Nata told Murphy that Slava, who had settled in the White Russian community of Shanghai, was lured back to the Soviet Union by false promises and thrown in a gulag. In fact, Nata knew her brother had not been lured anywhere. He was an NKVD intelligence officer. It turned out that her real father was an NKVD officer as well. Murphy failed to uncover any of this."

Within a few months of Nata's arrival in Tokyo, she developed a romance with Murphy's friend and patron, Ed Snow. Snow was working with Murphy and Yankovsky on the program to send Russian émigrés back into the Soviet Union as agents for the United States. The real story of Ed Snow's rise and fall is one of the most closely held secrets in the CIA.

Quentin Johnson, who worked with Snow, described the Washington State native as one of the finest CIA officers he ever knew. Like Marian Murphy, Snow's parents were White Russians. Snow could speak Japanese, Chinese, and Russian, and he was one of Allen Dulles's original CIA officers who never took a polygraph test. His career appeared to be unstoppable. Murphy took full advantage of Snow's old boy status.[7]

Snow pushed for a series of promotions for Murphy and another CIA man, Bob Anton, who was working undercover in Tokyo as an Associated Press correspondent with the name "Tom Ames." Murphy was called back to CIA headquarters and given a large promotion. As Accompura put it, "So his [Murphy's] name gets in the hopper and the next fucking thing you know he's in Washington and he's a GS-umpteen."

Meanwhile, Yankovsky was supervising agents who were being sent into the Soviet Union from the Far East with sophisticated radio equipment, much like the Munich operations with the NTS agents. Snow and Yankovsky selected all the agents. Like the operation in Munich, this one was penetrated from the start. "The casualty rate on these missions was about 100 percent," said Robert Crowley.[8]

Because the operations were such failures, the Soviet Division back at CIA headquarters decided to drop them. But Snow, as head of the Soviet Branch in Tokyo, ignored headquarters and, without proper authority, kept funding Yankovsky. Snow was officially reprimanded for not following orders, but he was neither the first nor the last CIA employee to divert funds because he believed in an operation, and his sin was overlooked.

Ed Snow's romance with Nata Sokolovskaya blossomed into marriage in 1952. Snow asked Tokyo Station Chief Robert Delaney for permission to marry, and CIA headquarters approved the marriage on the basis of David Murphy's work on Nata's bona fides. For Snow, the marriage seemed, at first, all he had hoped. Nata soon became pregnant and gave birth to a daughter. It took Ed Snow five years to understand that marrying Nata was the second great mistake of his life. The first was befriending Dave Murphy.

The trouble started when Nata began an affair with a Soviet military intelligence officer. This episode, Robert Crowley recalled, got both the "Office of Security and Angleton's attention." Angleton became so concerned when he learned of Nata's affair that he sent John Mertz, one of Harvey's former FBI associates who had joined the CIA, to Tokyo to conduct a counterintelligence investigation. According to Peter Kapusta, Mertz and Angleton did not tell Tokyo Station Chief Henry Hecksher they were conducting the investigation. Mertz wrote a report concluding that Yankovsky's behavior and that of his daughter should be watched.

Despite Snow's personal troubles, the CIA transferred him back to Washington and kept him on a career fast track. Dulles considered Snow's expertise on Soviet affairs so vital that in 1954 he put Snow in charge of all CIA assignments against the Soviets. Then, in December 1954, a GRU colonel and amateur tennis player, Yuri Rastvorov, defected to the British during a roaring snowstorm in Tokyo. Rastvorov was an anxious and jumpy defector. When his plane to London was delayed because of the weather, he became very nervous when his MI6 escorts started drinking.

Then one of them said something complimentary about Kim Philby, and it was all over. Rastvorov walked out of the airport into the snow, took a train back to Tokyo, and redefected, this time to the United States.

The CIA's Donald Morris was the young agent assigned to Rastvorov's case: "It was a blinding snowstorm. . . . Yuri [Rastvorov] was one of the first major defectors to walk in," Morris recalled. "He gave us the news that Stalin had the KGB and GRU working hand-in-hand for almost a year and half."[9] The CIA agreed to pay Rastvorov twenty-thousand dollars and flew him to Okinawa for debriefing. "Because he was a hot property," Accompura recalled, "as many of the big shots from headquarters wanted in on the act as possible, and that included Ed Snow, who at this time was high up in Soviet Operations, and also David Murphy. Snow walked into the room and he [Rastvorov] took one look at Andy Yankovsky, and that was it. He said he would not talk in front of Yankovsky, that Yankovsky was under KGB control."[10]

"Yuri wanted to disappear, and he said, 'Get me outta here! I won't talk to these guys,'" Robert Crowley added. "Then they separated him and got into his recollections, and his recollection was that these guys [Snow and Yankovsky] were controlled [by the KGB]. And he knew them. In fact, he wanted to get off the island, and he wanted to turn a different color."[11]

Angleton said it was this incident that started the clock ticking against Snow. Angleton began the slow investigation that finally culminated in 1959.[12] When Angleton finally presented his case against Snow and Yankovsky to Richard Helms and Allen Dulles, Dulles once again suppressed any hint of scandal. No charges were brought against either Snow or Yankovsky. Snow was asked to resign, and Quentin Johnson replaced him as head of Soviet Operations. However, Dulles gave Snow a letter stating that he was not resigning under a cloud and arranged a high-level job for him with Westrex Corporation in Japan and then with Litton Industries. Ed Snow died in California on April Fool's Day 1990.

The CIA kept Yankovsky as a contract employee and found him a cover job with TRW in the Far East. TRW held the contracts to build and operate some of the CIA's most important spy satellites. Yankovsky eventually became a multimillionaire. He died in San Francisco in 1978.

Former CIA colleagues of Snow's confirmed that the real reason Snow was not brought up on charges was because of the embarrassment to Dulles and the CIA if the story became public knowledge. Dulles believed that by hiding this mistake, as he had done with James Kronthal, he could control the damage. However, Angleton and Dulles compounded the damage by failing to properly investigate the vetting of Yankovsky. To make matters worse, Dulles continued to throw intelligence assignments to Snow in Japan.

According to William Corson, one of the jobs Snow did for Dulles after he left the CIA was to approve the bona fides of Lawrence Wu Tai Chin, who turned out to be one of the most damaging spies the People's Republic of China ever sent to the United States. "We know that Ed Snow signed off on Wu Tai Chin's bona fides," Corson said. "It kind of makes you wonder how many more were out there."

Meanwhile, according to Quentin Johnson, "Ed became leery of Murphy. After a few years he realized something was not right . . . and the relationship cooled off." By that time it was too late. It was largely because of Snow that Murphy had risen to stardom in Soviet operations. It was also because of Snow that Murphy ended up at Berlin Base.

CHAPTER FIFTEEN

COWBOYS IN BERLIN

D ESPITE DAVE MURPHY'S FAILURES in the Far East, his reputation back at headquarters was that of a hot shot, someone un-
afraid to take on the Soviets head-to-head. An incident from his Tokyo
days illustrates how he got his reputation.

The scene was a Tokyo apartment house. The hallway was dark, and
Murphy's adrenaline was going. He was about to complete a recruitment
operation that he had been working on with Ed Snow for months. Murphy's Soviet sources had told him about an NKVD agent who had grave
doubts about what was happening in the Soviet Union and was willing to
begin spying for the United States. Murphy, always ready to throw everything he had into an operation, had told his sidekick Bob Anton, another
cowboy CIA officer, that he believed he had a big fish on the line.

As the Soviet officer walked down the hallway toward his apartment
door, Murphy emerged out of the darkness and began his pitch for freedom. Suddenly the officer began screaming. Almost immediately, the local
police descended on Murphy. The ever-optimistic Murphy had been totally set up in one of the most embarrassing incidents in the history of the
young CIA.[1]

It later turned out that Murphy's bad luck with the Soviets did not
start with Andy Yankovsky. Behind the scenes was Igor Orlov. Ever since
Orlov's early contact with Murphy in Munich, the Soviet master spy had
tailored an approach to Murphy by the NKVD/KGB and the GRU to

make him worse than ineffective to the CIA. As James Angleton later learned, Orlov had reported back to Moscow that Murphy was confrontational in nature and totally willing to engage an enemy; also, that he was so full of self-confidence that he believed he could recruit even the most hardened Soviet officer. "The Soviets used that knowledge to take Murphy in twice," said Angleton. "The insidious thing . . . they were able to do was to confuse the Agency on what it thought about Murphy."

Murphy's hopeless and clumsy effort to recruit the Soviet intelligence officer in Tokyo was a direct result of what Orlov had told Moscow Center about his former American case officer. Murphy was hand-fed intelligence indicating that his target would be responsive to his overtures. Instead, an exchange of punches turned the failed recruitment into an international incident that made the Japanese extremely uncomfortable.

Murphy's failed effort in this incident was also all too typical of the early CIA. In the United States' headlong rush into the intelligence business, men like David Murphy and Bill Harvey were anxious to "make cases" and recruit Soviets. They lacked the patience to develop a great case, a great source. That was the main difference between the old Soviet service and the new American one. "We would try and recruit everything . . . and damn the quality. . . ," said Berlin Base veteran John Sherwood, "while the Soviets were notoriously reticent. While the KGB would go after an Army officer to get a radar system manual, they seldom tried our approach of trying to get every Russian with a diplomatic passport to work for them."[2]

The Soviets did not stop with Murphy. They also targeted Bob Anton, succeeding to the point that a Japanese FBI source accused Anton of being a Soviet agent. Then, in 1951, Snow arranged for his favorite team of Murphy and Anton to be moved to Munich.

In their new posting in Germany, despite the Tokyo disaster, Murphy and Anton were allowed to continue recruiting Soviet case officers. General Walter Bedell Smith, the former CIA director, "would have never allowed such recruitments," said Angleton. "It was a completely naïve approach. I suspect that whoever was giving Murphy his orders was taking them from Allen Dulles or Wisner, who did approve of such operations."

One of these recruiting efforts involved a Soviet officer, B.Y. Nalivaiko. Anton, posing as a writer named "Robert Gray," doing a book about the Soviet Union, had several preliminary meetings with Nalivaiko. Anton decided he had a live target when he learned that Nalivaiko was being reassigned to Vienna as a consul. Murphy and Anton thought Nalivaiko was already under their control, since he had slipped classified Soviet documents of marginal interest to "Gray" for his book.

After several social meetings between Anton and Nalivaiko in Vienna, Murphy and Anton decided to complete the recruitment. In early February 1952, Murphy, using the name "Colonel Francis Manning," traveled from Munich to Vienna for the big meeting. This time they selected a public place, just in case it was another setup. Neither intelligence service, they thought, dared risk a public altercation.

"Gray" arranged for himself and "Manning" to meet Nalivaiko at the Gartenbau, a fashionable café in postwar Vienna, located on the famed Ringstrasse. As it happened, the café was also adjacent to the Soviets' official garage in Vienna.

At the Gartenbau, Murphy confidently told Nalivaiko that "any time you want to defect, it could be arranged immediately."

Nalivaiko's face darkened. In a café crowded with NKVD officers, he tossed an entire stein of beer into Murphy's face. Murphy had been set up yet again. The NKVD officers jumped into action and held the Americans until the Austrian police arrived and took "Manning" and "Gray" into protective custody.[3] The Soviets embarrassed the CIA by publicly accusing them of trying to recruit their agents. Bob Anton, alias "Tom Ames," alias "Robert Gray," had come to the end of his usefulness to the CIA.[4]

But Murphy had not. "In a sense," according to Angleton, "the Soviets' personal operations against Murphy backfired. The truth is that Dulles and Harvey wanted people who would take on the Soviets. Murphy had done that. In some ways the Soviets caused Murphy to get the branch chief's job in Berlin."

David Murphy became Bill Harvey's most powerful assistant as the head of Soviet Operations at Berlin Base. But Murphy did not impress Anita Potocki, whom Harvey had brought with him from headquarters, or many other Berlin colleagues. "He came breezing in and was going to take over," Potocki said. ". . . I think that Murphy thought of himself as being much more talented than anyone else because he spoke Russian, and I think that he was after the chief's [Harvey's] job from the time he arrived there. . . . He was a very self-centered individual. He sought adulation from the people who worked for him. He was going to walk over corpses to get where he wanted to go."[5] (Murphy would not comment for this book. He wrote his own book about Berlin operations, *Battleground Berlin,* which makes no mention of many of the incidents described in this book. When asked to respond to his colleagues' comments, Murphy replied in an e-mail that a recent heart condition prevented him from discussing his CIA career. Additional e-mails went unanswered.)[6]

One of Murphy's first projects was to make sure agents being run by the Base understood where all the drop sites and mail addresses for recontacting agents were located. It had taken years for the case officers to set up these drops. They were for use in emergency situations only. If the Soviets learned the location of a drop site, they could identify U.S. agents just by watching to see who picked up information. Although Murphy was told such an all-out test would jeopardize all the drop sites, he continued to insist on it. Potocki and others at the Base were furious. The case officers, fearing for their agents, quietly began to rebuild the drop system.

Murphy's actions at Berlin Base caused his new colleagues more than one sleepless night. One evening, Potocki interrupted a bear of a man in the supposedly secure "Soviet Target Room," where she kept the pictures and dossiers on all the Soviets the Base wanted to recruit. The man Potocki surprised was one of Murphy's favorite contract agents, a man called Andy Hanfam (Andy Yankovsky), and he was looking at a picture of a Soviet agent that was lying in a file on a desk.[7] He asked Potocki where she had gotten the picture. Potocki, curious, asked him why he wanted to know. He told her that he had once met the Soviet. He then began backing out of the conversation. To Potocki, "It struck me as very, very peculiar as he was backing away from it."

Potocki went to Harvey and recounted the incident. Harvey told her he would follow up, but she realized that "Bill was so inundated with everything else that he couldn't follow it up."

Potocki had other grounds for worrying about Murphy. He insisted on sharing too much information with General Gehlen's West German intelligence organization at Pullach. He went from branch to branch within the Base to secure information, breaking all the rules of compartmentalization established to protect secrets. But Harvey, who liked Murphy's toughness, turned a deaf ear to Potocki's complaints.

George Kisevalter offers an additional explanation: "David Murphy was successful in Berlin Base because . . . Murphy knew how to con Harvey better than anyone else. 'Good morning, Doctor' [he'd say], and he'd always be there one minute before Harvey came in the morning. . . . That's his operational technique. Impress your boss; that's the whole operation."[8] But Kisevalter never questioned Murphy's loyalty. To Kisevalter, Murphy was simply an opportunist who stopped at nothing to get ahead.

Murphy did not shrink from trying to discredit those he thought were his chief competitors. It did not always work. One person Murphy targeted was Sig Hoeckster, the brilliant and well-liked scientific case officer at Berlin Base. During this crucial time of competition for superiority in atomic weapons, key Soviet uranium supplies came from East Germany. Hoeckster had a very special role debriefing sources who had any information about these facilities. "He probably worked longer hours than anyone at the Base," Paul Garbler said. "He would debrief his agents at night. . . . It was the only real intelligence the Base seemed to produce on a regular basis." But Hoeckster usually did not arrive at the Base until ten or eleven. "I happened to be standing outside Harvey's office," said Garbler, "when he and Murphy were in a discussion about Sig. Murphy said, 'You know this guy comes in late every morning. . . .' Harvey cut him off and told him to forget it. 'Leave Hoeckster alone.'" Harvey understood why Hoeckster came in late. After debriefing his agents, he spent most of the rest of the night watching female mud wrestling. It was his way of unwinding.

When Ed Snow arrived at Berlin Base for a visit, David Murphy handled the introductions. Potocki and others remember Snow working there for weeks. There were even rumors that he was going to be assigned to Berlin. That didn't happen. He closely examined every major case, debriefed Harvey and other Base officers, and left.

It took Harvey a year to get the bulk of his team in place, and, as John Sherwood put it, "I will tell you [he] had [a] collection of guys that just wouldn't stop."

Unfortunately, one of the things they wouldn't stop doing was indulging in sexual indiscretion. As Harry Truman knew, CIA Director Allen Dulles was an inveterate womanizer and he set the example. Station chiefs and base chiefs were turned into pimps when "Uncle Allen" came to visit. "It was a real problem and a real pain," according to William Corson. "There were terrible security implications. Allen Dulles would screw anything that wasn't tied down. This was the guilty knowledge that those at the top of the CIA shared: Did I sleep with the same woman as Dulles? Those were the real secrets these men had."[9]

BOB officers made certain Dulles had female company on his visits to Berlin. "In fact," Corson explained, "it was a security consideration. If he went out and picked up women, could you imagine what the KGB might have done?"

Donald Morris, the Annapolis graduate who wound up in Berlin, was amazed at some of the sexual activity going on at the Base. Even Theodore C. (Ted) Shackley—who was just under David Murphy in the Berlin Base hierarchy, and who many people there felt was more machine than human—took part. Shackley "was all business," Morris recalled. "Ted Shackley was a human computer. Very incisive. Nobody ever left his presence without knowing exactly what the hell he wanted and when he wanted it, which was usually yesterday." But off duty, "He had an affair with Case Officer Jim Burson's wife, Hazel, and she divorced Burson and married Shackley," Morris said. George Kisevalter said the one who suffered in the affair was Shackley's first wife, who was well liked in Berlin.

Another Berlin employee, John Sherwood, was originally sent to BOB because he had an affair with a colleague's wife in Munich. He had a reputation as a peerless recruiter and agent handler, and a shameless womanizer. Sherwood recalled the atmosphere at the Base: "Oh God, there were parties, and Drambuie was a nickel a bottle, and French cognac was fifty cents a bottle. . . . There was a lot of screwing of German girls. There were a lot of good-looking German women. And the attitude towards Berlin was always different. I mean, Berlin is Berlin, and by God, they all love us and it's okay." In retrospect, Sherwood believes the availability of women should have been seen as a security problem. But he added, "That is [as] if we had anything really to secure."

The most popular places for sexual encounters were the safe houses used and maintained by the CIA. These residences were supposed to be kept vacant for agent interrogation. No sensitive cases could be brought back to the same safe house a second time. In Berlin these commonsense security practices went by the boards. Not only were safe houses used for interrogations again and again, they were also used by BOB officers for sex. That meant Berlin Base officers could be identified and also blackmailed by the KGB.

"We had 30 safe houses, many of them villas," Sherwood recalled. "One night I had come back because there was a guy I hadn't been able to break. I hadn't been able to get him to talk to me."[10] Sherwood heard what was obviously a sexual encounter upstairs. Using the alias "John Black," he announced himself, with his bewildered agent in tow, only to see CIA officer Harold Chipman, dressed in a Goering-style leather coat, descend the staircase in the company of a platinum blonde. Chipman's nickname at Berlin Base was the "Omaha Bull."[11]

Then there was Walter O'Brien, who was married to one of the best-liked women at the Base, Betty Lou. O'Brien dated a German woman openly and even bragged about it to other Base employees. Sherwood said about him, "He was my friend, but he was a real first-class shit." When Betty Lou O'Brien came down with multiple sclerosis, Walter O'Brien walked out on her, according to Sherwood and others. It was all too much for Harvey, who transferred O'Brien to Munich. It was one of the few cases where Harvey acted to discipline sexual misbehavior.

David Murphy and Ted Shackley were at each other's throats a good part of the time. They were both vying for the approval and the attention of a man who had been practically turned into a god in the intelligence community. They were also competing to replace Harvey when he decided to go on to bigger and better things.

For Harvey, human chemistry was everything in a spy organization. For that reason, he was a tremendous man to work for. The same cannot be said for his deputies. Sherwood was dumbfounded when he first came to Berlin because Murphy would not give him an assignment that took full advantage of his flawless German. One night, Sherwood found himself talking to Marian Murphy at a party. "Murphy comes up to me and says, 'What are you doing with that German in that shitty job?' That's a dumb thing to say unless you are about to offer the guy a better job."

Sherwood's office was directly across from Harvey's on the second floor of Berlin Base, and he used the proximity to impress Harvey without really doing anything.[12] To Harvey, it looked as if he were working late when, in fact, he was writing love letters. Sherwood admits that he "played Harvey" the way he played his agents. "I don't feel good about that, because he was a very decent man. . . . I had this talent. . . . I took full advantage of it."

Sherwood believes that there are two kinds of leaders. "There are banyan trees, under which everything withers, and there are the enriching soils. . . . Harvey was rich soil. He bent over backwards to be generous. He had no feelings of personal insecurity. He was a very strange person, I think. . . . Remember, he must have grown up as this bug-eyed, really weird-looking kid who was probably smarter than anyone else. . . . That's not an easy life. . . . In fact, he was one of the few really decent people in the CIA."

Harvey allowed David Murphy to dominate the Base with his forceful personality and the fact that, as head of the Soviet Branch, his work interested Washington more than anyone else's. Shackley had the less-glamorous job of heading operations for Soviet satellites like Poland and Czechoslovakia. Almost from the day he arrived, the chemistry between Shackley and Harvey was right. Harvey treated Shackley like a younger brother. Although the two seemed nothing alike, Shackley, in his early thirties, even mimicked Harvey's use of FBI jargon and his B-movie approach to life. Shackley's lack of Ivy League credentials or family status endeared him to Harvey. Others at Berlin Base found Shackley less appealing.

Shackley's colleagues describe him as a loner and secretive. He moved through the Base with the stealth of a large shark. Shackley was deliberately impersonal and at times almost mysterious about his rather ordinary background. Some people thought he was an orphan, while others thought he was a football hero.

Shackley was not an orphan, but he did play football. Former teammate Edward Elssey said that Shackley was a top-notch tackle at Palm Beach High, was "as mean as sin," and "took no quarter from anyone." Shackley's nickname, "the Blond Ghost," did not come from his height and blond good looks. It came from his bureaucratic talents, which he used the way a surgeon uses a scalpel.

Shackley was not known for his sense of humor. One time, a visiting congressman and education snob asked the men how many were Phi Beta Kappa. All present raised their hands, including Shackley. George Weisz, who did not get along with Shackley, believed he was lying and convinced a young case officer to write a letter to the University of Maryland to see if Shackley was really Phi Beta Kappa. The response proved Weisz correct. There was no chapter of Phi Beta Kappa at Maryland when Shackley was a student. Weisz had his junior colleague post the letter from the university on the Base bulletin board. For days, Shackley was obsessed with discovering who put it there. When he found out, the junior case officer was transferred. It was this doggedness that Harvey liked best about Shackley.

THAT WAS BERLIN BASE in its "glory days." From this incubator came the men and women who were to dominate American intelligence for a generation. It was the graduate school for the best and the brightest in the CIA. The officers Harvey either inherited or recruited into Berlin Base determined how the CIA operated in hundreds of places throughout the world.

Harvey's deputy, Henry Hecksher, was first assigned to Berlin in 1945. Colleagues recall him as a man without any apparent self-doubt. Nicknamed "Fat Henry" after a local wurst stand he patronized, Hecksher was an absolutist when it came to operations against the Soviets. Before Harvey arrived, Hecksher served as acting chief of base. He believed in supplying Russian partisans like the NTS with weapons and other support and sticking with them even when an operation was obviously failing. He was not afraid of taking criticism from headquarters over some of his more aggressive activities. He was German-born and understood very well the oppression that was strangling half his homeland. Hecksher worked with Harvey less than a year before he was sent to Guatemala to help overthrow that country's regime. He later served as chief of station in Tokyo and in Santiago, running aggressive operations in both places.

After his tour in Berlin, Ted Shackley became one of the most important figures in American intelligence, running the two largest stations in CIA history. Lucien Conein—Wally Driver's old roommate from the early days of Berlin Base—forever changed the course of history in Vietnam. Hugh Montgomery, Harvey's utility man who dealt with the Berlin authorities, managed, despite periodic problems, a successful career in the CIA and, later, in the Department of State as deputy to the U.S. ambassador to the United Nations. David Murphy would become head of the CIA's Soviet Russia Division.

Samuel Vaughan Wilson, whom Harvey brought to Berlin from Munich, shuttled back and forth between the Pentagon and the CIA in jobs of increasing importance, until eventually he came to head the Defense Intelligence Agency. Paul Garbler later became the first chief of station in Moscow, one of the CIA's most sensitive jobs. John Sherwood later became a top official at CIA headquarters in Langley, Virginia.

Of all the men assigned to Berlin Base, no one handled more important cases than George Kisevalter. He and Richard Kovich became the two top Soviet case officers in the history of the CIA.

Harvey's team had the job survival instincts necessary to succeed in the highly competitive and often strange world of American intelligence. The men who served in Berlin were a diverse group with seething personal rivalries and egos that clashed more violently the closer they climbed to the top.

CHAPTER SIXTEEN

IGOR AND THE LADIES

⸻⋗●⋖⸻

IGOR ORLOV WAS LIKE A PRISM," said George Kisevalter. "People saw in him what they wanted to. David Murphy saw him as the Base's only great asset, who had successfully penetrated Karlshorst. To his case officers, he was the closest they would ever get to running a real agent. When a guy is making your career go, you don't ask a lot of questions."

Orlov seemed to try very hard to be everything the CIA wanted him to be. Most of all, he succeeded in getting his CIA handlers to think of him as their eyes and ears in East Berlin. Harvey and his case officers believed in Igor Orlov because the little man was imaginative, aggressive, and, above all, dependent. The more reliant an agent is on his case officer for survival, the more appealing he is. Orlov understood that the CIA selected agents who were at risk. Vulnerability gave case officers extra leverage to entice their agents to take more risks and to push them a little further than they might normally go.

Igor Orlov was a master at making it appear to Harvey and his colleagues that his day-to-day existence depended on them. Even his marriage, based on false documents, made Orlov and his wife dependent on Sam Wilson, his first case officer in Berlin, with whom he had also worked during his NTS and SBONR days in Munich. Orlov constantly reminded Wilson and his later case officers that without their help, he and his wife could not travel because they had no papers, and they could not work because they had no permits. This gave the case officers the illusion that Igor would do nothing to jeopardize their trust and help.

Wilson was a particularly generous and loyal case officer. Other case officers used and disposed of agents like Kleenex. Sam Wilson did not operate that way. Eleonore Orlov remembered the dashing young intelligence officer from Virginia as being "a very kind man." He looked after his prized agent, his wife, and, later, their children for more than a decade.[1]

Igor met Wilson at various safe houses around Berlin. During these meetings, Wilson gave Orlov his $500 monthly salary, huge by any standards in the early 1950s, and enormous for Berlin. "We were paid under the table," Eleonore Orlov remembered. "He would bring Igor's salary in cash," and the spy and his case officer would converse for hours in Russian.

Bill Harvey went along with Orlov's scheme to recruit Russian officers out of Karlshorst by compromising them with whores. Orlov's charm had its customary effect on Berlin's young women and made him a great success as the BOB pimp. "At his height," recalled Paul Garbler, one of Igor's later case officers, "Orlov was running 11 whores, and the bar he worked out of literally had a one-armed piano player."

Orlov used other methods besides his charm to recruit the young women. He sometimes used records that Berlin Base obtained from the West Berlin police to blackmail them, or he entrapped them into violating rationing or black-market rules, actions that carried severe penalties.

Sometimes Orlov brought his work home with him. Igor arranged for one of his whores, a favorite of a top KGB official at Karlshorst, to travel with her KGB man to Hungary and agreed to care for her three-year-old son while she was away. He told Eleonore he had brought the boy home from a refugee camp. "He told me his mother had decided to go back," Eleonore said. She found out the truth a year later when the prostitute returned to Berlin and reclaimed her son.

One day Igor came home and recounted in great detail his first meeting with "Mr. Ross" (Bill Harvey), describing him to Eleonore as "the big boss." They had met in a safe house in a seedy section of Berlin, with Sam Wilson making the introductions. Igor told Eleonore that he had requested additional help for his operation and that Mr. Ross had quickly agreed.

Meanwhile, once a week, Igor Orlov confidently strode into Soviet headquarters at Karlshorst, the four-square-mile Soviet ghetto in East Berlin. In a series of hideaway offices on an unmarked floor of the huge complex was the forward base of the GRU, Soviet military intelligence. Each week Orlov walked right in. The dapper little man assumed the carriage of a great Russian and announced himself as "General Orlov."[2] Bill Harvey's prize agent then sat down and reported on all his Berlin Base activities.

In 1954, Harvey decided that Paul Garbler would run the Orlov operation. Garbler took over from Wolfgang Rabinow, who followed Sam Wilson when Wilson was assigned to assist George Kisevalter with an important Soviet defector.

The decision to make Paul Garbler Igor Orlov's case officer looked good on paper. Garbler spoke fluent Russian, and he had a smoothness that Harvey liked. Unfortunately, Garbler was not an experienced case officer, and Orlov was a very experienced agent.

Paul Garbler, a carrier pilot in the war, was assigned to Korea with Naval Intelligence when the war was over. An avid tennis player, he had played in a Korean championship with George Blake, who later made headlines when he was captured at the British Legation in Seoul by the North Koreans and turned over to the Soviets. Garbler could have stepped off a Navy recruiting poster. Over six feet tall, he was handsome, easygoing, and addicted only to tennis and flying. He looked like the perfect Naval attaché, and this was his cover for years.

Garbler's first experience with the CIA was not promising. His commanding officer in the Navy told him the CIA was looking for good people to operate a station in Alaska. Garbler reported to the CIA and met two men, both of whom used false names. One, who had a Southern accent, said almost nothing. The other man, "kind of rumpled and roly-poly," Garbler noted, made the pitch to him about joining the CIA in Alaska.

The idea of an Alaskan CIA station seemed a little silly to Garbler at first, but the rumpled man explained that Inuits could be trained and sent across to Siberia as agents. That made sense to him, and, after receiving a few instructions, Garbler shook hands with both men and left for a 90-day training program. Garbler was destined to run into these men again.

At Berlin Base, he learned that the roly-poly man was Colonel George Kisevalter, and the taciturn Southerner was Sam Wilson.

In Berlin, Garbler maintained his Navy cover, this time as an overt intelligence officer. Most of the Berlin Base officers had cover jobs through either the State Department or the military. Garbler's identity as a Navy spy was known and accepted by the Soviets.

At Garbler's unforgettable first meeting with Bill Harvey, Harvey had ordered him to learn German. With great difficulty, Garbler finally found an East German refugee who agreed to teach him. The refugee did not speak English, so Garbler had to learn German by speaking Russian with his tutor. "I remember spending all winter . . . climbing up four flights of stairs. The guy had no heat. All I did was try to concentrate long enough and try not to freeze," Garbler recalled.

After six tough months of this, Garbler was finally ready to see Harvey again for his first assignment. To Garbler, it was clear that Harvey's intentions at Berlin Base were "to make certain it became known as an outpost for guys with testicles . . . a place where things happen." It was that attitude, spelled out again and again to Harvey's men over three-double-martini lunches, which played right into the KGB's hands.

Harvey told Garbler that he would be running the Orlov operation, and he explained that he had "major plans" for it. "Nothing," Harvey said, "is more important than trying to get our own agents recruited in Karlshorst."[3] He briefed Garbler on Orlov's use of women to compromise Soviet officers. "To be told you are to be running an operation involving 11 whores and a one-armed piano player was pretty interesting . . . ," said Garbler. "They wanted me to expand the operation. . . . They figured that with more girls, we had a better chance of recruiting more officers." At the outset of a CIA career that was full of hope and promise, Garbler had no way of knowing that he was walking into a nightmare that would dominate the rest of his life.

Garbler's first meeting at a safe house with Orlov, like his first meeting with Harvey, was unforgettable: "He was a tiny little man. He was perfectly proportioned with those piercing blue eyes and dressed to the nines. He was extremely formal. He was very businesslike. He had this way of capturing your attention. . . . We never developed a personal relationship. He seemed so very serious." It was the first of over one hundred safe house sessions between the two men.

From the start, Garbler found the Orlov operation strange. He did not understand why he had to deal with Orlov in German when he and Orlov both spoke Russian fluently.[4] It was one of many things he never understood about running the little man.

Garbler soon realized there were practical problems to being a "master pimp." The girls got pregnant, were arrested, or contracted social diseases, and, if Orlov could not handle a predicament, Garbler had to take care of it. For Garbler, AE CALVUS (in the CIA's system of cryptonyms, AE was the designator for Soviet cases, CALVUS for Orlov)[5] soon became his main reason for being. The girls became CALVUS 2 through 12, and the one-armed piano player CALVUS 13.

Normal security called for case officers to avoid meeting their agents outside of safe houses. But Garbler often had to bail his agent out of jail after long drinking bouts and take him home. That is how he first met Eleonore Orlov.

Garbler felt he had little control over Orlov. He did not know how Orlov paid his girls or even if he paid them. Mrs. Orlov was surprised to learn decades later that her husband was receiving several thousand dollars a month from Garbler. "I never saw much of that money; we lived very frugally," she said.

In Garbler's two years of running Orlov, only once did he bring a Russian over, and nothing much came of it. The operation reveals an important American weakness: a failure to understand that other peoples don't necessarily see things the same way Americans do. The Soviets successfully used American sexual ethics to entrap and blackmail agents into treason. The CIA assumed that the Soviets were susceptible to the same pressures. They weren't. "What Orlov did," John Sherwood explained, "was create this world through the American point of view. He actually convinced professional intelligence officers that Soviet officers would be responsive to blackmail for getting involved with West German girls. . . . That just wasn't something the Russians were going to be punished for. . . . In the end a lot of Russians just got a lot of sex."

Meanwhile, Orlov's file should have raised some questions, should have given Harvey and his deputies some warning that the little man was not totally trustworthy. "That never happened," said Garbler. "No one ever suspected Igor Orlov of anything in Berlin."

Garbler's statement is in direct contradiction to David Murphy's published memories of his Berlin days. Murphy wrote, ". . . at CIA headquarters and at the German [U.S.] Mission, continuing routine checks into his past revealed possible security breaches. Some accused Orlov of making up reports while he was associated with the Gehlen organization, for example, and others charged him with doctoring documents during his SBONR period." Murphy said that on April 20, 1954, the German Mission ordered BOB to drop Orlov as an agent.[6] Since Murphy was in charge of Soviet operations at BOB, it is curious he never shared that information with Orlov's case officer, Paul Garbler, or carried out the order to fire Orlov.

In fact, Murphy ordered Garbler to use Orlov to support other operations, too. In one case, when letters had to be sent to East Berlin post office boxes to reestablish contact with agents, Garbler handed them to Orlov to mail. Orlov mailed them—but only after notifying the GRU and KGB. By simply watching who showed up to claim them, the Soviets could discover and compromise the agents.

If Murphy suspected Orlov was a Soviet plant, as he said in his memoirs, then why did he expand Orlov's operations?

Eleonore Orlov was not happy in Berlin. Having tricked her into moving there, Igor kept her terribly isolated. The couple had few friends, and, for security reasons, the CIA made them move to a different house every three to four months. They even had to change their names again. Eleonore recalled telling Igor that the new name "must begin with a *K* because all our linens had a *K* on them [for Kopatzky]. . . . So Wilson gives us the name Koischwitz—Igor becomes 'Franz Koischwitz.'"[7]

When Eleonore became pregnant again, Igor demanded that she have another abortion. After all, illegally married displaced persons should not have children—it drew too much attention to them. That was the sacrifice that Igor Orlov made for his cause. As for Eleonore, Igor determined her sacrifices.

At first, though, she still had hope for a successful marriage, and in one way Igor's work drew the couple closer together. Because Igor never learned to type, Eleonore prepared all his agent reports. She was very much a partner in his CIA job. And, as she later said, "I was afraid of him, but I did love him."

Her efforts to find out more about his background yielded little information. Igor simply said that his father was a Soviet general who had been shot down and killed during the war. He never deviated from his cover story—never. He told her that his mother was alive, but he could not risk contacting her. "He said she taught English at an orphan school where the orphans of high-class officers were getting educated," Eleonore recalled. Everything Igor told her matched his well-crafted and fully developed cover story.

Eleonore said she accepted Igor's prostitution ring, but she felt some strain because of it. After all, "he was recruiting girls . . . beautiful girls. He had to meet them in all the West Berlin joints at night and get friendly with them."

"My husband was very handsome—almost beautiful—and interesting," Mrs. Orlov explained. "And so people liked him. All my landladies would fall in love with him. Oh, he is like the little prince; he had excellent manners. He had big blue eyes that were open and friendly. You liked him instantly." But now that Eleonore was totally dependent on him, he showed more and more of his dark side: "He could be very ugly if you didn't obey him. I know he was very jealous, so I didn't even dare to look at some people. I gave up everything. I had a lot of friends before I met Igor. . . . He insisted I give them up."

Eleonore especially missed Igor's émigré friends in Munich who had seemed to bring out his personality. Now all he seemed to care about was his call-girl operation. He insisted that Eleonore not make any new friends. "It is too dangerous," he told her when she suggested they invite someone over.

"Igor was a perfect spy. He didn't trust anybody, not even my mother, not even me," Eleonore said. She had trouble adjusting to her husband's paranoia. When they fought, she reminded him that she had given up her German citizenship to marry him. Was that act of love not enough to merit his trust?

Orlov's best friend during his NTS days in Munich was Vladimir Kivi, an Estonian. Eleonore and Igor were constantly in the company of Vladimir, who was much taller than Igor, and his petite Russian wife.

Eleonore's mother gave the Kivis a piano and other furniture to get them started. After Vladimir's young wife died during childbirth, he became more and more entangled in Igor's REDCAP operation (the code name for White Russians used in intelligence work).

Early in the days of running call girls at Karlshorst, Igor suggested that Sam Wilson bring Kivi to Berlin from Munich. With his good looks, Kivi was perfect for recruiting women for the prostitution ring. Wilson agreed, and Kivi arrived just a few weeks later. Orlov soon began to regret bringing his old friend to Berlin. Kivi had become a heavy drinker, and Orlov regularly complained to Eleonore either that he was not pulling his share of the workload or that he was not conscious enough of security. But those faults did not bother her. She enjoyed having their old friend around again. While Igor was serious and dour, Kivi was fun to be with, despite the loss of his wife, and he and Eleonore spent much time together. "We were mostly talking about his dead young wife or the child that survived her death and her growing up with her grandparents away from Vladimir. . . . It made him very sad," Eleonore recalled. But Igor grew jealous and accused Eleonore of having an affair with Vladimir. "Igor was so angry with me that he held his gun to my head," Eleonore recalled, and all he kept saying was, "You whore, you whore." She tried to reassure him, and eventually succeeded in calming him down, but the incident made her now realize that there were parts of his personality she would never understand.

Kivi wisely decided to stay away for a few days after that, but when a week had passed, Igor became increasingly worried. He suspected that Kivi had gone to see an old girlfriend from before the war and had gotten lost trying to find the Orlovs' apartment, since Kivi was totally unfamiliar with Berlin and they had no telephone for him to call. Igor went to hospitals, and even the morgue, and he finally told Eleonore that he was certain Kivi had been kidnapped and sent back through East Berlin. At that time, hundreds of Russian émigrés were being kidnapped by the KGB and taken into the Eastern Zone.

When the Orlovs finally found Kivi, it turned out that Igor's first guess was right. Vladimir had gotten lost in East Berlin and simply could not find his way back to the Orlovs' apartment. He showed Igor and Eleonore the instructions his girlfriend had given him to get to her apartment. The trip took over two hours by bus. Looking at the instructions, the Orlovs realized that the woman lived just across the East German line, off the Unter den Linden, the massive avenue that leads from the Brandenburg Gate into the heart of East Berlin.[8] A trip on the S-Bahn (the subway) to Friedrichstrasse followed by a short walk to her apartment took no more than 20 minutes.

A week later, on a pleasant night in October 1951, Vladimir came to see Igor and Eleonore again. The couple had planned to go to the movies that night, but Igor immediately gave in when Vladimir said he wanted to go see his girlfriend. Igor said that he and Eleonore would go with him to Friedrichstrasse and point him in the right direction. The three friends got on the S-Bahn and rode the few stops to Friedrichstrasse.

"Kivi and I walked from the station through the tunnel at Friedrichstrasse. Igor was behind us. By the time we came out of the tunnel, there were a group of men waiting for us," Eleonore Orlov remembered. The men jumped at the three friends and started beating them. "All three of us were attacked viciously. I screamed. My hat was torn off, and the buttons on my coat were gone. My lip was bloody. No one spoke a word. They were all military-looking guys . . . Russians, I thought." Eleonore spoke to Igor in German. "I told Igor, 'Shoot the guy! Do something!' Igor always carried a gun. He told me, 'I cannot. . . . If I shoot, we are all dead.'"

Eleonore urged him to at least say something. He asked her what he should say. She told him to "use Russian and pretend that he was a higher-ranking officer—name the general in charge. 'Just pretend you are part of this.' He said he could not. I begged him. I told him in German that I did not want to die in Siberia."

Igor walked away with one of the men and went to a telephone on a nearby street corner. "They kept switching positions on the phone. One would talk and then Igor," Mrs. Orlov said. "Kivi disappeared with the other men. They just took him away."

Finally, Igor returned with what he said was fare money from the Soviet soldier for the subway ride home. Igor told his wife that he had bluffed the Russians. When she asked about Kivi, Igor grew very angry. She recalled him saying very firmly, "Do not ever tell anyone about this! If you report it, no one will believe you." That night was another turning point in Eleonore's life with Igor. "From this day on Igor blackmailed me. I was never allowed to speak about Vladimir Kivi again. Igor said we had been photographed by the Russians. Any clothes I wore in old pictures with Kivi and Igor had to be destroyed. The clothes I wore that night—my coat, my black hat—had to disappear."

On that night, Eleonore realized that even her marriage to Igor was part of his operation. "I felt like I was no more to him than his Minox camera or his gun." Igor then sat down and methodically cut Vladimir Kivi out of pictures of the three of them in Berlin. "That's how easy it was for Igor to get rid of someone," Eleonore said.

She thought about that incident for many nights to come. Soon she started to wonder if Igor hadn't deliberately led their friend into jeopardy. "I never felt so alone as that week," she said. "I had dreams about Igor taking others who trusted him into East Berlin and leaving them for the Russians. They believed him because he worked for the CIA." For 48 years, Eleonore Orlov kept the secret of Vladimir Kivi. Tears ran down her face as she finally told the story.

After Kivi disappeared, Igor became even more remote. The CIA suspected for a short time that he might have been involved in Kivi's disappearance, but those suspicions soon faded. Harvey and Murphy kept using Igor because he was one of the few sources they had.

At one point in their moves around Berlin, the Orlovs had a neighbor named Werner Boch, a tall and handsome young man from Bressen in the Eastern Zone. He had come to Berlin to study chemistry at the university. Eleonore remembered him as a fun-loving man who loved to dance and go to classical music concerts. With her estrangement from Igor growing, she began spending time with Boch.

Returning from a concert one evening, Eleonore asked him, "Would you like to come in for some tea?" Boch grew visibly uncomfortable. He shook his head no and hurriedly said goodnight. He later told Eleonore that he had smelled Igor's cigarette smoke and knew he was hiding close by.

Puzzled, Eleonore went to her bedroom. Suddenly, Igor leaped from under the bed and began screaming at her. "I will sleep with him if you keep this up," Eleonore recalls telling her husband.

Igor then asked her, "How do you know he does not work for the Russians?"

Furious, the next day Eleonore waited for Boch to come home from the university and went to his room. She threw herself into his arms and

urged him to make the relationship more than platonic. Boch pulled himself away and suggested they leave the building for a walk. After looking
around cautiously, Boch became very serious. "You cannot—we cannot
do this," he told her. "Igor is very, very high up."

"What do you mean by high up?" Eleonore asked.

Werner looked around again. As they walked, he explained why he
was so afraid. "The last time I visited my parents in Bressen I took the
train home. On the train I walked through a first-class car, and I saw Igor
sitting in a first-class compartment with two Russian generals. I could not
believe it was him. They were being very respectful of him. They called
him 'General.'"

Eleonore told him, "You are crazy. You have seen too many spy
movies."

Werner, very upset, stopped and turned to her. "Where was your Igor
on those dates?"

Eleonore shook her head.

Boch then described in detail the tie, the cigarette case, and the kind
of cigarettes Igor was smoking that day. "He was in the Eastern Zone for
several days on that date," Mrs. Orlov recalled. "He liked a certain cigarette from Russia that he could get only in the Eastern sector; that's what
Werner said he was smoking. Finally, Werner was right about the dark
tie. I packed it for him for that trip. I knew he was telling the truth."

That was the end of the relationship between Werner Boch and
Eleonore Orlov. Werner was terrified, not only for himself and Eleonore
but for his parents in Bressen.

Now Eleonore truly had no way of escaping. If she did try to leave,
she would be penniless and stateless, with no work permit. There was
nowhere she could go that Igor could not find her. If anyone tried to help
her, he would be putting himself and his family in great danger.

Eleonore now had the guilty knowledge of her husband's betrayal. If
she went to the authorities, they would not believe her. Igor was, after all,
the CIA's star agent. Because she feared for her own life and felt no one
would believe her, she decided "it was better to say nothing."

By 1955, Igor Orlov finally felt secure enough for his wife to have a
child. Paul Garbler sent a dozen roses when the Orlovs' son was born.
Igor wanted to name the baby Robert Alexander Orlov. Eleonore

opposed giving her son a name drawn from what she thought was her husband's first alias, "Alexander Kopatzky." But Igor insisted on Alexander. The Russian diminutive is Sasha.

The last time Paul Garbler saw the Orlovs was to say good-bye after his reassignment back to headquarters in 1956. Garbler felt the CIA had gotten very little from the Orlov operation: "We spun our wheels a lot in Berlin. . . . I don't think we got much done." Garbler had paid Orlov tens of thousands of dollars in two years. He still has a book in German about Berlin that Eleonore Orlov gave him as a farewell present. Unfortunately for Paul Garbler, he had not heard the last of Igor Orlov.

CHAPTER SEVENTEEN

TUNNEL VISION

—————⊰•⊱—————

O F ALL THE PROJECTS the CIA launched in its early days, none held out more hope than intercepting Soviet communications. Many of the Allies' most stunning breakthroughs in World War II had involved intercepting Nazi communications, and the CIA expected to be just as successful against the Soviets in the Cold War.

Richard M. Bissell, an economist by training, went to work for the CIA soon after Allen Dulles was named director. Part of Bissell's job description was to develop new espionage technologies, including the authority to give a bureaucratic jolt to promising projects through funding and management support. His office became a hothouse for ideas and was responsible for the U-2 spy plane and, later, spy satellites. Like Frank Wisner, Bissell was an activist who believed that covert operations were the key to the CIA's success. Neither man understood nor had the patience for traditional espionage.

In 1953, the British attempted to win back the CIA's trust after the Burgess/Maclean defections by informing Wisner and Bissell of a major technological breakthrough. John Taylor, officially an employee of the British Postal Special Investigations Unit, in fact ran the electronics laboratory for MI5 and MI6.[1] His breakthrough involved wiretapping on a massive scale. Carl Nelson, one of the CIA's most brilliant researchers, incorporated Taylor's ideas into his own work.[2] The combination of the two technologies led to a bold and ambitious plan to bypass human agents and collect information on the Soviet Union electronically.[3]

When Wisner and Bissell flew from Washington to Frankfurt in late 1953 and summoned their new Berlin Base chief to a meeting, Bill Harvey had no idea what to expect. At the meeting, the two men told him about Nelson's breakthrough in converting electronic echoes off telephone lines into words and how the technology could be used to eavesdrop on a wide range of Soviet communications. Harvey was enthusiastic and proposed that the discovery be used to bug Soviet military communications at Karlshorst.

The first step was a technical test to see if tapping into the East Berlin telephone system would work at all. If the idea did work, a test tap would be made at the main telephone exchange to determine whether building a full-scale, operational system was worth the cost and the risk. Wisner told Harvey that Allen Dulles was uncertain about the plan. Wisner explained that if the preliminary stages proved successful, Dulles was more likely to approve full funding for the project.

Harvey's enthusiasm faded when tech chief Bissell told him that the project had to be run jointly with MI6. Harvey, obsessed with Philby's betrayal, believed there was a fourth, perhaps even a fifth, member of Philby's KGB spy ring still at work in British intelligence. "I agreed with Bill's caution," James Angleton recalled. "He thought operating jointly was too risky, but Bissell refused to listen to Harvey's warnings. He insisted that the project be run jointly." According to Angleton, Harvey did succeed in getting full authority over the entire project.

Harvey's first task was to find out where all the telephone cabling in Berlin was located to see if it was even possible to make the wiretaps. He used every resource of the Base, including asking Igor Orlov to get old telephone directories for Karlshorst—not an easy task in the Soviet system. Orlov tried to be as helpful as possible, hoping to learn why the Base was so interested in such mundane matters. He learned from his own sources on the West German intelligence chief's staff that they, too, had been tasked with providing details on the prewar Berlin telephone system.

The British briefed Harvey on a test of eavesdropping methods that had succeeded in Vienna,[4] a project called OPERATION SILVER. Harvey responded by saying: "Then this one will be GOLD." A planning and coordinating committee for OPERATION GOLD was set up, and soon the project became a reality. Since few people at Berlin Base were technically minded, no one except Harvey himself was on the committee. Among the members of the planning committee were Peter Luan, MI6's technical man in Berlin, and his urbane deputy, George Blake, the diplomat who had been captured by the North Koreans in 1950 and turned over to the Soviets.

George Blake's assignment to Berlin was his first overseas posting since he was released by the Soviets after his incarceration. Blake's colleagues in Berlin marveled at his comeback after being a prisoner of war under the toughest of circumstances.

Harvey did not brief any of the Berlin Base staff on OPERATION GOLD, apart from giving basic information to his deputies, Hugh Montgomery, Ted Shackley, and David Murphy. While various Berlin Base officers were assigned tasks related to GOLD, they were not told what it really was.

Harvey worked with General Gehlen's staff at Pullach, researching how the Berlin phone system was set up before the city was split in two by the occupying armies. Harvey learned that all the Soviets had done to take West Berlin out of the system was cut some of the old lines and reroute them.

Harvey also learned and reported back to Washington that Berlin was second only to Moscow in the Soviets' communications network. Every official government call made from Eastern Europe was routed through the central exchange in East Berlin. If a Soviet general in Prague called Moscow, the call went through East Berlin.

More important, Berlin was a "forward base" for the Soviets. Because their military was much more decentralized than the United States', Karlshorst was, in effect, the Soviet Pentagon for Europe and was headquarters for both the military and the KGB. Wiretapping the main communication lines to Moscow could be the ultimate intelligence coup.

Despite Harvey's misgivings about the British, OPERATION GOLD became an enormous Allied intelligence effort. The CIA's Carl Nelson designed the equipment that could decipher telephone messages, while West Germany's Pullach technicians worked for six months with old Wehrmacht and Luftwaffe diagrams of Berlin's wartime telephone system to set up the test tap. It was decided that America's young National Security Agency would process all the encoded signal traffic, while a special British laboratory at Earl's Court in London would process the bulk of the voice traffic. The CIA established a new technical services division to analyze the United States' portion of the take.

Once Nelson and the Pullach technicians had done their part, Harvey and Gehlen got an agent inside the East German telephone exchange to make the intricate cable hook ups to run the test tap. When that was accomplished, Harvey placed a CIA technician in a closet at the exchange to listen to the lines and determine whether the taps were likely to produce enough traffic to justify proceeding. The technician monitored and recorded three weeks of Soviet message traffic. The good news was that the test taps confirmed that the Soviets had left the basic lines in operation. The bad news was that a quarter-mile-long tunnel needed to be dug to reach them.

In January 1954, Harvey picked up a group of arriving CIA officials— Tracy Barnes and Mike Burke from the CIA's Frankfurt Station and Frank Wisner from headquarters. Wisner told Harvey that a skeptical Dulles had reluctantly approved the building of the tunnel. The CIA estimated the cost at $15 million. Harvey smiled and told Wisner, "The Krauts say they can do it for a third of that."[5]

Harvey's cover story to the mayor of West Berlin for building the tunnel was that the U.S. government wanted to do some geological work under the city because of fears that the Soviets might try to sabotage West Berlin's sewer system. The poor mayor was not told the real reason why the CIA wanted assistance in getting rid of vast amounts of dirt, and he quickly pledged his cooperation and silence. Later he was told that a secret underground radar system was being installed. That explanation was partially true.

Gehlen suggested to Harvey that they dig the tunnel on the southern rim of Berlin at Alt Glienicke, a key junction for telephone cables in East Berlin, and an excellent location for a clandestine operation for several reasons. It was a swampy, largely abandoned industrial area that had been heavily bombed during the war, and the only inhabitants were homeless refugees living in shacks they had thrown together. Finally, a new U.S. radar station was already under construction nearby. Since the Soviets were aware of the radar station, the new digging, the Allies thought, would not look suspicious.

The main telephone cables were buried under two feet of highway, 330 yards inside the East German border. This road was the main transportation link between Berlin and the Soviets' major East German military base. The plan was to dig some fourteen hundred feet to that road from the Western Sector. Harvey placed a couple of junior agents in the area to make certain that rumors about the new work did not spread.

A squeamish Dulles ordered only one change in Harvey's excavation plan, to avoid digging through a cemetery. In mid-November 1954, members of the Army Corps of Engineers arrived to dig the tunnel. They had made a full-scale mock-up of the tunnel in the New Mexico desert.

As the tunnel was being excavated, Harvey encountered nightmarish logistical problems. The worst of these occurred when workers breached old sewage lines, causing serious water problems and unexpected delays.

What really bothered Harvey, however, was that the East German police, the Vopos, seemed to take little interest in the construction. His subordinates assured him that the East Germans were convinced it was simply additional construction at the radar site. There were frequent planning sessions involving the MI6 team and Harvey's own team, both in Frankfurt and in Hitler's old Olympic Stadium in Berlin. George Blake, not long ago a Communist prisoner, acted as secretary and took notes during these sessions. Meanwhile, BOB was making the big move from its old mansion in Dahlem into much larger quarters at the U.S. Military Compound on Clayallee, and that was also very much on Harvey's mind.

The Berlin tunnel was a massive project 24 feet under East German soil. There were actually two tunnels: a short one that ended in the basement of the new radar facility (where workers packed dirt into wooden crates marked "electronic parts" and hauled them off), and the main tunnel, nearly eight feet in diameter and fourteen hundred feet long—longer than the Empire State Building is tall. The diggers removed 3,100 tons of dirt.

That winter Harvey often traveled down to the nearly finished site. The vista in front of him was not comforting. Above the entire length of the tunnel was a puddle where the snow was melting over the barren terrain, clearly marking the tunnel's outline. To keep the snow from melting further, Harvey ordered all heat turned off inside, which made working conditions even more difficult.

The tunnel was lined with prefabricated steel sections. Each section was welded to the next one, sealing and shoring up the tube as the work progressed. At the East German end was a series of three prefabricated metal rooms, giving the feeling of a submarine. Around and underneath the area that housed the eavesdropping equipment, diggers scooped out cavities where they could place explosives.

Each chamber had metal doors that closed automatically. The workers installed air-conditioning, electronic equipment, and a sophisticated switchboard in each chamber. All of this was linked by thick cabling that ran the length of the tunnel to a special electronic nerve center in the basement of the radar station. Once operations began, the heat from the several tons of electronic equipment caused groundwater to seep into the tunnel, and special pipes were added to remove the moisture.

Finally, MI6 specialist John Wyke headed into the tunnel and climbed down a ladder to a vertical shaft that took him to where he could reach the two thick telephone cables. He opened up the cables and began the laborious task of matching up over 450 pairs of wires. The most delicate part of the operation was to complete the tap without East German telephone operators noticing any degradation in the lines. Amplifiers and backup generators were used to make the taps undetectable.

The system went "live" in February 1955. Telephone calls were taped in the radar station control room, and they could also be monitored with a bank of headphones. The whirling tape recorders, amplifiers, filters, and cipher machines picked up conversations between the Soviet embassy, the KGB, the Karlshorst compound, and Soviet military outposts all over Europe. Duplicate tapes were delivered to Berlin Base and to MI6's Berlin office for shipment back to Washington and London. So much material came in that Berlin Base officers began to notice. "You didn't ask about it, but you had a pretty good idea of what it was," Paul Garbler recalled.

For Harvey and his team, the Berlin tunnel seemed a great triumph. Harvey's Hole, as it came to be known in the CIA, operated for a little over a year and produced vast amounts of material. But on March 26, 1956, British intelligence called Harvey and told him that the tenor of the telephone traffic had changed—for the last 10 days, the conversations, especially from Karlshorst, had been much more cautious than usual. People were talking in a way that indicated they knew someone was listening.

On April 21, the Vopos started digging near the tunnel. Then, at about 10:30 A.M., the alarm system went off. After several more hours, the Soviets got into the first chamber. In the interim, Harvey proposed to Washington that he blow up the tunnel. Headquarters cabled back: No.

When the Soviets got into the first chamber, they quickly deactivated the explosives. They later reported that a coffee pot was still on and the CIA operators inside had barely escaped. In fact, Harvey and his MI6 experts had removed the most important electronic equipment when the digging began the night before, along with all but one technician.

Harvey had ordered that a hand-lettered sign be placed on the door to the control room that read in both Russian and German: YOU ARE NOW ENTERING THE AMERICAN SECTOR. Harvey told his technicians that if they were faced with Soviets crossing into the American end, they should shoot if necessary to protect their retreat. Nothing so dramatic happened. The KGB never went through to the American Sector.

According to Hugh Montgomery, Harvey also ordered a .50-caliber machine gun set up at the tunnel's border between the East and West. When some Russians did approach the Western Sector, Harvey positioned himself behind the machine gun and pulled back the breech. The unmistakable metallic sound in the confined space was enough to stop the Soviets from advancing. When Harvey arrived back at Berlin Base, he found a black wreath tacked to his door in memory of Harvey's Hole. To most of the men and women of Berlin Base, the tunnel, though short-lived and expensive, was a marvelous success.

Many at CIA headquarters thought the Soviets would keep quiet about the discovery of the tunnel because it was too embarrassing. They thought the KGB would quietly close the tunnel down, and it would become just another bygone secret operation in the intelligence game. To the CIA's surprise, Soviet Colonel Ivan A. Kotsyuba, the local KGB chief, invited Berlin's press contingent into the tunnel for a tour. He took great pains to explain that the tunnel was discovered when an electrical line had to be repaired. He did not, of course, mention George Blake, nor did the CIA in its self-congratulations make the connection between Blake's note-taking and the appearance of the Vopos with shovels.

Bill Harvey basked in a rare moment for an intelligence officer. His enemy made his triumph public. For the next year, busloads of schoolchildren and "workers" were taken down in small groups to see the CIA's work. Some hundred thousand East Germans toured Harvey's Hole.

The CIA treated Harvey like a hero. Dulles flew him back to Washington and, in an elaborate secret ceremony, presented him with the Distinguished Intelligence Medal. Harvey's stock was never higher. Newspaper editorials praised the daring and cunning of the young spy agency. Berlin Base seemed to have fulfilled General Walter Bedell Smith's vision of West confronting East, and winning.

CHAPTER EIGHTEEN

A Defector at Last

On November 9, 1952, nine months after David Murphy got beer thrown all over him trying to turn a Soviet agent, the CIA finally got lucky in Vienna.

It was an unusually warm day for the time of year. An American diplomat and his wife decided to take a break from Christmas shopping and eat lunch in one of the city's best restaurants. As the couple parked their car, a stocky man in civilian clothes watched them. He waited for them to enter the restaurant and then looked down to verify that his hat hid a sealed brown envelope in his hand. Carefully looking around to make certain he was not being watched, Major Pyotr Semyonovich Popov made his move. He walked over to the parked car, dropped the envelope onto the driver's seat, and nonchalantly walked away.

Popov slipped around a corner and waited for the couple to emerge. When they returned to their car, he watched the diplomat pick up the envelope. It was addressed, in rough German, to "American Ambassador-Vienna." The diplomat put it in his inside breast pocket and, after dropping off his wife, quickly headed for the American embassy.

The diplomat personally handed the envelope to the CIA's chief of station, who found inside yet another envelope, addressed to "Chief of Intelligence." Inside that envelope was a typed letter in the Cyrillic alphabet.

The chief of station, Peer deSilva, and his new operations chief managed to get the letter translated. It contained a straightforward proposal.

The sender was offering the CIA a copy of the Austrian Armored Division's Table of Organization for three thousand Austrian schillings, then about one hundred and twenty American dollars.[1]

DeSilva immediately notified headquarters in Washington. Having waited years for a serious recruitment, Washington did not want to blow the opportunity to recruit a Soviet agent by leaving it to the "locals." However, Popov's note gave a two-day deadline, and there was not enough time to get one of the CIA's top Russian-speaking case officers to Vienna for a first meeting. Washington reluctantly authorized a Russian-born translator who was on the scene to handle it. They made certain, however, that a Russian-speaking case officer was in Vienna for the second meeting.

The station nearly sabotaged the defection at the outset by foolishly loading down the translator with heavy surveillance. In Vienna the Soviets routinely engaged in counter-surveillance. If they had suspected Popov and followed him, the sight of CIA onlookers might have caused his arrest before he even got to the meeting place.

After a three-hour-long session with Popov on November 12, Vienna cabled Washington saying that the Russian translator had confirmed Popov was who he said he was. What Vienna did not tell Washington was that the station chief wanted pictures, and a photographer with a Leica camera was hidden in the safe house. The camera's shutter was loud enough that Popov noticed it. He was also suspicious of the émigré translator and thought seriously of not coming back. He later told his handlers that he decided to return only because he figured that if he was already compromised, he had nothing to lose.[2]

Popov, the first of several important Soviet sources, was given the cryptonym AE MAX. The CIA in Washington told Vienna that a case officer was being dispatched from Berlin Base and was to have full charge of the case. The extent of Vienna's involvement from now on was only for support, if the case officer requested it. The case officer headquarters selected was, in fact, the first of an elite cadre of case officers who would travel the world for the CIA: George Kisevalter.[3]

Kisevalter was a Russian, born in St. Petersburg just before the Revolution. He had family connections to Vienna: His father and his French mother, a schoolteacher, had first met there when his father, an engineer in the czar's munitions department, was sent to Austria to buy mortars and artillery shells for Russia's war with Japan in 1905. After the Russo-Japanese War ended, the senior Kisevalter went to work for a prosperous munitions maker, and in 1915 was sent to the United States to operate a munitions plant for the czar outside Philadelphia. When the Revolution started, the senior Kisevalter applied to the U.S. authorities for citizenship for himself and his family, which was granted.

The Kisevalters settled in New York. They spoke Russian at home, along with French and English. George in due course graduated from Dartmouth College. During World War II, the Army Reserves called him for duty, and Army intelligence made him a liaison officer with the Red Army in Alaska, in charge of the Soviet pilots who were ferrying American-built planes to the German front.

It was there that Kisevalter got his first glimpse of Soviet security. The Soviet pilots came with "watchers," military intelligence officers who made certain they were not tempted by the "capitalists" during their stay in America. In two years and four months, the pilots flew 12,500 planes to Russia. Kisevalter spent most of that time keeping the unruly Soviet officers from defecting and smoothing over their annoyances at perceived slights. At one point, the base's supply of red-star decals ran out, and the pilots grumbled about flying "unfinished" planes back to the Soviet Union. Kisevalter, a very resourceful man, asked a local Texaco dealer for some of his red stars. The Soviets flew their planes home with the symbol of a capitalist oil company on their fuselages.

After the war, Kisevalter became the Pentagon's premier Russian expert. He was the officer who debriefed General Gehlen after Frank Wisner recruited him in Germany; the information Gehlen provided was Kisevalter's first real exposure to intelligence about Stalin's Russia. Soon thereafter, however, Kisevalter resigned from the military to try his hand at raising alfalfa in the Midwest. After a couple of years of quiet farming, he decided to accept an invitation to join the new CIA. There were fewer calluses in espionage, and that was part of the attraction.

When Kisevalter arrived at the CIA in 1949, the Agency's massive language-training effort was underway, but there was still an appalling shortage of operations staff who spoke Russian. Kisevalter's personal warmth, and the fact that he thought like a Russian and understood Russian culture, history, and literature, made him the CIA's star case officer. He was also without ambition and was therefore seen as nonthreatening by the CIA power structure. He looked nothing like the well-tailored CIA men from Harvard and Yale. As Paul Garbler noted later, he was perpetually wrinkled and rumpled. His profound affection for his Viennese wife's superb cooking meant he would never be sleek and svelte. Bill Harvey dubbed him "the Teddy Bear." Those who knew him well used the nickname; those who did not called him "Colonel."[4]

When George Kisevalter arrived in Vienna to meet Major Popov, he did not impress anyone at the station. Exhausted by a long plane trip from Tokyo, where he had been working the previous month, he looked more like an unmade bed than usual. He walked into Vienna Station and asked for a comfortable room and the tapes from the first meeting with Popov. He spent the night reviewing the tapes, making careful notes. He then interviewed the Russian translator who had attended the first meeting.

Now ready for the second meeting, Kisevalter made sure there was Russian vodka and plenty of food for a long session. The safe house he and Popov used was an apartment in the American Sector that featured a false wall, behind which two men ran taping equipment and a still camera.

Popov told Kisevalter that he came from Solnechnaya, from a family of farmers. He said his job in Vienna was to assist in preparing cover for Soviet agents crossing into the West illegally. "He spoke half-ass German," Kisevalter recalled. ". . . He was not a linguist but a peasant." Popov loved talking about farming techniques with Kisevalter, whom he knew as "Colonel Harry Grossman." Major Popov and Colonel Kisevalter quickly became great friends. Kisevalter's visits to see Popov in Vienna went on for three years.

Kisevalter later explained that the secret of this farm boy's success in the Soviet system was that Popov "was a dead shot with a rifle . . . which made his general radiant. He was an avid fisherman. He got along with the boys." It did not take Kisevalter long to realize that Popov was not very security conscious. He had to keep reminding the defector that he should make all phone calls from public phones, and that he must always say, "Max is calling." Although Popov had a wife and children and claimed to be happily married, he also kept a mistress, who was herself a very tough GRU agent. Kisevalter thought Popov took "god-awful chances sometimes."

As the GRU duty officer, Popov had regular access to the master safe where all GRU officers stored their work every night. For security, each officer had a personal wax seal. Over the course of several months, Popov brought Kisevalter originals of all the seals, and a CIA technician duplicated them on the spot. This allowed Popov to break into sealed documents, use a Minox camera to photograph the pages, and then reseal the documents and return them to the safe.

Kisevalter believed that money never really motivated Popov: "He just hated what the Soviets had done to Russia." Popov was paid through a numbered Swiss account, but he could collect the money only if he decided to leave the Soviet Union—and he never gave Kisevalter any indication that he wanted to leave. In addition to the Swiss account, Kisevalter brought him small gifts and, on occasion, sums of a few hundred dollars.

Even so, Kisevalter was always amazed at how little Popov asked for. As far as Kisevalter could determine, all Popov ever bought for himself was a used raincoat and some polyester shirts. He did want a little money for his mistress, whom he had met when he recruited her as a spy, and from time to time he asked Kisevalter for outlandish things to please her. "He wanted a collapsible canoe to take her on outings," Kisevalter recalled. He turned down this request because if Popov were seen by the Soviets with an American-made canoe, he would be unable to explain where he got it.

Within two years, Popov gave the CIA a detailed look at the GRU and its operations in Austria. The Popov case made Kisevalter a legend in the intelligence community.

In 1953, Popov went on home leave to his small farming town in Russia. Before he left, Kisevalter gave him several hundred dollars, and the two men set a date and time for their next safe house meeting in Vienna.

When the appointed time came, Kisevalter went to the safe house and waited. When Popov did not show up, Kisevalter started drinking, worrying about the most important—in fact, the only—Soviet asset the CIA had. Twenty-two days later, he was still waiting.

He had reason to worry. Soon after Popov returned home, Stalin died, and the leadership purges began. The Soviet Union was in political upheaval as Beria, Khrushchev, Molotov, and others jockeyed for power. Finally, however, a cheerful Popov returned. He brushed aside Kisevalter's concerns and regaled his case officer with stories about how he had spent his vacation. As well as Kisevalter knew Popov by now, he was still amazed at the man: During Popov's first leave in seven years, he had spent the three thousand rubles Kisevalter had given him on a cow for his brother. As Popov explained, "I have a crippled brother who is a book-keeper, so he gets paid the least of anyone in the whole cooperative. So now he has a CIA cow."

Next, Popov pulled out a sketch of a Soviet airfield near the Volga. "I drew this while I was fishing," he said. After a few glasses of vodka, Kisevalter learned that Popov had been promoted and assigned to a new unit. Popov then turned over detailed information about assignments and politics in GRU headquarters at Arbatskaya Square in Moscow.

In 1955, shortly after the treaty that made Austria a neutral country was ratified, Popov returned to Moscow. Kisevalter did not see him for over a year. Then Popov was reassigned to East Germany. After a tour in Schwerin, he was sent to Rostock, a Baltic town on the main train line to East Berlin.

Popov was the biggest and best double agent Berlin Base ever had, and George Kisevalter tried to resume contact with him to get the operation going again. Bill Harvey went to enormous trouble to outfit a Berlin safe house with the latest recording equipment for the anticipated meeting. No expense was spared, nothing was left to chance. Sam Wilson, Igor Orlov's former case officer, helped Kisevalter with the preparations.

Meanwhile, at a Rostock beer hall, Popov noticed two British officers having a bite to eat.[5] He waited until one of them went into the men's room and then followed him in. Popov passed a letter to the surprised officer as he stood at the urinal. Popov told the officer in accented German to deliver the letter to "Colonel Grossman" at the CIA in West Berlin. The British officer hesitated. He had strict orders never to accept anything from the locals while in the Eastern Zone. But something in his gut told him to accept the letter. Besides, he had no choice: By the time he had finished at the urinal, Popov was gone. On the way back to West Berlin, his colleague opened the envelope and discovered six pages of small handwriting in Russian.

The next day, the letter went to MI6. The regular MI6 translator was out for the day, so it was given to a Russian-speaking case officer. Helping the case officer with the translation was George Blake, the MI6 technical officer who had served on Harvey's tunnel operation. After reading the letter, Blake said, "Looks like Harvey has a good strong GRU case in the Eastern Zone."[6]

In his letter Popov asked for new signals so he could let the Americans know when he could meet them. Popov said that he would await the CIA's contact by standing in front of the German-Soviet Friendship Society in Schwerin at certain times for several days.

After reading the letter, the Brits turned it over to the Americans. At Berlin Base, Harvey brought in his Soviet branch chief, David Murphy, and asked him whom they should send on this mission. They put the list of signals and meeting sites on very thin paper that could be rolled up to the size of a piece of lint.

Harvey, Murphy, and Kisevalter settled on a 74-year-old East German postal worker to make a brush contact with Popov. The old man carried off the contact in front of the Friendship Building without a hitch. On the appointed day for the meeting, Popov came to Berlin and took the S-Bahn, getting off at the Am Zoo stop. He called in, and Kisevalter instructed him to go to the Hotel Kempinski. There, the two men got together and rode to the safe house at 3 Litzenseestrasse. Kisevalter told Popov that from now on he was to call him "Lieutenant Colonel Scharnhorst."

During the debriefing, Kisevalter learned that his Soviet agent was being promoted again, this time to the "illegals" section at GRU Opergruppe. Here, the most dedicated spies in the GRU were prepared for the most important missions abroad. This was the most important CIA target within Soviet headquarters at the Karlshorst. Popov was about to learn the identities and assignments of the men and women being sent under deep cover for operations that could last a lifetime.

The CIA's most important source in its brief history was now in East Berlin running the Soviets' most closely guarded operation in Karlshorst. The tunnel "success," the Popov case, and the promise of Igor Orlov made Bill Harvey and his colleagues believe that they had the Soviets on the run.

CHAPTER NINETEEN

THE ILLEGALS

—⇒❂⇐—

B ILL HARVEY, the former FBI agent, knew only too well that catching an illegal Soviet agent in the United States was, for the Bureau, nearly the equivalent of capturing a unicorn. Soviet intelligence selected and trained only the most capable officers as illegals. Their job was to use false identities to enter another country and then to penetrate that society by blending into the community and pretending to be average citizens. A Soviet illegal usually portrayed himself as very conservative politically and fervently anti-Communist.

The mission of the Soviet illegals started out small. Moscow's original intention was to keep them deep underground as "sleepers," and to use them only in time of war to replace "legal" spies using diplomatic cover, who could be expected to be ousted if war broke out. However, as time went on, the GRU and KGB expanded the role and eventually used illegals to service their most important spy rings and to conduct "wet affairs," the euphemism for assassinations and sabotage. The CIA and FBI used their top agents to try to find and capture Soviet illegals.[1] Unfortunately, the Agency and the Bureau did not always see eye-to-eye on procedures or follow the other's advice.

Popov's information told the CIA how the illegals system worked and alerted them to the spies' identities even before their arrival in the United States. This was the situation in the fall of 1957 when Popov signaled for an emergency meeting. He told Kisevalter he had been assigned to put

Mararita Nikolayevska Tairova through her final briefings before she was sent to New York to join her husband as an illegal in the United States.

Popov had both Tairova's travel name and her cover name in New York. He said that after her final processing, he would take her to Tempelhof Airport. From there, she would fly Pan Am to Frankfurt and then on to New York. Her travel name was "Mary Grodnik," and she was posing as an American returning from a month's holiday in Germany. Once in the United States, she would assume another name, Florence Grochowska, and pretend to be the daughter of a Polish-American family from Cleveland.

Trained by the GRU as a beautician, "she has no idea what she is doing," Popov told Kisevalter, ". . . and she drinks too much." Worse, from a professional point of view, her main reason for going to America was to check on her husband, an illegal working in downtown Manhattan. "She's hysterically jealous," said Popov. ". . . She says if she catches him with another woman, she is going to drag him by the hair back to Moscow."

Popov actually brought to one of his safe house meetings with Kisevalter, the suitcase Tairova was to carry to the United States. Inside were worn shoes from Bonwit Teller, lingerie from Macy's, and other items skillfully designed to convince U.S. Customs that this was an American coming home from a European vacation. But then, Kisevalter recalled, "He unscrews the mirror out of the suitcase, and there is three thousand dollars."

As Popov munched his sturgeon, he noticed that Kisevalter was not eating. "George, what is the matter?" he asked. A deeply worried Kisevalter explained that once the illegal arrived in New York, the CIA was obligated to notify the FBI that she was there. The Bureau would send agents to follow her. If she detected them, the trail could lead back to Popov.

Popov pushed back the plate of cold fish that he had barely started and told Kisevalter, "No matter what you do, there cannot be any surveillance of her in Europe or New York. All her training was designed to teach her to detect such surveillance. You must promise me that no such surveillance takes place."

Kisevalter replied that the FBI was always very careful, and it must be told. He explained that in Europe, holding back surveillance "isn't a problem. But in New York, we [have] to identify her and that is the only way you can do it."

When Kisevalter assured Popov that the greatest care would be taken, he meant it, but he was worried. Popov then asked Kisevalter where

Yonkers, New York, was. Kisevalter told him it was a suburb of New York City. Popov said there was also a KGB courier involved in the operation who was a barber on the ocean liner, the SS *United States*.

After leaving the safe house, Kisevalter took a series of cabs back to Berlin Base. It was well after midnight when he arrived. Harvey was at his desk, waiting. At first, Kisevalter and Harvey considered not telling headquarters about Tairova at all, but Harvey decided that was impossible. The two men got drunk that night as they drafted and tore up seven cables to CIA Director Allen Dulles. Finally, they settled on a cable that said: "We're on top of this. The illegals are going to do nothing we don't know about. If they hurt anybody, we'll stop it. You've got to go tell Hoover. If he finds out we knew about this when we did and we didn't tell him, we are going to have a political brush." The cable went on to describe how the case, if handled properly, gave the CIA and FBI the promise of unlocking the entire illegals network in the United States.

Harvey knew enough about the FBI from his years there to know that Popov was in danger, but he did not have the heart to tell Kisevalter and increase his concern. When Dulles received the cable, he did as his subordinates requested. Following the rules and mindful of the consequences if he didn't, he went to see Hoover and told him of the illegal Tairova's impending arrival and the importance of not letting her detect any FBI surveillance. Hoover quickly reminded Dulles that his responsibility for the operation ended when Tairova entered the United States. "I'll take care of it," Hoover told the concerned CIA director, who immediately notified Harvey that Hoover was creating problems.

For Kisevalter, what ensued was a horrible nightmare. "He [Hoover] brought in special agents from Chicago to New York so nobody would know them. Of course, these agents didn't know New York either. Not 30 agents, but three hundred."

Although the bulletin Hoover sent out to his New York field office cautioned the agents how important it was to avoid detection, the agents had never been up against a well-trained Soviet illegal. The bulletin went on to describe all the pertinent details of Tairova's arrival. "It was as if the Bureau put out a Welcome-to-America sign" for her, Kisevalter lamented.

On November 27, Tairova's flight arrived at then Idlewild Airport. The FBI quickly spotted the stocky woman with dishwater-blond hair at immigration. She took a taxi driven by an FBI agent to the Prince George

Hotel in lower Manhattan. On November 30, an FBI burglar broke into her room and searched it and her three suitcases. He found nothing unusual. When Tairova returned to her room later that day, however, she immediately spotted telltale signs of the break-in. She changed hotels and switched to her back-up identity, "Florence Grochowska," the Polish woman from Cleveland.

Hoover, desperate to show up the CIA, had made a fatal mistake in ordering the unlawful black-bag job on Tairova's hotel room. The FBI hoped to find some indication of her husband's real identity there. As Kisevalter put it, "We wrote the contents of the fucking thing from *A* to *Z*, everything. But no. They had to look. Now, you know, you can't fool any woman, let alone an intelligence agent. . . . But they had to search to see if what we said was in there was there."

On December 7, Tairova took a train to Yonkers and walked to the Park Hill Cinema and met her husband, Zhakob, in the nearly empty movie house. Zhakob embraced his wife. The couple returned by train to Manhattan, ate dinner in a seafood restaurant, and went to Zhakob's unassuming apartment on West 70th Street, not yet a fashionable part of New York in 1957. The next day, the FBI followed Zhakob to work and learned that his cover job was as a bookkeeper, and his cover name was "Walter A. Soja."

The FBI's round-the-clock surveillance continued through February 1958. At that point, Hoover became convinced that the couple was nothing more than low-level sleeper agents and ordered the surveillance cut back. With this decision, Hoover signed Popov's death warrant.

In Berlin, troubles were mounting for Popov from other directions. The Soviets reprimanded him for twice taking credit for the recruitment of his mistress. Although Popov never asked, Kisevalter told him that if he ever felt he was in danger, the CIA was prepared to resettle him and his family in the United States, reminding him that the entire family could sneak out on a weekend. Popov said his wife and children had no idea of his double life; it would be unfair to them to suddenly move them to the West.

On March 12, the FBI lost the Tairovs. The illegals the FBI thought so insignificant and poorly trained evaded the biggest counterintelligence surveillance in American history. The couple left New York on separate flights to Canada, met in Mexico City, and successfully made their way back to Moscow.

Four weeks after the Tairovs disappeared into Canada, Popov reported to Kisevalter in a state of absolute panic. The KGB counterintelligence section, the Second Chief Directorate, had sent a colonel from Moscow Center to investigate the charges that Tairova was now making against Popov. "The first thing he asked me," Kisevalter remembered, "was why didn't we arrest them, shoot them, anything but let them report back to Moscow." Popov reported that the woman said surveillance had started at Tempelhof. When Kisevalter assured him that it had not, Popov sarcastically asked if he should tell his GRU general that his CIA case officer said there was no surveillance.

Once again, Kisevalter offered Popov the opportunity to escape. Again he refused. Their next meeting was scheduled for the following month, and Kisevalter's heart sank when Popov signaled for a meeting ahead of schedule. Popov explained that he was being called back to Moscow on a West German spy case. Kisevalter did not bring up defection again; Popov had told him that he intended to stick it out, though he wanted to get out of illegals work and into something less stressful.

During this meeting, contact procedures were arranged so that Popov could send a message from Moscow. Kisevalter gave Popov a hunting knife and a fishing reel that opened up to reveal code pads and ink that required special chemicals to make it visible. After the meeting, Kisevalter and Popov got into a CIA car, and the driver dropped Popov off for the walk to the S-Bahn. Kisevalter had a sinking feeling as he watched the thick-waisted peasant walk away on that warm night in Berlin that he would never see his good friend again.

Russell A. Langelle, assigned to Popov in Moscow, was one of five CIA officers stationed in the Soviet capital. By American standards, Langelle was an experienced intelligence officer, but compared to the Soviets he was a rookie of the greenest sort. Langelle's job was to establish brush encounters with Popov every few weeks to exchange messages.

On October 16, Langelle took the number 107 Moscow city bus on his way to work. He was to make a brush contact with Popov on the bus just a block from the U.S. embassy, at Vorovskovo and Chaikovskovo streets. Popov was going to slip Langelle a palm-sized notebook containing details of his latest experiences. Langelle thought he was meeting Popov after Popov left his desk at GRU headquarters. He had no idea Popov, in fact, was on the bus after being in a cell at Lubyanka Prison, which backs up to Moscow Center.

Langelle looked out of place on the Moscow bus. He successfully bumped into the chunky Popov, quickly placed the notebook in his pocket, and got off at the next stop. Relieved, Langelle started to walk away. A black Zim automobile suddenly pulled in front of the bus. Three KGB men sprang from the car, grabbed Langelle, and pushed him into the limousine. He was taken to a nearby KGB office and "talked to" for several hours.

The KGB officers proposed that to save himself from career embarrassment, Langelle become a spy for the Soviets. Absolutely petrified, he refused to say a word. Finally, the officers gave up, told him to forget the incident, and dropped him off at the embassy, but kept his notebook.

Unaware of the CIA's activities in his domain, the United States ambassador to the USSR was under the mistaken impression that Langelle was the embassy security officer, his cover job. Langelle's report on the KGB's actions to the surprised ambassador led to an official U.S. protest.[2] In response, the Soviet Foreign Ministry told the State Department that it would be very foolish to make an issue of Langelle's detention.

Langelle was declared persona non grata and thrown out of the Soviet Union. According to William R. Corson, who conducted operations in Moscow on behalf of four presidents, "The CIA was showing its inexperience by assuming that you could hold any kind of meeting with an agent under suspicion in Moscow. It was a ludicrous idea."[3]

Not until 1962 was Popov tried for treason, put before a firing squad, and shot. To the last day of his life, George Kisevalter was haunted by the loss of Popov. "He thought he was going to go home and live among his equals . . . ," Kisevalter said. "We should have grabbed the family and evacuated them right away."

Although Berlin Base lost Popov, this first major Soviet defector had provided remarkable information to the CIA over his five years as an active source. He, together with the Berlin tunnel, secured the reputations of the men and women of Berlin Base with headquarters in Washington. By the end of the Popov operation, Bill Harvey had a hundred people working for him. Graduates of the Base were fanning out all over the world to run similar operations. At Camp Peary, the CIA's sprawling training facility near Williamsburg, Virginia, the Agency used BOB as the example of how junior officers were to do business. The successes seemed to keep on coming.

One December night in 1960, case officer Donald Morris was working late at Berlin Base. He and his colleagues were all on edge. Earlier in the day, they had received word that BE VISION was defecting. BE VISION was the CIA code name for Michel Goleniewski, the Polish intelligence service's liaison officer with the Soviets.[4] Goleniewski had contacted the CIA through a series of letters signed SNIPER, and now he was making the move to defect, bringing his mistress with him.

David Murphy decided to personally welcome BE VISION to West Berlin by picking him up in his Mercedes. Not long after Murphy left the Base, Morris received a phone call from Murphy, instructing him to get a car with German plates and go down to the meeting. "Dave Murphy had locked his keys in the trunk compartment of the car," Morris recalled.

Before being taken to Frankfurt for processing at the elaborate Defector Reception Center, Goleniewski, the head of Polish counterintelligence, made it clear to George Kisevalter and Anita Potocki that he did not trust David Murphy and wanted nothing to do with him.

In Frankfurt, BE VISION told his debriefers that the KGB had a Soviet agent, a technical type, in MI6. He said the Soviets were getting copies of MI6 documents from this source, whom the KGB had code named DIAMOND. BE VISION reported that this source had served in several posts, including Berlin. Frankfurt passed the information along to the British, who, after several false starts, concluded that DIAMOND was George Blake, the British diplomat who was captured by the North Koreans in 1950 and who had worked with the CIA on various occasions in Berlin.

MI6 recalled Blake from an Arabic course he was teaching in Lebanon on the pretext that he was being promoted. Once back in England, he was interrogated for days.[5] In the end, he confessed that he was in fact a Soviet agent.

The first operation he said he had compromised was Bill Harvey's Berlin tunnel. Blake also said he had given the KGB the location of a score of defectors, who were subsequently kidnapped and taken back across the border. In addition, he confessed to tipping off the Soviets to the Popov case. But perhaps the most damaging information George Blake had given the Soviets was the identity of most of the case officers at

Berlin Base. He had told Moscow who they were and, more important, what their weaknesses were.[6]

MI6 and the National Security Agency were at first skeptical of Blake's assertion that the tunnel had been compromised, given the volume of telephone traffic they had monitored. It took years, but eventually they concluded that once the tunnel was in operation, the Soviets had made certain that only low-level phone calls went through Berlin. They put on this elaborate charade so as not to tip off Harvey's men that they were aware of the tunnel, and to protect George Blake. The Soviets were surprised that he confessed.

During the entire period from the beginning of the tunnel operation in 1954 until Goleniewski's revelations, Berlin Base operated unaware of Blake's treachery. Once it was discovered, no executive of the CIA was about to admit the Soviets had penetrated its most famous operation. Even today, most accounts of the tunnel marvel at its great success.

CHAPTER TWENTY

THE HUNGARIAN DEBACLE

⸺⦿⸺

T HE RELATIONSHIP BETWEEN Berlin Base and General Gehlen's group at Pullach grew closer through the efforts of David Murphy as Soviet Branch Chief. Though several of his colleagues felt the relationship was risky, Murphy insisted that Berlin Base share much of its information with Gehlen. This material included important technical secrets as well as the identities of Berlin Base agents in East Germany. What Murphy forgot is that the Americans were not the only ones who understood how Hitler's former henchmen could be recruited for a Cold War intelligence service. The Americans were to pay the price for Murphy's overconfidence.

Hans Clemens had commanded the Gestapo in his hometown of Dresden before the war. Ruthless enough to become head of Hitler's SS liaison group in Rome, Clemens ordered the execution of 335 Italians at war's end. He was put on trial at Nuremberg and sentenced to four years in prison. When the embittered Clemens was released from prison and returned to Dresden, now in Soviet hands, his wife told him she had become the mistress of an NKVD colonel.

The two men talked, and the colonel proposed that Clemens become a Soviet agent, go to West Germany, and attempt to get a sensitive job. Clemens agreed but did not land a job that gave him access to sensitive material. He was fearful the Soviets would punish him for failing, but then in April 1951, his luck changed. On a train, Clemens ran into an old SS buddy, Willi Krichbaum. Krichbaum, a "cleansed" Nazi, was a top personnel official in Gehlen's operation at Pullach. He hired Clemens, the new Soviet agent, as a recruiter in Karlsruhe. Krichbaum was so pleased with Clemens's work that he brought him into the inner sanctum at Pullach.

Once in a position of power, Clemens hired two old friends and former colleagues, Heinz Felfe and Erwin Tiebel, also to serve as double agents. In November 1951, the Soviets gave Felfe the code name PAUL and started running his operation out of Karlshorst in East Berlin. Tiebel became a courier for Pullach; on the side, he carried stolen secrets to KGB contacts in West Berlin, who then delivered them to Karlshorst. In 1954, when the West German government formalized Gehlen's intelligence service as the new BND (Federal Intelligence Service), the Allies told Gehlen to get rid of all associates who had played major roles in the SS. Despite that order, Clemens and Felfe survived. Not only that, Felfe was promoted.

Felfe worked frequently with Ed Petty at the CIA Base in Munich and with David Murphy at Berlin Base. Felfe became a wonder in the BND because he seemed to know intuitively where the Soviets might try to penetrate. He was constantly unmasking low-level Soviet operations, such as a series of KGB agents in the U.S. Army.[1]

After exposing the Soviet agents, Felfe reported on his greatest feat, an operation in Aue, Czechoslovakia, called URANUS. Felfe told all about how he had infiltrated the local uranium mine, which supplied the Soviet Union's atomic weapons program. He backed up the story with pictures, production statistics, and supposed samples from the mine. Gehlen proudly told CIA Director Allen Dulles of Felfe and the operation and even sent Dulles some of the samples. Dulles was so impressed that he brought Gehlen to Washington as a reward.

It took more than a decade before the story was proved untrue and Felfe was unmasked, even though Anita Potocki in Berlin was suspicious from the start. When Potocki ran into Ed Petty at the Munich Base, she complained to him about one of her agents being arrested. "I tried to tell him there had to be a penetration in the BND, and it involved a case I was working on that got compromised, thanks to Murphy and his insistence on sharing it with the BND," Potocki recalled.[2] She remembered Petty replying, "Oh no, it can't be. How did you get to this?" Potocki explained that a leak in the Gehlen organization was the only way her agent could have been exposed. Petty did not take any action on Potocki's warning. In fact, he would later claim that he was the one who discovered Felfe's betrayal.[3]

The Felfe operation might have gone on for another 10 years if it had not been for the defection of Gunther Maennel, an East German intelligence officer who was brought directly to Camp King near Frankfurt for what turned out to be a very disturbing debriefing. Maennel exposed a series of KGB infiltrations of British, German, and American intelligence. Almost as an afterthought, he told his interrogators that there was a double agent in Pullach under the code name PAUL.

Gehlen did not believe his security officers when they told him his trusted Heinz Felfe was a KGB agent. It was Felfe himself who precipitated his own arrest. When he learned of the defection to Berlin Base of an important KGB assassin, Bogdan Stashinsky,[4] he immediately told his handlers at Karlshorst. The BND intercepted the message, and based on this and Maennel's information, Felfe was arrested.

Even from prison Felfe continued to do damage. The West Germans foolishly gave him the job of addressing magazine mailing labels while he awaited trial, and for months he managed to send out secret messages to the Soviets.

Most disturbing is the fact that Felfe's ability to deliver so impressed the CIA that it shared almost everything it had with him, despite Anita Potocki's attempts to convince Dave Murphy that "it just didn't seem very smart."

Instead of blaming Murphy for the disaster, Harvey defended him. To Harvey, the intelligence business was not black and white. "Sometimes you win a few, sometimes you lose," Harvey said to his critics. "[Murphy] is like Babe Ruth. He strikes out a lot. But when he hits one, he really hits one."

David Murphy was probably the most unpopular man at Berlin Operating Base until the arrival of the new Hungarian and East German Branch Chief, George Weisz, in April 1954.

Weisz was still as elegantly turned out as he had been the day in 1945 when he first met his future wife, Etta Jo, and Bill Harvey's future wife, C.G., at Carmel Offie's office in Frankfurt. John Sherwood said that Weisz "could have stepped out of a limo in Manhattan on his way to Merrill Lynch."

It didn't take Weisz long to earn the enmity of his colleagues. As Anita Potocki put it, "Weisz was one of those that went around cutting people's throats and stabbing them in the back." She said this was particularly true regarding case officers who were returning to Washington: Weisz always made certain when he took over a job that headquarters understood how poorly his predecessor had done. Wally Driver, who worked on several operations with "the Black Knight," as Weisz was known, remembered him as "a tough guy. He had all the personality of a fish just hauled up from three thousand fathoms."[5]

Weisz further alienated colleagues by bragging that he was already a high-ranking GS-15 when he arrived in Berlin. Driver recalled him saying at lunch one day that he "had done the agency a great favor by coming over from the State Department" and that his assignment was to "straighten out Harvey's operation." As for his own operation, instead of trying to disguise his background as the CIA had instructed him to do, he brought his theatrical and lively mother, Gizelle Breuer Weisz, to live with him and Etta Jo in Berlin.

Berlin Base colleague Sam Wilson believed part of Weisz's problem was that he was very insecure. Wilson described Weisz as "kind of the little guy on the outside looking in. He was sort of on the periphery of big things, but he never really made it" into the Berlin Base hierarchy.[6] (John Sherwood said this was because the hierarchy excluded Jews, but Wilson maintained that acceptance at Berlin Base had nothing to do with ethnic or religious background.) Whatever the cause, Weisz's behavior did not endear him to his colleagues. As Wilson put it, "George politicked very hard, worked very hard to secure assignments. . . . He was boring. The real pro does his goddamn job, and his superiors know his work and give him greater responsibility. . . . That's the kind of pro I understand."

To Wilson and others at Berlin Base, George Weisz asked too many questions about operations that he had nothing to do with and pushed too hard for information. "He was always curious about whatever I was doing . . . which I found distasteful," Wilson said. Wilson never questioned Weisz's loyalty, however: "I had nothing to go on." Wilson added, "I consciously, intellectually resist trying to stereotype someone because of commonly accepted racial characteristics. I really fight that in myself tooth and nail. It happens to me once in a while. It happened to me in the case of George. I thought, 'George, hey, you're acting like a frightened little Jew now. You know, you're an American. . . . Come off it.'"

Although not popular with his colleagues, Weisz was operationally effective. He was still a master at breaking people down. "I worked later on a specific operation with George," Driver recalled. "An East German girl had come out as a refugee and the operation got kind of complicated, and it began to look like a double operation. . . . He worked on the girl. And I'll tell you, in a matter of less than an hour he reduced her to absolute shreds."

Apart from his personality, two things dominate the Berlin Base alumni's memories of George Weisz. The first was that he traveled more in Communist countries than any other Berlin Base officer—so much so that, as Driver put it, "some people wondered if he was a mole." The second was his activity regarding Hungary. Weisz had regularly visited his Hungarian homeland ever since his arrival in Berlin—despite the fact that Berlin Base personnel were discouraged from contacting relatives in Eastern Europe, because if the KGB became aware of a connection, the relatives would be susceptible to blackmail. But Weisz really raised eyebrows when he went to Hungary at a time when it could not have been more dangerous or unusual for a CIA officer—shortly after the uprising in October 1956.

One reason Weisz was sent to Berlin in the first place and made his early trips to Hungary was that Frank Wisner was relying on Weisz's connections to aid Hungarian freedom fighters the CIA had been secretly training. Despite the loss of thousands of anti-Soviet Eastern Europeans over the years, Wisner and his colleagues were once again trying their luck at rolling back the Yalta agreement through covert action.

Wisner, the fiery proponent of clandestine action, had kept the CIA on a high wire with daring—and dubious—covert operations, which demonstrated that the Agency could change governments in Third World countries almost at will. In 1953, Wisner supervised the coup in Iran at the behest of CIA Director Allen Dulles and his brother John Foster Dulles, the secretary of state. The Dulleses had become annoyed when Iran's President Mohammed Mossadegh nationalized the British government's oil company there, claiming that Great Britain was stealing the bulk of petroleum profits from Iran. It was because of Wisner and the CIA that the Shah replaced Mossadegh and ascended the "Peacock throne," leading to political upheaval in later decades. But the prime example was Guatemala, where Wisner ordered the 1954 coup against the government of Jacobo Arbenz. Arbenz had annoyed the Dulles brothers first, by allowing the Communist Party to join his coalition government and then by expropriating four hundred thousand acres from the United Fruit Company. Berlin Base's Henry Hecksher arrived in Guatemala City dressed in lederhosen to play a major role in that coup.[7] His effort became the template for future covert operations.[8]

Dulles was enthralled with covert operations. He was called "the Great White Case Officer" because he was so fascinated by the details of these operations. Another reason why he favored covert warfare was that it sustained Congress's and the president's support for the new intelligence agency. When Dulles became the director of central intelligence, he promised President Eisenhower results in the battle against Communism. So far, however, the CIA was having little luck in its publicly announced goal of rolling back the Iron Curtain. The Soviets had largely refused to engage the CIA anywhere, including Berlin. The CIA had spent several hundred million dollars and had produced precious little in the way of real intelligence. An operation like Guatemala dazzled the politicians who controlled the CIA purse strings.

Since his OSS days during the war, Frank Wisner had been doing one difficult job after another. By 1956, the instability that Carmel Offie had taught him to disguise was starting to spin out of control. The pressure of a life of secrecy had broken other men, and now it was breaking him.

It could not have happened at a worse time. The Soviets had a new leader in Nikita Khrushchev, and the KGB was showing the world who was boss with the crackdown in Hungary. It was also an election year in the United States, and President Eisenhower did not want to risk a direct confrontation with the Soviets for political reasons. He had already refused to back the British, French, and Israelis over the Suez Canal in August, and he refused to back the Hungarians now.

In the middle of the Hungarian uprising, Wisner came through Berlin with his deputy, John Baker, on a tour of CIA stations and bases. When Harvey saw him, he told colleagues that Wisner seemed a little "strange." On his next stop in Vienna, Wisner monitored the Hungarian bloodbath, as the CIA had once again led thousands of freedom fighters to believe that the United States would help, only to abandon them to Soviet tanks. Wisner, who had watched helplessly for more than a decade as the Soviets cracked down on one Eastern European resistance movement after another, was crushed.

Back in Washington, at meetings of the Directorate of Plans (as the office in charge of all the CIA's covert operations was now called), Wisner became more and more emotional and unreliable. The once-confident and imaginative clandestine warrior became argumentative with old friends and started screaming when orders were not carried out to his satisfaction. His colleagues attributed his bizarre conduct to a serious case of hepatitis and a high fever that he had contracted on the trip. For the next year, Wisner operated as head of the Clandestine Services in this impaired mental condition.

Then, on an oppressively hot day in August 1958, employees in Clandestine Services, located in Building L along the Mall, noticed a commotion.[9] Shock registered on their faces as they watched an ambulance crew carry out their leader, Frank Wisner, in a straitjacket. For six months, doctors at Shepard Pratt Hospital in Baltimore gave Wisner electric shock therapy, without success. The father of American covert action never recovered.

Dulles kept Wisner on the payroll, first in London and then in Thailand. In October of 1965, his remarkable mind now twisted and bleak, Wisner put a gun to his head and blew his brains out.[10] The progenitor of the CIA's Clandestine Services, the man who had recruited General Gehlen after the war and supervised the importation of Nazi war criminals to the United States, was now part of the CIA's secret history.[11]

BILL HARVEY had the best espionage unit in the CIA, and he was still not satisfied with his team's performance. Too many case officers were producing too little intelligence. For one thing, the Base had run Igor Orlov for five years, and yet he had not produced one useful agent. Then, the relationship between Berlin Base and Gehlen's operation had been thoroughly exploited by the Soviets. Now, one of the biggest efforts of the Cold War, the Hungarian uprising, had failed on Harvey's doorstep. Later, the CIA's counterintelligence division determined that the KGB had learned from the Gehlen organization about the secret base outside of Munich where the CIA trained the Hungarian freedom fighters.

Had Bill Harvey looked into George Weisz's connections to the Hungarian government going back to his OPC days, he would have found another piece of the puzzle. Much of the support for a Communist government in Hungary had come from Jews who did not want to see the Nazis back in power. By 1956, Weisz had been trading information with members of that Communist government for a decade. To Weisz, America's role in the failed 1956 revolution was one more act of betrayal by his adopted country: In his eyes, many of the exiled Hungarian leaders trained by the CIA were nothing but Nazi collaborators trying to regain power.

Weisz's bitterness toward those who had betrayed the Jews in Hungary was at the very heart of his being. Yet Harvey never troubled himself with such personal information. He was not alone. None of Weisz's CIA bosses over the next 30 years ever really questioned his motives.

CHAPTER TWENTY-ONE

HARVEY HAS PROBLEMS

E VEN BEFORE THE RECALL of Popov to Moscow and the failure of the Hungarian uprising, there were signs of trouble at Berlin Base. "Agents were being rolled up by the dozen," George Kisevalter recalled, "and no one could figure out why." Between 1956 and 1959, more than one hundred Berlin Base agents were arrested or shot by the KGB and East German intelligence. As Bill Harvey and his men tried to piece together what was going wrong, even more agents disappeared.

"I sent my people out to help Bill do a CI investigation," James Angleton said, "but we could find nothing. We had the Office of Security go through Berlin Base headquarters in the U.S. Mission compound, but found no bugs or intercepts." It took the CIA's most experienced case officers years to figure out what was wrong.

One part of the answer proved to be Harvey's reliance on Hugh Montgomery to keep the peace with the local authorities and get favors from the police and the prosecutor's office. As it turned out, Montgomery had used one of his numerous police sources to run name checks for Base operations, including some of Igor Orlov's prostitutes. George Kisevalter eventually discovered that Montgomery's policeman had an office mate who was a Soviet agent. This individual gave the KGB the names on every file Montgomery's man pulled. Eventually, the man admitted that his office mate had full knowledge of his work for the CIA, and the office mate confessed to passing the information on to the Soviets.[1]

While Kisevalter got to the bottom of this facet of the mystery, one middle-level policeman did not account for anywhere near the number of agents who were lost. The other piece of the puzzle proved to be Harvey's greatest nemesis in Berlin, Markus Johannes Wolf.

Harvey had more trouble with the SSD—the East German version of the KGB, run by Wolf—than with the KGB itself. Wolf had spent a decade fine-tuning the SSD into a spy service that humiliated both the CIA and its West German counterpart, the BND. Wolf was so high in Moscow Center's confidence that the KGB gave the SSD the task of penetrating NATO, of which West Germany became a full-fledged member in 1956. By 1958, Wolf's spies had succeeded in burrowing into NATO via the BND.[2]

Wolf's most outrageous operation was his successful plan to infiltrate the camp of Germany's most popular politician, Willy Brandt. Wolf was well aware that Brandt had been on the CIA payroll for years. Harvey's wife, C.G., used Brandt's name to get favors from the police and other authorities. When a colleague at Berlin Base suggested to C.G. that she could get into trouble by using the future chancellor of Germany in such a cavalier fashion, her response was, "Oh hell, he works for Bill."

Wolf, too, thought it likely Brandt would replace the aging Konrad Adenauer as chancellor some day, and he devised a way to get one of his agents into Brandt's camp. The first step, finding someone in East Germany with strong ties to Brandt, was easily accomplished when Wolf found Dr. Ernst Wilhelm Guillaume. Contrary to Peter Sichel's assertion in the early days of Berlin Base, there was a wartime resistance movement in Germany, and Willy Brandt had been part of it. Dr. Guillaume was a doctor who had tended to his war wounds and hidden him from the Nazis.

Guillaume, now ill himself, lived with his son, Gunther, and daughter, Elsa. In post-war Germany, Gunther passed himself off as too poor to attend University, when in fact he was already a Captain in the new East German Army. Gunther had actually been sent to Kiev for a special KGB course offered to allied intelligence services. To build the cover, Gunther earned a living traveling from East Berlin to West Berlin clearing war rubble for new construction. It was during this period that he declared himself opposed to communism and the East German government and was embraced by the anti-communist political establishment represented by the Social Democrats in West Berlin. Gunther effectively became an SD party functionary. The SD was lead by Gunther's father's old friend Willy Brandt.

In a classic intelligence operation, Wolf recruited Gunter and put him through training as an SSD agent. Gunter's first task was to persuade his father to write to Brandt and ask him to give his son an "opportunity for a better life." In January 1955, Gunter received a response in a letter inviting him to West Berlin for a meeting. Brandt, a generous and appreciative man, offered the untrained Gunter a job as one of his three personal assistants.

The SSD's tutoring paid off. Gunter Guillaume became Brandt's most "loyal" assistant. Brandt, who left the Bundestag in 1957 and became the mayor of West Berlin, trusted him fully. Whenever Bill Harvey needed to inform Mayor Brandt of a CIA operation or request help, he or Hugh Montgomery dealt with the young and hardworking Gunter Guillaume.

When Brandt became Chancellor of Germany he assigned Gunther the job of reviewing all documents that came to Brandt. Guillaume copied everything and then passed them to his SSD case officer through drops, or through his wife Christel while she visited relatives in East Berlin. When a Russian KGB officer Vadem Belotzerkovsky received asylum in France he informed French intelligence that Guillaume was a Soviet agent. Brandt was informed and for nearly a year pretended that he still trusted Guillame. The BND arrested Guillaume in April 1974. A month later Willy Brandt said to the president of the West German Republic: "I accept political responsibility for negligence in connection with the Guillaume espionage affair and declare my resignation from the office of Federal Chancellor." Gunther Guillaume was convicted and sentenced to thirteen years. He was traded for political prisoners back to East Germany in 1982.

Despite its problems, Berlin Base kept its importance to the CIA because East Berlin and Vienna were the only two main entry and exit points for the entire Communist world. It was through these cities that technical merchandise was smuggled into the Soviet Union from the West, and Third World leaders were secretly brought to Moscow for education, indoctrination, punishment, and rewards. It was through these portals that double agents were whisked to Moscow for medals and pictures and then quickly returned to the field. In short, East Berlin had to be watched.

The pragmatic necessity of keeping track of the opposition replaced the earlier glamour and excitement of engaging the enemy.

Berlin Base in the late 1950s was as loaded with oddball characters as it was in its glory days. In the triumph of the Popov defection, George Kisevalter was carrying Berlin Base's reputation and workload on his considerable shoulders. "Kisevalter basically did everybody else's work for them. . . ," said John Sherwood. "It's a little bit like having Bronco Nagurski on your team." But Kisevalter did not like paperwork, and his assistant, June Sworobuck, had to follow him around to get him to pay attention to administrative details. "George could not spell the word *administration*," Donald Morris remembered.

Berlin Base's scientific case officer, Sig Hoeckster—the connoisseur of female mud wrestling whom David Murphy had tried to get fired—wasn't the only known CIA officer to publicly belong to the International Socialist Workers Party. Harvey was flabbergasted when Hoeckster was offered the job of secretary of the party, but Hoeckster saw no conflict. He simply said he was Austrian, not American.

Hoeckster did not know how to drive a car. When Washington dictated an economy move, he lost his driver and was told to learn to drive. "Well, a couple of gateposts and wrecked cars later . . . they went back to getting him a chauffeur," Wally Driver recalled. Hoeckster also had assistants to help him file reports. "He knew everything there was to know about mathematics and atomic energy. . . ," Driver continued, "but his English was not quite perfect. He couldn't type. He wouldn't learn."

Then there were the bon vivants in the social set. Freddy Vreeland, son of fashion arbiter Diana Vreeland, was a well-turned-out addition, at least sartorially, to the Base. Another fixture was Ace Rosner, a one-armed jack-of-all-trades who tooled around Berlin in a white sports car. Dick Montague, whose father was chief executive officer of the Borden Company, spoke flawless German, but, according to John Sherwood, his chief claim to fame was that "once a year he would rent the entire top floor of the new Hilton Hotel and throw a black tie for everyone in the Base."

One of the female characters was C.G. Harvey, who remained her husband's protector and confidante. "There wasn't anything Bill didn't tell her," George Kisevalter said. She saw herself as Berlin Base's kindly empress. In reality, she terrorized some of the younger officers and their wives. John Sherwood recalls his arrival in Berlin as beginning with an "audience with C.G. Harvey. . . . She was the official barrier. . . . We had tea and cookies." Both Sherwood and Morris found her an intimidating presence, and both men tried to stay on her good side. For decades after Bill Harvey's death, she helped perpetuate the mythology surrounding Berlin Base.

The main thing everyone remembers about C.G. Harvey is how she and Bill became parents to their daughter, Sally. One night, the Murphys found a basket containing an infant on their front porch. As Donald Morris tells it, "Of all people, Marian Murphy looks at the baby and says, 'What's that?' and C.G. says, 'It's a baby.' And her next words were, 'I am going to keep it.' She took it home. By this time it is about one in the morning. Everybody with a child under three at the Base was called. Cribs, bottles, sterilizers, diapers were arriving in relays, with copies of Dr. Spock. I think I contributed about 25 diapers. When I got there, C.G. had the baby. She was masterminding operations. There was a police official there, insisting the baby had to go to the police station for registration and everything else, and C.G. could put in a claim to adopt it. C.G. paid no attention to him. She picked up the telephone, dialed a number, and when the phone was answered, she just held the receiver out to the police officer. He found himself talking to Willy Brandt."

Grumbling from some of the wives at Berlin Base brought questions to Harvey from headquarters about the baby. "Needless to say, headquarters found this a little on the bizarre side and insisted that they check out at least who the mother was," Morris recalled. "The mother turned out to be a daughter of an East Berlin functionary. It was an illegitimate child. She and her mother did not dare tell her father about it since he was a German from the old school. She managed to have the baby, and she and her mother took it over and left it on the best-looking doorstep they could find. Her father never did know about her. The baby's father was also identified. . . . The father was just a young stud who had some ties to the KGB."[4]

BY 1959, BILL HARVEY was overseeing one hundred case officers and support workers, but they were doing mostly routine work. The cowboy days were definitely over. When an occasional defector or spy crossed over, Berlin Base hummed with activity for a time, but Harvey seldom called the troops at midnight anymore to meet at the Base motor pool "with heat" to cover some agent meeting that the case officer thought "might not be on the up and up."

Bill Harvey understood how the CIA was evolving and saw that the future was in covert action, not in espionage. Berlin Base had, by geographic circumstances, little hope now of conducting any business except traditional espionage, and it wasn't doing that very well. Harvey was painfully aware that Berlin Base was producing less intelligence of real value now than at any time since the tunnel, and he suspected that Washington was disappointed in the "take." He understood from his FBI experience that certain jobs lead to promotions and others didn't. As long as he stayed in Berlin, he was outside the CIA's power center. He had to come to terms with his Berlin job or do something about it.

ELEONORE ORLOV HAD HAD ENOUGH of her husband's secret life and wanted to go home to Munich. "What was the last name of my child? Kopatzky? Koischwitz? . . . I wanted to take my baby and go home to my mother . . . ," she recalled. "The CIA would not allow it. And Mr. Wilson said that the best thing is to get you American citizenship."[5] Sam Wilson offered Igor Orlov several alternatives. One was a lump-sum payment of $25,000 to begin a business in Munich; another was United States citizenship for the family. Eleonore urged her husband to take the money and start a business. Igor argued that their life had improved dramatically over the years with the CIA.

In the end, Orlov stayed with the CIA in Germany. Sam Wilson in Washington, Bill Harvey, and David Murphy arranged for him to be promoted to Frankfurt Station, and they promised to arrange American citizenship for his family. They made Igor a full-fledged case officer, running his own agents. Whatever doubts CIA headquarters had about Orlov in 1954 were forgotten. The failures and suspicions that David Murphy wrote about 40 years later never surfaced at the time.

Eventually, the Orlov family made their way to America, and the little man became the obsession of a generation of American intelligence higher-ups.

CHAPTER TWENTY-TWO

TRANSITION, ASSASSINATION, AND CONSCIENCE

I N THE FALL OF 1959, Bill Harvey made his career decision and returned to Washington. Shortly thereafter, Ted Shackley followed him, coming back to a slot in the Eastern European Division. David Murphy's years of flattering Harvey appeared to be paying off when he was named acting chief of base. But then, for the first time in his meteoric career, Murphy was stopped.

Harvey was really angry when CIA executive John Bross passed over Murphy and appointed Munich Chief William Hood to Berlin. Harvey had total contempt both for Hood and for Bross, the man who had failed to approve support for the East German insurgents back in 1953.

No one at BOB was reassured when Hood arrived in early December 1959, with two steamer trunks full of dress shirts. John Sherwood, who worked for Hood in Munich before he came to Berlin, said, "He corrected your clothes. He was great at parties. He played a lot of chess, loved charades, played good badminton, talked a fantastic game, and was never on the street—ever."

Hood and Harvey were as different as night and day. Hood reciprocated the contempt his legendary predecessor had for him. Hood had married well, and many colleagues believed that his older wife, Cordelia, was a good deal smarter about the spy business than he was. "Conspicuous consumption was Bill Hood's life . . . ," said Sherwood. "You could follow Bill Hood around and rewrite the theory of the leisure class."

Hood picked John Dimmer to replace Shackley as his deputy in charge of Soviet satellite countries. Dimmer was best known for his disconcerting habit of picking his cuticles so they were almost purple.

Hood's sole accomplishment as base chief was to replace the old-fashioned European water closets with American-style toilets and to install twin toilet paper dispensers. This earned him the nickname in German of "two-asshole Hood." In February 1960, two months after Hood's surprise arrival, he was just as quickly gone. This is when David Murphy finally became chief of base. "Hood was an example of the consuming and leisure class. He was married to a brilliant woman, who also worked for the Agency," John Sherwood said.

Donald Morris was one of the few officers in Berlin who admired David Murphy: "Murphy was usually doing nine things at once, and eight of them extremely well. He had a brand of infectious enthusiasm that was unreal. A secretary could go in there, and she would come out with a piece of paper that she thought was the most important document in the government. Dave was brilliant. The mind worked like nobody's business." However, Morris admits, "There was a feeling he wasn't entirely loyal to people under him, that if he got crossed or something, he wouldn't back them up." Yet Morris felt Murphy's talents were so great that this perceived lack of loyalty should be overlooked.

For John Sherwood, working under Murphy was a frustrating experience. Sherwood was annoyed that Berlin Base concentrated so much on the Soviets and ignored the East German military. He mounted an operation to penetrate the headquarters of the East German Ministry of Defense, located in the East Berlin suburbs. Within three months, he put together a network of agents and informants. From information they supplied, he pieced together the first sketch Berlin Base ever had of the headquarter's physical layout. To Sherwood's surprise, Murphy called him in and said, "All these fucking reports you are writing. . . this isn't our target." Sherwood said, "Well, shit, man, it is the East German Ministry of Defense." To which Murphy replied, "Give it to the Army."

Sherwood headed over to Army intelligence and, to his dismay, learned that the Army had not targeted the East German defense establishment either. "They had never done a thing," Sherwood recalled. He spent three months working as chief of operations on the project, which included using transport planes to overfly the area and put together the first detailed and often-frightening picture of the East German Army. Unfortunately, when a top Army intelligence official from Frankfurt made an inspection visit and found out a CIA man was running the operation, he ordered it shut down.

It was on Murphy's watch that the KGB showed just how tough it could be. The head of the KGB was now Ivan Aleksandrovich Serov, who had come to power in March 1954, during the tumultuous period following Stalin's death. He immediately set to work expanding the KGB's capacity for assassination. There was a botched attempt to kill anti-Soviet émigré leaders early in Serov's tenure in 1954, but soon thereafter he established the kamera, a special laboratory for exotic weapons research.[1]

Like any Party sycophant, Serov wanted to please his bosses. He turned the KGB's assassination department into a tool for political retribution. Under Serov, top Kremlin officials used the KGB to destroy anyone who displeased them. Khrushchev, who became secretary general of the Communist Party in 1955, while on the surface an anti-Stalinist reformer, did not hesitate to use Stalin's methods. Khrushchev gave the KGB and Serov the authority to kill anywhere in the world, as long as they used weapons that could not easily be traced to Moscow.

Serov formalized and enforced a policy requiring that all overseas assassinations be approved by a special secret committee of the Politburo. He and the members of the committee picked the targets. To oversee the assassinations, Serov selected Aleksandr Semyonovich Panyushkin, a former ambassador, and appointed him head of the First Chief Directorate, the KGB's foreign-operations department. Panyushkin's first task was to find a way, once and for all, to silence the NTS, the old anti-Soviet émigré movement that Igor Orlov had penetrated back in 1949. Penetration was not enough for Secretary Khrushchev. He wanted the leaders of the pesky group eliminated.

By the late 1950s, the NTS was mainly engaging in stunts and was, at best, a marginal threat to Communism's grip on power in Russia. One of its stunts involved an NTS operative approaching a Russian outside the country and telling him that the NTS "controlled" certain cities, including Moscow. To prove it, the operative told the bewildered Russian to go to a certain phone kiosk where he would find his name written on the wall. Though efforts like this were merely pathetic, the KGB still considered the organization dangerous because of its continued CIA funding.

Serov launched his campaign of action against the NTS in September 1956. One day, Bogdan Stashinsky, a Ukrainian agent, was shown into Serov's fourth floor office at 2 Dzerzhinsky Square. Waiting for him were Serov and Panyushkin, the assassination overseer. Panyushkin, who had a flair for the dramatic, personally presented a new weapon to Stashinsky and described to him his assignment in West Germany.[2]

Like Igor Orlov seven years earlier, Bogdan Stashinsky was to become a trusted member of an anti-Soviet group—in his case, the Organization of Ukrainian Nationalists.[3] Also like Orlov, he went to work for an exile newspaper in Munich, Lev Rebet's *Ukrainsky Samostnik*. While the CIA's interest in the anti-Soviet émigré movements had waned, Rebet and his colleagues were still a major thorn in Moscow's side. On October 12, 1957, Stashinsky walked into the newspaper's offices in Munich's Karlsplatz carrying a small leather suitcase. When Rebet came to the top of the staircase and greeted his employee, Stashinsky opened the suitcase, pulled out a strange-looking device, and pressed down on a pair of metal tubes. As Rebet looked down the tubes, they exploded, spraying seven cubic centimeters of hydrogen cyanide over his surprised face.

As promised by the KGB laboratory, the effect was immediate.

Rebet's mouth and nasal passages absorbed the poison, his heart stopped, and he dropped to the floor, dead. There was no sign of violence. Stashinsky swallowed an antidotal capsule as instructed, and successfully escaped. West German authorities thought the death suspicious, but with no evidence of murder, they listed the cause of death as a heart attack.

Effective as Serov was, in December 1958, Khrushchev replaced him as head of the KGB with his own man, Aleksandr Nikolayevich Shelyepin. A Communist Party hack of the highest order, Shelyepin had been an organizer in the Komsomol, the Communist Youth League. He had never worked in intelligence, and he lacked the patience and insight of a Chekist, as seasoned KGB agents often called themselves.[4] He did not want to know the human motivations of the other side; he simply wanted his adversaries out of the way. According to the assassin Stashinsky, the new KGB boss took an even greater interest in assassinations than his predecessor.

On October 15, 1959, Stashinsky waited in the vestibule of an apartment building on Munich's Zeppelinstrasse for Stephan Bandera. Bandera, the firebrand leader of the Organization of Ukrainian Nationalists, was a man particularly hated by the Kremlin, because he had worked for MI6 before the war, for the Nazis during the war, and he now worked for the CIA. When Bandera entered the vestibule, Stashinsky once again pressed the levers of the air gun and fired capsules into his victim's face. Bandera's death touched off a firestorm in the Soviet émigré community, but, once again, the cause of death was listed as natural.

From Munich, Stashinsky traveled to Berlin and crossed to the Eastern Zone, where he was summoned back to Moscow. The head of the KGB presented the successful killer with the Order of the Red Banner.

It was not until July 1961 that the CIA learned the true story of these assassinations. A month before the Berlin Wall went up, a married couple with East German identity cards identifying them as Josef and Inge Lehmann crossed from East Berlin into West Berlin and presented themselves to the U.S. Army CIC, which quickly notified Berlin Base. When a CIA interrogator arrived, Joseph Lehman stood up and identified himself as the KGB assassin Bogdan Stashinsky.[5] He verified his role in the assassinations with details that only the killer could know, and the following year he confessed to the crimes in court. He was not the last assassin the KGB sent to the West.

THERE IS NO BETTER EXAMPLE of American cynicism than the way the CIA risked and often sacrificed émigrés for its own purposes. The CIA recruited thousands of vulnerable refugees who fled their homes behind the Iron Curtain for a better life in the West, and used them with little thought for their safety. The CIA's reliance on schemes using anti-Soviet émigrés failed again and again, cost many human lives, and provided cover for Soviet agents like Igor Orlov.

Even in the most closely held CIA files, no accurate death toll of all these émigrés is available. Of the hundreds of agents trained and sent into the Soviet Union, there is no indication that a single one ever successfully accomplished his mission. In Poland, meanwhile, it turned out that WIN, the anti-Soviet Polish resistance group that the CIA backed with large resources, was a total Soviet operation. The Soviets themselves had created WIN to attract Poles who supported the West so that they could identify and then destroy them. The Soviets did this with appalling success.

Harry Rositzke, who ran most of the paramilitary operations against the Soviets from Munich, was ready to end behind-the-lines operations in

1955. Still, some CIA veterans like Donald Morris defend these operations, because "they kept the KGB occupied . . . confused."

John Sherwood's saddest experience showing this lack of regard for other people began when Richard Bissell, Deputy Director for Plans, visited Berlin Base. "We lined up in the second-story corridor, and in comes this man in a three-piece suit with a watch chain, the very embodiment of the establishment. And he addresses us. I turned to another guy and I said, 'Is this a board meeting of IBM?'" Sherwood remembered. Bissell announced to Sherwood and his colleagues that he had a special mission in mind. Bissell trumpeted: "We understand that there are some surface-to-air missile bases around Berlin. I would take it as a personal favor if you would begin to work on that."

Sherwood received the assignment and began one of the most ruthless operations in the history of Berlin Base. Using every tool available, he began to recruit hundreds of agents, mostly recent immigrants, to try to locate the surface-to-air missiles (SAM) and manuals for the SAM systems. According to Sherwood, "A lot of them did it because they felt they had just come out . . . and they thought, 'Jesus, if I don't do this, I am sunk. . . . I have got to do this to get out.'"

Throughout the very dangerous operation, one agent after another was arrested and beaten or shot. One agent had all his teeth knocked out. Torture was not unusual. But Sherwood kept up the recruiting. "I got so I could break these guys like a nut. I knew exactly what to say to them. I was so fucking slick. . . . I did it all day long; I did it at night." Each evening, Sherwood visited West Germans who had relatives in East German towns where the SAM sites were located and got them to write their relatives to ask for information or to invite them to come over for a visit. Then Sherwood attempted to recruit them. After a leisurely breakfast the next morning, he came into the Base with his report from the night before. He was so gung-ho that he urged David Murphy to put all case officers in Berlin on a night schedule. Murphy ignored Sherwood's request.

After several months of this, Sherwood succeeded in locating and obtaining photographs of all the SAM sites. His last task was to secure a copy of the SAM operating manual. He had recruited a very young West German with relatives in the town of Glau where the missile command was located. The manual was sure to be there, and the young West German agreed to try to get a copy.

It turned out that the entire town was home to a religious sect called the Weisenbergers. The young German told Sherwood that a book about the sect had been published with maps showing every building in town. With a copy of the book, he could get his relatives to point out which building the air defense forces used.

Sherwood cabled Washington, asking them to go to the Library of Congress for a copy of the book. Weeks went by. Leonard McCoy, the reports officer in the Soviet Division who was responsible for getting the book, did not respond to Sherwood's request. Sherwood managed to get the book independently and sent the young man on his very perilous mission. He was arrested. "If you are going from East Berlin into the Eastern Zone, it was like going into Alcatraz, really tough. . . ," Sherwood said. "That's where I was losing people. . . . They would agree to go back and see a relative to establish communications, and they would never come back out. They'd made some mistake."

It angered Sherwood that neither Harvey, Murphy, nor headquarters seemed to care what happened to these people. "Murphy didn't care at all. All he was obsessed with was the Russians. He told me one night . . . , 'John, you don't realize this, but the Russians know I have hurt them. They know how I've hurt them. My life is always in danger in this town.' . . . My metaphor for Murphy is a dark, dark night, lots of objects all over the lot. . . . Here is this huge halogen lamp that moves swirl-like. It illuminates everything. . . . Just as you're beginning to see, it moves off . . . a quick, shallow brain. That's all."

Later, when Sherwood returned to headquarters, he encountered Leonard McCoy. "I was steamed up a little bit because they didn't send a book or tell me about Glau . . . so I tracked McCoy down. I was sniffing around to see who cared. I was still sore because all these guys went to jail. . . . I went to McCoy and said, 'Look, here are the reports and you must be interested in these things.'"

McCoy's response surprised even Sherwood. He asked Sherwood why he should be interested in those reports since the CIA had had the SAM manual for two-and-a-half years. "He told me he got it from an Indonesian defector. . . . So we put all the people who worked on it in jail for nothing. There were about two hundred poor bastards. I worked my ass off for three-quarters of a year for nothing, absolute fucking nothing."

Even today, Sherwood hates to think about the agents who were beaten, arrested, or worse. "It's grotesque, isn't it? I'd wake up at four in the morning and I just couldn't get back to sleep. . . . I just felt like I was sick."

For Sherwood, that incident was a realization about his own life's work. "I was really a good case officer. I probably recruited as many or more people than any single guy. It was just a natural talent. I am as proud of it as one would be if he were a good second-story man. It is valueless virtue. . . . I searched for that redeeming factor, and I didn't find it."

CHAPTER TWENTY-THREE

WHAT WALL?

I N AUGUST 1961, just a year and a half after David Murphy took over as base chief, BOB underwent yet another transition when Murphy left for Washington and a top job in the Soviet Russia Division. His replacement in Berlin was William Graver, one of the tallest men in the CIA, with an ego to match.[1]

Graver, one of the Berlin cowboys under Bill Harvey, had served in BOB from 1954 until 1958, when he went to Washington to head the German Desk.

Former colleagues remember two things about Graver: his arrogance and his sexual appetite. John Sherwood recalls a typical conversation with Graver: "He told me one day he was really proud to find out that I was color-blind because he's color-blind. He had read some place that color-blind people are unquestionably genetically superior to others."

Graver's nickname, "El Supremo," came not from his six-foot-four-inch height but from his reputation for going to extremes to get women to sleep with him. When he was station chief in Vienna, Graver got Charles Malton, a well-educated and kindly man but not a very able officer, named as his deputy. The reason, according to Sherwood and confirmed by others, is that "Graver wanted to fuck his wife. It's that simple."

On the other hand, Graver had no use for women he didn't want to sleep with, like June Sworobuck, George Kisevalter's assistant. Sworobuck got to the point "where she hated Graver," according to Kisevalter, who added: "Oh yeah, he was a woman hater. A woman shouldn't get ahead." Sworobuck, a lawyer, eventually rose to a well-deserved executive position in the CIA.

Graver was also an ingrate, as he demonstrated when, during his tenure, Bill Harvey visited Berlin and got drunk. "And what do you think Graver did?" asked Kisevalter. "He writes home a cable protesting Harvey's behavior. . . . [Harvey] is the guy who put him there, and then he does this to him. That was Graver."

E. Allan Lightner, Jr., the senior American diplomat in Berlin, was fed up with Berlin Base. He had long ago concluded that it was producing very little intelligence. He was about to find out quite how little.

During the week of August 6, 1961, Graver was adjusting to life in Berlin, and David Murphy was tying up loose ends getting ready to leave. On Wednesday, August 9, a secret joint military and CIA group called the Berlin Watch Committee met at BOB. Graver viewed the committee as "a dull cultural event," and neither he nor Murphy attended the session that day. Instead, they sent John Dimmer to represent the CIA.

Colonel Ernest von Pawel—a West German officer whom Murphy had openly ridiculed—spoke forcefully to the group: "I know that some of you here disagree with my views, but I want to state them for the record. I believe that the East Germans and Russians are in the process of cordoning off the Eastern sector with some kind of system of barriers."

Since CIA officials were not allowed to travel in East Berlin or East Germany, and since Murphy's case officers had less than a dozen agents operating in East Berlin, the only reliable intelligence about East Berlin came from the joint American-West German Military Liaison Mission (MLM)—of which Colonel von Pawel was then the head. The MLM could drive to the Eastern Zone and inspect very limited portions of East Germany. Unfortunately, almost 60 percent of East Germany was out of bounds, and Stasi agents followed the MLM Jeeps in areas where they were allowed. Still, the MLM had learned enough to convince von Pawel that, as he told the meeting, a wall "would be erected to stem the flow of twenty-five hundred East German refugees a day into West Berlin." He explained that the East German authorities believed the country could no longer allow its population to hemorrhage to the West. He reminded everyone that Hitler had sealed in Warsaw's Jews. He reminded John

Dimmer in particular that the CIA had "never once managed to accurately predict what the Soviets' intentions in Berlin have been."

Dimmer, speaking for Berlin Base, said that Walter Ulbricht, the man in charge in East Germany, would "commit political suicide if he put up a wall."

Lieutenant Colonel Thomas McCord, head of the U.S. Army's military intelligence group in Berlin, spoke up next. He reported that one of his agents, a doctor and a functionary in the East German Communist Party, had learned the previous Sunday that West Berlin would be sealed off by August 13.

Dimmer knew that McCord had already made the same report to Murphy and Graver, who had dismissed it because the doctor seemed mistaken about unrelated matters. Graver ordered the report forwarded to Bonn Station, remarking that the source was so unreliable that no one would dare send it on to headquarters. And so Dimmer paid no attention to McCord. By the end of the meeting, only von Pawel and McCord were predicting the wall.

The next day, French intelligence passed on to McCord information they had received from Dr. Hartmut Wedel, an East German dentist with many patients in the SED, the East German ruling party. The French told McCord: "They are going to erect a series of barriers through all of Berlin." McCord dutifully passed this report on to Berlin Base, where it was treated as lightly as McCord's own source.

In Washington, the young president of the United States—still smarting from the Bay of Pigs disaster in Cuba four months earlier—was desperate for information on Berlin. He was calling the German Desk at the State Department so often that they began calling him disparagingly "our Berlin Desk Officer." Kennedy's instincts that the CIA and the State Department were withholding information from him were correct.

On Friday, August 11, four thousand refugees streamed through the Marienfelde camp. Reports Officer John Maypother saw the hysteria in the faces of those he hoped to recruit, but, like his colleagues at Berlin Base, he did not ask why.

On Saturday, an East German officer, Frank Steinert, who later defected to the United States and spent his last years in Virginia, was attending a birthday party for a Communist Party functionary along with other military officers, including Lieutenant Colonel Martin Luffler, who was in charge of a division of the National People's Army of East Germany.

After the buffet, instead of announcing a toast to the birthday boy, Defense Minister General Karl-Heinz Hoffmann gave the orders to implement the sealing of Berlin. "How could the CIA not have known?" Steinert later asked. "It just makes no sense to me."[2]

Berlin Base learned of the Wall at five-fifteen on Sunday morning. Graver and his men straggled in to the office. They did not discuss their fantastic intelligence failure. Graver's big concern was evacuation plans. "What if we are trapped?" he asked his incredulous colleagues. They patiently explained to Graver that the Soviets surrounded all of Berlin. If they chose to cross the border into West Berlin, Berlin Base personnel could not reasonably expect to escape, because the Western powers maintained only a token military presence. Although Graver did not get it, he had just presided over the passing of an era.

Neither William Graver nor his predecessors had a clue it may have been one of Berlin Base's own, George Weisz, who gave the Soviets the confidence boost they needed to put up the Berlin Wall.

When Weisz returned to Washington from his tour at Berlin Base, he resumed his work for OPERATION PAPERCLIP, the secret recruitment and importation of Nazis into the United States. The operation was controlled by a secret Army unit, the Joint Intelligence Objectives Agency (JIOA), and was run directly out of the Joint Chiefs of Staff.

Starting in 1955, the Soviets had targeted a U.S. Army major, William Henry Whalen, who drank too much on the embassy cocktail circuit. Whalen, deputy chief of the JIOA, was a quart-a-day alcoholic and deeply in debt. The Soviets believed he was highly vulnerable to GRU recruitment. What they wanted from him was information about the 361 Nazis brought in under PAPERCLIP.

According to FBI documents, on December 16, 1957, George Weisz received "Top Secret" military security clearance.[3] He needed the clearance for his assignment to the Defense Department to work with Colonel Whalen, as he now was, and the JIOA to coordinate efforts to get more Nazis out of Communist countries. In addition, Weisz's new job included helping the Defense Department and the CIA coordinate evacuation plans through the Washington Liaison Group in case the Soviets invaded West Berlin.[4] Knowingly or not, Weisz was assisting a project that was very significant to the Soviets.

In March 1959, Whalen, now a double agent for the GRU, met his Soviet contact at a shopping center parking lot in Alexandria, Virginia, and turned over reports on the Army's defenses in West Germany and West Berlin. The colonel sold out his country for a total of $14,000 over five years. During much of that time, Weisz was working with Whalen on the Berlin evacuation plans. By August 1961, the Soviets knew from Whalen that the United States had no plans for defending Berlin and in fact had very few military assets in the divided city. The KGB confidently told Nikita Khrushchev that the Americans had no realistic way of defending Berlin short of a suicidal nuclear exchange.[5]

Whalen and Weisz continued to work together until Whalen's arrest by the FBI in 1964. Justice Department files indicate that everything possible was done to avoid embarrassment to the Army and the CIA concerning Whalen's activities. A small part of Whalen's case file has now been released. It reveals that he pressured his colleagues for security information, which he supplied the Soviets.

It may be that Whalen's proximity to Weisz was an unfortunate coincidence. There was no serious security investigation to determine if Weisz or anyone else deliberately assisted Whalen's betrayal of the United States.[6] The CIA by that time had sent Weisz back to Frankfurt, where he continued to bring Nazis to the United States under the guise of national security. His career continued uninterrupted.

Berlin Base was evacuated all right, but not because of the Wall. Those few, like John Sherwood, who had wondered for some time what exactly the legendary Base was accomplishing, were now coming to power in the CIA hierarchy.

Ed Ryan, a former Naval attaché, replaced Graver as chief of base in 1963. It was Ryan's misfortune to have to explain to Sherwood, who by this time was deputy to John Limond Hart, Chief of the CIA's Western European division, that he felt Berlin Base should be staffed up to go after the Soviets one more time. Sherwood rejected the recommendation. When Ryan protested, Sherwood asked: "'How are you going after the Soviets? When they come over, they are like little raisins in pudding, not even raisins—one raisin in a huge pudding. How are you going to get them when they come through? Are you going to pick them up? You have no surveillance capability. We don't know who they are.' He [Ryan] didn't

like that, but I had him because I had the experience and he didn't."
Under Ryan, Berlin Base dropped down to 30 people from the hundred or
so in Harvey's glory days.

There was no rebirth of Berlin Base. Instead of being a launching pad
for those with "rockets in their pockets," as Sam Wilson had bragged, it
became a dumping ground for minor operatives who could not get assignments to the hot spots. The Berlin Wall was the ultimate and seemingly
permanent reminder that the top men in the CIA had gone up against the
KGB on the front lines of the Cold War—and lost.

The leftover agents from Berlin Base were shifted to Munich, where
they planted weapons caches and agents to be activated if the Soviets invaded Germany. "Yes," as Sherwood put it, "when you only have one act
you can do, you keep doing it."

None of this seemed to tarnish the reputations of the original boys
from Berlin Base. They were now America's intelligence leaders. Like
seeds sown in the wind, they drifted to Cuba, Vietnam, and Chile. Some,
like Ted Shackley and George Weisz, went back through Berlin for brief
tours. But most of the boys who had made their bones in Berlin eventually got to show their stuff all over the world. Their stuff wasn't much,
and the consequences were devastating.

CHAPTER TWENTY-FOUR

ASSASSINATION

AS FOREIGN POLICY

W HEN BILL HARVEY returned to Washington in the fall of 1959, he had great hopes. As victorious Berlin Base chief, he thought he had earned the top job at Soviet Russia (SR), the most prestigious division of the CIA. Without question, he had more experience against the Soviets than anyone in the Agency.

However, there was a problem. The head of SR was an administrative job, which meant Allen Dulles, Richard Bissell, and Richard Helms would have to rub elbows with Harvey on a daily basis. The idea of having Harvey, the man who tweaked the establishment by blowing the whistle on Philby, in that position did not appeal to Dulles, Bissell, or Helms. According to Robert Crowley, "They couldn't stand the sight of him. But Berlin Base was the shining faux jewel in the CIA's crown, so promoting Harvey's career without having to deal with Harvey was the methodology they followed."

Richard Bissell, head of covert operations, came up with the answer to this huge in-house dilemma. He told Harvey he had a far more sensitive and difficult assignment in mind for him. Bissell, now the Deputy Director for Plans after Frank Wisner's breakdown, told Harvey he wanted to use his experience against the Soviets to help with the most secret operation the CIA had ever undertaken. Although he did not tell Harvey this right away, the operation Bissell had in mind was the assassination of foreign leaders.

The fact of the matter was, the theater of direct confrontation between the United States and the Soviet Union had moved. Where center stage was once Berlin, now it was Cuba.

In 1959, after years of guerrilla fighting, Fidel Castro and his men ousted Cuba's corrupt dictator, Fulgencio Batista. Only after he took power in Havana did Castro openly declare what observers had suspected, that he was a Marxist who wanted to ally his country with the Soviet Union. This declaration drastically changed the geopolitical landscape for the United States. The Cold War was no longer a cloak-and-dagger movie being fought in distant places. The front line was now America's own backyard. At the CIA, Dulles and Bissell authorized Harvey to go after the Communists in Cuba even more directly than he had in Germany.

First, Bissell made Harvey the head of Staff D, the department responsible for communications intelligence. Harvey's Berlin tunnel experience, combined with his knowledge of Soviet operations, made electronic intelligence (ELINT) a logical assignment for him. It also made sense to his CIA colleagues, most of whom never learned the true nature of his work.

Only after Harvey had spent a few months on Staff D did Bissell introduce him to the CIA's war on Castro. Communications intelligence was really the perfect cover for Harvey's true job. At that time, nothing was more sensitive than communications secrets, so extra security—including a Marine guard posted outside Harvey's office door—did not awaken suspicions about Harvey's activities.

Bissell explained to Harvey that his job was to oust Castro from power. Under Harvey's control would be all the components for a two-pronged attack. First, Harvey himself was to set up facilities to recruit anti-Castro Cubans. Next, others in the CIA would train a brigade of these recruits to invade and free the island. After listening to Bissell, Harvey told colleagues that he believed the CIA had finally learned from its mistakes in abandoning the Ukrainians and Hungarians on those earlier missions. "This time they will follow through," Harvey asserted to a skeptical colleague.

The invasion was to take place at the Bay of Pigs in early spring 1961. Harvey's job was to provide intelligence and manpower to the military planners. He started by setting up a new CIA station in Miami with Ted Shackley, the first Berlin Base veteran Harvey brought into the project, as its organizer. During the next five years, Harvey reassembled the best of his Berlin Base team for Staff D, which eventually evolved into Task Force W.

Acting under Harvey's instructions, Shackley rented some old buildings at the University of Miami and put up signs that read: Zenith Technical Enterprises. Shackley patterned JM/WAVE, the Miami station, after Berlin Base. It grew to six hundred case officers and became the largest CIA base in the world. Much as Berlin Base case officers had interviewed East German and Eastern European refugees, these case officers interrogated the 2,800 Cuban refugees arriving in Florida every day. And just as most Berlin Base case officers did not speak Eastern European languages, many of the JM/WAVE case officers did not speak Spanish.

The second mission of Task Force W ran contrary to Harvey's entire education and upbringing as an attorney and man of law. It was a special unit called ZR/RIFLE, which put the United States in the business of murder.

Bissell instructed Harvey never to speak to Allen Dulles or President Eisenhower about this part of his new job. Bissell and others explained that it was essential for it to appear as if the president and even the director of central intelligence were out of the loop. Nothing about this part of the assignment should be put in writing; the less there was on paper, the less to deny if things went wrong.

Despite Dulles's desire for "deniability," he was deeply involved with Bissell in planning the assassination capability. Harvey's job was to prepare for "executive action," a euphemism that came back to haunt the CIA.[1]

The roots of ZR/RIFLE went back to shortly after World War II and Frank Wisner's Office of Policy Coordination. The OPC's mysterious Program Branch 7 (PB-7) was incorporated into the CIA along with the OPC. Its job, according to former CIA official E. Howard Hunt of Watergate note, was "the assassination of suspected double agents and similar low-ranking officials."[2]

PB-7's boss was Boris Pash, one of the more colorful figures in U.S. intelligence history. Pash—who also took credit for discovering actress Lana Turner at Schwab's Drugstore during his Hollywood days—was the security man who haunted Dr. J. Robert Oppenheimer during the research and development of the atomic bomb. Pash also headed the first military missions into Germany to bring back the Nazi rocket program. Although Pash denied that PB-7 ever carried out a murder, he did not deny that murder was part of its charter.[3]

Rumors about the CIA having a secret unit to kill people had circulated for years. Donald E. Denesyla, who worked in the Soviet Russia Division, recalled that while he was in training for the CIA, he and his colleagues were told "if we betrayed the Agency we would be hunted down and killed."[4] Denesyla said the officers running the training course "put a guy behind a screen who they described as a CIA operative who went after those who were not loyal. . . . It was very strange. I am not certain anyone in the class really believed it."

President Eisenhower authorized the first CIA attempt on a major foreign leader's life in April 1955. The target was Red Chinese leader Chou En-lai. The plan called for an Air India plane with Chou on board to blow up en route to a non-aligned nations conference in Bandung, Indonesia. Part of the assassination attempt worked: The freelancers employed by the CIA blew up the aircraft. Fortunately for Chou En-lai, he had switched to another flight.

Undaunted by this failure, the CIA decided to try a more focused approach against Chou. A 48-hour poison developed by Dr. Sidney Gottlieb—the man who Robert Crowley thought probably produced the poison that killed James Kronthal—would be placed in his rice bowl while he was attending the Bandung conference. The poison's delayed reaction time was just long enough for Chou to travel back to China and die there. William R. Corson, the leader of the assassination team, recalled that at the very last moment the order was rescinded. [5] According to Corson, "It was called off in the nick of time" by General Lucien Truscott to prevent embarrassment to the president.[6] To cover his own role, Dulles sent a follow-up cable to the assassination team saying that the United States does not engage in such activity.

The development of untraceable drugs to use for assassinations started in the Technical Services Division of the CIA under Archibald Roosevelt. Dr. Gottlieb worked for Roosevelt, developing everything from mind-control drugs to very efficient exotic poisons. According to the late CIA official, Miles Copeland, in 1957 Gottlieb, again with the approval of Dulles, impregnated the favorite cigarettes of Egyptian leader Gamel Abdel Nasser with yet another toxin.[7] Nasser apparently never smoked the spiked cigarettes. Later, Bill Harvey told associates he always believed that Gottlieb (nicknamed "Dr. Death" by his colleagues) "enjoyed his work a little too much."

Harvey and a handful of his Berlin Base officers formed the core of ZR/RIFLE. The code name was kept secret from even high-ranking colleagues. The efficiency Harvey had demonstrated when he first took over Berlin Base was back. It's true that his drinking problem continued. It had plagued him since his early years at the FBI and CIA with his first wife, Libby; did not stop with his second wife, C.G., in Berlin; and returned with him to the States. "But hell," as John Sherwood put it, "everyone drank in Berlin, everyone drank at headquarters. It didn't dawn on any of us it affected our work."

Harvey set about making ZR/RIFLE secure. He ordered that all communications about "executive action" be stored in a special one-ton safe in his office. This safe was in addition to three smaller safes Harvey used for his "communications work."[8] The CIA was never mentioned by name in any ZR/RIFLE documents or oral communications; instead, Harvey mandated that the Agency be referred to as KUBARK. The materials from the "executive action" files, released years later under the Freedom of Information Act and through the 1975 investigations by the Senate Select Committee on Intelligence, are chilling in their references. They detail a side to American policy that was much like the assassinations the KGB ordered against enemies of the Soviet state. The main difference is that while the methods employed by Bogdan Stashinsky and other Soviet assassins were simple and effective, the CIA's assassination attempts became entangled in a morass of complexity that even the most far-out fiction writer would find hard to imagine.

Harvey handled the recruitment of assassins under the rubric of an operation to steal electronic secrets from other countries. The rule was that no U.S. citizens could be recruited. James Angleton also instructed Harvey never to recruit Sicilians, for fear the CIA could be blackmailed by the Mafia. He recommended using Corsicans instead.

As Angleton later recalled, "Bill came to me for help in obtaining phony backdated counterintelligence files to 'prove' that assassins had connections to the KGB, not the CIA, if their deeds ever became public. This material would be released to friendly newspaper reporters when necessary." Angleton said that he also urged Harvey to propose assigning "executive actions" to friendly foreign intelligence services. "It was the only way to assure U.S. deniability. . . . If you had to conduct something like this, all you had to do was look at the Soviet pattern. They used Bulgarians, Czechs, and East Germans for wet operations."[9] In particular, Angleton recommended working through the CIA in South Korea.

One reason Harvey sought Angleton's advice about assassination procedures was that Angleton ran CIA liaison with Israel. "No service was wetter than Mossad," John Sherwood explained.[10] The primary advice Harvey got from Mossad was to recruit only non-Americans.

In 1959, the Eisenhower Administration decided that Congolese rebel leader Patrice Lumumba was a dangerous Marxist. Thus, Lumumba gained the honor of becoming ZR/RIFLE's first target. Harvey hired a pair of Corsican hit men and told them about Dr. Sidney Gottlieb's "African special," a toxin whose effects resembled those of an African fever. The idea was for the assassin to administer the potion as a "truth serum" during an interrogation after Lumumba was arrested. Lumumba would then come down with what appeared to be an African fever and slowly die.

Two hit men were selected for the mission. Harvey flew to Frankfurt Base to supervise the final briefing and training of one of the men. Neither assassin ever met the other. Only one of them would be selected to administer the poison. Harvey also dispatched Dr. Gottlieb to Europe, where he promptly shared the details of his mission with several colleagues who were not cleared to know about it. It did not take long for John Sherwood, still at Berlin Base, to hear about it.

Sherwood first met Dr. Gottlieb at Munich Base in the mid-1950s. Gottlieb had wanted to apply his black arts to fieldwork, so he had requested an overseas post as a case officer. After being turned down by dozens of CIA base chiefs who wanted no part of him, Munich Base Chief William Hood permitted him to come for a tour. "He was out in Munich, God bless him, to learn the trade. He came out as a case officer, a GS-16 case officer," Sherwood said. Sherwood and Gottlieb became friends, and their families spent a great deal of time together in Munich. Looking back on it, Sherwood said he should have realized that Gottlieb was using innocent human beings in CIA experiments, but "I thought the guy was a real family man. Hell, we used to go mountain climbing together."

In the fall of 1960, Sherwood heard from a colleague, Marvin Evans, a CIA lawyer based in Frankfurt who was visiting Berlin, that Lumumba was going to die in two weeks. "I said, 'Had Sid been through Frankfurt?' He said, 'Yes.' And I said, 'Okay.' We all knew what Sid was up to. . . . Sid was hand-carrying the stuff to Africa."

In September 1960, Gottlieb flew from Frankfurt to Leopoldville in the Congo to deliver the twin vials of toxin. In October, the CIA chief of station in Leopoldville presented Gottlieb's kits to the assassins, code-named QJ/WIN 1 and QJ/WIN 2. The CIA paid each man $7,200 in advance, plus expenses.

Neither Harvey nor his deputy, Justin O'Donnell, who abhorred the idea of assassination, had much faith in Gottlieb, his poison, or the plan. Harvey dispatched O'Donnell to the Congo to see if the U.S.-backed rebels could take care of Lumumba without involving the CIA directly. As it turned out, O'Donnell's mission became unnecessary. Lumumba was killed on February 12, 1961, after being captured by opposing rebels without CIA assistance. The hit men did not need to be activated.

O'Donnell warned Harvey that the CIA was going down a dangerous road with ZR/RIFLE. Harvey asked O'Donnell what his biggest fear was about using assassination to further U.S. objectives. O'Donnell, a thoughtful man, said, "If the United States engages in assassination as foreign policy, then we had better expect our targets to respond in the same way." Harvey did not have time to ponder O'Donnell's heartfelt prediction. President Eisenhower had decided to have another trouble-maker killed. Fidel Castro had moved to the top of the hit list.

IN THE SUMMER of 1959, Allen Dulles did an about-face in protecting the Agency and ordered a paper trail created to make President Eisenhower's decision to assassinate Fidel Castro appear to have actually originated at the CIA. Accordingly, Western Hemisphere Director J. C. King sent Dulles a memorandum suggesting that "thorough consideration be given to the elimination of Fidel Castro. . . ." The memorandum was followed by a meeting of the White House Special Group, a panel of National Security executives, in March 1960.[11]

At that meeting, the plan to eliminate Castro was expanded. Livingston Merchant, President Eisenhower's undersecretary of state for political affairs, first suggested getting rid not only of Castro but of the entire Cuban leadership, including Fidel's brother, Raul, and Che Guevara, the man Castro called the conscience of the revolution. The CIA representative at the meeting, General Charles P. Cabell, protested that Merchant's suggestion was "uncertain of results and highly dangerous in conception and execution. . . . It would have to be concluded that Mr. Merchant's suggestion is beyond our capabilities."

That Special Group meeting put on record what the president and Dulles had agreed to off-the-record. It also gave the president and his CIA director deniability. In fact, by the time Merchant made his suggestion to the White House Special Group that March, the CIA already had Harvey developing a working plan for Castro's assassination. Harvey understood from the time Task Force W was formed, that if Bissell's dream of a brigade taking back Cuba was to come true, the invasion must be accompanied by the assassination of the Cuban leader. Now, Harvey's career was on track. Once again he had the most important assignment in the CIA.

Bissell ordered Harvey to unleash Gottlieb and the Technical Services Division to prepare a series of chemical attacks on Castro. In July 1960, the CIA's Havana Station was shocked when headquarters notified it to put out the word that it would pay ten thousand dollars to anyone who assassinated Che Guevara.

Sheffield Edwards, the CIA's Director of Security (and the man who had warned Allen Dulles about James Kronthal), was a longtime friend of Harvey's. Now, Edwards had a not-so-bright idea: In keeping with CIA policy of hiring others to carry out assassinations, he suggested that the Agency get the Mafia to murder Castro. Harvey, the old street-smart FBI man, made the uncharacteristic mistake of believing Edwards when he described the Mafia as a monolithic, unified force.

Ignoring James Angleton's warnings about working with the Mafia, Harvey and Edwards took this proposal to Richard Bissell in August 1960. They convinced him that Castro's defeat of the mob-backed Fulgencio Batista meant the Mafia was losing hundreds of millions of dollars in gambling and other vice revenues from Cuba. Bissell gave his approval because he believed the mob was "well motivated to see that the job got done . . . to regain control of the casinos."

Harvey and Edwards told Bissell they would use a cutout (CIA front man) to make the contacts with the Mafia, and Bissell gave them the go-ahead. Edwards selected Robert Maheu, a former colleague of Harvey's at the FBI. The CIA had hired Maheu back in 1953 because it needed someone to do jobs that might have embarrassing repercussions. Under CIA auspices, Maheu set up a private investigations firm, Robert Maheu Associates.[12] He was paid a starting retainer of five hundred dollars a month, and he was permitted to take private clients.[13] In 1960, Maheu had just taken on an especially interesting client with the CIA's approval—the millionaire, Howard Hughes.[14]

Maheu's case officer was another ex-FBI man, James O'Connell. The decision was made for O'Connell and Maheu to approach the mob together. They were to say to the gangsters that Meyer Lansky, the mob's financial brain, would pay a handsome reward for toppling the man who had cost the Mafia so much revenue. The Cuban people knew that the mob wanted Castro dead, Maheu assured the CIA, and so the United States Government would not be blamed.[15]

Maheu went to Johnny Roselli, a "made man" in Hollywood, to propose the contract. Roselli, movie-star handsome himself, provided mob-managed entertainment to the casinos in Cuba and Las Vegas. Roselli suggested two mobsters with interests in Cuba who might do the job— Santos Trafficante of Tampa and Sam Giancana of Chicago.

Harvey's mistakes in Berlin were mistakes of omission: He failed to properly check out agents the Base recruited, like Igor Orlov, and he failed to follow up on legitimate complaints like the ones about David Murphy. He brought those same weaknesses with him to Task Force W. Harvey failed to get proper intelligence on either the mobsters Maheu recommended or the approach he proposed to take with them.

Had Harvey done his homework, he would have found out about Castro's real relationship with Trafficante and shut down the operation immediately. He did not know that Trafficante, in a power move against Meyer Lansky, had struck an early deal with Castro. In the years of guerrilla warfare against Batista, Castro received guns from Trafficante. In return, Castro promised Trafficante control of gambling in Cuba once the revolution succeeded. Trafficante also allowed Castro's supporters to bring heroin into Miami and sell it on his turf to help finance the revolution.

In addition, Trafficante masterminded scams for Castro's agents operating in Miami before and after the revolution. Each week, the winning Cuban National Lottery numbers from the previous week in Havana were used by Trafficante's numbers operators in Miami to allow Castro's agents in "Little Havana" to bet and win.

Trafficante moved quickly to solidify his control over the Cuban émigrés, who were mostly settling in Miami and in Union City, New Jersey. Much as the Soviets had slipped spies into West Berlin, Trafficante placed Castro agents among the refugees fleeing Cuba after the revolution. Most Cuban-Americans never realized that some of the most fervent anti-Communist émigré organizations were controlled by Fidel Castro's DGI, the KGB-trained Cuban intelligence agency. Nor did the CIA realize that among its recruits for its anti-Castro army were some of Castro's most loyal supporters.

Ricardo Canete, a Cuban-American, worked for Harvey's anti-Castro operation and became embroiled in Trafficante's criminal activity. He described how it worked: "Fidel needed money, and he needed information. A man out of the Cuban Mission to the UN named Fernandez ran the Cuban DGI [in the United States]. He took orders from Trafficante. It was clear by the late 1960s that drugs and protection being run through Little Havana were far more profitable than anything the mob had done in Cuba."[16]

Just how powerful Trafficante was became clear when, after the revolution, Castro arrested Meyer Lansky's brother, Jake. Trafficante personally intervened to get Jake released and the casinos reopened. Lansky now owed Trafficante.

Harvey was convinced that what held Roselli, Trafficante, and Giancana together was the promise of regaining control of the casinos if Castro were successfully removed. Just as Berlin Base lacked intelligence about the Eastern Zone and the Karlshorst compound, Harvey lacked intelligence from Cuba. He did not know that one of the gangsters he was hiring to assassinate Castro was, in reality, an ally of the Cuban leader.

One person who did have information on Trafficante's relationship with Castro was Harvey's old boss, J. Edgar Hoover. According to FBI files, Cuban exile leader Jose Aleman was an FBI informant and told the FBI of conversations with Trafficante where the mobster sounded "like Karl Marx."[17] Hoover never shared this information with Harvey or anyone else at the CIA.[18]

There was yet another problem with the CIA's scheme to use organized crime to assassinate Castro. Sam Giancana, the Chicago mob boss at the other end of Maheu's triumvirate, was at that time sharing a girlfriend with the Democratic presidential nominee, John Kennedy. Frank Sinatra had separately introduced Giancana and Senator Kennedy to Judith Campbell, a buxom and attractive brunette. Both Giancana and Kennedy began affairs with her during 1960.[19]

In September 1960, Harvey sent Maheu to meet with Johnny Roselli at the Brown Derby restaurant in Hollywood. Maheu had agreed to tell Roselli a cover story about a businessman wanting Castro killed. Instead, Maheu appealed directly to Roselli's pocketbook. He asked Roselli what it would be worth to Meyer Lansky to have Castro dead. Roselli said he would have to check with some people.

A week later, Maheu brought "Jim Olds" along to a second meeting. "Jim Olds" was Harvey's assistant, James O'Connell. He was present when Roselli, Giancana, and Trafficante accepted the CIA contract. Trafficante then told Maheu and O'Connell that Lansky wanted to add something to the arrangement: In addition to the $150,000 fee the CIA was paying, Lansky was offering an additional million dollars and safe passage out of Cuba for anyone who killed Castro.

The mobster was really putting something over on the CIA. There was no additional contract. Why would Lansky jeopardize his relationship with Castro when the casinos were still open for business? Trafficante was using the Agency so that Castro would never trust Meyer Lansky again. According to Ricardo Canete, the message got out fast. The CIA sent the information to its case officers, who, in turn, told agents at JM/WAVE, the CIA's Miami operation. Among those agents were the Cuban double agents Trafficante had planted there, who quickly brought the news back to Havana. "Trafficante knew that Castro would never trust the information if it came from him, so he made certain the source was believable," Canete explained.

During the meetings between the mob and the CIA, Trafficante agreed to serve as the courier for the operation and as the recruiter for the agents in Cuba who were to carry out the murder. The CIA was now conspiring directly with one of the men closest to Castro.

Harvey had confidence in very few people at CIA headquarters, and he especially disliked Sidney Gottlieb and his Technical Services Division. The exotic methods Gottlieb wanted to supply to the mob to kill Castro flabbergasted Harvey. He felt that if you needed a reliable instrument of

death, you should use a rifle, not some outlandish toxin. But Richard Bissell felt differently. He wanted to make certain that the murders of Castro
and his associates were not connected to the CIA, and he believed that
Gottlieb's potions would leave no evidence behind. He instructed Gottlieb
to prepare poisons that would penetrate the skin, dissolve in water, or im-
pregnate clothing, and he instructed Sheffield Edwards to give Gottlieb's
creations to the mobsters.

Meanwhile, Dulles made it clear to Harvey that Eisenhower wanted
Castro eliminated before the November elections. In early October, a
deadline was set for the murder. Under pressure from Dulles, Harvey decided not to wait for Dr. Gottlieb and the Mafia to take action. He went
ahead and ordered Ted Shackley to quickly recruit and train two Cuban
exiles for an assassination attempt using high-powered rifles.

Harvey asked Richard Helms to call Air Force Colonel L. Fletcher
Prouty and arrange for a small plane to fly the pair of Cubans from Eglin
Air Force Base on the Florida Panhandle to an airstrip on the outskirts of
Havana. Prouty agreed, and the two men set off on their mission. How-
ever, JM/WAVE was so penetrated by Castro's agents that the would-be as-
sassins were arrested by Cuban intelligence before they could fire a shot.[20]

CHAPTER TWENTY-FIVE

THE KENNEDYS
AS CASE OFFICERS

TO THE SURPRISE OF much of the CIA's leadership, John Kennedy defeated Richard Nixon in the 1960 election. The Agency had no idea about his relationship with Judith Campbell or Campbell's relationship with Sam Giancana. J. Edgar Hoover, who was aware of both the Giancana connection and of the CIA's activities, was saving the information for the moment when he might need something from the Kennedys.

Even though Allen Dulles was beholden to the Republicans, he hedged his bets as the election approached. Secretly, he briefed John Kennedy's right-hand man, his brother Robert, before the election, giving Kennedy an edge over Nixon when the subject of Cuba arose during their debates. After Kennedy was elected, Dulles maneuvered to gain his support. Much to Eisenhower's dismay, Dulles briefed the president-elect about the planned invasion at the Bay of Pigs and other sensitive operations before the outgoing president had a chance to do so. Dulles wanted to convince Kennedy how valuable he was in hopes that the young president would ask him to stay on as director of central intelligence.[1] His maneuvers worked.

Both Jack and Bobby Kennedy were impressed with the CIA. James Angleton had a personal friendship with the new president and thought he was too smart to be manipulated by Dulles. But Angleton also knew that the president and his brother were strongly attracted to covert operations. As things turned out, President Kennedy agreed not only to keep

Dulles on as DCI but also to continue the Cuban operations, including Bissell's projected invasion.

That invasion at the Bay of Pigs in April 1961 proved to be a tragedy of major proportions for the freedom fighters and a political nightmare for the United States. Bill Harvey was wrong in thinking that Bissell had learned from the mistakes in the Ukraine and Hungary. Bissell had learned nothing. Wanting to carry out the operation while maintaining American deniability, he and his team made mistake after mistake in the planning stage and in training the exiles. The resulting disaster turned the Kennedy brothers against Bissell and Dulles and ended their careers. However, like President Eisenhower in Hungary, President Kennedy was partly to blame. At the last moment, he assured the failure of an already flawed operation by ordering Bissell to cut back on the bomber attacks intended to incapacitate Castro's air force. As a result, supply ships were unable to unload ammunition, and the invaders had to surrender after a few days.

Despite his role in the disaster, Kennedy quickly concluded that the CIA and the military were not as competent as he had believed. He and his brother decided to take full control of all intelligence operations. President Kennedy named John A. McCone, a Republican shipbuilder and Catholic convert, as the new director of central intelligence. McCone picked Richard Helms to replace Richard Bissell as Deputy Director for Plans, the position Helms had long coveted. McCone saw his role as that of day-to-day caretaker. He kept himself above the nasty activities of Task Force W and other operations in the CIA's Plans Directorate. In reality, Robert Kennedy, the attorney general, ran the intelligence agency through the White House Special Group.

The Kennedys did not give up on the idea of ousting the Cuban regime. Instead of attacking Castro, however, they decided to build an alternative to the spreading force of Communism in Latin America. They wanted to compete with Communism by offering an American model as an alternative, cloning New Frontier-style democratic regimes around the Western Hemisphere. Robert Kennedy convinced his brother that the only way to prevent Communism from being exported from Cuba to the rest of Latin America was to develop an aggressive partnership among American business, the Catholic church, and the CIA. Although Jack Kennedy had won the election by the thinnest of margins, with his Catholicism an issue in the campaign, he secretly ordered the CIA to begin operations with the Jesuits in Latin America, especially in Chile.[2]

President Kennedy's Alliance for Progress became a giant cover operation for these political activities. However, the overt buildup of the U.S. presence in Latin America during the New Frontier was also spectacular. Large CIA stations were established in many capital cities. The CIA used an entire news organization, Copley News Service, as cover for its agents. Latin America had finally been taken back from the FBI.

Land reform in Chile was first seen as an issue by President Eisenhower. The president's brother, Milton Eisenhower, got conservative Chilean President Jorge Alessandri to begin modest efforts at land reform in 1958.[3] When Alessandri and the power structure started to resist this American pressure, President Eisenhower did something unprecedented. According to Edward M. Korry, ambassador to Chile from 1967 to 1971, Eisenhower threatened to withhold aid if reforms were not instituted. No American president had ever before linked land reform to U.S. aid in Latin America. Alessandri was furious.

In the same time period, the Vatican launched an effort to shore up its lessening influence in Latin America. In 1958, a high-level Catholic clergyman in Santiago wrote a letter to the Vatican urging it, as Korry put it, "to wake up to the threat posed by the alarming advances of 'Protestantism [the evangelicals], Marxism, and laicism [freemasonry].'" In response to this letter, Roger Vekemans, "a brilliant Jesuit priest and political organizer," was dispatched to Chile. According to Korry, "Vekemans set up a dynamic, continent-wide organization to resuscitate Roman Catholicism to compete with the three other forces."[4]

The Catholic church played a major role in President Kennedy's actions. As Korry put it, Kennedy in effect "forged a secret relationship between Latin Jesuits and the Kennedy Administration to fight the spread of Protestantism and freemasonry in Latin America. . . . When you consider that George Washington, Thomas Jefferson, Harry Truman were all Masons, you have to ask yourself, 'What in God's name [was] the CIA, on orders from our first Roman Catholic president, doing?'"[5]

A month after the Bay of Pigs, according to Korry, President Kennedy allocated U.S. relief funds to the Jesuits for these activities. The president and the attorney general also created a partnership with major American and multinational corporations to work with U.S. intelligence in Latin America. President Kennedy buttonholed David Rockefeller at a May 1962 meeting of the Harvard Board of Overseers and asked him what it would take to get substantial private investment in Latin America. Rockefeller told the president that businesses needed some kind of financial guarantee against political instability.

Out of that meeting came the idea of cheap political risk insurance underwritten by a branch of the Agency for International Development (AID). By the time Ed Korry arrived as ambassador to Chile in mid-October 1967, nearly one-quarter of all such insurance written anywhere in the world was on U.S. companies operating in Chile. Korry was so alarmed that he proposed and signed a secret agreement with the AID insurance writers in Washington that no further insurance would be written for Chile without special review.[6]

The Kennedys also created a far more sinister organization, the Business Group for Latin America, to carry out their plans.[7] The Business Group was, in fact, a CIA front established to funnel private funds to secret operations that Robert Kennedy thought important. Enno Hobbing, a former CIA officer, was its executive director.[8] The Group's job was to provide a cover organization to which corporations could contribute money to pay for bribes and other political activities in Latin America. Twenty years later, the Reagan Administration used many of these same methods for its ill-fated policy in Central America.

To punish the CIA for its mishandling of the Bay of Pigs operation, the Kennedy Administration moved the paramilitary operations that the CIA had conducted during the Eisenhower years to a special staff under Secretary of Defense Robert Strange McNamara. New-style warriors like General Maxwell Taylor and General Edward Lansdale became the military theoreticians for the Kennedy brothers. In particular, Lansdale was brought in to help address the Castro problem.[9]

Yet in many ways this was a change without a difference. Lansdale had been one of Frank Wisner's CIA operatives; he had waged war against the North Vietnamese and against anti-Marcos Communist rebels in the Philippines. And Harvey's men from Berlin Base began to play even bigger roles in the intelligence community. When Lansdale took over paramilitary operations against Castro, he made Sam Wilson, Igor Orlov's former case officer, his deputy.

After Richard Helms became deputy director for plans, he quickly called in Harvey and told him he was to take over the entire Cuba account. Harvey protested. He still wanted to run the Soviet Russia Division. Helms gave Harvey a pep talk about being the point man for the operation the White House considered far and away the most important intelligence activity at that time. Helms said he was certain that between Harvey at the CIA and Lansdale and Wilson at the Pentagon, the United States could instigate a popular uprising to oust Castro. Helms did not tell Harvey about a secret report sitting on his desk as he spoke. The report from the Intelligence Directorate stated that even if the assassination of Castro was successfully carried out, no popular uprising against Communism would follow.

Helms immediately sent out a cable to all stations and bases stating that Bill Harvey was in charge of Cuba. The new code name was OPERATION MONGOOSE. When Harvey later talked with Lansdale, he realized that his orders had not changed. His assignment was still to kill Castro.

Ian Fleming's spy novels were at the height of their popularity at the time, and President Kennedy was a great fan of James Bond. Kennedy asked Lansdale if the United States had a James Bond. Lansdale, a close friend of the president, brought Harvey over to meet him. For this meeting, Harvey left his guns at home.

The president grabbed Harvey's hand and congratulated him on his new assignment as head of OPERATION MONGOOSE. Harvey no longer wondered if Kennedy understood what his job really was. The president joked about whether the strange, pear-shaped Harvey had as much luck with women as James Bond. Harvey later confided to Angleton that he liked the president but could not stand Bobby.

After the Bay of Pigs, John Kennedy sent his brother Robert to the CIA to punish the Agency for its failure. Like so many others before him who had arrived behind those closed doors, Robert Kennedy fell in love with the world of espionage. Already fascinated with cloak-and-dagger operations and the intrigue of covert warfare, he was quickly seduced by being in on the secret knowledge the CIA offered. Bobby Kennedy met and got to know Bill Harvey, Ted Shackley, Sam Wilson, and other Berlin Base alumni. While his brother enjoyed hearing war stories from Berlin Base, Robert, always intense, became the force to oust Castro. He met with CIA officials daily. Despite the lesson he presumably learned from the Bay of Pigs, he was taken in by the illusion that the CIA understood more about the world than any other organization.[10]

Harvey soon began to realize how much the CIA was being micromanaged by the attorney general. The Kennedy brothers manipulated covert action at a faster rate than any other administration before or since. In the thousand days of John F. Kennedy's presidency, the United States conducted a record number of covert actions and assassination attempts. Not even Ronald Reagan in eight years in office came close.

Harvey repeatedly met with Thomas Parrot, the White House liaison with the CIA for OPERATION MONGOOSE. Harvey brought into the operation additional Berlin Base veterans, still among the few people he truly trusted at the CIA. Anita Potocki and her husband, Will, joined Harvey in the basement of the massive new CIA headquarters in Langley, Virginia. John Sherwood took charge of Task Force 80, which involved all operations outside of Miami.

Harvey had to rebuild everything the Agency had lost in the Bay of Pigs fiasco. Old Berlin Base hands like Lucien Conein became key to Shackley's Miami station. Shackley followed the old Berlin and Munich models and recruited Cuban refugees, turned them into agents, and sent them back to Cuba as spies.

Shackley recruited thousands of Cuban nationalists out of the émigré community, and the CIA trained them in sabotage and assassination. From these ranks came violent right-wing groups like Alpha 66 and Omega 7. From Keystone Point to Key West, the CIA purchased waterfront homes, converted small boats into attack gunboats, and sponsored hit-and-run raids on Cuba. It was untrue when Kennedy announced at one point that the relocation of refugees would be limited to Dade County. In fact, tens of million of dollars were spent to develop a covert capability against Castro from sites throughout the United States.

Shackley and his colleagues made the same mistakes at JM/WAVE that they had made in Berlin. Too many JM/WAVE case officers had little background in Cuban culture, just as Berlin case officers had little background in German and Eastern European cultures. Counterintelligence at the Miami station was almost nonexistent, so Santos Trafficante and Castro's intelligence service were able to penetrate it thoroughly, just as the

KGB had penetrated Berlin Base. As the Stasi and the KGB knew all about the Berlin tunnel and other Berlin Base operations, the DGI and KGB were fully aware of everything Task Force W was attempting against Castro.

John Sherwood found his assignment at Task Force 80 a complete nightmare. He warned Shackley that Castro had penetrated JM/WAVE "up the kazoo," but, as Sherwood said, "How would they know? Ninety percent of our guys down there didn't speak any Spanish. None of the branch chiefs knew the language." Because of DGI penetration, Sherwood so distrusted the Cuban community that he chose as translators Mexican Americans from New Mexico who were serving in the Air Force. "I tried not to have any Cubans near classified material, and I failed," Sherwood said.

CHAPTER TWENTY-SIX

KHRUSHCHEV'S GAMBIT

————⇒●⇐————

T HE RELATIONSHIP BETWEEN Bill Harvey and Ed Lansdale—
between the CIA and the Pentagon—soon deteriorated," William
Corson recalled.[1] "Harvey thought Lansdale was a military blowhard
who was good at telling the Kennedys what they wanted to hear but
seemed to create more paperwork than success. When Lansdale came up
with one harebrained scheme after another, he demanded that Harvey file
long reports on why he had not followed through."

Lansdale wanted the CIA to poison Cuba's sugar cane crop, but Harvey refused, explaining to the general that this would quickly be traced
back to the United States. Next, Lansdale wanted to place an exploding
seashell in Castro's favorite diving spot, and Harvey refused again. The
list of crazy plots went on and on: poisoned cigars; a diving suit for Castro impregnated with one of Dr. Gottlieb's poisons; a special powder that
would make all his hair, including his beard, fall out. Lansdale's bizarre
ideas, combined with Sidney Gottlieb's concoctions, kept coming across
Harvey's desk in a wave of murderous stupidity.

Justin O'Donnell, Harvey's deputy, finally had enough. He knew the
CIA had Harvey running operations to kill Castro and also leaders of
other countries. As Robert Crowley told it, Tracy Barnes, one of Richard
Helms's top men, gave a briefing to top CIA management in August
1961, updating them on what was new in covert operations. When
Barnes, as patrician as anyone in the CIA's old boy network, announced

that the CIA had purchased a cigarette factory in Africa as cover, O'Donnell simply snapped. He stood up in the back of the room and interrupted Barnes: "A cigarette factory in the middle of Africa? For Christ's sake! What in God's name are we going to do with it?"

There was silence. O'Donnell had violated the cardinal rule. He had talked back to the establishment. John Sherwood was there and went up to O'Donnell after the meeting. "I went up to smell him; I thought that he had to be drunk. I didn't smell anything. I told him, 'Don't ever commit regicide with a rubber knife.' . . . Three weeks later, he was out on the streets."[2] O'Donnell was the only CIA official to speak out against the assassinations. Now he was gone.

Every week, Lyndon Johnson, a very bored vice president, had a gossipy lunch with J. Edgar Hoover. After one of these lunches in 1961, Johnson told Walter Jenkins, his top aide, "Bobby Kennedy has turned the damn CIA over into some Murder Incorporated." In 1962, Johnson told others he thought the Kennedys were playing with fire. "Someone is going to try and get even," he predicted. His staff and friends wrote off Johnson's comments as "Lyndon's hyperbole." However, Johnson had reached the same conclusion as O'Donnell: Assassination as government policy could end badly.

Whenever Robert Kennedy complained that nothing was getting done, General Lansdale blamed Bill Harvey. In turn, Harvey began referring to Bobby Kennedy as "the little fucker." Lansdale had worn out his welcome with everyone but Kennedy. James Symington, one of the attorney general's Justice Department assistants, once called Lansdale the "All-American Boy Guerrilla Fighter" in front of his boss. Kennedy reproached Symington, describing Lansdale as a great warrior.[3]

Harvey worried that Lansdale was leaking every operational detail to the Kennedys. He was right. Robert Kennedy frequently usurped Harvey's authority by calling his Cuban agents in for secret meetings at the Justice Department. On several occasions, Kennedy and Lansdale went to Miami to meet with Harvey's agents and then instructed them not to tell anyone at the CIA about the meetings, including Harvey. Harvey was furious when he discovered that Kennedy was even calling junior agents and demanding reports. When he appealed to Helms and Lansdale for help, he got nowhere. All Lansdale offered was the strong suggestion that Harvey use a former Castro crony, Rolando Cubela Secades, for the assassination. The CIA had recruited Cubela, whom they code named AM LASH, when he left the Castro regime to finish his medical studies. But Harvey refused to use him. He was convinced that AM LASH was as extreme and unstable as any other member of Castro's revolution.

Harvey's operations against Castro continued but accomplished little. By now, Harvey had 60 agents-in-place in Cuba, but he so distrusted the CIA's files that he met with Hoover and asked him to help him keep track of Castro's DGI agents in the United States. Hoover warned Harvey that the DGI was infiltrating the CIA-backed Cuban nationalist movement at an alarming rate.

After meeting with Hoover, Harvey traveled to Miami. On April 21, 1962, he met Johnny Roselli, the handsome ex-con Robert Maheu had hired to assassinate Castro, at a bar at Miami International Airport for drinks. Harvey told Roselli that the Castro hit was his alone to orchestrate and that the CIA would give him whatever he needed to finish the job. Harvey told him that he was now working directly for the CIA, a more unforgiving group than Trafficante and Giancana. Roselli's assignment was to make certain that Tony Varona, a Cuban exile leader whom Bobby Kennedy had introduced to the president, found a way to serve Gottlieb's new and improved poison capsules to the entire Cuban leadership. Harvey then gave Roselli four of Gottlieb's now-perfected pills. Strangely, the two men became friends before the operation was over. Harvey found Roselli more honest than the people he had been dealing with in Washington.

On May 7, 1962, three top-ranking men in the CIA—Deputy Director for Plans Richard Helms, General Counsel Lawrence Houston, and Director of Security Sheffield Edwards—arrived at the Justice Department to brief Bobby Kennedy on the earlier assassination plots with the mob. They told the attorney general what they thought was the entire story: that the CIA had offered the mob $150,000 for Castro's murder. Kennedy, knowing about his brother's relationship with Judith Campbell, asked who the gangsters were. When he heard the name Sam Giancana, he hid his reaction. He looked at the men gathered in his office and, as Lawrence Houston later recounted, said, "I trust that if you ever do business with organized crime again—with gangsters—you'll let the attorney general know."

On August 11, 1962, Harvey attended a meeting in Secretary of State Dean Rusk's office along with President Kennedy's top national security aides, including Lansdale. Among the subjects they discussed was the Castro assassination. Harvey assumed nothing would be put in writing. Three days later, DCI John McCone summoned Harvey from the basement. To Harvey's horror, when he entered the director's seventh floor office, McCone waved a copy of a memo Lansdale had written about the meeting and demanded to know who had decided to kill Castro. It turned out that Helms had never briefed McCone on ZR/RIFLE. McCone explained to Harvey that he had embraced Catholicism and could be excommunicated if murder was done in his name. Harvey told McCone that he was simply following orders.

On August 17, 1962, Harvey sent John Sherwood to Miami with a message for Ted Shackley at JM/WAVE. "I walked into Shackley's office," Sherwood recalled. "He instinctively knows people he can't dominate. He has the pit-bull instinct, and he hated me from the very first time he saw me. . . . And he said right off the bat, pointing his finger at me, 'Sherwood, you think you're pretty fucking smart. I'm going to show you. I'll get you someday.'" All Sherwood wanted to do was give Shackley Harvey's message: "I was to tell Shackley that Bill Harvey says he's going to pay you that $5,800 in a couple of days." Sherwood assumed he was communicating instructions to Shackley for the Mafia assassination operation.

Sherwood returned to Washington wondering about Shackley's threat. He knew Shackley was jealous because Sherwood had succeeded in getting agents into Cuba while Shackley kept losing agents.

More than a year later, Sherwood realized that Shackley had followed through on his threat during another assassination attempt that went wrong.

This operation involved the Garcia family, who, through Garcia Shipping Lines, provided ships for the Bay of Pigs invasion. As Sherwood tells it, Eddie and Freddie Garcia and a dozen other Cuban émigrés "were going to go in and do in Castro in a suicide mission. . . . They were going to infiltrate at night and they thought they could find him and shoot him. A commando raid. I told them they were crazy. 'Fellas,' I said, 'you are in deep shit.' I trained them in combat. I trained them in arms out in the Virginia countryside. . . . One guy had [had] a very bad accident, and I told Eddie, 'You know, you should never have had a guy in a clandestine operation that has an outstanding physical mark [like a scar]. It's too easy to remember.'"

Sherwood warned the Garcias that their biggest problem would be making certain the commando team kept the operation a secret. "Cubans are just a little worse than most other people [about secrecy]. I said to them, 'I am going to tell you not to tell anybody about your relationship with me. . . . Don't tell a soul.' So he tells his best friend, the third one, same thing, and the fourth one's best friend is your worst enemy. That's Cuba." Sherwood gave the Garcias a final warning, "If you tell anyone that any of your people talked to anyone in Miami, they are dead and you are dead."

Several months later, Sherwood realized that Shackley had indeed gotten even. "He was deceitful and dishonest. He penetrated my operation, and the person who penetrated the operation was penetrated, and so the operation got known on the island, and ten guys got shot." Shackley wasn't trying to get the Cubans killed, but he never stopped to think what effect his games-playing might have. When the Havana newspaper clippings crossed Sherwood's desk, he saw the young man with the scar. "I still think of him," Sherwood said.

Another unhappy memory for Harvey and Sherwood was Lawrence Lunt, a Cuban rancher who owned a *finca* outside Havana. Lunt met Chip Bohlen, a Kennedy State Department official, at a party and offered to spy for the CIA in Cuba. Bohlen asked Harvey to handle Lunt, and Harvey assigned Sherwood. "I knew from experience that the guy was way out in the country, a hundred miles from Havana. What the hell could he do? *Our Man in Havana* [the Graham Greene novel] says it all." Despite Sherwood's misgivings, he recruited Lunt. The two men communicated through a very complicated system of secret writing. Sherwood— known to Lunt as "John Brighteye"—instructed his new agent to do nothing and wait until he got instructions from the CIA.

To Sherwood's surprise, Lunt wrote back that he was busy recruiting people. Harvey and Sherwood agreed that they had a potential lunatic on their hands, and they decided to decommission their new spy. Sherwood learned that Lunt's very rich wife was on a shopping tour in Europe and was going to return to Cuba through New York. In the Oak Room of the Plaza Hotel, Sherwood told Mrs. Lunt that the CIA was cutting off its relationship with her husband.

Several months later, a special private telephone rang in Sherwood's office, and a man asked for John Brighteye. To Sherwood's shock, it was Lunt. They met at Blackie's House of Beef in downtown Washington, D.C., and Sherwood told Lunt directly that he was no longer a spy. He asked Lunt why he was staying on in Cuba. Lunt told Sherwood he must come down to Cuba to see for himself. "I said, 'You bet your sweet ass, I would love to see the real Cuba.' He [Lunt] closes his eyes and says, 'The women.' I thought, 'You dumb fuck.' Girls were keeping him there." Not long after Lunt returned to Cuba, he was arrested for spying for the CIA. His Cuban girlfriend had turned him in. He ended up serving more than a decade in prison.

Despite the failures, the attempts on Castro continued. The CIA recruited Marie Lorenz, a German woman who was one of Castro's girlfriends. She also had a relationship with a Cuban exile, Frank Fiorini, one of Howard Hunt's operatives who later made headlines in Watergate as Frank Sturgis. Lorenz claimed she accepted two of Gottlieb's capsules from Fiorini and hid them in a jar of face cream. Later, when she returned to Havana, the capsules "melted. . . . It was like an omen. . . . I thought, 'To hell with it.'"

While these Keystone Cops assassination attempts were going on, Bill Harvey's intelligence agents in Cuba were sending in bits and pieces of other information that started fitting together to indicate that Khrushchev was up to something big. In September 1962, Harvey's agents reported that the Soviets were installing intermediate-range ground-to-ground missile sites in Cuba. Capable of traveling a thousand miles, the missiles could reach targets as far north as Washington, D.C. Each missile carried a three-megaton nuclear warhead, big enough to destroy any city. While Harvey had failed to kill Castro, this single bit of information should have assured his future in the CIA and the gratitude of the Kennedys.

To verify his agents' reports, Harvey went to McCone to get approval for coverage of Cuba by the U-2, the United States' super-fast, high-flying reconnaissance plane. McCone had little faith in Harvey's sources in Cuba, but he gave the U-2 order as a precaution. He thought such an inexplicable strategic grab by Khrushchev would be insane.

CHAPTER TWENTY-SEVEN

OSWALD IN MOSCOW

—————⊰•⊱—————

O N HALLOWEEN, 1959, three years before the missiles appeared in Cuba, a slight young man with a sneer on his face walked into the American Embassy in Moscow. He said he was a former United States Marine and had come to renounce his American citizenship. When he demanded to see a consular officer, the embassy staff ushered him into Richard E. Snyder's office. Snyder, although listed as a member of the diplomatic staff, in fact worked for the Central Intelligence Agency.

Snyder noted the sneer on the young man's face. He realized he was dealing with an arrogant individual when the former Marine said, "Here is a letter with my declaration."

Snyder accepted the handwritten letter and read the signature, Lee Harvey Oswald. Snyder thought there was something a little surreal about the young man—his demeanor just didn't quite add up. At first, Snyder tried to talk him out of defecting. "It was clear he was not interested in listening to me," Snyder later told superiors. "It was clear he had his own agenda."

When changing Oswald's mind seemed fruitless, Snyder moved on to obtain information about him. "So you were in the Marine Corps?"

"I served in Japan. I was a radar technician."

"Where in Japan?"

Growing impatient, Oswald said, "Here is my passport. I demand that you accept my passport and my rejection of my citizenship." Then, with a flourish that seemed forced to Snyder, the angry young man added, "Whatever knowledge I learned in the military I will share with my new countrymen."

Snyder gave Oswald a receipt for the passport and a phone number to call if he changed his mind. Oswald insisted again that the State Department formally accept his rejection of American citizenship and repeated that he intended to turn over to the Soviets information he had acquired in the Marine Corps.

Snyder felt Oswald had rehearsed the entire encounter before his arrival at the embassy. Very uncomfortable about it, Snyder quickly wrote a cable reporting the incident. The CIA's Office of Security received a version of Snyder's report. James Angleton's counterintelligence operation did not.

Given Snyder's strong sense that something was wrong, the Office of Security should have immediately asked to see the young man's Marine Corps file. It made no such request. As Angleton later put it, "That was the first disaster in a long series of disasters that were involved in this case." On file at Marine Corps headquarters, a few miles from the CIA, was a dossier showing that Oswald had been a radar operator assigned to Marine Air Squadron One in Atsugi, Japan. This information alone was enough to have alerted the CIA had they looked for it. It was from Atsugi air base that the CIA ran a squadron of its super-secret U-2 spy planes.

At Atsugi, Oswald's few friends had noticed that he often went to Tokyo on liberty and was extremely secretive about what he did there. He confided to one Marine buddy that he had fallen in love with and was dating a "hostess" at a Tokyo club called the Queen Bee, and he was also dating a Eurasian woman who spoke fluent Russian.[1]

The Queen Bee, where a bottle of champagne cost a hundred dollars, featured some of the most expensive prostitutes in Japan. Oswald, an enlisted man who made $85 a month, spent many nights there. His skeptical friends were flabbergasted when the Queen Bee "hostess" he had been dating visited him in Atsugi. She was beautiful. The 18-year-old Oswald seemed hardly the type to attract such an expensive bar girl. They were right. Not all the girls at the Queen Bee worked for the bar—five of the hostesses were also on the KGB's payroll. In fact, according to Angleton, the Queen Bee was one of the KGB's most intensive recruiting operations.

"Unfortunately," said Angleton, "we found out later that a number of CIA officers and U-2 pilots began relationships with hostesses in that bar."[2]

Eventually, the Marine Corps reassigned Oswald to the United States. By that time, he spoke and wrote basic Russian, though he had received no formal training. The remainder of his tour in the Marines he devoted to finding a way to get to Moscow.[3] While he was being processed out of the Marines in Los Angeles, the FBI photographed him meeting with Lieutenant Colonel Pavel T. Voloshin, a top KGB recruiter who was in LA with a Soviet dance troupe. The FBI placed the picture in a counterintelligence file on KGB "watchers" of cultural organizations visiting the United States. The FBI also took another picture of Oswald, this time as he was visiting the Cuban consulate in Los Angeles.

The FBI had no idea who the young man in their photographs was or whether his visits to Communist facilities had any significance. They did not share their information with the CIA.

Several years later, in Moscow, Snyder wondered about the young man. Yet he heard nothing back from his report to Washington. He wasn't surprised. It was routine for a field officer to hear nothing back from Washington.

The U-2 reconnaissance missions were a source of pride for the CIA. For James Cunningham, the CIA's "go-to" man running the logistics of the program, 1959 was another very good year for the U-2 operation, code named RACE CAR. The gliderlike, high-flying Lockheed planes took off from bases in Japan and Turkey and made long runs across the Soviet Union with impunity.

Some of the U-2s carried high-resolution cameras and photographed the Soviets' most secret installations. Others recorded military conversations and communications. These flights by Cunningham's civilian pilots, coupled with the work of the National Security Agency, gave the United States a close-up look at what had been a black hole for U.S. intelligence. The U-2 was the CIA's main contribution to technological intelligence and a big reason why the Agency continued to get congressional and presidential support.

The U-2 overflights were driving the Soviet leadership to anger, as George Kisevalter learned from Popov when the double agent was still in Berlin.[4] The Soviets had no idea how to stop them. Other American spy planes were, on occasion, shot down when they strayed into Soviet air space. But the U-2, relatively small and able to cruise at altitudes of over fifty thousand feet, flew over the heart of Russia and over its most secret targets without fear of attack.

Although the Soviets had made great strides in missile technology and had beaten the United States into space with the *Sputnik* launches in 1957, they could not counter this sophisticated form of reconnaissance. Soviet SAM missiles did not have the accuracy to hit a U-2 target. Stymied and frustrated, the Soviet leadership tasked the GRU and KGB to assist air defense in finding a way to shoot one of the planes down. To carry out this directive, the KGB focused on the air bases in Turkey and Japan, hoping to recruit a mechanic or a pilot.

After Oswald's defection, a series of attempts to sabotage U-2 operations on the ground occurred in Atsugi and in Adana, Turkey. In a Turkish attempt, Sarkis Soghanalian, a major international arms dealer, said that one of the suspects was Edwin P. Wilson, a CIA functionary who was later sent to prison for illegally supplying explosives to Libya and plotting to kill federal prosecutors. Wilson denies that he ever gave the Soviets access to the aircraft in Turkey, but Soghanalian maintains that the CIA's James Cunningham complained about the security problem.[5] The Soviets often used a two-source system to obtain American intelligence. If their agent was selling them false information, the second source would give the Russians some assurance of the veracity of the material. Bruce Solie of the Office of Security confirmed that there was an investigation into Ed Wilson's contacts with Turkish nationals working for the KGB and GRU at the time he was in Turkey.[6] Solie added that direct connections between Wilson and the KGB were not proven until 1968, when Wilson was observed socializing with a known Soviet agent.

Whether the attempt in Atsugi had anything to do with Oswald is not known for sure. Nevertheless, there may have been a connection among the Queen Bee, Oswald's visits with the KGB recruiter and the Cuban consulate in Los Angeles, and his access to U-2 secrets. Had anyone made these connections when Oswald defected in 1959, Angleton believed that the CIA could have pieced together the chain of evidence that connected the young defector to his job at Atsugi. But it did not.

Soviet authorities claimed they rejected Oswald's request to become a Soviet citizen because they thought he was too unstable. They also claimed that, after this, Oswald attempted suicide. Angleton believed that Oswald's odyssey to the Soviet Union was carefully planned by the KGB and that his suicide attempt and the Soviet authorities' reluctance to accept him were both part of an orchestrated cover story.[7]

After giving Snyder the impression that he was unstable, Oswald gave the same impression to a reporter from the North American Newspaper Alliance. It was almost as if he wanted to be on record as a flake. Once he disappeared into the Soviet Union, the CIA never seriously attempted to find out what he was up to.

Strangely, no American saw Oswald in the Soviet Union for more than a year. It turned out that the Soviets sent this man whom they did not want because he was too unstable to Minsk, where they gave him a luxurious apartment by Soviet standards, pay equaling that of a top military officer, and perks available only to members of the KGB or the nomenklatura. Angleton later became convinced that this was Oswald's reward for compromising the U-2. He believed Oswald went to the Soviet Union armed with details of U-2 radar images, flight trajectories, capabilities, and runway distances—all the information the Soviets needed to aim their missiles if they were ever to knock down the elusive aircraft.

CHAPTER TWENTY-EIGHT

SR-9

I N 1960, THE CIA'S Soviet Russia Division was in turmoil. The Soviets' Sputnik launches had given a stunned world the sense that the Soviet Union was on the move while the United States had been caught napping. Other Soviet advances in technology—especially in nuclear warheads and intercontinental ballistic missiles—confirmed that impression. In the 1960 presidential campaign, Senator Kennedy was scoring big points against Vice President Nixon by charging that the Eisenhower administration had allowed a "missile gap" to develop.

President Eisenhower hoped to repair some of the damage to his administration by getting an arms-control deal with the Soviets before the election. Accordingly, a summit meeting with Nikita Khrushchev was on the schedule for May in Paris. Then, on May 1, a Soviet SAM missile did what the CIA had assured President Eisenhower could not be done: It shot down a U-2 spy plane.

The U-2 shoot-down and the subsequent capture and trial of pilot Francis Gary Powers was a low point of the Cold War for the United States.[1] As with the Berlin tunnel, the Soviets did not try to hide the incident. Rather, they used it to embarrass Eisenhower, who had made matters worse by publicly denying the United States was spying on the Soviet Union. Adding to the embarrassment was the fury of Premier Khrushchev as he called off the Paris Summit at the last minute. The high-level diplomacy that was supposed to help Richard Nixon win the election had backfired.

To the CIA, the U-2 shoot-down meant that its most important technical tool was in the hands of the Soviets, along with its pilot. DCI Allen Dulles reacted by desperately trying to find new means of getting information out of the Soviet Union. By this time, the CIA was aware of so many Soviet penetrations of its operations that Dulles and other high-level Agency officials thought the only thing to do was to create a super-secret unit to operate separately within the compromised Agency. The unit was given the name Soviet Russia 9.

The idea behind SR-9 was to provide a wall of security so that in the future someone like George Blake could not get near an operation and compromise it. Robert Crowley put it best: "If you are inside the Capital Beltway, you are closer to the center of things than most of the world. If you work for the federal government, you are closer yet. If you work for the CIA, you are very close to the center of power. If you work in the Soviet Division of the CIA, you stand near the heart. But if you are one of the handful in SR-9, you are at the absolute center of the known intelligence universe."[2]

SR-9 consisted of a handful of the CIA's most trusted intelligence officers. It was designed to be an elite headquarters-based team that was ready in an instant to travel anywhere in the world to bring in a Soviet agent. The next time a Popov appeared, the local CIA base or station would be kept out of the case as much as possible. SR-9 would have full control.

SR-9 was technically in the Soviet Russia Division, which was headed by Jack Maury with Quentin Johnson as his deputy. Yet top Agency officials told Maury and Johnson that SR-9 did not answer to them. Instead, the unit was headed by Joseph Bulick, who reported directly to the Directorate for Plans through Richard Helms, Bissell's deputy. Bulick took this chain of command very seriously. As Paul Garbler later put it, there were "highly secret things that were going on that they wouldn't even tell Jack Maury about. I mean, that is the way Bulick operated."[3]

Maury later told subordinates, including Garbler, that he was told not to ask any questions about SR-9, even though it was in his division. Maury was thoroughly intimidated by Helms. Colleagues recall that during meetings with Helms, Maury, a tough ex-Marine who smoked a pipe, would actually begin to drool. James Angleton said that Helms used this emotional edge to run operations without Maury's knowledge.[4]

The CIA's best Soviet case officer, George Kisevalter, who had been traveling the world on various assignments, was shocked upon his return to headquarters to learn that he had a new assignment and a new boss. Kisevalter told Garbler and other colleagues that he could not understand why Bulick, someone with no experience, was placed over him. Bulick, who in fact was an expert on Soviet agriculture, had been given one of the most important jobs in the CIA. He operated within the CIA in much the same way Stalinists ran collective farms.

Kisevalter and SR-9's other top case officer, Richard Kovich, frequently worked closely together and were great friends.[5] Kisevalter had even asked Kovich to be godfather to the daughter he and his Austrian wife had adopted in Berlin.

Kovich was born near Duluth, Minnesota, in the Iron Range, where his father was a miner. According to Kisevalter, both of Kovich's parents were Serbian and ardent anti-Communists. Richard enlisted in the Navy at 17 and spent the war as a radio operator. He was recruited into the CIA out of the University of Minnesota because of his military background and his facility for languages. According to Paul Garbler, Kovich was "a very valuable asset . . . because he could go out and talk with a guy and get at his level and never have any problems with language or communication, and he's smart. . . ." Kovich and Kisevalter had the most important clandestine jobs in the CIA. They communicated with, cajoled, and worked with every major Soviet defector for more than a decade.

Paul Garbler's career took off after his stint at Berlin Base. After a successful tour as the CIA's chief of station in Stockholm, Garbler, well liked by Bill Harvey, James Angleton, and SR Division boss Jack Maury, was cleared for appointment as the CIA's first station chief in Moscow. (While there had been CIA operatives working in Moscow before—like Popov's contact, the ill-fated Russell Langelle—there had been no formal station.) As in Berlin and Stockholm, Garbler worked under Navy cover. He was assigned a staff of four officers.

One person who was not consulted on Garbler's appointment was Joe Bulick. Bulick, as Garbler put it, had been sending in "singletons to operate in Moscow." Bulick maintained security by not telling even the ambassador who in his embassy worked for the CIA. But because of his own lack of experience, he recruited inexperienced officers. That combination was a prescription for disaster in Moscow.

Neither Garbler nor Maury realized that Bulick had his own candidate for the first Moscow chief of station: another Berlin Base alumnus, Hugh Montgomery. As Garbler later reflected, "Having had Hugh in the pipeline and having all of a sudden been confronted with me, Joe was disappointed. And I don't blame him, you know. If they had gone around me like that, I would have tried to take some counteraction."[6] Bulick was eventually forced to accept Garbler in Moscow, but not without a battle.

In October 1961, after Garbler was appointed but before he left for Russia, Director of Security Sheffield Edwards called Garbler and Maury in for a meeting, at which Angleton was also present. Edwards, who had a disconcerting stutter, greeted Garbler and told him he could not go to Moscow because George Blake, the British traitor, had identified him to the KGB. George Kisevalter, who had been sent to London to review the damage Blake had done, had told Edwards that Blake had helped himself to files that identified several CIA officers, including Garbler. Edwards said the compromise took place when Maury, Garbler, and Quentin Johnson, who had replaced Edward Snow as director of operations in the SR Division, visited London and briefed the British on how to use tourists to collect intelligence.

It was clear that Joe Bulick felt this was his last opportunity to rescue the Moscow station job for Hugh Montgomery. To save his assignment, Garbler had to think fast. He argued that the KGB was so compartmentalized that he would be home from the assignment before the Soviets figured out that he and the man Blake had identified were the same guy.

Strangely, Edwards never asked Garbler about any other contacts with Blake. Since Edwards did not ask, Garbler did not volunteer information about a more bizarre series of incidents linking him to Blake. Years later, this silence did great damage to Garbler's career, but in the fall of 1961, he was on his way to Moscow, the hottest assignment in the CIA's world, and he did not want to ruin the opportunity.

What Garbler failed to disclose is that he knew George Blake in South Korea in 1948. Garbler was the assistant naval attaché in Seoul, and he and his wife, Florence, became friends with Sir Vivian Holt, an eccentric Englishman who was a minister at the British Legation there. Holt introduced Garbler to Sidney Faithful and George Blake, who also worked at the legation. Garbler and a U.S. Army major ended up beating Blake and Faithful in a match for the tennis doubles championship of

South Korea. When the Korean War started, Holt refused to leave the legation, and the North Koreans took Holt, Faithful, and Blake prisoner.

In 1954, the North Koreans released Holt and the others through Moscow and Berlin. Holt, who was extremely ill, told Garbler that Sidney Faithful was okay, but he did not respond when Garbler asked him about Blake. Garbler later said that he never ran into Blake while he was working at Berlin Base, despite the fact that MI6 sent Blake to Berlin in 1955.

There is no doubt that Blake could easily have told the Soviets who Paul Garbler really was. Between his association with Blake in Korea and his stint as Igor Orlov's case officer in Berlin, Paul Garbler was probably a blown operative before he ever got to Moscow.

Yet if Garbler was not the best choice for Moscow station chief, Joe Bulick's candidate, Hugh Montgomery, was even worse. Because Bulick had not been consulted on Garbler's appointment, "His counteraction," as Garbler tells it, "was to send Montgomery to be my deputy. I didn't have any choice in that at all."[7] Garbler, who had worked with Montgomery at Berlin Base, was not happy about the selection: "I never trusted him," Garbler said.

Montgomery, in many ways, was not one of the boys at Berlin Base. Among other things, he did not approve of the womanizing. Professionally, Montgomery had serious lapses as an intelligence officer. He had never guessed that it was through his source in the West Berlin police that so many Berlin Base agents were lost in the late 1950s—the connection that George Kisevalter eventually tracked down. And now Montgomery was heading to Moscow. His job, in effect, was to spy on the CIA's new station chief for the CIA.

As Garbler and his unwanted deputy headed to Moscow, Nikita Khrushchev's constant prodding of the United States was becoming a major concern to his colleagues. SR-9 was about to be overwhelmed with important cases.

CHAPTER TWENTY-NINE

THE KREMLIN
AGAINST KHRUSHCHEV

MULTIPLE THREADS were coming together for the CIA during the late 1950s and early 1960s.

A conversation James Angleton had with Kim Philby in Italy in 1960 haunted the counterintelligence chief. Philby told Angleton that the entire KGB was being restructured to penetrate Western intelligence services using its best operatives. Angleton did not have a chance to question Philby on how the targeting would take place or even why. Had Angleton had a better understanding of what was happening in Moscow at that time, his conversation with Philby would have made sense.

Nikita Khrushchev had clawed his way to the top of the Soviet Communist Party in 1955 and consolidated his hold on power with his denunciation of Stalin in 1956. In 1958, he became chairman of the Council of Ministers and premier. By that time, he had faced the reality that the Soviet Empire was on thin financial footing. The Warsaw Pact was too expensive to maintain. The ideological split with China was starting to develop and was costly. Khrushchev lurched from reform to reform trying to increase agricultural production, which nevertheless remained flat. His closest supporters in the nomenklatura began to question his erratic behavior, especially toward the United States. From every element of the Soviet power structure came serious questions about his reforms, together with attempts to undermine him.

One such attempt occurred on a clear June night in 1959 in Sweden when a tiny boat came hurtling across the Baltic Sea from Poland. The boat carried two unusual passengers, Nikolai F. Artamanov, a lieutenant commander in the Soviet Navy, and his Polish girlfriend. The handsome naval officer told Swedish authorities that he wanted to defect. He said he had been sent to Poland to help train the Indonesian Navy, and there he had met his girlfriend, Ewa Gora. He was afraid of being called home and separated from her, and he was also disgusted with the direction the Soviet leadership was taking under Khrushchev. Artamonov was brought to the CIA's then chief of station in Stockholm, Paul Garbler, who welcomed him as the most important Soviet defector in Cold War history.[1]

James Angleton in Washington approved Artamonov's defection when Leonard McCoy, a Soviet Desk officer and the same man who had stalled John Sherwood over the SAM manual, asked him to intercede with Allen Dulles to make certain that Artamonov became the property of the CIA rather than being co-opted by the Navy.

Artamonov was not the only member of the nomenklatura who thought Khrushchev was going off the rails. Other officials in Moscow were also acting to stop him.

One of these was Yekaterina Furtseva, the most powerful woman in the Soviet Union and Khrushchev's lover. She and her family, including her husband, Nikolai Firyubin, owed their positions to Khrushchev and had carried out many operations for him. It was her husband, along with KGB man Yuri Andropov, who had handled the Hungarian repression for Khrushchev in 1956. In recent years, Yekaterina, who was Khrushchev's Minister of Culture and a member of the Presidium, had gained power over the KGB. Deputy KGB Chief Vladimir Semichastny, to increase his chances of succeeding his mentor, Aleksandr Shelyepin, in the top KGB slot, "gave Yekaterina Furtseva anything she desired," according to William Corson. "He made her son-in-law a KGB officer. He allowed her to handle important case files. She loved all things American."[2]

As Paul Garbler was setting off to take up his new job in Moscow, Madame Furtseva was still Khrushchev's political supporter, but she was beginning to doubt his hold on power. She shared her concerns about Khrushchev with other wavering allies of the Premier, including Leonid Brezhnev and Yuri Andropov (who, like Furtseva, was an Americaphile). She even engaged in open conversations with Semichastny and top military officials about Khrushchev's increasingly bizarre behavior, which by now included his shoe-banging performance at the United Nations and his "We will bury you" threat to the United States.

Secretly, the Furtseva cabal began to meet to discuss how to get Khrushchev to act less erratically. At the same time, they began sending messages to the West.

In 1961, Vladimir Semichastny ascended from deputy to head of the KGB. One case that particularly interested him was the Artamonov defection. He assumed Artamonov was a traitor. His patron, Madame Furtseva, thought otherwise. She had learned that Artamonov, the son-in-law of Admiral Gorshkov, the head of the Soviet Navy, had left his wife behind in Leningrad. Furtseva understood that this information was power.

It was only years later that the CIA learned what Furtseva had guessed right away. Fearful that Premier Khrushchev's lurching policies could start a nuclear war, Admiral Gorshkov had decided to send his own message to the United States in the form of a very special messenger. Gorshkov first sent his handsome and brilliant son-in-law to Poland to build a cover story so that his defection to the West because of his mistress would seem believable. From Poland, Artamonov made his dash across the Baltic, beginning the journey that was to take him to America as an agent of influence.

For Admiral Gorshkov, the CIA was not the goal: The goal was the American Navy. Admiral Gorshkov wanted his son-in-law to let the U.S. Navy know that the Soviet Navy was not interested in nuclear war with the United States.

Philby's warning to Angleton that the Soviets were sending agents still had not registered with the CIA when Artamonov arrived. It wasn't until the next major "defection" occurred that the message got through.

Through the late 1950s, the rift between those in positive intelligence collection, like George Kisevalter[3] and Paul Garbler, and those responsible for counterintelligence, like James Angleton, had grown wider and wider. Angleton's role as chief of counterintelligence was to make certain the CIA was not penetrated by the Soviets. Although Allen Dulles and Richard Helms had total trust in him, others in the CIA believed he used his job to conduct witch hunts.

The security investigation of Edward Snow had alerted Angleton to just how easily the CIA could be contaminated. What Angleton did not see was that through his old relationship with Guy Burgess and Kim Philby, the Soviets were well aware of his own personality and attitudes. They knew that he had access to almost every secret communication, operation, and document the CIA had. The Soviets' penetration of General Gehlen's operation had taught them that penetration of CIA counterintelligence was the shortcut to obtaining important secrets.

Captain Artamonov, now renamed Nick Shadrin, dazzled the positive intelligence types with the information he gave them about the Soviet Navy. When another Soviet "defector" appeared on the scene, he arrived with a different target: James Jesus Angleton.

Anatoly Golitsyn, code named AE LADLE, defected in Helsinki in December 1961. Characterized by those who had to deal with him as unpleasant and egotistical, Golitsyn looked down on Soviet Russia Division's employees as errand boys and dopes. He made exorbitant demands for money, privileges, and perks. His most outrageous request was that he be allowed to bypass his handlers in the Soviet Russia Division and deal directly with Angleton. No one else in the CIA, he said, was smart enough or knew enough to question him.

Golitsyn was like no other defector in the CIA's short history. As a major in the First Chief Directorate of the KGB, he was almost too fortunate and too high up to have a reason to defect. But he was so loaded with details of KGB operations around the world that the Agency could not ignore him, and he maneuvered so skillfully through the CIA bureaucracy, using his keen mind and arrogance, that he was able to override objections and eliminate those who stood in his way. Before long, he actually got to see Attorney General Robert Kennedy. He talked to Kennedy "enough times to give us trouble," George Kisevalter remembered.

Golitsyn totally captivated the president's brother, who eventually had so much personal prestige invested in the defector that CIA doubters realized to raise any questions about Golitsyn's bona fides was to risk a career. In his boldest move to intimidate his CIA handlers, Golitsyn wrote a letter to the president, complaining that his handlers were deliberately keeping him away from Angleton and gave the letter to Robert Kennedy to deliver to the White House. To the horror of Joe Bulick and SR-9, Robert Kennedy told Golitsyn he would give his brother the letter.

George Kisevalter—who was so trusted that he had virtually the run of the CIA—was given the task of stopping Golitsyn's letter from reach-

ing the president. As Kisevalter tells it, "I met at a special place the director had up near the Marine Barracks . . . where they brought in Golitsyn.
So I told Golitsyn, 'Let's not write in English. . . . We'll use Russian. I'm
authorized to take your letter to the president. I will personally take it. As
a favor to you, I'll check it for you, if you like. Maybe you have something you want to smooth out.' . . . So he gives me the letter, and I read it
in Russian, and I say, 'Oh, boy, this is perfect,' because my mission was to
get him not to deliver it. I said, 'What a beautiful case. Perfect case of
blackmail.' He says, 'What?' I said, 'Blackmail.' He says, 'I'm making this
request for these number of hundred thousand dollars,' this and that and
the other thing, 'because who knows, another president may not go
through with the promises that the current president and his brother have
promised me.' I said, 'Fine. I'll give this to him. Then he'll know you're a
real, real son of a bitch.' Then he jumped across the desk. We had a
wrestling match. 'Give me the letter.' I say, 'No. No. I'll deliver it. I want
this. This is great. It'll really make a shit out of you.' . . . Christ, we
wrestled all over the floor. Naturally, he won; he got the letter."[4]

However, in the end, SR-9 had no choice but to turn Golitsyn over to
Angleton. Pressure from Robert Kennedy—who by this time was running
the CIA through the White House Special Group—was constant. And
once Golitsyn made his allegations about the CIA being penetrated,
Howard Osborne—an old friend of both Bulick and Angleton, who had
now replaced Jack Maury as head of the Soviet Russia Division—had no
choice but to relinquish him to the CI staff.

Robert Crowley later recalled that he suggested privately to Angleton
that Moscow Center might be attempting to penetrate the CIA by using
Golitsyn to exploit Angleton's mind-set. Beyond this, no one at the CIA,
including Crowley, had the courage to voice these concerns officially,
either to Angleton or to Deputy Director for Plans Richard Helms. Angleton later said the problem with LADLE was that his information was better than anything the Agency had. Vetting him was, in some ways,
beyond their abilities.

Until Golitsyn, Angleton never got personally involved with defectors. Golitsyn, renamed "John Stone" for his lucrative resettlement, became the only defector Angleton ever trusted. "With the single exception
of Golitsyn," said Ed Petty, a veteran of Munich Base who later worked
for Angleton at headquarters, "Angleton was inclined to assume that any

defector or operational asset in place was controlled by the KGB. That is why I refused to meet with Artamonov. I was sorry I ever facilitated him getting in."[5]

Angleton and his staff began debriefing Golitsyn. Among the first questions asked of a defector is whether he is aware of any CIA penetrations. Golitsyn smiled at his questioner—something that this very serious man seldom did. It was a chilling smile. "Your CIA has been the subject of continuous penetration . . . ," Golitsyn said. "A contract agent who served in Germany was the major recruiter. His code name was SASHA. He served in Berlin. . . . He was responsible for many agents being taken by the KGB."

Golitsyn's allegations sent James Angleton on a mad search for the penetration agent SASHA and, more important, for any officers he might have recruited inside the CIA to work for the KGB. Angleton was convinced that whoever had worked with SASHA, given him his jobs, and provided him with opportunities was probably also working for the KGB. SASHA had to be found.

The case officers targeted in the SASHA probe were never told they were being investigated. The investigations were conducted with such secrecy that few people were even aware of them. Reputations were destroyed, not by official inquiry, but by a wink and a nod between Angleton and a division chief. "People simply stopped getting good assignments and promotions," George Kisevalter said. John Sherwood explained that the methods used could be as subtle as suggesting to a division chief that he should read the security file on an applicant before hiring him. Slowly, Angleton's mole hunt began disrupting Agency operations. Richard Helms, preoccupied with the growing demands of our involvement with Vietnam, let him continue with it.

In Moscow, meanwhile, the meetings of the Furtseva cabal continued and expanded. Madame Furtseva "had the ability to make every one of them think she was doing it for their own good," William Corson said. "She also would report to Khrushchev and encourage his tough stance. She was playing everyone off each other."

CHAPTER THIRTY

PENKOVSKY REPORTING

❧

I T WAS ALMOST SUNSET in Moscow, one evening in August 1960,[1] when a pair of Americans walked out of the Lenin Library on Prospekt Marksa, not far from Red Square. They were walking up the sidewalk toward Manezhnaya when a slender, middle-aged man dressed in a well-tailored European business suit joined them. The man, speaking Russian, said, "Please keep walking." He then asked, in heavily accented and very halting English, "Do you understand Russian?" The two Americans, though fearful of a Soviet provocation, nodded that they did. They both looked down at a folder of dog-eared papers the Russian was carrying.

"Just keep walking as if we are old friends," the Russian said in his native language. "I am a Red Army officer. I would like to make contact with someone in the American Embassy. I have access to information of great importance to American intelligence. Just look at these documents." As he tried to hand them the file he carried, he saw fear in the eyes of both men.

The Russian understood that provocations by the KGB to Americans were common. If this was a setup and the Americans took the documents, the KGB could arrest them, embarrass the United States publicly, and perhaps trade them for Soviet spies who had been arrested in the West. Frustrated, the man looked at the apprehensive Americans and said in Russian, "If you are afraid to take my documents, then *please* take this letter to the American Embassy. It is very important."

By now, the strolling men had reached the streetlights west of the Alexander Gardens. The streets were crawling with military police. One of the Americans quickly took the letter, but the Russian was not finished. As the Americans walked away, he called after them in Russian, "Tell the embassy that I'll be waiting here for someone to contact me for the next seven evenings. Please do not forget." With that, Colonel Oleg Vladimirovich Penkovsky walked into the Moscow night.

This was not Penkovsky's first approach to the West. He had made similar overtures to other Americans, the British, and even to Canadians, but until now his offers were ignored.

The two Americans he approached this time did as they promised and brought Penkovsky's letter to the U.S. Embassy. When it reached the top-ranking CIA officer there (this was before Paul Garbler opened the first Moscow Station), he took off his jacket and tie and went to the top floor of the embassy. He nodded to the Marine guard standing outside a door, who stepped aside and let the officer pass into a large, secure conference room. Inside the conference room was an odd-looking, large plastic bubble. Inside this security cocoon was a small conference table and chairs. Supposedly air-conditioned, the bubble, in fact was miserably hot, especially in summer. The CIA officer closed the door behind him, sat down, and prepared a message recommending that the Penkovsky letter be ignored, as previous ones had been, on the assumption that it was a provocation and Colonel Penkovsky was an agent sent to do mischief.

When SR-9 in Washington received a copy of Penkovsky's letter, Richard Helms and Joseph Bulick disregarded the Moscow officer's advice and decided to investigate the possibility of pursuing Penkovsky. They started by asking the FBI and MI6 which Westerners had been approached by him in the past. MI6 reported that two British businessmen had been contacted and added the information that Penkovsky had served as a military attaché in Turkey in the 1950s. Based on that report, the CIA asked the British to pursue the case.

The Penkovsky case now took on a life of its own. The CIA was still using the long list of KGB penetrations into MI6 to make the British "cousins" feel guilty and beholden, at the same time keeping quiet about its own penetrations. By 1960, because of MI6's defections to the Soviet Union, the British had descended in status to junior partnership in Western espionage. They were forced to rely on the CIA for any major information about Soviet strategic forces.

By first treating the Penkovsky case as merely a provocation by a GRU agent and "nothing," the CIA could demand to see more and more British documentation without committing itself. Helms and his colleagues were not willing to risk a bet on Penkovsky until the British could show he was almost a sure thing. If that turned out to be the case, the British would be kept on hand as partners for one purpose only: to take the blame if Penkovsky proved less than the solid-gold discovery the CIA in fact thought he was.

The British pursued the case. They determined that Penkovsky had a cover job as deputy chief of the Foreign Section of the State Committee for Science and Technology. This committee was responsible for all scientific liaison outside the Soviet Union. Penkovsky's real GRU job was to meet with foreign scientists and businessmen at home and abroad and identify the ones he thought were ripe for KGB or GRU recruitment.

Penkovsky was a "talent spotter." Once he had a promising candidate, he would introduce him or her to a "colleague," who, in reality, was a KGB or GRU case officer. By keeping Penkovsky independent of the actual recruitment, the GRU managed to keep his cover intact. That is how Penkovsky met British businessman Greville Wynne.

Wynne represented half a dozen British firms selling industrial equipment to the Soviet Union, Poland, and East Germany. Penkovsky recklessly, the British thought, approached Wynne at a Moscow trade fair in December 1960.[2] He told Wynne, who feigned surprise, that he was fed up with Nikita Khrushchev and wanted to make contact with the CIA or MI6. Penkovsky correctly assumed that Wynne was debriefed by British intelligence on a regular basis.

In fact, Wynne was a longtime MI6 agent working under commercial cover. He carefully gave Penkovsky a preliminary debriefing as instructed by MI6. The two men agreed to meet again in London on Penkovsky's next trip there. In late March 1961, British intelligence notified Helms of the approach. Helms in turn told Bulick that Penkovsky would be at the Mount Royal Hotel near Marble Arch in London with the Russian trade delegation. MI6 arranged to put bugs in the rooms directly above the ones being occupied by the Soviets.

The CIA's carefully constructed plans to keep SR-9 operations totally secret now went out the window. The meeting with "the new Popov" quickly turned into a circus. On the evening of April 20, representatives of MI5 (the British equivalent of the FBI), MI6, and the CIA all waited at the Mount Royal for George Kisevalter to lead the four-man debriefing team. Kisevalter was in an ideal position because of his close working relationship with British intelligence in reviewing the George Blake damage.

When Kisevalter arrived, he realized that he and Penkovsky were the only ones present who spoke fluent Russian. "I was running it. Who the hell else spoke Russian? I did all the speaking. The other guys asked me in English and I translated. . . . The agenda was all written out in English."[3]

Kisevalter began the debriefing by asking Penkovsky his age. He learned that Penkovsky was in his early forties and came from one of the most distinguished families in the Soviet Union. His grandfather had been a famous judge prior to the 1917 Revolution. Unlike Popov, this man was no peasant: Penkovsky belonged to the nomenklatura. He had special store privileges, cars, a dacha in the country, and a life very much removed from that of the average Soviet citizen.

The first session, which was taped, lasted five hours. Penkovsky insisted that he absolutely believed Khrushchev was evil incarnate. He said that he had to do what he could to remove Khrushchev from power even if it meant betraying his country. As Kisevalter questioned Penkovsky, he learned that during World War II Penkovsky had been an aide to the man who later became the Soviet marshall of artillery, Sergei S. Varentov. This general, who was now in charge of the Soviet ICBM program, had been Penkovsky's mentor, and the two men were still close.

The CIA was woefully short of intelligence on the Soviet ICBM program when Senator Kennedy made his "missile gap" charge during the 1960 presidential campaign, and it had not been able to learn much in the months since. No technical intelligence interested the CIA and MI6 more than Russian rocketry. Early Soviet space successes, which had involved huge payloads by American standards, had demonstrated that whether or not there was a missile gap, there was certainly a payload gap.[4] Penkovsky had access to Varentov's secret files as well as to many of his deputies'. He was a dream come true.

The idea that a devoted Marxist was offering himself to the West with precisely the intelligence the CIA and MI6 were struggling to obtain should have caused someone to stand back and think about Penkovsky. That did not happen. MI5 counterintelligence officials did question why a colonel would have such high access to all this information, but Penkovsky had a ready answer. He said, through Kisevalter, that his uncle was a lieutenant general and that nepotism had its rewards even in the People's State.[5] When the counterintelligence people still expressed doubts, Penkovsky added that he had married very well: His father-in-law, Vasal Gaponovich, was a Red Army general.[6]

What should have been puzzling to Kisevalter and his colleagues was why a member of Moscow's elite was so bitter about Khrushchev that he would take absurd security chances and risk his life. They should have realized that Penkovsky was no volunteer and no ideologue. What they had on their hands was a messenger from the most conservative elements of the Soviet power structure—elements that wanted Khrushchev, the liberal reformer, removed from power. But even the experienced George Kisevalter did not see this.

In that first interview, there were other hints of trouble. Penkovsky, code named AE HERO, told Kisevalter that his father and an uncle had fought with the Whites against the Communists in the Revolution but had managed to survive and prosper. This statement should have raised a red flag. The Soviets were steadfast in their hatred of the White "counterrevolutionaries." They never allowed former Whites to become GRU colonels. On the Soviet side, the conservatives in the Kremlin knew that the CIA had complete faith in the Whites. They knew that if Penkovsky said there were anti-Soviets in his family tree, the CIA security people would have an easier time swallowing his fables.

If the men in the field were misled by their euphoria over Penkovsky, Angleton's CI staff back at headquarters should have been more objective and raised questions. Unfortunately, during these events Angleton was away in Arizona recuperating from a recurrence of tuberculosis, and his staff had little clout without him. [7]

To the American/British debriefing team, Penkovsky's information was the most valuable the West had ever gotten out of the Soviet Union. Penkovsky gave them an unforgettable view of the Soviet power structure. "Everybody was out for a fast ruble," as Kisevalter later put it, "not in terms of money, but in terms of goods from abroad. He brought back [to the Soviet Union] suitcases full." Greville Wynne, the MI6 agent, carried Penkovsky's selections from London back into the Soviet Union on his next "trade trip."

After the first debriefing, the CIA, MI6, and MI5 concluded that Penkovsky was real. They gave him the code name ALEX and decided to run him as a joint operation. They brought him back to their suite, where CIA technicians trained him to use a Minox and two other cameras.

The special cameras the CIA developed for Penkovsky were, according to Kisevalter, "a little bit bigger than a Minox. . . . We froze the F stop at 8. . . . You didn't need the focusing. He would take a piece of paper, and at seventeen-and-a-half centimeters from the document, he would automatically be in focus." Penkovsky was so effective with the camera that he shot the leader to get a total of fifty-five frames per cassette. Out of five thousand pages of "top secret" documents he photographed over the next two years, only one frame failed to come out.

The CIA trained Penkovsky to listen for one-way voice broadcasts. The CIA men knew that the KGB knew that the numbers broadcast over Radio Free Europe were messages to spies, but they trusted that the Soviets would not be able to identify individual spies or break the code. The messages were to be beamed to Penkovsky's Russian-made shortwave receiver from a transmitter in Munich. His handlers gave him a "one-time pad" that allowed him to translate the digits into a message that made sense. These pads were printed on very lightweight and, supposedly, edible paper, and there were only two copies of each pad: one for Penkovsky and the other for his case officer.

Had the CIA really studied what Penkovsky was saying, it should have seen the obvious: His message was that Kennedy could not trust Khrushchev's sanity. In a later session, on July 15, 1961, Penkovsky warned his debriefers that Khrushchev was bound and determined to win his battle with the West by rattling nuclear weapons. In that session, Penkovsky told Kisevalter that, on the basis of the summit meeting in Vienna in June 1961 (two months before the Berlin Wall went up), Khrushchev considered Kennedy a weak man who would back down before his threats. SR-9, instead of asking why their source was telling them how dangerous Khrushchev was, simply took the information and turned it into an acceptable intelligence product.

Angleton and his staff never raised a question about ALEX. Years later, Angleton said that the across-the-board information should have been a warning. In retrospect, he realized that the CIA had never asked the single most important question about any traitor: *Why?* What motivated him? "If you accept what he said, then the motivation was never enough."

CHAPTER THIRTY-ONE

NO QUESTIONS ASKED

M ORE THAN A YEAR after Lee Harvey Oswald appeared at the American Embassy in Moscow to turn in his passport, he wrote a letter to Richard Snyder, the CIA officer who interviewed him. In the letter, dated February 5, 1961,[1] Oswald said he wanted to redefect to the United States, and he wanted his passport back. The vitriolic young man Snyder had met in the fall of 1959 said that he was still a Marxist, but he now felt that the Soviet Union had abused Marxism for the personal gain of a few leaders.

Oswald and the American Embassy communicated by mail—all monitored by the KGB—for several months. By May, Oswald was demanding that the embassy not merely grant him the right to return home but accommodate his new bride, Marina, as well. Oswald's whirlwind courtship of Marina had taken just one month. Despite serious problems with Marina's identity that took nearly a year to resolve—and inconclusively—the State Department agreed to pay for tickets to the United States for the Oswalds.[2] On June 13, 1962, the couple and their infant child, June, arrived in New York aboard the SS *Maasdam*. Lee Harvey Oswald's mission for Yekaterina Furtseva was underway.

That same month, Yuri I. Nosenko, a KGB agent in charge of watching members of the Soviet delegation to the Geneva talks on nuclear weapons, launched a separate but related mission for his employer.

Like Penkovsky, Nosenko came from a leading Soviet political family, but unlike him, Nosenko had been in one scrape after another in his undistinguished life. While he was at the Frunze Higher Naval School—the Soviet equivalent to the U.S. Naval Academy—he had deliberately shot himself in the foot to avoid military service. Because he was the son of the late Ivan Nosenko, the Soviet minister in charge of shipbuilding until his death in 1956, the young Nosenko was grudgingly accepted into the KGB. There, he soon developed a reputation as a womanizer and drinker, and wore out his welcome among his father's old cronies. It took his mother's plea to the wives of the Kremlin powers, in particular the wife of Aleksei N. Kosygin, to save his career.

Even so, it was an extraordinary event for a high-ranking KGB officer from a distinguished family to volunteer, out of the blue, to help the CIA. Yet that is precisely what Yuri Nosenko did. In June 1962, he approached the CIA's Tennant Peter Bagley in Geneva. The KGB had picked the right CIA officer as Nosenko's target. According to Paul Garbler, there were few people in the CIA more "nakedly ambitious than Pete Bagley." Bagley came from a family of American Naval giants. His successful CIA career looked puny compared to the accomplishments of the other men in his family.

First, Nosenko told Bagley that he would like to work for the United States but that he could not defect to the West as long as his wife and children were in Moscow. Nosenko then gave Bagley valuable information in exchange for a small payment. Bagley was thrilled at what he thought was a great recruitment. Because Bagley spoke very little Russian, SR-9 quickly dispatched George Kisevalter to handle the debriefings.

Nosenko revealed to Kisevalter that he had served in the Far East and that in June 1958 he had been appointed deputy chief of a branch of the KGB that specialized in the recruitment of tourists in Tokyo and other cities. A year and half before Lee Harvey Oswald was arrested for murdering President Kennedy, Nosenko was telling the CIA that he was the man in the KGB who handled recruitments of people like Oswald.

Nosenko also provided his handlers some "chicken feed" (legitimate but unimportant or already known information given to establish one's credibility), including the fact that the U.S. Embassy code room in Bern, Switzerland, was bugged by the KGB. This information was of particular interest to Bagley, who had earlier been based at Bern Station. In the chicken feed was one item of real importance, a signal that Nosenko's controller was not the KGB, but another faction interested in making certain that the Penkovsky operation continue successfully. Nosenko warned the CIA that a drop site being used to support that operation should be abandoned.

Before Nosenko left the debriefing, he was given the usual contacts and one-time code pads. He was also given a special telegraph code that would, if the need arose, instantly set up an emergency meeting at a safe house in Geneva. Kisevalter had dutifully recorded the Russian's words on four hours of tape, which he transcribed back in the SR-9 offices at Langley. The transcripts were very closely held. Joe Bulick, Kisevalter's boss, was the first to review the material.

"Had the Soviet Russia Division not been overwhelmed with the Penkovsky case and Angleton not been totally consumed with the search for Golitsyn's SASHA," said Robert Crowley, "someone in a position of responsibility might have asked why Nosenko was sending this message. But no one did." Not that Angleton wasn't skeptical. After all, he trusted Golitsyn, who had warned him that the KGB would send a series of false defectors to try to discredit him.[3]

A former deputy to Angleton offers an even more disturbing scenario. Ed Petty believes that Nosenko and Golitsyn were both dispatched by the KGB. As Petty analyzes it, "Golitsyn had predicted that a person such as Nosenko would arrive with the KGB mission of discrediting Golitsyn. Given that Nosenko was handled as a dispatched agent, the true effect was to consolidate the position of Golitsyn. On the question of whether Nosenko was, in fact, dispatched, all the lengthy analyses overlooked the point that, given convincing evidence of the presence of a well-placed 'mole,' it is certain that a 'genuine' Nosenko, having returned to Moscow in 1962, would have never again been allowed to leave."

When Penkovsky met again in London with Wynne and Kisevalter, on July 15, 1961, he turned over several dozen Minox cassettes of documents he had photographed at Soviet General Staff Headquarters in Moscow. "The CIA thought they had struck gold," recalled Victor Marchetti, an intelligence officer at the time. After the first debriefing of Penkovsky, the CIA asked the American defense establishment to list every important question it had about the Soviet rocket program. Kisevalter now presented Penkovsky with the detailed and revealing shopping list, which alone was enough to do great damage to the American defense position. The questions told the Soviets exactly what the United States did not know about their programs.

At this second meeting in London, Kisevalter discussed with Penkovsky how he could make contact in Moscow in an emergency. British intelligence also assigned Penkovsky a regular Moscow-based MI6 case officer, Roderick Chisholm. Paul Garbler, who eventually became involved in the case in Moscow, later said, "Penkovsky returned to Moscow more than ever convinced that he was doing the right thing. The path he had chosen would be a long, lonely, twisted, and dangerous one."[4]

Penkovsky's photographs caused hearts to swoon at the CIA. The pictures delivered across-the-board intelligence that meant Penkovsky had access to all sorts of Soviet military secrets. Overnight, the CIA was transformed from an agency that had trouble getting a KGB telephone number in Moscow to one that had access to the USSR's most closely held secrets. At least, so the CIA believed.

In September 1961, Penkovsky traveled to Paris for a Soviet trade exhibit. Among his duties was escorting the wife of the head of the KGB. During his month in Paris, Penkovsky met often with his MI6 and CIA handlers. They helped him procure a long list of luxury items for his military bosses and their wives at home. Penkovsky's bosses seemed more interested in perfume, jewels, and silk shirts than in French industrial goods. As Garbler put it, "Where one stood in the Kremlin hierarchy appeared to be part and parcel with what one was able to acquire from abroad."

Penkovsky had other important assignments besides shopping. As Garbler explained: "Penkovsky's first assigned task was his cover job . . . to arrange for the trade exhibit. . . . This would have been a full-time job in itself for any normal person. Next, he was responsible to the local GRU resident." Penkovsky could undertake assignments for the GRU in Paris that other Soviets could not because he had better access and more freedom of movement. In addition, he was expected to try to recruit at least one of his French trade contacts as an intelligence asset for the GRU or KGB. Penkovsky had, according to Kisevalter, an amazing appetite for life as well as the energy to handle all the complications in his routine.

In Paris, Penkovsky gave the CIA its first look into the mind of the Soviet military leadership since World War II. He had procured almost all the answers to the CIA's list of questions about the Soviet Union's rocket and missile programs. He gave Kisevalter the information needed to break the GRU's code for communication with its field agents.

During these meetings, his MI6 handlers and Kisevalter showed Penkovsky a passport, officially stamped, that would be his if he ever needed to resettle in England. He was told that if he were in danger, he would be sneaked out of the Soviet Union in the hidden compartments of a series of cars, first to Hungary and then to England. In fact, the trip to Paris was Penkovsky's last trip to the West.

After Paris, communication between the West and Penkovsky was very dangerous. The KGB had twenty thousand officers in Moscow all looking for opportunities to make their careers. The KGB routinely conducted surveillance of all British and American diplomatic personnel. If a diplomat was suspected of being an intelligence agent, he received around-the-clock surveillance. As Garbler put it, "The KGB is prepared to put two- or three-man teams, each team operating in eight-hour shifts, which means nine KGB officers every 24 hours for each American target. . . . This is one reason there was no unemployment in the USSR."

Wynne continued his role as courier, bringing Penkovsky fresh film in exchange for his exposed film. But with every meeting, the CIA and MI6 risked exposure. In a fit of intelligence lunacy, British case officer Roderick Chisholm decided to use a totally untrained agent—his wife, Janet— as a conduit to Penkovsky in Moscow. After a brush meeting with Janet Chisholm on January 12, 1962, Penkovsky told Wynne that the KGB was following him.

It was only at this point when the Penkovsky operation was in trouble that Station Chief Paul Garbler was called in. Up until then, at Joe Bulick's insistence, Garbler had been kept out of the loop. It was Bulick's own man in Moscow, Hugh Montgomery, who was fully briefed on Penkovsky and reported directly back to Bulick.[5] As Garbler later put it, "Nobody even told me what they should have been telling me about what was going on with Penkovsky."

Now SR Division Head Jack Maury summoned Garbler to Hamburg. After filling him in on the background, Maury told an incredulous Garbler what Roderick Chisholm was planning: Janet Chisholm would dress up like a Russian, wheel her baby carriage to a nearby park, and wait until, as Garbler later put it, "Penkovsky throws something into the baby carriage or gives the baby some candy and the pass is made. I said, 'You guys must be mad.' Maury said, 'What do you mean?' I said, 'It doesn't make any difference if she dresses up like a Hottentot, when she comes out of that residence where she lives, they are on her just like that. Bang! They know who he is; they know who she is. And even if they didn't, they would be following her, particularly if she is dressed up like a Russian.' Maury reacted by saying: 'Oh shit. Is that right?' Garbler, now angry, said, 'Yes, that's right.'"

Penkovsky passed more film in Moscow at the Queen's Birthday reception at the British Embassy and at the Fourth of July celebration at the American Embassy. On July 5, Wynne had dinner with Penkovsky at the Beijing Restaurant in Moscow. The Beijing was full of patrons, most of whom were KGB surveillance officers watching Wynne and Penkovsky. Both men realized that evening that the operation had been compromised. Even so, Penkovsky refused to be secretly whisked out of the Soviet Union to England as planned. His behavior was much like Popov's during that last meeting with Kisevalter in Berlin.

At this point, the British turned the operation over to the CIA out of fear of its being further compromised. From then on, the way SR-9 ran the case can only be described as bizarre. Instead of letting Garbler, the man on the scene, handle it, Bulick insisted on controlling it from headquarters. Then, instead of using experienced CIA officers, Bulick picked John Aybidian, the State Department security officer for the U.S. Embassy, to handle drop sites. This turned into an operational disaster. Aybidian was already under constant KGB surveillance because he was the embassy security officer. He even had KGB officers on his staff, since he had hired some Russians for nonsensitive security jobs.

Penkovsky's last attempt to deliver film at a U.S. Embassy reception on September 5 failed because he did not recognize Aybidian in the crowd. A later drop was successful and significant: The Furtseva cabal had learned from the head of the Soviet rocket forces that Khrushchev had placed nuclear-tipped intermediate-range ballistic missiles in Cuba, within five minutes of American targets. The cabal was desperate to notify the United States before it discovered the missiles on its own. They did not quite succeed in that—Harvey had already passed on to John McCone what his own agents had uncovered—but the information Penkovsky provided allowed the CIA to pinpoint the flight paths of its U-2 planes.

In a meeting in Copenhagen, Howard Osborne, successor to Jack Maury at SR Division, told Paul Garbler to expect a signal from Penkovsky. Weeks went by, during which no one from the CIA or MI6 saw Penkovsky in any of his normal activities. Then, on October 11, Garbler received a signal, which he and Bulick's SR-9 team determined was genuine.

Garbler knew he would have to assign an officer to check the agreed-upon drop, which was in the vestibule of an apartment building. But Bulick, without telling Garbler, decided to have Montgomery send John Aybidian into the building the day before to check it for himself. When the untrained Aybidian went to the apartment building, he lit a match in the dark hallway, looked around, and left. Aybidian's action was an espionage no-no. With the KGB watching him, in this situation it was a catastrophe. It set a trap for whoever showed up the next day.

Garbler had no idea the drop had been compromised. Despite feeling uncomfortable about Bulick and Montgomery, he did not expect either of them ever to make this sort of fundamental error. Even more astounding, this was the drop site that Yuri Nosenko had warned, months before, had already been compromised. Why did Bulick ignore Nosenko's warning?

Garbler met with Penkovsky's case officer, David Jacobson, in the embassy security bubble. Garbler was worried that the drop was a trap, and he told Jacobson that if anything looked suspicious, he should discard whatever he had picked up. "I had a bad feeling about the whole thing," Garbler recalled.[6]

Jacobson saw no threat when he walked into the vestibule, but as he reached into the drop, five big KGB men grabbed him. They pushed him outside and into the back seat of a Volga. To his credit, Jacobson denied any wrongdoing, despite being confronted with the film cassettes in his possession.

Jacobson was quickly released to the embassy. He, Hugh Montgomery, and three others from the embassy—Robert K. German, Rodney Carlton, and Captain Alexi Davidson—were all declared persona non grata and thrown out of the Soviet Union.

On November 2, while Greville Wynne was in Budapest serving yet another MI6 operation, the KGB and its Hungarian counterparts arrested him and took him to Moscow. He was one of the last Westerners held in the Lubyanka prison before it was closed. Soon it grew clear that

Penkovsky and Wynne would go to trial together. In May 1963, the public trial began. Wynne said almost nothing. Penkovsky confessed, with little apparent remorse. Penkovsky's sentence was death by firing squad. Wynne received a sentence of 11 years.[7]

As Paul Garbler saw it, SR-9 and MI6 both "behaved like a bunch of Keystone Cops." Though Garbler had been proven right in not trusting Bulick's operation, it was Garbler and not Bulick who later paid the price. Had Bulick communicated with Garbler, they all might have understood that Penkovsky was no ordinary double agent.

Garbler said, "When Penkovsky first came in, he had reported to Kisevalter that the ultra-conservatives in the Politburo were frightened, terribly frightened, by Khrushchev's addiction to freewheeling nuclear poker. If there was any resistance by the Americans or the West to Khrushchev's try at nuclear blackmail, the orthodox Politburo members would probably retreat and leave Khrushchev out there on the point all by himself."

The question that the CIA failed to ask was: *Why* was Penkovsky bringing this message? *Why* suddenly, beginning with Penkovsky, with Golitsyn and Nosenko close behind, was so much information coming America's way? And, finally, *why* was Penkovsky willing to give his life to warn the Americans that Khrushchev was about to risk the end of the world?

CHAPTER THIRTY-TWO

HE FOUND THE MISSILES–
SO FIRE HIM

———◆———

AT CIA HEADQUARTERS, Sherman Kent, head of the Board of National Estimates, had the job of figuring out what was happening in Cuba. Like McCone, he believed that Harvey and Penkovsky were wrong: Khrushchev would not risk installing offensive missiles in Cuba. But on October 14, 1962, the U-2 reconnaissance pictures confirmed that there were indeed missiles in Cuba. They also confirmed the type of missiles and size of warheads that Oleg Penkovsky had reported. Kent and his colleagues were wrong.

For the first time since nuclear weapons were developed, the United States faced the real possibility that its retaliatory capability could be destroyed in a first strike. President Kennedy informed the nation of the crisis in a radio and television address on October 22 to an estimated audience of fifty million people.

Many in the Pentagon believed that a shooting war with the Soviets was unavoidable and therefore urged the president to act first, before the Soviets could activate the missiles. General Curtis LeMay, head of the Strategic Air Command, pressed for air strikes followed by an invasion of Cuba. Instead, President Kennedy imposed a naval quarantine to prevent any further weapons being delivered to Cuba. In the military's view, this just gave the Soviets more time to get the existing missiles operational. They continued to press for quick action.

Robert Kennedy chaired EXCOM, an Executive Committee of the National Security Council formed to deal with the crisis. The Kennedys, so enthusiastic at first about the CIA and then badly burned by the Bay of Pigs and the Berlin Wall, now took nothing for granted about the Agency. They feared that it might try to make up for the Bay of Pigs debacle by precipitating a war over the missiles.

They also were appalled at the lack of hard intelligence out of the CIA in Moscow. As Robert Crowley recalled, "The CIA did not understand why we were getting messages from these agents and defectors. Not one of us thought that there was a unity in the message. The first person to raise it was the president himself. During meetings with his brother and other aides he simply asked the question: 'How do we know that Khrushchev is in charge?' We had no answer for him."

Because the CIA missed the likelihood that Penkovsky had been dispatched to warn the United States, President Kennedy was forced to guess whether Khrushchev had simply lost his mind or whether he had placed the missiles in Cuba under pressure from Kremlin hard-liners. The country avoided nuclear war only because Kennedy guessed correctly and acted accordingly.

As the crisis spun further and further out of control, the KGB's Washington resident, Aleksandr Fomin, contacted ABC News diplomatic correspondent (and future UN Ambassador) John Scali. In a series of meetings at the Occidental Restaurant, Fomin expressed interest in setting up a back channel for negotiations. William Corson, who was working for Kennedy as an intelligence aide, recalled, "We would later learn that Fomin was sent directly by Semichastny. There was no question that the crisis was made worse with the loss of Penkovsky coming in the middle of it. Khrushchev turned to Fomin to let the Kennedys know that his hand was not the only hand at the Soviet tiller."[1] The theory that Khrushchev was not in total control was given credence by a conciliatory letter that arrived from him, only to be followed by a belligerent one.

Yekaterina Furtseva knew that Khrushchev was no madman and that his hold on power was indeed precarious. The most hard-line elements of the Politburo held the balance of power. Khrushchev had turned to Furtseva, with her connections in the KGB and in the nomenklatura, to get the message out. "She was the reason the back channel worked," said Corson.

Meanwhile, according to Corson, the CIA's inability to provide the president with even the fuzziest picture of what was going on in Moscow "convinced Kennedy that our government needed to concentrate on overt intelligence and rethink spending on covert operations."

In the midst of all the tension, Bill Harvey's good work in finding the missiles went by the boards when he ignored an order from the White House. The president wanted no Task Force W operations against Castro during the crisis. Robert Kennedy told McCone to suspend all operations, and McCone relayed the order to Harvey. After consulting with General Lansdale, however, Harvey concluded that the order did not include pre-invasion operations. He allowed the dispatch of more than 60 men from JM/WAVE to land on the island to be in place should an invasion be ordered.

When the attorney general learned of Harvey's actions from a source at JM/WAVE, he was furious. He summoned McCone and Harvey to a meeting and lashed out at Harvey, suggesting he was about to plunge the world into World War III. Harvey explained that Lansdale had asked for the agents, but Kennedy responded that he had checked, and Lansdale had done no such thing. Lansdale had lied to Kennedy, who believed him. Kennedy then told Harvey that he had 30 seconds to give him an explanation. As Harvey began to answer, Kennedy walked out of the room.

Right in the middle of the Cuban Missile Crisis, John McCone removed Harvey from Task Force W and OPERATION MONGOOSE. Bill Harvey, the legendary CIA figure, was finished. McCone said to an associate, "Harvey has destroyed himself today. His usefulness has ended."[2]

According to John Sherwood, Harvey was betrayed by one of his own. It was Ted Shackley, Harvey's Berlin Base deputy and the man who cost Sherwood his agents in Cuba, who tipped off Robert Kennedy about Harvey's decision to send people into Cuba. According to Angleton, Harvey "was convinced Shackley put the knife in." (Shackley refused to be interviewed for this book.) Shackley's career did not suffer like Harvey's for his part in the failed anti-Castro operations. Despite his poor performance, he began to play an even bigger role in the CIA.

McCone assigned Desmond FitzGerald, the head of the CIA's Far East Division—whom Harvey did not regard very highly—to take over the Cuban account. Task Force W became the Special Affairs Staff. One of FitzGerald's first actions, on Shackley's recommendation, was to reactivate AM LASH, Rolando Cubela Secades. Cubela was the questionable Castro confidant who had said he wanted to work for the CIA, but who Harvey had insisted was a double agent. Shackley and FitzGerald's decision to use Cubela set in motion a nightmarish chain reaction that could not be stopped until it finally played itself out, on November 22, 1963.

United States' foreign policy attention had begun to shift from Western Europe to the Western Hemisphere in the late 1950s, as Washington attempted to counter Castro's efforts to export his revolution. In resolving the Missile Crisis, Washington and Moscow reached a quid pro quo. Khrushchev agreed to pull the missiles out of Cuba, and Kennedy pledged not to invade Cuba or attempt to remove Castro. With that standoff, Cuba receded from the world stage. A new game took over the world arena: Vietnam.

U.S. INVOLVEMENT in Indochina had begun years earlier, under President Eisenhower, but events now took a new turn. The Kennedy brothers became increasingly convinced that Vietnam would remain a trouble spot as long as Ngo Dinh Diem was in power. In the summer of 1963, President Kennedy requested his new ambassador, Henry Cabot Lodge, Jr., to start preparing for a coup that eventually took place on November 1, 1963.

In Vietnam, as earlier in Cuba, Richard Helms relied on the men who had begun their CIA careers in Berlin. Yet one man who found no place in Vietnam was Bill Harvey. After he was relieved from OPERATION MONGOOSE, he was briefly considered for a position in Laos, but his stock was so low with Robert Kennedy that John McCone sent him to Rome, which was by this time a real intelligence backwater.

Harvey ended up in Rome because he had lost the will to fight the bureaucrats of the gentlemen's club. His great policeman's mind and his terrific memory were still there, but he felt humbled by his own mistakes and devoured by the aristocratic culture perpetuated by top CIA officials like Richard Helms. Harvey's superiors, most of whose entire intelligence knowledge amounted to less than his entries in his famous ledger in a given month, treated him badly. They had contempt for his odd shape, contempt for the cut of his clothes, but mostly contempt for his refusal to be like them and think like them.

His fitness reports from Rome portray him as a drunk. Ambassador Frederick Reinhardt, whom Harvey considered a fool, made every attempt to get rid of him. McCone, who always disliked Harvey, was happy to keep a list of his mistakes. David Murphy and Ted Shackley, eager to curry favor with Richard Helms, joined in the chorus. "Rome was Bill Harvey's cold storage" is how Paul Garbler put it.

Harvey suffered a bad heart attack in Rome. CIA doctors warned him to quit drinking and smoking, which he did for a while. He even managed to get some operations going—until he discovered that his cases were being sabotaged by a shadow Chief of Station Richard Helms had installed to work around him.

By this time, Helms had appointed Desmond FitzGerald, the man who replaced Harvey in OPERATION MONGOOSE, as head of the CIA's Operations Directorate. FitzGerald personally relieved Harvey from his assignment in Rome. Harvey, the outsider until the end, returned to Washington in disgrace as a public drunk. FitzGerald had so little understanding of Harvey that he actually expressed fear that Harvey might kill himself over the humiliation of being relieved as chief of station. Instead, before leaving Italy, Harvey threw a large going-away party for himself at the Rome Hilton.

At this party for the man once plausibly introduced to President Kennedy as "America's James Bond," Angleton gave him a hand-tooled holster for his .38. Harvey also received a stuffed ferret, because no one from Task Force W could find a mongoose. His subordinates put on a sketch of the life of Julius Caesar. At the end of the skit, someone yelled out to Harvey, "Who was Brutus?" With no emotion in his voice, Harvey simply said, "Bobby."

At CIA headquarters, the new director of central intelligence, Richard Helms, called a meeting in his famous, narrow seventh-floor office to discuss Harvey's future. Those present were Angleton, FitzGerald, and Lawrence ("Red") White, the Agency's executive director.[3] They weighed the many liabilities of Harvey's return to headquarters, and the others asked White, who did not know Harvey, to make it clear to him that if he slipped up once more, his career would be over.

THE SUCCESSFUL DEFUSING of the Cuban Missile Crisis had a profound effect on both John Kennedy and Nikita Khrushchev. The two men had been to the brink of nuclear war together and were determined never to come that close to the brink again. "A partnership, a thawing was taking place," as William Corson put it. Negotiations began for a treaty to terminate the testing of the giant nuclear weapons both sides had been testing with increasing regularity. As part of the quid pro quo that ended the crisis, a secret agreement was made to remove obsolete Jupiter missiles from Turkey.

However, as Corson added, "Both men had enemies that would not profit if the thaw continued." As in a Greek tragedy, the two men who knew the most about nuclear war were at risk because they were unwilling to consider it a rational policy.

CHAPTER THIRTY-THREE

THE LONG KNIVES

E ACH WEEK, Kennedy and Khrushchev moved closer to the first significant agreements since the advent of the Cold War. They even established a "hotline" for quick communication between Moscow and Washington.[1]

Khrushchev had concluded that the Cold War was bankrupting the Soviet Union, and the country could not survive without an end to the arms race. Meanwhile, emboldened by the resolution of the Missile Crisis, he began demanding more and more internal Soviet reforms.

Khrushchev did not conduct his activities in secret. One by one, he told the entire Soviet hierarchy what he had done and what he was planning—including the fact that his secret agreement with President Kennedy to end the Cuban Missile Crisis had gone beyond removing the missiles in exchange for a U.S. pledge not to invade Cuba. Kennedy and he had also agreed to deal with Berlin and with the entire issue of East Germany.

The opposition this stirred up within the KGB and the Soviet hierarchy escalated beyond anything Khrushchev foresaw or the CIA could discover. Khrushchev had always been the great survivor. He was enough of a politician, enough of a ward boss, to be able to cajole his colleagues to obtain the support he needed. But now, in the minds of Leonid Brezhnev and other Soviet leaders, Khrushchev's reforms threatened the very existence of the Soviet state. The agreement on Turkey did not sit well with the hard-liners in the Kremlin, and, as Edward Crankshaw later wrote, the premier's decision to reach an accommodation with Kennedy not just on Berlin, but on all of East Germany, told the hard-liners that he was "getting ready to sell Comrade Ulbricht down the river."[2] The decision on Germany finally turned even Madame Furtseva into an enemy of her old lover.

Furtseva was a creature of total ambition. Strong-willed and beautiful, she was in and out of Khrushchev's favor. Her authority over bureaucrats like KGB head Vladimir Y. Semichastny gave her enormous influence. She did not hesitate to bully the pliant Semichastny, threatening to replace him with his deputy, Vadim Tikunov, whenever he displeased her.

Throughout the Penkovsky operation, Furtseva had gone along because, as William Corson pointed out, it served her interests to play on all sides. But she became alarmed at Khrushchev's post-Missile Crisis reforms. To her and others of his sometime allies, Khrushchev seemed to be engaged not only in a perilous rush to accommodate Kennedy but also in dangerous domestic schemes.

Furtseva had vehemently disagreed with Khrushchev in 1961 when he began sending Moscow's best craftsmen to work on restoring buildings in rural areas. She eventually cowed him into bringing the artisans back to Moscow to work on her pet projects. However, their relationship was never the same afterwards. Now, as Khrushchev attempted to curb excesses in the lifestyles of the nomenklatura, he began to lose his last supporters in the Central Committee and the Politburo. Furtseva concluded that he was a dreamer, an impractical man.[3]

Madame Furtseva was a political pragmatist; she wanted to assure her own comfort and her children's future. She herself served on the Presidium, the ruling body of the Communist Party, and she was the Minister of Culture. Her husband, Nikolai P. Firyubin, was Deputy Minister of Foreign Affairs.[4] Their daughter, Svetlana, was married to Igor Kozlov, a KGB major and the son of Frol R. Kozlov.[5] Frol, one of Khrushchev's principal allies, had been rewarded with running Leningrad. Although Furtseva, Firyubin, and Kozlov owed all that they had to Khrushchev, their loyalty did not extend to risking their own futures by supporting his reforms.

The conspiracy to wrest power from Khrushchev was delayed but not stopped by the Missile Crisis. Led by Leonid Brezhnev, the conspiracy now included Furtseva, Firyubin, Firyubin's old friend Yuri Andropov, and other former Khrushchev cronies. Brezhnev was playing a delicate game: He needed Furtseva's influence over Semichastny at the KGB, but he was also promising the top KGB job to Yuri Andropov if the conspiracy succeeded. Brezhnev understood that if he could maintain Andropov's loyalty while he used Furtseva to manipulate Semichastny, he could control the KGB and take over the country.

The KGB had no interest in seeing Khrushchev's reforms succeed. As Brezhnev and Furtseva well knew, the greatest fear of the nomenklatura was losing their shopping rights in the special Beriozka stores, their dachas outside Moscow, and the thousand and one other perks that made life pleasant for those at the top of the Soviet system. They were willing to back whoever seemed likeliest to let them keep their privileges.

The conspirators understood that what gave Khrushchev his stature as a world figure was the unique relationship he had developed with John Kennedy. By resolving the Missile Crisis, Kennedy had made Khrushchev into a statesman. Brezhnev, as Semichastny later wrote, "realized that if Khrushchev lost his relationship with Kennedy, he would lose his support for remaining in power."

While Brezhnev had certainly succeeded in using Penkovsky to make Khrushchev look dangerous during the Missile Crisis, this success was only temporary. He had also used the arrest of Penkovsky to install his own loyalists in the GRU. Now Brezhnev was busy privately arguing that the man he had at one time accused of being a saber rattler had lost his nuclear nerve during his recent look into the abyss.[6]

BACK ON JUNE 26, 1962, before the Missile Crisis, two Dallas-based FBI agents interviewed Lee Harvey Oswald about his life in the Soviet Union. Oswald was uncooperative. He denied being approached by Soviet intelligence while in Russia, and when the agents asked him to take a polygraph exam, he defiantly walked out of the interview, making them more suspicious.

Then, on July 2, the FBI intercepted a letter from Marina Oswald to Vitaly A. Gerasimov at the Soviet Embassy in Washington. In the letter, Marina requested permission to return to the Soviet Union. The FBI found it significant that Mrs. Oswald had chosen Gerasimov to write to: He was not only a consular officer but also a top KGB case officer. The FBI suspected that Marina Oswald might not be just the innocent young wife of a confused ex-Marine. More letters came from the Oswalds, all addressed to Gerasimov.

During the 1950s and 1960s, James Angleton administered an illegal program, code named HT/LINGUAL, to intercept letters from the Soviet Union and its Eastern European satellites and keep records on the people who received such letters. Now HT/LINGUAL intercepted a letter to Marina Oswald from Igor P. Sobolev, a KGB official who had served in Europe. Angleton's subordinates notified the FBI of the unusual piece of mail.

On August 16, 1962, two FBI agents followed Lee Harvey Oswald to a parking lot in Dallas. They tried again to interview him, but he was even more hostile and uncooperative than he was in June. Later that summer, his mother, Marguerite, became concerned because he was spending very little time with his family since his return from Moscow. He seemed to her almost totally involved with the Russian émigré community in Dallas. When she asked him why he had come back from the Soviet Union, he told her, "Not even Marina knows why I returned."[7]

That fall, at about the same time as the Cuban Missile Crisis ended, a strange man named George De Mohrenschildt began to take an active interest in Lee and Marina Oswald. No one seemed to know how he and the Oswalds met, or understand why a wealthy Dallas businessman would take such a paternal interest in the strange young couple. De Mohrenschildt started pressing his friends to supply the Oswalds with housing and jobs. He gave the Oswalds money. He also portrayed the couple (falsely) as being estranged.

De Mohrenschildt later told author Edward Jay Epstein that he had been asked by the CIA to keep an eye on Oswald—an assertion that James Angleton denied. In 1983, the police reported that De Mohrenschildt had committed suicide. No one ever got a clear explanation of his relationship to the Oswalds.

Some assassination theorists build the case that De Mohrenschildt's occasional contacts with U.S. intelligence demonstrate that Oswald was working for the CIA. Angleton, however, maintained that De Mohrenschildt worked for the KGB and that he was the Oswalds' control officer.

George De Mohrenschildt was born in Mozyr, Russia, in 1911. He claimed that his father was killed in the Russian Revolution. FBI files indicate that in 1941, now in the United States, he was arrested for making a sketch of a naval facility in Port Arkansas, Texas. By the end of World War II, the FBI had concluded he was an NKVD agent.

De Mohrenschildt developed a reputation as a top petroleum engineer. The FBI and CIA both believed his engineering success resulted from Communist connections. He was invited to Soviet receptions and worked for a time in Yugoslavia, but he carefully cleared all his activities with the CIA and was voluntarily debriefed by the CIA after each trip. He clearly was at home on the international scene. He married well—four times.

In the spring of 1960, De Mohrenschildt and his wife of the moment disappeared from view. De Mohrenschildt told friends and his wife's family that the two of them were going to drive to the tip of Latin America, but they actually wound up, in April 1961, just a few miles from the training base in Guatemala that the CIA had used to prepare for the Bay of Pigs invasion. By October 1962, De Mohrenschildt was back in Dallas and had befriended the Oswalds. In April 1963, De Mohrenschildt suddenly left Dallas for good, his work with Lee Oswald apparently over. James Angleton came to believe that this was when the KGB handed Oswald off to Castro's intelligence service, the DGI.

A week later, Oswald took a bus to New Orleans. There is evidence that he orchestrated a street fight there purposely to establish an arrest record. Within a few months, he established himself as a Castro sympathizer. He began telling associates he considered Castro's revolution more true to Marxism than the Soviet system.

At the same time, he also became deeply involved with the anti-Castro movement in New Orleans and with a number of Cuban émigrés connected to New Orleans crime boss Carlos Marcello. Marcello had been included with Santos Trafficante and Sam Giancana in the 1960 CIA contract to kill Castro.

Oswald was openly associating with rabid right-wingers involved in OPERATION MONGOOSE, including pilot David Ferrie, who had done contract work for the CIA, flying émigrés to CIA training camps. Oswald also spent time at the Habana Bar in New Orleans, a hangout of the most extreme anti-Castro Cuban émigrés. His meetings with right-wing Cuban refugees continued through the fall of 1963.

Angleton believed Oswald's efforts to be seen with anti-Castro Cubans in New Orleans "indicated to me that he was trying to provoke them into a confrontation. . . . Perhaps his goal was to report to DGI on their activities. More likely is that he had been duped into the assignment by his Russian handlers. The idea would be to link him to Castro and not to the Soviet Union."[8] In the summer of 1963, Oswald perhaps went to Mexico City to apply for a visa to Cuba. There, he is supposed to have visited both the Cuban and Soviet embassies. There is a paper trail for a Lee Harvey Oswald in Mexico, and there were even witnesses who claimed they rode with him on a bus to Mexico City. However, when these witnesses looked at pictures of Oswald, they had trouble confirming it was the man they had met. The CIA, which was photographing everyone going in and out of the Soviet and Cuban embassies in Mexico City at the time of Oswald's visit, first released what it said were pictures of Oswald. The man in the pictures was much heavier than the slender Oswald and bore no facial resemblance to him. The CIA later conceded that the man in the pictures was not Oswald but refused to say who it was.[9]

In spite of President Kennedy's post-Missile Crisis promise not to remove Castro, OPERATION MONGOOSE remained operational. Desmond FitzGerald, using the talents of Berlin Base veterans Ted Shackley in Miami and John Sherwood in Washington, kept the push on despite continuing failures. To Sherwood, mired in the madness of OPERATION MONGOOSE, "The Kennedys were basically criminals. Their father was a crook. He should have been in Leavenworth."

Because so many attempts against Castro were bungled and the Cuban community was so infiltrated with Communist agents, the KGB was completely aware of ZR/RIFLE and OPERATION MONGOOSE.

For Brezhnev, the elements had finally come together. Kennedy's assassination was to be conducted by Cuban intelligence as a matter of simple retribution. As Donald Denesyla, one of Golitsyn's CIA handlers, put it, "Khrushchev would realize that there was nothing he could do, except hope to hold onto power."

The first public hint that Khrushchev was in serious trouble came on November 12, 1963, when Frederick C. Barghoorn, a close friend of President Kennedy, was visiting Moscow. Walter Stoessel, the deputy chief of mission in Moscow, gave a cocktail party for Barghoorn at the U.S. Embassy. As Paul Garbler remembered the incident, "Barghoorn was being given the red carpet treatment. It came time for Barghoorn to leave. He had to go back to the hotel, and Stoessel said, 'Well, why don't you take the ambassador's car back?' . . . So Barghoorn[10] gets into the Cadillac and he goes back to . . . the Metropole Hotel. He is getting out of the ambassador's Cadillac . . . when he is accosted by this guy that shoves a big rolled-up set of blueprints into his hand. . . . The Cadillac hasn't pulled away from the curb yet when these two guys jump on him and say, 'We got you!' They were hauled off to KGB headquarters . . . in a cab."

President Kennedy was furious when he heard about Barghoorn's arrest. As Garbler tells it, "The information got to Kennedy, and he blew his cork. I mean, he really got madder than hell. He got on the hotline to Khrushchev. Khrushchev was out of town, and Brezhnev was acting for Khrushchev. . . . So Kennedy talked to Brezhnev and said, 'You have to understand, this is a personal friend of mine, and I am going to take great umbrage if you haven't got him out of jail within an hour. He is not the kind of guy who is going to run around looking for rocket sites or anything like that. He is a very nice, quiet academic.'" At a news conference on November 14, Kennedy said, "His arrest is unjustified. I repeat again: He was not on an intelligence mission of any kind."[11]

According to Garbler, Brezhnev called Khrushchev and told him about the call from Kennedy. "So [Khrushchev] comes rushing back up from the Crimea . . . and Brezhnev tells him the story. Khrushchev says to him . . . , 'You are the biggest shithead I ever met in my life. Do you know that? Did you approve of the KGB [doing] this utterly stupid damn thing?' And Brezhnev said, 'Yes.' And Khrushchev says, 'I ought to kick your ass all the way back to the Crimea. You call President Kennedy on the telephone and tell him he's out of jail. Call the American Embassy and tell them to go get him.'"[12]

Garbler found the incident funny at the time. He did not connect it with anything sinister. In retrospect, the dizzying series of events that were about to engulf the United States began with the arrest of the president's old friend.

The Barghoorn incident, like the Penkovsky reports, made Khrushchev look like a loose cannon. It should also have set off warning bells at the CIA that Brezhnev, not Khrushchev, was in control of the KGB.

Brezhnev was dealing directly with Semichastny's ambitious new deputy, Aleksandr I. Perepelitsyn. Perepelitsyn had suggested to the

Politburo a series of KGB assassinations, which Khrushchev had stopped. "We had gotten reports of these operations," said Quentin Johnson, who was the CIA's Soviet Operations chief at the time. "We knew Khrushchev had stopped some of these assassinations from being carried out at the last minute."[13]

Meanwhile, in November 1962, Desmond FitzGerald had decided that Bill Harvey's decision not to use AM LASH—Dr. Rolando Cubela— had been hasty. Harvey had told his colleagues that he was suspicious of Cubela, and Angleton said that he personally warned FitzGerald that Cubela was a double agent. FitzGerald refused to heed these warnings and began to deal directly with Cubela. While FitzGerald was bragging in staff meetings about how he had recruited Castro's personal friend to murder the Cuban leader, CIA and Army phone intercepts were recording the fact that Pavel Yotskov and Valery Kositkov, KGB officers in Mexico City, were also in contact with Cubela. Cubela was clearly reporting everything to Moscow.

Desmond FitzGerald demonstrated unbelievable operational stupidity when he personally met with Cubela in Paris on October 29, 1963. Cubela asked FitzGerald for the CIA's backing in a coup against Castro. FitzGerald said he would have it. Cubela then asked for a high-powered rifle with a scope on it and a second weapon that would allow him to kill Castro at close range. A date was set—November 22, 1963—for Cubela to meet FitzGerald and receive the close-range weapon: a ballpoint pen inserted with a hypodermic needle loaded with a poison called Black Leaf 40.[14]

Brezhnev and Perepelitsyn understood the depth of humiliation Fidel Castro felt over OPERATION MONGOOSE and the resolution of the Cuban Missile Crisis. Khrushchev had dismissed Castro's complaints, pointing to the agreement he had secured with Kennedy not to invade Cuba once the missiles were pulled out. Castro was not impressed by the agreement: What good was the United States' promise not to invade Cuba if he himself was hunted down and killed?

It was Castro's resentment and fear that Brezhnev and Furtseva exploited. The idea was to make certain that the operation to kill John F. Kennedy was carried out by the DGI, not the KGB. The United States might still blame the murder on Khrushchev: After all, Khrushchev's defeat at the hands of Kennedy in the Missile Crisis was motive enough for the CIA and FBI to suspect him of having ordered a "wet affair." But that did not bother the conspirators as long as the KGB itself did no more than aid the DGI by supplying willing resources like Lee Harvey Oswald.

CHAPTER THIRTY-FOUR

BLOOD BRINGS BLOOD

———⟫●⟪———

ON NOVEMBER 22, 1963, the conspiracy to remove Nikita
Khrushchev from power took its most celebrated victim. The Cold
War turned hot for a moment when the American president was shot
dead in Dallas. Amid all the speculation about the events of that day, the
people who knew most about it had powerful incentives to keep their
knowledge to themselves. As the American people watched the events of
that weekend on their television screens, the cover-up of mistakes, screw-
ups, and great crimes began.

The Kennedy family themselves did not demand a great inquiry into
the president's death. The fact that John and Robert Kennedy had behaved like real-life versions of a mob family had to be kept quiet.

Lyndon Johnson, for his part, was politically astute enough to know
that if he told the truth about the Kennedy brothers, the messenger
would be hated more than the message. He also feared that if an inquiry
proved the Russians were involved, the resulting outrage could lead to
demands for war.

As for the security agencies, the CIA and FBI were busily withholding
information from each other and from other government agencies. For one
thing, the CIA had not passed along to the Secret Service the grim information that Angleton's favorite defector, Anatoly Golitsyn, had brought with
him. According to Donald Denesyla, who was assigned to keep Golitsyn
company, Golitsyn said that the KGB had become active in "wet operations

again. . . . One of the things he [Golitsyn] told us was that because of the Eisenhower Administration efforts against Castro, Nixon was targeted for assassination. It is apparent that when the Kennedys continued with the same activity, the plan was simply continued."[1]

The CIA was no more open with its information after November 22. Angleton later said that within a few days of the Kennedy assassination and the killing of Lee Harvey Oswald, the CIA had information linking Castro to the killings, but that it deliberately withheld it from the FBI on national security grounds. One key CIA document, finally released to the House Select Committee on Assassinations in 1977, detailed the getaway plans of a suspected assassin; on the CIA routing slip for this document someone had scrawled, "I'd let this die a natural death as the Bureau is doing." The FBI, it turned out, had information on unusual DGI activity in New Orleans, Dallas, and Mexico that it never checked. Both agencies withheld their information from the Warren Commission.

Even among those with the greatest access to information, there are different and sometimes conflicting theories about what happened. Angleton maintained that Castro sent three DGI agents to Dallas in the days before November 22. In Angleton's theory, agents Policarpo and Casas, plus a third man whom Angleton would not name, separately worked their way to Dallas, where they met up and carried out the assassination. Angleton believed that Oswald's role was solely to convince Castro that the murder was a joint KGB/DGI wet operation. "Oswald was never aware of the others," Angleton said. "Telling him would serve no purpose."

Eyewitnesses told the House Select Committee on Assassinations that they saw a man who looked like Oswald leave the Texas School Book Depository and get into a white Rambler station wagon.[2] These witnesses said the driver appeared to be a Cuban between 25 and 35 years old—a description that fits either Policarpo or Casas.

Casas's and Policarpo's escape route is on the public record. After the assassination on the afternoon of November 22, the Border Patrol closed the roads to the Mexican border, but nothing was done to stop small airplane traffic. Documents released by the CIA reveal that an Air Cubana flight from Mexico City to Havana that evening was held up for five hours. The CIA noted that on the next day, the Mexico City airport was teeming with Cuban and Soviet diplomatic officials. At 11:10 P.M., a man (later identified as Casas) went directly from a twin-engine plane that had just arrived from the United States onto the Air Cubana flight without going through Mexican customs.

A document released by the CIA to the House Select Committee revealed some of the movements of the other man, Policarpo. On November 20, he was in Tampa, where he obtained a tourist visa for Mexico. On November 25, he registered at the Roosevelt Hotel in Mexico City. Two days after that, he cleared Mexican customs using an expired American passport and a special temporary visa issued by the Cuban embassy in Mexico City. Policarpo was the only passenger aboard an Air Cubana flight to Havana served by nine crew members.

Hours after Kennedy's murder, President Johnson dispatched William Corson to Dallas to begin an investigation. Corson, who ended up working for the Warren Commission, believed that Policarpo's role was to make certain Jack Ruby carried out the assignment to eliminate Oswald. "That's the only explanation for the chance he took in staying in Dallas those extra days," said Corson.

A CIA document dated December 9, 1963, reported a conversation between a CIA source and Casas's aunt.[3] The aunt said: "Miguelito has just arrived from the United States. He was in Dallas, Texas, on the day of the assassination of Kennedy, but he managed to leave through the frontier [town] of Laredo. . . . A plane brought him to Cuba. . . . He is one of Raul's men. . . ." CIA agents in Cuba also reported that Casas was suddenly flush with money.[4] Investigators eventually learned more about his background. Although the Casas family was poor, Miguel and his older brother were smart. Both learned Russian and went to Moscow for training. After they returned to Cuba, the older brother got Miguel into a sabotage unit of the DGI, where his ratings were remarkable. According to Angleton's own investigation of the assassination, Raul Castro personally selected Miguel for the mission.

After the Barghoorn incident, Premier Khrushchev returned to the Crimea to resume his vacation and was still there on November 22. Once again, Brezhnev was in charge at the Kremlin. He called Khrushchev himself to tell him of Kennedy's murder. According to William Corson, the news hit the Soviet premier hard. "Khrushchev was trapped in the Crimea by terrible weather," said Corson. "He was rushed back to Moscow in a special sealed train—one that does not stop to pick up passengers along the route—so he could sign the condolence book."[5]

That same day, Moscow Station Chief Paul Garbler was in England meeting with London Station Chief Archibald Roosevelt. Garbler was "ordered back to Moscow because," as he later put it, "at that time we thought it might be a wider conspiracy." Garbler added that, although the CIA knew Oswald had lived in the Soviet Union, neither he nor his colleagues were ever asked to look into Oswald's activities there.

Lyndon Johnson's Oval Office recordings indicate that he was convinced the Soviet Union was behind the Kennedy assassination, and Angleton, who personally briefed Johnson, confirmed that the president remained convinced of that until his death.[6] President Johnson also told a number of people, including his chief of staff, Joseph A. Califano, that Kennedy was assassinated because Castro was seeking revenge.

Lyndon Johnson, who knew only bits and pieces of the truth, understood that he did not have the political capital to demand that the whole story be revealed. He was determined, however, to put "Murder Incorporated," as he called the CIA's assassination operations, out of business. When, in 1964, Richard Helms officially informed the new president of the CIA's operation against Castro, Johnson ordered Helms to shut it down. [7]

It took President Johnson two years to finally put a stop to CIA assassination plots. A popular American president was dead. But just as the CIA's assassination capability did not begin with Kennedy, it did not end with him either.

In March 1966, Rolando Cubela was put on trial for treason in Havana. He confessed his role with the CIA and demanded to be shot. In the course of his testimony he said that he had continued to work for the CIA through 1965—more than a year after Johnson ordered Helms to shut down the operation. Secretary of State Dean Rusk was incensed and demanded an explanation. In a memorandum replying to Rusk, Helms wrote that the CIA was "not involved in a plot with AM LASH to assassinate Fidel Castro." Almost 10 years later, testifying before the Senate Select Committee on Intelligence (the Church Committee) in 1975, Richard Helms described the outright lie to Rusk as "inaccurate."[8]

Desmond FitzGerald, now running Cuban operations as the CIA's Western Hemisphere Division chief, told subordinates when he visited the CIA's Buenos Aires Station in 1964, "If Jack Kennedy had lived, I can assure you we would have gotten rid of Castro by last Christmas." The lesson that should have been learned from Dealy Plaza was lost on the CIA hierarchy.

To make matters worse, the creator of the murder capability, former DCI Allen Dulles, decided to volunteer to help investigate President Kennedy's murder.

Dulles, fired by the Kennedys in 1961 for his role in the Bay of Pigs debacle, was not one of the prestigious group originally selected by Lyndon Johnson to serve on the investigating commission headed by Chief Justice Earl Warren. According to William Corson, the former spymaster "lobbied hard for the job." Once appointed, Dulles wasted no time installing himself as the intelligence expert on the Warren Commission.

Dulles tasked Corson, who had commanded Dulles's son in the Marine Corps during the Korean War, to investigate the Jack Ruby angle. After his investigation, Corson concluded that organized crime was not behind Ruby's murder of Oswald. In retrospect, Corson came to believe that "it is entirely possible I was sent on an assignment which would go nowhere. I spent a year. . . . Allen Dulles had a lot to hide."[9]

In the weeks following the assassination, major changes took place in the CIA. At one point, Paul Garbler was summoned to Rome from Moscow. He thought the purpose of his trip was another routine meeting with Howard Osborne, the Soviet Russia Division chief. When Garbler arrived at Bill Harvey's villa, where a party was in progress, he was shocked to learn from other guests that not Osborne but David Murphy, his nemesis from Berlin Base, was now in charge. Murphy had achieved the post Harvey had longed for. When Garbler learned that Murphy was the new Soviet Division chief, he and his wife left without greeting Murphy or his wife.

Richard Helms had appointed Murphy just before Kennedy's murder, and Murphy quickly picked Pete Bagley as his counterintelligence deputy. The entire Soviet Division was soon filled with Murphy loyalists. Quentin Johnson and other officials who considered Murphy less than a Soviet expert were on their way out.[10]

Bagley, who had happily recruited Yuri Nosenko just a year and half earlier in Geneva and passionately defended the recruitment afterwards, had undergone a great change of heart. Bagley was one of the few people in the Soviet Russia Division with a keen interest in counterintelligence. As the SR Division official who dealt directly with James Angleton, he came to worship Angleton professionally.

According to Leonard McCoy, by then a top reports officer in the Soviet Division, Angleton asked Bagley to come to his office one Saturday in December 1963.[11] In a single weekend, Angleton turned Bagley around on Nosenko by taking him into the inner sanctum of counterintelligence and showing him the transcripts of Golitsyn's debriefings, in which the defector warned about agents being sent to discredit him. When Angleton eventually introduced Bagley to Golitsyn, the conversion was complete.

A month after Kennedy died, Bagley wrote a memo predicting that Nosenko, his own recruit, would prove to be a dispatched agent[12] and warning that he might return at any time. Almost on cue, Nosenko activated his emergency code and signaled for a meeting in Geneva. Nosenko, who had agreed to operate as an agent-in-place in the Soviet Union, was now calling for help.

Igor Orlov and Eleonore Stirner in a rare, early photograph taken while the Soviet double agent began dating his future wife in Munich.

After Orlov's CIA-arranged marriage ceremony.

Eleonore Stirner as proud Nazi youth and star athlete.

Werner Boch, the young chemical engineering student who dropped a flirtation with Eleonore after a train trip to East Germany on which he spotted Igor in a full Soviet Officer's uniform. Boch told Eleonore, but she could never bring herself to tell CIA authorities.

Igor insisted he and Eleonore visit the Soviet War Memorial in East Berlin.

Eleonore Orlov at Hitler's Olympic Stadium in November 1953 with a friend. This site became the secret meeting place for planning Harvey's Berlin tunnel operation. George Blake, KGB agent, attended those sessions.

Robert Orlov and his mother as he prepares for school.

A rare photograph of the Soviet case officers working under William King Harvey at Berlin Operating Base (BOB).

Samuel V. Wilson, case officer and friend to Igor Orlov, spent most of his career in Soviet operations. He is President Emeritus of Hampton Sydney College in Virginia.

Paul Garbler, Igor Orlov's case officer and the CIA's first station chief in Moscow.

John Sherwood and friend near Berlin Operating Base. Sherwood said that, under Harvey, the main activity the case officers at BOB were good at was womanizing.

Yakterina Fursetseva, the most powerful woman in the Soviet Union, handled Lee Harvey Oswald when he was in Russia. Her son-in-law, Igor Kozlov, was dispatched as a double agent.

James Jesus Angleton, the CIA's long-time Chief of Counterintelligence, at the end of his career.

Edward M. Korry, the United States
Ambassador to Chile, blew the whistle on
the CIA wrongdoing that led to an end to
the longest running democracy in Latin
America in 1973.

Edward M. Korry, President Salvadore Allende, and
Pat Korry at La Moneda Palace in Santiago, 1971.

George Weisz and his mother when the
family still lived in Hungary.

George Weisz and his mother, father,
and sister before he went off to war and
a double life.

Etta Jo and George Weisz after their
wedding and before embarking on
their Cold War honeymoon to
Hungary.

George Weisz in 1975 when he served as Chief of Station in Vienna during the disappearance of Nick Shadrin.

Weisz's Pentagon pass gave him access to the most secret vault in the building as he worked on his mole hunt in the days before his death.

Nikolai Artomonov and Ewa Gora in Poland in 1959, shortly before Artomonov defected to the West and became Nick Shadrin, triple agent. Shadrin "disappeared" in Vienna, Christmas 1975.

George Weisz (center) as head of the Department of Energy's Security and Safeguard's office. In this job, Weisz had access to America's most important nuclear secrets and facilities.

George Weisz on his beloved farm a few weeks before his mysterious death. At the time, Weisz was looking for a KGB mole inside the Reagan White House.

Weisz's body after his death from carbon monoxide poisoning. Maryland State Police ruled his death a suicide despite overwhelming evidence to the contrary.

One of the things that didn't add up: The ignition was found in the off position by authorities. That would have been impossible for Weisz to do if he committed suicide.

The contents of Weisz's fireplace included highly classified notes concerning his mole activities. The condition of his farmhouse raises suspicions that Weisz might have been held against his will before his death.

CHAPTER THIRTY-FIVE

HOOVER SAVES PHILBY

———⟫•⟪———

THE LOSS OF THE PRESIDENT caused Angleton to reexamine everything he took for granted. Always haunted by the spector of Philby over his own career and the CIA, Angleton said, "I began to wake up. I began to think about what we might be facing."

It began as a simple precaution. Golitsyn's information about a "third man" in MI6 had rekindled Angleton's fears that his old friend Kim Philby might be a mole. Using his strong connections to Mossad, Angleton got the names of CIA and Defense Intelligence Agency employees with whom Philby was socializing in Beirut, where he had been since 1956. When the name of Beirut-based CIA Officer William Eveland showed up repeatedly in these reports, Angleton grew concerned and reopened the case that was essentially closed in 1955.

Bill Harvey had been Philby's nemesis back in 1951, when the disappearance of Burgess and Maclean first cast doubts on the master spy. Harvey had gone on to other things, but his old boss, J. Edgar Hoover, remained obsessed by the case. At the time, Hoover was furious that MI5 did not come up with enough evidence to destroy Philby. He was further enraged when the CIA was unable to prove continued contacts between Philby and the Soviets after Philby left the United States and returned to England.

Deputies of Hoover, including Sam Pappich, attributed Hoover's strong feelings about Philby to the two men's closeness during Philby's

time in Washington. They had met at dinner parties and had worked together in the search through the VENONA intercepts. "I think the director felt a little foolish and felt he had been had," said Pappich. "Hoover
had a long memory."[1]

Hoover had been as much an Anglophile as Donovan, Dulles, and the
other leading OSS men and had enjoyed a strong relationship with his opposite numbers at MI5. That relationship led Hoover down a trail with
devastating unintended consequences.

On a bright spring day in 1954, Vladimir Petrov, a Soviet intelligence
officer, defected to the West in Canberra, Australia. A London newspaper
with ties to MI5, *The People,* reported that the defector was contradicting
the British government's official theory about the defection of Burgess and
Maclean. Although filled with speculation and mistakes, the newspaper
article forced the Foreign Office to respond. Petrov's charges were that
Burgess and Maclean were not simply two lone diplomats who had defected, but were part of a wider conspiracy within MI6 and that a fellow
conspirator, a "third man," had survived and remained as an agent-in-
place in British intelligence.

Hoover was energized by this news. "He became convinced it was
time to reveal Philby to the world," Robert Crowley said. "Philby being
on his heels and pensioned out of MI6 was not enough. Hoover wanted
him destroyed."[2]

Hoover made personal calls to several newspaper reporters. His firm
rule with the press was that he was not to be quoted. He told the reporters that the FBI had learned the reason Burgess and Maclean disappeared when they did is that Philby had tipped them off that they were
under investigation and urged them to flee to Moscow. When reporters at
the New York *Herald Tribune* and San Diego *Union*—two newspapers
where Hoover had close ties—did not publish his tip, his staff contacted
an FBI stooge at the International News Service (INS).[3]

Hoover, in 1955, wrote a memorandum to the file[4] stating he had revealed to the INS that Philby had a drinking problem at the time he was
assigned to Washington, and that he had access to the most secret information there. Hoover mistakenly told the INS that Philby had to be escorted back to London by MI5 after Maclean and Burgess defected.

Hoover warned the INS that Philby would sue if they wrote a story.
A way to avoid a suit, he suggested, was to have Philby named in Parlia-

ment. Under British law, comments in Parliament, as in the American Congress, are exempt from libel laws. Hoover offered to work with the INS and put them in touch with a British newspaper with close ties to MI5, *The Empire.*

The INS sent their man to London to meet with Jack Fishman, editor of *The Empire,* who in turn attempted to persuade Labour members of Parliament to ask Prime Minister Anthony Eden's government about Philby during the Prime Minister's Questions. When this ploy did not work, Fishman, under Hoover's guidance, leaked the story to the New York *Daily News's* London Bureau. On October 23, 1955, the *Sunday Daily News* named Philby as the "third man in the Burgess and Maclean case." Two days later, Marcus Lipton, a member of Parliament with long suspicions of Philby, rose at question time and asked, "Has the prime minister made up his mind to cover up at all costs the dubious third-man activities of Mr. Kim Philby . . . ?"

Hoover, finally successful in getting Philby's name out, cabled the FBI's legal attaché in London to say that he would now have to provide "information on Philby to certain high U.S. government officials." Hoover thought he had designed a foolproof scenario to force the British into a full-scale investigation. He did not understand either the ongoing feud between MI5 and MI6 or the role of the British class system in all the events surrounding Philby.

Foreign Secretary Harold Macmillan, who considered the intelligence services little more than policemen, asked Sir Dick White of MI5 to write a paper on the whole subject. The letter accompanying White's paper revealed Hoover's role in orchestrating the leak, which stirred up anti-American sentiment in Parliament and deflected calls for further investigation.

Macmillan ordered British intelligence to end Philby's pension, thus removing him from the official payroll. At the same time, Macmillan took a step in the other direction. On November 7, 1955, he rose in Parliament and said, "No evidence has been found that Philby was responsible for warning Burgess or Maclean. While in government, he carried out his duties ably and conscientiously. I have no reason to conclude that Mr. Philby has at any time betrayed the interests of his country or to identify him as the so-called 'third man,' if indeed there was one." In exchange for accepting dismissal, Philby was publicly cleared.

Hoover was flabbergasted and furious. He had hurt his own credibility with the media and further damaged his relationship with the CIA. More important, MI5, unable to find evidence to arrest Philby, watched their target being cleared in the most public way possible.

The next day, a sober, calm, and witty Philby held a press conference to revel in his exoneration. He was on top of his game and handled the press with ease. Most of Britain believed he was innocent. Hoover, humiliated, ordered the Bureau to close its file on Philby. The date was December 29, 1955.

Thanks to Hoover, British intelligence decided to put Philby back to work. The Macmillan deal prevented him from being hired as a staff officer but did not prevent the Secret Intelligence Service (MI6) from hiring him as a freelance agent. By July 1956, Philby was back in the spy game, this time as an agent in Beirut working undercover as a journalist.

BEIRUT IN THE LATE 1950s was a remarkable, cosmopolitan city. Philby's assignment as a reporter for the *Economist* and the *Observer* allowed him to routinely meet with CIA officers and other high-ranking CIA executives. He met with Angleton several times during this period and used those opportunities to reassure his American friend of his innocence.

When in 1960 Philby's old friend Nicholas Elliott became SIS station chief in Lebanon, he immediately increased Philby's access to secret information. That same year, Sir Dick White, author of the report for Macmillan five years earlier, was plucked from MI5 to become head of the SIS. He was shocked to see that Philby was back on the SIS payroll.

White decided to resolve the Philby case once and for all. He began by sending Philby on assignments in the Eastern Bloc, feeding him real and false information, and tracking his activities closely. It was a risky strategy. As William Corson, White's friend and colleague, put it: "White did not know if Philby was guilty, but he had to find out. He understood that if it turned out badly, it could mean the end of an effective SIS."[5]

Kim Philby had endured five years of persecution in England. Yet through it all—through all the drinking, womanizing, and failed marriages—he had remained the consummate intelligence officer. He had even inadvertently discredited America's most visible surviving anti-Communist, J. Edgar Hoover. Now the tests became more severe as the assignments from London flowed. A new marriage and family did not deter Philby's bosses; they worked him very hard.

One of Philby's closest friends in Beirut was George Blake, the KGB agent who had so far escaped detection and was running the SIS's Arab Language School. Suddenly, acting on information provided by the Polish defector Michel Goleniewski, the British called Blake back to London in April 1961 and arrested him. Philby said he was convinced Blake had been brainwashed in North Korea.[6] The suddenness of Blake's arrest made him openly wonder if the MI5 investigation into his own activities was starting up again.

In fact, MI5 and the SIS had agreed to step up the investigation of Philby after Angleton's Mossad contacts turned up an old Philby family friend as a witness against him. With information dating back to the 1930s, MI5 and the SIS finally had enough to confront Philby yet again. Finally, on January 10, 1963, Nicholas Elliott, his old friend and current boss, arrived in Beirut from London carrying with him a prosecutor's brief.

In what Elliott thought would be a tough hostile interrogation, Philby simply confessed. Elliott was empowered to offer him complete immunity if he agreed to reveal all his contacts and other KGB agents in the services. Elliott urged him to write down his confession. Philby asked for time to think it over.

This was a ploy to hold Elliott at bay while he activated an escape plan to Moscow. Stalling for time, he gave Elliott false written information that cleared Anthony Blunt of suspicion. He also falsely named others in MI6 as working for the KGB. Everything Philby gave Elliott was a lie.

At the end of a week, Elliott had gotten no real confession from Philby. Philby refused to return to England for further questioning, and Elliott foolishly flew home without him. On January 23, in the midst of a rainstorm, Philby left his wife, Eleanor, and their son, Harry, and boarded a Russian freighter docked in Beirut. Four days later, he arrived in Moscow. It took MI6 months to figure out what had happened.

Golitsyn had been right. His information finally revealed one of the greatest spies in Soviet history. However, in May 1963, when Philby's defection became known, the mole in the American service called SASHA had still not been caught.

CHAPTER THIRTY-SIX

HAUNTING ANGLETON

A YEAR PASSED after Philby escaped from Beirut to begin his new life in Moscow as a general in the KGB. In a note to Robert Crowley, Angleton wrote, "There was not an hour I did not think of the damage he could do after he defected." For Angleton, the paranoia that is the occupational hazard of the counterintelligence officer was heightened by the death of his president and by Philby's betrayal. He later said, "I came to believe that the events that would lead to my own downfall at the CIA and the successful cover-up of the Soviets' involvement in the Kennedy murder were orchestrated by Philby."

What happened to the CIA during its so-called "dark period" from 1961 through 1975 began with the defection of Golitsyn and his chilling talk of penetrations. It entered a new phase with the final defection of Philby, who arrived in Moscow in the midst of the internal plotting against Khrushchev. Evaluating their position after the assassination, the Soviets made an assessment: If only Angleton in the CIA was questioning the Soviets' role in the Kennedy murder and if only Angleton was convinced SASHA was dangerous and had to be tracked down, then who better to manipulate Angleton—and to discredit him—than Philby? Who better to make Angleton look like the CIA's Joseph McCarthy? Who better to depict a paranoid Angleton looking under every desk for a Communist mole? The real cause of the "dark period" was Angleton's fear of his old friend.

Two months after President Kennedy was murdered, David Murphy sent Pete Bagley back to Geneva to keep the appointment with Yuri Nosenko. However, because Bagley's command of Russian was poor, SR-9 sent George Kisevalter along with him.

Angleton was not happy that Murphy sent Bagley back to Geneva. After all, Bagley, no longer simply a case officer, was now the top counter-intelligence official in the Soviet Division. Kisevalter was not thrilled either. He did not think much of Bagley or his abilities as a case officer, and, on the basis of the memo Bagley wrote after his meeting with Golitsyn, Kisevalter felt that Bagley had already made up his mind about Nosenko.

It was a cold wintry afternoon in Geneva when Yuri Nosenko, self-confident but harried, arrived at the suburban apartment where Bagley and Kisevalter were waiting for him. The large, gregarious man was very nervous. Bagley asked sharply why he wanted to defect now, when he had said in their previous meeting that he would never leave his wife and children back in Moscow. When Kisevalter translated the question, Nosenko gave a familiar answer, "I have been summoned back to Moscow. I am afraid they may be aware of my relationship to U.S. intelligence. . . . I want to defect. I cannot wait." Once again, every word was recorded on tape.

Kisevalter took charge of the conversation and tried to put Nosenko at ease. As they talked, Bagley saw Kisevalter turn serious. His Russian was not good enough to understand that the men were talking about the assassination of John Kennedy. Nosenko was reminding Kisevalter that he had been in charge of recruiting Americans in Moscow. He said he had detailed knowledge of the KGB's relationship to Lee Harvey Oswald during the time Oswald lived in the Soviet Union. Kisevalter turned to Bagley and explained what Nosenko had said. Both Kisevalter and Bagley were full of questions.

"Did you recruit him for the KGB?" Kisevalter asked. Nosenko said he had not. He said Oswald was so unstable, so "strange" that the Soviets had decided to pass on recruiting him.

Then Nosenko dropped a bombshell. He said that the decision not to recruit Oswald was made not by the KGB, but by Yekaterina Furtseva. For the KGB to pursue Oswald after she had given orders not to would have been foolhardy.

Kisevalter and Bagley both tried to talk Nosenko into not defecting but remaining in place and working for the CIA in Moscow. They realized that as Foreign Minister Andrei Gromyko's "watchdog," Nosenko was potentially a source of valuable information. However, the Oswald material was too sensational and too important to risk, and Richard Helms made the decision, based on Kisevalter's advice, to bring Nosenko to the United States.

Back at headquarters, George Kisevalter celebrated with David Murphy and Joe Bulick. They finally had a credible source on Oswald. Leonard McCoy and the Soviet Division's other experts all concurred with Nosenko's view that no one would go near Oswald once someone as powerful as Furtseva was involved.[1]

James Angleton did not join in the celebration. To him, the reality was setting in that Lee Harvey Oswald had attracted the attention of those at the highest levels of the Soviet government. Furthermore, Nosenko's assertion about Furtseva sounded like precisely the sort of thing he would have been instructed to take to the West if the Soviets had plotted against Kennedy. Angleton even wondered if Brezhnev had arranged for Furtseva, Khrushchev's old lover, to handle the Oswald case as a way of tying Khrushchev to Oswald. Angleton argued that extra care should be taken to keep Yuri Nosenko isolated from CIA operations until his bona fides were thoroughly checked. He was convinced that the KGB had sent Nosenko, just as Golitsyn had predicted.

Donald Denesyla, one of Golitsyn's handlers at the time, had a more cynical view about Helms's decision to allow Nosenko into the United States: "He decided to allow Nosenko to come in, to sweep Kennedy's murder under the rug. It was all part of the cover-up. . . . Nosenko cleared the Russians, and the CIA had no real capability to decide if the Russians had done it or not."

Slowly, the battle lines over Nosenko were drawn. David Murphy, accepting the views of his SR-9 unit, believed Nosenko was real. Angleton and Bagley, in counterintelligence, were aligned with the Office of Security in suspecting Nosenko and his motives. Howard Osborne, now chief of security, decided to sweat the truth out of Nosenko using isolation and hostile interrogation.

IN OCTOBER 1964, Brezhnev was ready to act. The coup against Khrushchev took place while the premier was on vacation at the Black Sea. Aleksandr Shelyepin, whom Khrushchev had fired from the KGB three years before, used his connections to give Brezhnev control over the secret police. Then Vladimir Semichastny, whom Khrushchev had elevated to KGB chief in Shelyepin's place, refused to help his old patron. By the time Khrushchev was summoned back to Moscow by his Party comrades, he knew it was all over.

Khrushchev knew the game—he had played it himself. One by one, his comrades in the Presidium stood up and listed his sins. They blamed him for every problem in the Soviet Union as well as for losing control of Castro. When they were finished, he stood up and told them bluntly that the Soviet Union would spin apart if peace were not made with the West. "We do not have the luxury of being timid," he told them. They voted, and he resigned all his posts. Khrushchev's vision of the future—a new world order that he and Kennedy would forge together—would never become reality. He understood that his dreams, like those of so many others, had died in the motorcade in Dallas.

About the time Khrushchev was ousted, James Angleton was shocked by another event linked to the late president.

ON THE EVENING OF October 12, 1964, Angleton and his wife, Cicely, were invited to a poetry reading at the house of an old friend, the artist Mary Meyer. Meyer's dreams had died in Dallas, too.

Twenty years earlier, just out of Vassar, Mary Pinchot as she was then, had married a promising young man, Cord Meyer, who later became one of Allen Dulles's top clandestine executives at the CIA. Mary Meyer came to hate her husband's job, and in 1956, she divorced him and moved to Georgetown to start a new life. That new life included a love affair with John Kennedy, which ended only with his murder. While Kennedy had many affairs while in the White House, Angleton insisted that the president and Mary Meyer "were in love. They had something very important."

The day of the poetry reading, Cicely Angleton called her husband at work to ask him to check on a radio report she had heard that a woman had been shot to death along the old Chesapeake and Ohio towpath in Georgetown. Walking along that towpath, which ran near her home, was Mary Meyer's favorite exercise, and Cicely, knowing her routine, was worried. James Angleton dismissed his wife's worry, pointing out that there was no reason to suppose the dead woman was Mary—many people walked along the towpath.

When the Angletons arrived at Mary Meyer's house that evening, she was not home. A phone call to her answering service proved that Cicely's anxiety had not been misplaced: Their friend had been murdered that afternoon. The Angletons went to the nearby home of Mary's sister, Antoinette, then married to *Newsweek's* Washington bureau chief, Benjamin C. Bradlee. They comforted the family and helped them make funeral arrangements.

As police later reconstructed that day's events, Mary had painted in the morning and at about noon had set off on her daily walk. It was cool outside. When the police were called to the murder scene, they found her dressed in slacks and an angora sweater. A detective commented that she was beautiful, even after the gunman had put two bullets into her. She was two days shy of her forty-fourth birthday. The D.C. police, always willing to cooperate with the government on potentially embarrassing matters, quickly arrested a local black man for killing Meyer.

A police officer had found the man, Raymond Crump, Jr., soaking wet, not far from the murder scene. Crump claimed that he had drunk some beer and fallen asleep and that he woke up only when he slid down the bank of the canal into the water. A jacket fished out of the canal after the shooting fit him. An eyewitness said the killer was black and was wearing that very windbreaker.

The next weekend, the Angletons, along with others of Mary's friends, began searching through her townhouse. They were frantically looking for a diary she had kept—really a sketchbook—which included details of her love affair with John Kennedy. Despite an exhaustive effort, they failed to find it.

A few days later, Antoinette Bradlee found the diary and many personal letters in a metal box in her sister's studio. It was hard to see how the earlier searchers could have missed it. Had it been removed and then replaced? James Angleton, who was close to Meyer's sons, was given the diary and letters for safekeeping.[2] He allowed some people to reclaim letters they had written to Meyer, but he told everyone that he had burned the diary. He had not. In July 1978, he said, "I kept it for her children. . . . You must understand that it was a personal, not a professional, responsibility."

Questions raced through Angleton's mind. Did the death of a woman in whom the late president might have confided have anything to do with the Soviet penetrations that Golitsyn had warned about? Had someone in

Kennedy's inner circle been compromised? Was Hoover's FBI, which kept track of such personal matters with astonishing competence, the Soviets' source? Had the Soviets penetrated the FBI as well as the CIA? Had other leaders besides Kennedy been targeted?

Golitsyn's first warnings when he defected were of a series of assassination plots by the KGB against Richard Nixon and various Western European political leaders. Golitsyn argued that the death of British Labour Party leader Hugh Gaitskell of a massive infection had come not from natural causes but from poison by a KGB assassin. The purpose of the Gaitskell assassination, said Golitsyn, was to install Harold Wilson as the new party leader. Golitsyn asserted that Wilson was under Soviet influence.

Fear that the Kennedy murder was the result of an international conspiracy faded in the minds of most Americans as President Johnson took control of the government. Angleton, however, believed there was a connection between Philby's presence in Moscow, the death of Mary Meyer, and the story that Nosenko was telling about Lee Harvey Oswald. "He believed it and would not let go of it," Ray Rocca, his longtime assistant, said in 1987. For Angleton, the nagging belief that Kennedy had been murdered by the KGB became an obsession. His mole hunt became very much a search for Kennedy's murderers. Said Angleton: "In counterintelligence you begin to rely on instinct because facts are so easy to manipulate."

On July 29, 1965, the case against Raymond Crump, Jr. for the murder of Mary Meyer went to the jury. After 11 hours deliberation, he was acquitted of murdering the president's former mistress. Who shot and killed Mary Meyer remains a mystery.[3]

CHAPTER THIRTY-SEVEN

THE SEARCH

FROM THE TIME of the Kronthal betrayal, the CIA continually faced challenges from the KGB. It was James Angleton's job to make certain the CIA was not penetrated, and by 1964 he was convinced that he had failed. He also believed the Soviet Union was using Yuri Nosenko to cover up its role in the murder of John Kennedy. It was this view that put Angleton up against the most powerful and enduring figure in American government: J. Edgar Hoover.

The Kennedy assassination was the darkest stain ever on the record of the FBI. Warning after warning about Lee Harvey Oswald had slipped through the FBI's fingers. They had failed to notify the Secret Service of Oswald's strange activities. They had ignored the dangers implicit in the letters Marina Oswald had sent to KGB officials. The Bureau's follow-up investigation was no better. Now it was under enormous pressure to solve the Kennedy assassination.

Yuri Nosenko, with his message about Oswald, was a godsend for J. Edgar Hoover. His arrival in the United States coincided with the convening of the Warren Commission, and the FBI was given access to him in order to further its investigation of the assassination. William Branigan, who ran FBI counterintelligence at the time, sent his two best men, Elbert ("Bert") Turner and James Wooten, to a Virginia safe house to question Nosenko,[1] who repeated to both men the story he had told

George Kisevalter and Pete Bagley in Geneva. The reports they submitted went up the FBI's chain of command to Hoover.

Nosenko's assurances that Yekaterina Furtseva herself had stopped the KGB from recruiting Oswald gave Hoover the evidence he needed to clear the Soviets of complicity in the Kennedy murder—and, even more from Hoover's point of view, clear the FBI of gross negligence. Hoover took this raw, unverified, and untested intelligence and leaked it to members of the Warren Commission and to President Johnson. Without checking with Angleton or with CIA Security Chief Howard Osborne, Hoover told President Johnson and Chief Justice Warren that the Soviets had not recruited Oswald. Hoover had the backing of former CIA Director Allen Dulles for this story. Dulles became Hoover's partner on the Commission in covering up the intelligence community's negligence prior to the Kennedy murder.

Warren Commission members accepted Nosenko's message without question and with great relief. William Corson, who participated in the investigation, said it was clear that Earl Warren was not pushing certain issues. According to Corson, the investigators wanted to put Marina Oswald through a serious interrogation, but when she came to give her testimony, the Chief Justice treated her in a protective, "almost fatherly fashion."[2]

Among senior government officials, only James Angleton continued to express the belief that the Kennedy assassination was not carried out by a lone gunman. Angleton was furious with Hoover for leaking the raw and unproven information from Nosenko. "Such inflammatory and untested information had an unfortunate impact on the Warren Commission members," Angleton said in a memo to Hoover and the Commission. Angleton wrote that Nosenko was no longer considered credible and that the CIA's Office of Security was taking over the case from the Soviet Division. It was at this point that Angleton asked Howard Osborne to cut off all FBI access to Nosenko. This was the first shot fired in the war between Angleton and Hoover—between the CIA and the FBI.

For Hoover, Angleton's action was a grave blow. Hoover wanted to demonstrate that the FBI had not failed, either through ignorance or through oversight, to take actions it could reasonably have been expected to take to forestall the assassination. Nosenko was his best hope. Without access to Nosenko, the Bureau could not make its case. All the top FBI and CIA people connected with these operations now acknowledge that relations between the two agenices were, as CIA/FBI liaison official Sam Pappich put it, "the worst they had ever been."

Angleton was not merely trying to undermine an old antagonist. His distrust for Nosenko was genuine and went deep. This distrust had initially sprung from Anatoly Golitsyn's warning to the "fools at the CIA" that frauds like Nosenko would be sent to discredit him. But other reasons had cropped up in the course of Nosenko's association with the CIA. The first of these, according to author David Martin, was a falsehood Nosenko told when he defected.[3] He told Pete Bagley and George Kisevalter that he held the rank of lieutenant colonel in the KGB. His proof was a tattered travel card he said was issued to him when he was on a KGB mission. Angleton showed the card to Golitsyn, who quickly identified it as a fraud. Nosenko then admitted he had lied about his rank and was never more than a major.

Angleton's problem was not with Nosenko's exaggeration of his rank. That was a common enough lie to inflate a defector's importance and thus, his bargaining power. What startled Angleton was that Hoover, who had so large a stake in Nosenko's credibility, claimed that SCOTCH, an important double agent at the United Nations, had confirmed the rank, which made it appear as if the entire Nosenko defection was a KGB creation. Angleton later uncovered SCOTCH (or FEDORA, as he was known to the FBI) as a KGB deception. These events gave Golitsyn even more credibility.

As Angleton continued to investigate, he found more evidence against Nosenko. The National Security Agency concluded that Nosenko had lied in saying he wanted to defect because he had gotten a recall message from Moscow. The NSA told Angleton that it had been monitoring Nosenko's communications, and no such message was ever intercepted. It was this last bit of evidence that Angleton used to convince Richard Helms and others in the CIA hierarchy that Nosenko should be incarcerated until his reliability could be determined.

At Camp Peary, the CIA's training base for new agents outside Williamsburg, Virginia, construction began on a tiny cement-block house for Nosenko. Under the supervision of the Office of Security and Pete Bagley from the SR Division, Nosenko was incarcerated under harsh conditions. He was not permitted outside at night because the CIA feared that, with his naval training, he would be able to look at the stars and figure out where he was. Nosenko, then 36, spent the next three years being sweated by experts from the Office of Security. Everything he said, every answer he gave, was picked apart.

For George Kisevalter and others in the Soviet Division, the treatment of Nosenko was shameful. "What he [Angleton] had done to Nosenko," said Kisevalter, "is a crime beyond anything that we, as Americans, would stand for . . . to torture a person for nothing." To Kisevalter, the irony of the United States using Soviet methods to force a confession that never came was something he could never forgive.[4] What Kisevalter and Angleton's other critics did not understand was that Angleton believed Nosenko was part of the Kennedy assassination conspiracy.

The tension between counterintelligence types and positive intelligence types has surfaced again and again in the course of this story. In the early 1960s, the tension escalated into guerrilla warfare. At the bottom of it was James Angleton's reliance on Anatoly Golitsyn.

The men of the Soviet Division were appalled by Golitsyn's influence over Angleton, and the defector's personal demeanor did nothing to win them over. As Kisevalter saw it, "He's a con man. . . . He thought, 'I could bullshit Americans.' And he did. And he decided, 'I'll use Angleton because he is the softest;' he's a con artist. And a con artist is always the biggest sucker for another con artist." Kisevalter was especially disgusted with Golitsyn's unending appetite for money. As Kisevalter put it, "He thought the streets in the United States were paved with gold . . . and that we were millionaires." Kisevalter offered the following story to support his charge: The Office of Security, which tended to be sloppy in its handling of defectors, took Golitsyn out for a haircut in Vienna, Virginia, where, to the horror of his CIA handlers, he ran into an old KGB colleague who had defected years before, Peter Deriabin. The Soviet Division eventually decided that since the two men now knew about each other anyway, why not officially bring them together and see what they said?

The CIA got a safe house "and they bugged the whole thing inside and out . . . ," Kisevalter recalled. "Golitsyn came with his wife and daughter and Deriabin came alone." To the CIA's dismay, the only thing the Golitsyns and Deriabin talked about was how much money they had gotten out of the CIA. The meeting ended with Deriabin screaming at Golitsyn's wife, Svetlana. Kisevalter remembered the laughter as the CIA officers listened to the tape. Soon enough, there would be very little that they found funny about Golitsyn.

Kisevalter started getting indications that Golitsyn was taking material that he picked up in his SR debriefings or from Angleton and reselling it as new information to the British, the Canadians, and the French. Kisevalter decided to test him. The test involved a Radio Moscow correspondent, Belitsky, a Soviet Jew recruited by the CIA in Brussels during the 1960 World's Fair. Belitsky, code named AE WIRELESS, had cut off contact with the CIA after the Cuban Missile Crisis. Nosenko told Kisevalter that Belitsky was really a KGB agent. He proved his knowledge of the case by describing, in detail, the gold watch and money that George Goldberg, Belitsky's CIA case officer, had given him during the operation.

When Golitsyn first defected in December 1961, he was asked about the bona fides of an agent fitting the description of AE WIRELESS, and he told his interrogators on tape that he knew nothing about the man. Now, in 1964, Golitsyn was in England, and Kisevalter asked the British to question him about Belitsky. This time Golitsyn had all the answers. "That son of a bitch began to regurgitate all the stuff we gave him on the case," Kisevalter said. But this incident "did not faze Angleton."

Kisevalter believed that Angleton had lost all judgment with regard to Golitsyn. Among other things, Golitsyn had led Angleton to worry about whether or not the Sino-Soviet split was real, an idea that the Soviet Division ridiculed. But much more important were the mole investigations, which in Kisevalter's view had become a witch hunt: "illegal wiretapping, illegal surveillance . . . all of this based on Golitsyn." Kisevalter faulted Richard Helms for allowing things to go too far: "Like General MacArthur, [Helms] was very loyal to his subordinates. If anything went wrong, he would take the blame. 'I didn't catch it, and I am the boss,' [he would say] . . . . Angleton had snookered him."[5]

Some on Angleton's own staff agreed. The only proven KGB penetration Golitsyn ever uncovered was George Pacques, a low-level NATO press official in Paris. If Golitsyn were a sent agent, giving up an agent like Pacques was a small price for the KGB to pay.

Angleton was no fool, however, and his trust in Golitsyn was not based on blind faith. Golitsyn had passed test after test. The British had shown him over two hundred real NATO classified documents and salted the file with 50 phony documents. Golitsyn picked out all the real documents and claimed he had seen every one of them in the hands of the KGB. It was a frightening and convincing performance. According to Angleton, Golitsyn was right more often than he was wrong, and "his answers made sense to me. . . . When he didn't know, he said he didn't know. That was very unusual for a defector."

And so, driven by Golitsyn's assertion that the KGB, as part of a "master plan," had penetrated all the NATO intelligence agencies, Angleton set off on a full-scale hunt for moles in the CIA. Whether or not Golitsyn was real, he could not have done more damage if he had been sent straight from KGB headquarters.

In the search for moles, Golitsyn started by asking to see security files on CIA case officers, on the grounds that something in the files might jog his prodigious memory. Angleton claimed he was very selective in giving Golitsyn access and that the individuals whose files Golitsyn saw were already too exposed for further operations. Even so, giving a defector such access was unheard of, and some on Angleton's staff protested.

This is how "the Golitsyn serials" began. Before the search was over, 14 CIA officers were accused of being Soviet agents. In the process, the CIA was torn apart.

Golitsyn's principal focus was on the Soviet Division, and particularly the super-secret SR-9 operation. The SR Division was a natural place to look for moles, since it would logically be the KGB's first target. The division had also been open in its distrust of Golitsyn from his first appearance.

For George Kisevalter and SR-9, what followed was Kafkaesque. Richard Kovich, Kisevalter's friend and able associate, became the subject of the first Golitsyn "serial." The case against Kovich began when Golitsyn, reviewing SR-9 personnel files, saw that Kovich's first name was actually Dushan (the Serbian equivalent of "Richard"). As Kisevalter tells it: "So this goddamn Golitsyn says, 'I think there was a Dushan who was a spy; that's his code name. He's a mole in American intelligence.' . . . With this bullshit, this guy [Kovich] was blackballed."

Another charge involved a supposed KGB agent in the CIA who had changed his Polish real name. Never good on specifics, Golitsyn finally settled on the name Klibanski. Klibanski turned out to be Peter Karlow, a son of German immigrants and a veteran of Berlin Base. In the fall of

1962, acting on Golitsyn's charges, the CIA's Office of Security set about destroying Karlow's professional life. Neither Angleton nor Karlow's immediate boss, Richard Helms, would call off the dogs. By 1963, Karlow was forced to resign. According to his friend George Kisevalter, since there was no real evidence against him, an expense money dispute was the reason given for his resignation. Years later, the CIA decided Karlow was innocent. They could not restore his lost career, but they did give him a medal and his long-denied pension.

At one point, Golitsyn went so far as to ask for the security file on George Kisevalter, but even Angleton would not allow that. No single man was more beloved in the CIA than "the Teddy Bear." "He wouldn't dare touch George," Paul Garbler said. "Helms would have never allowed it."[6] But while Angleton's reluctance to go after Kisevalter was instinctively correct, it again demonstrated a serious weakness in the entire counterintelligence mind-set of the CIA. Kisevalter was beyond investigation, whereas Kovich and Garbler, who did not share his popularity, could be professionally ruined. "It was similar to the decision at the start of the CIA not to polygraph certain members of the CIA's old boy network," said William Corson. "This attitude made any hope for respect for serious security in the CIA impossible."[7]

From Kisevalter's perspective, what was so insidious about the way Angleton, Helms, and Osborne conducted their mole hunt was that they never gave their victims a chance to defend themselves. They never even told the subject that he was undergoing a security investigation.

From Angleton's perspective, an officer who was under suspicion must not be warned. Like Kim Philby, "he could warn others, and they might escape."

CHAPTER THIRTY-EIGHT

CLOSING IN ON SASHA

———⟫●⟪———

W HILE THE "Golitsyn serials" were wreaking havoc in the Soviet Division, the real mole Golitsyn had fingered—SASHA—was still at large. In 1964, when Nosenko defected, he also claimed there was a KGB agent who had infiltrated U.S. intelligence in Germany. Just as Angleton was closing in on the identity of SASHA, however, Nosenko insisted the mole had penetrated not the CIA but the United States Army. That information delayed the investigation by precious months while Angleton kept pressing Golitsyn and Nosenko for more details.

Later that year, according to Angleton, Golitsyn suddenly and rather mysteriously remembered enough new details for Angleton to pinpoint SASHA as someone who had been an agent in Munich and Berlin in the early 1950s. Angleton finally narrowed his mole search down to one possibility: Igor Orlov. Orlov's recruitment alias had been "Alexander Kopatzky," and Sasha is the Russian diminutive of Alexander.

As Angleton studied the Orlov file, his faith in Golitsyn was reaffirmed, and he became convinced that Nosenko's Army theory was a deliberate effort to protect SASHA by pointing the investigation in the wrong direction. In Munich and Berlin, Orlov had known officers who now held important jobs in the intelligence community, especially in the CIA's Soviet Division. The investigation of Igor Orlov became the main thrust of the Golitsyn serials. Orlov himself, however, had fallen through the cracks. No

one at Langley knew where to find him, including his old case officer, Sam
Wilson, who back in 1956 had brought the Orlovs to America.

Igor and Eleonore Orlov first saw America on April 12, 1956, an unusually hot spring day. They were greeted by Pete Sivess, a big Ukrainian
ex-major-league pitcher, and his wife, Ellie, who were in charge of hosting
defectors and agents for the CIA. At the airport, a State Department official
carried the family's papers in a file sealed with wax and a red ribbon. With
the official's help, they bypassed U.S. Customs and Immigration. "We got in
a big black limousine. . . . Peter and Igor spoke Russian on the way to the
farm," Mrs. Orlov remembered. "I thought I was in Russia." Ashford Farm
was an old estate, not in the best repair, along the eastern shore of Maryland. Its isolation made it an ideal place both to debrief defectors and to
train agents. The mother tongue at Ashford Farm was Russian.

One of the Orlovs' first nights in America they spent in sheer terror.
The old mansion's alarm system started sounding in the middle of the
night, and emergency floodlights suddenly came on. The Orlovs thought
it was an attack, and they were going to be killed. In fact, a local sheep
farmer had walked onto the property trying to find a lost lamb. Ellie
Sivess greeted the terrified farmer as she had been instructed: "Walk no
farther—there is a minefield." The farmer, more frightened than the Orlovs, quickly retreated.

During the day, Igor learned CIA tradecraft—all the basics of being a
CIA case officer. He had come a long way since the night when he was
shot out of the sky by the German Army. As he patiently learned CIA
tradecraft, he was, in reality, a full colonel in the KGB.

The Orlovs' first son, Robert Alexander, had been born early in 1955,
and Eleonore was pregnant again when the family came to America. As
her August due date approached, the CIA moved the Orlovs into a safe
house at a fashionable Georgetown address, 3301 O Street, N.W. The
safe house had servants, including a maid, Emma Roland. It was also
completely bugged. The Orlovs were not permitted to have visitors or to
go out much. Mrs. Orlov's doctor was the same one who later delivered
Caroline Kennedy at Georgetown University Hospital. For security reasons, the CIA selected a French-speaking nurse who did not understand
English or German to assist in the delivery. Mrs. Orlov gave birth to a
blue-eyed son the couple named George. When the Orlovs returned to
Frankfurt in October, they carried one young American citizen with them.

In Frankfurt, the Orlovs had a government-supplied apartment and car and shopping privileges at the U.S. commissary. Despite their new life, little had really changed between them. If anything, Igor's violence and secrecy became more intense. In their Berlin days, he had relied on the three years of English that Eleonore had studied in her youth to produce his agent reports; now, although he still had not learned English, he would not let his wife type his reports—he typed them himself in Russian.

At Frankfurt Station, Igor worked with Nick Kozlov, one of the first Russian émigré officers recruited by Sam Wilson for American intelligence. Kozlov had spent some time in the United States, spoke reasonable English, and seemed to the Orlovs to get favored treatment from the CIA. Both Orlov and Kozlov worked for Lieutenant Colonel Sasha Sogolow.

Igor became more and more troubled by Nick Kozlov's activities; he told his wife that Kozlov lied about working overtime and was stealing expense money from his agents. Even though Eleonore begged Igor not to do it, he began sending reports of what he considered to be Kozlov's improper behavior back to CIA headquarters. But the letters never reached the CIA—Sogolow simply intercepted them and waited for an opportunity to rid the CIA of Igor Orlov.

The CIA gave Eleonore security clearance for a job in its mail-opening operation, which helped financially. However, Igor was constantly traveling to recruit agents, and with Eleonore no longer his secretary, the couple had even less in common than before. During one of Igor's trips, in February 1957, Eleonore decided to go see the film *Sayonara,* starring Marlon Brando. It was late in the evening when, "in a romantic mood," Eleonore returned home from the film by streetcar. A man sitting across from her asked why she was smiling. She told him that it was her first outing since she had stopped nursing her son. The man, who approached Eleonore much as Igor had on a Munich streetcar years before, talked about his own children. He turned out to be a former merchant seaman and the technical director of the Frankfurt Opera.

The man rode with Eleonore to her stop and kissed her hand as they parted. He said he hoped to see her again, but she said that since she was married, that would not be possible. That Sunday, however, they met again by chance in a nearby park where their children were playing. "This is destiny," she remembered him telling her. She later recalled, "I was kind of happy to have this little affair because it took my mind off all the other problems." It was a secret life away from politics and spying.

From then on, when Igor was out of town, Eleonore would meet her friend at the opera. He gave her opera tickets, and she used her PX card to bring him gin and cigarettes. Sometimes, if the weather was warm, they sat and talked in a dark corner of the park. She told him nothing about the clandestine life of which she was a part. They talked about "measles and problems with children. . . . We talked about the kind of things that a normal couple would talk about. . . . Igor could[n't] care less about children. . . . He could have died for them, but he would never touch them. He was very distant."

As he walked past her house on his way to his job at the opera, Eleonore's friend always whistled a melody from the opera being performed that evening. "I would know it was him, and so I tiptoed out to the balcony and blew him a kiss," she said.

In 1958, young George Orlov became ill with what doctors diagnosed as tuberculosis. He needed better medical care, and the Orlovs also needed to reenter the United States to keep their citizenship process current. For whatever reason, Sam Wilson had never told them that the director of Central Intelligence had the power to grant the family citizenship with the stroke of a pen. Yet all Wilson did was help them start normal immigration procedures.

In any case, the Orlovs left for Washington where they discovered George's illness was a simple infection. While they were gone, Eleonore's friend sent her a playful postcard to her Frankfurt home, saying he missed her at the opera, and he missed his gin from the PX. When the Orlovs returned to Frankfurt after three weeks in the States, a new maid Igor had hired gave the postcard to Igor. True to form, he never showed it to his wife. He simply took it and put it in a safe at the office that he shared with Kozlov. "He never told me he suspected anything," she said.

In the summer of 1959, Igor went to Vienna on a three-week mission to the International Youth Festival to meet several of his Soviet agents. He wore a full disguise, including lifts to increase his height, a mustache, and glasses to hide his piercing blue eyes.

When he returned to the office, he found that someone had gone through his part of the safe: Four pieces of mica he had placed in it to detect tampering were on the floor. Inside were the names of more than three dozen current agents he was operating, as well as details of a score of other operations, but the only item missing was Eleonore's postcard. Orlov asked Colonel Sogolow if he should file a report reflecting his opinion that Nick Kozlov had gone through his things. Sogolow, who frequently socialized with Kozlov, told him it would not be necessary.

In the fall of 1959, Sasha Sogolow went to the Orlovs' apartment during the day accompanied by military policemen. "Mrs. Orlov, you are in trouble for bartering American goods," Sogolow said. The military police took her to be polygraphed for dealing in the black market, but she refused to answer questions. She was fired from her job as translator, and over the next year she underwent a major security investigation, including several more polygraph examinations. In the end, Sogolow could only prove that Eleonore had twice given her friend bottles of gin and American cigarettes in thanks for the opera tickets. Eventually, the investigators concluded that her flirtation had no national security implications.

Igor, however, believed there was more to the arrest of his wife than concern over the black market. He was convinced that Nick Kozlov and Sasha Sogolow were attempting to destroy his career because he had accused Kozlov of committing fraud. Once the Office of Security cleared Eleonore of any serious wrongdoing, Igor demanded that Sogolow come home with him and personally tell Eleonore she could have her job back. Sogolow climbed the flights of stairs to the Orlovs' apartment and made the apology.[1] This episode did nothing to enhance Orlov's future in the CIA.

Orlov repeated his charges that Kozlov not only padded overtime reports but also cheated on expenses. When Sogolow asked for evidence, Orlov said that Kozlov, instead of giving his agents expensive Minox cameras, gave them much cheaper versions and pocketed the difference. Sogolow assured Orlov he would look into these matters and urged him not to file any more reports with headquarters. Orlov's dislike for Kozlov got back to Sam Wilson, who later said, "Orlov tried to blame and blacken Nikolay Kozlov. The two of them didn't get along very well at all."[2]

Why Orlov was so determined to get Nick Kozlov is an important question. Had his Soviet controllers asked him to destroy Kozlov's reputation with the CIA? Eleonore Orlov saw no indication that her husband was meeting with the Soviets since their Berlin days, when Werner Boch told her about seeing Igor with Soviet and East German generals on the train. But now, in 1959, Igor suggested something totally unprecedented: a winter vacation for the family.

Igor and Eleonore, with the boys in tow, motored from Frankfurt all the way to Grindelwald, Switzerland. Eleonore asked Igor why they had to travel so far for snow, but he insisted it be Switzerland. Then one day, Eleonore recalled, "Igor said there was a hole in the muffler of the car, and he had to take it to the mechanic and get it fixed. . . . He was gone for the full day. I knew he was lying. . . . He went to meet the Russians."

For Eleonore, who was already under a cloud with the CIA, her husband's activities were terrifying. If Igor was doing something wrong, her family's citizenship and their livelihoods were in jeopardy. In the summer of 1960, Igor again proposed a family vacation, this time to the Chiemsee, a mountain lake in eastern West Germany. He drove the family first to Munich for a visit with Eleonore's mother and then on to the isolated mountain retreat. "On the second day there," Eleonore recalled, "Igor said that he had to go back to Frankfurt; the CIA had called him back in an emergency. . . . I later learned the house we were staying [in] had no phone. . . . I knew in my heart he was meeting with the Russians again." A week later, he returned to take the family back to Frankfurt.

In November, Igor told his wife that Sasha Sogolow had called him into his office and said that he had good news: Igor was being promoted, this time to a job in the United States for the new Defense Intelligence Agency (DIA). Nick Kozlov urged Igor to take the new assignment. With first-class passage booked, they packed all their worldly possessions, and on January 15, 1961, the Orlovs stood at the rail of the SS *America* as it passed the Statue of Liberty in New York harbor. While the family watched the magnificent view, one of the ship's officers came searching for Igor. He handed him a cable, which Eleonore had to read because Igor's English was so poor. It said: FOR INAUGURATION NOT POSSIBLE TO COME TO WASHINGTON. STAY IN NEW YORK.

Totally confused because they had no idea what "inauguration" meant, the Orlovs took their car off the ship and drove in the snow to Washington, where they found that because of the Kennedy inauguration, the entire city was booked. They finally found a motel room at midnight in Manassas, some 30 miles away in what was then the Virginia countryside. This difficult journey was only the beginning of their nightmare.

On this trip to the United States, there was no welcoming party, no safe house with servants, no State Department official to clear away red tape. No one from the CIA even returned Igor's telephone calls. With a growing sense of panic, he called Sam Wilson, his former colleague and friend, to find out why the Defense Intelligence Agency seemed never to have heard of him. Wilson was surprised: "I was at Fort Bragg . . . with the U.S. Army Special Forces when he gets me on a long distance telephone call from Alexandria." Wilson told Orlov that he was no longer in a position to be of much help.

Eleonore Orlov called the only person she knew in America, Emma Roland, the maid who had worked for them in the Georgetown safe house during their 1956 trip. In turn, Mrs. Roland contacted the CIA. Over the next six months, the Orlovs' hopes of a new life were crushed. Igor's old colleague Nick Kozlov had gotten the DIA job that Igor thought he was getting. To make matters worse, the Orlovs still did not have their citizenship.

The CIA assisted them in getting the boys into a Lutheran school and offered them a few thousand dollars to help them resettle. When it was suggested that Igor use some of the money to take a Berlitz course in English, he angrily turned the money down.

Desperate, the diminutive Orlov took a job moving furniture. Then, during a family outing along the Potomac River, he ran into an Army enlisted man who suggested that he go to work at night as a driver for the *Washington Post* delivering newspapers. The job paid $60 a week. At the suggestion of their landlord in Alexandria, the Orlovs also opened a small picture-framing gallery. Igor worked nights delivering newspapers, and during the day he made picture frames. Eleonore contacted the CIA and asked for the resettlement money Igor had turned down. When she told Igor she had the money, he instructed her to return with the boys to Germany and find him a job there.

In November 1962, Eleonore Orlov left for Munich with her two boys. She was still not an American citizen. Complicating matters further, her secret life with Igor made it impossible for her to satisfy the German bureaucracy regarding the details of her personal history, and so she was unable to get a job. Igor sent her money every month; she did not know that he was selling their possessions to do so. Eleonore and the boys had to rely on friends and family for food and shelter. Finally, Igor wrote to Eleonore, begging her to return. However, he suggested that, before leaving Germany, she should try to get him a job at Radio Free Europe in Munich as a last resort, since it was a CIA front and Igor had worked there years before.

Had Eleonore Orlov understood the details of her husband's life, she would have known that the odd treatment she received when she went to Radio Free Europe was a hint of worse to come. By the time she contacted the broadcasting service in July 1963, the CIA had realized they had lost track of their old agent. They were looking for him everywhere. When Eleonore proposed her husband's name for a job, the personnel department at Radio Free Europe urged her to ask him to come in, in person, as soon as possible. She thought this was strange.

CHAPTER THIRTY-NINE

THE NET WIDENS

O NCE ANGLETON WAS CONVINCED that Igor Orlov was SASHA, he put together a team to explore the former agent's elusive history. The team included the FBI, because, by statute, the Bureau was responsible for all counterintelligence investigations inside the United States. J. Edgar Hoover even agreed to make his Washington field office and counterintelligence staff available for the mole investigation. Despite this seeming generosity, nothing had happened to restore relations between Hoover and Angleton, and Angleton did not set much store by the six FBI agents Hoover provided.

From the CIA, Angleton chose Bruce Solie, his main asset in the Office of Security, and Pete Bagley, the only man he seemed to trust in the Soviet Division. This small group trained all their investigative firepower looking into the backgrounds of both Igor and Eleonore Orlov. They also began examining the career of every CIA officer who had been in contact with the Orlovs.

Angleton began by looking at Orlov's activities at Berlin Base, particularly when he ran the 11 whores and the one-armed piano player at the Karlshorst Bar. He also looked at Orlov's two key case officers in Berlin, Sam Wilson and then Paul Garbler. To Angleton, Wilson's long history of kindness to the Orlovs might indicate a major problem.

Sam Wilson's CIA assignment in Berlin ended in 1954 when he rejoined the Army, where he became a top officer in the Green Berets at

Fort Bragg, North Carolina. Then, when President Kennedy took OPER-
ATION MONGOOSE away from the CIA and put it in the hands of
General Edward Lansdale at the Pentagon, Lansdale picked Wilson as his
top aide.

One day during the mole investigation in 1963, Francis M. Hand, the
CIA's liaison to the Secretary of Defense's office, called Wilson in and told
him Angleton wanted to talk to him. That day was, as Wilson later put it,
"a very painful part of my educational upbringing."

In Wilson's account, "Hand . . . said, 'I gave his [Angleton's] secretary
your telephone number, and you may be hearing from him today or tomorrow.' The phone rings shortly thereafter. Angleton says, 'I am sending
a guy with a file. Take time to look at it. You'll find it very interesting.'
The guy comes all the way from Langley down to the Pentagon, up to the
suite of McNamara and Gilpatrick, and threw whoever was in my office
out and sat down and spent two hours going through the file. . . . Made
me very sad 'cause I could see where things had gone wrong. . . . My hair
was kind of going up like this [standing straight up], seeing this guy
[Orlov] was a rat fink all the time."

After reading the file, Wilson said he concluded that Orlov's defense
would be "he was still anti-Soviet and was doing this [spying for the Sovi-
ets] because he was determined to fight against the Soviets and the only way
he could do it was by pretending to work for them." Wilson said he was relieved that Angleton, whom he now considered a friend, had warned him
about Orlov. Wilson recalls thinking, "Boy, that was a close one. Wilson,
you know, you nearly got hit by a truck. But that was Orlov. . . ." However,
there are nagging questions about Wilson's recollections—especially the fact
that, by his account, he was informed that Igor Orlov was a Soviet agent a
year or more before Angleton finished his investigation. Since Wilson was
one of the first to work with Igor Orlov, it would be very surprising if
Angleton informed him of his probe before it was completed.

The other prime candidate for the mole was Paul Garbler, Orlov's case
officer for two years. When the Office of Security began its investigation,
Angleton remembered Garbler's insistence that George Blake's defection
should not prevent him from being posted to the Soviet Union. The Office
of Security, meanwhile, had learned that Garbler knew Blake in Korea,
something Garbler did not mention before his posting to Moscow. As the
first CIA station chief there, Garbler was in charge during the Penkovsky

debacle, the Cuban Missile Crisis, and the Kennedy assassination. Hence, Angleton concluded, Paul Garbler had to be a serious mole suspect.

In the spring of 1964, Garbler, then still the Moscow station chief, met with his boss, David Murphy, in Europe. "Murphy asked me what I wanted to do when I ended my tour in Moscow. I told him I wanted to go to the Army War College. Dave said, 'You can't go there. You are a spy, not a soldier.' He then said, 'How about coming back to Washington as my deputy?'"[1] The two men shook hands on the new job. Garbler was returning from Moscow with high hopes.

Before leaving Europe, he and his wife, Florence, went on a skiing trip to Zurs, Austria. Garbler took a nasty fall while skiing and suffered a severe head injury. He was recuperating at a clinic in Innsbruck when CIA security became alarmed and moved him to an Air Force hospital in West Germany. He was then transferred to Bethesda Naval Hospital for another three weeks of treatment.

Finally, in July, he returned to CIA headquarters. The man he was supposed to replace as Murphy's deputy had not yet received his new overseas assignment, so Garbler was named chief of operations for the Soviet Russia Division. "When I first came home, I was in pretty bad shape," Garbler said. "I had lost a lot of weight, and I don't think my head was working as good as it should have."[2] At his first Division staff meeting, when he began to tell his colleagues how great it was to be back among friends after the skiing accident and a lonely assignment in Moscow, Murphy interrupted him and said curtly, "Let's have none of that. Have you got anything else to say?"

Surprised at Murphy's tone, Garbler then gave a standard debriefing. He also went through a polygraph examination, in which he was asked if he had had any sexual encounters or was under the control of the KGB. He had no idea this polygraph test was any more significant than the dozen he had taken before. He thought it was just more Office of Security flutter. He passed, just as he had when he returned from all his other overseas assignments. He did not know that he had returned to headquarters in the heat of the battle over Nosenko and Golitsyn and in the middle of the search for the mole.

Although Garbler was well aware that Joe Bulick's SR-9 team had kept things from him in Moscow, neither he nor his colleague Richard Kovich had a hint that they were both now being investigated by Angleton. "I was totally isolated from all of that stuff when I was in Moscow," he recalled. "Nobody ever told me anything. Nobody even told me what they should have been telling me about what was going on with Penkovsky."

In his ignorance, Garbler was very pleased with his new Operations job. He enjoyed sitting at a desk reviewing cables and giving various bases operational instructions. About three weeks into the job, a cable that seemed unusual came across his desk late one night. Garbler felt that the cable disclosed too much classified information. "Fortunately, the fellow who drafted the cable was still here. . . . I called him on it, and he said that Dave [Murphy] wanted it to go out that way. He warned me not to make waves."

The next morning, Garbler, a direct man always leery of Murphy's actions, walked into the SR Division chief's office and raised his objections to the previous evening's cable. Murphy was very cool and said, "Maybe you don't belong on this team."

Garbler, astonished, looked at his old Berlin Base colleague and said, "From the way this place is being run, that's probably a good idea."

Garbler also worried that Murphy had put Pete Bagley in charge of counterintelligence for the Soviet Division. He had no way of knowing that Bagley was working with Angleton on the mole hunt. Garbler worked it out long afterward and said, "Bagley is directly in line for upward mobility in the SR Division with me and Kovich out of the way. Here comes this guy [Garbler] out of Moscow, and he's going to be the deputy chief of the Division. Don't you think that when Golitsyn puts his finger on Kovich and Garbler, that this was a God-given opportunity for the most ruthlessly ambitious guy I have ever met in my life?"

Until that moment, Garbler had never considered Bagley serious job competition. "See, CI in the Soviet Division was nothing," Garbler explained. "We were all focused on positive intelligence and recruiting Soviets. Recruiting a Soviet was the ultimate objective of the whole SR Division." But Garbler had a feeling that Murphy and Bagley were somehow conspiring against him. Then, "to Dave's credit, he found me a good job, not as good as I had, but a good one." By the fall of 1964, Garbler was working at his new job as chief of operations in the new Western European Division.

Garbler enjoyed this job and seemed back on a strong career track at CIA headquarters. That is, until Bagley and Angleton came into his life again. He was called into the office of Thomas Karamesines, one of

Richard Helms's deputies, and was told he had a new assignment: to share his extensive Moscow experience with officers in training at Camp Peary. Garbler was dumbfounded. "He told me that Charlie Kaitak, an old friend, was about to leave Camp Peary. Hell, I had just had lunch with Charlie the week before. He and his wife were set for another year down there." Garbler later learned that his transfer to the training base was at Angleton's request, though this does not make much sense. If Garbler were the mole, as Angleton suspected, why did Angleton put him in a job where he knew every new recruit in Clandestine Services? Nonetheless, that's where Garbler went. "I really had very little to occupy me [at Camp Peary]," he recalled. "I taught a couple of classes in operational procedures. I participated in every one of the exercises."

Garbler, one of the few officers who had been face-to-face with the Soviets on their own turf, thus became a casualty of Angleton's mole hunt. At Camp Peary, he still did not know he was considered a security risk. No one confronted him or gave him a chance to face his accusers. He was merely pushed out of the way.

MEANWHILE, THE OTHER HALF of Angleton's SASHA team, the FBI, followed the Orlovs for months. Working under the direction of Joe Purvis, the Bureau's Washington field office tracked the family to the picture framing shop in Old Town, Alexandria. FBI agents, posing as customers of Gallery Orlov, found nothing in Igor's behavior to indicate he was a Soviet spy. Nonetheless, in April 1965, at Angleton's insistence, the FBI raided the Orlovs' house and shop. The Orlovs' nightmare was about to deepen.

At the time of the raid, Igor was told to report to the FBI's Washington field office every day for questioning. At no point did he hire a lawyer or attempt to get outside help, according to the agents who questioned him. Their approach to Orlov was not gentle. Agents slowly doled out to him the details the mole investigation had uncovered and asked him if he had attempted to recruit Garbler, Wilson, Murphy, and others from Berlin Base. He denied every charge. He claimed that when he parachuted into Germany he had no intention of working for the Soviets again.

At one point, the FBI agents thought he was going to confess that he had been blackmailed into working for the Soviets when a fellow NKVD penetration agent discovered his real identity in Munich after the war. But

Orlov would not confirm this. He was questioned about the disappearance of Vladimir Kivi, the Estonian NTS officer who had vanished from Berlin. By now, the CIA had learned that Kivi had ended up in the gulag. Orlov denied knowing anything about it.

When Eleonore Orlov refused to take a polygraph examination, the FBI warned Igor that if she continued to refuse, they would have no choice but to arrest him for espionage. It was all a bluff. The FBI had no real evidence. To make matters worse, the CIA never turned over to the Bureau the results of Mrs. Orlov's polygraph tests in Frankfurt in 1959. When Igor called the agents' bluff, they decided not to bring Eleonore in for questioning, a major misjudgment. If they had, they might have figured out that Igor Orlov was no ordinary suspect.

The agents did hit Orlov with one piece of information that startled him: His mother was alive and well and living in Moscow. He had not seen her since 1944 and did not know she was still alive.

The next afternoon, May 10, 1965, Orlov left FBI headquarters as usual and went to his night job delivering papers for the *Washington Post,* whose building happens to be located across an alley from the rear of the Soviet Embassy. While Orlov was loading his truck, he saw a Russian official directing trash removal through a back door. He dashed from the newspaper's loading dock and told the man in Russian that he needed help. The man invited him in and led him to a small reception room with a large mirror on the wall, through which, it later turned out, he was photographed.

The FBI missed it all. The Bureau normally shot still and motion pictures of everyone going in and out of the Soviet Embassy. However, they had no camera at the back door, and the FBI man watching the front door was suffering from the flu that evening and had to leave his post periodically to go to the bathroom. An automatic camera got a picture of Orlov leaving the embassy, but it was misfiled. This combination of mishaps cost the FBI an important piece of evidence.

When they finally did realize he had been at the embassy, Orlov told them he had gone there to tell the Soviets he feared his mother might be harmed because of his problems with U.S. intelligence. He said he told the Soviets that his father was a hero of the Great Patriotic War, as he was himself, and implored them to watch out for his mother. None of this was truc. According to Angleton, that evening Orlov "gave them very important information about contact codes for a group of Soviet illegals he was servicing."

Nor is that all that Igor Orlov accomplished that night. According to Eleonore, he fully expected to be arrested for espionage, and since he had been operating under a false identity in their interests for 23 years, he believed that the USSR should help his family if he were arrested. The Soviets readily agreed. He had no idea that it was the Soviets who had caused all of his current problems through Golitsyn and Nosenko.

Right after Orlov left the embassy, the KGB resident there sent a cable to headquarters in Moscow and received his instructions the next day. He picked up the phone, called the Department of State, and told the Soviet desk officer that a man named Igor Orlov had come to the embassy asking about help for his ill mother in Moscow. The State Department routinely notified the FBI, which then attempted to locate a picture of Orlov entering or leaving the embassy. Having misfiled the photo, they could not confront him.

The night before what Igor thought was his last interrogation before being arrested, he told his wife he would not see her again. "'They will arrest me,'" she remembered him saying. "He said he had made all the arrangements. He said to me, 'Leave everything here. Take nothing with you. Leave your car at the boys' schoolyard. Take a taxi to the shopping center in Alexandria. At 2 P.M. this afternoon, there will be a black limousine. The Russians will take care of you. They'll know what to do.'"[3]

Eleonore did not want any part of it. She argued with her husband. "I told him we do not speak Russian." Igor replied, "If they arrest me, how will you manage? How will you eat?" The next day, Eleonore dropped Igor off at the old Post Office building in downtown Washington. Instead of following his instructions, she went to her Lutheran pastor to seek his advice. She even asked friends to raise the boys if she had to escape with Igor. In the end, she made the decision not to go to the shopping center to meet the Russians.

The FBI interrogated Igor harshly about his visit to the embassy. He replied that he feared for his mother. What the FBI agents should have been asking themselves is why the Russians had called the State Department to let them know about Orlov's visit. Even Angleton had no idea the

Soviets were giving up Igor Orlov to support the credibility of Golitsyn and Nosenko. They were willing to sacrifice Orlov for the next and most important penetration operation of all.

After hours of merciless questioning, agent Courtland ("Court") Jones and the others saw they could not get enough evidence to arrest Orlov. What finally clinched his freedom was a phone call from the Soviet Embassy asking the State Department if the United States had sent Orlov there as a provocation. The FBI politely thanked Igor Orlov and told him the investigation was over. He was free to go back to his normal life.

While Eleonore was greatly relieved when Igor returned home that sunny spring afternoon, he was angry with her. "You should have gone. You have loused up our life. . . ," Igor said. She responded, "I am sick of it all. I would rather jump from a bridge with my children, but since I am not so crazy, I just didn't go. By the way, I have a cat giving birth to four kittens. You don't leave a kitten in the house just born." Igor said it did not matter for now. The FBI had told him he had been cleared.

Even so, Igor Orlov became so embittered and frightened that, according to his wife and son, he stopped leaving the house. He never could bring himself to trust Eleonore, and now his violent jealousy surfaced in strange ways. He refused to drink the coffee she made, telling her she might poison him. He did not trust her marital fidelity and once held a gun to her head trying to get her to confess to an imagined affair with a young picture framer he had hired.

Meanwhile, although the FBI cleared Orlov of being a Soviet agent, James Angleton did not. As soon as the FBI informed him they could not arrest Orlov, Angleton listed Orlov as a penetration agent and continued going after almost everyone who had been associated with him.

Even though the Bureau considered the Orlov case closed, they continued surveillance of the little man because of Angleton, who was too powerful to buck. As a way of making amends to Orlov for what they considered an injustice, FBI agents Court Jones, Joseph Purvis, and others routinely had their pictures framed at Orlov's gallery. By the mid-1960s, much of Orlov's business came from FBI agents.

There was one incident in this period that troubled Eleonore Orlov deeply. Many of the Austrian and German prints and paintings the gallery sold came from her contacts in Germany. Although the Orlovs had very little money, Eleonore was able to arrange credit with a number of artists in Bavaria, one of whom was Hans Proquitter, a Munich painter famous for his mountain scenes. He let the Orlovs pay him a small amount of money over a long period.

One afternoon, before the first shipment was unpacked, a man walked into Gallery Orlov. "He had a trace of an East German accent, but he was an ordinary, middle-aged man," Mrs. Orlov recalled. The man surprised her by asking for "any Hans Proquitters you may have." Eleonore wondered about his request, because they had not advertised the works, and there was no way for the man to know about the shipment. "Igor then came in and quickly said to the man, 'Let me show you where we do the framing.' They disappeared into the little framing shop through the garden."

An hour later, the two men came out. The German took a Proquitter away with him. Eleonore asked her husband if the man had paid the hundred dollars for the small painting. Although money was very tight for the Orlovs, Igor said, "He'll send us the money." He never did. And Igor never complained about it. "It was very strange," said Mrs. Orlov.

Gallery Orlov also attracted an amazingly well-connected group of CIA and State Department clients. Averell Harriman was a frequent customer. Eleonore recalled that Harriman "loved our work. . . . He would even send packages over to the gallery that included shoes and clothing for Igor." The only problem: Harriman was tall. Nothing in his "care packages" fit the diminutive Igor.

Angleton was already suspicious of Harriman for other reasons. Although his investigation of Harriman, code named DINOSAUR, never yielded enough proof to go after the former governor and power broker, Angleton believed that Igor Orlov was Harriman's back channel to the KGB.

By the mid-1960s, Angleton's mole hunt had frozen CIA operations against the Soviets everywhere. As William Colby, then head of the Far East Division, put it, "Everything stood still. We had become an intelligence service that wasn't collecting any intelligence."[4] Years later, when Colby became director of the Agency, he used this as one of his reasons for firing Angleton. However, as the record from Berlin onward shows, the CIA had almost no effective human operations against the Soviets.

Their real successes relied on technology. The Soviet Division had no real agents, and Angleton's probe had no real effect on America's intelligence capabilities. Former Berlin Base officer John Sherwood put it best: "You have to have operations against the Soviets for Angleton to stop. What his investigation did was stop *attempts* at operations."[5]

CHAPTER FORTY

THE PERFECT OPERATION

W HEN JOHN MCCONE stepped down as DCI in 1965, President
Johnson appointed Admiral William Raborn to succeed him. A
few months later, Johnson decided to replace Raborn with Richard
Helms. Helms had built a career on his political and social skills. One of
his priorities as director was to walk a tightrope between not agitating
Angleton and keeping him from shutting the CIA down.

Angleton's power at this time was enormous. His strength came
partly from Helms's confidence in him and partly from the connections to
Mossad that Kim Philby had urged him to make so many years before. In
effect, Angleton was operating his own intelligence service through the Israelis, and often, the intelligence Angleton gathered through these sources
was taken more seriously than the CIA's own field reports. Yet time was
running out for Angleton. Brezhnev and his fellow conspirators were
pushing him hard, and Angleton was in danger of becoming the boy who
cried wolf once too often.

The first of "the Golitsyn serials" was the investigation of Richard
Kovich. However, Angleton did not have enough evidence to prove Golitsyn's allegation against Kovich until a bizarre series of events from the
early 1960s came to his attention.

In 1962, Richard Kovich was one of two CIA agents dispatched to
Pakistan to meet KGB Major Igor Kozlov. Their assignment happened to
coincide with Yuri Nosenko's first contacts with Pete Bagley in Geneva.

Kovich had no way of knowing that this routine assignment would come back to destroy his career.

Major Kozlov began by telling U.S. intelligence he disliked Khrushchev's methods. This was the same message expressed by Colonel Penkovsky two years earlier. What made Kozlov an especially attractive potential recruit was that his father, Frol R. Kozlov, was a Khrushchev intimate.

Kozlov's pragmatic pitch was also appealing: He would provide information on KGB personalities in exchange for details on the activities of Soviet defectors in America. The quid pro quo was simple: The CIA would get information it needed, and he would get promotions within the KGB.

As promising as Kozlov was, the recruitment never took place. Even though Kozlov was visible to observers in subsequent years, he never recontacted the CIA. Neither Richard Kovich nor anyone else in the CIA understood that his 1962 approach was merely another move in Brezhnev's plan to get rid of Khrushchev. Kozlov himself never knew why he was ordered to make contact with the CIA. To him, the visit to Pakistan was just another incomplete mission in his career. To Kovich and Kisevalter, Igor Kozlov was simply one of many cases SR-9 was trying to develop after the loss of Penkovsky.

In the late 1950s and early 1960s, the great Soviet technological edge in space began to disappear. The combination of *Sputnik,* massive Soviet nuclear tests, and the Cuban Missile Crisis had awakened America from a slumber induced by the presumption of scientific superiority. In 1964, Brezhnev found that his successful removal of Khrushchev came with a large price tag: Having won the support of the KGB and the military, Brezhnev now had to reestablish Soviet dominance.

According to Angleton, by mid-1966 the Soviet military was demanding a concerted effort by Moscow to provide the technical and scientific information it needed to modernize its forces. As Angleton later put it, "The Soviets had neither the money nor the technology to arm the motherland to a standard competitive with the United States." Their best hope was not to spend large sums on research and development, but to use their intelligence services to steal Western technology.[1] Brezhnev ordered the KGB and GRU to start stealing on a massive scale.

All this was taking place against a backdrop of further changes in the Kremlin. After taking control of the government, Brezhnev immediately began to shed former Khrushchev supporters who had participated in his plot. The KGB director who betrayed Khrushchev, Vladimir Semichastny, was on his way out, and Yuri Andropov, who had been proving his effectiveness in Vietnam, was ready to collect his long-awaited reward and assume control of the KGB.

Yekaterina Furtseva was anxious for her daughter and her two-year-old granddaughter to prosper during the coming changes. She knew she had to help her son-in-law, KGB Major Igor Kozlov, whose career had stalled after his powerful father's death in January 1965. As a major in the Inspectorate Division of the First Directorate (Foreign Intelligence Operations), Igor Kozlov had hardly made an impression on the KGB power structure. His hope of being sent to Washington as a top KGB officer was dashed when a colleague, Oleg Sokolov, got the assignment instead. Kozlov's mind was razor sharp, but he had little of his father's political flair. He had relied on his father's connections to make his way in the KGB. Although the younger Kozlov's contacts with the CIA in 1962 were carefully orchestrated, they did little to burnish his chances of rising above the rank of major.[2]

Madame Furtseva saw her chance. She knew Brezhnev was growing worried about public doubts in America about the Warren Commission's conclusion that Lee Harvey Oswald had acted alone. Brezhnev, mindful of the American press, thought it was only a matter of time before the KGB's and the DGI's role in the murder would emerge. As Angleton put it, "When Yuri Nosenko was discredited inside the CIA, Brezhnev knew that something had to be done. Since Nosenko's bona fides were unacceptable to the CIA, the KGB needed to send another messenger who could assure the Americans that Russia played no role in Kennedy's assassination."

In March 1966, Igor Kozlov's career was put back on track when his powerful mother-in-law arranged a very important temporary-duty assignment to Washington. His job was to make contact with the CIA again and convince it that the KGB had nothing to do with the Kennedy assassination.

Nosenko had won his way into the United States by telling the CIA and FBI that he had personal knowledge that Furtseva had ordered the KGB to have no contact with Lee Harvey Oswald. He lost credibility because he was caught lying about smaller matters. Now Furtseva's son-in-law was in a position to keep Brezhnev in the family's debt for years. Since Igor Kozlov had already made contact with the Americans and given them reason to believe he could be recruited, he was tailor-made for this brief but vital assignment.

As the Soviet "journalist" Victor Louis (who in fact worked for both Israeli and U.S. intelligence) later described the scene, Yekaterina Furtseva invited Igor Kozlov for a walk along the snow-covered road that led to her government-provided dacha outside Moscow.[3] She explained to her son-in-law the importance of his mission to Washington. She told him that not only Yuri Nosenko, but entire departments of the KGB had been purposely led to believe she had prevented Semichastny from recruiting Lee Harvey Oswald, but that Angleton and others in the CIA had not believed Nosenko. Unless the Americans could be convinced there was no high-level Soviet involvement in the Kennedy assassination, Brezhnev feared war with the United States.[4] She needed someone to step forward who the CIA would believe was in a position to know the truth about Oswald. Only then could Angleton's investigation be stopped before it implicated the Soviet leadership.

The details of Igor Kozlov's mission were complicated and brilliant. First, Kozlov would confirm to the CIA Golitsyn's charges that Igor Orlov, the picture framer, was in fact the infamous SASHA. This information would give him credibility with Angleton and the others who sided with Golitsyn. Kozlov would also carry the same message Golitsyn's rival, Nosenko, had brought: Oswald had not been recruited by the KGB. This time, however, the KGB would let the CIA know through other channels that Kozlov was related by marriage to the person who had supposedly blocked the recruitment of Oswald. As Angleton later pieced the story together, if the KGB could deliver this information through one of his regular, trusted sources, "they would rightly believe that I would accept Kozlov. They did it brilliantly." Angleton added, "There was no immediate reason not to trust Kozlov."

The second phase of the Kozlov mission was designed to solve Brezhnev's other problem: providing the Soviet military with the technology it needed to compete with the West. This phase of the operation involved the recruitment of Commander Nikolai Artamonov, the Soviet naval officer who had defected to the United States in 1959. Artamonov had been living in Virginia under the name Nick Shadrin and working in a small Defense Intelligence Agency translation unit (the same one that Igor Orlov thought he was going to work for in 1961). In this second phase,

Kozlov was to demand that the CIA give him Shadrin as payment for the Oswald and SASHA information.

The public story of Nikolai Artamonov—that he had been found guilty, in absentia, of "traitorous acts" against the motherland and sentenced to death by firing squad—had nothing to do with reality. Artamonov—the son-in-law of Admiral Sergei G. Gorshkov, the father of the Soviet Navy—was no traitor. He had been working as a spy for the Soviet Navy all along. As Nick Shadrin, he was "an agent of influence" in the United States.

To Igor Kozlov, this was a stunning revelation. Kozlov understood that if he could "recruit" Shadrin, he would surpass all his rivals in the KGB—which was precisely his mother-in-law's objective.

Much had to be done to prepare Kozlov for the mission. He was to get a briefing from a very special man before he left for Washington. The briefer had extensive experience working in Washington and with Angleton and would serve as his case officer.

BY APRIL 1966, Court Jones, the head of counterintelligence in the FBI's Washington field office, was under pressure from J. Edgar Hoover to close down the investigation of Igor Orlov.[5] Jones and his immediate boss, William Branigan, agreed that the surveillance of Orlov was a waste of valuable manpower. As Branigan put it, "Even if Igor Orlov had been SASHA, what harm could the man do now? He was driving a truck and making picture frames." Jones and Branigan both believed in Orlov's cover, and they were very wrong.

Over at the CIA, meanwhile, Angleton had finally convinced Richard Helms that Berlin Base veteran David E. Murphy might be a Soviet agent. Murphy had stood aside and let Paul Garbler be ruined by allegations he never got a chance to deny. Now, with the help of the ambitious Pete Bagley, David Murphy, the head of the powerful Soviet Division, faced the same fate.

Murphy had run Igor Orlov in Munich and Berlin, but those connections had only prompted the investigation. It was Murphy's history in Korea and Japan, especially his suspicious role in clearing the bona fides of Andy Yankovsky's family and his involvement with Ed Snow, that convinced Angleton Murphy could not be trusted.

Unlike Paul Garbler and Richard Kovich, however, Murphy could not be shunted aside to some out-of-the-way job and ignored. He was in a position to fight back. He had risen far since he was Sasha Sogolow's jeep driver in Japan and had detailed knowledge of the less than pristine behavior of many in the top echelons of the CIA, including former Director Allen Dulles. Besides, to hide Murphy away would tip the Soviets that the CIA suspected him of being a mole.

Instead, Murphy was allowed to finish his three-year tour as head of the Soviet Division and was then given an overseas assignment as chief of station in Paris. However, Murphy's hopes of being effective in Paris were crushed when, without warning, Angleton told his counterpart in the French Security Service that Murphy was under investigation as a possible Soviet agent.[6] Angleton defended the decision to tell the French, saying, "It was my responsibility to let the French know. He may have been incidental, but we were penetrated, and he ran the penetration agent. My job was to protect the CIA. Fairness didn't enter into it."

Pete Bagley, who had led the investigations into Garbler, Kovich, and now Murphy, harbored dreams of replacing Murphy as head of the Soviet Division. But Helms, increasingly burdened with Vietnam, wanted no one with that much ambition running a major division. Instead, Helms installed Rolfe Kingsley, a man who could never be accused of rocking the bureaucratic boat.[7]

By mid-1966 the Soviet Division of the CIA was at a standstill. Angleton and the Office of Security had stopped all Soviet recruitment. The most aggressive case officers were shuffling papers or undergoing security investigations. Angleton continued to badger Hoover and the FBI over their acceptance of Nosenko. As William Branigan put it, "It got to the point where anyone who accepted Nosenko's view of Oswald, or who believed Nosenko, was suspect."[8] That is exactly how Igor Kozlov's new case officer, Kim Philby, thought Angleton would react.

CHAPTER FORTY-ONE

THE SON-IN-LAW

———⟶●⟵———

IN EARLY JUNE 1966, the telephone rang at Richard Helms's home in Georgetown. Helms's estranged wife told the caller, who did not identify himself, that Mr. Helms was no longer at that number. When the caller finally tracked Helms down, he said he was KGB Major Igor Kozlov, and he wanted to work for American intelligence. He explained that several years earlier he had talked with two CIA officials in Pakistan, both of whom he named by their code names. They were Gus Hathaway and Richard Kovich. He advised Helms that he would call back in two hours. After that, he would be out of touch.[1]

Helms called James Angleton at his home in Arlington. Angleton told Helms that under no circumstances should the Soviet Division be brought into the case, because of the possible mole there. Instead, Angleton suggested that Bruce Solie, from the Office of Security, work with the FBI on the case. Angleton contacted Solie, and when Kozlov called Helms back, Helms arranged a meeting between Kozlov and Solie for that afternoon.

Bruce Solie was the picture of an ordinary man. He worked strictly "by the book" and was well aware that the CIA could not legally "run" Igor Kozlov while he was in the United States. Solie, who got along well with the Bureau, immediately called Bill Branigan, the head of Soviet counterintelligence at the FBI, and told him about the upcoming meeting.

Branigan, who looked like the 1940s actor William Bendix, did not need another Soviet case. J. Edgar Hoover's preoccupation with Soviet penetration had now shifted to subversion from within by anti-Vietnam War protesters, student radicals, and black activists. As a result, Branigan was left with just a few agents to work against the Soviet and Eastern Bloc "diplomats" and "commercial representatives" in the United States who were, in reality, Communist agents. At the time of Solie's phone call, Branigan had only about 20 agents to cover the hundreds of Soviet Bloc agents operating in Washington.

One of Branigan's men, Courtland Jones, was packing his bags for a vacation in North Carolina when Branigan called him. Jones and his family were preparing to drive to their summer retreat at Kitty Hawk, along the Outer Banks. Branigan told Jones about Igor Kozlov and asked him to suggest a code name for their new Soviet contact.[2] Jones suggested KITTY HAWK.[3] The two FBI men decided that Bruce Solie should go alone to the first meeting.

Court Jones called Bert Turner, his most experienced CI agent, and assigned him to work with Solie; Turner eventually became one of KITTY HAWK's case officers in the United States.[4] For the KGB, Bert Turner was an unexpected bonus. His career had taken a downturn following the bureaucratic errors the FBI made in investigating Lee Harvey Oswald before the assassination. Having been bounced from the top ranks at headquarters to the Washington field office, he, as much as anyone in the FBI, wanted to prove the Soviets had nothing to do with the Kennedy assassination. In Bert Turner, KITTY HAWK gained a receptive audience.

At their first meeting, Igor Kozlov impressed Bruce Solie with his command of English. Solie found him to be a cut above the typical KGB agent in manners and refinement. "He was a very intelligent individual," Solie later said.[5]

Kozlov explained that he was on a temporary embassy inspection mission that would last 65 to 70 days. He said that normally he was assigned to "KR" (Kontra Razvyedka)—KGB counterintelligence. He offered to work for the CIA inside the KGB in exchange for material that could "get me the promotions I want."[6] With the CIA's help, he said, he would have no trouble climbing to the top ranks of counterintelligence in the KGB, which in turn would place him in a better position to assist the CIA. Like Nosenko when he first approached the West, Kozlov said he had no desire to defect to the United States.

Then KITTY HAWK got to the heart of what he wanted. His main assignment while he was in Washington that summer, he said, was to recruit a former Soviet Naval officer who had defected seven years earlier, Captain Nikolai Fyodorovich Artamonov, a.k.a. Nick Shadrin. Kozlov asked the CIA to assist him in recruiting Shadrin.[7]

Solie asked Kozlov why the CIA should help him in this recruitment. Kozlov replied that if the CIA gave him Shadrin, he would assist the CIA in its mole investigations. Because he was responsible for finding ways to penetrate the CIA, he said, he knew the identities of all the moles. Solie, who by now had spent several years on the mole investigation, tried to get Kozlov to offer some details, but Kozlov refused to say anything more until he got an agreement from the CIA. He added that he would feel more comfortable dealing with his earlier CIA contacts and again identified Berlin Base veterans Richard Kovich and Gus Hathaway by the cover names they had given him in Pakistan in 1962. At no time, now or later, did Kozlov mention his family connections back in the Soviet Union in order to to prove himself.

Before leaving their meeting place, Kozlov and Solie made arrangements for another contact within a few days. When Solie returned to his office at CIA headquarters, he wrote down in longhand on a yellow legal pad his notes of the meeting. He made a list of everything Kozlov had said that gave him cause for concern. Then he called Angleton and Branigan and briefed them.

Angleton was apprehensive about KITTY HAWK from the start. Here was an agent who had come in with previous contacts with two CIA case officers, one of whom was under suspicion as a Soviet agent, and both of whom had served at Berlin Base with SASHA. Now this KGB man wanted to recruit back a former Soviet Naval officer, whose first contact with American intelligence had been Paul Garbler, another suspected mole. In this conversation with Solie and Branigan, Angleton decided to let Kozlov meet with Gus Hathaway, the other case officer he had met in Pakistan, for a single session. However, Angleton ordered that under no circumstances was Kovich to be involved.

As Angleton and his staff studied Kozlov's approach, Angleton remembered that he himself had had more than a passing involvement with Nikolai Artamonov at the time of his defection. Angleton's approval was key to his coming to the United States and to his acceptance by American intelligence.

WHEN ARTAMONOV WALKED INTO the American Embassy in Stockholm in 1959, Paul Garbler was ending his tour there. At that point, Artamonov and Ewa Gora, his young Polish lover, had been in the hands of the Swedes for several weeks. Garbler remembered that Ewa was wearing a dress he could almost see through.[8] Because Garbler was very much a Navy man as well as a CIA officer, he was able to prevail on the Naval Attaché's Office at the embassy, which provided him with a transcript of Artamonov's debriefing by the Swedish government.

Garbler sent the raw Artamonov material to CIA headquarters as a coded message and identified Artamonov as an NIP, an individual with National Intelligence Potential.[9] At headquarters, the message went to Leonard McCoy, the dour Soviet Division reports officer who monitored a broad range of Soviet subjects. McCoy said he feared that the Swedish government, to avoid political problems, might send Artamonov back to the Soviet Union, so he took matters into his own hands.

Without informing his boss, Soviet Division head Jack Maury, McCoy bypassed the protective procedures the CIA used to prevent penetrations and made his case directly to James Angleton.[10] Without an appointment, McCoy went to see Angleton and convinced him to pressure Director Dulles into asking the Swedish government to send Artamonov to the United States. Angleton told McCoy to wait in his outer office while he called DCI Dulles. Angleton then called McCoy back into his office and told him that Dulles would tell Olof Palme, then an aide to the Swedish prime minister, that Artamonov was coming to America.[11]

First, though, Artamonov was sent to the CIA's Westport defector processing operation in Frankfurt. McCoy's bureaucratic sleight of hand caused the center to be less cautious than they would normally be. Since Artamonov had the endorsement of both Allen Dulles and James Angleton, the processors rushed Artamonov and his girlfriend through the procedures, even though they both failed several polygraph exams. From that day on, there was an assumption on the part of every agency that dealt with Artamonov that someone else had properly cleared him. Angleton's hasty action allowed a defector who otherwise was suspect to be welcomed into the CIA.[12]

To make matters worse, Angleton, in the hopes of arranging for his favorite defector, Anatoly Golitsyn, some friendship that might stop him from leaving the United States and going to England, decided to bring him together with Shadrin, as Artamonov was by then known. From a security standpoint, bringing two top defectors together on a social basis was very dangerous. If they were double agents, the friendship gave them a chance to compare notes. The CIA bugged both men's homes, but the Russians frequently went for walks together, sometimes joking about the monitoring.

The last time Golitsyn and Shadrin saw each other was in 1963, when Golitsyn gave Shadrin a dog and a color television set before he left the United States for England. The last communication between them was in late 1964, when Golitsyn called Shadrin from Canada, and the two men spoke for over an hour.[13] When Golitsyn returned to the United States a year later, he told Angleton that Shadrin was more than likely a Soviet agent.

Now James Angleton was wondering: Why did Kozlov want Shadrin? He concluded that KITTY HAWK wanted to impress his Kremlin bosses. If Kozlov could recruit Nick Shadrin, then the KGB could make an example of Shadrin to show that no defector was unreachable. The other factor was, Shadrin had already outlived his usefulness to the CIA. Angleton's decision to use him to aid KITTY HAWK was made on the coldest possible basis: Shadrin could be sacrificed.

Neither James Angleton and the CIA nor Bert Turner and the FBI had any way of knowing that once they were on the hook with KITTY HAWK, the real purposes of the Kozlov mission could go forward. Kozlov could now clear the KGB of any involvement in the Kennedy assassination and use Nick Shadrin to get classified information from the United States, not only right under the CIA's and FBI's noses, but with their help and approval. Brezhnev had promised the Soviet military Western technology, and thanks to Kozlov, he would soon be able to deliver.

The FBI assigned to Bert Turner a slightly younger partner, James Wooten. Turner handled Kozlov, and Wooten handled Shadrin.[14] Because

Kozlov's tour of duty in the States was for less than three months, the FBI needed to know all it could about him in a hurry.

Immigration records revealed that Kozlov was in the United States on a temporary-duty visa under diplomatic cover—that much checked out. He had come into the country with a man named Vladimir P. Zaystev, which rang no warning bells because the FBI misidentified Zaystev. According to Angleton, it took almost a year for the FBI to discover that Kozlov's traveling companion was one of the most aggressive and feared KGB operatives ever sent to the West. If they had found that out at the time, the FBI would have delved more vigorously into Igor Kozlov's background and motives.[15]

The next meeting with KITTY HAWK was scheduled within a week of the first. In the meantime, James Wooten contacted Nick Shadrin and told him about Kozlov.

At the meeting, Gus Hathaway and Bruce Solie introduced KITTY HAWK to Bert Turner.[16] Kozlov asked Solie if Shadrin had agreed to the recruitment. On the basis of what Wooten had reported, Solie told Kozlov that Shadrin "would not run away if he were approached." Kozlov then began completing his mission as instructed by his mother-in-law.

Once the FBI and CIA gave him Shadrin, Kozlov kept his promise to help with the mole hunt. He verified to Turner what Golitsyn and Nosenko had said years before about SASHA, but he went much further. He stated without reservation that SASHA had been the KGB's recruiter at Berlin Base, and he flatly identified SASHA as Igor Orlov. He said Orlov was using his little framing gallery for drops, and he added that Orlov's wife, Eleonore, was part of the spy team.

Solie and Turner were convinced that KITTY HAWK was lying, because the FBI's investigation had shown no evidence of current activity by Igor or Eleonore Orlov. When KITTY HAWK detected his handlers' doubts, he said, "If you do not believe what I am telling you, then you know he visited the Soviet embassy through the back door on May 10, 1965." He handed the intelligence officers a photograph taken by the KGB through the mirror that day.

Solie and Turner replied that if Orlov had gone to the embassy, the FBI would also have his picture. Kozlov, in his most confident voice, told them, "Look again. You did take his picture. The KGB made sure he left through the front door." Within a week, the FBI confirmed that the picture had been taken, but, because the photographer was ill at the time, it had been misfiled.[17]

The KGB had set the bait for Angleton once again. KITTY HAWK confirmed what Golitsyn had said about SASHA. The Orlov investigation that Hoover wanted closed was now reopened, this time on a bigger scale. Angleton began to believe that KITTY HAWK was real.

Igor Kozlov saved for the next meeting his most shocking revelation: He had personal access to information that could conclusively prove Nosenko had been assigned the Oswald case by the KGB, but, because Oswald proved so unstable, any attempt at recruiting him was forbidden.

Angleton was furious when he got the report of this meeting. As James Wooten put it, "Anyone supporting Nosenko in Angleton's eyes had to be not just a plant, but part of a KGB conspiracy." Angleton now concluded that Kozlov was a sent agent and could not be trusted.

Over at the FBI, however, this report had the opposite effect: To Hoover and his men, Kozlov's verification of Nosenko was electrifying. Hoover had been so worried about the Warren Commission, which he had tried to talk President Johnson out of forming, that he had ordered his agents to collect derogatory information on Commission members which he could leak to the press should the FBI be treated badly in the final report.[18] Now, KITTY HAWK's information meant the FBI could finally close the book on the Kennedy assassination. The Bureau's slipshod investigation and Hoover's own absurd performance before the Warren Commission could all be swept aside. Thanks to KITTY HAWK, Hoover dodged the bullet that should have ended his long career. He was not about to allow Angleton to win this one.

For Hoover, there was no time for analysis. The FBI had only five weeks left before KITTY HAWK's assignment would end. The caution that Solie showed at the start of the operation disappeared as Bert Turner and the FBI pushed ahead.

AT THE FIRST MEETING between Nick Shadrin and Igor Kozlov, Kozlov told Shadrin—supposedly sentenced to death for treason—to tell the FBI that a pardon could be arranged if he could prove his loyalty to the Soviet state. Kozlov then told Shadrin to tell the FBI that he would be expected to supply top-quality naval intelligence from the Department of

Defense and the CIA to prove his loyalty to the Soviet Union and to earn his acceptance back into the fold. Kozlov said that for their next meeting, Shadrin should bring a full report on all the defectors and Soviet émigrés he was working with in the translation unit.

Shadrin had no difficulty doing as he was told. In the effort to support Igor Kozlov, the Americans gave him the classified materials he wanted. According to the FBI's Bill Branigan, the orders to do anything necessary to protect KITTY HAWK came directly from J. Edgar Hoover.

At their second meeting, Kozlov showed Shadrin a picture of Nosenko that the KGB had taken in the Maryland suburbs and asked him to obtain the addresses of Nosenko and Anatoly Golitsyn. Shadrin replied that he did not have access to either one but would attempt to get them. KITTY HAWK also told Shadrin to become friends with Nick Kozlov, his colleague in the translation unit, with a view to recruiting him.[19]

KITTY HAWK held five meetings with Shadrin before his assignment in Washington ended. At one of these, he warned Shadrin that under no circumstances was he to go near Igor Orlov, who he explained was a longtime Soviet agent. Shadrin later told his "wife," Ewa, to stay away from Orlov's gallery.[20]

At their last meeting, KITTY HAWK said that the KGB wanted to continue to receive details on the émigrés with whom Shadrin worked, and he instructed Shadrin on the specific kinds of classified naval documents the KGB expected—above all, communications material concerning American submarines. When James Wooten debriefed Shadrin later that afternoon, he assured him there would be no problem getting the information KITTY HAWK wanted.[21]

Though Igor Kozlov and Nick Shadrin met only half a dozen times, the CIA/FBI operation ran for years, as Shadrin fed thousands of pages of real secrets to his Russian handlers in the hopes of keeping KITTY HAWK as the CIA's man in the KGB. Peter Kapusta, who at this time was a counterintelligence official in the Soviet Bloc Division, later said that he received a formal complaint from a senior analyst in the Strategic Research Division about the secrets being given to Shadrin in "amounts that stagger the mind." Kapusta, who had been told about Shadrin's polygraph failures years before, said, "The CIA and FBI gave Shadrin a legitimate, legal way of meeting with the Soviets on a regular basis. They gave the Soviets access through Shadrin to the U.S. secrets they needed to build their Navy. And they gave him amounts of material that could not be reduced to photography."[22]

In addition to the documents he passed, Shadrin prepared memos for the KGB on U.S. intelligence plans for dealing with the Soviet Navy. Throughout the time Shadrin was working as a double agent, he received many speaking invitations in the U.S. and made many new contacts from these appearances. In addition, he began to seriously court high-ranking government officials. He had close friends at Naval Intelligence and the State Department.

Sam Wilson, by now a lieutenant general in the Army, was well acquainted with Shadrin during this period, and the two men were thought to be friends. Later on, Wilson claimed he "never sought Nick out socially. The only times I ever went to lunch with Nick . . . was when he was asking for it." Wilson recalls one particularly uncomfortable incident. "I went over to the old Post Office building to see someone there . . . and there was Nick, and he jumps up and gives me a big embrace in front of everybody. Hell, I don't know Nick that well. . . . He was not one of my close friends. He would have people think that he was."[23]

At the end of the summer of 1966, KITTY HAWK went back to the Soviet Union, and the FBI lost control of the operation. To complicate matters, Angleton's insistence that the Soviet Division be kept out of the case meant that the CIA had almost no resources to run KITTY HAWK overseas. When Bert Turner attempted to keep track of KITTY HAWK in Moscow through Bruce Solie at the CIA, Solie had to rely on Angleton himself for information. The sightings of KITTY HAWK were infrequent. "He was never available. Visible, but never available," said Ambassador James E. Nolan, Jr., who later evaluated the case for the FBI.

Eventually, the CIA learned that Igor Kozlov had won his promotion to lieutenant colonel and a coveted post in the KGB's Second Directorate, where he was assigned to a cover job with the International Atomic Energy Agency, escorting Soviet delegations traveling around the world. With this news came the hope that the FBI or CIA would have more meetings with KITTY HAWK.

James Angleton remained skeptical of Igor Kozlov. He argued, "KITTY HAWK's tradecraft was better than that of 90 percent of our own agents. . . . KITTY HAWK seemed to anticipate the CIA's questions too well, and he had ready answers for them." He also had too much information across too many divisions in the KGB. "There was no reason for him to have that kind of access," Angleton said, "no reason, above all, for him to know anything about the Oswald case. "Kozlov's job was counterintelligence for the KGB," Angleton said, "not the recruitment of Americans."[24]

Angleton's initial reason for keeping Kozlov away from the Soviet Division was his fear of a mole there. As the case developed, he had a second reason: "I wanted to send a message to the Soviets that I was really taking Igor seriously and was taken in by him, by virtue of the fact that I kept his identity from the SB [Soviet Bloc] Division."

Some time after KITTY HAWK returned to the Soviet Union, one of Angleton's friends in Israeli intelligence told him that Lieutenant Colonel Igor Frolovich Kozlov had married the daughter of Yekaterina Alekseyevna Furtseva in 1964. The Mossad source provided pictures of the happy family. Angleton's arguments that Kozlov could not have had access to such a wide range of classified material were refuted by the identity of his mother-in-law. Kim Philby knew exactly what it would take for Angleton to change his mind about Kozlov and how to deliver this information to him. Angleton acknowledged to his assistants that once the Israeli reports came in, "I had nothing left to seriously challenge Kozlov's bona fides."

When word of the Kozlov-Furtseva relationship reached Bruce Solie, the normally reserved security man immediately called William Branigan at the FBI to tell him the news. For the FBI, the name Furtseva was not new. They had heard it from the lips of Yuri Nosenko in 1964, before Angleton cut off their access to the defector. For Bruce Solie, the new information about Kozlov meant that Nosenko had been telling the truth all along. Eventually, CIA Director Richard Helms asked Solie to write a report clearing Nosenko. This had a profound effect on Angleton.

The news about Kozlov's mother-in-law was all that Hoover needed to write off any talk about Soviet involvement in the assassination of John F. Kennedy. Meanwhile, keeping KITTY HAWK on the right career path became more important than ever for both the FBI and the CIA. KITTY HAWK was officially listed as the United States' most highly placed Soviet agent. Hoover and his subordinates believed they had developed the greatest source in the history of the Cold War.

WHEN KIM PHILBY defected to the Soviet Union, he did not have up-to-date secrets to share: He had something better. Philby understood the characters of Angleton and Hoover, the two men assigned to protect the United States from the Soviets. That knowledge helped the Soviet Union checkmate Angleton and Hoover. The Soviet fingerprints on the Kennedy assassination were wiped away.

CHAPTER FORTY-TWO

FATAL COUP IN VIETNAM

—————

BY 1966, THE CIA was on a war footing. On President Johnson's orders, the Agency's attention had shifted from Castro and his Cubans to an even more determined people: the Vietnamese. The Kennedy assassination and even Angleton's mole hunt were beginning to pale compared to the new enemy in the Far East.

Not yet a nightmare, the Vietnam adventure actually began much earlier—in 1954, when President Eisenhower decided that the United States could replace France as the colonial power in Vietnam. By the time John F. Kennedy assumed the Vietnam portfolio, the Pentagon brass were "already pushing for a big show and a bigger war," according to William Corson, who served several tours in Vietnam and Laos.

Corson and Kennedy got to know each other when Kennedy visited the Far East as a senator and Corson was there on assignment for President Eisenhower. In April 1962, the Kennedy White House brought Corson to Washington from Laos to brief the president. As Corson later put it, "Kennedy had already lost faith in the CIA. Crisis after crisis was hitting him. It was in the middle of it all he asked me to brief him on what the Agency was doing in Vietnam. He asked because he no longer trusted what he was hearing from the military or up the river at Langley. He caught them in lies."

Corson was in a unique position at this point to tell the president what was really going on. "We were in the middle of investigating a

Soviet mole at the top of ARPA [the Advanced Research Projects Agency]," Corson said. "I had wiretap authority across the board. As a by-product of the mole investigation, I soon learned that my fellow officers wanted a war. They had picked Vietnam and were doing everything they could to sell it to Kennedy."[1]

Corson gave the young president his own Vietnam observations in what Kennedy himself dubbed the "no shit" briefing. Corson started at the beginning: "I told him that Lucien Conein was the first CIA man in Vietnam." Conein, a Berlin Base veteran, had arrived in 1954. Rugged, tough, called Luigi by his Berlin Base pals, Conein had come a long way from doing name checks for Peter Sichel in the early days at Berlin Base.

Born in France, Conein was raised in the American Midwest. He fought the first part of World War II with the French Army.[2] When the Germans overran France, he joined the OSS and distinguished himself by parachuting into Indochina and leading raids against the Japanese Imperial Army as the mythic "Lieutenant Laurent." After the war, first in Nuremberg with Ted Shackley and later at Berlin Base, Conein tried to set up various paramilitary operations behind the Iron Curtain, without much success.

Conein arrived in Vietnam just after the French decided to call it quits following the loss of the garrison at Dien Bien Phu. The armistice signed in Geneva on July 21, 1954, divided the country at roughly the 17th Parallel. The South was in the hands of the pro-French emperor, Bao Dai, and the North in the hands of the Communist liberation fighter, Ho Chi Minh (who, as it happens, had worked with the OSS against Japan in World War II). The partition was supposed to be temporary: Included in the Geneva Accords was a provision for democratic elections for a new, unified country by July 1956.

President Eisenhower made the political decision not to replace the French Army with a large American military presence so soon after Korea, but he badly wanted to prevent the country from going Communist. He and DCI Allen Dulles knew that paramilitary expert Edward Lansdale had successfully stopped a Communist takeover in the Philippines. They wanted him to repeat that success in Vietnam.

Lansdale in turn picked Luigi Conein because, unlike so many in the CIA, Conein had actually operated against an enemy in Asia. His Indochina experience and his expertise in unconventional warfare made him a natural for this operation. Lansdale and Conein, together with some one hundred American soldiers, made up the Military Assistance Advisory Group for Vietnam.

General Lansdale's task was to create a pro-American, anti-Communist government based in Saigon. His first job was to find a leader who was acceptable to the United States, who had not cooperated with the French, and who was truly anti-Communist. Lansdale chose Ngo Dinh Diem, an American-educated Roman Catholic, and convinced the emperor, Bao Dai, to appoint Diem as his prime minister. In exchange, the CIA gave the emperor a handsome stipend to ease his endless exile on the French Riviera.

Lansdale understood that a leader acceptable to the United States might not be the choice of the Vietnamese people in the elections called for in the Geneva Accords. Whether or not a majority of Vietnamese favored Communism, they honored Ho Chi Minh as the man who had led the war of liberation against the French. If the election were between Diem and Ho, Diem did not stand a chance. And so, the United States government set about inserting itself into a democratic election because it did not like the potential outcome.

One of the CIA's tools in this operation was another provision of the Geneva agreement, the resettlement provision. By May 1955, every Vietnamese had to choose whether to live in the North or the South. The CIA gave its men a blank check to resettle enough Catholics in the South to create a political base for Diem. It was an outlandish scheme that nevertheless worked. The CIA spent $100 million moving nearly a million Vietnamese from the North to the South. World War II hero General Claire Chennault conducted the evacuations using his Civil Air Transport, which he ran for the CIA from Taiwan.

One of Conein's jobs was to create a sense of panic and terror over what life might be like for those who remained in the North. Conein worked with Catholic bishops who convinced the more gullible members of their flock that the Blessed Virgin was moving south and they had better follow her. Conein also orchestrated the publication of an almanac that featured well-known Vietnamese astrologers predicting a wide variety of disasters under Communist leadership. Conein's most effective propaganda involved the distribution of leaflets showing where the United States planned to drop atomic bombs if civil war broke out.

Lansdale and Conein succeeded in convincing six hundred thousand Catholics to move below the 17th Parallel. By the time Civil Air Transport and the U.S. Seventh Fleet completed the relocation, 65 percent of the North's Catholics had fled to the South. Unfortunately, these included nearly four hundred thousand Vietnamese who had been affiliated with the colonial French, including government bureaucrats and military personnel. These refugees were a problem for Diem and his CIA handlers because they saw themselves as more French than Vietnamese. Also among the refugees were more than fifteen thousand[3] Vietminh sent by Hanoi to settle in the South and live there until called upon. As in Berlin Base's failure to detect Soviet agents like Igor Orlov and Miami Station's failure to find Castro's agents among the fleeing Cuban refugees, the CIA failed to detect thousands of enemy agents in South Vietnam, a fatal mistake.

Since the election of a non-Communist regime for the whole country was a lost cause, Lansdale and Conein decided to use the resettlement for a second purpose: to plant agents and weapons behind Communist lines to be activated in the event of a civil war. These stay-behind agents used CIA-supplied counterfeit North Vietnamese currency (piasters) to live on. The counterfeit money also helped destabilize the North's economy.

Conein was the case officer for a Filipino priest imported into Haiphong, ostensibly to run a soup kitchen and a staging area for the evacuation. In fact, the priest was in charge of distributing the counterfeit funds to the stay-behind agents. It did not take long for Ho Chi Minh's government to discover the priest and try to kill him. Although he personally survived several attacks, many other agents were uncovered and executed. The CIA fared no better in these stay-behind operations in Vietnam than it had in Germany and Korea.

Lansdale and Conein then went to work turning Ngo Dinh Diem into an effective political force. The good news was that Diem, for all his faults, was strong, and in a country that hated the French colonizers, he was very much anti-French. Yet even though he personally detested the French, his army and civil service were French-trained and were still under French influence.

Under Conein's instructions, Diem and his brother, Ngo Dinh Nhu—who was the real political brains behind the regime—started plotting against their political enemies. As William Corson later told President Kennedy in his "no shit" briefing, "While Ho Chi Minh enjoyed firm control over the North, Diem competed not only with the five to ten thousand Communist stay-behind agents, but also with two armed religious sects, the Hoa Hao and Cao Dai. Diem also faced the French-dominated civil service and army, as well as the Binh Xuyen, Saigon's version of the Mafia. Of all the local opponents, the Binh Xuyen was the most dangerous to Diem."

In the 1950s, Allen Dulles and his brother, John Foster Dulles, were still not certain Diem was the leader they wanted. On April 27, 1955, John Foster Dulles decided to replace Diem on the advice of Ambassador General J. Lawton Collins, who claimed that Diem's unwillingness to compromise with his enemies—including the thugs in the Binh Xuyen—doomed his regime. Diem learned that the U.S. government was abandoning him from his own spies in Washington. He confronted Lansdale and Conein, who had received the order but not acted on it.

The day after Dulles called for Diem's removal, twenty-five hundred members of the Binh Xuyen began to fire mortars into the prime minister's palace. Conein and Lansdale led a 12-hour battle and beat back the Binh Xuyen, who were mauled and fled into Saigon's Chinese-dominated suburb of Cholon.

The incident silenced Ambassador Collins. It was years before the American government again seriously considered replacing Diem. Washington called Lansdale back for reassignment. Eventually, he became executive secretary to the interagency group making policy for OPERATION MONGOOSE. Lucien Conein was in and out of Vietnam over the next decade as Diem's case officer and mentor. Conein was, for all intents and purposes, the CIA's main fixture in Vietnam. Although he never got the top job, he outlasted Saigon Station Chiefs John Anderson (1956), Nick Natsios (1957–60), and even William Colby (1960–62).

The Geneva Accords mandated national-unity elections by 1956. As the time approached, CIA headquarters ordered Conein to make certain that the elections did not happen. Taking his cue from Allen Dulles, Conein convinced Diem to simply refuse to schedule elections, which Diem did, stating that there was no point discussing elections as long as the Communist North did not permit "democratic liberties." His spokesmen added that he did not consider himself bound by the Geneva agreement, since he had not signed it. Instead of national-unity elections with the North, Diem called a referendum in the South offering a choice between himself and Bao Dai, which Diem won overwhelmingly. In October 1955, he declared himself president and announced that elections for a National Assembly would take place within a year. Conein suddenly found himself midwife to the Republic of South Vietnam.

William Corson later told President Kennedy that the CIA had created a government. They had done it in the hopes that a Catholic minority, led by Diem, could create a strong enough economy to discourage Communism from taking root in the South.

With Conein's help, Diem rigged the first elections for the new National Assembly in 1956, in which his supporters won 112 of the 123 seats. Over the next three years, President Diem, who thought of himself more as a benign dictator than as a democratic leader, continued to refuse North Vietnamese initiatives for national-unity elections. The Communists began to realize that war was the only way they would win a voice in South Vietnam's government. On July 8, 1959, the Vietnamese civil war claimed its first American lives, when two members of the Military Assistance Advisory Group were killed outside of Bien Hoa, 20 miles northeast of Saigon. William Colby, who was then deputy chief of station in Saigon, reported that the CIA had no advance warning.[4] Six months later, on January 26, 1960, the Communists attacked an Army post near the Cambodian border, and the war began in earnest.

Conein and Lansdale's efforts in Vietnam were a disaster. Conein, for all his abilities at waging war, had little understanding of two thousand years of Vietnamese history. In a country where a majority of the people were Buddhist, he helped create a government backed and supported by the Vatican. One of the major lobbyists on behalf of Diem and his regime was Francis Cardinal Spellman of New York. Diem might as well have called his new country the Catholic Republic of Vietnam. [5]

As events unfolded, Conein and his CIA colleagues in Vietnam, numbering about 40 by 1959, failed to tell headquarters at Langley that the Catholic minority, spurred on by Diem's brother, Ngo Dinh Nhu, and his wife, Madame Nhu, had become the oppressors of South Vietnam's Buddhist majority. Increasingly stringent restrictions were placed on Buddhists' religious practices, and then, in the spring of 1963, the government issued an order forbidding public celebrations on the Buddha's birthday,

May 8, partly because that day was also the anniversary of the fall of Dien
Bien Phu, a major Communist holiday. All these events gradually transformed the country into a major world hot spot.

"By 1963," as William Corson put it, "Diem and Vietnam were President Kennedy's main problem." The Kennedy brothers' decision to overthrow Diem had been building for a year when, on May 8, thousands of
Buddhists demonstrated in protest against the government and were bru-
tally repressed by the South Vietnamese Army, on Ngo Dinh Nhu's instructions. A grenade attack killed nine Buddhists.

When the Buddhists launched a storm of protest, Diem responded by
making some concessions, including compensation to the families of the
nine Buddhists who were killed. Then on June 11, a Buddhist monk,
Thich Quang Doc, aided by hundreds of fellow monks, set himself on fire
and died in front of American cameramen. Over the next few months, six
other Buddhists set themselves afire. As the self-immolations continued,
Madame Nhu earned the nickname "The Dragon Lady" for her remark
that the monks were "barbecuing themselves."[6]

Although Diem promised President Kennedy he would leave the Buddhists alone, Diem's CIA-trained Special Forces increased their harass-
ment and attacks. Diem refused to separate himself from his hard-line
brother and sister-in-law. CIA head John McCone argued forcefully that
Diem was the only leader who could hold South Vietnam together, but
Robert Kennedy decided that he could not support so repressive a regime,
despite strong protests from some military advisers, the CIA, and the
Catholic church.

The CIA and the Pentagon began searching for someone more cooperative to replace Diem. In the summer of 1963 President Kennedy authorized his new ambassador, Henry Cabot Lodge, Jr., to order Saigon
Station Chief John ("Jocko") Richardson to prepare for a coup.

The coup was designed to be bloodless. Neither Diem nor his brother
were to be harmed. President Kennedy gave the order to evacuate the two
men and their families out of Vietnam to safety. While political murder
was not Kennedy's policy in this case, it was the policy of others in the
U.S. government. The events surrounding the coup in Saigon were not coincidental to other events playing out in the United States in 1963.

Luigi Conein thought he was running the coup. The plan was for him,
the minute the coup began, to convince Diem, Nhu, and their families to

go to Taiwan for a brief exile. Conein was to call Diem to tell him what was happening and then meet the brothers and their families at a safe house in the Cholon suburb. From there, he was to see them safely to the airport and their flight to Taiwan. A hitch developed when the coup was temporarily thwarted by Diem and Nhu's intelligence agents, who, having penetrated Saigon Station, learned about it. They began a public newspaper attack on the CIA.[7] Eventually, however, Conein was able to obtain Diem's cooperation in his own removal from power.

On November 1, 1963, Diem and Nhu received the call and went to the appointed meeting place, a Catholic church in Cholon. Then a series of events took place that had nothing to do with President Kennedy's orders or Lucien Conein's plans. As Diem and Nhu got into an Army personnel carrier for the ride to the airport, they were shot to death. Conein said that when he heard about it, he "was shocked at the killing of Diem and his brother; it had never been part of the CIA plan."[8] Corson later said he never believed either Conein or Kennedy was responsible; when Kennedy learned of the murders, Corson said, he was as "angry as I ever saw him, absolutely shaken."

Who changed a nonviolent coup into the murder of Diem, Nhu, and a Catholic priest accompanying them? To this day, nothing has been found in government archives tying the killings to either John or Robert Kennedy. So how did the tools and talents developed by Bill Harvey for ZR/RIFLE and OPERATION MONGOOSE get exported to Vietnam? Kennedy immediately ordered Corson to find out what had happened and who was responsible. The answer he came up with: "On instructions from Averell Harriman. . . . The orders that ended in the deaths of Diem and his brother originated with Harriman and were carried out by Henry Cabot Lodge's own military assistant."

Having served as ambassador to Moscow and governor of New York, W. Averell Harriman was in the middle of a long public career. In 1960, President-elect Kennedy appointed him ambassador-at-large, to operate "with the full confidence of the president and an intimate knowledge of all aspects of United States policy." By 1963, according to Corson, Harriman was running "Vietnam without consulting the president or the attorney general."

The president had begun to suspect that not everyone on his national security team was loyal. As Corson put it, "Kenny O'Donnell [JFK's appointments secretary] was convinced that McGeorge Bundy, the national security advisor, was taking orders from Ambassador Averell Harriman and not the president. He was especially worried about Michael Forrestal, a young man on the White House staff who handled liaison on Vietnam with Harriman."

At the heart of the murders was the sudden and strange recall of Saigon Station Chief Jocko Richardson and his replacement by a no-name team barely known to history. The key member was a Special Operations Army officer, John Michael Dunn, who took his orders, not from the normal CIA hierarchy but from Harriman and Forrestal.

According to Corson, "John Michael Dunn was known to be in touch with the coup plotters,"[9] although Dunn's role has never been made public. Corson believes that Richardson was removed so that Dunn, assigned to Ambassador Lodge[10] for "special operations," could act without hindrance.

Neither Corson nor Kennedy knew in 1963 that James Angleton was also worried about Averell Harriman and had begun a highly secret counterintelligence investigation code named DINOSAUR. This investigation continued throughout the rest of Angleton's CIA tenure. "There was a strong circumstantial case that Harriman was at least an agent of Soviet influence and maybe much worse," Angleton said.

Angleton became convinced that Harriman's role in the coup was motivated by more than a policy difference with Kennedy. Angleton believed that the Vietnamese assassinations were designed to throw American policy in that country into chaos. That was certainly their effect. "The U.S. never really recovered from that coup," said Corson, who later returned to Vietnam as a Marine commander.

Harriman's actions made no one happier than Yekaterina Furtseva's friend, Yuri Andropov, who was running Vietnam operations for the KGB. Andropov understood that the murders of the Vietnamese leaders destroyed U.S. policy. Averell Harriman set in motion in Saigon, without the president's knowledge, a series of events that doomed all future U.S. efforts in Vietnam.

CHAPTER FORTY-THREE

THONG NHUT STREET

———⟶⊶⊷⟵———

S AIGON STATION occupied the top three floors of the American Embassy on Thong Nhut Street. As the United States found itself sucked
further and further into the military abyss, Saigon Station's 40 case officers ballooned to four hundred and eventually reached more than a thousand. Three thousand additional agents worked for the CIA in other
bases around the country in "pacification" efforts.[1]

Many of the case officers sent to Saigon were veterans of Berlin Base,
and, predictably, the mistakes from Berlin were repeated in Vietnam as
they had been in Cuba. The major difference was the cost. Instead of several thousand Germans, Hungarians, and other Eastern Europeans who
were sacrificed to mistaken policies, the toll here was 58,000 American
lives and hundreds of thousands of Vietnamese. Yet the policy continued
long after the American public had had enough.

The choice the CIA bosses made in sending veterans of Berlin Base
to run operations in Saigon almost guaranteed the defeat that was taking
shape for the United States. Frank Snepp, who did two tours at Saigon
Station, wrote: "Many of the case officers who ended up in Vietnam
were old German or Latin American hands with no knowledge of the
country and no interest in developing any. Yet within a month or so of
their arrival and without any language training whatsoever, they often
found themselves exiled to a godforsaken outpost in Vietnam's western
highlands or in the delta, responsible for recruiting agents, gathering

intelligence, and administering an amorphous new program for saving the country, known as 'Rural Development.'"[2]

Rural Development is a bland description that barely hints at the activity conducted under the rubric of Civil Operations and Rural Development Support (CORDS). The idea was that, in guerrilla war, military action was not enough. As Lyndon Johnson put it, America had to "win the hearts and minds" of the Vietnamese people. CORDS was a carrot-and-stick program designed to disrupt Communist guerrilla forces in the South (the Viet Cong). It gave rural Vietnamese an economic reward for wielding the stick against the Viet Cong under a separate program called PHOENIX. CORDS was originated by CIA man Robert W. Komer in the early days of the Johnson Administration. When William E. Colby went to Vietnam in 1968 to run CORDS as Komer's hand-picked successor, he was given the rank of ambassador, an indication of just how important the United States government considered these programs to the success of its war effort.

To receive their rewards under PHOENIX, the South Vietnamese were supposed to smoke out Viet Cong cadres, capture them, and turn them in to be interrogated. Unfortunately, Vietnamese who wanted to collect the rewards paid little attention to actual evidence in determining whether or not someone was a Viet Cong leader. More and more, the interrogations gave way to torture and assassination. With the blessing of Saigon Station's Berlin veterans, PROJECT PHOENIX turned into a grassroots, Asian version of OPERATION MONGOOSE, with the United States government unintentionally funding the assassinations of thousands of innocent Vietnamese. Instead of winning their hearts and minds, the program caused many Vietnamese to hate their American allies. They viewed the United States as a sponsor of the worst kind of terrorism.

Berlin Base veteran Sam Wilson, already under investigation in James Angleton's mole hunt, returned to Asia where he had been a war hero two decades earlier. In 1941, as little more than a boy, he had walked seven miles in the rain from his rural Virginia home to join the National Guard. He wound up fighting with Merrill's Marauders in Burma. He received the Silver Star with Oak Leaf Cluster.[3] His Vietnam assignment was not nearly so heroic.

On paper, Wilson was chief of the Pacification Program of the Agency for International Development (AID). In reality, he worked with the first level of the assassination programs (Internal Corridination and Exploitation or ICEX) part of both CORDS and PHOENIX. In 1966, Wilson, having volunteered to demonstrate how CORDS could work, put together a "model" AID team in Long An province. Washington regularly received reports praising Wilson's efforts as a great success, but, within a year, Wilson left Vietnam in disgust, convinced the United States could not win the war. However, because he still had career ambitions both in the Army and in the intelligence community, he kept his mouth shut.

At the war's height, Vietnam was a tapestry of operations run by the military, the CIA, and the Agency for International Development. The connections the Kennedys had formed between the Pentagon and the CIA over Cuba had now matured into a joint military and intelligence collaboration.

Tens of thousands of civilian Americans who arrived in Vietnam began to treat the beleaguered country as a dependent colony of the United States. "We were regarded by the Vietnamese people as imperialists, not partners or saviors," said John Sherwood, who served a tour of duty as chief of covert action in Saigon. The Duc Hotel, an Asian version of Howard Johnson's, provided a temporary billet for newcomers three blocks from Saigon Station. Lucien Conein's long CIA career ended when a wild party he gave at the Duc Hotel in 1967 turned violent (although Conein remained on the CIA payroll as a contract officer). Higher-ups like William Colby, who spent nearly 12 years in Vietnam, used a private club, Le Cercle Sportif, as the center of their social lives in Saigon. The club was built for the colonial French back in the days when Saigon had the ambience of Paris rather than a decaying Tijuana. Here, the chiefs of station and visiting base and branch chiefs ate, swam, and played tennis as Vietnam burned. Many of the waiters were spies for the North Vietnamese or the Viet Cong.

U.S. Army Colonel Tullius Accompura—who had served in Korea and Japan with David Murphy and Ed Snow—arrived in Vietnam in 1965 to work with Peer De Silva, a West Point graduate who was then chief of station. He remembers De Silva as essentially a decent man who "couldn't tell Monday from Friday."

Accompura's job, under military cover, was to get close to one of the honest members of the South Vietnamese government, Air Force Major General Nguyen Ngoc Loan. Loan, a mid-level Air Force officer when Diem was overthrown, became an understudy to Air Force Commander (later Premier) Nguyen Cao Ky, who put him in charge of the Vietnamese National Police. "Loan was a patriot, completely committed to his country," Accompura said. William Corson agreed. According to Corson, "Loan was one of the few leaders who knew what he was doing and why he was doing it. . . . He was far too independent for the politicians who were running the war, yet he probably wanted the best for the Vietnamese people."[4] He was also too independent for most of the men at Saigon Station. He believed that the South Vietnamese Army had to treat the war as its own to win or to lose if it ever hoped for victory.

Saigon Station was like Berlin Base in too many ways. The lack of counterintelligence, the lack of attention to detail, the philandering and drinking-all contributed to the fantasy picture the CIA wove about what was going on in Vietnam.

The situation got much worse with the arrival in 1966 of John Limond Hart—former chief of the CIA's Western European Division—as chief of station. Tullius Accompura described Hart as "bad, bad, viciously bad." The two men had worked together in Korea much earlier in their careers. By the time Hart got to Vietnam, his personal weaknesses had gotten the better of him.

Sherwood said of Hart, "I know when he was in Vietnam . . . he was on pills and drugged up half the time. . . . Often, I had to get up during the night because I was the guy responsible for the political stuff. . . . I was up there writing a cable, and I always wanted to let John know if I was going to send out something important."[5] Sherwood said he found his boss incoherent a good deal of the time.

In Berlin, Sherwood had spent his time wondering what went wrong. Now he was doing the same thing in Saigon. Nothing had changed. The CIA was using the same methods and telling the same lies, only this time it was providing intelligence for American soldiers to depend on in battle. During the course of the war, the CIA was slowly revealed as a professional fraud. It failed to collect the numbers—the hard intelligence. It signed off on blatantly false intelligence provided by General William C. Westmoreland and others who were hoping to promote the war at home. The CIA became party to what Walt Rostow, the Bundys (William and McGeorge), and Robert McNamara were selling to Kennedy and Johnson. The result was that Vietnam did more than divide the country: It planted seeds of distrust between the American people and their government.

The most graphic illustration of CIA failure occurred in January 1968. The Agency had been confidently telling the White House that Saigon was the one place the Viet Cong could not strike. Sherwood, who still liked to get out of the station and onto the street as he had in Berlin a decade before, thought otherwise. What he saw made him believe Saigon was very vulnerable to attack. When he returned to Washington that January, he sat down and wrote a report saying so. Since he had served as chief of covert operations in Saigon, he could not be completely ignored.

When DCI Richard Helms received Sherwood's paper, he scheduled one of his famous director's luncheons in his private dining room at Langley. Present in addition to Sherwood were Helms; Cord Meyer (ex-husband of Mary Meyer who had been killed on the towpath in Georgetown); William Colby, who was preparing to go back to Vietnam in charge of CORDS; and George Carver, who spent more than a decade in Vietnam, and was COS at the time. In keeping with the mind-set of the CIA hierarchy, the elegant luncheon was served by black waiters. "The agenda was my paper," Sherwood recalls, "and the guest of honor was Phil C. Habib, with whom I had worked amicably and agreeably in Vietnam" when Habib was counselor for political affairs to the U.S. Embassy. Habib proceeded to call Sherwood's paper alarmist and unnecessary. After the paper had been thoroughly skewered, Helms led his guests down to the situation room. As Sherwood tells it: "We go down to the situation room, and there are maps and colonels and majors and all kinds of assholes running in and out. This little slick kid has put all this together—something to keep Helms's ass from being caught in a sling. . . . We are standing there . . . when a major comes up and says, 'Mr. Carver, sir, I have a cable for you. The embassy in Saigon is under siege.'"[6] The Tet offensive was underway. To his dismay, Sherwood was right.

The CIA's unpreparedness for the Tet offensive was typical of the incompetence Sherwood had witnessed during his career, and it was again costing lives. Only this time, they were the lives of American servicemen. The CIA's self-deluding assertion that the Viet Cong could not operate in Saigon proved deadly. Up until the first bullets were fired, the CIA hierarchy refused to believe the warnings and real intelligence, even from its own men. Fortunately for the United States, General Loan's police held the presidential palace and the radio station—although American officials never forgave him for ordering his troops to abandon the U.S. Embassy in order to defend the presidential palace.[7]

CHAPTER FORTY-FOUR

THE CIA AND THE DRUG LORDS

———⊰•⊱———

THE EERIE SIMILARITIES between Berlin Base in the 1950s and Saigon Station in the 1960s only increased as Bill Harvey's boys from Berlin were tapped for the biggest jobs in Vietnam.[1] Berlin Base alumni Ted Shackley and George Weisz ran Saigon Station between 1968 and 1971, when Vietnam still could have avoided complete disaster. But Shackley and Weisz had not changed.

After Berlin, Harvey had rescued Shackley from obscurity in the Eastern European Division to join in the pursuit of Castro. As chief of station in Miami, Shackley recruited agents, made contacts, and developed relationships that he continued over the next three decades, often with grievous results for the United States and for other, smaller countries. He also shafted his old mentor, tipping off Bobby Kennedy that it was Bill Harvey who had sent agents into Cuba during the Missile Crisis.

Both in Berlin and Miami, Shackley, nicknamed "the Ice Man" and "the Blond Ghost," was willing to carry out almost any order without questioning it. He made himself an expert in handling out-of-pocket operations and keeping them from being traced back to the CIA. These "off the books" operations gave him a reputation for being tough and cunning, much like Bill Harvey. But Shackley had a bureaucratic side that Harvey lacked. Shackley was, at heart, cautious. If he sensed that an operation could hurt his quest for power, he bailed out or placed the blame on someone else.

In 1965, after OPERATION MONGOOSE and the follow-on programs against Castro were phased out, Shackley was named chief of base in Berlin. But his new rabbi, Desmond FitzGerald (the same man who removed Bill Harvey from Rome), had a bigger plan for him, and that was to run the CIA's secret war against the North Vietnamese in Laos. Shackley's immediate boss was William Colby, at that time chief of the Far East Division, and his specific assignment was to manage the Hmong tribesmen through a local warlord, General Vang Pao.

In Laos, Shackley made use of a loyal cadre of Cuban refugees whom he had recruited in Miami and who remained on the CIA payroll as career spies. Also in Laos, Shackley first worked with Edwin P. Wilson, the man who Sarkis Soghanalian said was paid off by the KGB in the shootdown of Francis Gary Powers's U-2 spy plane. Wilson was a CIA front man, owning and operating scores of businesses used to hide Agency operations. Later on, Wilson, Shackley, and Shackley's Miami deputy, Tom Clines, became business partners in ventures involving Libya that made headlines in the early 1980s and sent Wilson to the federal penitentiary.

Shackley's men didn't all make headlines, but they got around. Felix Rodriguez had tagged along on the Bolivian Army's successful hunt for Che Guevara in 1967. Frank Fiorini (a.k.a. Frank Sturgis) was later arrested as a Watergate burglar, as was E. Howard Hunt, known to the Cubans as Eduardo. Rafael "Chi Chi" Quintero, along with Shackley and Clines, played a major role in the Iran-Contra operation. These men bribed foreign leaders, moved tens of millions of dollars, and formed the cadre of a private, shadow spy organization within America's official intelligence service.

In Laos, Ed Wilson worked with Shackley's deputy, David Morales, a Yaqui Indian who was famous for his hard drinking and his willingness to take on outrageous missions for Shackley. According to Wilson, Morales actually led the capture and assassination of Che Guevara, for which Felix Rodriguez liked to take credit. Morales was "Shackley's man in Germany, at JM/WAVE during MONGOOSE, and in Laos. He would do anything for Shackley—from blowing up a radio tower in the Dominican Republic to paying off the drug lords. He was totally devoted to Shackley."[2]

The colorful Special Operations expert, General John K. Singlaub, chief of Military Assitance Command Vietnam Special Operations Group (MACV-SOG) in Vietnam, also worked with Shackley and his team in

Cambodia and at the secret CIA air base at Udorn in Laos. These men in turn worked for the ambassador to Laos, William Sullivan (he was later ambassador to Iran at the time the embassy was captured by radical students). In Vientiane, the capital of Laos, the CIA ran an office that assisted the Air Force in picking bombing targets; it was here that Shackley got to know a brilliant Air Force pilot, Richard Secord.

The relationships Shackley developed during his time in Laos eventually made him one of the most powerful men in the CIA, because he and his associates held a common secret: The CIA was in an alliance with Laotian drug lords against the North Vietnamese and the Pathet Lao, Laos's own Communist guerrilla army. Once again, the CIA was in business with the mob.

As Ed Wilson explained it, "It was never the CIA's intention to get in the drug business, but the smugglers had information they needed."[3] In Laos, the war effort against the Communists was inextricably tied up with the drug trade. Working out of Vientiane, Shackley ran the Hmongs' war effort at a time when the Hmong were involved in the drug trade. Hmong leader General Vang Pao was fighting for full control of the opium trade and used the opium income to finance his war against the Communists.

Santos Trafficante—the Tampa-based mobster who had accepted the contract to kill Castro for the CIA when he was, in reality, a Castro spy—was now the biggest importer of China white heroin in the world and General Vang Pao's biggest customer. The fact that Shackley was working with an opium smuggler who was doing business with a man who had played a role in the murder of John F. Kennedy seemed to bother no one in the CIA. "Shackley's a practical man," Wilson said.

During the years at Berlin Base, Lucien Conein and Ted Shackley did not have to worry about drugs: In Berlin the currency was sex, forged identity papers, or good old-fashioned money. The nasty secret of the early phase of the Vietnam War was that Conein's clients, Ngo Dinh Diem and Ngo Dinh Nhu, were at the Vietnamese end of the Corsican heroin trail. What the CIA had taken over from the French colonial administration in Vietnam was the Southeast Asian drug business.

That our Laotian allies were in the illegal drug business did not come as a shock. For many years, the CIA had been allowing rebel armies it supported and dictators it backed to engage in drug dealing to finance operations.

In 1950, when Chiang Kai-Shek's CIA-backed Kuomintang (KMT) scattered in defeat from the Yunnan province of China into Burma, the CIA created a pair of front companies to supply and finance the KMT soldiers. One of these, based in Taiwan, was Civil Air Transport (CAT), the predecessor to Air America (the airline used in the massive Vietnamese resettlement in 1954 to 55). General Claire Chennault, organizer of the Flying Tigers during World War II, was put in charge of CAT as well as of Taiwan's other air service, while his wife, Anna, spent her time in Washington lobbying for more aid for her husband's activities against the Communist Chinese.

Chiang Kai-Shek's men, funded by the CIA in the hopeless notion that they could retake mainland China, became the foot soldiers of the Asian drug armies. They persuaded Burmese farmers to switch from growing food to supplying the raw material for the drug cartel. In Bangkok, the CIA put Paul Helliwell (later the paymaster for Shackley's anti-Castro Cubans) in charge of Sea Supply Corporation, the CIA shipping firm, which used CAT planes to deliver weapons and food to Burma and fly out drugs—operations paid for by American taxpayers.

Hundreds of tons of opium and heroin were carried from Burma into Taiwan and Thailand on these CIA flights. In his book, *The Politics of Heroin in Southeast Asia,* Alfred McCoy explained how the city of Chiang Mai in northern Thailand became to drugs what Chicago is to agricultural commodities.[4] Jim Thompson, the so-called "Thai Silk King" (who in fact was a CIA officer), had recruited General Phao, head of the Thai police, to accept the KMT Army's drugs for distribution. Later, Thompson mysteriously disappeared on a weekend holiday. A few years later, his sister, who was investigating his death, was murdered, gangland fashion, in a wealthy suburb of Wilmington, Delaware.

By the time Lucien Conein and Ed Lansdale arrived in Vietnam in 1954, the Corsican Mafia was already using Saigon and paying its officials for the export of heroin. At the same time, James Angleton was working with French intelligence and the AFL-CIO's International Division to make certain that the Corsican Mafia, not the Communists, took control of important French ports like Marseille. American taxpayers unwittingly created the security the French Connection drug traffickers needed to import and export illegal narcotics.

By the 1960s, Santos Trafficante was doing business with the Laotian warlords and also with Ngo Dinh Nhu, who collected protection money for allowing the Hmong and Meo tribesmen in the highlands of Vietnam to farm opium poppies. These Montagnard tribesmen, who fought more bravely than any other group of Vietnamese, were rewarded with free transportation on Air America for their opium crop. According to the Drug Enforcement Administration's John J. O'Neill and others, the policy was not to stop the drug business in Vietnam but to win the war. River boats openly transported opium paste, which looks like wax beehives, from the highlands down to Vietnam's delta, where the vast amounts of water needed to process the paste into heroin were readily available.

According to William Corson, who served as a paymaster for the Montagnards, "There was never any real effort for a serious investigation of the CIA's role in this. I can tell you that we had Air America pilots who were tempted by the money. During the war, the CIA faced the same corruption we see in drug enforcement today. There was just too much money involved." Air America pilots often got drunk and violent. According to Robert Crowley, once when two of them shot it out in Bangkok, the station chief decreed that the dead pilot be buried on the grounds of the CIA station to avoid public attention.

Many GIs not only got hooked on heroin but also became pushers. Dover Air Force Base in Delaware, which served as the main East Coast mortuary during the Vietnam War, became a Mafia haven. The main method of shipping drugs back to the United States was to hide them in the thousands of military caskets being sent home.

Ted Shackley's bosses at the time—William Colby, William Wells, and Desmond FitzGerald—were so pleased by his performance in Laos that, in 1968, they named him chief of station in Saigon. Only in his forties and having been chief in Miami, Shackley gained the distinction of heading the two largest stations in CIA history. True to his calculating reputation, Shackley distanced himself from CORDS and PHOENIX, knowing full well they were not the kind of programs an ambitious bureaucrat wanted on his résumé.

Having rewarded Shackley with his new posting, headquarters promptly assigned his old Berlin Base adversary, George Weisz, as his deputy.

In 1964, Weisz had become chief of station in Bonn, one of the CIA's less glamorous outposts, and in late 1967 he volunteered to join the growing list of Berlin Base veterans sent to Saigon. As George Kisevalter described it, the assignment of George Weisz to Saigon was bizarre. "He'd be there as the number two man, which already displeased him. He had to work with Shackley, whom he hated. He was jealous of him."

Frank Snepp, who served in Saigon at the same time, said Weisz "really viewed himself, I think, as chief of station in Saigon. He didn't like taking orders. He was a wheeler-dealer. You could say there was sort of a Weisz-Shackley rivalry. Shackley had to rein him in a few times. I don't think there was any love lost."[5] Their egos, their ambition, their bureaucratic survival instincts made Weisz and Shackley very much alike.

Although the relationship between Weisz and Shackley was not pleasant, Weisz for the most part didn't let it interfere with his work. While officially he was the deputy chief of station, he functioned more like the chief of operations in Saigon. According to Tullius Accompura, if there was bad news, Weisz usually had to give it.

Weisz's main job was running clandestine operations to penetrate the Viet Cong and the North Vietnamese government and armed forces. Weisz personally took on the chore of recruiting diplomats from Eastern Bloc countries who were politically close to North Vietnam and had vital information. He was also in charge of approving the lists of suspected Viet Cong to be targeted for assassination. He also assisted in the secret war in Laos—his tattered passport is the only public record of his comings and goings into Vientiane.

George Weisz, never popular with his subordinates (in a later posting he was called "Napoleon" behind his back),[6] lived up to his reputation as a very formal, tough taskmaster. Kisevalter remembered what happened when Weisz first arrived: "Now he [Shackley] sent some officers out to meet Weisz. He's met by a couple of station officers, and the first thing he does is to bawl the hell out of them. They're not wearing ties. It's a hot day—they were in shirts. Weisz, getting off the goddamn plane, bawls them out. Imagine that."

All that Weisz and Shackley failed to learn about the intelligence business in Berlin was repeated on a personal level in Vietnam. Few wives were allowed in Saigon. Weisz, Shackley, and others traveled on occasional weekends to Hong Kong, where their families lived at a safe distance from the war zone. Eventually, Shackley moved his wife, Hazel, and their daughter, Suzanne, to Saigon. Etta Jo Weisz came to Saigon on some holidays, when the couple would entertain, and Weisz's mother remembers him bringing a group of high-ranking Vietnamese intelligence officials on a trip to the United States during this period. But mostly, there was little contact between Saigon-based CIA officers and their families. Weisz's son, Donnel, became more and more troubled during his father's absences.

Shackley quickly reverted to old habits in Vietnam. As Frank Snepp put it, "Shackley, an ambitious technocrat, was not satisfied with Station accomplishments, and throughout his tenure . . . , he continually pushed Station personnel to 'recruit, recruit, recruit'—that is, bribe, inveigle, and hire anyone and everyone to work for us as agents. By the time he was through, the Station's spy roster had swollen impressively, and the stream of intelligence reports flowing back to Washington had reached a record five hundred per month. Only some time later, in 1974, as the CIA was frantically trying to clarify Hanoi's ceasefire strategy, were we able to realize what havoc Shackley's zeal had visited on us: Over a hundred of the VC (Viet Cong) 'agents' who had been recruited during his reign were discovered to be fabricators, clever Vietnamese entrepreneurs who knew nothing of Communist plans but had been able to patch enough information together from newspaper stories and soup kitchen gossip to keep us supplied with what looked like valid intelligence, at great cost to the U.S. government."[7]

As in Berlin and Miami, the cost of relying on false agents with bad information was paid not only with money but also with blood.

CHAPTER FORTY-FIVE

Losing Vietnam

UNDER TED SHACKLEY, Saigon Station became a sea of inflated cases and inaccurate intelligence assertions. The station also spied on those who were supposed to be America's allies. Shackley himself became the de facto case officer to General Dang Van Quang, security adviser to Nguyen Van Thieu, who became president in 1967. The station also had the head of the National Police, General Nguyen Khrac Binh, under its control. Shackley frequently cited these two officials as top-flight sources, ignoring the more realistic input from the tougher and more independent General Loan.

For Peter Kapusta, Vietnam brought back another bad memory—David E. Murphy, whom Kapusta had known both in Japan and in Germany.[1] Murphy was prospering as Paris Station Chief despite Angleton's warning to the French government that he was a suspected Soviet agent. Because Kapusta and Tullius Accompura shared Angleton's suspicions, they became increasingly concerned when Murphy in Paris kept demanding huge amounts of classified material from Vietnam.

By 1968, Murphy's main job was supervising the bugging of the meeting rooms and living quarters of North Vietnamese officials who were in Paris for the peace talks, which began under President Johnson and continued throughout President Nixon's first term. Considering that Murphy was operating in a friendly city, he had surprisingly few successful operations against the North Vietnamese or the Soviets, according to classified CIA reports on the performance of his station. A secret CIA inspection report in 1969 stated: "My feeling is that everyone is aware of the major difficulties here . . . the tendency to become involved in lengthy speculative exercises, particularly in the covert action area. . . . Certainly, the history of the Paris station efforts against the Soviet target is not a happy one. This statement is supported by the fact that even today the inventory of agent assets is low. . . ."[2]

In 1971, Peter Kapusta was the CIA's top hostile interrogator of non-military North Vietnamese intelligence officers at the National Interrogation Center in Saigon. His colleague John Bodine handled military intelligence interrogations. One day, Bodine came to Kapusta with a plea for help. Something about a North Vietnamese captain he was interrogating did not ring true. Kapusta began to work on the case. It did not take him long to establish that the "captain" was, in fact, the North Vietnamese general in charge of counterintelligence. The general turned out to be one of the most important prisoners the United States ever captured in Vietnam.

David Murphy, still under investigation by Angleton, arrived in Saigon at almost the same time, to brief the station on the status of the Paris peace talks. Murphy stayed in Saigon two weeks and, according to Kapusta, did all he could to learn the identity of every high-ranking North Vietnamese prisoner in the CIA's hands—including the mysterious captain.[3]

While the United States was trying to extricate itself from Vietnam through peace negotiations, it was also ostensibly preparing the South Vietnamese to carry on by themselves. In fact, the Nixon Administration wanted a stable regime in place so that its unacknowledged abandonment of South Vietnam was not so obvious. Henry Kissinger's Nobel Peace Prize was not for making peace but for orchestrating a drawn-out surrender.

It was no secret in Saigon that Nixon and Kissinger's visit to China in February 1972 signaled the end of American participation in Vietnam. Colonel Accompura delivered the news to General Loan that the war was over and that "China would dictate the terms of the outcome." For men like Accompura and William Corson, the deaths that took place in Vietnam after 1971 were a tragic waste.

Accompura was about ready to go home to the States after his three-year tour ended in 1968 when General Loan came to see him. "The reason I stayed on was because during the Battle of Tet he [Loan] told me, 'Look, you are the only fucking guy who knows what is going on. You are the only guy I can trust. You are the only guy I can talk to. Don't go home.' He said, 'I will assure you that I will change this fucking thing.' Well, he was on the verge of doing it. Don't forget he saved Saigon during Tet. If it hadn't been for him, it would have been over. Saigon would have fallen like that," Accompura said, snapping his fingers.

Loan was the one-legged general whose cold-blooded methods were seared into the world's consciousness forever after the Tet offensive. Few Americans recall that his police saved Saigon; what is remembered is the news footage of Loan personally shooting a Viet Cong prisoner in the head. Loan watched without emotion as blood spurted from the man's skull and his body dropped to the ground.

General Loan grew to hate the CIA. After the Tet offensive, Shackley, Weisz, and others at the station predicted the United States was on the verge of a great victory. Loan thought this was nonsense. He was convinced the United States would abandon the South Vietnamese.

Accompura believed Loan was one of the few Vietnamese who realized that, for the South to survive, it had to have the grit to fight the war without the United States. Only if the South Vietnamese displayed real independence did they have any chance for victory. With the gradual eclipse of Premier Ky by President Thieu, Loan found himself having less and less influence. And then, four months after Tet, in May 1968, any hope that Loan could save Vietnam ended with a gunshot. As Accompura tells it, "He was hit by a .22 caliber bullet in the artery of his leg. . . . He was finished. . . . That morning I told him, I said, 'Don't leave the palace,' because every time he heard a shot fired, he'd put on that vest and jump out there. He was going to lead the troops. . . . I just walked away. I was so damn mad, I just walked away."

Loan did not die. A few days later, George Weisz called Accompura and told him that Loan was asking for his case officer. Weisz then told Accompura that the America government "wants to get rid of this guy. . . . They were hoping he wasn't going to survive," Accompura recalled.

Vietnam was full of ghosts for Berlin Base alumni—the mistresses, the enemy agents, the flood of false intelligence. Also, many Berlin Base veterans went to Vietnam for the wrong reasons. The saddest of these men was Herbert W. Natzke.

Natzke had finally made chief of base in Berlin when Berlin was no longer important. Having seen the horrors of battle, fighting the Germans in World War II, Natzke urged his son Nick not to join the Marines. Nick ignored his advice, joined up, and served a successful tour in Vietnam.

Then, over his father's protests, Nick signed up for a second tour. In Berlin, Natzke learned that his worst fear had come true, and his son was dead. Heartbroken, he had a German craftsman make two triangular wooden boxes—one for his son's flag and the other for his son's remains. He then asked for an assignment to Vietnam. As George Kisevalter tells it, "And in he goes to Vietnam, to go to the place where his son was killed, which was near the 17th Parallel, where the goddamn heavy artillery of the 175th that the Soviets gave the North Vietnamese were bombing the living hell out of the Marine position. Well, he found out where his son was killed, a hole in the ground or something. How else are they going to mark it? He had a miserable time in Vietnam. He was going crazy, motivated by this. . . ."[4]

When Ted Shackley was due to leave Vietnam in 1971, George Weisz was picked to succeed him. In March 1970, Paul Garbler—who at this time was back in Langley, working in the operations office of the Directorate of Plans—saw the order go out nominating Weisz as COS/Saigon. As Garbler tells it, Weisz's "reply came back, 'I'll take the job if you make me an 18,'"—then the top civil service grade. Garbler was amazed that Weisz was even nominated for the CIA's most important station. "I don't think George was that smart," said Garbler. "As a matter of fact, that's another one of Richard Helms's blind spots. For some reason, he fastened onto George." And now Weisz was arrogantly refusing to take the post unless he was promoted to a civil service super-grade.

Weisz must have known that the CIA could not raise him to a GS-18, because that would have given him a rank equal to higher-level U.S. officials in Saigon, including the ambassador to CORDS. "Anyone in the government would have known that," said William Corson. ". . . Weisz was knowingly making a demand the CIA could not deliver on."[5] Why did a blatantly ambitious man pass up the chance to head the world's largest CIA station? The full answer did not come to light till much later, but even at the time it was clear that, as Corson put it, Weisz had become "especially cozy with members of the International Control Commission from Soviet Bloc countries, including Poland and Hungary. It was no secret these guys were intelligence agents, operating under the guise of bringing a negotiated settlement to the war."

When Langley refused Weisz's demand and he officially turned down the position, it went to Thomas Polgar, a fellow Hungarian refugee. Typical of the CIA's personnel choices, Polgar had plenty of operational experience in Europe and Latin America, most recently as chief of station in Buenos Aires, but no Asian experience. Subordinates disliked him almost as much as they did Weisz. Berlin Base alumnus Wally Driver recalled that Polgar had a fine personal history—among other things he had taken risks to smuggle Jews out of Hungary at the end of World War II. But despite his courage and his intensity, Driver said, "Tom Polgar is a snot. He was a pain in the ass." During his German days, he called subordinates in for "demeaning" debriefings. According to Driver, Polgar did not "give a purple shit whether people liked him or not."

Tragically, his intelligence gathering was no better than his personal behavior. Orrin DeForest, chief interrogation officer of Military Region Three in Vietnam, said that he could "not understand the way Polgar thought. We did know that Polgar had become close to a Hungarian colonel for the International Control Commission. We knew this colonel was feeding Polgar information that a negotiated settlement was likely, with a coalition government being set up. . . . This belief . . . caused him [Polgar] to order us not to evacuate Vietnamese who had assisted, sometimes valiantly, the CIA. These people would be killed if they were left behind. We had a situation where Polgar was delaying everything because he believed this Communist colonel."

Every month, the *Intelligence Digest* gave an "A" rating to intelligence that came out of talks between Polgar and the colonel. "God, it made me wonder when I saw them," DeForest said. "Polgar, a Hungarian, speaking Hungarian to a Hungarian colonel, who we knew was an intelligence officer. Who did he think was slicking whom?"

Wittingly or not, Weisz and Polgar, on the basis of information from their Eastern Bloc sources, set up a catstrophe that was difficult to comprehend. In DeForest's headquarters in Bien Hoa alone, nearly six hundred CIA employees were left to the mercy of the North Vietnamese because Polgar believed his suspect source. The same nightmarish scene was repeated in scores of places throughout South Vietnam after the United States abandoned the country in 1975. The net effect was that, after the fall of Saigon, thousands of CIA agents, case officers, and workers were rounded up by the Communists, tried, and either sent to reeducation camps or executed.

In 1970, Wally Driver was between assignments. As a deep-cover agent, he was not easy to place. Normally a person in his position would be sent to graduate school, but Driver was getting too old. He had heard that Tom Polgar was in Washington, and although they had never been close, "I asked permission to see him socially. . . . I explained my lonely, long-lasting search for a job. . . . We saw each other two or three times. One time, he says, 'Oh, I have an idea. I am going out to Saigon in a few months as chief of station. There is a case out there we call "the French doctor operation" that I have been watching, and we haven't been able to crack it. It is a French physician that was recruited in Paris about 15 years previously by the GRU. We know that he has a penetration in President Thieu's palace. We know he can communicate by short-wave radio, but we don't know who his operator is. We don't know who the agent is, and we don't know how he communicates with the doctor or how the doctor gets the stuff off the radio operator.'"

Polgar told Driver, "I think maybe you can do that for me, so I will see if I can get you out to Saigon. But this is between you and me. This isn't going to be on any of the paperwork. It's just between us."

When Driver left Berlin on April 7, 1971, there was still snow on the buildings. Dressed in a winter suit, vest, and coat, he arrived at Ton Son Nhut Airbase to find that it was 104 degrees. He went to the Majestic Hotel in Saigon under his well-established cover as a magazine photographer. "I got my own visas for Saigon. . . . By that time . . . I had been in *Life, Look, The Saturday Evening Post.* . . . When I was working, I was really working. . . . I was real." Driver spent his first few days getting his journalistic accreditation without going through the CIA's "central cover" operation.

On his fourth day in Saigon, the Station sent a young Jewish officer over to see him. There was very little the officer could do for Driver, but in the course of their conversation he told Driver how unhappy he was as a family man at Saigon Station. Almost everyone there had taken up liaisons with local Vietnamese women. "He was married," Driver recalled. "He didn't screw around, and he was appalled by people who did."

To Driver's surprise, everyone in Saigon seemed to know Ted Shackley and what his job was. When Shackley wanted to see his new deep-cover operative, he sent a courier to the Majestic, and a nervous Driver would meet Shackley in another hotel somewhere else in the city. Shackley told Driver that he would be in charge of a series of agents working under commercial cover.

When Polgar arrived in late April to take over from Shackley, Driver, a disciplined agent, did not call him. After several days had passed and he still had not heard from Polgar, a worried Driver typed a message on a three-by-five card—"Why haven't I heard from you? Wally"—and sent it to Polgar through a CIA courier. He sent it a second time, but got no reply.

Finally, to his surprise, he was summoned to the new chief of station's house for a get-acquainted dinner party for all of his agents. Driver protested the risk of blowing his cover with such an appearance, but Polgar did not relent. He tried to reassure Driver by saying that he and his agents could arrive at timed intervals through various entrances in light disguises.

During the party, Driver finally took Polgar aside and reminded him of the French-doctor assignment. After several minutes of conversation, a frustrated Driver gave up and spelled it out. According to Driver, Polgar responded, "My God, I forgot." It turned out that the French-doctor spy ring had already been broken by using a grid to locate the radio transmitter. Although the problem had been solved, Polgar forgot to tell Driver, who simply wrote the experience off.

For Tullius Accompura, Saigon had an unreal atmosphere not conducive to fighting a serious war. "How the hell can you have a war when you have Saigon and everybody is having 'ooh la la' . . . the good life? Correspondents used to sit up there in the Majestic Hotel and write about those poor bastards getting blown up. You know, you had generals who had their mansions, and they would come in from there and bivouac. So the whole damn thing was so artificial. In fact, I used to tell them to declare the damn place an open city."

According to Accompura, Vietnamese mistresses were commonplace: Many American government officials kept one. Accompura came to believe that "had this war been somewhere where the women may not have been so attractive to Americans, it might have only lasted six months," not 20 years. John Sherwood found Saigon "like Berlin, except worse. . . . There were some restraining influences in Berlin. Those were gone in Vietnam."[6] William Colby, still married to his first wife, did not bring his family when he returned to Saigon in 1968 as ambassador to CORDS. According to Accompura, Colby "had a girlfriend. He was screwing some [Vietnamese] senator's wife." Accompura said that General Creighton Abrams also got involved with a Vietnamese woman. "Christ, I took Abrams out of a situation that he allowed himself in. He was a very decent, devoted kind of guy," who was so chastened by the incident, according to Accompura, that he converted to Roman Catholicism.

Even in a place teeming with illicit sex, Polgar's activities dominated Saigon Station gossip. Wally Driver remembers seeing Polgar openly walking down the street "with one of his Vietnamese gals."[7] Accompura said of Polgar, "From the day he arrived in Vietnam . . . and I am not just trying to moralize . . . everywhere he went they used to have to set up the girls for him. This . . . was his suddenly found sexuality. . . . They had an interpreter pool of gals, all Vietnamese, who eventually came here [to the States], who were available."

The boys from Berlin Base mostly managed to survive and get out of Vietnam, and technically, the country's collapse did not happen on their watch. Sam Wilson returned for a while to the Army, to run the Eighty-Second Airborne at Fort Bragg. Then, in 1971, he was appointed military attaché in Moscow, where Yekaterina Furtseva developed a fondness for him. George Weisz, Ted Shackley's longtime enemy, had given up Saigon for the much lesser job of base chief in Berlin. Shackley himself returned to Langley to head the Western Hemisphere Division. Lou Conein retired from the CIA. By 1974, only three hundred CIA officers worked out of Saigon Station.

Tom Polgar was the last CIA chief of station in Vietnam. In January 1975, he visited Orrin DeForest's base at Bien Hoa. The war was lost, but Polgar made a remarkable speech to DeForest and his colleagues. In his heavy Hungarian accent, he said, "I want you to know that everything is going okay. We don't see any problems in 1975. Our reading is that the situation is under control."[8]

According to Driver and others, Polgar had been reinterpreting the Order of Battle information coming in from the field in order to make it fit his preconceived notions of what he wanted to send on. Driver said, "Whether this was at his own behest or that of the U.S. Ambassador, I don't know." At the end of the war, General Loan was so furious at the Americans for betraying the South Vietnamese that he went to Polgar and threatened to use the Saigon militia, which he controlled, to kidnap top American officials and turn them over to the North Vietnamese.[9]

The last chaotic hours of the Vietnam War are an appropriate symbol of the way top CIA management treated the people of Vietnam. A three-man Vietnamese crew was bravely keeping a satellite communications link going between Saigon Station and Langley. The CIA promised these men evacuation and admittance to the United States for their courage. As helicopter after helicopter took off, the danger for the communications crew increased.

The last message that Thomas Polgar sent from Saigon Station was hardly worth risking the lives of these three loyal men. At 3:20 A.M., April 30, 1975, Polgar said: "It has been a long and hard fight and we have lost. . . . The severity of the defeat and the circumstances of it, however, would seem to call for a reassessment of the policies of niggardly half measures, which have characterized much of our participation here despite the commitment of manpower and resources, which were certainly generous. Those who fail to learn from history are forced to repeat it. Let us hope we will not have another Vietnam experience and that we will have learned our lesson. Saigon signing off."

William Colby—who by then was director of central intelligence—sent Polgar a message almost simultaneously: "As we approach the end of communication with Saigon, I would like to record the Agency's pride and satisfaction with the job its representatives did there. . . . The courage, the integrity, dedication, and high competence the Agency displayed in a variety of situations over these years has been fully matched and even surpassed by your performance during the difficult final phase. . . . Your Government has profited immensely from the accuracy and breadth of your reporting. . . ."

In the end, the three Vietnamese communications men did not make it onto the last American helicopters out of Vietnam. A top CIA official scratched their names off the list and added the names of two of his Vietnamese mistresses. According to Tullius Accompura, only one of the three men survived his years in a "reeducation camp." The Vietnamese women who provided sexual favors to the CIA official became American citizens.

CHAPTER FORTY-SIX

Nixon Versus Kennedy's Ghost

E VEN WHILE the Vietnam War was still on, there was another focus of CIA attention, and that was Chile.

At one time, Chile was the most successful democracy in Latin America. Since its birth as a nation in 1818, it had fewer revolutions than any other country in the region. All this changed when the United States intervened in Chile's 1958 presidential election.

The Eisenhower Administration was pleased with the new president, the conservative Jorge Alessandri. It was less pleased that liberal Christian Democrats, led by Eduardo Frei, were gaining support, and, far more disturbingly, a Marxist Socialist, Salvador Allende Gossens, had made a strong showing, winning more than a third of the vote. Even before Castro took power in Cuba, Marxism had planted roots in Chile through the ballot box. That was the main reason why President Eisenhower began pressing Alessandri for land reform.[1]

Then, in May 1960, a massive earthquake struck Chile. The need for relief was enormous, and Eisenhower used the opportunity to press Alessandri further, linking U.S. aid to the reform proposals. According to Edward M. Korry, who became ambassador to Chile seven years later, it was unprecedented for Washington to impose conditions of this sort in dealing with a friendly head of state south of the border.

This seemingly well-intentioned decision by President Eisenhower launched a series of actions by him and his successors, Presidents

Kennedy, Johnson, and Nixon, that plunged the United States into a debacle for itself and a tragedy for the people of Chile. What started as a project to help the land-poor people of Chile, by 1970 had turned that country into a political battlefield where Richard Nixon waged war with John Kennedy's ghost.

It was just a few months after Chile's 1958 election that Fidel Castro came to power in Cuba. He and Allende became friends, and soon the Chilean was head of OLAS, Cuba's political organization in Latin America.

Under the Chilean constitution, the president served a six-year term and could not succeed himself. As Chile's 1964 election approached, the Kennedy Administration saw there was a serious danger Allende would become the first freely elected Marxist anywhere in the world. Kennedy started diverting U.S. aid money into clandestine operations in Chile—not through a State Department official or even a CIA officer, but through the articulate and handsome Jesuit priest from Belgium, Roger Vekemans, whom the Vatican had dispatched to Chile in 1958.

Ralph Dungan, Kennedy's White House aide on Latin America, later confirmed that he brought Vekemans to the Oval Office for a secret meeting in May 1963, after first introducing him to CIA Director John A. McCone.[2] Meeting Vekemans deeply affected the young president. In Ambassador Korry's view, "Kennedy would have trouble not thinking of this fellow [as] being superior in every way to him. He could articulate in English as well as John Kennedy. He had a profound knowledge of history, of philosophy, of sociology. Kennedy liked him, was impressed by him, and allocated to him the money, in secret, to keep Chile from falling under Castro and Communist influence."

Vekemans urged Kennedy to meet Eduardo Frei, the Catholic church's candidate for president of Chile. Dungan secretly brought Frei to the White House to meet Kennedy. After this meeting, Frei was the New Frontier's candidate. The CIA was authorized to spend $3 million to assist him and his Christian Democratic Party—which was patterned on the Christian Democratic parties of Western Europe—in the 1964 election.

The Business Group for Latin America was also put into action to defeat Allende and elect Frei. Robert Kennedy orchestrated the spending of large amounts of money collected from 37 business friends of David Rockefeller. The attorney general used all his clout to get the cooperation of heads of corporations that did business—or wished to do business—in Chile.

During the Kennedy years, Ralph Dungan ran much of the covert activity in Chile out of the White House. When Lyndon Johnson took over, he decided Dungan could accomplish more on the spot in Santiago, the Chilean capital. Johnson named Dungan ambassador to Chile in 1964, in time to manage the local end of the effort to elect Frei. Ambassador Dungan made use of CIA money-laundering organizations, including the Henry J. Schroeder Bank and Trust Company and a front company called Deltec Ltd., set up specifically for the operation. The CIA also worked in conjunction with Agustin Edwards, a well-connected conservative Chilean and the publisher of *El Mercurio*, Chile's largest daily newspaper. Others who worked to elect Frei included American copper companies, the Catholic church, Swift and Company, and the Latin American subsidiary of the International Meat Packers Union.

The meat packers and the Swift company were interested because there was a severe meat shortage in Chile in the months leading up to the election. The CIA convinced the Chilean people that all was well by getting Swift to smuggle meat into Chile from Argentina. Thirteen years later, Dungan defended his action. "I had to see that Frei got elected," he said. "It was something the president really wanted. . . . Our efforts were benign. They really made an attempt to improve the lot of the Chileans. When we brought food in for the '64 election, it was no different than a ward heeler giving away turkeys for an election here."[3] In the end, Frei won big, with a 54 percent majority.

Once Frei was installed in power, Dungan set to work remodeling the Christian Democratic Party. Soon it looked and sounded like a Chilean version of Kennedy's New Frontier or Johnson's Great Society. Dungan's successor, Ed Korry,[4] wrote that Dungan "was described in Washington and Santiago as the only American member of the Frei cabinet."

To his credit, Frei carried out many reforms, particularly in the areas of education and health. But the Christian Democratic Party did not have a majority in the Congress, and both the Left and the Right combined to vote down many of Frei's measures.

The real Kennedy aim had been to guarantee a Christian Democratic dynasty in Chile like the one that emerged in Italy after World War II, and this meant holding on to the presidency in the 1970 election. However, under the Chilean constitution, the highly popular Frei could not succeed himself, and his would-be Christian Democratic successor, Radomiro

Tomic, was not a promising candidate. A party debate raged on how best to face the coming challenge, and in late 1966, a split developed between Frei's supporters and the Catholic church, represented by Father Vekemans. Dungan became more and more personally involved in the effort to buttress Frei's faction. As Korry later learned, "Dungan arranged for the CIA to start a biweekly newspaper. He had some Frei ministers, including his defense minister, on the CIA payroll. He pressured Anaconda Copper Company to hire Christian Democrats to replace others." Frei and Dungan had the same confessor, Father Renato Poblete, who was on the staff of Santiago's cardinal. According to Korry, Poblete was the most influential Chilean cleric and the chief rival of Vekemans.

Edward M. Korry took over as ambassador in late 1967. Korry was a veteran newsman whose award-winning career had mostly been spent in Europe, first with United Press and then with the Cowles organization. His first ambassadorial appointment had been to Ethiopia in 1963.

When Korry arrived in Santiago, he found that "we [the United States] had arrogated to ourselves the responsibility for every facet of Chilean life—agriculture, education, health, finance, production, savings and loans, police, and the military. I had the legal obligation to report annually on some 50 different lines of activities involving U.S. tax dollars." Korry was responsible for overseeing some $2 billion (in 1968 dollars) of loans, investment guarantees, and other forms of largesse to a country with only eight million people. In addition, Dungan had promised the Chilean Air Force that no black Americans would serve in Chile. Shocked, Korry quickly reversed this policy.

Not long after taking over, Korry cabled the State Department (with copies to the National Security Council and the CIA) saying that "the incestuous intimacy is hurting us both" and announcing his intention of disengaging "very quietly and prudently." Much to the Pentagon's annoyance, he began to press Washington to slash U.S. military missions in Chile.[5] He cut the U.S. military presence in Chile to a minimum, even eliminating the Air Attaché plane that flew him and other American diplomats.

Despite Korry's best efforts to limit U.S. interference in Chile, many connections continued. At a farewell luncheon in early 1968 for the CIA's deputy station chief, who was returning to Langley, Korry was surprised to see that the guests included several Chilean notables and a Maryknoll priest, Miguel d'Escoto.[6] Years later, the Los Angeles-born d'Escoto became the foreign minister of Marxist Nicaragua.

Another guest at the farewell lunch was Father Vekemans. One of Ambassador Korry's first acts had been to cut off the access the Belgian priest enjoyed. "After I met him," Korry said, "I did not see him for three years. He came to me then to complain that the Agency for International Development [AID] was going to audit his books," and the books were not in order. Korry called the head of AID and stopped the investigation to protect Dungan and the White House from embarrassment. Years later, the U.S. General Accounting Office said $400,000 earmarked for "population studies" was missing. "In fact," Korry said, "it was used to bribe Chilean politicians who supported the church.

"The GAO said there was criminality," Korry continued. "But you have to place responsibility on Dungan and Bobby Kennedy. They were the architects of all this. When Dungan testified to the Senate, he lied and got away with it." In 1975, Dungan told the Senate Committee set up to investigate CIA plots: "When I was ambassador to Chile, U.S. covert activities in Chile were not extensive, and most were irrelevant and not directed to Chilean political institutions."[7]

In 1968, Korry learned that the CIA and the Defense Intelligence Agency's efforts were not limited to Chile. In early 1964, Lyndon Johnson had ordered the Defense Department and the CIA to secretly back a military coup in Brazil against President João Goulart. It was done quietly and successfully, scarcely attracting the attention of the media. An American armada was dispatched to let the Brazilian military know that the U.S. government backed the coup. The United States had helped to eliminate an elected government, following the precedent it set in Chile.

The CIA was already wary of Ed Korry before he arrived in Santiago. When he was ambassador to Ethiopia, he learned from a young Agency officer that the chief of station was fabricating reports to Langley. As Korry recalled, "The subordinate had told me in the greatest confidence his boss was imagining or inventing some reports the tiny station was filing to Washington. Since I was convinced that the CAS [chief at station] was drinking far too much, that his work product was of no value to the embassy, and that I knew of no covert operation worth a damn for us in Ethiopia, I cabled via the back channel used for such matters to voice my criticism."

Korry found himself attending a hearing in Washington chaired by the third-ranking CIA official, Lloyd George, an ex-FBI man. George attacked Korry for not providing proof, but Korry refused to reveal his source. In the end, the station chief was reassigned. Korry later learned that he was "dried out" by the Agency and resumed his career as a sober, effective official. But the CIA never again trusted Korry.

Just months before Korry's arrival in Chile, the CIA appointed Berlin Base alumnus Henry Hecksher as the new Santiago station chief. After leaving Berlin, Hecksher had gone to Guatemala City and played a major role in the 1954 coup against Jacobo Arbenz. For his success in Guatemala, the CIA rewarded him with a string of other Latin American jobs. Tom Polgar, who by 1967 was station chief in Buenos Aires, assisted Hecksher in a variety of harebrained schemes.

About a year after Korry arrived in Santiago, Hecksher came to him with a major problem. A Bolivian government minister who had been on the CIA payroll was threatening to expose the network of current CIA agents in Bolivia and to reveal the man who had been in charge of hunting down and killing Che Guevara. As Korry tells it, the defector, Interior Minister Antonio Arguedas, "announced in northern Chile, where he was received by Allende, then president of the Chilean Senate, that he was going to name every CIA agent in Bolivia. Hecksher asked me to intervene, since the Agency had failed to make a dent with the Chilean Minister of Interior."

In fact, the Chilean minister had put Arguedas into "protective custody" when he found out it was not only the CIA that had an interest in him: Castro had dispatched BARBAROSSA, the legendary head of Cuban intelligence, to Santiago to take custody of Arguedas. "Hecksher asked me—he had never before sought my intervention—to arrange for Arguedas's handler in the Agency to be allowed to talk to him, no more, for an hour in his cell. I arranged it. Arguedas then agreed to the Chilean proposal that he fly to Spain, where he could do what he wished. [DCI] Helms, Hecksher, and [Secretary of State] Rusk then asked me to convince the British to give Arguedas a visa, since the CIA had learned in Madrid that the Cubans intended to grab him there. Arguedas flew with a Chilean guard to Madrid. The Cubans tried but failed to get him. He was transferred at Madrid airport immediately by the Agency to a plane for

London." Arguedas did eventually get to Cuba to talk about who was involved in the capture and murder of Che Guevara, but too late to do serious damage to the CIA.

Despite the Kennedy/Johnson efforts to create a Christian Democratic dynasty, the Chilean Congress and electorate remained divided into three factions: the moderate Christian Democrats led by the lame-duck President Frei; a right-wing coalition led by former President Alessandri (who, having been out of office for a term, was eligible to run again); and a left-wing coalition headed by Allende. Since Frei could not succeed himself, he and his party made good on a promise to support Radomiro Tomic in the 1970 election. Tomic had been Frei's ambassador to Washington, where he had convinced the American Catholic establishment and many others that he could beat Allende and Alessandri.

Korry warned Washington that Allende's support came "ironically, not only from the usual organized labor vote, the urban slum dwellers, the intellectuals, the teachers, but, critically, from the Freemasons of the PR"—the centrist Radical Party. In the embassy, only Korry (according to his deputy, a career diplomat) thought Allende had a good chance to win.

Fidel Castro, meanwhile, was taking a growing interest in Allende. He sent one of his top intelligence officers to Chile to help Allende organize for the election. That officer, Luis Fernandez Ona, had met Allende's favorite daughter, Beatriz, when she went to Cuba for training under a Socialist Party program. Beatriz, an extreme Marxist, married Fernandez during his stay in Chile.[8] According to Korry, Allende himself at this time was becoming much more the captive of violent and extreme elements in the Marxist world. He received financial support from the Soviet Bloc, but the powerful left wing of his Socialist Party looked to Maoist China. This perceived threat energized the anti-Allende forces both in Chile and in the United States.

As Chile's 1969 congressional campaign began, CIA Station Chief Henry Hecksher, now in Korry's confidence, pushed the ambassador to spend the $350,000 authorized for anti-Allende candidates. Korry angered Hecksher by bucking the CIA culture of payoffs and duplicity and spending just $50,000, spread among dozens of candidates. He also managed to end all but two unbreakable CIA subsidies to Chilean politicians, paid, in effect, as pensions ever since 1964. Still, it took a while for word to get around. According to Korry, a year before the 1970 presidential election, representatives of Allende, Alessandri, and Tomic each secretly came to him in search of a million dollars in U.S. contributions.

IN THE LATE 1960s, the United States itself was going through one of the most tumultuous political periods in its history. In the midst of escalating protests over the Vietnam War, President Johnson was challenged for reelection, first, by Senator Eugene McCarthy and then by the former attorney general, now Senator Robert Kennedy. At the end of March, Johnson stunned the American public by pulling out of the race. The question of whether Robert Kennedy could win the nomination became moot when he, like his brother, was brought down by an assassin's bullet. Richard Nixon eventually defeated Vice President Hubert Humphrey and former Democrat George Wallace for the presidency.

Nixon's paranoia about the Kennedy brothers and his keen interest in covert operations combined to produce disastrous results in Chile. Nixon had discovered on a trip to Latin America in early 1967 that the Kennedys had used Chile as their laboratory for the creation of a Pax Americana. Almost from Nixon's first day in office, his staff started badgering CIA Director Richard Helms for detailed information on the Kennedys' operations. "It was as if Nixon was shadowboxing dead men," said Korry. "Anything Kennedy stood for, he [Nixon] was automatically against. . . . He felt that he could do exactly the same thing as the Kennedys, but, in fact, the Kennedys could get away with it, and he couldn't."

For Korry, the first days of the new administration offered a look into Nixon's troubled mind. Even before Nixon was inaugurated, he had done everything possible to signal his opposition to President Frei and the Christian Democrats and to make it clear that he wanted Jorge Alessandri to return to the presidency in 1970. Now, two key State Department nominees sent word down the ranks, as Korry put it, "that Nixon . . . wanted the scheduled state visit by Frei annulled, and that there would be little or no fresh money for Chile. The office director at State informed me by private, confidential letter. I told no one." Korry added: "Nixon was settling scores with the Kennedys by crossing Frei's name off the list of heads of state to be invited to Washington that year."

When the CIA produced a National Intelligence Estimate highly critical of Frei, Korry protested in a series of tough cables. In one of these, he said that a campaign in support of the Right in Chile would only help Allende and his Communist supporters get elected. He tried to make it clear to President Nixon that the United States faced "three lemons" as candidates and that the aged Alessandri and the noisy Tomic would each much rather see Allende win than the other.

Early in the Nixon Administration, CIA officials realized that the ego-driven National Security Adviser, Henry Kissinger, was now in charge of covert operations. Robert Kennedy's old Special Group, designed to bring together high-level officials to respond to specific crises, became the Watch Group, chaired by Kissinger. Korry was invited to several Watch Group meetings. He did not know that when he and several others left the room, the Watch Group immediately converted into the super-secret Forty Committee, also chaired by Kissinger.

The Forty Committee was one of the most powerful organizations in government: All U.S. covert operations overseas required its approval. Within this committee, the true decision-making group consisted of Undersecretary of State U. Alexis Johnson, Nixon's favorite official at State; DCI Richard Helms as well as the number two man at the Pentagon; and Kissinger.

One of Helms's greatest tactical successes had been in keeping the paramilitary side of United States covert activities under the aegis of the Defense Intelligence Agency (DIA). "This is how he kept his tunic clean," Robert Crowley explained. "The CIA-DIA partnership was one of many ways the CIA hid the dirtiest and most vile of its operations. It gave the Agency deniability." In 1975, when Senator Frank Church's Select Committee held its hearings on CIA transgressions, many Americans believed they were learning all there was to know about the CIA's "family jewels," its darkest secrets. But the real dark secret is how the CIA became the public whipping boy while military secrecy was used to protect even more damaging operations.

For Helms, the DIA arrangement meant no decrease in power. He was very much the director of central intelligence—the person who oversaw all U.S. intelligence activities, not just the CIA. The other intelligence agencies deferred to him. And, if an operation failed or was exposed, he could deflect blame and responsibility. As Berlin Base veteran John Sherwood put it, "This was his most well-developed talent."[9] However, it was a talent that failed to protect him as the disaster in Chile spun out of control.

When Richard Nixon first met Ed Korry in Ethiopia in 1967, he offered him a job as an aide, and Korry turned him down. Now, in 1969, Korry heard from Acting Assistant Secretary of State Pete Vaky that he was the only Kennedy/Johnson appointee to be retained in the new Republican administration. Then Korry was told that Nixon had canceled a $20 million loan to Frei's government that had been approved months before. Korry cabled Washington: "If you are trying to destroy Christian Democracy and to elect Allende—your worst enemy, whose hero is Castro . . . if you are trying to provoke a reaction by the Christian Democrats against the copper companies for whom we have $500 million in taxpayers' money on the line . . . you will have a reaction."

Korry was not surprised when the State Department quickly telephoned to say he was being fired. However, his views so impressed the new assistant secretary of state for Inter-American Affairs, Charles Meyer, a former Sears executive, that he intervened and asked Nixon if it was true Korry was being fired. As things turned out, Chile did not get the loan, and Korry kept his ambassadorship. In retrospect, he probably wishes he hadn't.

Korry's most striking action involved U.S. copper companies operating in Chile. When the companies' Washington supporters tried to get special U.S. protection for their profits, Korry opposed them. Instead, he offered a breathtaking proposal to deal with the basic problem of American ownership of most of Chile's copper.

Copper provided 89 percent of Chile's earnings abroad and 15 percent of its national budget. Korry learned that President Johnson, when he began to feel the financial pinch of the Vietnam War, had leaned on President Frei to sell the U.S. one hundred thousand tons of copper at far below the world market price. Of course Frei agreed, but his action negatively affected the price of copper and seriously hindered the Chilean economy. Korry reckoned that the U.S. copper properties were sure targets for nationalization and that U.S. taxpayers, through the insurance underwritten by AID, might be on the hook for hundreds of millions of dollars. He urged the companies to make a preemptive deal by offering Chile 51 percent ownership of their businesses.

Ironically, it was Frei who balked at the proposal. "When I began to talk to Frei about this problem," Korry recalled, "he was shocked. He said he had given JFK, LBJ, and Dungan his word that in return for the huge amounts of fresh investment by the companies to modernize . . . he could not try to change the rules again." He had just signed agreements with the United States after three long years of tedious negotiation for fresh copper investment. "How can I reopen the matter?" he asked. As Korry recalled, "I replied that I only wished him to start thinking about an inevitable problem that affected his country and our relations more than any other."

Few Chileans or Americans understood that Ralph Dungan, following the Kennedy/Johnson model for Latin America, had sought to squeeze the Chilean military budget to its lowest level ever. Under Chilean law, the military got a small percentage of the country's take from all copper exports. Korry believed that giving Chile a fairer share of copper profits would help quiet an increasingly mutinous military. He also felt that "the additional funds would help the anti-Communist government to expand social services, improve education, etc."

Before Korry could make any headway, the leaders of Chile's other parties began to clamor for a new deal with Anaconda and Kennecott. After many weeks, with negotiations bogged down in public insults, Korry began to act as a secret mediator. The deal he brokered was unprecedented. Chile got effective control (51 percent) of Anaconda and Kennecott. Both paid huge windfall-profits taxes to Chile, recompensing Chile for the profits it lost when it helped President Johnson in 1966. Ironically, the *New York Times* and *Washington Post,* in hailing the agreements, praised the U.S. government for staying out of the negotiations.

Unfortunately, Korry's accomplishment, good though it was for U.S. taxpayers and the people of Chile, threatened the bottom line of the multinational corporations that were the CIA's longtime partners. Nixon was working with Kennedy's secretive Business Group for Latin America, now rebaptized the Council of the Americas. The Council's executive committee was made up of some of the richest and most powerful men in the United States, including some of Richard Nixon's biggest supporters and closest personal friends. Korry did not understand the extent to which the Council, led by men like Harold Geneen, the president and chairman of the board of International Telephone and Telegraph (ITT), and Donald Kendall, president and CEO of Pepsico, preferred the old ways of doing business in Chile. Geneen did not want to have to sell ITT's Sheraton Hotels or its majority holdings in the Chilean Telephone Company to the

Chilean government. He, like most U.S. businessmen, did not like the Christian Democrats, particularly their new candidate, Tomic. They wanted Alessandri to win in 1970.

On April 10, 1970, José de Cubas, the CEO of Westinghouse International, and Charles J. Parkinson, chairman of the board of Anaconda, called on Korry's boss at the State Department, Charles Meyer, and proposed a joint campaign to back Alessandri in the upcoming elections. They offered $500,000 in campaign funds. Meyer did not definitely reject the multinationals' proposal, but he refused to give them a commitment.

At this point, former CIA Director John McCone, now on Harold Geneen's payroll as an ITT board member, became the chief lobbyist for the effort. McCone, who had elevated Richard Helms to the position from which he finally got the CIA directorship, called on his old employee and, with the White House's blessing, pushed the CIA to get behind Alessandri.

When Korry learned of this "Anaconda proposal," he responded with a withering cable that called Alessandri the "candidate of the rich" and said he did not need U.S. funding. If Alessandri won, said Korry, any U.S. donation would make Washington susceptible to the demands of his government for his entire six-year term.

Both Korry and Meyer thought Korry's cable killed the proposal. Not so. Korry was no match for Harold Geneen. Geneen had backed the 1964 effort against Allende and had not been happy with Frei in the years since. According to Robert Crowley, who handled corporate relations for the CIA at the time, "Geneen had the connections to get what he wanted. . . . He wanted the CIA to support Alessandri, and he was tired of Korry getting in the way."

CHAPTER FORTY-SEVEN

DON'T CROSS GENEEN

Although it had other businesses, the core of ITT's multinational empire was still its global communications network. ITT handled enormous amounts of U.S. government communications, including most of the secret communications for U.S. facilities abroad. Furthermore, ITT had the technology to tap into almost any phone conversation in Europe or Latin America. This made Harold Geneen very valuable to the CIA and the National Security Agency. William R. Corson, who was charged with protecting U.S. communications intelligence, said that Geneen even had considerable power over who ran the NSA.[1]

Geneen pressed hard to get an ITT-approved official appointed director of the NSA during the Johnson Administration, and President Johnson agreed. As the name of the proposed NSA director was circulated, the Administration was under tremendous pressure from several members of Congress close to Geneen to hurry the appointment along. However, according to Corson, who had previously investigated the director-designate, Johnson's choice was a suspected Soviet agent. Corson ran a two-year investigation that discovered that William Charles Godell was part of a Soviet spy ring at the highest levels of the Pentagon's most secret office—The Advanced Research Projects Agency. To make certain Godell was never given a government job again, Godell was indicted and convicted for violating an obscure statute about misspending appropriated funds. "It amounted to an Al Capone kind of case. We did not have the ability to charge him with espionage because the man he was handing off documents to had been either murdered or committed suicide. So this charge was substituted." The appointment was finally dropped.[2]

ITT did not lose its special relationship with the government when President Nixon took office. In fact, Geneen had even closer ties to Nixon than he had to either Kennedy or Johnson.

Especially after the fight over the "Anaconda proposal," Geneen did not trust Korry, and his deputies worked closely with the CIA to circumvent the ambassador. By the spring of 1970, ITT had stepped up its campaign in support of Alessandri. Two ITT officials—Harold Hendrix, a raspy-voiced former Miami newspaper reporter who had long been on the CIA payroll, and Robert Berrellez, a former Associated Press man—were secretly meeting with a CIA operative known as "Felix." Felix, with the assistance of Santiago Station Chief Henry Hecksher, was illegally feeding the ITT men Korry's views on the coming election. In July 1970, armed with the ambassador's confidential exchanges with his station chief and with the State Department, Geneen asked for a meeting with Richard Helms, who sent William Broe, then head of the Western Hemisphere Division, in his place. Geneen offered Broe a million dollars through ITT's Brazilian subsidiary to support Alessandri and stop Allende.

Broe told Geneen that, while the CIA itself could not accept the money, it could suggest how best to use it—a fine distinction. Broe made arrangements to advise ITT on how to get the money to the right people in Chile, while Geneen continued to lobby Henry Kissinger for more direct government action.

During a meeting of the Watch Group on June 27, 1970, Kissinger said: "I don't see why we have to let a country go Marxist just because the people are irresponsible." When Korry was told of the comment, he realized that the Nixon Administration cared less about democracy than keeping the Communist Allende out of power and protecting the profits of its corporate friends.

Henry Hecksher was doing everything he could to reinforce the conviction in Washington that the conservative Alessandri would beat Allende. While Korry and his staff were reporting that if Alessandri won, it would be by a small margin, Hecksher was sending back inflated predictions of an Alessandri landslide.

At one point, Hecksher confronted Korry directly. As Korry tells it, Hecksher, "a proper Prussian gentleman," warned the ambassador that "my aloof, hands-off approach to the elections would be read by Chileans as a signal that the U.S. didn't care if Allende and the Communists came to power, [and] wasn't that contrary to U.S. policy and to my mission as a U.S. ambassador? Of course, he was correct. So, for the elections—and these are the actual verified figures of what was expended and spent as opposed to what was authorized in principle at the beginning in the discussions—the CIA spent $90,000 for a propaganda campaign." Korry says Hecksher's team spent an additional $40,000 on minor covert activity, bringing the total expenditure on the 1970 election to $130,000.

Korry continued: "I cabled State that the campaign would probably deliver votes to Allende—the techniques I had first seen with the 'Red Terror' scare posters with Russian tanks as a young correspondent in Italy in 1948. Moreover, I notified Washington during the last month of the election campaign that I had discovered the CIA's confident predictions of an Alessandri triumph were based on a census from 1960 and were meaningless. The embassy, by contrast, predicted a narrow Alessandri triumph over Allende with Tomic a distant third."

The White House, meanwhile, was also pressuring Korry and his deputy, Harry Shlaudeman, to do more to prevent Allende's election. For Korry, the time leading up to the election was "spent weaving, ducking, toadying, misdirecting, and tarrying to prevent the U.S. from being involved. It was dangerous, I knew, to try to be smarter than everyone else in Washington, but I thought I had succeeded in preventing any covert interference."

Of course, ITT and the CIA were far from the only ones trying to influence the election. As Korry put it, "Some Socialists had joined the rightists to plot with the Chilean generals to bring down Frei. The Communists were using large subsidies from abroad to buy and sell senators and deputies in the Chilean Congress, to blackmail key public figures, and plant agents in the other parties. Fascists were receiving help from Brazil to make trouble for Frei. And my hands-off, low-profile policy was abetting the process, as my CIA station chief reminded me."

Five weeks before the election, Korry finally sent Washington a "contingency plan" which the State Department had demanded weeks earlier, detailing what U.S. policy should be if Allende won.[3] Titled "Fidelismo Without Fidel," the plan predicted with about 98 percent accuracy Allende's probable actions in his first two years as president. The plan made no mention of covert activity or approaches to the Chilean military. "I had repeatedly reported to Washington that the Chilean military would follow a politically neutral course," Korry recalled.

Before the report arrived in Washington, Kissinger cabled Korry, asking what the policy should be if Allende won. The message from Korry was "cool but correct." Shortly after that, another cable arrived from Washington, this one from State, asking about the possibility of Chilean military action. Korry cabled back that such a course "was an utterly hollow hope doomed to failure."

On September 4, 1970, Korry's fears proved correct. Allende won with a plurality of 36.4 percent against Alessandri's 34.9 percent, while Frei's dismal stand-in, Radomiro Tomic, received only 27.8 percent. Washington was in shock. "It was [as] if they actually believed their own polls," Korry said.

Complicating matters was the fact that lame-duck President Frei had taken it upon himself to contact President Nixon and suggest that more be done by the United States, on the grounds that if Allende were elected, the "extremists he fronted for" would take control of Chile. "Frei sent a tendentious message to Nixon through a visiting State Department official," Korry recalled. "Since I was translator, I immediately interjected the bottom-line question: 'Are you asking the U.S. to intervene in some way?' Frei replied, 'No, only propaganda.' Frei added that he did not fear Allende's own instincts, but the men around him were another story. Allende's closest intimates—his daughter Beatriz, his two drinking cronies, and his mistress-secretary—were each very dedicated Castroites, and the Communist Party, as his allies and the architects of the divide-and-rule approach to Allende's opposition before the election, was regarded by Moscow as the one Communist party in Latin America that was well and reliably led."

The message, including Frei's "No, only propaganda" reply to Korry, was read by Kissinger and Nixon as an invitation. Nixon's staff suggested to Korry that perhaps the United States should consider a military coup. Korry cabled back that such a knee-jerk reaction could only backfire.

Almost immediately after the election, Korry heard from *El Mercurio* publisher Agustin Edwards, leader of the CIA effort against Allende in 1964. Edwards wanted to know what the United States was going to do to stop Allende, whose election still had to be ratified by the Chilean Congress. "I told him, 'Absolutely nothing,'" Korry recalled. ". . . When he said, 'What about military action?' . . . I said, 'We will observe and report.'" Edwards told Korry that he was leaving Chile and that his family was already out. Korry did not know that Edwards had a close relationship with the Rockefeller family and with Donald Kendall of Pepsico and that, through Kendall, Edwards was to meet with Attorney General John Mitchell and make his case for U.S. intervention in Chile. If the ambassador and the State Department would not cooperate, then Edwards would find someone like Mitchell who would.[4]

On September 14, Mitchell, Kissinger, Kendall, and Edwards had breakfast together. John Mitchell understood ITT's concerns. He was also well aware, as was President Nixon, that ITT had promised $800,000 to help underwrite the GOP national convention in San Diego in 1972[5] and had promised additional funds for the president's reelection campaign. Two hours after the meeting, President Nixon personally called DCI Helms and told him to prepare and implement a plan to stop Allende from assuming the presidency. Nixon told Helms he was to take any action necessary.

Helms, no lover of covert warfare, could think of one other possibility, and that was to stop Allende by having the Chilean Congress vote against ratifying his presidency. To throw Korry off the scent, the CIA cleverly gave its tacit support to a far-fetched scheme the Christian Democrats had concocted to block Allende's ratification and eventually return Frei to the presidency. The Christian Democrats' scheme, labeled by Korry "the Rube Goldberg gambit" because of its complications, appealed to the CIA because it helped shield the real covert action going on through ITT.

The plan was to have the Christian Democrats in the Congress vote against Allende and then vote for Alessandri, the close second in the popular vote. Alessandri, in exchange for political concessions by the Christian Democrats, would resign after taking the oath of office. That would allow Frei, still the most popular politician in Chile, to get around the constitutional ban on two consecutive terms and run directly against Allende in a new election.

On September 15, the CIA approved this nutty last-ditch effort to block Allende. Korry, though dubious, encouraged belief in the plan, in the hope of holding off more extreme intervention from Washington. The CIA also suggested to ITT that it pay off Chilean deputies and senators to vote against Allende. Washington sent Korry a secret message instructing him to call on President Frei and offer him $250,000 to use for that purpose. Korry ducked the assignment, convinced that bribes would not work.

At almost the same time, Korry's military aide, Colonel Paul Wimert, told him that three top Chilean generals wanted to know from Korry what they should do about Allende's election. "Shlaudeman and I drafted a one-paragraph message for Wimert to read to the generals from me," Korry recalled. "It praised the professionalism of the Chilean armed forces, their patriotism and discipline, and pointed out they were responsible to the orders of their commander-in-chief, the president, and Frei was that for the next two months." Korry's message to the generals got back to Washington with predictable results. "They had assumed, wrongly in this case, that I had presented to Frei the $250,000 offer . . . and that I was pressuring Frei. I deliberately chose to avoid telling them what I was not doing, as Hecksher belatedly discovered."

On September 16, Richard Helms informed his subordinates that an "Allende regime was not acceptable to the United States." Helms was in a dilemma. He remained gun-shy of covert operations, but Nixon had given him a direct order. In the end, he authorized a two-track policy to prevent Allende from coming to power. Track I was the Rube Goldberg political plan, in which the unwilling Korry worked with his superiors at the State Department in "paper chasing" exercises on never-implemented ways to get the conservatives and Christian Democrats to come together to defeat Allende. Meanwhile, the Forty Committee had the full cooperation of the CIA's Hecksher and the embassy's military attachés in keeping from the ambassador all word of Track II—the real CIA/ITT plan. This involved encouraging the Chilean military to stage an armed coup. As a secret CIA memo blandly reported, "The second approach was designed to try to prevent Allende from taking power, when and if the constitutional route would not succeed."[6]

Benny Holmes, the manager of ITT's Chilean operations, was overtly working on Track I, funneling ITT money to members of the Chilean Congress. Ironically, Holmes was a Masonic Lodge brother of Allende, whom he liked and who he predicted would be better in office than the Christian Democrats. Meanwhile, the CIA was putting together a special, very secret task force for Track II, the armed coup.

By September 15, Korry was growing concerned. He had learned that in direct contradiction to his orders, Hecksher had been working with members of Patria y Libertad (Fatherland and Liberty), a militaristic, neo-Fascist group that used torture to enforce its views. The group's patron saint was militant Brigadier General Robert Viaux.

The previous fall, Viaux had tried to foment rebellion in the military, leading a 24-hour uprising at the Tacna Artillery Regiment in Santiago to protest poor pay and equipment. After this incident, Viaux was placed on parole and "retired" from the Army, and Korry ordered all Americans in Chile to stay clear of him. But under Berlin Base veteran Hecksher, Santiago Station secretly arranged for Viaux to meet with ITT's Hendrix and Berrellez to assist him in drumming up support in the Chilean military. Also contained in this volatile mixture was General Viaux's beautiful and ambitious wife, whose activities, according to Korry, had been monitored by Allende's agents for more than a year. "She had an Evita personality complex," said Korry. ". . . She was a very attractive woman. And she was even stronger than strong men."

Later that same week, Korry walked into the office of his deputy, Harry Shlaudeman, and found Henry Hecksher there. "I made some unimportant comment to the effect that I wish I knew what Frei would do about the Rube Goldberg gambit," Korry recalled, "and suddenly, and totally out of character, Hecksher, a Prussian by birth and very conscious of authority, blew up. I knew this guy for three years. He angrily asked why I didn't arm-twist Frei. He knew, he said, that I had reported to Washington I was pressuring Frei when I was not. Well, I gave him 24 hours to renounce, once and for all, any thinking like that or leave the country forever. And he immediately crawled back. When he left the room, I asked Shlaudeman, 'Is it possible there's something going on behind our backs?'" Shlaudeman promised to look into it. When Shlaudeman got back to Korry, he reported that embassy officers had seen no sign of any unusual CIA activity.

Even so, Korry remained suspicious. On September 25, he sent cables to Kissinger and to the State Department warning, as he later put it, "that if anybody is thinking like that [allowing the CIA to support military intervention], it would be a disaster. I asked permission to come back and brief the U.S. Congress." He was told that under no circumstances was he to leave Chile.

By this time, Korry had barred Berrellez and Hendrix from the embassy, but it was too late. They had already learned about the secret cable ordering him to offer Frei the $250,000, and they sent a telegram to ITT in New York saying: "Late Tuesday night, Ambassador Edward Korry finally received a message from State Department giving him the 'green light' to move in the name of President Nixon. The message gave him maximum authority to do all possible—short of a Dominican Republic-type action—to keep Allende from taking power. . . . We know that the army has been assured full material and financial assistance by the U.S. military establishment . . ." The ITT executives had confused the Track I bribe with what they knew of Track II. The CIA and the Defense Department had shared more information and worked more closely with two corporate executives than with the United States ambassador.

Not everyone was playing the same game. While the CIA was advising Berrellez and Hendrix to finance Major Arturo Marshall and other supporters of General Viaux, an Agency officer was telling Korry that Marshall was behind a series of bombings around Santiago and was out to kill Allende. Korry informed Chilean Defense Minister Sergio Ossa, his official contact with Frei, that Marshall was the designated assassin of Allende, and Marshall was arrested.

Korry believes these actions may have caused Washington to hit the panic button. He learned later that his military attachés received a message on September 28 from the deputy director of the DIA, General Jammie Philpott, authorizing DIA and military personnel in Korry's embassy "to work closely with the CIA chief or, in his absence, his deputy, in contacting and advising the principal military figures who might play a decisive role in any move which might, eventually, deny the presidency to Allende. DO NOT, REPEAT NOT, advise the ambassador or the Defense attaché of this message or give them any indication of its portent. In the course of your routine activities, act in accordance with the ambassador's instructions. Simultaneously, I wish—and now authorize you—to act in a concerted fashion with the CIA chief. This message is for your eyes only, and should not be discussed with any persons other than those CIA officers who will be knowledgeable. CIA will identify them."[7] Hecksher promptly acted on those orders, calling a meeting of his own staff and the embassy military staff and telling them to have no further discussions with Korry concerning their operations to prevent an Allende presidency.

Korry also learned later that Sergio Ossa had formerly been on the CIA payroll. Korry's conversation with Ossa found its way to Langley not long after Ossa reported it to President Frei. Ossa told someone in the CIA's pay that, as a secret CIA memo later put it, President Frei "did manage to confide to several top-ranking military officers that he would not oppose a coup, with a guarded implication he might even welcome one."[8] Ossa's report encouraged Kissinger and Helms to take a more direct path.

On Friday, October 9, fifteen days before the Chilean Congress was due to vote on Allende's ratification, Korry cabled Kissinger and the number two at State, Undersecretary U. Alexis Johnson, "that if anybody is thinking of playing around with the Chilean military, it will be worse than the Bay of Pigs." Korry closed the cable by asking again for permission to come home.

When Kissinger read this cable, he immediately concluded that Korry had discovered Track II. Korry was told to fly to Washington and report to Kissinger at the opening of business on October 13.

That Tuesday morning, Korry found himself telling the National Security Adviser, "that only a madman would deal with the military in Chile." In retrospect, it seems that as Korry pressed this argument, Kissinger became more and more convinced he knew about Track II. Suddenly, Kissinger asked Korry if he wanted to see the president. Surprised, Korry said, "Yes," and Kissinger led him to the Oval Office.

As soon as Korry and Kissinger took their seats, Nixon launched into a mirthless tirade concerning Allende. "'I am going to smash that son of a bitch,'" Korry remembers Nixon saying. "He said [Allende] was going to ruin the Chilean economy, and he went on and on. He looked to me for applause when he got through with this monologue, and that's when I said to him, 'Mr. President, I have not changed. You were kind enough to say to me when we started this interview that I tell it like it is. Therefore, you will not take it amiss, I hope, if I say you are dead wrong.'"

As Korry tells it, Nixon paused for a moment and then looked up at him "with that sort of half smile on his face as if to say, 'Well, this guy has gone nutty again.' And then he motioned for me to speak, and I said, 'I have not changed my mind about Allende, but you could have a self-fulfilling prophecy,' and I ended by saying that it was lunacy for anybody to think anyone could now prevent Allende from coming in."

Korry asked Nixon to explore whether the United States could get along with Allende. He suggested that Nixon send a congratulatory message once Allende was confirmed by the Chilean Congress, then send a normal U.S. delegation to the inauguration, and finally allow him, as ambassador, to begin talks with the incoming governmental team to resolve any specific problems. Korry recalls telling Nixon that, "'Just as it takes two to tango, Mr. President, it takes two to make war,' and that it would be unseemly for the president of the United States, the most powerful democracy on earth, to get involved in a personal vendetta with the head of a country of only some eight million people down near the South Pole."

Korry remembers Nixon seeming "strange but friendly" after the encounter. Korry went immediately to the State Department to see his boss, Charles Meyer, and U. Alexis Johnson. They expressed doubt when Korry said he thought he "may have turned around the president." But Korry did unknowingly achieve one thing that day. He provided great relief to Kissinger and Nixon. They were now convinced he knew nothing of Track II.

Korry remembers Kissinger's role with some anger: "Henry, coming out of a German background, is always obsequious in front of wealth and power. He used me to say what he thought because he didn't have the moral courage to do it. The next day he brought me, in a rare act, into a [Watch Group] meeting."

Richard Helms was not present at that Watch Group meeting on October 14, because he was in Brazil directing Track II activities and being briefed, along with Tom Polgar, by Henry Hecksher. Helms and Polgar learned that the CIA was still going forward with Track I, funneling one million dollars from ITT in Brazil to Chilean lawyers to buy votes against Allende in the Congress. But, should the vote-buying fail, Hecksher and the DIA operatives in Chile were also working with key elements in the Chilean military on separate coup plots. At this time, they thought any coup had to be completed prior to the ratification vote, scheduled for October 24.

Back in Washington, Korry sat and listened as Thomas Karamessines, the CIA's deputy director for Plans and chairman of the Chile Task Force, briefed the Watch Group on the political situation in Chile. U. Alexis Johnson interrupted and asked Korry for his views. Korry once again urged that no one look to the Chilean military or anyone else to reverse the election results. Allende would be president, he told the group with emphasis.

Korry left for Santiago at the end of the week, feeling the danger of U.S. intervention was past. He was not aware of what happened when the Watch Group meeting ended, and the Forty Committee's discussion of the CIA operations began.

Early in the Track II planning, Sergio Ossa had warned Henry Hecksher of a major obstacle to letting the Chilean military handle Allende: the Army Chief of Staff, General René Schneider. A military man in the best tradition, Schneider was committed at all costs to maintaining civilian control. He would not take part in any plan to oust a democratically elected leader. Now it became the CIA's official policy to get this man out of the way.

The secret CIA memo quoted previously concluded: "After early October—absent any evidence that Frei was responding, politically speaking, to artificial respiration—a military coup increasingly suggested itself as the only possible solution to the Allende problem."[9] The memo went on to point out "that the Army was central to a successful coup, and, as long as General Schneider remained head of the Army, the Army could not be counted upon." Because Frei refused to pressure General Schneider, the CIA foolishly decided to support General Viaux's plan to kidnap him and his loyal deputy, General Carlos Prats, until the coup could be pulled together. After the kidnap, Hecksher's CIA and DIA operatives planned to take the two men across the Andes to Argentina.

Korry did not know that his own military attaché, Colonel Paul Wimert, had grown closer and closer to the right-wing extremists in the Chilean military. Now, on instructions from Hecksher, Wimert made plans to supply weapons to a crony of General Viaux's, General Camilo Valenzuela, from stocks the CIA maintained in Brazil and Argentina. A horse lover, Wimert went riding with General Valenzuela and promised him "several submachine guns, ammunition, a few tear-gas grenades, gas masks, all of which were provided, plus $50,000 for expenses (which was already passed on demand)."[10]

Unfortunately, as in Berlin, the CIA was not very good at concealing its plans from the opposition. As Korry had warned Washington repeatedly, the MIR (Leftist Revolutionary Movement), a Cuban-backed paramilitary organization with ties to Allende's Socialist Party, had penetrated Viaux's organization and learned of the plot to kidnap General Schneider. The CIA later acknowledged in an internal document that: "All activities of retired Army General Viaux were being carefully scrutinized by both Allende and General Schneider during this period . . . because he [Viaux] was a known dissident with some residue of influence in the Army."[11]

On October 6, General Viaux told the CIA he was ready to launch his coup with the abduction of Schneider on "October 9th or the morning of 10 Oct; but was in need of paralyzing gas grenades."[12] The DIA and the CIA both went searching for grenades, but neither agency had any.

On October 12, the day Korry arrived in Washington for his meeting the next morning with Kissinger, the CIA concluded that Viaux's plan could "create an unpredictable situation which could result in civil war and considerable carnage." Despite that somber warning and despite Korry's blunt talk with Nixon and Kissinger, the plan went forward. DIA headquarters in Washington sent a message to the CIA's Santiago Station saying: ". . . Sponsors regret that technical factors and time limits preclude meeting Viaux's two direct requests, the air drop and the 'paralyzing gas.' (Frankly we don't have the latter). . . . What sponsors can promise in lieu of above is financing. . . . We promise to finance any successful attempt by Viaux to obtain them. . . . Separate and distinct from above, sponsors will pledge up to $250,000 for 'insurance purposes.'"[13] That message also included a reference to a second coup plot, independent of Viaux's plans.

The Viaux coup was delayed and rescheduled for October 17. On October 14, Hecksher reported that "military units in Concepción and Valdivia were ready to move against the government. . . . Last week, General Viaux appeared to be the only military leader committed to blocking Allende. Now, we are beginning to see signs of increased activity from other military quarters . . . even President Frei. . . . The prospects for a coup may have improved significantly in the past 24 hours. . . . President Frei and Minister of Defense Ossa have not yet abandoned the possibility of finding a military solution for blocking Allende."[14]

On October 15, before leaving Washington, Korry met again at the State Department with U. Alexis Johnson and Charles Meyer to draft a congratulatory telegram for Nixon to send to Allende. That same day, Hecksher reported to Langley: "General Viaux intends to kidnap Generals Schneider and Prats" within the next 48 hours "in order to precipitate a coup."[15] But by that time Henry Kissinger and his deputy, Alexander M. Haig, were starting to fear that Viaux might not be the right man to launch the coup. Three days after Korry's Oval Office appearance, Kissinger and Haig began to retreat from the plans they had previously approved. On October 16, Kissinger instructed Thomas Karamessines to "defuse the Viaux coup plot."[16]

A sense of fantasy runs through that whole week's message traffic. A CIA memo to file dated October 16 reads: "Although Henry Hecksher will be advised to discourage him from launching a coup without additional support from the regular military, it's conceivable that Viaux will not heed this advice and will move anyway, thereby undermining the possibility for a subsequent broad-based coup. If this should occur, we could be confronted tomorrow morning with a coup attempt which, despite its outcome, will significantly alter the political and military situation—if successful for the worse."[17]

That same day, CIA and DIA headquarters sent out another message reaffirming "the firm and continuing policy that Allende be overthrown in a coup. It would be much preferable to have this transpire prior to 24 October but efforts in this regard will continue vigorously beyond this date. We are continuing to generate maximum pressure toward this end utilizing every appropriate resource."[18] This message ordered Santiago Station to contact Viaux and ask him to join forces with other coup efforts.

The kidnapping and the coup were now planned to begin on October 22. The plan was to invite Generals Schneider and Prats to a stag party, where they would be kidnapped and taken to Argentina. But that is not what happened.

At 8:15 A.M. on October 22, General Schneider, on his way to Army headquarters, was attacked by machine-gun fire and fatally wounded.

Hecksher immediately ordered Viaux to go out in public to establish that he was not a party to the assassination.

Despite Schneider's murder, Hecksher still believed the coup could take place. His hopes now rested on General Valenzuela, the man with whom Colonel Wimert went horseback riding, and who was in charge of the Santiago garrison. Back at Langley, Karamessines agreed: Despite the murder of General Schneider, the coup should proceed. On October 23, Hecksher cabled Washington that a "coup climate exists in Santiago." However, Frei and Alessandri were getting cold feet. They could not deny the fact that, despite ITT's and the CIA's best efforts, Allende was still the democratically elected president of Chile. The Congress ratified Allende's election on October 24, by a vote of 153 to 35, and the CIA at last became convinced that the opportunity for a coup had passed.

Richard Helms was very careful to distance himself from the plot he had approved. He told colleagues that it had no more than a 10 percent chance of succeeding. In fact, Helms grossly overestimated the chance of success: The Viaux plot was doomed from the start. Washington had paid no attention to Korry's repeated warnings that Allende sympathizers had thoroughly penetrated Viaux's organization and that Allende would know every detail about any plots by the CIA, American corporations, or the White House. Korry had also pointed repeatedly to the extreme views of leftists in Allende's own party, who would welcome a coup attempt as a pretext for a violent Maoist-type revolution. Korry had reported by cable that Allende had made a pre-election deal with those extreme Socialists.

Now, after the killing of Schneider, Allende went to the Chilean military and offered them a deal. In return for letting the military plotters off with light punishment, and for meeting the opposition's demands that he uphold democracy, Allende wanted all the details of the involvement of the CIA, the Pentagon, and any corporations. And that's what he got.

Nor was this the end of the disaster for the CIA. As Korry put it, "The supreme irony, in this thicket of ironies, is that the generals . . . turned over to Allende's men all of the dossiers that my military attaché and the CIA had been feeding their friends in the Chilean military for years. Not only did they furnish him our knowledge of Castro's agents in Chile, but in other parts of Latin America as well."

Korry believed that he had at least succeeded in preventing the United States from being involved in the Viaux coup attempt and the murder of Schneider. He had no idea that Hecksher and his superiors had gone ahead with their mad schemes on White House orders. Allende, believing at first that Korry had taken part in the plotting, demanded his immediate removal as ambassador. However, he changed his mind later and let Korry know it.

CHAPTER FORTY-EIGHT

BLOOD AND JUDGMENT

———⋙●⋘———

URING THE HEIGHT of the coup efforts in Santiago in mid-
October, Korry and Meyer found themselves in an endless tug-of-
war with Kissinger over the congratulatory message Nixon should send
to Allende.[1] Finally, after the plots all failed and Allende's election was
ratified, Nixon permitted Meyer to attend the inauguration, but all he
was authorized to say to Allende was: "The United States extends its con-
gratulations to the people of Chile for having held a democratic election."
Meyer was so embarrassed, according to Korry, that he murmured the
words when he spoke to the new president. Allende, a very savvy politician, immediately called a press conference and announced that Nixon
had sent him a very significant message of friendship.

Once Allende was installed in the presidential palace (the Moneda),
Ambassador Korry quickly set about attempting to establish relations
with the new Chilean administration and met with Claudomiro Almeyda,
Allende's Maoist foreign minister. From Washington, Charles Meyer's
deputy, John Crimmins, telephoned Korry, reprimanding him and asking
him why he had defied instructions to stay clear of Almeyda. Korry told
Crimmins that given the taxpayer money at stake in Chile, a relationship
"seemed in order."

In the early months of 1971, Korry launched a series of negotiations
with the Allende regime designed to forestall the expropriation of American properties. Korry explained to Allende that if his government would

agree to buy out ITT's, Anaconda's, and Kennecott's interests for an amount equal only to the taxpayers' insurance on them, roughly five hundred million dollars, then the United States could arrange credit at favorable terms for Chile. By May 1971, Allende had agreed to try a model transaction for a small U.S. copper company, Cerro. In all, they agreed on more than a dozen amicable buyouts, including the Chilean properties of ITT, Anaconda, Kennecott, and Bethlehem Steel.

Unfortunately, Allende had paid too high a price to his own left wing in order to get the presidential nomination. He had given veto power to Senator Carlos Altamirano, the head of the Socialist Party. Now, Altamirano exercised that power, forcing Allende at the last minute to cancel the model deal to buy Cerro Copper. Nor could Allende persuade Altamirano to accept Korry's scheme of paying the value of the insurance guarantees to Anaconda, Kennecott, and ITT in return for U.S. Treasury backing for Chilean bonds.

In addition to his political weaknesses, Allende also was not flawless personally. According to Korry, "He was a very likable man, but he was a man who took bribes. In fact, he knowingly had his subordinates and several of his cronies take bribes. One [bribe] of $800,000 from one European-owned company bought a good deal for it. Another was arranged through a lawyer for Cerro. And ITT gave funds through a Chilean senator named Jacopo Shaulson, nicknamed 'The Fatman.'" Allende also had problems with liquor and prescription-drug dependency. He acquired his new home by expropriation and bedded the former owner's wife, as well as the wives of several of his upper-class political supporters.

Korry also found that Allende was not well versed in policy or political theory. "The Allende I knew," Korry said, "had not read a book in 25 years on any subject. He was a fundamentally decent man who wanted to bring about a true revolution . . . [but] Castro had nothing but intellectual contempt for him and showed it again and again. He told him he was a bloody fool if he did not destroy the bourgeoisie, because if he did not, and if he did not transform the armed forces into a reliable tool for the revolution, they would beat him back. Castro was correct."

By early 1971, Allende's forces had control of all the national television stations, 80 percent of the radio stations, and nearly all the major papers. *El Mercurio* was still independent, but the once-proud, pro-American paper had been reduced from 80 pages to just six. "After the election," said Korry, "and after Allende's team began to use extreme, illegal pressures in an attempt to gain control of all significant press and media, as the embassy officers—not CIA—and I documented in many cables, I proposed covert funding so that Frei's party could buy a small radio station, so that the party, as Chile's largest, could continue to have funds as well." Korry also proposed keeping *El Mercurio* afloat.

Because of these initiatives, Korry, as Hecksher informed him, was at the top of an assassination list compiled by the most extreme supporters of Allende, the Cuban-backed MIR. The second name on the hit list was Frei's former vice president, Edmundo Perez-Zujovich, the man who had helped Korry and Hecksher in the Arguedas case. In July 1971, Perez-Zujovich was machine-gunned to death in his automobile. His last act was to save his daughter's life by shoving her down on the car floor out of the range of fire.

"I was advised repeatedly of the dangers," Korry recalls. "I sent Shlaudeman to the Minister of the Interior, who had expressed concerns that I was riding in my official car with a reading light in the evening, walking through the center of town. I said to tell him I was a guest in his country; it was his responsibility to insure my safety, not mine. . . . My purpose, as I told Washington in cables, was to show the U.S. was calmly going about its business." Korry had reluctantly accepted a retired Chilean police detective to chauffeur him, but he often found a way to detach the detective.

As Korry had predicted, Allende soon took the country's economy into a period of runaway inflation. In the spring of 1971, Korry testified to a House committee in Washington that Allende's unlimited printing of money to win popular support posed the greatest danger to his government and to Chile. Korry was under no illusions about how much attention the U.S. government would pay to anything he said. The State Department seemed to look upon him as a Nixon man, while the White House and the CIA distrusted his independence. The CIA told him very little, and that did not change when Henry Hecksher was replaced by Ray Warren as chief of Santiago Station.

In March 1971, Korry received a visit from *New York Times* foreign affairs columnist C. L. Sulzberger, an old friend. Sulzberger came to lunch, and, over coffee, he leaned toward Korry and asked if he could have a word with him in private. Korry suggested they talk in front of his wife, but Sulzberger insisted they go to a "secure place." "We walked into the library and he put his lips to my ear, in my own house, as if the place were bugged, and said, 'I understand you stopped a military coup in Chile.' I thought he was thinking about the Dominican Republic-type invasion. I looked at him and I said, 'Cy, that's ridiculous.' And then he put his lips to my ear again and said 'unimpeachable sources' told him that I had stopped it. I said that was absolutely nonsense. I still, of course, had no idea that there had been a plot actually started behind my back."[2] Sulzberger and the *Times* had been told what no one had told Korry.

Later in 1971, the ubiquitous Ted Shackley, fresh from Vietnam, came into the picture. In his new job as director of the CIA's Western Hemisphere Division, Shackley had to pick up the pieces after the failed coup. Shackley's work in OPERATION MONGOOSE made him the perfect choice for Richard Nixon's plans for Chile. Thanks to Henry Hecksher, the soil in Chile had already been plowed, and Shackley had easy ground to till. The newly arrived Santiago Station Chief, Ray Warren, less action-directed and more politically oriented than Hecksher, kept up the CIA's contacts with the Chilean military.

Meanwhile, elsewhere in the world, there were major changes in East-West relations. In 1970, Allende had received a great deal of support from Moscow. Now, according to Pepsi's Donald Kendall, in return for détente—and especially for the promise of a Strategic Arms Limitation Treaty—Nixon and Kissinger had gotten the Kremlin's permission to deal with Allende as they wished. Korry learned that the Russians refused Allende's plea in late 1971 for more than half a billion dollars to bail out the country's economy. Kendall called the Soviet abandonment of the first freely elected Marxist president "the first fruits of détente." The Chinese, who were also in negotiations with Kissinger (the famous Nixon-Kissinger visit to China would take place in February 1972), also refused Allende any cash for his fractured economy.

Korry assumed, wrongly, that the CIA, like him, was reporting back to Washington on the points of vulnerability in Allende's presidency and on the opposition's plans. He was also wrong in assuming that no CIA plotting was underway. Ted Shackley, the heir to Robert Kennedy's policy in Latin America, began methodically to replace the CIA assets lost in Chile and the rest of Latin America when Allende's forces learned all their names. To do this, he turned to the Cuban nationalists he had recruited for OPERATION MONGOOSE and then used again in Laos. He readied these men for a new effort to overthrow the Chilean government.

On October 15, 1971, President Nixon pulled Ed Korry out of Chile and replaced him with career diplomat Nathaniel Davis. Charles Meyer cabled Korry, suggesting that he go back to Africa as an ambassador until things in Chile "quieted down": Nixon wanted no one to learn what he was attempting—let alone planning—for Chile. Korry refused the Africa posting.

After Senator Altamirano blocked Allende's buyout negotiations with Korry, he and his allies on the far left pressured Allende into expropriating ITT's mines as well as those of the big copper companies, all without compensation. The expropriation insurance written by the Overseas Private Investment Corporation (OPIC) forbade American companies from interfering in the domestic politics of other countries, and the CIA concealed from OPIC the truth about the political activities of ITT and the other companies. In fact, the Nixon White House pressured OPIC into paying the insurance claims, which eventually cost U.S. taxpayers hundreds of millions of dollars, just as Korry had feared. He refused to accept this outcome quietly and made himself extremely unpopular by alerting the Justice Department and by seeking court actions by the United States government.

Meanwhile, the Allende regime's move against the multinational corporations, combined with the large number of foreign Communists operating in Chile, caused the CIA to gather its resources to back his removal. Although by the summer of 1973 Chile's economy was collapsing under Allende's failed Marxist measures, Shackley did not wait for Chileans to resolve matters on their own. His Western Hemisphere Division orchestrated yet another coup attempt.

Though Shackley left his post before the coup unfolded, it was his team that set it in motion. This time, the man the CIA backed to take over the government was General Augusto Pinochet Ugarte, Allende's friend and fellow Freemason, who had just replaced General Prats as Army chief of staff. Allende was so fooled by the coup that he told supporters on the morning of his overthrow that he believed Pinochet, his Masonic brother, would be the savior of his Popular Unity government. When he learned the truth, Salvador Allende, remaining in the Moneda even as it burned, shot himself in the head.

Pinochet established a military dictatorship that engaged in every form of torture. The CIA helped train Pinochet's secret police, the dreaded DINA, and the CIA suggested that DINA hire some of Shackley's Cubans for its murderous operations. In 1976, DINA sent Michael Vernon Townley, an American who had been deeply involved in CIA-sponsored activity during the 1970 efforts against Allende, to the United States on a recruiting mission. Two of the Cubans whom Townley recruited were Dionesio Suarez and Virgilio Pablo Paz, both of whom were affiliated with Omega 7, the anti-Castro terrorist group. In addition, Suarez had once tried to fire a mortar shell into the United Nations building in New York City.

Paz became a hit man for an ongoing operation supervised by the head of DINA, Colonel Manuel José Contreas Sepulveda. Code named CONDOR,[3] this was a plan to kill vocal foes of the Chilean junta living in exile. CONDOR also provided an assassination capability for several other governments, including the Bureau of State Security in South Africa.

The assassinations began in October 1974 with General Carlos Prats, General Schneider's deputy and later chief of staff, and his wife, Cora, as the first victims. They were killed in a car bombing in Buenos Aires, where they were living in exile. In March 1975, Pinochet's henchman ordered the hit team to kill Defense Minister Oscar Bonilla, who had recently fallen out with Pinochet. Bonilla died along with five other people when the helicopter in which they were passengers blew up. On October 6, 1975, Paz himself fired shots at former Christian Democratic leader Bernardo Leighton and his wife, Ana, as they strolled down a street in Rome. Fortunately, the couple survived the shooting. Shackley and his colleagues had created a Frankenstein monster.

In the midst of these murders in 1975, Colonel Contreas journeyed to Washington and was welcomed by Deputy CIA Director Vernon Walters in a series of secret meetings at CIA headquarters.[4] While in the United States, Contreas traveled to Miami and met with Cuban exile leaders.

The murders later came home to the United States. In Washington, D.C., on September 21, 1976, Virgilio Paz and Dionisio Suarez, directed by Michael Vernon Townley, planted a bomb in the car of Allende's former ambassador to the United States, Orlando Letelier. Letelier had settled in Washington and was working with the far-left Institute for Policy Studies. He was driving two American colleagues to work. Ronni Karpen

Moffitt sat next to him in the front seat, and Moffitt's husband, Michael, sat in the backseat. As the car approached Sheraton Circle along Washington's Embassy Row, Michael Moffitt later recalled, there was a hissing sound, and a moment later the bomb went off. Letelier's lower body was severed—the blast turned him completely around in his seat. Ronni Moffitt showed no outward sign of injury, but her carotid artery had been severed, and she drowned in her own blood. For the second decade in a row, the CIA's use of murder, this time through a surrogate intelligence service, had come home to the United States. Innocent Americans were paying for the CIA's actions in Chile.

What role Richard Helms may have played in the DINA assassination spree has long been debated. Unwelcome publicity over the 1970 Chile venture, combined with his failure to cooperate with the Nixon White House about Watergate, brought his carefully cultivated CIA career to an end before DINA came into being. Helms was fired as director of Central Intelligence in November 1972, and packed off to Tehran as ambassador to the Peacock throne. By the time of the Letelier murder, he was supposedly long out of the CIA—although the station chief in Tehran repeatedly complained that Helms seemed to be running his own intelligence operations out of the embassy.

In April 1976, William Zylka, a New Jersey businessman[5] and operative for the CIA, escorted Colonel Contreas to Iran to meet with Ambassador Helms. Zylka had a long relationship with the CIA through Eisenhower Treasury Secretary Robert Anderson, who informally ran dozens of businessmen as Agency assets; another of them was Zylka's friend William Casey, who later became DCI during the Reagan Administration.

Zylka said later that he was not invited to take part in the meeting between Helms and Contreas. "Bob called me and said that he needed a favor," Zylka recalled. "This Chilean needed to be brought to Tehran to meet with Helms. My job was getting the colonel there. I arranged and paid for his plane tickets and his hotel bill. At the embassy I was asked to pose for a picture with the colonel, because there was something wrong with the exterior surveillance cameras. I did that, and I got him back to Chile after the meeting." Five months later, Letelier and Ronni Karpen Moffitt were dead. Colonel Contreas remains wanted for the Letelier/Moffitt murders to this day.

In 1973, Senator Frank Church called Richard Helms back from Iran to testify before the Senate Subcommittee on Multinational Corporations about the CIA's dealings with ITT. Under oath, Helms lied to the subcommittee repeatedly. The subcommittee staff also pressured Ed Korry to testify, in the mistaken belief he was part of the 1970 coup attempts. Senator Church's counsel, Jerome Levinson, and his deputy told Korry, in effect, that if he did not agree to testify against Kissinger and Nixon, he would be targeted for a perjury investigation. Korry persisted in saying he knew of no U.S. coup or ITT involvement. However, nothing came of Levinson's threats for the moment. By this time, the Watergate investigation was heating up, and it was ITT's domestic payoffs to Nixon, not its involvement in Chile, that grabbed the headlines.

In 1975, Senator Church chaired a new Senate Select Committee set up to investigate CIA plots, particularly in Chile. When the new CIA director, William Colby, began to divulge to this committee the "family jewels"—the accounts of the CIA's darkest secrets, compiled on Colby's orders—Levinson then made Korry a public target. He leaked to the press that Korry had committed perjury by denying any awareness of the CIA-White House plot to thwart Allende's inauguration. He fingered Korry because the ambassador had refused to reveal what, in fact, he did not know. Levinson was also worried that Korry could reveal activities in which the Kennedy and Johnson administrations had engaged in Chile at a time when Levinson himself was serving there as an AID appointee.

The *New York Times* and *Washington Post* printed the libel on their front pages without attempting to contact Korry or otherwise verify it. Then Levinson told his newspaper chums that Korry's name was being sent to the Justice Department for contempt proceedings. Reporter Seymour Hersh of the *Times* published this new invention of Levinson's on page one, again without investigation.

Ed Korry's life was ruined by these false, planted stories. He counted on the Church Committee to clear his name. Again, his confidence in decency was unfounded. Kissinger, Helms, Dungan, Meyer, Davis, and everyone else testified in secret before the senators. Kissinger—by then secretary of state in the Ford Administration—negotiated a deal with the Kennedy camp and with Democratic presidential hopeful Senator Walter Mondale, a member of the Church Committee, to prevent Korry from appearing. The ambassador was categorically promised that he would be permitted to testify during the months of secret hearings and was even invited to do so by Committee letter. Two Committee investigators, who came to Korry's home for pre-testimony in mid-1975, divulged to him the existence of the 1970 plot after having established his own lack of knowledge. However, the Church Committee barred Korry until after it had disseminated its findings to the world. Months later, he was allowed to speak under oath to committee lawyers, in secret, with no senators present.

Blocked by the senators, the CIA, and Kissinger, Korry wrote a letter to Gerald Ford's attorney general, Edward Levi, pointing out that crimes might have been committed in connection with a Chile cover-up and in connection with ITT's OPIC insurance claim for one hundred million dollars.

With this letter to Levi, the protective cover was finally ripped away from Richard Helms, the CIA, and Henry Kissinger. A Justice Department investigation began. By November 1977, a federal grand jury was ready to indict the former CIA director on multiple counts of perjury and obstruction of justice. Only after massive lobbying of the Carter Administration by such Washington powers as Clark Clifford—and after a threat from Helms to reveal state secrets and take Kissinger and numerous other public officials down with him—did the Justice Department allow Helms to cop a plea. With apparent contrition, Helms appeared before an angry Judge Barrington Parker and received a two-year suspended sentence. When he emerged from the courtroom and stood before the press, his demeanor changed. He said later at a luncheon organized by former CIA colleagues that he would wear the conviction for withholding information from Congress "as a badge of honor."

Helms attended the luncheon of the Association of Former Intelligence Officers, where he received a round of applause for his defiance. David Atlee Phillips, one of the architects of the Chile disaster, passed around a wastebasket to collect money to pay Helms's fine. Paul Garbler, whose career had been derailed by Angleton's mole investigation, was among those present. Garbler, who knew that Helms had stood by and let his veteran officers be destroyed by Angleton's mole hunt, did not put money in the wastebasket.

Any further investigation into Harold Geneen and the CIA was squelched on national security grounds. No one went to jail for what the United States did to the Chilean people. Ted Shackley escaped prosecution in the ITT case because his knowledge of American embarrassments

was, like Helms's, too extensive to risk a trial. Instead, Shackley was promoted, to assistant deputy director for Operations. The man who knew
too much was rewarded for his guilty knowledge.

Other CIA officials, including many of the boys from Berlin, lied to
Congress at the time, and the CIA still denies its level of responsibility for
the destruction of Chilean democracy. Instead of learning from its enormous blunder, the CIA hid its activities, only to return to its failed methods later on in Central America—again with tragic consequences.

The only American official to suffer in this whole ugly ordeal was Edward Korry, the man who tried to prevent the tragedy. His colleagues,
both in government and in the press, turned against him. Both Democrats
and Republicans in Washington wanted to conceal their administrations'
actions in Chile and the involvement of their constituencies—the bankers,
the corporations, and the Catholic church. As for the journalists, they did
not want to spoil their good guy–bad guy story by revealing the 11
months of honest negotiations Korry had carried on with Allende's government. Korry had sacrificed everything to integrity. In 1971, angered
and frustrated over the lack of justice, he left public life to live in self-
imposed exile.

WHY DID THE American citizenry know so little of the CIA's debacles?
Why did it take until the mid-1970s for Americans to begin to learn how
much had gone wrong? One of the reasons the CIA's incompetence and il-
legalities remained unknown was the complicity of the men who published the newspapers and magazines and ran the television networks.
From the Sulzbergers in New York to the Copleys in San Diego, such cooperation was common. The details varied by organization. Copley actually had CIA agents as correspondents; the Kennedy Administration cited
national security to keep the Sulzbergers' *New York Times* from exposing
the ill-fated Bay of Pigs invasion before it took place. Rewards were given
to reporters who covered things up. The corruption of the media by the
intelligence apparatus was not even debated in our society until 1977,
when news organizations finally got around to examining themselves.

Ed Korry, a former newspaperman, had friends throughout the
media, including Abe Rosenthal, then the managing editor of the *New
York Times*. Rosenthal had known Korry since they both were award-
winning journalists in Europe in the 1950s. But in 1975, Rosenthal al-

lowed his star reporter, Seymour Hersh, to destroy Korry in print. The following year, when a little-known reporter reinvestigated Korry's story for a far less potent newspaper than the *Times* and learned that Korry was right and Hersh wrong, Rosenthal did not correct the record. Even after Hersh admitted on television that he had been "mistaken" and that he had "punished" Korry, Rosenthal did nothing.

Instead, Korry was allowed to twist in the wind. His best earning years were lost because Hersh's lies kept him from getting major positions. When the able *New York Times* correspondent John Burns tried to write the truth in 1975, Rosenthal spiked his story. Not until February 21, 1981, did a rare front-page retraction appear under Hersh's byline. In several thousand words, Hersh grudgingly revealed that Korry had not been part of Kissinger's and Nixon's Track II conspiracy against Salvador Allende.

Korry got this retraction not because Rosenthal or Hersh had a sudden attack of conscience, but because Hersh needed Korry as a source for the book he was writing about Henry Kissinger, *The Price of Power.* Korry refused Hersh an interview unless Hersh wrote a retraction. So Hersh told Rosenthal he had "new evidence," which was a fresh falsehood.

The truth is that the owners of the big media had received so many favors from the national security establishment that they were unwilling to expose it.[6] The fact that not even the great *New York Times* had the courage to tell Korry's story is especially troubling. Only because Korry persisted under the most difficult personal circumstances was the truth revealed about what the United States did to Chile.[7]

CHILE WAS PART of the natural progression of CIA disasters that began with Berlin Base. Abetted by the CIA, General Pinochet eradicated Communism in Chile by eradicating democracy. The Chilean middle class, tired of political trouble and wanting only to live well, welcomed Pinochet. For the poor and for those, like General Schneider, who cherished Chile's civil traditions, it was another story. At night, the children of Santiago's barrios—wearing masks so the police could not identify them—threw chains over the big towers carrying high-voltage wires; sparks lit up the sky as electricity was cut off to huge sections of the city. Rocks and burning tires blocked passage to the barrios that ringed the city. Here Pinochet's secret police shot priests and children.

Meanwhile, Pinochet built a home in the hills of Los Condes. The $25 million mansion is surrounded by guards and video cameras and looks more like a suburban hospital than a home.

Despite the rash of murders and disappearances in Chile, despite the end of democracy, free speech, and basic human rights, the CIA's cooperation with Pinochet continued throughout the Nixon, Ford, Carter, Reagan, and Bush administrations. Pinochet retired as president in 1989 but remained in control of the armed forces. In 1991, the Chilean government released a report saying that Pinochet was responsible for the deaths or disappearances of more than two thousand Chilean citizens. In 1998, Judge Baltazar Garzon of Spain caused an international sensation by having Pinochet arrested in London and held for extradition to Spain to stand trial for his crimes.

President Clinton personally ordered the release of twenty thousand pages of documents revealing the United States' role in supporting Pinochet and his secret police. These documents, made available in July 1999 through the National Archives, show that American officials routinely reported to their superiors the horrendous details of Pinochet's regime, without changing the U.S. government's support for him. Chile is the clearest example of how much damage American foreign policy can do when it places commercial interests ahead of justice.

CHAPTER FORTY-NINE

WEISZ IN GERMANY

———※◆◆————

W HEN GEORGE WEISZ returned to Berlin Base in 1971 and let
Tom Polgar, his good Hungarian friend, take Chief of Saigon Station, his colleagues were shocked. Weisz, as ambitious as any man in the
Operations Directorate, could hardly have thought going back to Berlin
was a good career move. The Base, downgraded further and further after
the Wall went up in 1961, now had only 20 agents. Sam Wilson recalls arriving in West Berlin from Moscow in 1972 to meet an agent he had been
attempting to recruit. "I was surprised to go back to Berlin and find George
there as chief of base," Wilson said. "It had shrunk. It was a shadow of
what it had been back in those active days when there were 29 different intelligence agencies swirling and pulsating through the night streets of
Berlin." In fact, Weisz had another agenda that was more important to him
than promotions. Unknown to the CIA, he had another master.

In Berlin, Weisz became reacquainted with State Department official
Felix Stephan Bloch, who at that time was assigned to the American Mission in West Berlin. Having first met in the 1960s while Weisz was chief
of station in Bonn, the two men struck up a friendship. Bloch confirms
that the relationship was not merely professional: "We frequently socialized. . . . My wife, Lucille, and George's wife were friends."[1]

Eighteen years later, Bloch was fired from his State Department job as
a suspected Soviet agent. On May 14, 1989, French counterintelligence-
la Direction de la Surveillance du Territoire—photographed him handing

a black briefcase to a known KGB agent after dinner at Le Meurice restaurant in Paris. News of Bloch's suspected spying dominated the headlines throughout the summer of 1989, thanks largely to then ABC News producer James Bamford.[2]

Neither Bamford, the State Department, nor the FBI knew that Bloch and George Weisz were friends—or why that was important. Bloch was simply fired. He never publicly brought up his relationship with Weisz as a defense, nor did he say he had done favors for Weisz on the assumption he was assisting in official CIA business. However, he later acknowledged that his predicament may have begun with his friendship with Weisz, the most mysterious of Bill Harvey's boys from Berlin Base.[3]

Felix Bloch and George "Napoleon" Weisz had much in common and were both unpopular with their colleagues. Both cultivated friendships with top-ranking officials in the countries where they served, making their own ambassadors very nervous. Both had a weakness for expensive, hand-tailored clothing. Both had secret sex lives outside their marriages and kept mistresses.

Like Weisz, Bloch came from a European Jewish family that had settled in New York City—in the Blochs' case, after escaping from Nazi-controlled Austria. Bloch and Weisz both believed their careers suffered because they were foreign-born and Jewish. Although some insiders disagree, others affirm that European Jews were not treated well in the CIA or the diplomatic corps. Berlin Base veteran John Sherwood said, "You cannot dismiss the issue of anti-Semitism in the CIA. It was there, especially in Berlin, and it was real."[4] George Weisz's daughter, Nikki, claims that plans to send her father to Oslo as station chief were scrapped because the U.S. ambassador to Norway disliked Jews. As the Agency had encouraged him to do, Weisz let many of his CIA associates believe he was German, not Hungarian. He emphasized that his mother was born in the United States, never disclosing that her parents returned to Hungary when she was only six months old.

Felix Bloch had the perfect cover for a spy. Like Soviet double agent Oleg Penkovsky, he was a "trade specialist," which gave him a legitimate excuse for meeting foreigners and traveling throughout East Germany. When Weisz reconnected with Bloch, he decided Bloch would be a perfect courier for some of his operations.

By this time, Germany was no longer officially occupied territory. East Berlin was the capital of the German Democratic Republic, and the United States had an office there. In 1974, Weisz's tour of duty ended, and he returned to Washington. In the same year, Bloch was transferred from West Berlin to East Berlin. According to State Department and CIA officials, Weisz remained in contact with Bloch from Washington. Bloch believed he was working with a top-flight intelligence officer involved in official CIA business. Had he known a little more about George Weisz, he might have thought he had fallen through the intelligence looking glass.

Weisz's behavior toward Sam Wilson in 1972 made Wilson wonder about Weisz's loyalty. Wilson had never felt professionally close to Weisz: "I don't think we ever ran any operations together. . . . Oh, I guess we had a drink or two from time to time and maybe a cup of coffee . . . but we never had any close professional association and practically no social ties." That is why Wilson was startled, on his arrival in Berlin, at the level of Weisz's friendliness: "I came in on business, and he was extraordinarily helpful. Very, very helpful. . . . He extended himself more on my behalf than I had any basis to anticipate . . . on the grounds of our former personal association. There was kind of a big hug, old-home week, and so on, and what can I do for you?"

Wilson immediately detected that Weisz was trying to learn the specifics of his operation. "He was extremely curious about what I was up to," Wilson recalls. "And I didn't particularly enlighten him. I tried not to be rude, but I was not about to spill my guts. I sort of had this feeling that George—he was a little antsy; he seemed a little bit insecure at the time. And I figured, 'Man, if I unloaded on him, he'd be a hero tomorrow morning because he would immediately turn around and report this.'" Weisz's curiosity bothered Wilson: "To put it mildly and politely, what he's doing is not in good operational taste," but he wrote it off as the kind of behavior that always kept Weisz, despite his high rank, from being a real insider in the CIA.

Weisz's Berlin staff was assisting Wilson in his operation, which was to meet a potential recruit in a West Berlin restaurant. One of the big questions in intelligence is whether or not to put surveillance on a meeting place to determine whether your recruit is blown or whether he has compromised you. Wilson asked for no on-site surveillance. He wanted to put his recruit at ease during the meal. "While I am right in the middle of this damn thing, George, who knows generally where I am but doesn't know the details, comes sauntering through while I'm sitting somewhere talking to someone having a meal. George comes sauntering through, and the fellow gives me the fisheye. And he [Weisz] comes by the table and keeps on going."

It was an operational mistake that the greenest novice does not make, let alone one of the most experienced men in the CIA, and above all, one who was long known to the Soviets. If they were following Wilson's target and saw Weisz on the scene, they would immediately know it was a recruitment. And if Wilson's Russian target knew Weisz, seeing him go by the table was a shocking warning that someone else, perhaps the KGB, was also aware of what was going on. Weisz risked an entire operation with his presence.

Wilson was furious and spoke to Weisz later. "I challenged him, and he says, 'Well, I was just doing a little countersurveillance,' and I said, 'I didn't ask you to.'" Wilson went on, "'Friend, don't ever do that again. Don't ever do that again!' . . . It was bad tradecraft; wrong tradecraft."[5]

Wilson, however, made no official report about Weisz's interference. Much as in Vietnam, where he saw mistakes but did not report them because he did not want to cause trouble, Sam Wilson took no action. In fact, years later, he gave Weisz a glowing recommendation to the FBI.

Had James Angleton been aware of the 1972 incident, he later said, he would immediately have begun an investigation of Weisz's personal history. Instead, Sam Wilson's silence allowed the event to go unnoticed. Weisz continued to claw his way up the CIA ladder, with remarkable results.

CHAPTER FIFTY

PINK SLIP FOR ANGLETON

———⊰●⊱———

I N 1972, PAUL GARBLER, banished to Port-au-Spain, Trinidad, returned to Washington, determined to find out why his career had been
sidetracked. An old friend visiting him in Trinidad had told him his problems stemmed from a personal security issue. Having never been questioned about his relations with Igor Orlov or confronted about his
activities, Garbler had no idea what it might be. He had simply been removed from the vortex of CIA activity and shunted aside. He had not
been considered for assignment in the biggest base of all, Vietnam, where
so many of his colleagues were prospering.

For Garbler, the periods between unimportant assignments were pure
torture. "By this time, you know, people are wondering. I am sort of a
pariah. I turn up at the water fountain in the corridor, people are talking,
and they all turn and walk away. . . . I come into the office, they turn the
papers over. All this kind of stuff." Garbler remembers exercising in the
CIA gym on the mat next to Richard Helms. Helms did not even acknowledge his presence. Garbler was the CIA's version of toxic waste.

Now he decided to press the issue, and he believed the man who
could best advise him was his old boss from Berlin Base, Bill Harvey. Garbler was so out of the loop he had no idea Harvey's own career had plum-
meted. He went to Langley and, searching the building for Harvey, he
heard rumors from Helms's staff that Harvey's mind was gone, that he
had left the CIA and joined a Washington law firm. In an out-of-the-way

corner, Garbler finally tracked down his old chief, still employed by the CIA. "He was in an office," Garbler recalled, ". . . just a big broom closet. He's a big bulky guy sitting at this little tiny desk. I went in and sat down and said, 'Bill, I don't know what the fuck is going on. This is some kind of weird scenario. Nobody will tell me what's happening. Really, I am not coming to you to tell me what's going on. I am coming to ask you what I should do about it.' And he looked at me for maybe 10 or 15 seconds and said, 'I can't help you.' That was the end of it."[1] Looking back, Garbler later realized that Harvey was powerless to help anyone: "Angleton was involved all the time in trying to destroy him. . . . Bill knew that."[2]

Garbler knew he was the subject of some vague security charges. He wanted to get to the bottom of it and was not prepared to give up. "I thought I had slipped up somewhere, and I just wasn't aware of it. But, you know, I could lay out fitness reports from headquarters I got while in Moscow, while I was in Trinidad, while I was at the Base. All this just didn't make any sense to me. So I said the only thing I can attribute it to is that there has got to be something here that involves security, and I want it laid out on the table so I can make sure everybody knows it is not true."

Garbler confronted Richard Helms and his deputy, Tom Karamessines, and demanded that he be cleared and given Vietnam or another CIA post of some significance. After long hours of discussion, Helms and Karamessines agreed. They did not tell him the specific charges against him. Instead, Karamessines offered him chief of station in Oslo. Unfortunately for Garbler, James Schlesinger replaced Helms as director before the appointment could be acted on and overruled it on "technical grounds." Unknown to Garbler, it was Angleton who stopped the appointment, on security grounds.

Eventually, Garbler was sent back to Stockholm, the same station where he had served in the late 1950s. It was a decision typical of Schlesinger: Reassignment of an agent to a place where the officer had previously worked undercover is considered an insult to the host country. That did not matter to Schlesinger or Angleton. Paul Garbler remained far from the real action, and that was the point of the assignment.

The irony was, by 1973, Angleton's mole hunt had thrown American intelligence into chaos, while the real mole, Igor Orlov, had survived the most relentless assaults. Soviet intelligence seemed to have dropped Orlov, presumably convinced that he had no further value after his interrogation by the FBI in 1965, even though Hoover's CI staff could find nothing on him. And so, the little man still worked in his framing shop, outwitting the CIA's chief of counterintelligence.

The FBI agents who visited the gallery had largely become friends with Igor and Eleonore Orlov and their two boys. Yes, reports were still filed, but the FBI thought Igor Orlov was a dead end, an Angleton fantasy. "We felt badly about barging in the place every time Angleton made noise," said the FBI's Courtland Jones. "It got to the point where we just went through the motions."

In the early 1970s, Angleton called for yet another round of polygraphs for the Orlovs, but he came no closer to proving what he suspected and feared. As his longtime assistant Ray Rocca put it, "He believed that Orlov was the top KGB control for every important illegal and agent the Soviets had in the American government. He was totally frustrated by the FBI's inability to make the case and Hoover's refusal to open new case files on people Angleton had tied to Orlov, including Averell Harriman."

William Branigan, the FBI's chief of counterintelligence during this period, said: "We would get requests to open new cases, and they would automatically be refused by Hoover." Sam J. Papich, former FBI/CIA liaison and Angleton's friend, confirms that Angleton feared Orlov was still spying: "Jim thought after the initial charge, Orlov became bullet-proof and could get away with it now."

Angleton was so focused on his mole hunt that he failed to notice what was going on around him in the Nixon Administration. In the summer of 1972, the White House was wildly scrambling. The "plumbers" unit—originally formed to plug leaks concerning Administration actions in the Vietnam War—had been caught breaking into the Democratic National Committee's offices at the Watergate Hotel. Each White House attempt at damage control led to new, unforeseen consequences.

Meanwhile, Senator Frank Church's Foreign Relations subcommittee was starting its investigation into the ITT-CIA connection in Chile, and it wanted Richard Helms to testify. As President Nixon reached into the CIA to make changes, Angleton was about to lose the job security he had enjoyed ever since the Kronthal incident.

In November 1972, Nixon summoned Helms to Camp David. Helms's bureaucratic survival instincts were finally about to fail him. The man Bill Harvey had called "the boy diplomat," the careful career spook covered in Teflon, was out of his dream job. Nixon sent Helms off to Iran and attempted to put in place a CIA management team more amenable to using the Agency for illegal domestic operations.

James Schlesinger, Helms's replacement as director, was one of the most disliked men in the history of the CIA. Although his tenure lasted only months, he appointed as his deputy a man with a very similar personality, William Egan Colby, who succeeded him as director in 1974. Colby ran the CIA for only two years, but he accomplished his one major goal: the removal from power of James Jesus Angleton.

On the most basic question of counterintelligence, Colby and Angleton were diametrically opposed. Colby refused to accept the idea that the CIA was penetrated, and Angleton was obsessed with it. Colby was not particularly concerned about the injustices to Berlin Base veterans Garbler, Kovich, and Murphy, which Helms did little to redress in the weeks between his firing and his departure for Tehran. Nor did Colby care one way or the other about Igor Orlov. What did worry him was Angleton's treatment of Nosenko and the effect the Golitsyn serials had on CIA morale and operations.

Angleton had convinced first Helms, and then Schlesinger, that many of the CIA's failures were linked to Soviet penetrations. But as Colby saw it, "Angleton could not explain to me in a rational way what he was doing. When I took over, this man had shut down operations. . . . Penetrations are a concern, but . . . the fear of penetrations [can] shut you down. We were shut down by fear."[3]

Colby also had personal reasons for hating Angleton. A few years earlier, Angleton had begun a security investigation into Colby because, while Colby was in Vietnam as head of CORDS, he had taken a mistress with ties to the Vietminh Communists. However, the roots of Colby's hatred go back much further. Although he didn't write a word about it in his autobiography, *Honorable Men,* he and Angleton had become rivals long before, during the 1948 elections in Italy.

Both men were involved in the CIA's effort to keep the Italian Christian Democrats in power at a time when the Communists were threatening victory. Angleton played a major role in funneling ten million dollars in CIA funds to the Christian Democrats. During the same period, according to both Angleton and William Mazzocco, who later served with

Colby under Ambassador Clare Boothe Luce, Colby met repeatedly with members of the Communist Party.[4] Angleton claimed that Colby failed to report these contacts in writing—as CIA regulations require—and Angleton humiliated Colby by reporting them to headquarters. The Office of Security dismissed Colby's failure to file the reports as an oversight, but the incident meant that Colby knew, firsthand, how it felt to be subjected to Angleton's suspicions, and he did not like it.

One of the few things on which Angleton and Colby did agree was the acceptance of Yekaterina Furtseva's son-in-law, KGB Lieutenant Colonel Igor Kozlov, as a legitimate CIA double agent. Colby approved the whole KITTY HAWK operation, which the CIA had been running with the FBI, including the use of Nick Shadrin, the dashing Soviet Navy defector, to supply real secrets to the Soviets in order to prove to Colonel Kozlov's Moscow bosses that he had truly "recruited" Shadrin.

This operation took a new turn when Furtseva, whose role in Soviet politics was of compelling interest to Angleton, became a star of Nixon and Kissinger's détente. Furtseva became very close to Nixon officials in Moscow, especially Berlin Base alumnus Sam Wilson, who was serving as the military attaché at the American embassy. According to embassy colleagues, Lieutenant General Wilson, who cut a handsome figure in his dress uniform, was besieged with flowers and phone calls from KITTY HAWK's mother-in-law.

The fact that she had played a major role in the overthrow of her former lover, Nikita Khrushchev, and was now using a family member to convince the United States that the Soviets had nothing to do with JFK's murder, should have raised suspicions. But the goal of better relations with the Soviets was the heart of the Administration's new policy, which the CIA backed: True to form, it did not keep an objective, analytical eye on the situation. America's critical intelligence faculties were suspended in support of the Nixon-Kissinger détente.

The dismantling of Angleton's empire began as Colby, still head of Clandestine Services, waited in limbo for several months for his Senate confirmation as director. Working with Kissinger and with the acting DCI, General Vernon Walters, Colby participated in the decision to take the so-called Israeli account away from Angleton.

For a quarter century, Angleton had lobbied for the Israelis, used their exceptional intelligence agents, and shared with them the fruits of

American technology—from spy satellite photographs to uranium and plutonium for their nuclear weapons program. Colby understood—as did Kissinger and Ted Shackley, by now assistant deputy director for Operations—that the Israeli account was a large source of Angleton's power. For one thing, it had given him special access to five American presidents. Now they would take it away from him. According to Robert Crowley, "Israel was removed from its special status and lumped into the CIA's Near East Division, which Mossad considered filled with Arabists. The Israelis, who credit their national survival to their intelligence organs, quickly ascertained that their relationship with the CIA would never be the same again."

For the government of Israel, the loss of James Angleton was a major blow, but one for which it was prepared. The Israelis had other friends in the U.S. intelligence community. Colby and Kissinger's changes in the CIA included cutbacks in Clandestine Services, as a result of which many of the CIA's most experienced officers were out of work and embittered. These officers, including key men who had served at Berlin Base, were ripe for recruitment for freelance work. Colby and Kissinger did not foresee that their downsizing would lead to the creation of a shadow CIA, which by the 1980s was not only working for the Israelis but also was involved in covert operations from Central America to Iran. Its activities, although partially exposed in the Iran-Contra scandal in 1986, continue to this day.

Because Colby was still unsure of his own power, he took his time in forcing Angleton out completely, until in December 1974, he was ready to strike. He did so not by calling Angleton in and firing him, but by leaking a story to Sy Hersh of the *New York Times* (the same reporter who had gotten Ambassador Korry's story wrong) to the effect that Angleton had run the CIA's secret mail-opening campaign. The resulting uproar forced Angleton and his top assistants to resign. The irony is that while the mail-opening program was run from Angleton's office, he had nothing to do with it. Still, in one sweeping stroke of Colby's axe, Angleton's mole investigation officially ended.

Angleton, however, did not clear out his desk, climb into his black Mercedes, and drive away from Langley until almost a year after his resignation. According to Robert Crowley, Angleton, totally convinced the Agency was penetrated, made a momentous decision. He arranged with a handful of trusted friends, including Crowley, to carry the most important counterintelligence files he possessed away from Langley in their briefcases. Included in that material were the names of suspected Soviet illegals whom Igor Orlov was servicing and officials in the United States government whom Angleton believed worked for the Soviets.

By the time Angleton's successors took possession of his office, the counterintelligence files in the special room next door had been sanitized. The accusations that had left 14 careers in shambles—Angleton's damning memorial—had been removed. From his house in suburban Virginia, Angleton continued the mole hunt with whoever would help him. Colby never asked him why he believed certain CIA officers were compromised. It was a profound oversight that had immense consequences.

Angleton's departure meant an end to any semblance of counterintelligence in the CIA. Colby selected George Kalaris and Leonard McCoy to replace Angleton. Neither of these men had any experience in the convoluted world of counterintelligence, and they both agreed with Colby's philosophy that the important thing was to recruit, recruit, recruit. Practically everyone in the CIA was encouraged to recruit agents. Whether or not the agents were real could be sorted out later.

At Gallery Orlov, Igor continued to entertain new customers, many of whom came from the Defense Intelligence Agency, Army intelligence, the Department of State, and the CIA. His customers also included a handful of the KGB's most important and protected agents. Now that Angleton was out, the little man really was bullet-proof.

CHAPTER FIFTY-ONE

WHO NEEDS
COUNTERINTELLIGENCE?

⟢⟢⟢

PAUL GARBLER returned from his second assignment in Stockholm
unwilling to wait any longer for an explanation of what had gone
wrong in his career. Leonard McCoy was the first person to tell him that
Angleton was suspicious of him because he had been Igor Orlov's case officer in Berlin.[1] McCoy urged Garbler to seek redress. As Garbler tells it,
"Leonard said, 'Did you ask for any money?' I said, 'Money? Money?
What are you talking about? No, I didn't ask for any money.' He said,
'Go write them a memorandum right now and tell them you want compensation for all the years that you have been a GS-16 and all the mental
anguish you and your family have suffered.'"[2]

Garbler followed McCoy's advice, and, after a series of meetings
with old colleagues, his long stay out in the cold began to end. Garbler
demanded that the CIA's inspector general investigate what had been
done to him. On August 8, 1977, John F. Blake, the acting deputy director of the CIA, wrote Garbler: ". . . I associate myself completely with
the IG [Inspector General] findings that the previously raised security
issue has been fully resolved in your favor. . . . Even at this late date I
also acknowledge and regret the adverse effect the now-resolved security
questions have had on your career. Your feelings of frustration and bitterness are understandable, and I am only sorry there is no way to turn
back the clock."

Richard Kovich's status as an outcast took longer to resolve. In the end, it took an act of Congress to compensate the former star of SR-9, the super-secret unit within the intelligence service.

One of the first cases the new counterintelligence staff tried to reactivate after Angleton's departure was KITTY HAWK. Colonel Igor Kozlov had shown no interest in pursuing the case after he returned to the Soviet Union at the end of his brief visit in 1966, according to FBI counterintelligence official James E. Nolan. Despite attention to the case, the CIA was unable to make contact with him in Russia. When his mother-in-law, Yekaterina Furtseva, visited the United States in 1972, the FBI and CIA hoped that Colonel Kozlov would be in her entourage, but he was not.

Angleton, for his part, had been content to let the KITTY HAWK case slow down, never trusting Kozlov fully but forced to let the case go on because of Kozlov's relationship with Furtseva. Then, two months before Angleton's resignation, Furtseva died, taking most of her secrets to the grave.[3] Those who plotted against Khrushchev and who knew the secrets about President Kennedy's murder were, one by one, aging and dying, moving beyond the reach of any intelligence service.

With Angleton gone, Kalaris and McCoy pushed to get KITTY HAWK going again. They still hoped that Colonel Kozlov would one day give them a mother lode of information on the Kremlin.

For Leonard McCoy, the case had a basic conflict of interest. At the American end of the KITTY HAWK operation was the defector Nick Shadrin, a.k.a. Nikolai Artamonov, and McCoy was the young reports officer in the Soviet Russia Division who bypassed normal security procedures in order to bring Artamonov to the United States. Now, a few years later, McCoy was running Shadrin in conjunction with the FBI.

There was a further complication. Perhaps if James Angleton had still been at the CIA, he might have learned what McCoy and Kalaris did not: that Felix Bloch and George Weisz had a series of meetings with Igor Kozlov in Vienna and then Berlin between 1971 and 1975.

WILLIAM COLBY'S RELIANCE on personnel who had served at Berlin Base included George Weisz. Colby named Weisz chief of the Foreign Intelligence (FI) staff of the Directorate of Operations in late 1973 and, a year later, promoted him to director of Operations under his old rival, Ted Shackley.[4] According to Sam Wilson, chief of Foreign Intelligence is "potentially a very powerful job. . . . The chief of FI, along with the DDO [Director of the Directorate of Operations] and the deputy DDO—they were kind of the wheels in the arena, and the fourth man, of course, was the Chief of CI." George Weisz had passed up a chance to run the CIA's most important station in the early 1970s—Saigon—in order to return to Berlin as chief of base. Now, the CIA was transferring him back to Langley as chief of FI.

Almost immediately after coming home from Berlin, Weisz did something out of the ordinary. He began obtaining the highest levels of security clearance for nuclear weapons. By the spring of 1975, Weisz was in a position to access details about the state of the American nuclear arsenal, even though his job responsibilities at that time barely touched on nuclear weaponry.[5] Before long, however, he had become the CIA's liaison with the Defense Department, the State Department, and the Department of Energy on matters dealing with the proliferation of nuclear materials.

None of this was important to Etta Jo Weisz. What mattered to her was that she was finally home. Her husband had not lived in the United States for more than 13 years of his entire life, and their children were as comfortable in Europe as in America. In fact, their daughter, Nikki, had stayed in Berlin to study dance. But Etta Jo vowed that Berlin was her last overseas assignment. She later recalled telling George, "The next time I go out of this house, it will be feet first." Their suburban Maryland home had suffered $16,000 damage from tenants over the years.

Like hundreds of other CIA marriages, the Weiszes' relationship was strained by the pressures of the job. According to George's mother, who lived with the couple from time to time during their overseas postings, George and Etta Jo stopped sharing a bedroom by the 1960s. During their second tour in Berlin, Etta Jo recalled, she and other Base wives spent weekends in Majorca "every four or five weeks" for the sake of their "sanity" and to get away from the social obligations of Berlin Base. Like many other CIA wives, Etta Jo grew to hate the Agency.

By the early 1970s, all the Weisz children were living away from home. Nikki was in Berlin, and the younger son, David, who bears a startling physical resemblance to his father, was already following in George's footsteps: He had done very well in college and was now embarked on a diplomatic career. The elder son, Donnel, suffered the most from the instability of a CIA family, according to his grandmother. Ironically, it was when the family was living in Hong Kong that Donnel first experimented with drugs, while his father was traveling back and forth to Laos, assisting the opium warlords there. By 1974, Donnel had been in a serious car accident, had a string of academic and professional failures, and was dealing drugs. To his great embarrassment, George had to ask his CIA superiors for help when Donnel got into trouble with the police for his drug activities.

In the spring of 1975, when George Weisz had been back at Langley for a year and a half, he met Dr. Robert Kupperman, a terrorism expert who was engaged in several major studies for the U.S. government. Kupperman, a rotund and dour man, was a close friend of Nick Shadrin. Shadrin collected officials who had access to top-secret information with the same determination with which he added firearms to his extensive collection. Kupperman was one of many well-connected friends of the charismatic Soviet agent.

With a background in strategic weapons, Kupperman had earlier served as chief scientist for the Arms Control and Disarmament Agency. His consulting job at the time Weisz met him was to create horrible scenarios about terrorists getting hold of nuclear weapons.[6] Coincidentally, Weisz's new responsibilities included formulating a CIA response to the emerging international terrorism threat. Kupperman recalled, "I knew George first in '75 when I was running government-wide studies of terrorism. George was then chief of staff on the ops [operational] side of the Agency. . . . I met George around the spring of '75 when the study started. I don't remember exact dates. George was involved in the study."

If Kupperman is right about when he and George Weisz got to know each other, their friendship must have been based on some very brief encounters. Weisz's diplomatic passport shows that he spent most of April and May that year in Mexico, Bolivia, Panama, Peru, and Venezuela, assisting Ted Shackley in restaffing Latin America after the Chile debacle, during which Castro's DGI learned the identities of most CIA officers in Latin America and their principal agents.[7]

Etta Jo Weisz recalled just how busy her husband was in the spring of 1975 as he toured nearly all the major Latin American stations. She said George was not a man to make friends quickly; she thought it unlikely that he and Kupperman could have become close over so short a time. The two men did not seem to have much in common other than being Jewish.

Suddenly, in August 1975, although Weisz had one of the top half-dozen jobs in the CIA, he was selected to go to Vienna, Austria, as the new station chief. Etta Jo was unprepared when her husband came home to tell her he had accepted another overseas post. She recalled that she and her son David were sitting in the living room when George came in and said, "Well, I'm glad you're both sitting down. . . . You're going to Vienna." Etta Jo told George she had no intention of going anywhere. She had hoped that George's top-level headquarters assignment would bring them back together. She had barely finished getting the house back in order from their second tour in Berlin, and she had just begun a new government job of her own.

Angry and hurt by her husband's decision, Etta Jo refused to give in, although she reluctantly agreed to get her diplomatic passport renewed and have a CIA physical. George told her he would return at Christmas to take her back to Vienna with him, since he was certain that by that time she would change her mind.

Weisz's sudden assignment to Vienna came as a shock not only to his family but also to many in the top echelons of the CIA, including Sam Wilson, by now deputy director to the intelligence community. "George tended to maneuver and tried to manipulate his way in," Wilson said. "So when he went to Vienna, I thought, 'George, either you've pulled a couple of coups I don't know about or you've gotten on the right side of somebody and have talked them into it. . . .'"

As Kupperman tells it, "George, around the summer of '75, told me he was going to become station chief in Vienna and wanted to introduce me to others in the Agency who'd take his place on the series of studies I was running. George went off, I presume to Vienna. I received some correspondence from George wanting me to come . . . about terrorism stuff, and he wanted to introduce me to the Ministry of Interior and a variety of other things, and just to get together socially."

If Weisz did tell Kupperman about the Vienna station job, he was violating CIA security. In any case, the curious relationship between Robert Kupperman and George Weisz was about to take a new turn. What makes their newfound coincidental friendship stretch all credulity is the fact that Vienna had been selected for the long-awaited reactivation of KITTY HAWK.

The CIA had just learned that Colonel Kozlov had a new assignment from the KGB. He would be traveling back and forth to Vienna on a regular basis, escorting Soviet scientists to International Atomic Energy Agency (IAEA) meetings there. Leonard McCoy and Nick Shadrin's FBI handlers agreed to try to arrange a meeting between Shadrin and KITTY HAWK, the first since 1966, in Vienna, just before Christmas 1975. McCoy and Kalaris asked George Weisz to attempt to become KITTY HAWK's new case officer.

So here was Kupperman, one of Nick Shadrin's closest friends, striking up a friendship with a top CIA official, who would be running the CIA station in the city where Shadrin was about to undertake his most important assignment for the United States. Kupperman claimed there was never any mention of Shadrin or KITTY HAWK in any of his conversations with Weisz. "Nick's name never came up," Kupperman said.

AFTER THE ISRAELIS lost the services of James Angleton, they cast about for someone to replace him. In the fall of 1975, according to Robert Crowley, they settled on Ted Shackley. DCI Colby and Shackley's immediate boss, Director of Operations William Wells, evidently were unaware of Shackley's activities with the Israelis or else tacitly approved them.

Crowley was convinced there was a connection between George Weisz's sudden assignment to Vienna and Shackley's new unofficial role with the Israelis. "The two men worked together their whole careers. There was a rivalry. But when this sudden appointment came, Shackley, who was technically George's boss, could have objected, but didn't." In fact, Shackley's relationship with the Israelis may explain why George Weisz was assigned to Vienna so soon after his return to headquarters.

Why the urgency? In 1974, Weisz, as head of the Foreign Intelligence staff, had learned that a new and closer relationship on nuclear matters was developing between the French and Saddam Hussein's Iraq. The Iraqis were offering the French tens of millions of dollars in contracts in exchange for nuclear technology, starting with a 70-megawatt commercial atomic reactor and a smaller research reactor. The Iraqis named the project Tammuz, after a Canaanite god and the month in the Arabic calendar when Saddam Hussein's Ba'ath Party took power in 1968.

This intelligence in unabridged form first found its way to Israel through Weisz. Months later, the Israelis received a version of the information through a new, official cooperative arrangement with the CIA, via the station chief in Tel Aviv.

The information the station chief gave them was so truncated compared to Weisz's full report that the Israeli government grew seriously alarmed. The Iraqis were Israel's most threatening neighbor. For them to gain nuclear weapons, though significant to the United States, was a matter of national survival for Israel. George Weisz, a reliable source for Israel for decades, was the obvious choice for the task of discovering the details of the French-Iraqi nuclear partnership.

For any intelligence officer, Vienna was a terrific assignment. Its proximity to the Iron Curtain, Austria's neutrality, and the fact that the CIA and the KGB both had a history of bold operations there made it one of the most important stations in the world. After the Berlin Wall went up, Vienna replaced Berlin as the frontline station in Europe. The United States' Vienna embassy had a staff of more than five hundred, and the CIA contingent ranged between 50 and 70 officers during the three years Weisz headed the station.

Because so many countries and international organizations were represented in Vienna, intelligence targets were plentiful. For the CIA, the key target was the International Atomic Energy Agency, located in facilities outside the old city. Here, scientists from countries with nuclear energy programs, as well as government officials and spies, came together to control the proliferation of nuclear materials.

If nuclear material that could become weapons grade was getting into the hands of terrorists, Vienna was an excellent place to find out. The IAEA was responsible for policing the use of commercial and research reactors and materials that might be diverted for military purposes—although it was an open joke that the two hundred IAEA inspectors were not permitted to inspect in Pakistan, India, Israel, and South Africa, all areas of real concern. Weisz's job, both for his American employer and for Mossad, was to find out if IAEA inspectors had looked the other way on French exports to Iraq.

The idea was to have Weisz penetrate the old boy network in the nuclear community and learn how non-strategic nuclear material was being upgraded to bomb-grade material in small research reactors with the complicity of countries like France. This is why Weisz applied for every major nuclear security clearance the year before he left for Austria. This is why he became the CIA's representative on matters of nuclear proliferation. And some CIA officers believe this is why he ended up being friends with Dr. Robert Kupperman: They believe Kupperman was Weisz's go-between with the Israelis. In answer to this, Kupperman will only say that he has consulted in Israel and that he and Weisz were friends.

CHAPTER FIFTY-TWO

CHRISTMAS IN VIENNA

AS GEORGE WEISZ was preparing to leave for Vienna, the CIA and FBI were jointly preparing for Nick Shadrin's meeting with Igor Kozlov. The old rivalry between the two agencies—complicated by lingering effects of James Angleton's mole hunt—made the planning seem more like a performance of Peter Sellers's Inspector Clouseau than an expertly run intelligence operation.[1]

Even with Angleton's departure, the CIA still considered KITTY HAWK's original case officer, Richard Kovich, too much of a security risk for so sensitive a mission and chose instead the German-born officer Cynthia Hausmann as Shadrin's case officer in Vienna. They also selected Gardener "Gus" Hathaway, the Berlin Base veteran who had met Kozlov years before in Pakistan, to be on the scene to reassure him if he arrived as they hoped.

The difficulties began almost immediately. First, Shadrin's FBI case officer, James Wooten, objected to Cynthia Hausmann accompanying Shadrin to Vienna. He complained to his superiors that she had been "blown" by the author Philip Agee in a sensational book published earlier that summer.[2] In answer, the CIA insisted Hausmann's identity being known to the KGB would not endanger Shadrin. FBI official Neil Sullivan felt the whole thing got out of control. "I didn't know who the hell was really controlling the Shadrin operation. Supposedly, it's Jim Wooten in the Washington field office. But to me, after the thing developed, it seems like everybody and his uncle had control over the operation."

Then, Eugene Peterson, the FBI's deputy for counterintelligence, learned that the CIA's Bruce Solie was not part of the operation. Solie was the agent who had first met with Kozlov in Washington in 1966, but he was not known to the Soviets. Solie was not even aware there was to be a meeting in Vienna. At the FBI's insistence, Solie, in charge of the Igor Orlov mole hunt, replaced Hathaway, well-known to the KGB because of his previous service in Moscow and Berlin.

A few days before Shadrin went to Vienna, Hausmann reported to the FBI that Vienna Station planned to place agents at fixed points to observe the meeting. The FBI, fearful that CIA agents would be spotted by the Russians and endanger Shadrin, canceled this surveillance. Hausmann failed to tell the FBI that the cathedral steps, where the meeting was to take place, were in clear view of the U.S. consulate, making a fixed-point observation a simple matter.

George Weisz arrived in Vienna on September 29, 1975, replacing Hugh Montgomery, his old colleague from Berlin Base. In December, Weisz put Vienna Station on full alert and cancelled most of the station personnel's leave for the weekend before Christmas. CIA officers were planted among the embassy staff with job titles that had nothing to do with their real assignments.

On December 17, Cynthia Hausmann arrived at the embassy and went directly to Weisz's fourth-floor office in the Peripheral Reporting Section.[3] Weisz moved the meeting from his office to "the bubble" in case of eavesdropping by the Soviets. In Vienna, the bubble was located directly over the ambassador's third-floor office. Hausmann and Weisz went over final arrangements, including Hausmann's announcement to Weisz that the FBI wanted no surveillance at all, even from fixed points.

Having completed these arrangements with Cynthia Hausmann and cancelled most of his new subordinates' Christmas leave, Weisz himself bizarrely left Vienna at almost exactly the same time Nick Shadrin arrived. Weisz's plane was still sitting on the ground at Vienna's International Airport when Shadrin's flight, delayed a day by a massive snowstorm, arrived at 2:00 P.M. on December 18. According to George Weisz's passport, he arrived at Kennedy Airport in New York later that same day. Curiously, although he was in the United States over the holidays, he called no one in his immediate family.

Nick Shadrin met with the Soviets on December 19 and again on December 20. Then he disappeared—apparently kidnapped by the KGB. The Russians later "admitted" that Shadrin "died" in a kidnapping operation from an overdose of chloroform as he was being whisked away from Vienna behind the Iron Curtain.

In fact, the Shadrin operation in Vienna was run by the KGB and Mossad; the CIA and FBI preparations were simply ornamental. Nick Shadrin was not attempting to ferret out KITTY HAWK, as American intelligence thought. He was going home. His mission was over. While the rest of the world thought he had been kidnapped by the Soviets, in reality, he was returning to his Russian wife, Elena, and their now-grown son. Kozlov was not even in Vienna for the meeting; the FBI and CIA had been totally fooled.

The scheme to get Nick Shadrin back to the Soviet Union by making it look like a kidnapping arose from a deal between the KGB and Mossad. Years before, Yekaterina Furtseva's careful planning for her son-in-law's operation against Washington had required that Angleton's Israeli sources confirm for him that Kozlov was real. According to Angleton, that confirmation came through a trusted Mossad agent in early 1967. Since that time, the Israelis had kept tabs on the KITTY HAWK operation both in the United States and the Soviet Union. When they learned of the Soviets' operation to repatriate Shadrin, they saw an opportunity to make a trade. They told the KGB that they would not expose the Shadrin operation if the Soviets agreed to release several key Jewish dissidents they were holding. Weisz made the final arrangements for Mossad before he left Vienna on December 18.

Weisz's departure just before this major CIA operation took place was absolutely uncharacteristic of him, according to colleagues like Sam Wilson. But the Israelis knew that if Weisz stayed in Vienna, the controversy over Shadrin's disappearance might draw unwelcome attention to their single most valuable asset in the CIA.

Nick Shadrin's behavior before he left for Vienna indicates he had no intention of returning to the United States.[4] He gave one of his cherished rifles to his office mate, East German defector Frank Steinert,[5] and he gave an expensive pistol to Polish defector Richard Odin.[6] Steinert later discovered a map of Vienna in Shadrin's desk with the section for the Vienna Woods cut out. The day he disappeared, Shadrin rented a car at the Bristol Hotel where he was staying and drove 22 miles, presumably to familiarize himself with the area.

George Weisz's friendship with the manager of the Bristol Hotel proved invaluable in making certain nothing went wrong.[7] The exchange of Nick Shadrin for several Soviet Jews took place in the Vienna Woods after Shadrin's second meeting with the Soviets on the evening of December 20. Weisz was able to tell the Israelis there would be no CIA surveillance, and the operation took place while Cynthia Hausmann was dining and drinking with an old colleague, Stanley Jeffers, in his Vienna home.[8]

The Shadrin disaster should have ended George Weisz's career, but it did him no harm at all. Because he had not run the meetings himself, Weisz was able to put the blame for the "blown" operation on the counterintelligence divisions of the CIA and the FBI. He went so far as to meet with Ewa Shadrin's lawyer, Richard Copaken, and later with *Reader's Digest* editor-at-large Henry Hurt, and was candid and relaxed as he gave them his cool professional view of the incompetent interlopers from Washington. Naturally, he made his own role seem innocent and entirely plausible.

To this day, the Russians and Mossad continue to cover up the Shadrin exchange. Neither service wants the CIA to know that its mortal enemy and its presumed ally colluded to serve their own mutual interests and embarrass the CIA.[9]

The Israeli intelligence services could be fearsome enemies but great friends, and starting in late 1975, they provided Shackley's people with material that made the Operations Directorate look very good. Meanwhile, George Weisz began an active program in Vienna that was not confined to picking up the gossip at IAEA cocktail parties and cultivating State Department officials involved with the IAEA. He also penetrated the nuclear inspection staff, recruiting international inspectors with the help of Mossad and officials in Austria's Interior Ministry.

To Sam Wilson, still working for William Colby, Weisz on his occasional visits to Langley was a man "whose personality ran hot and cold. . . . He could be very, very warm, and then all of a sudden there was almost as though he was another individual—began to back up, he'd hit the switch in his warm field."

During this period, Wilson said, "George would come back from Vienna and invariably sit there in my outer office until I was free in order to come in and sit and chat. I sensed this guy was feeling very lonely and very much on the outside, and I always tried to be decent to him. And the result was I had the feeling he just kind of glommed onto me. . . . I had a rear entrance to my office. I'd go out the rear entrance and go do something and come back, and George would still be sitting there, and, 'Well, George, glad to see you,' when I had been sitting inside the office and just didn't have the time to spend with him. That's a cruel thing to tell you. . . . He just wanted to talk. He was kind of brooding; he was unhappy. If I had to pick one word that would strike me, he seemed, again, psychologically very insecure, very insecure. I would talk about light, frivolous, humorous, funny-bone-rattling things, and I could hardly get a smile out of him. He never did have much of a sense of humor, but it seemed to me to have just about gone. The other very minor thing, and I may be reaching a little bit for this—always curious, always kind of probing as to what's really going on and, 'Have you heard about such and such?' . . . I don't like for anybody to do it."

At the end of January 1976, President Ford fired William Colby. For the next year, the CIA was run by the loyal patrician Republican, George H.W. Bush, who was as fascinated by covert operations as the Kennedy brothers had been. Bush fancied himself a foreign policy expert, and because he went to Yale and was a member of the Skull and Bones Society, he considered himself cut from the same cloth as the founders of the CIA. In many ways, Bush and the CIA were a match made in heaven.

Bush was seldom at the Langley headquarters, leaving most of the administrative work to his executive assistant, Hank Knoche, a man with no experience in covert operations. Away from the office, Bush became friends with many top Agency officials, ranging from Security Division Chief Robert Gambino to DDO William Wells and ADDO Ted Shackley.

In this environment of absentee management, Ted Shackley thrived. According to Robert Crowley, Shackley "understood that Wells would make a fool of himself. . . . He went around blaming all the bad things that were happening to Clandestine Services on Wells." While Shackley had the trust of those in covert operations, Wells was not taken seriously. Because of his frenetic approach to life, his nickname at the Agency was "Bugs Bunny."[10]

Meanwhile, Shackley made the Israeli account his own. He kept the relationship personal, as Angleton had done. According to Crowley and other Agency officials, Shackley told no one in the chain of command anything he was doing with respect to Israel.

Shackley had many close calls in his career but always survived. He was not held accountable for his roles in OPERATION MONGOOSE, Laos, or Chile. Now he found himself at a high enough level to influence intelligence policy. He introduced George Bush to many of his old Cuban friends in Miami. A decade earlier, they had been the heart of the CIA's anti-Castro effort. Now, they were a powerful political force Bush could use in his quest to fulfill political ambitions that went beyond the CIA.

For George Weisz, life in Vienna was very good. If he felt disappointment at Etta Jo's decision not to join him, it did not last. George, long a womanizer, at age 57 met Cheryl Thomas, a tall, leggy brunette half his age, at the Marine Corps ball a month after his arrival in Vienna. The two quickly became lovers. They may have believed no one knew about their affair, but, according to CIA officer Stanley Jeffers, "They were the talk of the station."

Why Cheryl Thomas was attracted to George Weisz is hard to fathom. Handsome in his younger days, when he reminded C.G. Follich of Charles Boyer, he was by now bald and paunchy. He was not rich—his wife did not remember him ever making more than his government salary. And he was no more popular in Vienna than he had been in Berlin, Saigon, or Langley; his subordinates continued to call him "Napoleon" behind his back.[11] And yet, although there were a number of younger and more eligible men around, Thomas set her sights on Weisz. Perhaps his European charm and formal manners appealed to her. Or perhaps it was something else.

Cheryl Thomas refused to discuss her relationship with George Weisz for this book. We do know that she was a secretary in the political section of the American Embassy, where a number of CIA officers were "employed." Judging from her professional history, it is possible that she herself was working not for the State Department but for the CIA. She carried a top-secret clearance and had several other clearances not normally granted to secretaries. Her previous assignments in hot spots like Jakarta and Beirut seem to be beyond the luck of the draw in the State Department secretarial pool.

In any case, George Weisz loved Vienna. Also, Vienna was close enough to Berlin so that he made frequent trips to see his daughter, Nikki, who by now was operating a dance school there. His visits to Nikki also gave him cover for contacting Felix Bloch, his recruit of several years earlier. Weisz found it easy to operate behind the back of Wiley T. Buchanan, the U.S. ambassador to Austria.

In November 1976, the defeat of President Ford by Jimmy Carter was a great disappointment to George Bush. According to Sam Wilson, Bush had hoped to stay on as CIA Director. Hank Knoche, who accompanied Bush to Plains, Georgia, to meet with Carter after the election, said: "I think that he would have been willing to . . . and he was never asked."[12]

Instead, Carter selected as the new director Admiral Stansfield Turner, with whom he had attended the Naval Academy.[13] Turner made a serious attempt to clean up after his predecessors' evasions and illicit activities, but he was as ill-suited for intelligence work as anyone who ever walked into the CIA. His appointment began a war between the Carter Administration and the old boys in Clandestine Services that raged until Carter's defeat four years later.

America had a new president, and across the world, Israel had a new prime minister, Menachem Begin. Begin, a revolutionary and terrorist in his younger days, was now a tough old politician who wanted to keep the Palestinians in check and Israel secure. His first priority was to stop relying on the United States to apply diplomatic pressure on France for selling fuel to the Iraqis for reactors they were constructing. Instead, Begin ordered Israeli military intelligence (Aman) and Mossad, the Israeli equivalent of the CIA, to coordinate plans to stop the Iraqi reactor projects. George Weisz's role was major: It was up to him to find out about the reactors' construction and fueling timetables.

Jimmy Carter owed his election in large part to significant support from the American Jewish community. One of his most important supporters was Milton Wolf, a Cleveland construction magnate and a leading light in the United Jewish Appeal, one of the most politically powerful pro-Israeli organizations in America. Wolf, a tough, smart, and savvy man, was Carter's choice for ambassador to Austria. For George Weisz, the arrival in Vienna of Wolf as his new boss made his job that much easier.

The Israelis did not rely solely on Weisz, however. They had a new agent, Jonathan Pollard, who was attempting to obtain American satellite pictures of the Iraqi reactor site. These were the same kinds of pictures that for years Angleton had regularly supplied to Israel but Stansfield Turner stopped.

CHAPTER FIFTY-THREE

AFTER ANGLETON

—⟶●⟵—

AFTER THE MASSIVE CIA scandals uncovered by Senator Frank Church and investigative reporters, the CIA worked harder at burnishing its image than at reforming itself. With Congress's approval, the new, kinder and gentler CIA decided to compensate with money and apologies the officers targeted by Angleton for investigation. With CIA management concentrating on public relations, the KGB, GRU, and a host of other friendly and unfriendly services rushed in to exploit its weakness. In the decades at the end of the twentieth century, Angleton's worst fears were realized.

The first incident, in September 1976, was the disappearance of CIA employee John Arthur Paisley while sailing on Chesapeake Bay. At first, the CIA announced that Paisley was a low-level official. Later, it turned out he was a top strategic expert. The body eventually recovered from the Bay did not match his description.

Other incidents ranged from the disappearance of Edward Lee Howard in 1985 to the arrest and conviction of Aldrich Ames in 1994. Howard was a double agent who slipped through an FBI dragnet, vanished in the New Mexico desert, and surfaced in Moscow a year later. Ames was a counterintelligence officer who started selling information to the KGB in 1985 and continued the relationship with the post-Soviet Russian intelligence service, the SVR. He is thought to be responsible for the deaths of at least 10 blown agents.

For a while, CIA embarrassments were occurring so frequently that the late-night talk shows had a field day with jokes about Agency security. Adding to the humiliation was that the security risks were uncovered not by expert police work but by angry informants. In one instance, the CIA's Hong Kong Station Chief was entertaining girlfriends in more than a dozen safe houses. His suspicious wife hired a private investigator who supplied her with photographic evidence of her husband's affairs. The wife, not following Agency rules, sent the entire package via regular mail to DCI Stansfield Turner. As it turned out, her breach of security scarcely mattered, because the private eye's regular employer was the intelligence service of the People's Republic of China. As a result, the entire CIA operation in Hong Kong was blown.

Careless security habits spread to the highest levels of the CIA. While George Bush was DCI he signed out a copy of the operations manual for the Keyhole 11 (KH-11) spy satellite, the country's most secret system, and never returned it. President Clinton's DCI, John Deutch, required a pardon from the president for using a government laptop computer loaded with sensitive state secrets to surf on the Internet, risking the exposure of the secrets.

Following Angleton's removal, the CIA's new counterintelligence team was so focused on discrediting him that they actually commissioned a study to prove that if there was a KGB mole in the CIA, it could have been James Angleton himself. Selected to do the study was a former Ottawa Station Chief, Cleveland Cram, who had a horrendous relationship with Angleton. In 1967, when Cram was in Ottawa, Angleton suspected that James Leslie Bennett, security officer for the Royal Canadian Mounted Police, might be a Soviet agent. This accusation put Cram in a rough position, and Angleton compounded his problems by ordering the various security tests on Bennett be conducted inside Canada.

Another former Angleton deputy, Edward C. Petty, independently working for Angelton's successors, filed a secret report concluding that Angleton was probably capable of being a Soviet agent. "It was as if the counterintelligence office had been reconfigured to demonstrate I was crazy, insane," Angleton later said. His old friend Bruce Solie added: "After Angleton was out of power, many people felt that if they could discredit him, then their own mistakes would be mitigated."

The activities of Cram and Petty constituted just about the entire CIA counterintelligence effort during the 1970s, as the Agency made the decision to all but ignore external threats and only pursue positive intelligence cases. Even after Shadrin's disappearance in Vienna and the infamous case of Christopher Boyce—a young man working for TRW in California who systematically sold the Soviets our most precious spy satellite secrets—counterintelligence remained dormant.

Coincidentally, Director Stansfield Turner was one of the high-level government officials Shadrin had cultivated when he was in the United States, and the two men had developed a close friendship.[1] After Shadrin's disappearance, there were several internal investigations, including one by the President's Foreign Intelligence Advisory Board (PFIAB). However, neither the PFIAB nor the Senate or House intelligence oversight committees ever questioned Turner about his relationship with Shadrin.

WHILE ANGLETON'S MOLE HUNT closed down some operations at the CIA, the new counterintelligence team, Leonard McCoy and George Kalaris, opened up other operations in ways that were often disastrous. For example, when the Russians tried to determine whether the KH-11 spy satellite manual that Christopher Boyce had sold them was real, they found a young CIA clerk, William Kampiles, who agreed to feed them confirming documentation. Kampiles went to Kalaris to tell him what he had done, claiming it was his own "counterintelligence operation." Kalaris delayed telling the FBI about the incident. That delay gave the Soviets precious time to further compromise the multibillion-dollar spy satellite fleet.

The CIA's failure to thoroughly vet its own people even caused a hero to be murdered.

Army Warrant Officer Ralph Sigler—code name GRAPHIC IMAGE—was the most successful double agent in American Army history. Because of him, the Soviets spent tens of millions of dollars in the belief that fake or doctored secrets he gave them were real. Sigler was exposed when a turf war broke out between the FBI and Army intelligence.

The FBI at that time was proudly touting its "turning" of Soviet illegal Rudolph Herrmann, a prize agent the FBI is protecting to this day. In 1976, the FBI began a secret effort to recruit the Army's Sigler to service Hermann.

Tragically, a young clerk from the CIA who transferred to Sigler's Army intelligence unit at Fort Meade was working for the Soviets and compromised at least six valuable national intelligence assets before he was discovered.

In the case of Sigler, the clerk benefited from a botched-up security investigation. In April of 1976, Sigler was given an Army polygraph test, which he failed because he had been told by the FBI not to tell the Army about his work on the Herrmann case. The clerk sent Sigler's name through to Moscow Center. The Russians so trusted Sigler as their own agent in the Army that, when they learned of his duplicity, they ordered a "wet" team to interrogate and kill him.

The wet team seized the opportunity of the Army's own interrogation of Sigler to do its work. At one point, Sigler was left alone in his Holiday Inn room between polygraphs, and the Soviet team moved in. They tortured him and then killed him by electrocution. The Army was shocked at what happened, but instead of investigating, they instituted a clumsy cover-up, telling Sigler's widow that her husband had committed a bizarre form of suicide. Weeks later, without explanation, the Legion of Merit arrived, awarded posthumously.

The question the counterintelligence investigators should have asked about Siglers' death was: Who was running the Soviets' operation? The low-level clerk played a necessary role, but someone else had to communicate with the Soviet illegals, who, in turn, sent in the wet team. Someone had to know U.S. intelligence from the inside. Neither CIA security and counterintelligence nor the FBI ever figured out how the illegals received their communications. Yet the answer was sitting in a small art gallery on King Street in Alexandria, Virginia.

Between 1974 and 1982, Igor Orlov disappeared from the CIA's and FBI's radar screens. The most effective agent in Soviet history, the man responsible for tearing apart the CIA, was all but ignored. "This was an oversight that cost my best double agent his life," said retired Captain Noel Jones, who ran Sigler and the Army's double agent operations in the 1970s. A top Army intelligence official who has reviewed the case file said: "The rat in Army intelligence who gave up Sigler to the Russians had a case officer. That case officer communicated using Orlov to get the message out to dispatch the team to kill Ralph. Orlov was used to communicate with illegals. Because the FBI had Sigler working with a former Russian illegal they had recruited and never notified the Army, Sigler was left wide open to being discovered by the Russians. . . . The KGB was onto the illegal[2] being turned by the FBI. They connected him to Sigler and decided to send him a message by killing Sigler."

In Noel Jones's view, by the late 1970s, counterintelligence was in "complete chaos." There were a dozen blown operations, less dramatic than the Sigler case, but all with FBI and Army connections. There was a growing fear that the mole might be very high up the intelligence ladder at the CIA, the FBI, or the White House. As Jones put it, "No one knew who they could trust. That's why they were looking for a mole in the Army, in the White House, everywhere. They began to panic."[3]

The frequent raids that Angleton had asked the FBI to conduct on Gallery Orlov in 1965 had produced lists of clients who got pictures framed or bought art there. Copies of the records of those raids were left in dusty file boxes at the FBI's Washington field office. Whether for lack of manpower or lack of interest, no one looked at the files for years. When, much later, a FBI agent finally went through them, he discovered some very disturbing patterns.

The most remarkable thing was that almost every major name in FBI and CIA counterintelligence and security had been a customer at Gallery Orlov. Igor Orlov had the identities of almost the entire United States counterintelligence apparatus to use as he wished.

The abandonment of the Orlov investigation allowed the Soviet Union's most senior spy in the United States to build his own communications network. He was easily able to establish contact with Soviet and Eastern Bloc illegals, using his picture framing and art import business as a cover. The kinder, gentler CIA that dumped Angleton also ignored Orlov.

Eleanore Orlov always feared that behind her husband's anger and jealousy was the possibility he was the man the CIA and FBI were looking for. A hundred inexplicable visitors and strange incidents caused her to build a wall in her mind so she would not think about Igor as the ultimate Russian spy. "Igor never left the shop and was suspicious of everyone who came into the shop," she said. She remembered how hard he worked delivering newspapers, doing anything he could to make extra money. "If he were such a great spy, wouldn't the Russians take better care of him?"

she pleads. When she is reminded that Igor told her the Russians would evacuate the entire family when the time came, all she will say is she can't believe it.

In late 1978, General Orlov was entrusted with a case that was fast spinning out of control. The agent was of great importance to the Soviet Union, but he was a man of divided loyalties, who had to be brought back under discipline. This man was that very complicated individual, George Weisz.

CHAPTER FIFTY-FOUR

THE ATOMIC SPY

———⇒⊛⇐———

W ITH THE CHANGE in administrations, a new ambassador came
to Austria. President Carter's appointee, Milton Wolf, arrived in
Vienna in July 1977. He and his family liked George Weisz from the start.
"For some reason or other we did develop a very close relationship. . . .
Perhaps it was because we were both Jewish," Wolf said, adding that for
his first eight months in Vienna he did not know Weisz was Jewish.[1] The
Wolfs were aware of George's adulterous relationship with Cheryl
Thomas, and they became friendly with her.

As a result of what happened to Ambassador Korry in Chile and because of other independent CIA activity revealed by the press and Congress, President Carter ordered that henceforth all CIA operations must
be conducted with the full knowledge of the ambassador. This action by
Carter and Turner angered Clandestine Services. Ambassdor Wolf
quickly called a meeting with the officers at Vienna Station to discuss the
new orders.

Over the time he and Weisz worked together, Wolf remembered only
once when he disagreed with Weisz and ordered him to stop an operation. In reaction, Weisz told Wolf he would appeal to Turner, and Wolf,
certain of his political standing, told him to go ahead. Unexpectedly, that
confrontation seemed to strengthen rather than weaken their relationship.

Wolf found Weisz a "meticulous" man in his work and his personal
life. Weisz was "a pro's pro," Wolf said. ". . . He was smooth as silk in a

social situation. George got along well with the Jewish leaders that passed through Vienna." Could Weisz have been working for the Israelis? "It wouldn't surprise me," said Wolf. If there was an Israeli connection, "I don't think it would be anything official," Wolf said, although he added: "I assume anytime something came up that involved the Israelis that I reported to Washington, I would presume they [the CIA and State Department] would pass on the information to the Israeli government. . . . I wouldn't do it myself, of course. . . ." Wolf concedes that he acted as a conduit between the Israeli ambassador and the Austrian government more than once. "I knew every time the Israeli ambassador got into trouble with the Austrian government officials. The Israelis never had a real good relationship with the officials there. . . . Many times I went over and straightened the Austrians out for the Israeli ambassador. He couldn't get an appointment to see them sometimes."

George Weisz's life in Vienna seemed secure and happy. But in late June 1978, as part of State's job rotation policy, Cheryl Thomas returned to Washington, where she went to work in the personnel office responsible for assigning cover identities for the CIA's clandestine overseas officers. Then, just a few months after Thomas left Vienna, the CIA "fired" George Weisz.

What was supposed to be the end of Weisz's intelligence career came on August 11, 1978, with a classified cable from John N. McMahon, the new deputy director under Stansfield Turner.[2] The cable congratulated Weisz on his retirement and praised him for his 37 years in national security. It said that his work in an "extraordinarily sensitive and difficult technical operation in 1976 is one of several which you have added to the lore of intelligence." McMahon had the unhappy responsibility of carrying out Turner's cutbacks in personnel.

According to Robert Crowley, Turner was able to blame his gutting of the Operations Directorate on the "cost reduction exercises" begun under William Colby. William Wells and Ted Shackley were asked to present a list of the people they would fire if they were faced with various levels of cost reduction. It was Wells, according to Crowley, who actually gave Turner the list, and he acted upon the recommendations.

By the end of 1978, Wells and Shackley themselves were among the casualties. Shackley, though he prospered under George Bush, could not escape the taint of scandal under Turner. He fell victim to the former head of U.S. Naval intelligence and future director of the National Security Agency, Rear Admiral Bobby Ray Inman. Inman was beloved by the congressional oversight committees for the illusion of candor he created. He was extremely skillful in his use of the media, particularly in a series of press leaks linking Shackley to Edwin P. Wilson, the arms dealer and CIA front man.

The first leak appeared as a front page story by Bob Woodward in the *Washington Post* in April 1977. In this story, Wilson, who ran several CIA proprietaries, was falsely portrayed as a renegade CIA man who had supplied parts for the bomb that killed Orlando Letelier. It turned out that Wilson had nothing to do with the Letelier case, but the prosecutors had become obsessed with his activities. They learned that in the spring of 1968 he had been transferred to naval intelligence after a Soviet agent working in a Senate office blew his CIA cover. Later, when press reports appeared saying Wilson had become a multimillionaire running guns, Inman gave more interviews. He said that when he was the head of naval intelligence and wanted to fire Wilson, Ted Shackley called him and urged him not to.[3]

Before Turner was done, 823 experienced members of Clandestine Services were fired,[4] and the animosity toward Carter and Turner (who by now had the nickname Standstill Burner) was intense. Years later, during the second Reagan Administration, Shackley resurfaced in ways that, had Turner been more astute, might not have happened.

When Weisz was "fired," it appeared that he was being forced out because of the Carter Administration's budget cuts. But the letter "retiring" Weisz was not all it seemed. Ambassador Wolf, who considered Weisz a good friend, was shocked and angered by the firing. "I can't tell you how surprised I was," Wolf said. "He came in one day and said he was being called back and retired. I was very upset. . . ." Wolf wanted to intercede with the White House: "I wanted to go to bat for him. I wanted him to stay in Vienna. He acted very strange. He told me the bottom line was that these were the rules of the game. . . . I think I could have kept him in Vienna. I was close with the president, Hamilton Jordan [Carter's chief of staff], and Stu Eisenstadt [the domestic policy adviser]."

Ambassador Wolf was right: He could have kept Weisz in Vienna. However, just as in Saigon, when he turned down the station chief's job and took Berlin instead, George Weisz had other plans.

Three months after Cheryl Thomas returned to the States, so did George Weisz, "fully retired" from the CIA. Oddly enough, his records show no break in federal service. He became a Department of Defense consultant with no change in income. The double life that George Weisz had been living in Vienna continued.

George and Cheryl shared a condominium in Gaithersburg, Maryland— miles from the Department of State but fairly close to Germantown, Maryland, home of the nuclear weapons program run by the Department of Energy. George never told Etta Jo about Cheryl or the condominium. This strange man kept three residences. He slept in the basement of his and Etta Jo's Chevy Chase home several nights a week, stayed with Cheryl other nights, and spent the rest of his time at the 33-acre farm he had bought, against Etta Jo's wishes, just before his last Berlin posting.

From time to time, George Weisz stopped by Gallery Orlov to look at the wonderful collection of European prints. To outward appearances he was no different from any other customer who enjoyed the quaint little gallery. In those days, the section of Alexandria where Gallery Orlov was located was not particularly fashionable. The small framing room and the garden behind the gallery were wonderful places to hold a meeting or receive a coded message. The message the KGB had for George Weisz when he returned home was not a welcome one. It was a reminder that he had yet another master.

George Weisz's assignment on behalf of Israel did not end in Vienna. Robert Kupperman, the scientist and arms expert who met Weisz a few months prior to his assignment to Vienna and then did not see him for three years, thought so highly of him that he introduced him to Donald Kerr, head of the Department of Energy's Defense Programs Division. In a 1988 interview, Kerr could not remember how or when he met George Weisz, but he thought it was through Robert Kupperman.[5]

At that time, the head of the Nuclear Safeguards and Security program at the DOE was the very experienced Admiral Harvey Lyon. A tough-minded engineer, Lyon was trained by Admiral Hyman Rickover in the nuclear weapons business. Now, to create an opening for George Weisz, Kerr orchestrated the firing of Lyon. William Bartells, who worked at the Energy Department, said, "No matter how it has been described, Harvey Lyon was canned in a hurry."[6] Kerr and Kupperman were jointly responsible for propelling Weisz, a man they barely knew, into the single most sensitive job in America's nuclear establishment.

Harvey Lyon did not think very highly of Kupperman. As a consultant, Kupperman was paid to devise scenarios in which terrorists captured a nuclear weapon. In Lyon's view, "He tended to be full of overreaction. He could drum up impossible scenarios to make his point." Lyon added: "Kupperman was an instant expert on large terrorist acts that never came about. . . . I did not trust the man." Admiral Lyon said that is why he refused to grant Kupperman access to U.S. nuclear secrets.

Unfortunately, Kupperman had more influence with Kerr than Lyon did. Getting rid of Lyon and putting Weisz in charge gave Kupperman access to any information he wanted.

Admiral Lyon made no bones about his opinion of the access Weisz was given to sensitive information. "He was obviously on the inside of our military manufacturing and fabrication of our nuclear weapons program. He had access to it all—to all of the facilities and all of the plants. He sat in on all the planning committees. If he made a point of doing it, he could find out the details of every type of warhead we had: the numbers in stock, the manufacturing difficulties, and their yields. In that position, he had a free run of laboratories, production facilities, and insight into all of the plants. He could effectively walk through anything unhampered. . . . He had control of approving security clearances. Any decisions that came up that were controversial would come to him."[7]

According to one of Weisz's deputies in the Nuclear Safeguards program, Tom Isaacs, Weisz had access to files on any employee or contractor connected to the department. The opportunity for recruitment on behalf of Mossad was tremendous. Weisz could call any likely candidate into his office and say with a straight face that he was recruiting for the CIA when, in fact, he was recruiting for another intelligence service. Such a "false flag" recruitment was exactly what had happened to Weisz himself in Hungary just after the war.[8]

The Atomic Energy Act requires the FBI to conduct a new security investigation of anyone appointed director of the Nuclear Safeguards program. On January 5, 1979, then FBI Director William Webster appropriately ordered an investigation of Weisz but told his agents that it had to be completed by January 15, hardly enough time to conduct a serious probe of

Weisz's long history.⁹ FBI agents rushed to interview people who had ever been associated with Weisz. Five days before Webster's deadline, they spoke to Lieutenant General Sam Wilson.

Wilson, who had accumulated so many doubts about his old Berlin Base colleague over the years, chose, for whatever reason, not to share them with the FBI. He did not tell the agents who interviewed him about Weisz's strange behavior in Berlin or his "bad operational taste" in snooping about for classified information.

Instead, Wilson told them that George Weisz was "the epitome of the professional intelligence officer." The FBI gave the words of General Wilson, who was, after all, a former head of the Defense Intelligence Agency, unusual weight and authority. According to the FBI report, Wilson "advised that the applicant has always demonstrated the highest standards of character, associates, morals, reputation, and loyalty to this country, and he would, without any hesitation or reservation, highly recommend him for a post of trust and responsibility with the U.S. government."¹⁰ Sam Wilson looked the other way for George Weisz, the atomic spy, just as he had looked the other way in Vietnam and during OPERATION MONGOOSE.

CHAPTER FIFTY-FIVE

MOLE IN THE WHITE HOUSE

———✦———

WITH A SUDDENNESS that his new colleagues at the Department of Energy found jarring, George Weisz assumed his post as director of the Nuclear Safeguards and Security program on January 15, 1979.[1] Admiral Lyon recalled, "The people I worked with out there were quite startled and upset at the appointment of Mr. Weisz." According to Samuel T. McDowell, who worked in the department at the time, "Weisz came out of the blue. . . . No one expected someone like him."[2] However, unlike most people who worked with Weisz, McDowell did not find the change all bad: "Weisz was casual and relaxed. Easy to talk to. He liked to entertain, and he enjoyed a good time."

Leonard M. Brenner was serving as Harvey Lyon's top deputy when "Lyon was very suddenly forced out and replaced with Weisz."[3] Weisz asked Brenner to stay on and run the day-to-day operations as one of his two deputies. Unlike McDowell, Brenner had the usual reaction to Weisz, finding him extremely strange. Brenner, who is Jewish, asked Weisz if he also was Jewish. Weisz lied, saying he "absolutely was not." According to Brenner, many on the staff speculated that Weisz was using the job at the Department of Energy as cover. On one occasion, Weisz asked Brenner if he could arrange for some non-DOE officials to attend several overseas meetings and not use their real names. Brenner later said that as far as he knew nothing ever came of Weisz's request.

Brenner also found the relationship between Weisz and his other deputy, Tom Isaacs, very odd. According to Brenner, Isaacs acted more like Weisz's boss than his deputy. Brenner remembered that, on several occasions, "Tom Isaacs threatened Weisz, in my presence, over various issues . . . and Weisz backed down. . . . I thought Weisz would stand Isaacs against the wall, and he didn't. . . ."

It was not long before Weisz's subordinates discovered that their new boss had no advanced degrees in math, physics or engineering, or any experience in nuclear safeguards or materials handling; nor did he have even the slightest technical aptitude. To these able technocrats, Weisz was a cipher they could not break. As Brenner put it, he was a "total misfit for the job. . . . He told me he had been an economist. . . . Others had told me he had been a spy. He was extremely secretive."

Weisz made it abundantly clear from the start that he was mainly interested in the international implications of the program. He wanted to be continually briefed on all activities in this area, and he attended almost all international meetings. He also made it clear that his priority was the issue of nuclear proliferation: He wanted all information the department had about countries on the verge of getting nuclear weapons. According to Tom Isaacs, who had also worked with Weisz at the CIA, Weisz was in the right spot. He was head of the office that designed instruments and devices to detect hidden nuclear weapons materials.

George Weisz seemed to enjoy his new job. He was overseeing a $70-million-dollar budget and was able to throw himself into the issue of curtailing Third World nuclear proliferation—a compatible goal with the interests of Israel. Sam McDowell, Weisz's speechwriter, said, "He was a good speaker. He knew how to handle himself. He would take cues from other speakers."

George Weisz lost no time making friends with officials of the French nuclear energy program. He dealt with Michael Levy, secretary general of the French Ministerial Committee on Nuclear Security, and with Guy Jeanpierre, Weisz's counterpart on the French Atomic Energy Commission.[4] He also struck up a friendship with François Delobeau, the director of military applications for the French atomic energy program. Weisz's colleagues say that, during his first months on the job, he looked for any excuse to travel to Paris. As McDowell put it, Weisz "always wanted to go to Paris. He kept in close touch with the head of French security. They struck a close relationship."[5]

Because of Weisz's position in Nuclear Safeguards and Security, it was a relatively simple matter for him to make tours of specific French nuclear facilities, such as the secure warehouse at Seyne-sur-Mer, where the Tammuz reactor cores Iraq had purchased were being stored prior to their shipment to Baghdad. By the first week in April 1979, Weisz had supplied the Israelis enough details on security at the warehouse that a Mossad commando team soon succeeded in blowing up both reactor cores.[6]

The French government was furious about the Mossad operation. It immediately announced that new cores would be prepared and shipped to Iraq to complete the agreement. Ironically, the French turned to Weisz for advice on how to prevent such penetrations in the future.

The close relationship between Weisz and the French made Admiral Lyon and others worry. "My personal concern about the French," said Lyon, "and I think it is still true, and it was particularly true at that time, [is] if you gave them anything, you could be certain that it would be in the Soviet Union within 24 hours." Until Weisz's appointment, according to Lyon, the United States had never shared nuclear military or safeguard secrets with the French.

Among his many responsibilities, Weisz was now in charge of perhaps the most secret team in the U.S. government, the Nuclear Emergency Search Team (NEST). If a terrorist or hostile group threatens the United States or any friendly country with nuclear blackmail, or if nuclear material is stolen and the theft is deemed life-threatening, then NEST is dispatched from its Nevada headquarters and goes to the scene equipped with the latest techniques in antiterrorism and nuclear detection.

Usually, when weapons-grade nuclear material goes missing, it is not through theft but through production loss or careless inventory. However, this was not the case in early 1979, when the manager of General Electric's nuclear energy plant in Wilmington, North Carolina, received a telephone call demanding ransom for missing nuclear material. A quick check revealed that weapons-grade uranium had in fact been stolen from the plant in sufficient quantity to make a crude nuclear device. If the telephone extortionist were a serious terrorist, hundreds of thousands of people were in jeopardy. The brand new director of Nuclear Safeguards quickly dispatched NEST, which, assisted by the FBI field office in Charlotte, North Carolina, tracked down and arrested the extortionist and recovered the uranium.[7] George Weisz and his team were commended for their achievement.

Weisz also had access to sophisticated security measures like the Optical Telephone Isolator, designed to thwart the latest in KGB eavesdropping techniques.[8]

Although Weisz's colleagues at the Department of Energy were never officially told of his affiliation with the CIA, they heard bits and pieces about him from others in the intelligence community and correctly guessed his past. To Sam McDowell, who accompanied Weisz on a number of trips abroad, Weisz's actions were often inexplicable. "Weisz would travel at every opportunity he got," said McDowell, but "would bow out of high-level meetings and disappear sometimes for hours and for days." McDowell added, "I swear I surmised he was still on the CIA payroll." Weisz would not talk about what he did when he disappeared. "Not a word," said McDowell.

One worrisome aspect of Weisz's behavior was his telephone conversations with his son David. According to McDowell, Weisz spoke with David fairly frequently when he was overseas. McDowell gathered from Weisz that David was a State Department official working in Moscow. Leonard Brenner added that Weisz sometimes used his trips overseas to meet his son. However, the Weisz family later insisted that David was then in Afghanistan, not Moscow, on a Department of State assignment. Etta Jo Weisz, who now detested the CIA, said that George and David had both promised her that David would never join the CIA. In fact, David Weisz, who declined to be interviewed about his father, was assigned to Moscow in 1981. The security implications are enormous. If the Soviets were aware of David's relationship to George, David would be highly vulnerable to blackmail and recruitment.

George's personal life was a well-guarded secret around the office—and not only the existence of Cheryl Thomas. When Sherry Cooper, Weisz's secretary, innocently asked her new boss if Mrs. Weisz would be accompanying him to a British Embassy reception, Weisz shot back, "There is no Mrs. Weisz." In fact, he and Etta Jo remained married, and he still spent a few nights a week at their Chevy Chase home. Most weekends, he drove out to the isolated farm in Frederick County, Maryland.

Etta Jo, who had opposed buying the farm a decade earlier, seldom went there. Cheryl was the one who frequently went with him, according to Dale Young, the caretaker who lived in an old tenant house on the property. "They always came in separate cars," Young said. A few colleagues at the Department of Energy were invited to the farm from time to time, and Weisz entertained foreign nuclear experts there, including the French.

According to McDowell and others, one of Weisz's favorite nuclear facilities was Brookhaven National Laboratory on Long Island. Weisz liked to combine his business at Brookhaven with visits to his mother and sister in New York City. George's mother remembers a chauffeur always waiting outside in a car during these visits.

At Brookhaven, Weisz became friendly with Herbert Kouts, one of the few energy officials in whom he confided—not always accurately, however. From conversations with Weisz, Kouts gathered that "both George Bush and James Angleton had been instrumental at putting Weisz where he was."[9] Since Angleton had been out of the CIA for more than four years when Weisz was appointed Safeguards director, this claim seems to have no basis.

Then, in March 1981, a drama played out in the halls of Congress. President Reagan had just taken office, and his new, activist CIA director, William Casey, and Casey's totally unqualified deputy director, Max Hugel, went to the Senate Select Committee on Intelligence with what some committee members considered an outrageous proposal. Casey told the committee that the French and the Soviets were both actively assisting Saddam Hussein's regime with the construction of a nuclear reactor at Osirak, 10 miles from Baghdad. The Soviets, in an effort to make Saddam Hussein their client, were pouring millions into the project. The idea Casey and Hugel floated to the committee was that the United States should undertake a covert operation to destroy the Osirak reactor.

Many of the senators were aghast. The United States could not secretly bomb another sovereign country, they said. Furthermore, since September 1980, Iraq had been at war with Iran, the United States' bitter enemy, which had held our Tehran embassy staff hostage for 444 days. One member of the committee at the time[10] insisted that Casey and Hugel were told in no uncertain terms that such a destructive operation could not be approved.

On April 13, Casey arrived in Tel Aviv to meet with his Israeli counterpart, the head of Mossad, Major General Yitzhak Hoffi.[11] Casey brought with him a wealth of spy satellite photography as well as information on air defenses in Iraq. By now, Israel and the CIA had reached a new level of cooperation. Of course, neither Casey nor Hugel knew of George Weisz's arrangement with the Israelis. The United States' Director of Nuclear Safeguards and Security had already warned the Israelis that 26.4 kilos of weapons-grade uranium 235 was about to be installed in the Iraqi reactor.

On Sunday, June 8, the Israeli Air Force flew the longest mission in its distinguished history and bombed the Osirak reactor. To assess the effectiveness of the attack, Israel asked the CIA if they could see pictures of the reactor and of Baghdad's air defenses taken by the Keyhole 11 orbiting spy satellite. When Casey refused, Israel used Jonathan Pollard's access to TALENT (satellite photography) material. Also, the DOE's analysis of what the radiation sensors aboard Keyhole 11 picked up made its way to George Weisz.

If the reactor were destroyed, the sensors should show signs of radioactivity. To Weisz's shock, there were none. Had Saddam Hussein been warned of the attack? Did he know in advance to protect his precious nuclear material? Through Weisz, the Israelis began to understand that the Reagan administration had a two-tier policy. While Casey was helping the Israelis on one side, others in the administration were secretly assisting Saddam Hussein in his war against Iran.

The administration was using Miami-based arms dealer Sarkis Soghanalian as its conduit to Iraq.[12] On his aircraft Soghanalian regularly flew agents of the CIA and administration intermediaries from Miami to Baghdad. It was Soghanalian who informed the administration that the Israelis were illegally supplying Iran spare parts and small weapons made under U.S. license, some of them classified. He brought back to the United States some of these weapons and systems, including night vision devices for tanks that the Iraqis had captured from the Iranians.

As the Reagan Administration pressed forward through the summer of 1981 with its plan to sell AWACS (Airborne Warning and Control System) surveillance aircraft to Saudi Arabia, the Israelis understood that their arrangement with Casey was not exclusive. There were other influences on the administration's Mideast policy. With this realization, George Weisz became more important to them than ever.

The two men who laid the groundwork for the AWACS sale were Air Force Major General Richard Secord and Marine Lieutenant Colonel Oliver North. Both had worked for General John Singlaub under Ted Shackley in Laos. Their connection to Shackley led to a scheme to trade arms through Israel for U.S. hostages being held by Shiite Muslim terrorists in Lebanon. In this scheme, they used the Israelis' long-term business relationship with Iran.

Even though the Israeli attack on the Baghdad reactor was not 100 percent successful, the information George Weisz supplied may have saved Israel from nuclear annihilation. Weisz himself, though, was now out in the open for the first time in his careful career. As a result, the KGB soon figured out exactly who was supplying the Israelis with inside information. When the French passed to the Soviets details about Weisz's previous contacts, the KGB decided to reaffirm an old relationship.

Meanwhile, Democratic Congressman John Dingell, whose Energy and Commerce Committee oversaw the Department of Energy, began seriously looking into Weisz's activities. According to Peter Stockton, committee investigator at the time, Weisz was reprimanded for his extensive foreign travel. Weisz aide William Bartells said the congressional scrutiny made Weisz "look real bad."

Two years earlier, Donald Kerr, after rushing to install Weisz at DOE, had left Washington to head the Los Alamos National Laboratory. According to Herb Kouts, Weisz, who was never comfortable as a bureaucrat, soon went head to head with Kerr's replacement, Duane Sewell.

Now, thanks to the congressional investigation, Sewell was in a position to downgrade Weisz's status, informing him that he would no longer report directly to the assistant secretary for Energy Programs, but to his deputy. Weisz counterargued that his job was too important to be downgraded. Sewell responded by taking away all his inspection responsibilities. A furious George Weisz wrote a letter about the security dangers inherent in Sewell's action. He showed Herb Kouts a copy of the "sharp letter," and then, according to Kouts, "George left just before being fired." Donald Kerr says he "thinks" Weisz was forced to resign as head of Safeguards and Security in October 1981.

However, the Kerr-Kupperman-Weisz connection did not end when Weisz left the Energy Department. Afterward, he was given consulting contracts with Los Alamos and Brookhaven, where he continued to work with his good friends Kerr and Kupperman.

In 1981, one of the first projects Ronald Reagan approved as president was the design and construction of the W-88 nuclear warhead. With explosive power ranging up to nearly half a megaton, the W-88 was small enough so that several of the devices could be put atop a submarine-launched Trident missile or loaded onto an air-launched cruise missile. Reagan wanted quick production of the warheads to counter an open threat from the huge Soviet SS-18 "city busters." The idea was that a single missile could carry up to eight independently programmed W-88s, which could each wipe out an SS-18 launch site deep in Soviet territory.

The only problem was, the W-88s were too heavy, and the missile carrying them could not fly the weight far enough to reach its targets in Russia. To lighten the weight, the designers used regular explosives and less protective shielding and made other sacrifices in order to get the W-88 deployed quickly. The design details were among America's most important secrets in the early 1980s, and George Weisz had access to them. The W-88 design was worth a great deal both to Russia and to China.

We now know that the W-88, originally believed compromised in 1989 during the Bush Administration, was lost much earlier. Donald Kerr, director at Los Alamos while the W-88 was being developed, and Robert Kupperman continued to give Weisz full access to the facility after he left the DOE. Ironically, in the year 2000, the man in charge of all computer and technical evidence in the W-88 espionage case against Wen Ho Lee was Donald Kerr, who became head of the FBI's troubled main crime laboratory in 1997. In August 2001, before the FBI's new director, Robert Mueller, took office, CIA Director George Tenet appointed Kerr head of the CIA's Directorate of Science and Technology, one of the Agency's most important and sensitive jobs.

In 1981, President Reagan put General Richard Stilwell, an old intelligence hand, at the heart of all military intelligence programs as the deputy undersecretary of Defense for policy. The intelligence collected by the National Security Agency, Army intelligence, and the Defense Intelligence Agency all came under Stilwell's control. According to Robert Crowley and others, Stilwell held "the keys to the kingdom."

The Reagan Administration gave Stilwell the task of reviewing all Pentagon intelligence policies. One of his first actions was to head up a damage assessment team that went to England to review the 12-year-long hemorrhage of secrets out of the Government Communications Headquarters at Cheltenham. GCHQ is the British equivalent of the National Security Agency, with which GCHQ's electronic eavesdroppers work closely. When code clerk Geoffrey Arthur Prime came under investigation for sexually assaulting a young girl, the authorities learned he had also been selling details from U.S. microwave and surveillance satellites to the KGB, at about the same time that Christopher Boyce was selling them information about the satellites themselves. Boyce was the TFW clerk and FBI agent's son made famous in the book and film *The Falcon and the Snowman*. Boyce had a pet falcon; the "Snowman" was his partner Andrew Daulton Lee, who also dealt cocaine.

On his return from England, General Stilwell wrote a controversial report downplaying the damage Prime had done. "He made it sound as though all Prime had done was give the British a bad cold," said Crowley. In fact, according to Crowley, Prime was one of the most damaging KGB double agents in history.[13]

Stilwell faced yet another major problem, this one involving the FBI and Army intelligence. In 1981, the FBI decided to run a joint operation with the Army in which an Army officer who was a longtime double agent against the Soviets would be assigned to the newly built U.S. Embassy in Moscow. The American agencies suspected that the KGB had bugged the embassy from top to bottom during construction, and they desperately needed to get someone inside the KGB to find out. It was a very dangerous assignment but, they thought, an important one.

The Americans' hopes were dashed when a KGB colonel who was working for the United States tipped his Army intelligence control officer in Berlin that the KGB was planning to murder the Army officer as soon as he arrived in Moscow. The Soviets had found out he was a double agent and knew all about the operation. Only a handful of people at the highest levels of the FBI and the Army had known about the plan to send the officer to Moscow. This meant that someone at the very top of American intelligence was working for the enemy.

The White House, on orders approved by the president, instructed Stilwell to investigate how and where the leak occurred. Stilwell was told to include even the White House in his investigation.

One of the seasoned professionals Stilwell hired to conduct the investigation was the man with very high security clearances, George Weisz. General Stilwell later said he could not remember how Weisz came to his attention, but he recalled that he decided to hire Weisz "because he knew the Red [Communist] side of the chess board. . . . Someone informed me that an outstanding professional man was leaving the CIA, and there might be a role for him." Stilwell said that Weisz "was a very impressive man, not only on the written record, but his deportment . . . with a great fund of knowledge."

In May 1982, seven months after Weisz left the Energy Department, he began making occasional visits to room 3C-276 at the Pentagon. That office suite included a super-secret vault, where Weisz would sit and read. According to Stilwell and his deputy for counterintelligence, Britt Snider (who eventually became the CIA's inspector general), Weisz's job was to review old intelligence files and attempt to answer the questions, who was the high-level mole and how were the Russians doing it? Among the files in that vault were horrendous stories of lost agents, including Army Warrant Officer Ralph Sigler.

Again, some of Weisz's new colleagues thought he was strange. Snider, at that time a young lawyer who had distinguished himself in the Watergate investigation, thought it was odd that someone like Weisz was willing to work in an unairconditioned vault without the normal perks of a super-grade bureaucrat.[14]

Weisz's handwritten notes indicate that he was conducting a "national-level study on vulnerability to penetration—the White House."[15] His notes also reveal he was studying the entire United States counterintelligence hierarchy, including the FBI, which was under suspicion because of the Moscow embassy leak.

General Stilwell was later asked to go over Weisz's notes. The notes indicated Weisz was contacting high-level White House officials, including Reagan Science Adviser George Keyworth. "Weisz had more notes on my job than I have,"[16] Stilwell said. He wondered: "Why would Weisz be looking into the presidential science adviser? I never tasked him to do that. . . . This just wasn't part of his job."

One answer could be that the Soviets were pressuring their agents to learn as much as they could about "Star Wars," Reagan's Strategic Defense Initiative, which aimed to research, build, and deploy a satellite defense system against incoming ICBMs. Keyworth was a disciple of Edward Teller and the leading proponent in the Reagan Administration of Teller's scheme to shoot down Russian missiles. Weisz had been involved at the Energy Department in protecting some early Star Wars technology. Tom Tucker, the Pentagon official to whom Stilwell recommended Weisz for a permanent job, found it ironic that "a general who found [a] Red under every bed may have brought one in to advise him."[17]

CHAPTER FIFTY-SIX

MOLEKILL

⎯⎯⫸⏣⫷⎯⎯

D URING THE SUMMER of 1982, George Weisz spent one week a
month consulting on terrorism and security issues at Los Alamos,
where he met routinely with Robert Kupperman and Donald Kerr.[1] He
also spent several days a month at Brookhaven National Laboratory. The
rest of his working time he hung around the Pentagon vault. According to
General Stilwell, Weisz retained all his security clearances and had access
to the total U.S. inventory of secrets. In fact, Stilwell eventually revealed
what many had guessed, that Weisz never officially left the CIA, even
while he was at the Energy Department. That is why some of his behavior
in the early fall of that year should have attracted serious attention.

According to the account Cheryl Thomas later gave the Maryland
State Police, on Monday, October 11, she told Weisz she wanted to
break off their seven-year romance.[2] She said she wanted some time
alone to think things over. On October 18, according to the travel schedule Weisz sent Gwendolyn Jolly in General Stilwell's office, he went to
Los Alamos and spent a few days as usual consulting on security matters. On October 25, he went to the doctor for treatment of a ganglion
cyst. On October 27, he asked colleagues in General Stilwell's office to
witness his new will. According to Etta Jo Weisz, it was not unusual for
George to review his will—he did so every time he was about to undertake a long overseas assignment. Normally, his personal lawyer, Tom
Sippell, attended to such matters.

On Thursday, October 28, Weisz left for Brookhaven, and the next day, following his usual pattern, he went to his family's apartment in New York City. His weekend plans included putting down a new floor in one of the closets and taking his mother, then a lively 86, out to dinner on Saturday night.

From the beginning of the visit it was clear to his family that something was wrong. George normally loved the Hungarian food his mother cooked, but on Friday evening he asked her to fix him an ordinary hamburger because he was trying to take off weight for an upcoming physical. When his sister, Suzanne Gottlieb, returned home from work that evening, George seemed to be in the mood to talk. Suzanne remembered thinking that he did not look very well. "He was dieting. . . . He had lost about ten pounds," she said. George suggested they go for a walk, but Suzanne said she was tired, and, anyway, it was too cold for a walk.

The next morning, George got an early start on his mother's closet floor. After Suzanne, who was working that Saturday, left the apartment, he began making telephone calls. Among them was a call to a bank in Gaithersburg, Maryland, to make certain that a $5,000 transfer from his savings account to his checking account had gone through to cover a check he had written to Cheryl Thomas—a strange gesture for a man who had just been rejected by the woman he loved.

George then received a call from Cheryl. That morning, he had told his mother for the first time the story of his seven-year relationship with Miss Thomas. "He said it was his fault," Gizelle Weisz recalled. ". . . 'I will tell you the whole thing is my fault.' He said he promised to marry her, but he wouldn't divorce Etta Jo."

Mrs. Weisz had never seen her often imperious son so emotional as he was after this phone call. Cheryl Thomas later told the police it was not until November 4 that she told George she had begun a relationship with another man out of frustration over George's refusal to divorce Etta Jo. However, Gizelle Weisz remembers her son saying, "'She told me that she fell in love with somebody who wanted to marry her.'" To Gizelle's shock, George then told her Cheryl was still on the line. He asked his mother to pick up the phone and plead with Cheryl not to leave him. "Go in and talk to her," he said. Mrs. Weisz remembered thinking, "How can I talk to somebody I never know, I never heard of, I never knew of?"

"What can I tell her?" she asked her son.

He said, "'Just go in and say anything. Anything! Just tell her to wait for me. Everything will be different.'"

For Gizelle Weisz, her son's love affair was a total surprise. She suspected George had known other women over the years, but she and her son had never discussed anything like this. "What can I say? What can a mother say to try and bring them together? He was 64 years old. A 64-year-old man, what can I say?" Mrs. Weisz awkwardly asked Cheryl Thomas, a total stranger, not to leave her son.

When Gizelle put down the telephone, she tried to comfort George. She told him to calm down and be reasonable. She also asked him how a grown man, in the spy business, did not know anything about this other man until after he had sent Cheryl $5,000.

Suddenly, George told his mother he had to go. He said he would be back the following weekend to finish her closet floor, but he could not stay that day: "I have to go. . . . I have to talk to her. . . . But she's right, I should have divorced Jo four years ago. Now it's too late." Gizelle Weisz watched helplessly as her only son, whom she loved deeply, left the family apartment distraught. Suzanne later said, "You could not threaten George. Especially a woman could not threaten him. He was a serious man. He was not a young kid threatened by a woman. But something must have happened."[3]

Gizelle and Suzanne tried to call him during the following week, but he did not respond to the messages they left on his answering machine. They finally called Etta Jo, but she told them not to worry—George was often traveling.

It later turned out that from New York he had gone to the Maryland farm. On the following Tuesday, November 2, his caretaker/tenant, Dale Young, told him that the chimney in the tenant house had caught fire. There was no serious damage, but George said he wanted to install a smoke detector.

Two days later, George failed to show up for an appointment with his lawyer, Tom Sippell, to draft another new will. On Sunday, November 7, George had two guests on the farm, an elderly man who used a cane and a woman fitting Cheryl Thomas's description.[4] Dale Young ran into Weisz and his guests at the farm's pond, where Weisz introduced them. Young later said, "George always acted strange . . . but this time he was different." That same day, Young noticed the gray Honda Civic George had bought for his daughter, Nikki, parked in the garage.

The following week, George again did not return phone messages. On Friday, November 12, his neighbors, Mr. and Mrs. Kenneth Brunner, thought it strange that he failed to wave to them, staring straight ahead when they drove past him in their car.[5] That evening, Young saw lights on inside the farmhouse, although he did not see Weisz himself. The next afternoon, Leigh B. Brownell, Dale Young's girlfriend, noticed a strange smell, which she thought was a noxious gas. Young dismissed her worries, attributing the smell to a lingering odor from the chimney fire.

By now, George's mother and sister were frantic. They had not heard from him in two weeks, and Mrs. Weisz could not believe George had failed to keep his promise to return and fix her closet floor. She made Suzanne continue to call Etta Jo and urge her to check on George.

By this time, Etta Jo was also becoming concerned, but severe arthritis prevented her from making the 45-minute drive to the farm. Finally, on Monday morning, Etta Jo, her concern mounting, called the only person she could think of to check on George—his insurance agent.

Carroll Stottlemyer had written insurance for George for several years, but the two men were not friends.[6] Stottlemyer assured Etta Jo he would drive up to the farmhouse, which he did around four that afternoon. He knocked on the door, but no one answered. His recollection of what happened next is apparently not totally clear, as he has given several different accounts. According to police records, however, he initially said that he looked through the closed garage door and saw Nikki's Honda with a yellow garden hose leading from the exhaust pipe through the hatchback and into the passenger section. Stottlemyer called Etta Jo and urged her to call the police to come and investigate. When she tried to get more information from him, he simply repeated that she should call the police right away.

Corporal Neil Healine of the Maryland State Police answered the dispatcher's call. Dale Young agreed to accompany him to the garage. Strangely, Stottlemyer apparently had not seen what Young and Healine now saw: a lifeless body sitting in the driver's seat of Nikki's car.

The state trooper noted that the outside garage door light was on and that the door was unlocked. So far, it was a classic suicide scene. A 16-

foot piece of ordinary half-inch yellow garden hose ran from the Honda's exhaust pipe, wedged in place by a screwdriver, through the hatchback window, and over the backseat. The end of the hose was next to where the body was in the driver's seat. Next to the exhaust pipe were some hand tools and a deflated air mattress.

According to the police report, Young identified the slumped-over body as Weisz's,[7] although he later said, "There was a definite doubt in my mind that it was him."[8] For starters, Young had never seen Weisz in sunglasses, yet the dead man had on a pair of dark aviator glasses. The police noted that there was a convenience-store cup of cold coffee on the roof of the Honda. Also, the ignition was turned off when Young and Healine arrived. A copy of the *New York Times* dated November 5 was draped over the Honda's steering wheel, as if, according to the police report, "the deceased had been reading the paper." But why would anyone intending to kill himself buy a cup of coffee and read a week-old *New York Times* while waiting to die? Why was he wearing sunglasses inside the garage? And if it was suicide, who had turned off the car's ignition? The evidence did not add up.

The body looked bloated, and there was a contusion on the forehead. The lips gave off a reddish mucous material. Rigor mortis was observed only in the fingers. Dr. R. J. Thomas arrived on the scene, examined the body, and ordered it sent to the Frederick Memorial Hospital morgue. Police took, as evidence, the Honda and a briefcase found in it.

Inside the briefcase was a note the police insisted was George Weisz's suicide note. They carefully quoted it out of context in their report: "Please contact Ft. Detrich or Ft. Ritchie. I am a retired Army officer, entitled to military medical privileges." The note in its entirety indicated Weisz thought he might survive whatever happened to him. It went on to say, "Also call Mrs. Etta Jo Weisz," and gave her address and phone number and those of the lawyer Tom Sippell. In an entirely different handwriting at the bottom of the note was the phrase, "I am tired."

The police then searched the house. Their report said there was no evidence of forced entry and that the residence was "found to be secure and nothing unusual observed." According to Young, however, "There was a lot of things that I remember were wrong. They found the clip to his 9 mm, but never found the gun. They found a lot of burned papers and books in the fireplace. . . . He just didn't live that way." The trash in the fireplace also included TV dinners, for which Weisz had open contempt. Although the report said "nothing unusual observed," the police were suspicious enough to bring a mobile crime laboratory to process the scene.

While Corporal Healine was still at the farm, the phone rang: It was Etta Jo asking what had happened to her husband. Healine told her that a state trooper was on his way to her house with information. Thirty minutes later she called again, saying that no trooper had arrived, and she wanted to know what had happened. Healine told her her husband was dead.

Etta Jo later told the police that George had returned from a trip to Los Alamos on November 5 and had gone up to the farm after spending the night at their house in Chevy Chase. She informed them that George worked for the CIA, the Defense Department, and the Department of Energy.

In New York, George's mother and sister, still unaware, were desperate for information. Mrs. Weisz suggested that her daughter call Nikki in Berlin. "And I got Nikki on the phone, and she was hysterical," Suzanne recalled. "And I knew. Nikki said, 'Don't you know what happened to my dad? My dad died.' And I screamed out, 'Died!' And with that, Mom fainted. . . . She [Nikki] asked me, 'How do you know Daddy's dead?' I said to her, 'What are you talking about? I don't know. I'm calling you to find out what happened to your father.'"

Suzanne then called Etta Jo to tell her that the family was on its way to Washington. She was taken aback when a stranger who answered the phone told her, "We don't think you should come. The family wants to be alone." Suzanne, furious, replied, "What the hell are you talking about? Who the hell are you to tell me not to come to my brother's house?" Then Donnel Weisz came on the phone and said, "This is not your brother's house, this is now my house." He threatened to have the police waiting to throw his aunt out of the house if she came.[9]

Nevertheless, the women journeyed down. When they arrived, Donnel lived up to his threat and refused to let them into the house. Two days later, with George's side of the family in hotels, David returned from overseas, and Donnel gave way to his younger brother.

Despite Nikki and Donnel's belief that the dead man they saw was not their father, other family members identified Weisz and quickly arranged to have the body cremated. Etta Jo wanted no announcement of her husband's death in the newspaper. No obituary appeared in the *Washington Post*.

Although George Weisz worked with hundreds of people over the years, only his family was present at the memorial service. Not one colleague from the CIA was notified of his death or invited to the service. George's nephew, Phil, remembers only a piece of driftwood lying in place of a casket. The drug-dazed Donnel gave a disjointed eulogy, which so upset his grandmother that she collapsed and had to be taken outside.

The police investigation into the death of George Weisz continued. On November 16, the police played three cassette tapes found in and near his answering machine. Several of the messages expressed anger at him for not returning calls. Strangely, some of the angry messages were from Cheryl Thomas. Corporal Ronald N. Herring called Thomas at the State Department, identified himself, and asked her if she knew Weisz. According to the police report, she seemed to sense something was amiss. When Herring told her that George was dead, she broke down and cried.

When she had recovered enough to ask Herring how George had died, Herring told her, adding that he needed to do a more complete interview with her in person. They met that evening, and Cheryl told Herring that she and George had first met in Vienna sometime in 1975. She said that from that time on they had lived together overseas and in the United States and were very close. Herring pressed her about the last time she had seen George, but she said she could not remember. Herring attributed this to her emotional state at the news of his death.

Cheryl then said she first told George she wanted to break off their relationship on October 11. She said the last time the two were together at the Gaithersburg condo was on November 4, and that is when she told George she had met another man. As the police report put it, George then told her that "he won't live without her."[10] Cheryl refused to give Corporal Herring the other man's name, saying there was no need for him to be involved, and Herring did not press her.

Cheryl told Herring she had made it clear to George that she was frustrated because he would not divorce Etta Jo. However, she also said that the last time she visited the farm, on Halloween, he showed her a piece of paper listing financial arrangements between him and Etta Jo, which seemed to indicate he was ready to proceed with a divorce.

In her interview with Corporal Herring, Cheryl Thomas also tossed in the statement that George had seemed disenchanted during the past six months, because he was being "downgraded and eased out of the Department of Energy in favor of younger men."

The State Police began to accept Thomas's version of events and came to the conclusion that Weisz had committed suicide over the end of their love affair. No one else who knew George Weisz believed that this 64-year-old man of the world committed suicide because his mistress had broken off their relationship.

Donnel Weisz told police that when he visited the farm in late September, he found his father "somewhat disillusioned with everything in general and with the federal government, especially since leaving the CIA. He stated his father was not the American patriot he used to be. However, Donnel did not believe his father was depressed."[11]

Gwendolyn Jolly of General Stilwell's intelligence unit gave police an important lead they did not follow up. She told them about the will Weisz had asked her and some office mates to witness. She added that a few days later, Weisz called in sick with bronchitis. Weisz was seldom sick in his long career, and Jolly said he "sounded more tired than sick."[12] Jolly maintained that Weisz gave no indication of being despondent or remotely suicidal. The only police witness who said Weisz was capable of suicide was Cheryl Thomas.[13]

Other evidence was overlooked or handled carelessly. Tom Sippell says he told the police that Weisz did not show up for his appointment on November 4 and never called to cancel, and that this was totally out of character. This information never appeared in the police report. And what about the will Weisz had asked his office mates to witness just eight days earlier?

Was George Weisz alone in his farmhouse that last week when no one could reach him? He recorded a message on his answering machine indicating he was having trouble retrieving his messages. Did someone force him to record that message to buy time? Then there was the fireplace full of trash—including those TV dinners. To Weisz's children, it began to look as if he might have been held in the house against his will.

Above all, there were the questions about the death scene—including doubts about the very identity of the dead man.

On December 15, 1982, the Maryland State Police produced a final report stating that George Weisz had committed suicide, and they closed the case. They cited the autopsy conducted in Baltimore, which failed to disclose any indications of foul play.[14] That same autopsy, however, also failed to indicate identifying features, such as a scar in the abdominal area and the absence of a gallbladder.[15] Weisz had had his gallbladder removed in a U.S. military hospital in Germany in 1978, and as anyone who went through gallbladder surgery prior to the 1980s can attest, the old type of surgery left a very large and unsightly scar. Assistant State Medical Examiner Hormez R. Guard noted no such abnormality.

Dr. Guard later said that before he began the autopsy, the State Police told him it was a clear case of suicide: "I was told there was a clear-cut suicide note." When the full contents of the Weisz note were shown to Guard, he said he had been misled. "When I opened the abdomen, I must admit I was not careful to look for the gallbladder, because I thought it was an obvious suicide.[16] He said if he had known the family had raised questions about the dead man's identity, he would have ordered a full dental comparison. If he had known there was a question of foul play, he would have proceeded more cautiously.[17]

The State Police's failure to inform Dr. Guard of these doubts and questions is especially curious since two nights after they discovered George Weisz's body, they paid a second visit to Dale Young. They were concerned about the Honda's ignition key. Young said the state trooper "looked up and said, 'Why did you turn the car off?' It took a second for it to hit me, but I said, 'Hey buddy, you can get the F out of my house.' It made me mad, and he calmed me down and he said, 'Hey, that was the way I was trying to get a reaction out of you.'"

The Soviets were expert at teaching the art of "suicide" to their assassins. One country that benefited from such training was Saddam Hussein's Iraq.

In the 1980s, arms dealer Sarkis Soghanalian regularly flew Americans from Miami to Baghdad. According to Soghanalian, he once even brought an American physician to Baghdad, courtesy of Ronald Reagan, to examine Saddam Hussein's back.

Soghanalian also flew Iraqi officials, including top intelligence agents, to the United States. "I flew people in and out at the CIA's request," Soghanalian said. "I did it as a favor to the government. I did not ask questions." Since the Iraqi visitors traveled on phony passports, it is impossible to ascertain who they were, how long they remained in the United States, or where they went, but some of them were in the Washington area when George Weisz died. Did they torture and kill Weisz, much as a Soviet team six years earlier had tortured and killed America's premier double agent, Army Warrant Officer Ralph Sigler? Sigler's murder ended CIA illusions that the KGB would not dare target American agents in the United States. If the Soviets believed Weisz had endangered their relationship with Iraq, at that time a major customer, they may have issued the wet order.

Guilt, puzzlement, and fear are Ambassador Milton Wolf's emotions when he thinks about his old friend George Weisz—guilt, because he was always too busy to get together with Weisz on his visits to Washington. "Yes, he wanted me to come and meet him in Washington," Wolf said. ". . . He kept in touch after I came back from Vienna. . . . He kept calling me up once a month until this thing happened, and then I was filled with remorse that I had not taken the time out to see him. I believe he wanted to tell me something." Wolf does not believe George Weisz killed himself.

Wolf found it strange that he never heard from Cheryl Thomas. "She never called me," he said. "She knew the extent of our relationship." Weisz had never told Wolf the couple was having difficulties.

Then there is the matter of Felix Bloch. It was Milton Wolf who interviewed Bloch for the Deputy Chief of Mission job he got in Vienna. During the summer of 1989, when the headlines were full of Bloch's suspected spying, Bloch was followed by the FBI and the media all over Washington. Wolf is convinced that those bizarre scenes were not what they seemed: "They don't have to have six or eight guys walk three feet away from him to make sure he is not going to leave the country. . . . Those people were three or four feet away from him every place he went to keep him from being kidnapped or killed. That was my opinion from the beginning."

Felix Bloch, though dismissed, was never arrested for espionage. The favors he did for George Weisz in Berlin, in Vienna, and after Weisz returned to the States, never became an issue in the FBI investigation of Bloch's loyalty. In fact, no one ever asked Bloch about George Weisz. Chances are that no American official wanted to hear his answer.

On the day President Clinton left office in 2001, he decided not to release Jonathan Pollard from prison. One reason was that Pollard had refused to name any other Americans spying for Israel. But Robert Crowley and William Corson believed George Weisz was probably the spymaster behind a long list of Israeli spy cases, including Pollard's. In an interview

General Stillwell said about Weisz: "The irony was, we had him searching for the mole."

The nuclear information Weisz provided Israel, including what he knew of the W-88 warhead, would have been a tremendous windfall for any government trying to catch up with the United States in missile technology. And as Israel's relationship with Russia cooled during the 1980s and 1990s, its closeness to China increased. By the end of the century, the Israelis were actively engaged in transferring to the People's Republic of China, technology the United States had supplied them in joint weapons manufacturing. The most notorious instance was the Lavi fighter, developed with billions in U.S. tax money. It came as a major shock when U.S. spy-satellite photography revealed that China and Israel had taken the U.S./Israeli technology and put it into production. The Israelis also transferred U.S. cruise missile technology to the Chinese, who later sold some of their missiles, the C802s, to Iran. Currently, these missiles are a direct threat to even the most sophisticated of American ships.

General Stilwell wondered why George Weisz was snooping around the White House, and specifically around those associated with Star Wars. Why did Weisz refer to George Bush's Iran-Contra middleman, Don Gregg, in his handwritten notes? Why, as Britt Snider wondered at the time, was Weisz spending so much time in that hot, dusty vault in the Pentagon? One possible answer is that the Soviets had threatened to reveal his spying for Israel, in order to blackmail him into providing details of Stilwell's evaluation of the Prime case, the mole in the FBI, Iran-Contra, and Star Wars. In this scenario, once the KGB had learned what it wanted, it let the Iraqis know who was responsible for the destruction of the Osirak reactor.

Yet the Soviets were masters at murder carefully executed to make it look like suicide. Why the discrepancies in the death scene? Was it designed, as with Ralph Sigler's death, to send the strongest message possible to other double agents?

All of the above assumes that the body found in the Honda was George Weisz. There are no indications of a Shadrin-type disappearance, but the Soviets (or someone else) may have had reasons for wanting Weisz alive but in their control.

The mysteries surrounding the most mysterious alumnus of Berlin Base did not end in November 1982.

CHAPTER FIFTY-SEVEN

THE END OF THE COLD WAR

⸻⸺⸻

I MAGINE A SECURITY COMPANY that has one client, and imagine that that client faces one principal security threat, a threat so potentially devastating that the client provides unlimited resources to protect his secrets. As the years become decades, the security company is given more and more resources—billions of dollars in resources—to protect the client. During that period, the company is caught in a series of scandals ranging from perjury and embezzlement to multiple murder, but the client overlooks all of that because the company is so good at the job it was hired to do.

Now, imagine the client discovers that many of the company's employees have been working for the very enemy the company was hired to protect against. Finally, imagine that one day the enemy suddenly disintegrates, and all the things the company had warned its client about turn out to be wildly at variance with reality. Over the years, the client has spent trillions of dollars based on the information the company provided about the enemy, but the company had got it all wrong.

If a security firm in the private sector were involved in a sham of that magnitude, lawsuits and prosecution for criminal fraud would surely be the result. And yet that is precisely what the CIA did to its clients, the American taxpayers. Ironically, we were all so happy to see the Soviets go that we failed to examine what went wrong at the CIA. Senator Daniel Patrick Moynihan was one of the few who spoke out publicly about how the CIA failed to predict the fall of the Soviet Union and thus caused us to spend billions on weapons we didn't need to defend ourselves against the rotting superpower.

The truth about what happened at the CIA during the last years of the Cold War is actually far more complicated and devious than Moynihan knew. During the Reagan and Bush administrations, it was a matter of policy for the Agency to lie to the American public and to Congress. Being called idiots and incompetents meant little to the men at the top of the CIA. These men were so committed to their own bureaucratic survival that being called names was just the price of doing business when they got caught in a lie.

It is an irony that the CIA's least powerful component, the underfunded and often ignored Directorate of Intelligence, had been making it clear to the higher-ups since the 1970s that the Soviet Union was rotting from the inside out and would ultimately collapse under its own weight. This was an analysis the higher-ups did not want to hear. To the all-powerful Directorate of Operations, any cheapening of the enemy was a threat to the CIA's power, prestige, and congressional funding. When DCI Stansfield Turner publicly discussed this aspect of the CIA culture before Congress, he was portrayed as a weak Jimmy Carterite and a man not worthy of the brotherhood.

The CIA did not like President Jimmy Carter, with the result that disloyalty to the commander-in-chief became rampant during his administration. The wolves in Clandestine Services went for the president's jugular, and eventually destroyed his presidency. In 1980, many officals from Berlin Base—some retired, some not—began to work for the election of George Bush and, later, for the Reagan-Bush ticket. Secrets detrimental to Jimmy Carter made their way to the Reagan campaign. Even members of Carter's own national security team, notably Robert Kimmet and Robert Gates, joined in. Rumors of secret Republican meetings with the Iranians about the Tehran embassy hostages were all over Washington during the campaign, and they were true. Only the meetings did not take place in Paris as reported, but in Spain. The CIA's top management had a long history of telling presidents what they wanted to hear—as we have seen repeatedly throughout this book—but starting in 1980, domestic political maneuvering became the Agency's main activity.

In 1976, George Bush was heartbroken at not being selected to continue as DCI when Jimmy Carter was elected. That non-hiring of George Bush gave momentum to the creation of a CIA in exile. This was a group of out-of-work agents that started to form with Colby and Kissinger's 1975 cutbacks in Clandestine Services. On All Hallows' Eve 1977, Bush's successor, Admiral Turner, speeded up the process by taking an even bigger axe to Clandestine Services. The unofficial leader of the exiled spooks was Berlin Base's Ted Shackley. His relationship to George Bush eventually resulted in the Iran-Contra mess during the Reagan presidency.

By the time Reagan and Bush took office, they had a choice of two CIAs they could do business with—one that required oversight by Congress, and another off-the-books group made up of the old boys. The odd group out in this spooky world was the Intelligence Directorate, where brilliant and dedicated officers poring over economic and other open data about the Soviet Union had put together a picture of a nation coming undone.

When the Carter Administration tried to make minor cuts in the Pentagon's budget at the end of the Vietnam War, the Joint Chiefs of Staff went to Capitol Hill and made ominous speeches saying Carter was opening a "window of vulnerability" to the Soviets. By the 1980s when America's military buildup against the Soviet Union was at its height, any data not conforming to the Reagan party line was left out of National Intelligence Estimates. When Senator Moynihan blasted the CIA for gross incompetence after the fall of the Soviet Union, he mistook treachery for incompetence. He denigrated the CIA's analysts for a deception orchestrated not by them but by the White House and the CIA's compliant political leadership.

The lasting damage from this deception was not the waste of tax money spent on defense against a hollow Soviet Union but the erosion of CIA independence. The agency that Harry Truman reluctantly allowed to exist had become, by the end of the Cold War, an extension of the White House National Security Council.

The total scope of the damage became evident in March 2001 when the CIA released the so-called "Princeton Papers"—19,160 documents that reveal some of the chicanery that went on during the Reagan and Bush years. The Princeton Papers clearly show that CIA management ignored the Directorate of Intelligence's analysis on such subjects as the

sincerity of Mikhail Gorbachev's reforms. To the bitter end, CIA management clung to its preconceived view of a powerful Soviet Union and could
not bring itself to heed its own experts. When the Soviet Union abandoned its Third World responsibilities and called its once blue-water navy
back to port, the CIA leadership concluded that it was a political ploy
and not a pullback of Russian forces throughout the world.

The Princeton documents include a report by one official that says
the massive Soviet military buildup the CIA was predicting in the 1980s
was not possible, because the Soviet economy could not handle such a
high level of expenditure and would collapse. CIA management refused to
allow this minority view to be distributed with the National Intelligence
Estimate. Not until the Princeton documents were released was the author of that minority report, Douglas J. MacEachin,[1] quoted publicly as
saying that, by 1986, the National Intelligence Estimates produced by the
CIA were not "realistic assessments."[2]

As William R. Corson put it: "All the operations, all the billions
spent, all the bodies we left around the world, all the lies to our countrymen, our friends, our families, our allies—in the end we failed at the mission. The mission was to keep track and predict what the Soviet Union
was up to. At that we failed. My old colleagues will not appreciate what
I am about to say, but I will say it anyway: We deluded ourselves into believing that intelligence was more meaningful than information. We confused degree of difficulty with the value of the information. The really
important information was sitting in front of our noses because it
seemed insignificant. Our problem was that we could not discern what
mattered."[3]

While the CIA was giving the country misleading estimates about the
military power of the Soviet Union, the FBI was committing a more dangerous folly. The Bureau, inheriters of the bulk of counterintelligence responsibilities from the CIA in the post-Angleton era, failed to listen to its
most qualified counterintelligence expert.

Tom Kimmel was convinced that the FBI he so loved had been penetrated by Russian intelligence. A senior agent with decades of investigative experience, Kimmel also had direct personal experience of the effects
of government stupidity and deniability. Kimmel's grandfather, the late
Husband Kimmel, was the admiral in charge at Pearl Harbor the day the
Japanese attacked in December 1941. Admiral Kimmel was not a political

admiral, and so he became the fall guy for the failures of U.S. Naval intelligence and its politically well-connected senior officers.

The young Tom Kimmel saw his dad, who had a distinguished naval career of his own, fight to clear his father's name. Tom watched with amazement as special interests within the Navy, and even some historians, conspired to make certain that the Pearl Harbor tragedy remained a stain on his grandfather's reputation. Growing up, Tom learned that government documents often contain lies; he understood how hard it is for people in government to always tell the truth.

Now in the late 1990s, at the end of his FBI career, Tom Kimmel had to make a choice. From all he saw in the Bureau, he knew that the Russians had somehow penetrated the FBI. Secret material that was getting into Russian hands was not all from the CIA through its mole, Aldrich Ames. For one thing, in the early 1980s, the FBI had burrowed a tunnel under the new Soviet Embassy in Washington—a la Harvey's Hole 30 years before in Berlin. By 1985, it was clear the Soviets had found out about it. The question for Kimmel was, how?

Kimmel had friends throughout the intelligence community, and unlike many FBI officers, he was trusted by people at the CIA. He knew that Soviet penetrations of the CIA were handled with self-delusion and lies by Agency top management, and it was exactly the same in his own shop. He knew there had been suspected moles at the top levels of FBI counterintelligence since the mid-1970s. Now, as retirement loomed, Tom Kimmel concluded that he and the Bureau could no longer afford to ignore the obvious.

Intelligence officers are reluctant to speak out about moles and enemy penetrations for fear of being "Angletonized" and portrayed as raving troublemakers. For all of James Angleton's specific mistakes, by the late 1990s it was clear in counterintelligence circles that he was right about the big picture. Double agent after double agent had been uncovered in the American intelligence services. Now, at Christmas 1998, Tom Kimmel was moved to sit down at his computer and write a most unwelcome document.

Kimmel put on paper his theory that Aldrich Ames was not responsible for all the intelligence losses, since some of the lost information was held only in FBI files. As Kimmel's friend William R. Corson put it, "The real damage does not come from what the CIA has access to, but from what the FBI would offer. Those domestic files offer the potential to target people for recruitment through their weaknesses . . . and that includes people who work for the FBI."[4]

Two and a half years before Robert Hanssen was arrested for spying for Russia, Kimmel concluded that there was at least one mole in the FBI's ranks. In January 1999, FBI Director Louis Freeh was present for a briefing by Kimmel. Freeh did not like Kimmel's conclusions. To start a mole hunt inside the FBI now after all the recent botched cases including Oklahoma City, Waco, and the Olympic bomber was not the legacy Freeh or his top staff wanted to leave behind. Kimmel's paper was seen as "a live grenade by Freeh," according to a member of his staff. Almost immediately, those closest to Freeh began denigrating Kimmel's work. They insisted that his suspicions were wrong—the culprit had to be inside the CIA. As Kimmel later told the *New York Times,* "I wasn't saying that I knew there was a mole in the FBI. I was saying, in effect, you can't rule out that possibility. I thought it was more of a possibility than they did. They were saying that we think the focus of our investigative efforts should be on the CIA."

After Ames went to prison in 1994, new mole-hunting teams at both the FBI and the CIA went to work. Their first catch was Earl Edwin Pitts, an FBI agent who, it turned out, had begun to spy for Moscow in 1987; he was sentenced to 27 years in a plea-bargain deal. Pitts told the FBI after he was arrested that Hanssen had hacked into a counterintelligence computer in his presence. The FBI ignored what Pitts said. Then, in late 1996, the FBI and CIA mole units developed Russian sources who pointed fingers at CIA officer Harold J. Nicholson. The Russian sources told the FBI that Nicholson had begun spying for the post-Soviet SVR in 1994.

With the arrest of Nicholson, the mole-hunting teams thought they had finished the job. However, Kimmel and other serious investigators at the FBI did not see how any of the incarcerated traitors could have information about the FBI's tunnel. Kimmel began to study all the cases again in great detail. Working with veteran counterintelligence agent Peter O'Donnell, he read through thousands of pages of Bureau files. The one case that stood out was Earl Pitts. The Russians had treated Pitts almost with contempt. Kimmel concluded that Pitts may have been deliberately sacrificed to make the Americans think they had captured the mole when, in fact, Pitts was a worthless decoy. This was not news Kimmel's bosses wanted to hear.

Robert Hanssen, a 25-year FBI veteran, was arrested on February 18, 2001, and later indicted on multiple counts of espionage and treason. The Justice Department says that Hanssen began spying for Moscow in October 1985, and that he was the one who informed the Russians about the FBI's tunnel. Hanssen's wife told the Bureau that she believed she caught her husband spying much earlier. With Hanssen's capture, Kimmel was vindicated. However, the Bureau's decision to ignore him in 1999 meant that Hanssen operated freely for two more years while his colleagues looked in the wrong places for the double agent.

After Hanssen's arrest–and plea bargain to life in prison—the next question is: Who got Hanssen his job in counterintelligence? Was there a mole of an earlier generation at the FBI? "The laws of probability and circumstantial evidence indicate there was," a colleague of Hanssen's admits.

The fact that Robert Hanssen's arrest came as a big surprise was a function of an American intelligence establishment that had completely ignored its counterintelligence program.[5] The idea that a Russian agent in the FBI went to the same church as the director of the FBI must have been especially humorous to Hanssen's SVR controller, since he was probably another FBI or CIA official.

The Hanssen case would not have come as a surprise to James Jesus Angleton. Angleton was convinced at the time of the Igor Orlov mole hunt that the Bureau had "to have been compromised. There was simply no other explanation for their inability to make the case against Orlov."

EPILOGUE

ON SEPTEMBER 10, 1999, a few of the remaining boys from Berlin Base and their aging opposite numbers from Russia and East Germany gathered in Berlin for an orgy of memories and self-congratulations. All of them were keeping alive the myth that Berlin Operating Base was the CIA's Camelot. For three days, the old spooks met in the glow of rose-colored memories and celebrated the release of six hundred pages of classified CIA documents pertaining to BOB.

David E. Murphy, the controversial CIA officer who managed to sidestep many intelligence disasters during his career, was the first to do this myth-making in public with his book, *Battleground Berlin*[1], published two years earlier. In his book, Murphy argued that Berlin Operating Base was never penetrated. He treated Igor Orlov as a minor figure, and his colleagues gathered in Berlin that day followed suit. That was how the CIA's official historians and those with vested interests in keeping the myth about BOB intact have spun the Orlov case. The theme was, "Mistakes were made, but hey, we won the Cold War."

As the old boys toured Stasi Headquarters and the KGB Station at Karlshorst and enjoyed roundtable discussions with titles like "Berlin in the Wilderness of Mirrors: Agents, Double Agents and Defectors," a large bucket of cold water was about to be dumped on their heads.

The cold water came from England. It was in the form of a new book presented by the British Secret Service, containing a collection of material from KGB files in Moscow. This was not the reassuring rubbish that has been coming from KGB "files" since the end of the Cold War. It was not the sanitized nonsense Murphy based his book on. This material came from the raw files of the KGB's First Chief Directorate, the agency responsible for Soviet operations against the West.

The material came from the personal archives of the KGB's head librarian, Vasili Mitrokhin, who really did have access to the KGB's greatest secrets. On an almost daily basis for 10 years prior to his retirement in 1985, Mitrokhin systematically removed key files from storage and copied their contents on paper. He hid these handwritten documents in his shoes, under his shirt, and in his pants, and snuck them past the KGB guards. At his home in the far suburbs of Moscow, he carefully typed up the pages. At first, he hid the typed material in old suitcases and trunks. As the files accumulated, he began to hide them in milkcans and buried them in his backyard. For a decade, he worked at copying this record of the dark heart of the KGB.

In 1992, as the old Soviet Union was falling apart, this scholarly man packed several thousand pages of transcripts, took a trip to Latvia, and approached the Americans with great care. At the U.S. Embassy in Riga, he told the CIA duty officer he had important documents and wanted to defect and collect a CIA pension. The CIA Station sent a cable to Langley. Headquarters thought about it and concluded Mitrokhin had no value because he was a librarian, not a spy. Besides, his documents were just his copies and could be forgeries. Not surprisingly, word went back to Riga that the KGB man and his files were not worth a CIA pension.

Meanwhile, word of Mitrokhin and his documents reached the CIA's chief of counterintelligence, Paul Redmond. Redmond knew at once that Mitrokhin should be recruited. His material could help the FBI clear many espionage cases. Above all, the Golitsyn serials could be ended once and for all. However, like Jim Angleton decades before him, Redmond did not win many fights with upper management. The answer was still no.

Was this yet another blunder by CIA leadership, or was it fear—fear that the documents this man had might expose the whole sham of the CIA?

Mitrokhin had read many times in the KGB files of the CIA's tradition of bad judgment. And so, when the rejection came from Langley, he gathered his papers and went to the British Embassy. There, a female officer of the Secret Intelligence Service (MI6) quickly realized the importance of Mitrokhin's documents. After grueling interviews and small and big tests, Mitrokhin became an MI6 agent. He was given the code name KURB.

We know the Mitrokhin material is real because it fills in the gaps in Western files on major cases through 1985. Also, the operational material matches Western electronic intercepts and agent reports. What MI6 got for a little kindness and a pension was the crown jewels of Russian intelligence.

The September 1999 publication of *The Sword and the Shield: The Mitrokhin Archive and the Secret History of the KGB,* by Mitrokhin and MI6's favorite historian, Cambridge Professor Christopher Andrew, turned modern intelligence history on its collective ear. The Mitrokhin archives thoroughly debunk the myth of U.S. intelligence superiority. More to the point for readers of *The Secret History of the CIA,* they contain conclusive evidence that Igor Orlov was exactly who James Jesus Angleton believed he was, a superior Soviet agent who had contaminated Berlin Base and those who ran him.

What Angleton discovered about Orlov through his own investigation came much closer to the contents of the KGB files than to official CIA files. One difference is that the KGB files give Orlov's real name as Aleksandr Grigoryevich Kopatzky—the name Orlov told his wife was an alias given to him by a German general after he was captured in 1943[2]— and that he was born in the city of Surozh in Bryansk Oblast in 1923.[3] In other respects, though, the KGB information on Orlov and Angleton's information match precisely.[4]

However, there is some bureaucratic protection of the Soviet star agent in the Soviet files. Mitrokhin and Andrew quote the files as saying: "While in a German hospital he agreed to work for German intelligence." Angleton's investigation concluded that Orlov's capture was his mission into Germany. The files agree on one point: In 1945, Orlov got where he was supposed to be. "During the last two months of the war," Mitrokhin and Andrew write, "he served as an intelligence officer in General Andrei Vlasov's anti-Soviet Russian Army of Liberation, which fought the Red Army in alliance with the Wehrmacht. At the end of the war, Kopatzky was briefly imprisoned by the American authorities in the former concentration camp at Dachau. . . . Despite his service to the NKVD, Kopatzky's anti-Soviet credentials seemed so well established that he was invited to join the American-supervised German intelligence service established in 1946 at Pullach, near Munich."[5]

For those who believe that the new Russian intelligence service, the SVR, is candid about the Cold War, Andrew and Mitrokhin write: "The SVR still regards the Kopatzky case as extremely sensitive. It insisted as recently as 1997, that no file exists which suggests that Kopatzky, under any of his aliases, ever engaged in 'collaboration . . . with Soviet intelligence." Mitrokhin, "however, was able to take detailed notes from the bulky file which the SVR claims does not exist. The file reveals that in 1949, Kopatzky visited the Soviet military mission in Baden-Baden and was secretly transported to East Berlin where he agreed to become a Soviet agent." The file Mitrokhin copied went on to describe Igor's operations against anti-Soviet émigré organizations like SBONR.

The SVR file confirms that Orlov, as his wife feared, was responsible for the kidnapping of Estonian Vladimir Kivi in the fall of 1951. As reported by Andrew and Mitrokhin, Orlov "did enormous damage to Agency operations in Germany for more than a decade. . . . No fewer than 23 KGB legal operational officers and one illegal 'met and worked with him'—a certain indication of how highly Centre rated him."

After Angleton began to close in on Orlov in 1965, the KGB decided to pull their star agent and his family out of the United States and send him back to Russia. The plan, according to Orlov's SVR file, was to publicly acknowledge his role against Germany and the United States between 1943 and 1965. However, on the day when Eleonore Orlov refused to go to the shopping center where she and the boys were to be picked up,[6] she singlehandedly stopped Moscow Center from carrying out its plan to have Igor go home and write his life story.

The SVR files show that Orlov remained a KGB agent-in-place in the United States until 1978, when this author wrote a newspaper article about Angleton's mole hunt that discussed Orlov. According to the SVR files, the KGB stopped all contact with the little man at that point. However, according to a current file made available for this book through confidential sources, Orlov was kept on the KGB payroll through his death in May of 1982. As cancer was killing him, he instructed Eleonore to contact the Soviet government when he died so that he could be buried at home. Mrs. Orlov has made three trips to Russia in recent years as a tourist and to bring Igor's cremated remains home. She has said, "Now that this has come out maybe they will find a place for him in the Kremlin wall."[7]

On January 6, 1988, Eleonore Orlov answered an after-hours knock on the gallery door. Two FBI agents told her they were there to conduct a raid. They were following up on yet another Soviet defector, Yuri Yurchenko, who had come over with a familiar and concocted story: The

Soviet Union did not recruit Lee Harvey Oswald, and, oh by the way, the late Igor Orlov and his two sons, Robert and George, were and are Soviet agents. Despite Yurchenko's claims, there was no evidence that either Robert or George had ever done anything for the Soviets. The FBI agents conducting the new investigation into the Orlov family did not know of the earlier investigations. Since that raid, Eleonore Orlov continues to be visited by the FBI from time to time. When she kids them about Yurchenko returning to the Soviet Union after just a few months working for the CIA, they have nothing to say.

Paul Garbler, the case officer who suffered most for his association with Orlov, is fed up with the self-congratulations over the accomplishments of Berlin Operating Base. "Nothing was accomplished there, nothing," said Garbler. "In retrospect, Igor's success does not surprise me. The Russians were far more experienced at this line of work than we were."

The KGB files will result in many new espionage investigations. What they will tell us about the most important Cold War case of all remains to play out.

Starting weeks after President Kennedy's assassination, the KGB sent a series of defectors, as well as Yekaterina Furtseva's son-in law, Lieutenant Colonel Igor Kozlov,[8] to tell us that Lee Harvey Oswald was not working for the KGB. Who sent these defectors to America? Who knew the American system well enough to understand that any suspicion of a Soviet role in JFK's murder had to be stopped immediately? The answer, Angleton believed, was his teacher, mentor, and tormentor, Harold "Kim" Philby. For three years after he defected, Philby, we now know, was working closely with Russian intelligence, but not at KGB headquarters. Why? Angleton became convinced that Philby had been taken over by a group of Russian insiders led by Leonid Brezhnev and including Furtseva and future KGB chief, Yuri Andropov. They were the people who decided to dump Nikita Khrushchev. At the time, Philby complained to friends who visited him from England that the KGB seldom contacted him.

Angleton believed that Philby's usefulness to the insiders was as a sounding board to tell them how the United States would respond if the Russians were shown to have played a role in JFK's murder. Angleton was convinced that Philby was behind the propaganda campaign, now confirmed in the Mitrokhin materials, in which the KGB leaked stories that the CIA was behind the Kennedy murder. Angleton said in 1979, "The

KGB would have never had the sense to use the countermeasures they did without Philby giving them instructions." Angleton believed, that after Philby served his purpose, his use to the Soviets was limited, and he could even have seemed dangerous to them.

For years, the KGB maintained that Philby played no active role in their organization. However, a 1999 book by Rufina Philby, who married Philby years after these events happened, demonstrates that he was actively in contact with Soviet intelligence officials until his death on May 11, 1988.⁹ However, the book also demonstrates that Philby was being watched more than honored. It was as if the Russians feared he might spill some great state secret.

James Angleton, written off as a crank and a madman by his critics, had the hardest job in the CIA: keeping the enemy out. What he learned before his death was that we were our own worst enemy.

When I ventured to his pleasant house in Arlington in late 1985, I found him coming to grips with this thought. "I realize how I have wasted my existence, my professional life," he told me. He was not bitter—just uncomfortable with the thought. His entire being told him that his beloved intelligence community had been penetrated by the Soviets with agents of great skill. He understood why his colleagues in the CIA eventually grew tired of his mole hunts and his efforts to try to protect the place. "I was always the skunk at the garden party, and even your friends tire of that," he said.

The last time I saw James Angleton, his face, always thinner than thin, had changed little, even though the cigarettes he would not give up had destroyed his lungs with cancer. The other cancer that was eating away at him was the suspicion and fear that came with his job. He was a man estranged by his career from his wife and children and dying in total emotional isolation.

Within the confines of his remarkable life were most of America's secrets. "You know how I got to be in charge of counterintelligence? I agreed not to polygraph or require detailed background checks on Allen Dulles and 60 of his closest friends." His monologue would stop only for a sip of tea or a violent fit of coughing. "They were afraid that their own business dealings with Hitler's pals would come out. They were too arrogant to believe that the Russians would discover it all." The real problem,

Angleton concluded, was that "there was no accountability. And without real accountability everything turned to shit."

All the trappings of Angleton's legend were gone by this time, except for his love of exotic tea. But now, this man who had struck fear into most of his colleagues—this man who had been able to end a CIA career with a nod or a phone call—unassuming house in Arlington seemed empty. "You know, the CIA got tens of thousands of brave people killed. . . . We played with lives as if we owned them. We gave false hope. We—I—so misjudged what happened."

I asked the dying old man how it all went so wrong.

With no emotion in his voice, but with his hand trembling, Angleton replied: "Fundamentally, the founding fathers of U.S. intelligence were liars. The better you lied and the more you betrayed, the more likely you would be promoted. These people attracted and promoted each other. Outside of their duplicity, the only thing they had in common was a desire for absolute power. I did things that, in looking back on my life, I regret. But I was part of it and loved being in it. . . . Allen Dulles, Richard Helms, Carmel Offie, and Frank Wisner were the grand masters. If you were in a room with them you were in a room full of people that you had to believe would deservedly end up in hell." Angleton slowly sipped his tea and then said, "I guess I will see them there soon."

Angleton has been portrayed as a lunatic and even a torturer, and, as this book has documented, he did harm to many loyal colleagues. However, I hope this book also clarifies who he really was and gives the reader a sense of the man whose life's mission was to protect the CIA from the enemy. As he told me, "Sometimes you can find the real enemy right in the mirror."

At the end, he seemed grateful for the release his lung cancer brought him. "I am afraid that whatever sins I have committed in my life," he said as he sipped his tea, "have now come home to roost. . . . I am fundamentally a failure. I failed to protect the CIA, because there was no real desire to secure the place from the Soviets. I never understood the great advantage the Russians had over us. . . . As Americans we just hold no real value in secrecy. God, it was such a simple explanation."

NOTES

CHAPTER 1

1 The files of CIA official Robert Crowley, entrusted to the author prior to Crowley's death in October 2000, contain much of the classified history of Beria's reign over the NKVD.

2 "The assistant" is the name U.S. intelligence used to protect the identity of the highest ranking Soviet intelligence officer who ever came under U.S. influence. He reported on a weekly basis to a U.S. Army intelligence officer stationed in Moscow, and his reports eventually ended up in the files of former CIA officials Robert Crowley and the late James Jesus Angleton. After the war ended, the assistant stopped reporting. Attempts by the CIA to recruit him between 1947 and 1953 were unsuccessful. Robert Crowley noted that his cooperation during the war was "directly related to his desire to see Russia prevail over Germany." James Angleton concluded the assistant cooperated on orders from Beria, who used the assistant to court the United States for increased war aid.

3 See also chapters 4 and 5 of Christopher Andrew and Oleg Gordievsky's *KGB: The Inside Story*; John Costello and Oleg Tsarev's *Deadly Illusions*, the most illuminating work on the fate of the Red Orchestra; and "Wooing the Russians" in *The Service: The Memoirs of General Reinhard Gehlen*.

CHAPTER 2

1 From Orlov's NKVD file.

2 The Kopatzky dossier would eventually contain tens of thousands of pages, broken into many files. In total, these files remained one of Russia's last great Cold War secrets. Notes from a version of these files were taken by Vasili Mitrokhin for his book, *The Sword and the Shield: The Mitrokhin Archive* with Christopher Andrew. None of the original identification history of Sasha was included in this version of the dossier.

3 The quotes come from the interrogation files of Orlov, his mother, and his father, incorporated in his NKVD dossier.

4 According to the interrogation reports of colleagues of Ivan Navratilov, he bit-
   terly complained about Stalin's purges in the intelligence service.
5 From the performance evaluation by Sasha's NKVD superior during this period,
   from files supplied by James Jesus Angleton.
6 From Orlov's classified file.
7 From James Angleton's personal records of the Orlov debriefings.
8 From a series of interviews with Eleonore Orlov between 1988 and 1999.
9. From the German debriefing reports of Igor Orlov, taken from the files of James
   Angleton and Robert T. Crowley.

CHAPTER 3

1 From Igor Orlov's personal papers.
2 From CIA Office of Security and Office of Counterintelligence interviews conducted in 1963–1966 with surviving members of the Vlasov forces.
3 The following account was compiled from debriefings of Orlov found in his
   closed NKVD file.
4 Lasnov was captured in 1945 and repatriated to Russia. The NKVD interviewed
   him in September 1946.
5 Interview with James J. Angleton.
6 Interview with George Kisevalter, CIA case officer to General Gehlen. Kisevalter
   and James Angleton looked at Orlov's role with the Vlasov forces after the defection of Anatoly Golitsyn in December 1961. Eleonore Orlov also provided background in a series of interviews, including one on July 6, 1988.
7 According to General Gehlen and others from the German General Staff.
8 General Reinhard Gehlen wrote in his autobiography, *The Service: The Memoirs
   of General Reinhard Gehlen:* "Hitler saw Vlasov at most as a propaganda tool to
   weaken the Soviet armed forces; promises might be given to him and deserters
   who came over to join him, but on no account should these promises be kept."
   General Gehlen believed that this shortsightedness might have cost Germany victory in the war.
9 From Gehlen, *The Service.*
10 Ibid, p. 11.
11 While Gehlen's relationship with U.S. intelligence during the 1940s and 1950s has
   been the topic of half a dozen books, it was not until September 2000 that the
   CIA admitted the relationship with the Nazi general. The CIA's acknowledgment
   of this relationship came in response to a Freedom of Information Act request by
   researcher Carl Oglesby. This was done under pressure from the Clinton Administration under the Nazi War Crimes Disclosure Act.
12 Orlov was important for two reasons: First, much of Gehlen's Soviet intelligence
   came from debriefings which Orlov had arranged—debriefings of Vlasov partisans as well as captured Russian intelligence officers; and second, Orlov had pro-

vided much of Gehlen's direct information about NKVD methods and operations. This second point was crucial to the success of the new West German–United States partnership, because the Americans wanted authentic information, and Gehlen knew that Orlov could provide it.

13 From the still highly classified files on the Orlov case in the archives of the SVR.

CHAPTER 4

1 An excellent biography is *Gentleman Spy: The Life of Allen Dulles*, by Peter Gross.

2 Hopkins had the dubious distinction of being the man FDR designated as the target for Stalin's frustrations.

3 From a series of interviews with Robert Crowley between 1989 and 1997.

4 From a series of interviews in February 2000.

5 From CIA records in the personal files of Robert T. Crowley, a deputy of James Critchfield, a U.S. Army officer who conducted Nazi recruitments.

6 The German postwar press was well aware of Gehlen's activities: "It seems," the Frankfurter *Rundschau* editorialized, "that in the Gehlen headquarters one SS man paved the way for the next and Himmler's elite were having happy reunion ceremonies."

CHAPTER 5

1 Later in the war, Angleton was upset to learn that Pound had been committed to St. Elizabeth's, a public mental hospital in Washington, D.C.

2 From an interview in March 1999.

3 From an interview with James Jesus Angleton, June 1976.

4 Comments written by Philby's Soviet control. From Philby's files now in the archives of the post-Soviet Russian intelligence service (SVR).

5 See Phillip Knightly's *The Master Spy*.

6 At that time, Palestine was controlled by Great Britain, and the British were refusing to issue entry permits to most Jews.

7 From a series of interviews with Angleton between 1976 and 1986.

8 Angleton was first exposed to the idea that there should be a Jewish state while he was a student at Yale. Professor Norman Holmes Pearson and his then very radical ideas deeply influenced the young Angleton. The men Angleton befriended included Teddy Kollek, later a renowned mayor of Jerusalem, and Reuven Shiloah who founded the Mossad, the Israeli intelligence service.

9 See Kim Philby's *My Silent War* and David Martin's *Wilderness of Mirrors*.

10 From a series of interviews with James J. Angleton between 1976 and 1986.

CHAPTER 6

1 On a cold Monday morning in early 1941, a maid at the Hotel Bellevue near Washington's Union Station opened the door to begin cleaning the room. To her

horror, inside the room she found the body of a man who had apparently blown a huge hole in his head with a .38 revolver. The night before, February 10, he had registered under the name Poref, but his papers said his name was Samuel Ginsburg and that he was born in the USSR. The metropolitan police were convinced it was a suicide. In the room was one suicide note to his lawyer, Louis Waldman, in English, asking him to help his wife and child; another note, in Russian, to his wife, Toni, telling her he loved her but "must go"; and a third note, in German, to a friend asking for help for his wife and son.

In reality, the man who died that night was General Walter Krivitsky, the former chief of Soviet military intelligence in Europe, who had defected in 1938. His death was no suicide. Shortly after Krivitsky had predicted that Hitler would form an alliance with Stalin, Hitler's government dispatched an assassin to kill him. The local newspapers made a sensation out of Krivitsky's death. Hoover wrote on a request to investigate the case a firm "No"—he would not be "baited by newspaper promotional tactics." After all, the FBI was supposed to protect the United States from foreign enemies. If it admitted that an enemy agent had killed a defector on American soil, it would be admitting to a huge failure in U.S. security. It was better to leave the death a suicide.

Whittaker Chambers had defected from the Soviet cause the same year Krivitsky left Europe. Krivitsky had urged Chambers to speak out about the spy network he had once worked for. Chambers met with Assistant Secretary of State Adolf Berle at his northwest Washington, D.C., home and told his story. Chambers listed the names of the spies, including Alger Hiss. Although the White House informed Hoover of Chamber's allegations, he dismissed them. A week before Christmas 1942, the Chambers' case was closed. Had Hoover done his job, he would have learned not only about Hiss but also that Krivitsky could identify a mole in the British Secret Service. That mole was Harold "Kim" Philby.

2 From the divorce-trial transcripts of Elizabeth and William Harvey, Jr.

3 Donovan told this story to scores of former OSS colleagues. He felt that Dulles had grown so bored with life as a Wall Street lawyer that he was engaging in intelligence fantasies.

4 See Peter Grose's *Gentleman Spy: The Life of Allen Dulles*. Grose makes a significant contribution detailing Dulles's behind-the-scenes dealings after he left the OSS.

5 See *The Old Boys: The American Elite and the Origins of the CIA*, by Burton Hersh, a lively and well-documented history of the origins of the CIA.

6 Interview with William R. Corson on January 9, 1991.

7 Dozens of counterintelligence files describing Offie and his role were among the papers of both Robert Crowley and William Corson.

8 As we will see in later chapters, the name "Sasha" ran throughout James Angleton's efforts to root out the mole who so completely penetrated the CIA's defenses.

CHAPTER 7

1 Based on a series of interviews with WAC C.G. Follich, who later became the wife of William K. Harvey.

2 The author obtained a copy of Weisz's classified CIA and State Department files and his open Army file.

3 Based on interviews with Weisz's sister, Suzanne Weisz Gottlieb, and his mother, Gizelle Breuer Weisz, as well as other relatives.

4 According to colleague Garston W. "Wally" Driver.

5 Interview with C.G. Harvey on April 19, 1988.

6 Interview with Gizelle Weisz on February 12, 1988.

7 Interview with Suzanne Weisz Gottlieb on February 12, 1988.

8 James Angleton, Robert Crowley, and William Corson all shared their views of Weisz in the series of interviews described in the preface. The author came into possession of their personal files on Weisz that reflected their conclusions.

9 Counterintelligence officials are divided on this. Angleton believed it was possible. Crowley and Corson were convinced that Weisz understood he was working for the Russians all along.

10 Officially, OPERATION PAPERCLIP ended in 1947; in reality, it went on until 1973. See Linda Hunt's excellent history of OPERATION PAPERCLIP in *Secret Agenda*.

11 Interview with Etta Jo Weisz on February 2, 1988.

12 Etta Jo remembered their honeymoon trip as a "harrowing experience. . . . People were furious. . . . People had really tried everything in the world to get into Hungary to see their relatives, and they wouldn't let anybody in. But they [George Weisz and the Communist Hungarian officials] had become friendly during all of these negotiations, and they put it right through." Mrs. Weisz spoke in an interview on February 2, 1988.

13 Interview with William R. Corson on April 12, 2000.

14 The late E. Allan Lightner Jr.—he died in 1990—remembered Weisz working for John J. McCloy in "an intelligence capacity." (Interview with Ambassador E. Allan Lightner Jr. on February 18, 1988.) Lightner said that Weisz visited camps set up for displaced persons. "We wouldn't call them concentration camps, but they were pretty close to it," Lightner explained. Weisz sifted through a sea of humanity looking for specific technical and intelligence experts in the camps or leads to where they might have gone.

15 From an interview of Lightner conducted by Charles Lewis, then with ABC's *20-20*, on November 3, 1984.

16 From a series of interviews with Suzanne Gottlieb.

CHAPTER 8

1 From a series of interviews with Eleonore Orlov between July 6, 1988 and October 3, 1999.

2 From an interview with Eleonore Orlov on April 10, 2000.

3 The post-Soviet Russian intelligence service (SVR) still regards the Orlov case as very sensitive. According to former KGB archivist Vasily Mitrokhin, "It insisted as recently as 1997 that no file exists which suggests that Kopatzky, under any of his aliases, ever engaged in 'collaboration . . . with Soviet intelligence.'" Mitrokhin, according to his 1999 book with Christopher Andrew, *The Sword and the Shield: The Mitrokhin Archive,* says he "was able to take detailed notes from the bulky file which the SVR claims does not exist. The file reveals that in 1949 Kopatzky visited the Soviet military mission in Baden-Baden and was secretly transported to East Berlin where he agreed to become a Soviet agent." The file Mitrokhin copied went on to describe Igor's operations against anti-Soviet Russian émigré organizations like the SBONR (see chapter 9).

4 Interview with Peter Kapusta on March 17, 1988.

CHAPTER 9

1 From a series of interviews with William R. Corson during 1989–90.

2 Interview with Wally Driver on October 13, 1990.

3 After being made an agent in Berlin by the CIA, Igor had his salary upped by the KGB (successor to the intelligence side of the NKVD) to 500 marks a month and worked under the codenames ERWIN, RICHARD and HERBERT, according to Vasili Mitrokhin.

CHAPTER 10

1 Interview with William R. Corson on June 4, 1990.

2 Adding to the legend of the Harvey/Hoover feud was a 1949 Hoover memo. In that year the atomic spying of Klaus Fuchs at Los Alamos was revealed. Meanwhile, the FBI discovered that in 1945, Harvey had been given a translation of a captured German document recommending that Fuchs be apprehended because he was a Communist agent. Had this document been acted on, the Soviet spy network would have been revealed several years earlier than it was. Hoover, supposedly furious, ordered an investigation. To reinforce the view that the two men were at odds, Hoover wrote: "In possession of the document was Supervisor W. K. Harvey up to the time of his resignation in the late summer of 1947. This material became delinquent in that it was not being handled on a current basis due to the shortage of personnel. After the resignation of Mr. Harvey, this material was reassigned, the delinquent handling of the material was corrected. . . ."

3 Interview with Paul Garbler on February 3, 1990.

4 Interview with William Corson on January 9, 1991.

5 From a series of interviews, described more fully in the Preface, at the Army and Navy Club and Duke Zeibert's original restaurant in Washington throughout the

late 1970s and early 1980s. Angleton often used me the way a case officer would use an intelligence agent. It was years later that I discovered that he had tried to get me to bring to a conclusion a series of CI cases left unfinished after his firing in December 1974.

6 See David Martin's *Wilderness of Mirrors* for an overview of how Harvey closed in on Philby.

7 From a 1986 telephone interview with Teddy Kollek.

8 Kollek gave his version of these events in 1987 at the dedication of an Israeli memorial to Angleton, a year after Angleton's death from lung cancer.

9 See Dan Raviv and Yossi Melman's *Every Spy a Prince.*

10 From page 166 of Philby's *My Secret Life.*

11 The best and most complete history of this period can be found in William R. Corson's *The Armies of Ignorance.*

CHAPTER 11

1 Interview with William R. Corson, January 2000.

2 A former head of the CIA's Soviet Russia Division, who asked that his name not be disclosed. The interview was conducted in November 1997.

3 From the files of William R. Corson.

4 From a series of interviews with Robert T. Crowley during 1990–1995.

5 From the Corson files on Kronthal and a series of interviews with Corson conducted in December 1999.

6 William Corson first revealed details of the Kronthal case in his book *Widows,* co-authored by Susan and Joseph Trento. New information found in files from the Corson and Crowley estates establishes what happened at the Dulles home that night.

7 Interview with Hank Knoche on February 18, 1988.

CHAPTER 12

1 Harvey related those views to both William R. Corson and Robert Crowley.

2 From a series of interviews with George Kisevalter.

3 From a series of interviews with John Sherwood.

4 From a series of interviews with Paul Garbler.

5 Interview with Donald Morris on March 20, 1990.

6 Interview with Eleonore Orlov on July 10, 1988.

CHAPTER 13

1 See chapter 11, "The Cold War After Stalin," in *KGB: The Inside Story,* by Christoper Andrew and Oleg Gordievsky.

2 From the CIA files of Robert Crowley.

3 See *Crowns and Trenchcoats,* David Chavchavadze's autobiography.

4 According to Ambassador E. Allan Lightner Jr., John Bross was the legal adviser to John J. McCloy's intelligence unit in Germany at the end of the war. Interview with Lightner on February 18, 1988.

5 From the CIA records of Robert Crowley.

6 Case officer notes from Orlov's secret SVR file.

7 The first CIA Moscow Station opened in 1961 with Paul Garbler as station chief.

8 This was especially true in the final years of the Soviet Union, when information provided by military intelligence caused the Russian Army to side with those advocating democracy over Communism.

CHAPTER 14

1 Interview with George Kisevalter on April 18, 1988.

2 Interview with Peter Kapusta on November 22, 1990.

3 "Bona fides" is intelligence jargon for confirming a defector's character and background. It is supposed to be a rigorous process that makes certain someone coming into the country is not a Soviet agent with plans to report back to Moscow. Once bona fides are accepted, the defector is trusted.

4 Interview with Peter Kapusta.

5 Interviews with Tulluis Accompura, Peter Kapusta, and other former Army intelligence officers.

6 See *Molehunt* by David Wise, p. 222.

7 Interview with Quentin Johnson and other former colleagues of Ed Snow.

8 Interview with Robert Crowley on January 3, 1991.

9 Interview with Donald Morris on January 8, 1991.

10 Interview with Tulluis Accompura on January 17, 1991.

11· Interview with Robert Crowley on January 8, 1991.

12 The head of CIA Counterintelligence, James Angleton, became so concerned after learning of Snow's wife's affair that he finally ordered an investigation. He sent John Mertz, one of Harvey's former FBI associates who had joined the CIA, to Tokyo to conduct a counterintelligence investigation. According to Peter Kapusta, Mertz and Angleton did not tell Tokyo Station Chief Henry Hecksher they were conducting the investigation. As Mertz kept digging, he learned that none of the agents that Snow's "father-in-law," Yankovsky, sent into the Soviet Union were ever heard from again. In 1956, Mertz wrote a report concluding that Yankovsky's behavior and that of his daughter should be watched.

CHAPTER 15

1 This account is based on interviews with James J. Angleton, several Tokyo colleagues of Murphy, and several official but still secret accounts of the incident.

2 Interview with John Sherwood on December 3, 1990.

3 The *New York Times* carried stories about the incident in its editions of February 6 and 7, 1952.

4 Robert Crowley later discovered that Anton had managed to stay on the CIA payroll for years. "First they turned him over to Dr. Nu, who is the head of the Psychiatric Branch. And, of course, Dr. Nu is on the twelfth chapter of his book and welcomes the opportunity to put Gray on the couch. He had no interest in reconstituting him. They finally tell Anton they are going to pay him by the month for a year to get on the ground and run. We had already moved him to Los Angeles where he was playing golf and enjoying the sun. Every month, I sent someone over with the check and a reminder that this was number such and such, and the checks were dwindling down. . . ." Crowley soon learned that Anton had pull, despite his apparent uselessness to the CIA, when Lyman Kirkpatrick, a powerful CIA executive, called Crowley and ordered him to continue issuing the checks. "We kept paying him and moving him for a very long time," Crowley said. Anton also began using his CIA alias "Robert Gray" in the United States.

5 Interview with Anita Potocki on November 28, 1990.

6 From an exchange of e-mails with Mr. Murphy in March 1999.

7 Anita Potocki, who Harvey brought with him from Washington, was in charge of a very special records room set up in Berlin Base. Harvey had found that it was often impossible to get a simple name check on a potential recruiting target from Washington. If an agent was recruited and Harvey sent back the name to see whether or not the CIA had a file on him, the clerks at headquarters might check one or two possible spellings and then reply that no information was found. Russian names are especially difficult because of transliteration. Easily dozens of possible spellings needed to be checked, but seldom were. And so Harvey decided that Berlin Base needed its own file system, which Potocki ran.

8 Interview with George Kisevalter on April 18, 1988.

9 Interview with William R. Corson on January 17, 1991.

10 Interview with John Sherwood on November 14, 1990.

11 Interview with George Kisevalter on April 18, 1988. Chipman's ex-wife, Starr, later married David Murphy after Marian died. The Chipmans did not have much happiness. According to George Kisevalter, tragedy struck the couple twice. On July 4, 1960, at a Berlin Base Independence Day celebration, their little daughter's dress caught fire and she burned to death. Years later, a second daughter, who grew up to be a beautiful young woman, visited Mexico with a hunting party and was accidentally shot to death.

12 Sherwood spent his first months at Berlin Base dismantling Frank Wisner's "stay behind" program. He soon discovered that most of the hidden weapons and supply stores had been long ago liquidated for profit by the CIA's not so devoted agents.

CHAPTER 16

1 Interviews with Sam Wilson and Eleonore Orlov. Wilson stopped contacting the Orlovs only when a subordinate to James Angleton warned Wilson in 1964 that Orlov was under investigation by the FBI.

2 Based on information supplied by a former high officer of the Soviet High Command at Karlshorst who asked that his name not be revealed.

3 Interview with Paul Garbler.

4 This bizarre requirement was never explained. In earlier dealings with Orlov, the Army CIC and, later, the CIA both used Russian. Mrs. Orlov insists that she heard Garbler and her husband speak Russian together, but Garbler said that never happened.

5 The true identities of cryptonyms are among the most precious of CIA secrets. George Weisz, who later joined Berlin Base, kept a list of agents' cryptonyms in his personal papers.

6 See pages 242–243, *Battleground Berlin,* by David E. Murphy, Sergei A. Kondrashev, and George Baily.

7 Interview with Mrs. Eleonore Orlov on July 10, 1988.

8 Ibid.

CHAPTER 17

1 See *Spycatcher,* by Peter Wright and Paul Greengrass for the MI6 view of the Berlin Tunnel operation.

2 According to Robert Crowley, Nelson was never properly credited for his technical breakthroughs. Years after the Berlin tunnel was declared a major success by the CIA, the director called Nelson to his office to receive a reward for his work. He thought he was probably going to get a medal and a large cash payment. Instead, the director gave him $100 and a certificate. It nearly broke his heart.

3 In charge of this special project for Dulles was the CIA's Staff D under Frank Rowlett.

4 They told him that in 1949 MI6 had purchased a house in a Vienna suburb and, using the ruse of resurfacing the driveway, had dug a 40-foot-long tunnel to the middle of the street where phone cables ran back to the Soviet Union. MI6 then successfully wiretapped the cables and intercepted Soviet telephone communications for two years. Carl Nelson was in Vienna at the time and studied this wiretap system.

5 According to Robert T. Crowley.

CHAPTER 18

1 For Vienna, the walk-in was a godsend. The justification for spending tens of millions of dollars to set up CIA stations was that they were needed to recruit Russians. Richard Helms, at CIA headquarters, put it clearly when assigning William

Hood to Vienna as station chief: "Your job is to recruit Russians. Until we've done that, we've failed. I don't care how many reports the Station sends in on the Czech Communist party or the Hungarian order of battle. Our basic job is to penetrate the Soviet establishment." "That never happened in Vienna," John Sherwood later said. "The fact of the matter is, the only significant thing to ever take place in Vienna of a positive nature was when Popov sent his letter." Hood, who would later chronicle the Popov affair in a CIA-approved book, described events in Vienna to Sherwood as "dull" before and after Popov.

2 See *Mole,* by William Hood.

3 This section is based on an interview with George Kisevalter on April 19, 1988, and on the personal papers of George Kisevalter and his Popov debriefing reports.

4 Much of the background material is from an unpublished 1981 article by Paul Garbler titled "Reflections on the Teddy Bear."

5 By agreement among the four occupying powers, designated French, British, and American representatives could inspect and make observations in East Germany, as Soviet representatives could in West Germany. These British officers, from the Potsdam Mission, were on such a tour.

6 Interview with George Kisevalter.

CHAPTER 19

1 The classic disaster involving an illegal is the case of Army intelligence agent Ralph Sigler and Soviet illegal Rudolph Hermann. The story is told in detail in Chapter 53 of this book and in *Widows,* by William Corson, co-authored by Susan and Joseph Trento.

2 See the *New York Times*, October 19, 1959.

3 Corson worked in secret operations, on loan from the United States Marines, for Presidents Truman, Eisenhower, Kennedy, and Johnson.

4 As AE was the designator for Soviet cases in the CIA's system of cryptonyms, BE was its designator for Polish cases.

5 Terence Lecky was the MI6 interrogator who broke Blake.

6 Blake was sentenced to 41 years in prison for treason. In 1966, after he had served six years, a Soviet-aided faction of the Irish Republican Army broke him out of Wormwood Prison, and he escaped to the Soviet Union.

CHAPTER 20

1 One name Felfe turned over in the summer of 1952 was that of Captain Michael R. Rothkrug, who had left the Army in 1951 to set up a business in West Berlin. In fact, Rothkrug sold worthless secrets to anyone who would buy them. Sacrificing low-level agents to give credibility to more important agents was standard KGB practice.

2 Interview with Anita Potocki on November 28, 1990.

3   Interview with Ed Petty on April 5, 1988.

4   See Chapter 22 for an account of Stashinsky's career.

5   Interview with Wally Driver in October, 1990.

6   Interview with Sam Wilson on June 14, 1988.

7   According to several Berlin Base colleagues.

8   The "successful" coups were already giving Wisner fits, as he made the discovery
    that the CIA was subject to blackmail by those who "helped" us. In Iran, Wisner
    was forced to pay off most of the top clerics to keep them in line. Meanwhile,
    General Walter Bedell Smith, at first privately furious over the coup in
    Guatemala, ended up on the board of directors of the United Fruit Company.
    That action set a pattern for former CIA directors joining companies that partici-
    pated in covert actions with the CIA. United Fruit got their property back after
    the coup, and Smith never publicly spoke out against it.

9   The park area that is the approach to the Vietnam War Memorial.

10 Interview with William R. Corson on January 10, 1991.

11 In 1958, after Frank Wisner left Washington, two of his deputies, Richard Bissell
    and Richard Helms, became the chief rivals for control of Clandestine Services, by
    then officially called the Directorate of Plans. Helms—whom Bill Harvey called
    "the Boy Diplomat," because he felt that Helms was trying to rein in nearly every
    operation Harvey wanted to run—remained as Chief for Western Europe, while
    Bissell was Dulles's choice for DDP (Deputy Director for Plans). Helms was vastly
    different from Bissell. He was a cooler character, a man who was able to deflect
    decisions and blame to the point of driving his subordinates to distraction. Al-
    ways the pragmatist, Helms seemed constitutionally incapable of taking a stand in
    arguments between subordinates. But during his tenure as Bissell's deputy, Helms
    did have one conviction: He was going to get Bissell's job.

CHAPTER 21

1   Interview with George Kisevalter on July 13, 1988.

2   "Wolf understood that NATO bickering caused the various members to put every-
    thing down on paper," Robert Crowley explained. "Memo after secret memo was
    written. . . . Wolf understood that to write memos you have to have secretaries, and
    that is who he targeted, the NATO secretaries." Wolf trained and sent the best-
    looking Aryan gigolos he could recruit to seduce women working in NATO. West
    German secretaries were easy targets because of the shortage of German men after
    World War II. Wolf also sought high-level penetrations. He looked for good recruits
    wherever he could find them. He went after Gehlen's BND with a vengeance.

3   When Brandt became chancellor in a coalition government, Guillaume had access
    to a complete range of NATO secrets, including the location of American nuclear
    weapons in West Germany. That sort of information gave the Soviets an enor-
    mous advantage in the event of a sabotage effort, if they planned to attack. To

make matters worse, Guillaume did not steal documents on a wholesale basis as most spies do. His position allowed him to simply turn over summaries of top-secret NATO reports to the SSD. Wolf's experts and Moscow Center reviewed the summaries, told Guillaume which full documents they wanted, and Guillaume ordered the documents in Brandt's name.

In 1973, the BND learned that Guillaume and his wife were traitors. Brandt, who knew nothing of the betrayal, was quietly told. Before closing down the operation, the CIA and BND seeded "Program of Transactions" lists with detailed reports of early cruise missile guidance research. According to Robert Crowley, the Soviets spent tens of millions trying to develop a cruise missile based on the information Guillaume gave them. The doctored material forced the Soviets to waste resources.

Guillaume and his wife were traded to the Soviet Union for several East Germans who were loyal to the West. Guillaume received the Order of Lenin for his exploits. Willy Brandt's career was shattered.

4 When Harvey returned to Washington, he showed a picture of the little girl to James Angleton. The usually somber counterintelligence boss looked at Harvey and said, "Have you had her checked out? She could be sent." Harvey, not amused, grabbed the picture back.

5 Interview with Eleonore Orlov on July 10, 1988.

CHAPTER 22

1 See Peter Deriabin and T. H. Bagley's *The KGB Masters of the Soviet Union,* pp. 361-362.

2 Georgi Okolovich was an NTS leader particularly hated by the Kremlin. In February 1954, the MGB, forerunner to the KGB, sent Captain Nikolai Kholkov on a mission to kill him. Kholkov had a girlfriend in West Germany and no desire to return to Moscow. Instead of carrying out the kill, he confessed to Okolovich and presented him with the poison bullets he was supposed to use. For a detailed history of Soviet émigré operations, see E.H. Cookridge's comprehensive *Gehlen: Spy of the Century.*

3 From Stashinsky's 1962 confession and trial transcript.

4 The Cheka, a forerunner of the KGB, specialized in sending agents into an enemy camp specifically to gain the trust of its leaders. Many KGB agents liked to call themselves Chekists.

5 See General Reinhard Gehlen's *The Service* for his account of Stashinsky's confession, pp. 240–241.

CHAPTER 23

1 According to several of his colleagues.

2 Interview with Frank Steinert, March 23, 1988.

3 FBI File #116-62428 on George Weisz.

4 The Liaison Group had a more delicate job as well. The group was responsible
for keeping track of and evacuating valuable ex-Nazis if their locations suddenly
became dangerous.

5 What seems likely is that Weisz supplied much of the intelligence about the CIA's
role in Berlin to Whalen, who, in turn, fed it back to his Soviet case officer. It is
also possible that the Israelis advised the Soviets of Weisz's importance. It was
then that the KGB demanded that Whalen bring Weisz back to the Pentagon so
Whalen could debrief him about CIA activities in Berlin to share with the Soviets
in preparation for the Berlin Wall. However, it appears that Weisz did not know
his new boss was selling out the safety and possibly the lives of Weisz's Berlin
Base colleagues.

6 A plea bargain was struck by the Justice Department to cover up Whalen's role in
bringing in war criminals. In an outrageous deal, Whalen accepted a 15-year sentence and was allowed to retain all his benefits and retire, despite his treason.

CHAPTER 24

1 Allen Dulles was always very careful to distance himself from Agency assassinations. Thomas Powers told the story in his biography of Richard Helms how
Armin Meyer, then head of the CIA's Office of Near Eastern Affairs, saw Dulles
bristle when someone suggested that then Iraqi leader Abdul Karim Kassem "be
gotten rid of." Kassem had about as much charm as Saddam Hussein, and the
suggestion seemed like a good idea to those at the meeting. Dulles, seemingly of-
fended by the very thought of such an act, lectured the group on how it was not
in the American character to engage in assassinations. The fact that Dulles was already organizing a hit squad within the CIA merely confirmed that "Uncle Allen"
was an artful liar. See Powers's *The Man Who Kept the Secrets*, p. 128.

2 *New York Times* interview, December 26, 1975.

3 Interview with Boris Pash in August, 1983.

4 Interview with Donald Denesyla on March 14, 1991.

5 Ironically, General Truscott was the top U.S. military commander in Germany
during part of Harvey's tenure as Chief of Berlin Base. Truscott's job at this point
was to make certain Dulles and the CIA did not do anything to surprise or embarrass President Eisenhower. When Truscott learned of the plan, he went straight to
Dulles, who sent a cable to the assassination team calling off the murder.

6 An excellent account of CIA assassinations can be found in William R. Corson's
The Armies of Ignorance.

7 See Copeland's *The Game of Nations*, p. 202.

8 See David Martin's *Wilderness of Mirrors*.

9 From a series of interviews with James Angleton between 1977 and 1980.

10 Interview with John Sherwood on December 14, 1991.

11 The White House Special Group was composed of administration and intelligence officials who formulated policy for presentation to a component of the National Security Council for approval.

12 Interview with Robert A. Maheu on February 18, 1988.

13 The retainer was more than most senior CIA case officers made in salary in those days. Maheu shared office space with Carmine Bellino, the accounting whiz who helped the Kennedys go after organized crime when John Kennedy was in the Senate. Jim Hougan's book *Spooks* contains a wonderful chapter about Maheu titled "The Master Spook."

14 The CIA had found Maheu effective in previous operations. At the CIA's request he had bugged Aristotle Onassis's apartment in a scheme to prevent the Saudi government from giving the Greek shipping magnate exclusive rights to carry their oil in his tankers. Maheu was no Boy Scout. He had produced a blue movie called *Happy Days* that featured a look-alike actor portraying Indonesian President Achmed Sukarno.

15 Maheu had a local Washington, D.C., connection to the mob. District of Columbia boss Joseph Nesline was contacted for help, according to former Washington Police Detective Carl Schoffler, who spent his career chasing Nesline. It was Maheu's overture to Nesline that began the fateful process. (From a series of interviews with Carl Schoffler between 1978 and 1981.)

16 From a series of interviews with Ricardo Canete between 1983 and 1985.

17 See George Crile's May 16, 1976 article about Aleman in the *Washington Post*.

18 See Jim Hougan's *Spooks*. In 1978, when Hougan first revealed suspicions about Trafficante working for Castro, the CIA and the Justice Department issued blanket denials. By the 1980s, when Ronald Reagan was fighting his new war against Castro, evidence was made public that both sides had been engaging in narcotics trafficking for decades to fund their activities.

Castro's island had also become a refuge for fugitives from the United States, including former Nixon associate Robert Vesco and former CIA gun runner Frank Terpil.

19 Kennedy met Judith Campbell at a party at the Sands Hotel in Las Vegas on February 7, 1960, when he was just six months away from his party's presidential nomination. Sinatra never told Kennedy the woman he was sleeping with was also the bed partner of a very tough mobster on the FBI's ten most wanted list.

20 Daniel Schorr's *Clearing the Air,* p. 148.

CHAPTER 25

1 President Eisenhower was infuriated by Dulles's "briefings" of the President-elect because Eisenhower thought Dulles was unnecessarily sharing sensitive information with Kennedy. On November 17, 1960, Eisenhower's military aide, General Andrew J. Goodpaster, informed Dulles that there were limits on what he should

provide Kennedy. Goodpaster pointedly reminded Dulles that Eisenhower was in charge until January 20, 1961. Goodpaster did give Dulles permission to brief Kennedy on "operations related to Cuba." Memorandum for the Record by Goodpaster dated November 17, 1960, from the Dwight D. Eisenhower Library.

2 According to James Angleton, Ralph Dungan (Kennedy's White House aide on Latin America), and others.

3 Interviews with Ambassador Edward M. Korry June 1976 through July 2001.

4 Letter written by Korry to the author on May 30, 1999.

5 Series of interviews between 1976 and 1987. Material from these and other interviews about U.S. intelligence activities in Chile appeared in the Wilmington, Delaware, *News Journal* between 1976 and 1982.

6 This insurance component of AID was written into law through a bill sponsored by Senator Jacob Javits (D-NY) creating a small government agency, the Overseas Private Investment Corporation, which is still operating.

7 From the still classified secret history of the Council of the Americas.

8 Author's interview with Enno Hobbing in December 1976. Hobbing left the Council of the Americas in 1975. Officially, he retired from the CIA in 1954. The author has obtained the unpublished history of the council called "More Than Profits, The Story of Business Civic Action in Latin America," written by Hobbing.

9 Lansdale remains a controversial figure among intelligence historians. His life was fictionalized in Graham Greene's *The Quiet American* and William Lederer's *The Ugly American.*

10 Robert Kennedy actually turned down his brother's request that he shift from running the Justice Department to heading the CIA. The president then officially gave Robert responsibility for the entire intelligence community, in addition to his job as attorney general.

CHAPTER 26

1 Corson conducted operations involving assassinations for three presidents.

2 Interview with John Sherwood on December 14, 1990.

3 See David Martin's *Wilderness of Mirrors,* p. 136.

CHAPTER 27

1 Author Henry Hurt did a good job researching Oswald's activities in Japan and his Marine Corps background for Edward Jay Epstein's breakthrough book, *Legend: The Secret History of Lee Harvey Oswald.* Hurt's own book, *Reasonable Doubt,* gives a thorough account of many events surrounding the Kennedy assassination.

2 From extensive interviews in 1977 and 1978.

3 The best account of this period of Oswald's life is in Epstein's book, cited above.

4 Interview with George Kisevalter on April 18, 1988.

5 Series of interviews with Sarkis Soghanalian in 2000 and Edwin P. Wilson in 1991–1992.

6 Interviews with Bruce Solie in 1988.

7 From a series of interviews with Angleton in 1977–1978, 1985.

CHAPTER 28

1 Years later, not long before his death in a more prosaic plane crash, Powers told family members that he believed it was Lee Harvey Oswald who supplied the Soviets with the information they needed to shoot down his U-2. Sarkis Soghanalian said flatly in an interview that "[Edwin] Wilson put a transponder aboard Powers's aircraft that allowed it to be shot down."

2 Interview with Robert Crowley on January 8, 1991.

3 Interview with Paul Garbler on February 4, 1990.

4 John M. (Jack) Maury was a former Reserve officer assigned as the assistant naval attaché in Moscow at the time of Hitler's invasion of Russia in June 1941. He stayed on to help out with the Lend-Lease program and, because he spoke Russian, was advertised within the CIA as an "expert" on all matters Soviet. Maury's attitudes and statements later on about the ineptness of Congress in providing oversight of the CIA did little to help promote better understanding of the real problems of intelligence collection. Maury once said, "One distinguished member apparently has never been quite clear on the difference between Libya, Lebanon, and Liberia, and when answering his questions on what's going on in these countries, a witness can only guess as to which of them he has in mind. . . . The older members also occasionally suffer from a decreasing attention span and, particularly in afternoon sessions, are prone to intermittent dozing. Also, failing faculties sometimes take their toll." These comments and others in like vein can be found in John M. Maury, "CIA and the Congress," *Congressional Record*, Vol. 130 No. 117, September 18, 1984.

5 Interview with George Kisevalter on April 19, 1988. (Richard Kovich declined to be interviewed.)

6 Interview with Paul Garbler on February 4, 1990.

7 Interview with Paul Garbler on February 3, 1990.

CHAPTER 29

1 For a complete examination of the Artamonov case, see William Corson's, Susan and Joseph Trento's *Widows*.

2 Yekaterina Alekseyevna Furtseva was born in 1910 in Vyshniy Volochek, west of Moscow. After studying chemical engineering in Leningrad and Moscow, she went to work as a weaver. By 1930, she was a member of the Communist Party and the secretary of her local Komsomol committee. She worked her way up through the Party until she became a member of the Central Committee in 1956

and a member of the Presidium in 1957. Khrushchev named her Minister of Culture in 1960. She traveled widely, starting with a trip to Peking in 1954 as a member of the Soviet delegation to the fifth anniversary celebration of the Chinese People's Republic. Later trips, mostly with official delegations, took her to Yugoslavia, England, India, Austria, France, Denmark, Italy, Poland, Rumania, Bulgaria, Japan, Mongolia, and finally to the object of her fascination, the United States. She died on October 25, 1974.

3 Interview with George Kisevalter on April 18, 1988.
4 Ibid.
5 Interview with Edward Petty on July 21, 1988.

CHAPTER 30

1 This account is based on interviews with American and British intelligence officers involved in the case.
2 An excellent account of Wynne's activities can be found in Nigel West's *The Circus*.
3 Interview with George Kisevalter on April 18, 1988.
4 See *Prescription for Disaster*, by Joseph Trento and Susan Trento.
5 Penkovsky said that his uncle, Lieutenant General Valentin A. Penkovsky, had gotten on the wrong side of Stalin but was resurrected when the war began to go badly for the Soviets.
6 General Gaponovich.
7 Interview with James Angleton in 1978.

CHAPTER 31

1 Obtained under the Freedom of Information Act.
2 Outlined in great detail in Edward Jay Epstein's *Legend: The Secret Life of Lee Harvey Oswald*.
3 For a detailed version of Nosenko's defection see Epstein, cited above.
4 From Paul Garbler's unpublished manuscript about the Penkovsky case.
5 Interview with Paul Garbler on January 21, 1991.
6 Interview with Paul Garbler on December 20, 1990.
7 Eventually, Wynne was traded for Soviet illegal Gordon Lonsdale, an alias. Lonsdale's true name was Konon Molody.

CHAPTER 32

1 Corson handled the most sensitive missions for President Kennedy, as he had for Presidents Eisenhower and later Johnson. At the time of the Cuban Missile Crisis, he was in India working with the Soviets to stop a war between China and India that had been triggered when an Indian officer went insane from altitude sickness.
2 See David Martin's *Wilderness of Mirrors*, p. 144.
3 Ibid, pp. 188–189.

CHAPTER 33

1   From memoranda and histories available at the Department of State and the John F. Kennedy Library.

2   See p. 286 of *Khrushchev: A Career,* by Edward Crankshaw.

3   From William R. Corson's and Robert Crowley's files on Furtseva.

4   Nikolai Pavlovich Firyubin was born in 1908. He was educated at the Ordzhonikidze Aviation Institute in Moscow and went into aviation engineering. He had joined the Communist Party in 1929, and by 1940 he was party secretary for the Moscow Oblast. Firyubin's diplomatic career began with a posting as counselor to the Soviet Embassy in Czechoslovakia in 1953; he soon became the ambassador to Czechoslovakia, and in 1955 he became ambassador to Yugoslavia, where he signed the Soviet–Yugoslav agreement on cooperation in peaceful uses of atomic energy—the first of many international agreements he would help negotiate. In 1957 he became deputy minister of foreign affairs and was given the rank of Ambassador Extraordinary and Plenipotentiary. He headed the Soviet delegations to talks in, among other places, Afghanistan, Australia, Albania, Poland, Hungary, Pakistan, and Ceylon, and to various UN meetings in Geneva. In 1966 Brezhnev named him secretary general to the Policy Advisory Committee of the Participating Members of Warsaw Pact. He died on February 12, 1983.

   Source: *Prominent Personalities in the USSR,* edited by Edward L. Crowley, Andrew I. Lebed, and Dr. Heinrich E. Schulz.

5   Frol Romanovich Kozlov was born on August 18, 1908, in the Ryazan Oblast. Educated at technical institutes in Leningrad and Moscow, he became a metallurgical engineer, working at plants in Kasimov and Izhevsk. He joined the Communist Party in 1926 and served on his factory Komsomol committees. From 1941 to 1944 he coordinated arms production and deliveries to the front. After the war he worked in the Kuybyshev Oblast, and by 1949 he was Party organizer at the Kirov Plant in Leningrad and an official of the Leningrad Oblast Party Committee. In 1952 he was named to the Central Committee of the CPSU, and in 1962 to the Presidium. From 1958 to 1960 he was first deputy chairman (directly under Khrushchev) of the Soviet Council of Ministers, and from 1960 to 1964, secretary to the Central Committee of the CPSU. He died on January 30, 1965.

6   From a series of interviews with James Angleton.

7   Edward Jay Epstein's *Legend: The Secret Life of Lee Harvey Oswald,* p. 171.

8   James Jesus Angleton interview.

9   In Mexico, whoever the man who called himself Oswald was, he presented detailed accounts of all his protests, interviews, and arrests in New Orleans to try to get an immediate visa to Cuba. After he had made three visits to the Cuban consulate, he became increasingly unpleasant, Cuban officials asked him to leave. On November 3, in Dallas, Oswald wrote another letter to the Soviet Embassy in

Washington, asking for their help in getting a visa to Cuba. In the letter he indicated that he had not used his real name in Mexico City.

10 Barghoorn had been a consultant with the CIA, which was probably the pretext for the arrest.

11 See p. 845 of *The Public Papers of the Presidents: John F. Kennedy 1963*.

12 Interview with Paul Garbler on February 3, 1990.

13 Interview with Quentin Johnson on January 25, 1991.

14 From a partially released CIA memorandum on OPERATION MONGOOSE.

CHAPTER 34

1 Interview with Donald E. Denesyla on February 15, 1991.

2 Photographs of the car were taken that day. In his book, *Reasonable Doubt*, Henry Hurt presents detailed information about other possible Cuban involvement in the assassination.

3 CIA documents regarding Casas, dated January 24, 1964 (CIA 491-201); January 25, 1964 (CIA 491-201); and January 27, 1964 (CIA 510-199).

4 CIA report titled "Information Possibly Connected with the Assassination," dated November 2, 1964 (CIA 979-929 AX). The routing sheet is CIA document number 979-929 AX.

5 Interview with William R. Corson on January 10, 1991.

6 Conversations President Johnson had with senior senators, including Richard Russell of Georgia, reflect this fear.

7 Lyndon Johnson Papers, The Johnson Library, University of Texas.

8 Daniel Schorr's *Clearing the Air*, p. 147.

9 From a series of interviews with William R. Corson between 1988 and 1991.

10 Quentin Johnson became chief of station in Copenhagen.

11 Interview with Leonard McCoy on August 4, 1988.

12 Interview with Ed Petty on July 14, 1988.

CHAPTER 35

1 From a series of interviews with Sam Pappich in 1988–89.

2 From a series of interviews with Robert T. Crowley.

3 Phillip Knightley's *The Master Spy* gives an excellent account of this part of Philby's life.

4 From the FBI, through the Freedom of Information Act.

5 Corson became acquainted with White during more than a dozen joint U.S./British operations.

6 According to his KGB file.

CHAPTER 36

1 See "Yuri Nosenko, CIA" by Leonard V. McCoy, published in the fall of 1987 in the *Central Intelligence Retirees' Association Newsletter*.

2 See "The Mysterious Murder of JFK's Mistress" by Phillip Nobile and Ron Rosenbaum, in *New Times Magazine*, July 9, 1976.

3 See the very complete biography, *Mary Meyer: A Very Private Woman*, by Nina Burleigh.

CHAPTER 37

1 Interview with William Branigan on January 27, 1988, and with James Wooten on March 23, 1988.

2 Interview with William R. Corson on February 17, 1991.

3 See Martin's *Wilderness of Mirrors*, chapter titled "No Innocent Explanation."

4 Interview with George Kisevalter on April 18, 1988.

5 Ibid.

6 Interview with Paul Garbler on February 24, 1991.

7 Interview with William R. Corson on January 10, 1991.

CHAPTER 38

1 This account is based on interviews with Eleonore Orlov. Lt. Col. Alexander Sogolow died before I could get his version of these events. Nick Kozlov declined to comment because he still works for the United States government.

2 Interview with Sam Wilson on June 14, 1988. At the same time Orlov was going after Kozlov, so were the Russians. According to Wilson, "the Soviets endeavored on several occasions to get to Nikolay Vasilovich Kozlov and either recruit him or get him to return home. . . . His uncle was asking about him and his uncle was a very influential man and all would be forgiven."

CHAPTER 39

1 Interview with Paul Garbler on February 24, 1991.

2 Interview with Paul Garbler on February 2, 1990.

3 Interview with Eleonore Orlov on July 10, 1988.

4 Interview with William Colby on June 6, 1988.

5 Interview with John Sherwood on December 3, 1991.

CHAPTER 40

1 Ironically, it was Khrushchev, not Brezhnev, who recognized that the Soviets were capable of great technological achievement. In the mid-1950s, the first Soviet ICBMs shocked the West with their enormous lifting power.

2 As a major in the Inspectorate Division of the First Directorate (Foreign Intelligence Operations), Kozlov had hardly penetrated the KGB power structure.

3 See chapter twelve of *Widows*, by William R. Corson, Susan Trento and Joseph Trento.
   As Angleton later quoted Louis, KGB head Semichastny had informed Furtseva that Brezhnev had had her house bugged, and so no important conversations

were ever held inside the house. Louis, the sometime Soviet middleman to Western journalists, was Furtseva's neighbor and longtime family friend; his presence in her house that afternoon was not unusual.

4 Fears paralleling those held by President Johnson, as we have seen.

5 Interview with Courtland Jones on April 14, 1988.

6 Murphy's abandonment of Kovich and Garbler only delayed Angleton's move against him. Angleton claimed in a 1978 interview that he had cleared his notification to the French with Richard Helms. Others at the CIA believed that after Angleton had spoken to the French, Helms was forced to accept Angleton's action. It was a fait accompli.

7 Kingsley, despite later protestations, never interfered with Angleton's mole investigation or made any attempt to protect anyone in his division. In fact, Kingsley did not speak out against Angleton's actions until years later, after Angleton's death.

8 Interview with William Branigan on January 27, 1988.

CHAPTER 41

1 From the secret files of the FBI agent in charge of the Kozlov case.

2 Interview with William Branigan on January 27, 1988.

3 Interview with Courtland Jones on April 14, 1988.

4 Elbert "Bert" Turner declined a request for an interview.

5 Interview with Bruce Solie on January 28, 1988.

6 From his FBI debriefing interview.

7 Interviews with William Branigan on January 27, 1988; with Courtland Jones on April 14, 1988; and with William Lander on February 27, 1988.

8 Interview with Paul Garbler on February 3, 1990.

9 An NIP (National Intelligence Potential) message from the field is guaranteed to get the attention of headquarters, for the obvious reason that the individual so named may be able to shed light on the critical question: "Are hostilities imminent?" No matter the "potential" of an NIP case, there are procedures to be followed to prevent false information or disinformation from entering the intelligence system. If these procedures are not followed, there is no telling where the mischief will lead. In the Nick Shadrin case, the NIP procedures were violated from the very beginning, and the results were totally predictable.

10 Interview with Leonard V. McCoy on July 27, 1988. McCoy insists that "the Soviets have never sent an intelligence officer to penetrate the CIA" and said he took the step of appealing to James Angleton to bring Shadrin into the United States, because "I was at the end of my rope. I really thought there was nothing more we could do to get this guy here."

11 Interview with Leonard V. McCoy on January 21, 1988.

12 Shadrin's contract as a special consultant entitled him to be compensated at the equivalent of a GS-11, Step 5. This amounted to approximately $9,000 per annum in 1960. The GS-11 status, roughly equivalent to the military rank of lieutenant commander, enabled Admiral Rufus Taylor to use Shadrin as a cat's paw in some of the internecine battles in naval intelligence as well as the intelligence community at large. Shadrin was identified as a former Soviet Naval Officer with unique qualifications in naval science, tactics, marine engineering, and ordnance, both conventional and nuclear.

Nick and Ewa Shadrin purchased a modest Arlington house with a payment for his services from the CIA and lived like any suburban working couple. Shadrin's $9,000 salary barely covered Ewa's dental school expenses and the costs of setting up housekeeping.

When Shadrin was transferred to the Office of Naval Intelligence (ONI) after a year and a half with the CIA, opposition came from William Abbott, the civilian head of counterintelligence at ONI. Abbott was convinced that bringing a defector into the core of ONI was bad policy. But since Angleton himself had cleared Shadrin, Abbott's objections were ignored.

13 Interviews with Ewa Shadrin.

14 The FBI had one major problem with Shadrin. Since he had become a naturalized American citizen in 1965, the FBI had no leverage, legitimate or otherwise, to pressure him into accepting their presumably very dangerous assignment to become a "counterspy" for the Bureau. Shadrin could have told the FBI he simply had no interest in the matter, and that would have been the end of it. When Shadrin agreed to become an FBI double agent without a moment's hesitation, his FBI handlers should have realized something was wrong.

15 Interview with Eugene C. Peterson on July 28, 1988. Peterson was William Branigan's assistant at the time of the KITTY HAWK approach in June, 1966.

16 The KGB feared that they could be arrested if they dealt with the FBI, since the FBI has the power of arrest, and the CIA does not. KITTY HAWK insisted that he deal with the CIA only.

17 According to Courtland Jones, prior to the information from KITTY HAWK, the only evidence the Bureau had that Orlov had gone to the Soviet Embassy was from a surveillance team that had been watching Orlov.

18 Interview with William Branigan.

19 See chapter 4.

20 At their final meeting in a supermarket parking lot not far from Shadrin's home, KITTY HAWK gave Shadrin an envelope. In it were two letters—one from his wife in Moscow (Admiral Gorshkov's daughter) and one from his son. There also were pictures of both of them. His son was as tall as he and looked like Nick when he first became a Soviet naval officer. Shadrin read the letters, studied the pictures, and then, as the rules were set down, returned them to Kozlov.

21 John T. Funkhouser, who debriefed Shadrin when he first defected, had been a designer with the old Navy Bureau of Ships. Shadrin's appearance in 1959 dramatically enhanced Funkhouser's and the CIA's knowledge of the Soviet Navy. Now, Funkhouser was assigned to supply the information Shadrin needed to feed back to the KGB in support of the KITTY HAWK operation. Funkhouser acted as a conduit to Shadrin for U.S. Naval secrets that came from the Pentagon through the CIA's Office of Strategic Research.

22 Interview with Peter Kapusta in March, 1988.

23 Interview with Lt. Gen. Samuel V. Wilson on June 14, 1988.

24 From a series of interviews with James J. Angleton.

CHAPTER 42

1 From a series of interviews in January 1999.

2 See page 9 of Neil Sheehan's *A Bright Shining Lie: John Paul Vann and America in Vietnam.*

3 See Carlyle Thayer's monograph, "War by Other Means."

4 See the "Strategic Hamlets" chapter of William E. Colby's *Honorable Men: My Life in the CIA.*

5 Neil Sheehan, in *A Bright Shining Lie*, explained: "Vietnamese converts to Catholicism had been used by the French as a fifth column to penetrate precolonial Vietnam and then had been rewarded by the colonizer for their collaboration. They were popularly regarded as a foreign-inspired, 'un-Vietnamese' religious sect. With the French leaving, the Catholics were naturally seeking another foreign protector."

6 Madame Nhu toured the United States in the fall of 1963 and further alienated the American people with her unbelievably callous statements about the opposition.

7 Articles from the Diem controlled press in Saigon "were clearly coming from Dien's office" according to a 1963 State Department Cable.

8 From a series of interviews with Lucien Conien.

9 Dunn, who retired to Washington as a lobbyist, refused this author's attempts to interview him right up to his death in 1998.

10 From a January 1999 interview with William R. Corson.

CHAPTER 43

1 From official rosters obtained by the author.

2 See p. 12 of Frank Snepp's *Decent Interval.*

3 A description of Wilson's accomplishments as it appears on a Web site for the Army Ranger Hall of Fame: Lieutenant General Samuel V. Wilson is inducted into the Ranger Hall of Fame for heroism, extraordinary achievement, and continued service to his country and the special operations community. General Wilson

began his special operations service with the Office of Strategic Services and subsequently with the 5307th Composite Unit (Provisional), popularly known as Merrill's Marauders, in the China-Burma-India Theater during World War II. As a highly decorated combat veteran, General Wilson returned to the United States, where he entered the Army's Foreign Area Specialist Training Program. Upon completion of the program, he was assigned to various tours involving the Iron Curtain countries and the Soviet Union. His expertise was recognized quickly and he was assigned to several high-level positions within the Department of Defense and Department of State. As a general officer, some of his assignments included: Assistant Division Commander (Operations), 82d Airborne Division; United States Defense Attaché to the Soviet Union; Deputy to the Director of Central Intelligence; and Director of the Defense Intelligence Agency. General Wilson's expertise in the area of special operations has been recognized and he remains a consultant to the Secretary of Defense and the Congress for matters concerning both special operations and intelligence.

4 Interview with William R. Corson on March 13, 1991.
5 Interview with John Sherwood on December 3, 1990.
6 Ibid.
7 Interview with General Loan in 1984.

CHAPTER 44

1 Except Harvey himself, who was never permitted to serve in Vietnam.
2 Interview with Edwin P. Wilson on May 26, 1991.
3 Interview with Edwin P. Wilson on March 16, 1991.
4 Published in 1972 by Harper and Row.
5 From an interview between Frank Snepp and Charles Lewis, then of ABC's *20-20*.
6 According to Stanley Jeffers, who served under Weisz at Vienna Station.
7 From p. 13 of Frank Snepp's *Decent Interval*.

CHAPTER 45

1 Interview with Peter Kapusta on November 22, 1990.
2 From a report prepared for John Limond Hart when he was Chief of Western Europe.
3 According to Kapusta, the CIA never cracked the general.
4 Interview with George Kisevalter on April 18, 1988.
5 Interview with William R. Corson on March 26, 1991.
6 Interview with John Sherwood on December 10, 1990.
7 Interview with Wally Driver on October 18, 1990.
8 See p. 249 of *Slow Burn*, by Orrin DeForest.
9 See p. 288 of Frank Snepp's *Decent Interval*.

CHAPTER 46

1 See chapter 25.

2 Interview with Ralph Dungan in November, 1976.

3 Interview for the Wilmington, Delaware, *News Journal* in October, 1976.

4 Series of interviews with Edward M. Korry between 1976 and 2001 and his personal letters, papers, and records.

5 From a 1968 cable from Korry to the Department of State.

6 Interview with Korry in 1983 for a Cable News Network broadcast.

7 From Dungan's testimony before the Senate Select Committee on Intelligence in 1975.

8 From CIA document #39979, dated March 30, 1972, prepared for the Director of Central Intelligence and giving the history of the Castro–Allende relationship.

9 Interview with John Sherwood on December 4, 1990.

CHAPTER 47

1 Interview with William Corson on January 14, 1991.

2 Famous Washington spy attorney Plato Cacherous was the prosecutor in the case Corson investigated. Godell ended up living in prosperity in Newport Beach, California. Ironically he and Corson died in the same year.

3 Korry presented the full text of this plan in Chile during a visit in 1996. It was the first time it had been disclosed to the people of Chile.

4 During the Allende years, Kendall gave Edwards a job in the United States as a vice president of Fritolay, a subsidiary of Pepsico.

5 This offer came to light during the election campaign, and the convention wound up taking place in Miami Beach.

6 "Subject: Special Mandate from the President on Chile."

7 Obtained under the Freedom of Information Act, Message 14648, dated September 28, 1970.

8 From Page 16 CIA Document #41388, dated November 16, 1970.

9 Ibid.

10 From CIA Document #41391, dated November 18, 1970 Page 22.

11 From CIA Document #41392, dated November 18, 1970 Page 20.

12 From CIA document #10949, dated October 28, 1970.

13 October 12, 1970 classified message "CITE HEADQUARTERS."

14 From a CIA document titled "Track II" dated October 14, 1970.

15 CIA document, dated October 15, 1970 entitled "Track II."

16 From a CIA document dated October 16, 1970 entitled "Track II."

17 Ibid.

18 "CITE HEADQUARTERS" message dated October 16, 1970.

CHAPTER 48

1 Korry supplied the author a copy of the final draft.

2 Korry said the newsman had come to Chile directly after he had published an interview with Nixon in the *Times* and had talked to Kissinger. Years later, Korry learned that Sulzberger had seen Helms as well. See "Killers" from the February 24, 1980 Sunday Wilmington, Delaware *News Journal.*

3 Based on FBI documents and interviews with FBI officials including Robert Scherer, who investigated the CONDOR operation for the FBI.

4 From FOIA documents released by the CIA on Chile.

5 Zylka was indicted in 2001 for bilking investors of the Evergreen Mutual Fund of Florida for loans made to mines he and his family controlled.

6 Sy Hersh was so disturbed the Wilmington *News Journal*, a medium-sized paper in Delaware, was examining his reporting on Chile that he called the reporter and said to him: "You have no business reporting on this story. You should turn your sources over to me . . . I work for the *New York Times,* this is our story . . . No one will believe you. You will be laughed out of journalism." The author was the reporter Hersh called.

7 I first requested these documents from the CIA in 1976 when I broke the Korry story as a newspaperman. It was not until 12 years later that the CIA more or less honored my request, sending me thousands of pages, many of which had been totally blanked out. With the cooperation of a number of former CIA officials, I have managed to fill in the blanks.

CHAPTER 49

1 Interview with Felix Bloch on April 4, 1991.

2 James Bamford is the author of the groundbreaking book *The Puzzle Palace*, about the NSA, and the producer of numerous investigative television pieces on national security.

3 Interview with Felix Bloch on April 4, 1991.

4 Sherwood is particularly sensitive to the issue, because he was accused and later cleared of being anti-Semitic.

5 Later, Wilson returned to Washington as William Colby's liaison to the general intelligence community.

CHAPTER 50

1 Interview with Paul Garbler on February 2, 1990.

2 Bill Harvey's last appearance on the public scene was his testimony on OPERATION MONGOOSE before the Church Committee in 1975. He died of a heart attack on June 7, 1976.

3 The author spent many hours discussing Angleton with Colby during a series of interviews from 1976 through 1994.

4 Interview with William Mazzocco in September 1988.

CHAPTER 51

1 Series of interviews with Paul Garbler between 1990 and 2000.

2 Interview with Paul Garbler on February 3, 1990.

3 Furtseva's fatal "heart attack," a surprise to all who knew her, came after a scandal involving misappropriated funds for the construction of yet another dacha.

4 George Weisz's employment history is taken from federal personnel form 171, which he prepared in 1981.

5 FBI documents show that George Weisz received his nuclear "Q" level clearance on March 7, 1975.

6 Interview with Admiral Harvey Lyon, former Director of Safeguards and Security at the Department of Energy, on April 17, 1991.

7 Weisz also continued to play a major role in servicing TRIGON, a high-level Soviet Foreign Ministry official recruited in Bogotá, Colombia, under the direction of Ted Shackley. TRIGON was Aleksandr Dmitryevich Ogorodnik. He had been sexually entrapped by the CIA while on assignment in Bogotá and blackmailed into becoming a mole. TRIGON was considered a very important agent because of his job in the Global Affairs section of the Foreign Ministry.

CHAPTER 52

1 Based on interviews with CIA officer Stanley Jeffers, FBI Agent James Wooten and Wooten's report on the case, the secret records of the President's Intelligence Advisory Board review of the Shadrin case as well as for attribution interviews with other participants in the operation.

2 *CIA Diary: Inside the Company* was published in June 1975.

3 Robert T. Dumaine, under official cover as an embassy political officer, was present at this meeting. Dumaine, in Vienna since August 1973, was in charge of Soviet operations there. Previously, he served with Sam Wilson in Moscow, where he received high ratings as acting chief of station.

4 According to extensive interviews with his wife, work associates, and friends.

5 Interview with Frank Steinert on March 23, 1988.

6 Had the FBI and CIA better examined the bait they used to reel in KITTY HAWK, they might have realized there were dozens of warnings something was wrong. Shadrin and his companion had failed their polygraph tests when they first defected. His CIA-created marriage to Ewa was not a happy one. The FBI never took the precaution of polygraphing Shadrin as they usually did routinely with double agents they ran jointly with Army intelligence. Had they done that, they might have realized the magnitude of the intelligence disaster they cosponsored for nine years.

7 One of Weisz's colleagues was amazed several years later when he traveled to Vienna with Weisz to meet a prominent Viennese resident. The manager of the Bristol Hotel's eyes lit up when he saw them. Weisz's colleague, thinking the reaction

was to his Austrian friend, watched the manager bypass them and enthusiastically greet George Weisz.

8 Interviews with Stanley Jeffers in August 1988.

9 Years later, Francis Meehan, who was deputy chief of mission in Vienna at the time, told Ewa Shadrin's lawyer, Richard Copaken, that the Shadrin disappearance was a matter of a man wanting to go home. Meehan said he had learned this from former East German lawyer Wolfgang Vogel, who brokered many spy swaps between West and East. Meehan, who later became U.S. Ambassador to East Germany, trusted Vogel, who was godfather to one of his children.

When the 1989 book, *Widows,* was published, revealing that Shadrin returned to Moscow voluntarily, Copaken received a series of mysterious telephone calls from individuals who said they were connected to Israeli intelligence and who confirmed that Shadrin had been part of a trade between the KGB and Mossad.

10 From interviews with John Sherwood and Robert Crowley.

11 According to Stanley Jeffers.

12 Knoche went on to say: "We were invited down to Plains two or three days after the election. George and I and Dan Murphy (who was the admiral that was in charge of the Intelligence Community staff) and a couple of others flew down to Plains. We were to have a three-hour session with Carter and [Vice President–elect] Mondale to brief them on the state of the world as we saw it. And I was going to describe some of the covert activities that we had underway. We had three hours down there with them which turned into eight. We were there well into the evening. A fascinating session. And when we arrived on the scene, George asked if he could see the two of them (Carter and Mondale) privately before we got into the briefing, and they were gone about ten or fifteen minutes. On their way back, Bush told me that what he had told them was that he wanted to resign effective inauguration day. He wanted them to know it. And they . . . That was perfectly acceptable to them. And I told George how I felt about it. I said . . . the . . . thing is, you have done the very thing that none of us wanted to see associated with this, you have politicized it. You have, in effect, opened it up to a political assignment for the new administration. And he recognized that. Life is a series of ups and downs, and you have to calculate where you come out in between the up side and the down side. And so that's what he did."

13 Theodore Sorensen was Carter's first choice, but he proved to be too controversial to get confirmed by the Senate.

CHAPTER 53

1 Personal correspondence between Shadrin and Turner obtained by the author.

2 According to the FBI, Rudolph Herrman is still in protective custody.

3 Interview with retired Army Captain Noel Jones in 1988.

Chapter 54

1 Interview with Milton Wolf on January 22, 1991.

2 Cable dated August 11, 1978, obtained under the Freedom of Information Act.

3 The interview with Inman took place in his Pentagon office in the spring of 1979, when I was the national reporter for the Wilmington *News Journal* in Delaware.

4 According to Robert Crowley, Turner was able to blame his routing of the Operations Directorate on "cost reduction exercises begun under Colby."

5 Kerr was interviewed in the spring of 1988 but, through his secretary, refused a request for a second interview.

6 Interview with William Bartells on February 29, 1988.

7 Interview with Admiral Harvey Lyon on April 17, 1991.

8 See chapter 7.

9 FBI teletype dated January 5, 1979 from Webster to field offices in Washington, Alexandria, Baltimore, New York, and San Francisco.

10 Richmond, Virginia, Field Office file 116-18130 of the FBI's investigation of George Weisz.

Chapter 55

1 From Weisz's government personnel file.

2 Interview with Samuel T. McDowell on May 4, 1988.

3 Interview with Leonard M. Brenner on April 17, 1988.

4 From Weisz's personal address books.

5 Interview with Samuel T. McDowell on May 4, 1988.

6 See the chapter, "The Art of Adventurism" in Dan Raviv and Yossi Melman's *Every Spy a Prince*.

7 NEST activities are top secret. Information about this incident was found in a letter dated March 6, 1979, from FBI Director William H. Webster to Weisz, congratulating him on the success of the NEST team he dispatched. The letter was obtained under the Freedom of Information Act.

8 Letter dated September 11, 1980 from William A. Bayan, then head of the FBI's Technical Services Division.

9 Interview with Herbert Kouts in February 1988.

10 This man is still in the Senate and has asked that his name not be used.

11 See p. 253 of Joseph E. Persico's *Casey*.

12 Series of interviews with Sarkis Soghanalian and interviews with intelligence officials of the Iraqi government conducted in Badhdad in 1984.

13 Interview with Robert Crowley on April 25, 1991. According to Crowley, the damage assessment team also included Berlin Base veteran Hugh Montgomery. After his stint as Vienna Station Chief preceding Weisz, Montgomery was briefly given a top security post at the Department of State. He quietly left that job when

sensitive State Department files began showing up on schoolyard playgrounds and at Lorton Prison outside Washington, D.C.

14 Interview with Britt Snider in the spring of 1988.

15 From the personal papers of George Weisz.

16 Interview with General Stilwell on March 9, 1988.

17 Interview with Tom Tucker on April 26, 1991.

CHAPTER 56

1 Interview with Robert Kupperman.

2 Maryland State Police report containing the interview with Ms. Thomas.

3 Interview with Suzanne Gottlieb on February 12, 1988.

4 According to Dale Young.

5 Interview with Mr. and Mrs. Brunner in March 1988.

6 Interview with Carroll Stottlemyer on April 17, 1991.

7 Maryland State Police number 20936, dated December 14, 1982, nearly a month after the incident.

8 Interview with Dale Young.

9 Interviews with George Weisz's mother, sister, nephew, and niece on February 12, 1988.

10 Maryland State Police Report #20936.

11 Ibid.

12. Ibid.

13 Ibid.

14 Maryland State Police Final Report on the Death of George Weisz.

15 George Weisz's Post Mortem Examination, case number 82-2182.

16 Interview with Dr. Hormez R. Guard on April 26, 1991.

17 There was nothing new in the Maryland State Police pushing Dr. Guard for a suicide determination. In 1978, they pushed for suicide in the case of suspected CIA mole John Arthur Paisley. Dr. Guard was in the office when Paisley was brought in. "I was convinced he [the man thought to be Paisley] was done away with . . . ," Guard later said. "I was shocked when Dr. Russell Fisher, the State Medical Examiner, refused my request to handle the Paisley case, and assigned it to Dr. Steven Adams, a young resident in training. . . . He [Adams] came to me for help, saying he was in over his head, but Fisher made it clear he didn't want me to have anything to do with the case." In the end, Adams identified the corpse, a man four inches shorter and some thirty pounds lighter, as John Arthur Paisley. It was also clear to Dr. Guard that the fatal gunshot wound was not self-inflicted. In light of the public humiliation the State Police suffered over the Paisley case, their actions in the Weisz case seem even more inexcusable and puzzling.

CHAPTER 57

1 Douglas J. MacEachin, deputy director for Intelligence at the CIA from March 1993 until June 1995, joined the Agency in 1965 and for 24 years worked mainly on research and analysis of Soviet and European security affairs. He was director of the Office of Soviet Analysis from 1984 until March 1989, when he became special assistant to the Director of Central Intelligence for Arms Control.

2 The *Washington Post,* Sunday, March 11, 2001, p. A-15.

3 Interview with William R. Corson in January 2000.

4 Series of interviews with William R. Corson in November 1998.

5 Noel Jones, the Army captain who oversaw GRAPHIC IMAGE, the operation that ended with Ralph Sigler's murder, suspected that FBI counterintelligence was out of control from the mid-1970s on.

EPILOGUE

1 *Battleground Berlin: The CIA vs. KGB in the Cold War,* by David E. Murphy, Sergei A. Kondrashev, and George Bailey.

2 Eleonore Orlov says she heard the name Igor Orlov for the first time when her husband was sworn in as a U.S. citizen.

3 See chapter 2. Mitrokhin did not have access to Beria's most secret file.

4 Including his service as a lieutenant in Soviet intelligence from August 1941 until he was wounded and captured by the Germans in December 1943.

5 See pp. 148–149 of *The Sword and the Shield.*

6 See chapter 39.

7 Interview with Eleonore Orlov on September 16, 1999.

8 See chapter 40.

9 *The Private Life of Kim Philby: The Moscow Years,* by Rufina Philby with Mayden Peake and Mikhail Lyubimov.

SELECT

BIBLIOGRAPHY

———————

Abramson, Rudy. *Spanning the Century: The Life of W. Averell Harriman 1891-1986.* New York: Morrow, 1992.

Agee, Philip. *Inside the Company: CIA Diary. New York*: Stonehill, 1975.

Andrew, Christopher. *For The President's Eyes Only: Secret Intelligence and the American Presidency from Washington to Bush.* New York: Harper Collins, 1995.

Andrew, Christopher, and Oleg Gordievsky. *KGB: The Inside Story.* New York: Harper Collins, 1990.

Andrew, Christopher, and Vasili Mitrokhin. *The Sword and the Shield: The Metrokhin Archive and the Secret History of the KGB.* New York: Basic Books, 1999.

Ash, Timothy Garton. *The File: A Personal History.* New York: Random House, 1997.

Baedeker's Berlin. New York: Prentice Hall Press, 1987, 1988, 1990.

Bamford, James. *Body of Secrets: Anatomy of the Ultra-Secret National Security Agency–From the Cold War Through the Dawn of a New Century.* New York: Doubleday, 2001.

Beschloss, Michael R. *The Crisis Years: Kennedy and Khrushchev, 1960–1963.* New York: Edward Burlingame Books, 1991.

Burleigh, Nina. *A Very Private Woman: The Life and Unsolved Murder of Presidential Mistress Mary Meyer.* New York: Bantam Books, 1998.

Bush, George. *All the Best, George Bush: My Life in Letters and Other Writings.* New York: Scribner, 1999.

Chavchavadze, David. *Crowns and Trenchcoats: A Russian Prince in the CIA.* New York: Altantic International Publishers, 1990.

Colby, William E. *Honorable Men: My Life in the CIA.* New York: Simon and Schuster, 1978.

Colitt, Leslie. *Spymaster: The Definitive Story of Markus Wolf.* Reading, MA: Addison-Wesley, 1995.

Cookridge, E.H. *Gehlen: Spy of the Century.* New York: Random House, 1971.

Copeland, Miles. *The Game of Nations: The Immorality of Power Politics.* New York: Simon and Schuster, 1969.

Corn, David. *Blond Ghost: Ted Shackley and the CIA's Crusades.* New York: Simon and Schuster, 1994.

Corson, William R. *The Armies of Ignorance.* New York: Dial Press, 1977.

Corson, William R., and Susan B. Trento and Joseph J. Trento. *Widows: Three Spies and the Wives They Left Behind.* New York: Crown, 1989.

Costello, John, and Oleg Tsarev. *Deadly Illusions: The KGB Orlov Dossier Reveals Stalin's Master Spy.* New York: Crown, 1993.

Crankshaw, Edward. *Khrushchev: A Career.* New York: Viking, 1966.

Crowley, Edward L., and Andrei Lebed and Heinrich E. Schulz, eds. *Prominent Personalities in the USSR.* Metuchen, NJ: Scarecrow Press, 1968.

Crozier, Brian. *The Rise and Fall of the Soviet Empire.* Rocklin, CA: Prima/Forum, 1999.

DeForest, Orrin. *Slow Burn: The Rise and Fall of American Intelligence in Vietnam.* New York: Simon and Schuster, 1990.

Deriaben, Peter, and T. H. Bagley. *The KGB: Masters of the Soviet Union.* New York: Hippocrene Books, 1990.

Dorril, Stephen. *MI6: Inside the Covert World of Her Majesty's Secret Intelligence Service.* New York: Free Press, 2000.

Dungan, Nelson V. N. *Secret Agent X Counterintelligence Corps.* New York: Vantage Press, 1989.

Epstein, Jay Edward. *Deception: The Invisible War Between the KGB and the CIA.* New York: Simon and Schuster, 1989.

———. *Legend: The Secret Life of Lee Harvey Oswald.* New York: McGraw Hill/ Reader's Digest Press, 1978.

Garbler, Florence Fitzsimmons. *CIA Wife.* Santa Barbara, CA: Fithian Press, 1994.

Gehlen, Reinhard. *The Service: The Memoirs of General Reinhard Gehlen.* New York: Popular Library, 1972.

Goulden, Joseph C. *Fit to Print: A.M. Rosenthal and His New York Times.* Secaucus, NJ: Lyle Stuart, 1988.

Greene, Graham. *The Quiet American.* New York: Viking Press, 1956.

Grose, Peter. *Gentleman Spy: The Life of Allen Dulles.* Boston: Houghton Mifflin, 1994.

———. *Operation Rollback: America's Secret War Behind the Iron Curtain.* Boston: Houghton Mifflin, 2000.

Hamilton, Norman R. *Accused: R. Craig Smith: The Spy Left Out in the Cold.* Bountiful, UT: Horizon Publishers, 1987.

Hersh, Burton. *The Old Boys: The American Elite and the Origins of the CIA.* New York: Scribner, 1992.

Holober, Frank. *Raiders of the China Coast: CIA Covert Operations During the Korean War* Annapolis, MD: The Naval Insitute Press, 1999.

Hood, William. *Mole: The True Story of the First Russian Spy to Become an American Counterspy.* New York: Ballantine Books, 1983.

Hougan, Jim. *Spooks.* New York: Morrow, 1978.

Hunt, Linda. *Secret Agenda: The United States Government, Nazi Scientists, and Project Paperclip.* New York: St. Martin's Press, 1991.

Hurt, Henry. *Reasonable Doubt: An Investigation into the Assassination of President John F. Kennedy.* New York: Holt, Rinehart, and Winston, 1985.

Knightley, Phillip. *The Master Spy.* New York: Knopf, 1989.

Kornbluh, Peter, ed. *Bay of Pigs Declassified.* New York: The New Press, 1998.

Lederer, William, and Eugene Burdick. *The Ugly American.* New York: Norton, 1958.

Mangold, Tom. *Cold Warrior: James Jesus Angleton: The CIA's Master Spy Hunter.* New York: Simon and Schuster, 1991.

Martin, David. *Wilderness of Mirrors.* New York: Harper and Row, 1980.

Mitrovich, Gregory. *Undermining the Kremlin: America's Strategy to Subvert the Soviet Bloc, 1947–1956.* Cornell, NY: Cornell University Press, 2000.

Murphy, David E., and Sergei A. Kondrashev and George Baily. *Battleground Berlin: CIA vs. KGB in the Cold War.* New Haven: Yale University Press, 1997.

Newman, John M. *JFK and Vietnam: Deception, Intrigue, and the Struggle for Power.* New York: Warner Books, 1992.

Parrish, Thomas. *Berlin in the Balance 1945–1949: The Blockade, the Airlift, the First Major Battle of the Cold War.* Reading, MA: Addison-Wesley, 1998.

Perry, Mark. *ECLIPSE: The Last Days of the CIA.* New York: William Morrow, 1992.

Philby, Kim. *My Silent War.* New York: Grove Press, 1968.

Philby, Rufina, with Hayden Peake and Mikhail Lyubimov. *The Private Life of Kim Philby: The Moscow Years.* Moscow: St. Ermin's Press, 1999.

Pincher, Chapman. *Their Trade Is Treachery.* New York: Bantam Books, 1982.

Powers, Thomas. *The Man Who Kept the Secrets: Richard Helms and the CIA.* New York: Knopf, 1979.

Raviv, Dan, and Yossi Melman. *Every Spy a Prince.* Boston: Houghton Mifflin, 1990.

The Public Papers of the Presidents: John F. Kennedy 1963. Washington, D.C.: U.S. Government Printing Office, 1964.

Riebling, Mark. *Wedge: The Secret War Between the FBI and CIA.* New York: Knopf, 1994.

Romerstein, Herbert, and Eric Breindel. *The Venona Secrets: Exposing Soviet Espionage and America's Traitors.* Washington, D.C.: Regnery, 2000.

Russell, Dick. *The Man Who Knew Too Much.* New York: Carrol and Graph Publishers/Richard Gallen, 1992.

Sayer, Ian, and Douglas Botting. *America's Secret Army: The Untold Story of the Counterintelligence Corps.* New York: Franklin Watts, 1989.

Schorr, Daniel. *Clearing the Air.* Boston: Houghton Mifflin, 1977.

Seale, Patrick, and Maureen McConville. *Philby: The Long Road to Moscow.* Middlesex, England: Penguin Books, 1978.

Sheehan, Neil. *A Bright Shining Lie: John Paul Vann and America in Vietnam.* New York: Random House, 1988.

Snepp, Frank. *Decent Interval.* New York: Random House, 1978.

Thayer, Carlyle. *War by Other Means.* Monograph. Allen and Unwin, 1989.

Trento, Joseph, and Susan Trento. *Prescription for Disaster.* New York: Crown, 1988.

Warner, Roger. *Backfire: The CIA's Secret War in Laos and Its Link to the War in Vietnam.* New York: Simon and Schuster, 1995.

Weinstein, Allen, and Alexander Vassiliev. *The Haunted Wood: Soviet Espionage in America—The Stalin Era.* New York: Random House, 1999.

West, Nigel. *The Circus: MI5 Operations 1945–1972.* New York: Stein and Day, 1983.

Whymant, Robert. *Stalin's Spy: Richard Sorge and the Tokyo Espionage Ring.* New York: St. Martin's Press, 1998.

Wise, David. *Molehunt: The Secret Search for Traitors That Shattered the CIA.* New York: Random House, 1992.

Wright, Peter, and Paul Greengrass. *Spycatcher.* New York: Viking, 1987.

Wyden, Peter. *Wall: The Inside Story of Divided Berlin.* New York: Simon and Schuster, 1989.

Zubok, Vladislav, and Constantine Pleshakov. *Inside the Kremlin's Cold War: From Stalin to Khrushchev.* Cambridge, MA: Harvard University Press, 1996.

INDEX